Provisioning Paris

The provisioning cycle (Deutsches Brotmuseum)

Provisioning Paris

MERCHANTS AND MILLERS IN
THE GRAIN AND FLOUR TRADE
DURING THE EIGHTEENTH CENTURY

STEVEN LAURENCE KAPLAN

Cornell University Press

ITHACA AND LONDON

This book has been published with the aid of a grant from
the Hull Memorial Publication Fund of Cornell University.

Copyright © 1984 by Cornell University Press

First published 1984 by Cornell University Press.
Published in the United Kingdom by Cornell University Press Ltd., London.

International Standard Book Number 0-8014-1600-0
Library of Congress Catalog Card Number 84-7004

Printed in the United States of America

Librarians: Library of Congress cataloging information
appears on the last page of the book.

The paper in this book is acid-free and meets the guidelines
for permanence and durability of the Committee on Production
Guidelines for Book Longevity of the Council on Library Resources.

59,910

To the memory of the grandparents of

Laurence George Charles and Renée Stéphanie

Preface

*C*ereal dependence conditioned every phase of social life in old-regime France. Grain was the dominant sector of the economy; beyond its determinant role in agriculture, directly and indirectly it shaped the development of commerce and industry, regulated employment, and provided a major source of revenue for the state, the Church, the nobility, and large segments of the Third Estate. Subsistence needs gave cereal dependence its most telling expression. The survival of most of the people turned on the availability of grain. Yet nothing was more uncertain than the harvest, and even an apparently abundant harvest could not allay anxieties, for the process of distribution was fraught with perils, both natural and man-made.

The provisioning imperative decisively marked the social organization, public administration, and ideology of old-regime France. Daily life turned on the need to procure bread. Working people saw themselves preeminently as consumers rather than producers and fixed obsessively on the subsistence question. (And most peasants were buyers rather than sellers of grain, so it should not be imagined that food distribution concerned only the towns and cities.) The dread of shortage and hunger tormented the police as well as the people, and forged curious ties of solidarity between them. No task preoccupied central and local administrators more doggedly than the obligation to assure an adequate supply of grain, flour, and bread at prices accessible to the laboring poor. Provisioning was a political issue, for the people held the government accountable for their survival, and government at all levels acknowledged this responsibility. No issue had greater mobilizing or destabilizing power than scarcity, or the fear of it. The government's commitment to the consumer interest (identified as *the* public interest) had weighty implications for the economy, for it circumscribed the incentives that were available to agriculture and the freedom that was available to commerce.

Despite the centrality and urgency of the grain question in everyday life, astonishingly little is known about grain (and flour) commerce, especially in the Paris region, where the presence of a vast city teeming with hundreds of thousands of poor consumers made the subsistence problem particularly acute. We are aware of the crucial importance of grain prices in shaping the evolution of the eighteenth century, but we do not know how those prices were made on and off the marketplaces. Somehow we have come to dissociate prices from the objects they describe, the signifier obscuring the signified. And, concomitantly, we have come to assume instinctively that prices are significant only in the long run, and thus are at some distance from *lived* social life. When we advert to the grain question, it is usually in reference to the tragic poetry of the crises rather than to the prose of the ordinary years. We call those years ordinary because they consist of endless and reassuring repetition of the same gestures; yet we have only a vague idea of what those gestures are and how they are articulated into a structure of everyday life. We have rushed to endorse the thesis that the "old demographic regime" gave way to a new one toward the end of the reign of Louis XIV, but we have been slow to test it by examining some of the possible explanations: improvements in market organization and linkage, innovation in technology, improved administrative practices. We have had a bountiful harvest of monographs and a heated debate on agricultural production, but we have paid almost no attention to the grain after the yield is calculated. We have had histories of rural France and histories of urban France, but little about the most telling economic, social, and political exchange that linked town and country. In some way or other, grain is present in all the scholarly literature on the old regime, but often in a surprisingly remote, abstract, and ritually emblematic fashion. If we occasionally encounter grain outside the farms, it is safe to say that we almost never happen upon flour; and on the basis of the internal evidence in some of the most impressive studies we would be hard pressed to discover that either was required to make bread.

I offer this book as a contribution toward remedying that neglect. It focuses on the institutions and the actors of the provisioning trade for Paris. Its aim is to follow the story of grain from the time the peasant threshed it until the moment that the baker took delivery of it in the form of flour. A subsequent study concentrating on the bakers of Paris will pick up the provisioning process from the acquisition of grain and flour to the consumer's inscription on the loaf of the sign of the cross.

Much of this work is devoted to mapping uncharted terrain: identifying and locating the critical actors and institutions, illuminating the environment in which they operated, and discerning the relations that joined and disjoined them. The absence of landmarks and the elusiveness and intractability of the data made the task doubly onerous. My greatest frustration was that I was not able to get to know the merchants, millers, brokers, and market officers more intimately. I would have liked to follow them into the *suqs* and *pasars* of the Parisian hinterland or into Zola's "stomach of Paris," into the sort of market-place that Malinowski called a "dramatic museum of the day," where "the people, their material objects, values and customs [were] on exhibit."[1] My material has confined me, however, more or less to the ethnographic periph-ery. The dialogue I established with my informants and their universe is vicarious or indirect or inferential. I simply could not answer many intriguing questions about motivation, trading methods, market preference, relations with clients, matrimonial strategies, income, investments, attitudes toward the regulations and the regulators, commercial rivalries, bookkeeping, lan-guage and literacy, and so on. I am inclined to think that the only path to thicker description will be through village- and town-level monographs based largely on local notarial and judicial records—where they are extant and accessible.

Despite its unevenness, my mapping has enabled me to delineate and analyze the elementary structures of the provisioning trade as they fared across the eighteenth century. This book begins with a discussion of ideology and institutions: the rationale for regulation, the practices of "police" and the administrative agents charged with the police of provisioning. The second chapter concerns the raw material itself: the ascendancy of wheat in Paris, the methods for selecting wheat and flour, and the problems of quality control and conservation. Chapter 3 explores the character of the grain trade in general and then focuses on the environment peculiar to the Parisian trade, including the supply zones from which the capital drained most of its grain and flour and the flow of merchandise into the metropolitan markets.

The next two chapters examine in detail the institutions and agencies of the grain trade. Chapter 4 is concerned with the merchants operating on the rivers and selling on the ports, who were traditionally perceived as the most active, the wealthiest, and the most indispensable to the provisioning of the city. Challenged by bakers and merchant-millers during the eighteenth cen-tury, the port merchants proved unable to sustain their dominant position. Chapter 5 surveys the grain trade at the central market called the Halle. Infinitely more discreet than their port counterparts, the Halle-based traders

1. Bronislaw Malinowski and Julio de la Fuente, *La Economia de un sistema de mer-cados en Mexico*, cited by Scott Cook and Martin Diskin, eds., *Markets in Oaxaca* (Austin, 1976), p. 7.

are often hard to distinguish from the country traders and even from some of the *gros laboureurs*. The grain supply was highly fragmented; the crowd of *laboureurs* and *blatiers* accounted for a critical portion of it.[2]

When I began to look at the provisioning of Paris, I had no intimation that flour would loom so large. The general economy of this book reflects the lessons I learned. Chapter 6 presents the miller and his machine. It discusses the work place and the work force, the comparative advantages of water and wind energy, the search for alternative means of power, the problems of mill construction and maintenance, and the cost and strictures of mill leases. Chapter 7 considers the miller in the public sphere: his reputation, his role in the community, his relations with the police, and his rivalry with fellow millers. A central theme is the shift from custom to merchant milling. In Chapter 8 I try to estimate the size of the Paris milling pool and its productivity. Chapter 9 is a study of miller families and fortunes.

In Chapter 10, in an effort to explain why the flour trade became so important, I trace the emergence of the flour merchants and their rise to prominence. The police encouraged them yet at the same time remained uneasy about their very dynamism. The records of the business failures of flour merchants point to some of the weaknesses of their commerce.

Chapter 11 links the commercialization of milling and the triumph of flour on the one hand with technological innovation, the political economy of liberalism, and the new science of subsistence on the other. I investigate the origins of economic milling, a strikingly modern conception of milling that promised myriad social benefits. I contrast the patronage that this practice elicited from the royal government and the scientific and "economic" communities to the resistance it triggered among millers, bakers, and certain public officials. Finally, I try to measure its diffusion and impact.

In many ways the bakers were responsible for the triumph of flour. They were the group least satisfied with the traditional provisioning arrangements. They chafed against their dependence on the port merchants and against the constraints on their commercial freedom. Chapter 12 shows how the bakers first plunged into the grain trade and then shifted into a new relationship with their millers.

The brokers also played a significant role in the commercialization of milling by fostering the market connection between bakers and flour merchants. Chapter 13 scrutinizes the origins of the institution, the changing character of recruitment, and the business methods of the brokers. It takes stock of the efforts of the police to reform the brokerage, which they viewed as the guarantor of the sanctity of the Halle market. The officials called measurers and porters were the object of the other major reform enterprise at

2. Frequently used terms, such as *laboureur* and *blatier,* have not been italicized in the text.

the central markets. In Chapter 14 I stress their deep involvement in the everyday provisioning trade, whose secrets they knew better than anyone else. Relentlessly under attack, the measurers and porters revealed an amazing capacity for survival.

I am indebted to a host of archivists and librarians too numerous to name who assisted me in my *dépouillements* in Paris and in the provinces. For their enduring friendship as well as their guidance, I must single out François Avril of the Bibliothèque Nationale, Jean Dérens of the Bibliothèque Historique de la Ville de Paris, Odile Krakovitch of the Archives Nationales, and Yves-Marie Bercé, formerly of the Archives Nationales, now professor of modern history at the Université de Reims. For providing me with important documents I am grateful to Micheline Baulant of the Ecole des Hautes Etudes en Sciences Sociales, Lucien Bresson of the Centre Régional d'Etudes Historiques et Documentaires de l'Ouest Parisien at Mantes-la-Jolie, Jean-Louis Jouastel of the Mairie de Corbeil, and Geneviève Dufresne of Chartres. For having introduced me to computer-assisted research, I am obligated to Douglas Van Houweling, now at the Carnegie-Mellon University, a demanding and compassionate teacher. Michael Strong, a friend and former student, now at the University of Pennsylvania, kindly helped me with computer and statistical work. For precious research and editorial assistance, I am pleased to express my appreciation to Eric Aguiar, Andrea Kane, Cynthia Koepp, Sylvia Rosman, and Elise Yousoufian, all present or former students at Cornell University. My friends Louis Bergeron of the Ecole des Hautes Etudes en Sciences Sociales and Yves Lequin of the Université de Lyon II graciously procured maps for me. Bergeron engaged me in many fruitful discussions about milling and provisioning, from which I learned a great deal.

Six friends subjected my manuscript to a searching reading: Daniel Baugh, Davydd Greenwood, and Peter McClelland, all colleagues at Cornell, and George Grantham of McGill University, Darline G. S. Levy of New York University, and Jacques Revel of the Ecole des Hautes Etudes en Sciences Sociales. I am deeply grateful to them for their generosity and counsel. As usual my dear friend Mary Ann Quinn saved me from myriad errors of style and substance and taught me a great deal about the subject in which I pretend to be a specialist. I benefited from the wise editorial advice of Lawrence Malley of Cornell University Press. The managing editor of the Press, Marilyn Sale, collaborated with designer George Whipple to improve the manuscript in many ways. The Deutsches Brotmuseum of Ulm-Donau and the Musée du Blé at Verdun-sur-le-Doubs kindly furnished iconographic documentation. To my wife, Jane, who read and proofread, and Laurence and Renée, who photocopied thousands of pages and kept me loving and puckish company, I say thank you. My years of research in France would not have been possible without the generous assistance of the National Endowment for the Humanities, the Ecole des Hautes Etudes en Sciences Sociales, and the Humanities Council and the Western Societies Program of Cornell University.

STEVEN LAURENCE KAPLAN

Ithaca, New York

Contents

5   The Grain Merchants at the Paris Halle   185

6   The Mill and the Miller   221

7   The Miller and the Public   264

CONTENTS   15

Illustrations and Tables

17

Provisioning Paris

CHAPTER 1

Provisioning Paris: Market Principle and Marketplace

The Subsistence of the People

"*T*he subsistence of the people is the most essential object that must occupy the administration," wrote Jacques Necker, minister, *philosophe*, banker, and grain speculator.[1] Save for two brief interludes, this commitment to the consumer-people of France was the uncontested tenet of public policy during the old regime. It was founded on the conviction that social stability could be guaranteed only by guaranteeing the food supply. History seemed to prove beyond a doubt that hunger and dearth had "preceded, prepared and caused" grave, sometimes fatal disorders in Rome, Constantinople, and China. Without order, government could not endure and society could not hold together.[2] The prerequisite for order, in the words of an eighteenth-century provincial administrator, "was to provide for the subsistence of the people, without which there is neither law nor force which can contain them."[3]

To assure an adequate food supply was not only in the interest of the government, it was its obligation, according to the doctrine (or covenant) that

1. Necker to Sartine, 14 February 1778, Archives Nationales (hereafter cited as AN), F[11]* 1, fol. 258.

2. Nicolas Delamare, *Traité de la police* (Paris, 1705–38), 2:566; *Journal de l'agriculture, du commerce, des arts et des finances* (January 1772): 48; Jacques Necker, *Sur la législation et le commerce des grains* (Paris, 1775).

3. Bertier de Sauvigny, "Observations sur le commerce des grains," Bibliothèque Nationale (hereafter BN), manuscrits français (hereafter cited as ms. fr.) 11347, fol. 228.

gradually developed to define relations between governors and governed. The people would "submit" provided their existence was safeguarded. This obligation became a responsibility and an attribute of paternal kingship: what more solemn duty could a father have than to enable his children to enjoy their daily bread? It was something the monarch was expected, even required, to carry out.[4]

All (consumer-) subjects were theoretically equally dear to the king, but the mission to provision the capital had primacy over all others, because of the government's conviction that "outcries of need there would be more dangerous than anywhere else and would set a fatal and contagious example."[5] Political experience had demonstrated well before the eighteenth century that it was cheaper to take a risk with food supply in the provinces than in Paris. The capital's population was immense, between 600,000 and 700,000 around mid-century, and the vast majority of its inhabitants led extremely arduous and uncertain lives. They were more likely to react collectively and violently to threats to their subsistence than to any other danger. A Parisian uprising, it was believed, could overturn the government. Thus, Paris was permitted to "devour" a substantial chunk of the kingdom because, as an author of a treatise on the police observed, without the special administrative advantages that the capital enjoyed "one would have trouble imagining that there are sources capable of meeting the needs of this vast pit."[6]

Even for Paris, however, the king was supposed to be only the victualer (or, as the revolutionaries put it, the baker) of last resort. It was not the government's intention actually to furnish consumers with grain or bread, nor indeed did the public expect it to. The government was not equipped to take over the primary food suply; it intervened through regulation. The burden of public authority was not to feed the people but to make sure they would be fed. This distinction implied a fairly simple division of social labor. Producers grew the grain; theirs was the responsibility, aided by a host of intermediaries, to distribute it. The government had to make sure that it reached the public in "due time," in good condition, and at a price accessible to the bulk of consumers. Authorities tracked grain from the time it was seeded until bakers made it into bread, watching its movement from hand to hand and trying to keep it optimally visible and reassuringly ubiquitous by enforcing certain rules of conduct and exchange. This surveillance and regulation was called the police of provisioning. But the actual task of provisioning was left to commerce.

4. Steven L. Kaplan, *Bread, Politics and Political Economy in the Reign of Louis XV* (The Hague, 1976), 1:5–8.

5. Louis-Sébastien Mercier, *Tableau de Paris* (Amsterdam, 1783), 4:203; Delamare, *Traité de la police*, 2:828; Regnaud, "Histoire des événements arrivés en France depuis 1772," BN, ms. fr. 13747; anonymous memorandum to controller-general (1784), AN, F[11] 294–95.

6. N.-T.-L. Des Essarts, *Dictionnaire universel de police* (Paris, 1786–90), 1:329. See also Kaplan, *Bread, Politics and Political Economy*, 1:34–35.

Commerce and the Market Principle

Commerce drew its power and derived its rationale from the *market principle*.[7] The market principle signified a system of relations in which prices were determined by the impersonal forces of supply and demand, regardless of the site of the transaction, and in which these prices allocated resources, income, and outputs. Predicated upon a global scheme of endless self-adjustment, the market principle demanded an untrammeled freedom of action for commerce. Interference of any sort would shatter its coherence and jeopardize its mission. Commerce thus required a quasi-institutional independence vis-à-vis the basic structures of social control. Its eighteenth-century partisans, of whom the physiocrats were the most vociferous, justified this autonomy on the grounds that the market principle, consisting of the "holy" and "imprescriptible" rights of property and liberty sanctified by nature's law, was anterior to all forms of social organization. Less sophisticated eighteenth-century exponents of commercial liberty, such as grain growers and merchants, understood the market principle more or less viscerally in terms of their right to dispose sovereignly of what they owned without any limitation and to realize maximum profits from their capital, their cunning, and their risk-taking courage. Concordant with human nature, self-interest was the calculus of the market principle, without regard to social or political or moral factors. Since the sum of all interests was ineluctably congenial and since the outcome of their interplay was necessarily socially beneficial, the perspective was reassuring.[8]

The police by and large grasped the logic of the market principle, but recoiled from it because it frightened them. They worried about its apotheosis of and dependence upon selfishness and its lack of social accountability. They were suspicious of its animus against public authority. To some extent they may have shared the ageless and widely held belief that there was something

7. My reading of market principle and marketplace in the context of the eighteenth century is inspired by Karl Polanyi, *The Great Transformation* (New York, 1944); Karl Polanyi, "The Economy as an Instituted Process," in Karl Polanyi, Conrad M. Arensberg, and Harry W. Pearson, eds., *Trade and Market in the Early Empires* (Chicago, 1957); Karl Polanyi, *Primitive, Archaic and Modern Economies,* ed. George Dalton (New York, 1969); Karl Polanyi, *The Livelihood of Man,* ed. Harry W. Pearson (New York, 1972); Paul Bohannan and George Dalton, eds., *Markets in Africa* (Evanston, 1962).

8. See Claude-Jacques Herbert, *Essai sur la police générale des grains, sur leurs prix et sur les effets de l'agriculture* (London, 1755), in E. Depitre, ed., *Collection des économistes et des réformateurs sociaux de la France* (Paris, 1910), pp. 7, 21, 57, 95; Pierre-Joseph-André Roubaud, *Représentations aux magistrats* (London, 1769), pp. 398–401; Nicolas Baudeau, *Avis au peuple sur son premier besoin* (Amsterdam and Paris, 1768), pp. 72–73; Pierre-Paul Lemercier de la Rivière, *L'Intérêt général de l'état* (Paris, 1770), pp. 64–65; Pierre-Samuel Dupont de Nemours, "Vrais principes du droit naturel," *Ephémérides du citoyen,* 3, première partie, no. 2 (1767): 102–3 and deuxième partie, no. 2: 131–33, 160–61, 167; J.-P.-L. Luchet, *Examen d'un livre qui a pour titre: "Sur la législation et le commerce des bleds"* (n.p., 1775), pp. 40–41.

odious about the merchant. If the provisioning trade were left strictly to commerce, they were convinced, society would live in constant peril. Frequently commerce discharged its task of distribution proficiently. At any moment, however, it was capable of provoking disarray and panic. Prompted only by "amour-propre and immoderate cupidity for a sordid profit," merchants time and again offered grain "only when they wished." They did not hesitate to use their enormous leverage to "promote public misfortune" in order to profit from it. They caused artificial dearths or aggravated real ones by hiding and hoarding, by purchasing futures, by recklessly outbidding all rivals, and by spreading news that was at once incendiary and demoralizing. The police classified all these practices under the rubric "monopoly." There was no more serious antisocial crime, for it struck down thousands of innocent people. Monopoly was the fruit of liberty run amok. Yet in the police view it was not at bottom a distortion of the market principle but its most complete expression.[9]

The police did not blame commerce for this behavior, for it was "in the very nature" of the trade. In some kinds of exchange it was tolerable and even advantageous to allow the market principle, with all its risks, free reign. In most sorts of trade, shortage, tardiness, fraud, and other defects or vices caused harm or inconvenience only to individuals, and never in mortal doses. The police were unwilling to permit the business of provisioning to become just another business, however. Grain was an item of "first necessity," ultimately a matter of life or death, for millions of consumers, whereas other goods merely complemented subsistence or enhanced pleasure. In the provisioning trade, "the least error almost always affected the public," menacing the whole community at its most vulnerable point.

The police attitude toward commerce and toward merchants was deeply ambivalent. On the one hand, provisioning was fundamentally a commercial operation and traders were absolutely necessary to do the job. On the other hand, the market principle was dangerous and unreliable, and the grain trader was somehow even more rapacious and untrustworthy than any other merchant, for who but vicious men would choose to speculate on the subsistence of their fellows? Provisioning could be confided to commerce only ambiguously, conditionally, and incompletely. Since society depended on it for survival, the police conceived of grain commerce as a kind of public service, and imposed restrictions upon grain traders that other merchants escaped. The grain merchant's obligations to the public would sometimes require him to set aside his self-interest. He had to be satisfied with a "just and legitimate gain" (even as he had to respect, on occasion, the imperative of the just price). Implicit in the police vision of the grain trade was the notion that the grain

9. For this paragraph and the next two, see Kaplan, *Bread, Politics and Political Economy,* 1:52–59, 62.

held by a merchant (or producer) was not perfectly and exclusively his own to dispose of as he saw fit. As the primary source of subsistence, grain was a "common good" upon which society had certain claims. Since the police had no reason to believe that the merchants would honor those claims voluntarily, they elaborated a set of rules that defined the way in which the trade was to be practiced.

Police and the Marketplace

To the market principle, the police opposed the *marketplace*—as a physical location and as a congeries of prescriptions that were rooted in (but not necessarily confined to) the market as a designated site. The market principle implied no sacrosanct place of exchange; the marketplace demanded physical concentration of goods and actors at a fixed place. The market principle required freedom from control and constraint, whereas the marketplace imposed surveillance and regulation. The one celebrated improvisation, the other routinization. The market principle was fundamentally private in ethos and operation, the marketplace quintessentially public. Transactions according to the market principle were closed (or covert) and occurred in open social space, while marketplace exchange was open and occurred in (en-)closed space. The market principle measured success in terms of profits; the test of marketplace success was public tranquillity.

Defined as a principle, the market was elusive: it was at once everywhere and nowhere; it was threatening because it was in some sense untouchable, unclassifiable, mobile. Defined as a place, the market was something that the police could invest and control. In a concrete, functional sense the marketplace as a physical site served as the linchpin of the regulatory apparatus. In a more general way the marketplace as an *idée force* and as a symbol of engagement embodied the police ideology. There was no single more important regulation concerning the provisioning trade than the requirement that all transactions occur in the marketplace.[10] This was the best guarantee of honesty and efficiency, not only in the view of the police but also in that of old-regime (and revolutionary and postrevolutionary) consumers, for whom market participation was the supreme test of civism. By concentrating the supply and rendering it visible and by making transactions transparent, the

10. Royal declaration of 19 April 1723, BN, Collection Joly de Fleury (hereafter cited as Coll. Joly), 1829, fols. 302–3; Archives du Département de la Seine et de la Ville de Paris (hereafter cited as Archives Seine-Paris), D5Z carton 9; Des Essarts, *Dictionnaire*, 1:19, 330, 402; Delamare, *Traité de la police*, 2:790–97; Edme de la Poix de Fréminville, *Dictionnaire, ou Traité de la police générale des villes, bourgs, paroisses et seigneuries de la campagne* (Paris, 1758), p. 72; Duchesne, *Code de la police, ou Analyse des règlements de police* (Paris, 1767), p. 99; William Mildmay, *The Police of France* (London, 1763), p. 99; BN, Coll. Joly 1312, fol. 117.

marketplace satisfied the deepest expectations of the consumer-people. Even the (constantly revocable) derogation accorded to registered Paris merchants permitting them to operate outside the marketplaces of the supply zone was conceived as part of a larger marketplace strategy that aimed at giving the edge to metropolitan merchants over their local competitors (even as it enabled Parisian authority to supersede local authority) and at guaranteeing the hegemony of the central or final marketplace of the capital over the subordinate collector-marketplaces. Other regulations, for example those dealing with licenses for merchants and passports for grain and flour, emanated from the marketplace even if they were meant to govern the space outside it. In some way or another, everything pertaining to the police of provisioning revolved around the marketplace.

The marketplace, as I construe it, was the consecrated space of neither capitalism nor carnival. No Smithian invisible hand ministered providentially to the needs of the parties involved. The marketplace bore the unmistakable imprint of the hands of the police (although the authorities placed a high premium on discretion). Unlike Bakhtin's "free place," the marketplace of the police was a preeminently official venue, structured, organized, regulated (at least in theory). Bakhtin's marketplace, infused "with unofficial spirit," was a post of subversion, derision, and laughter. It defied cooptation as well as control: "it enjoyed a certain extraterritoriality in a world of official order and official ideology." The marketplace of the police was devised precisely to refuse extraterritorial privilege and to enshrine the official world view. Yet the official spirit of the marketplace was no less "with the people" than the unofficial marketplace that Bakhtin so brilliantly evoked.[11]

The police intended the marketplace not to throttle commerce but to domesticate it and moralize it, not to obliterate the market principle but to correct it. The police designed the marketplace as a way of articulating the requirements of trade with the needs of state and society. They tried to incorporate certain features of the market principle while excluding or tempering others—a gesture denounced as futile and hollow by the advocates of the market principle, who insisted that it had to be taken as an indivisible whole. For them, liberty was entirely incompatible with the marketplace of the police. If the authorities engineered the marketplace to prevent monopoly (i.e., to prevent liberty from degenerating into license and libertinage), the proponents of the market principle contended that it was precisely the marketplace (i.e., too little liberty) that caused or nurtured monopoly. Unalloyed, the market principle was utterly corrosive of the marketplace as physical site, as world view, and as apparatus of control. It made the marketplace superfluous, save as an occasional matter of convenience. If the marketplace

11. Mikhail Bakhtin, *Rabelais and His World*, trans. H. Iswolsky (Cambridge, Mass., 1968), pp. 153–54. On the noneconomic functions of the marketplace, see also Bohannan and Dalton, eds., *Markets in Africa*, pp. 15–19.

was erected as a dike to contain the burgeoning tide of the market principle, its adversaries scorned it because that tide was irresistible. Goods tended to flee the marketplace as the market principle attempted to assert itself. Thus the *pays de cocagne* of certain grain and flour merchants—those capable of profiting from this kind of freedom—was the space outside or between the established marketplaces.

In theory, the more pervasive the market principle, the less the economic importance of the marketplace as a site of transactions, and the less its political and ideological importance as a concept and institution of social organization. In part, viewed from today's vantage point, the market principle was underdeveloped in eighteenth-century France because the economy was underdeveloped. Yet is was also underdeveloped because it was self-consciously resisted, and the marketplace loomed large as one of the vehicles of this resistance. The marketplace was the sign of a certain kind of backwardness (to the extent that the market principle was on the side that we conventionally call "progress") and the mark of a certain kind of vitality (to the extent that the French were trying to grapple with one of the most agonizing problems of modernization).

In old-regime France, the social organization was not submerged in the market principle, as it is in most modern "market" societies today. Rather, the distribution of certain goods—in particular grain and flour—was determined by the social organization. Embedded in the social and political institutions, the provisioning trade could not escape certain rules and controls that expressed values to which Frenchmen by and large subscribed. The marketplace stood for the priorities resulting from this type of governing code. When, on several occasions, liberalizing reformers sought to disembed the grain and flour trade from the traditional social organization (or free the promethean market principle from the chains of the marketplace), the immediate consequences were catastrophic.[12]

Exciting and Containing: From Theory to Practice

Marketplace exchange was the police (and the popular, or consumer,) norm: this was the way the provisioning trade was supposed to work according to regulatory theory. Market principle exchange was the way the merchants wanted the provisioning trade to work, and the way the police (and the consumer-people) feared that it would indeed work if the official rules were not obeyed (or not enforced). How in fact did the provisioning trade work?

A twentieth-century economist might suggest that the forbidden practices were neither evil nor dangerous but rational and beneficial—that, more

12. See Kaplan, *Bread, Politics and Political Economy,* chaps. 4, 5, 7, 9, 10, 12.

efficiently than the police methods, they got grain and flour into the hands of those most able to make effective use of them, and that they passed the risks of holding stocks in unstable markets to those most willing to bear them. The economist might be tempted to argue that the market, following the market principle, functioned much better than the police believed and that the main culprit in the story was not the libertine merchant or liberty run amok but the authorities, whose actions undermined confidence and generated insecurity and who failed to make a pretty good market work even better by providing more complete information, better public goods (notably in transportation), and uniformity in weights and measures. The police and the people, the economist might add, believed that they lived in a (market) world of combinations in restraint of trade and of monopoly prices and monopoly profits, but in fact their world was quite competitive, with relative ease of entry and other conditions that usually obtain in the neoclassical model.

Our economist might very well conclude that there were two worlds in the eighteenth century: a world of self-indulgent myth and delusion, associated with what I have called the marketplace, or the police ideology ("phantoms," said their archenemies the physiocrats), and a world of hard-nosed, self-adjusting reality, associated with the market principle, or with unfettered commerce.[13] I am inclined to acknowledge the existence of multiple, often rival or contradictory realities. The way in which the police, and the consumer-people, represented the world to themselves constituted a powerful reality that shaped every aspect of the provisioning process, including price making. From this perspective, it is of little consequence that what the police perceived as a "monopoly" price may have at bottom been nothing more than a modern economist's new equilibrium price. The interesting question is not whether the police were right or wrong, but why they saw things as they did. Yet I do not want to suggest that the police reality was somehow inferior to the economist's because it was essentially psychological or "subjective" as opposed to "objective." The police framework was not necessarily fatally flawed. Many of their doubts and fears about provisioning were the fruit of distortion and exaggeration: perceptions refracted by ideology (a combination of "prejudices" and "ignorance," observed the physiocrats).[14] Many others,

13. Herbert, *Essai sur la police générale des grains,* p. 4; speech of Creuzé-Latouche, 8 December 1792, in *Archives Parlementaires* (Paris, 1879–1894), 54:682.
14. Controller-general Laverdy to procurator general, 4 December 1765, BN, Coll. Joly 1131, fol. 9; Laverdy to same, 23 October 1766, BN, Coll. Joly 1109, fols. 145–46; Turgot to intendant of Alençon, 19 September 1774, Archives Départementales (hereafter cited as AD) Orne, C 89; Roubaud, *Représentations,* pp. 39, 80, 93; "Avis du Parlement de Dauphiné," *Ephémérides du citoyen* (1769), 7:156; Turgot, "Lettre circulaire aux officiers de police dans les lieux où il y a des marchés de grains," 15 February 1766, AD Haute-Vienne, C 479.

Nor were the police and the people the only ones to see things this way. Large numbers of intelligent men of good will distrusted what we would call (in twentieth-century terms) market solutions and assumed that to each problem there corresponded a "police" solution.

however, were warranted by the structural conditions of the grain and flour trade in the eighteenth century. Nor should we assume that the neoclassical outlook was or is a value-free recipe for universally desirable development or "progress." In physiocracy, its early expression, and its later, more refined avatars, neoclassical economics is as much an ideology as an analytical tool, and in this sense is flawed in some of the same ways as the police view. It is perhaps futile to apply the same categories of analysis to the police and neoclassical models—while the latter sees the issues in economic terms, the former regards them above all in social and political terms. We return to the point of departure of the police: provisioning was too delicate and too imperious a task to relegate to the economic domain, that is, to entrust to the market principle.

The story of the grain and flour trade is to a large extent the story of the tension between the marketplace and the market principle, the story not of a battle between the forces of Darkness and the forces of Light, but of the shifting relationship between two theories and two (or more) realities. It would be a mistake to infer from the timeless and merciless strictures of the police regulations, or from the self-serving propaganda of the physiocrats, that the police operated in a mindlessly and mechanically rigid and oppressive fashion. The authorities themselves understood the need to reconcile regulation and liberty, which they recognized as "the soul of commerce."[15] They knew that the cost of overpolice was sometimes as onerous as the cost of overlaxness. Even as they anguished over the dangers of allowing the merchants too much freedom, they worried about "disgusting" them and stifling commerce. The officials responsible for provisioning internalized the tension between marketplace and market principle.

The problem was to find the proper dosage. In theory the police never veered from their commitment to the marketplace; in practice their position was often temperate, tolerant, and flexible. Delamare, the celebrated police theorist, who drew on his long experience as a field agent, recommended a differential police of provisioning: one police for periods of abundance, another for middling years, still another for dearth, and a fourth style of police for famine.[16] During "normal" years—most of the period with which we are concerned—the Paris authorities practiced benign neglect. They neither repudiated procedures that had been fully assimilated by the trade nor condoned blatantly illicit activities, and they refrained from rigorously executing many of the regulations and permitted others to lapse into virtual desuetude. The traditional controls, especially the mosaic of rules fixing all transactions at the official market sites, the procurator general of the Paris Parlement, one of the highest judicial and administrative officials in the realm, informed the provincial and local authorities, "are not to be strictly executed when there is

15. Delamare, *Traité de la police*, 2:775.
16. Ibid., p. 794.

no dearth to fear." He openly avowed that these regulations "hamper the grain trade" and should only be used with extreme discretion. In everyday practice he urged officials to avoid "authoritarian ways" and to "close your eyes" when they encountered violations of the marketplace code that did not threaten the public interest.[17] Often the police abstained from coercive measures not out of indulgence for the merchants but rather to avoid provoking "alarms" and "anxieties" among consumers. The authorities were sufficiently self-critical to ask themselves whether the classical remedy would not, in the specific circumstances at hand, prove worse than the disease.[18]

The evidence indicates that officials very often followed this remarkably subdued and supple line throughout the kingdom. Trading practices deemed monopolistic in periods of stress frequently passed for reasonable commercial operations in more tranquil times; an action only became monopolistic to the extent that it maimed the public interest. The police in the Paris region generally rebuffed price fixing, not from scruples about violating the property rights of dealers—the physiocrats branded *taxation* "theft"—but because they felt that it did more harm than good. Although they had no sympathy for merchant "abuses," along with their mentor Delamare they had no interest in running "a forced commerce."[19] A real liberty was accorded the merchants, but this liberty was not a right derived from nature but a concession granted conditionally by society. It remained contingent on the good faith of the merchants and on supply conditions.[20]

In theory—perhaps even more tellingly in rhetoric—the marketplace and the market principle were at antipodes. In practice, the opposition was less harsh and unremitting. The tension between them was partly resolved in time (merchants were allowed much more freedom in good periods than in bad) and partly in space (certain areas were more hospitable to liberty than others). In some ways the marketplace and the market principle adjusted to and accommodated one another. Merchants and authorities shared in a certain complicity. The merchants learned never to attempt certain transgressions and when to venture others, and incorporated certain controls into their daily practice. The police were surprisingly opportunistic and elastic—

17. Procurator general to fiscal procurator of Charly, 23 November 1757, BN, Coll. Joly 1107, fols. 6, 7; BN, Coll. Joly 1130, fols. 156–57 and 2418, fol. 177.

18. Kaplan, *Bread, Politics and Political Economy,* 1:78–80.

19. Delamare, *Traité de la police,* 2:922–34; BN, ms. fr. 21647, fols. 64–74; Duplessis to procurator general, 2, 5 January, 21 September 1726, BN, Coll. Joly 1118, fols. 5, 8–9, 206–7; Jacques St.-Germain, *La Vie quotidienne en France à la fin du grand siècle d'après les archives du lieutenant général de police Marc-René d'Argenson* (Paris, 1965), pp. 208–9; *Ephémérides du citoyen* (August 1767), cited by Georges Weulersse, *Le Mouvement physiocratique en France de 1756 à 1770* (Paris, 1910), 1:538.

20. *Journal économique* (May 1752): 121–27; AN, K 908. Cf. Louis Viala, *La Question des grains et leur commerce à Toulouse au dix-huitième siècle* (Toulouse, 1909), pp. 29–30.

doubtless in part because the marketplace arsenal they held in reserve gave them a sense of deep strength. They were also divided among themselves on a number of major issues. There was no consensus, for instance, on dispensation accorded Paris dealers to operate outside the market sites.[21] The merchants appreciated and profited from the distinctions made between law and usage.

But the police of provisioning was still in many ways a forbidding system. The market principle never operated beyond the shadow of the marketplace. Dealers still had to live in great uncertainty about the future, comply with many vexatious rules, and face inconsistencies in police attitudes in different places as well as at different times. Even though officials frequently overlooked the rules in easy periods, they often enforced them vengefully in hard times, as if to atone for their indulgence. Even in times called normal, the prospect of dearth, of tomorrow, preoccupied everyone.

The Hierarchy of Police Administration

Who were the stewards of marketplace authority and ideology? Who exercised the police of provisioning?[22] The king held the supreme police power in the realm. Royal legislation devised or reaffirmed the general rules meant to govern the provisioning trade throughout the kingdom. The monarch invested regional and local officials with authority to enforce these rules and more broadly to assure the provisioning of their areas. Intermittently, several of the royal councils reviewed the state of subsistence, discussed problems concerning the trade, and adjudicated disputes. During periods that required extraordinary measures of relief and regulation, the king often became personally involved.

The king's chief deputy for all domestic affairs, the controller-general, directed a sort of superministry that embraced everything pertaining to the economy, finance, public works, public assistance, and general administration. For most of his business, the controller-general circumvented the royal councils and worked directly with the king or in intimate ministerial committee. His recommendations were carefully prepared by specialized bureaus, one of which was called the grain department, known also as the bureau of subsistence or the department of abundance. Managed by an intendant of finance or commerce and staffed by clerks who provided a continuity of

21. "Mémoire contre la Déclaration du 9 septembre 1737," BN, ms. fr. 21635, fols. 168–69; Missonnet to procurator general, 31 July, 30 October 1752, and 2 April 1753, BN, Coll. Joly 1112, fols. 114, 192–93; Foucaud to procurator general, April 1757, BN, Coll. Joly 1113, fols. 240–41.
22. The following discussion of the character and composition of the different levels of police is drawn from Kaplan, *Bread, Politics and Political Economy,* 1:14–42.

expertise by surviving ministerial changes, this bureau collected data on production, consumption, and prices and assessed the mass of information upon which the minister based his decisions. The controller-general tried to anticipate deficits and surpluses and facilitate regional distribution. In emergencies he coordinated regional and local efforts to cope with scarcity and organize relief measures. Interested in every dimension of the grain and flour trade and of the provisioning police, he kept track by corresponding with the provincial intendants directly responsible to him and with a host of lesser officials.

Yet despite his omnicompetence, and to some degree because of it, the controller-general had little influence in day-to-day provisioning business. In part this was a matter of policy, for the government conceived of subsistence as a preeminently local problem. But this policy itself betrayed the government's inability to deal with this vast and infinitely complex matter. Moreover, the sweeping scope of his duties made it impossible for the controller-general to delve deeply into the intricacies of provisioning. The field administrators were the real protagonists of the police of subsistence, the custodians of the marketplace. The controller-general, sometimes assisted by a secretary of state, played the role of deus ex machina, swooping down on the stage when the drama demanded his intervention.

The intendants of the *généralités,* administrative divisions that cut across the old provinces, constituted the first line of royal provisioning police in the field. Seconded only by a small corps of subdelegates and inspectors, the intendant depended on a staggering array of local officials, each of whom retained considerable autonomy. He expected them to make most decisions on their own, with reference to the common fund of rules that had hardly changed for generations and in light of specific circumstances. With the aim of unifying control procedures or quashing abusive practices, he sometimes issued interpretative decrees that clarified or redefined the meaning of existing laws and customs. He exercised his greatest leverage by regulating the circulation of grain and flour across time and space. He had the power to accelerate or to impede or even prohibit the flow of merchandise within the *généralité*. In certain situations, the intendant took it upon himself to prevent the "export" of grain and flour outside the boundaries of his circumscription, as a result jeopardizing the well-being of neighboring provinces. Intendants clashed bitterly over matters of policy and jurisdiction. A king's man par excellence, the intendant was nevertheless capable of defying royal instructions that he believed placed *his* consumers at risk. The intendant of Paris was the provincial chief least competent and least disposed to obstruct royal will, largely because of his propinquity to Versailles. He also had the least influence in provisioning affairs because his jurisdiction did not include the city of Paris—the capital was subject to no intendant, though the lieutenant general of police performed many of his functions—and because the police administration of the capital exercised extensive authority in the hinterland.

The police powers considered so far emanated directly from the king and fit into a pyramidal hierarchy that extended from the apex to the more than thirty *généralités*. There was, however, yet another major police authority, exercised on the regional scale by the thirteen regional courts called *parlements*. Though royal in origin, the parlements owned a generous measure of institutional and constitutional independence and practiced a sort of parallel police vis-à-vis royal administration, sometimes complementing it, sometimes supplanting or challenging it. The most familiar levers of parlementary power were the captious tactics by which the courts subverted royal legislation, by overt opposition (refusal to register) and by more subtle devices (judicial decisions, filibustering, inadequate publicity), or remolded it to conform to their own needs or views. Much of this was a matter of adaptation rather than obstruction, for the crown gave the courts fairly wide latitude in the interpretation and implementation of royal legislation.

Less well known was the parlements' authority to enact quasi-legislative decrees called *arrêts de règlement*. In this capacity they acted on their own initiative and on their own terms rather than in reaction to measures taken by the central government. Unless the king's council decided to quash their regulatory decrees on grounds that they contradicted new or existing royal legislation, they had "force of law" within each *ressort*. They dealt with a sweeping range of issues affecting public, private, and criminal law as well as police affairs. The acts by which the Paris Parlement limited bakers in a dearth period to making only two sorts of bread and by which the Dijon Parlement placed an embargo on the removal of grain outside its jurisdiction were *arrêts de règlement*. Whereas the rights of registration and remonstrance gave the parlements significant political influence, this quasi-legislative power to render arrêts enabled the sovereign courts of justice to function as authentic regional governing institutions.

Another powerful instrument of parlementary police was the juridico-administrative apparatus directed by one of the court's leading magistrates, the procurator general. It was particularly important in the Parlement of Paris, whose procurator general commanded great prestige and whose jurisdiction stretched over a third of the kingdom. The procurator had *substituts* in scores of towns and hamlets scattered throughout the *ressort*. These deputies, often called royal procurators *(procureurs du roi),* functioned as local officers of justice and police as well as representatives of the parlement. They regarded the procurator general as their protector and as the authority to whom they were ultimately accountable. Many of them kept him closely informed on general affairs such as the state of the market and the price of grain as well as on matters of justice. They often solicited his advice and instructions for the proper conduct of affairs; he was supposed to keep them posted on changes in laws, regulations, and procedures and he gave them specific orders either in his capacity as a superior police official himself or as the spokesman for the court. The *substituts* constituted an extraordinary network of grass-roots intelligence and enforcement. In many instances the procurator general was better informed than the intendants or even the controller-general, and better placed than they to see his commands executed.

The Paris procurator general was also the organizing force behind the informal "assembly of police," composed of the first president of the Parlement of Paris, the lieutenant general of police, and the *prévôt des marchands* as well as the procurator, which met sometimes monthly, sometimes weekly to discuss all matters pertaining to the administration of the capital and took a special interest in subsistence questions. The lieutenant general reported on the state of public opinion, the situation in the Halles or central markets, the conduct of the bakers, and the conditions in the markets and the farms of the nearby hinterland; the prévôt told his colleagues about the port markets and the river trade; and the procurator passed on data from his *substituts* on the harvests, stocks, and market conditions throughout the *ressort.* The officials assessed the situation and tried to decide upon a common course of action (or inaction). Decisions did not come easily, for the prévôt and the lieutenant were bitter rivals, and both resented the "tutelage" which the first president in the name of parlement pretended to exercise over them. On balance, the assembly of police seems to have been fairly successful in coordinating general policy for the police of provisioning, at least during the first half of the reign of Louis XV, the only period for which the minutes of the meetings survive.

Primary responsibility for the police of the capital's subsistence resided in the *lieutenance générale de police.* Created in the 1660s to deal especially with matters concerning the security of the city, the lieutenance rapidly assumed responsibility for a sweeping range of functions embracing "everything which treats of the public good."[23] The maintenance of order remained the constant preoccupation of the lieutenant general, but order in the broadest sense: the order that obtained not merely from the repression of crime but in particular from the establishment of social conditions that made life bearable for the majority of inhabitants. The regular supply of a sufficiently copious and cheap quantity of bread commanded the lieutenant general's unswerving

23. On the origins and mission of the lieutenance, see BN, ms. fr. 8118; Edme Béguillet, *Description historique de Paris et de ses plus beaux monuments* (Paris, 1779–81), 1:253–55; A. Gazier, ed., "La Police de Paris en 1770, mémoire inédit, composé par ordre de G. de Sartine sur la demande de Marie-Thérèse," *Mémoires de la Société de l'histoire de Paris et de l'Ile-de-France* 5 (1878): 31–32; Marc Chassaigne, *La Lieutenance générale de police de Paris* (Paris, 1906); Charles Desmaze, *Le Châtelet de Paris, son organisation* (Paris, 1870); Jacques St.-Germain, *La Reynie et la police au grand siècle, d'après de nombreux documents inédits* (Paris, 1962); Pierre Clément, *La Police sous Louis XIV* (Paris, 1866); F.-A. Isambert et al., eds., *Recueil général des anciennes lois françaises depuis l'année 420 jusqu'à la révolution de 1789* (Paris, 1821–33), 18:100–103; Voltaire, *Le Siècle de Louis XIV: Oeuvres complètes* (Paris, 1878), 14:503; Alan Williams, *The Police of Paris, 1718–1789* (Baton Rouge, 1979).

attention. He reviewed the subsistence situation in depth four times a week, just before and after the official market days, and kept his eye on events in between. One of the bureaus of his secretariat focused exclusively on provisioning affairs, one *commissaire* and an inspector worked virtually fulltime on grain and flour marketing, while others carried out specific assignments bearing on the provisioning trade, and numerous special agents (including market measurers and porters, police agents called *exempts,* officers of the *maréchaussée* or rural constabulary) gathered intelligence in the capital and in the supply zones. The lieutenant general oversaw and in some sense directed the entire provisioning process. He kept track of entries into Paris, but his jurisdiction was by no means limited to the city barriers. His *droit de suite* permitted him to pursue suppliers into the barns, granaries, farms, and inns of the hinterland. His authority superseded that of local officials; much to their outrage, he was not loath to use it to favor the needs of the capital more or less without regard to the local costs. In day-to-day terms, the lieutenant general decided on the mix of market principle and marketplace. As a judge as well as an administrator, he set the mood for the enforcement of the rules. To the extent that there was any long-term planning, it took shape in his office. In consultation with the controller-general and the procurator general, he commanded the crisis center in periods of dearth.

The prévôt des marchands, who presided over the municipality (*bureau de l'Hôtel de Ville,* composed of city councillors called *échevins*) contested the hegemonic claims of the lieutenance, specifically in the domain of subsistence and more generally in affairs involving economic, social, and cultural life.[24] Protesting that its titles were as old as those of the monarchy, the prévôté bitterly denounced the ruthless encroachments of the upstart lieutenance. For the most part its resistance proved vain, although it always found some pretext to sustain its pretensions and illusions.

The prévôté drew its greatest strength from its traditional association with waterborne commerce. By and large the lieutenance ceded the prévôté the administration of the ports and the traffic on the rivers. The prévôt des marchands was in no position to set provisioning policy, but he was allowed

---

24. On the clashes between the lieutenance and the prévôté, see "Affaires générales de la police" (1753), Bibliothèque Historique de la Ville de Paris (hereafter cited as BHVP), ms. 29736; Denis Diderot et al., *Encyclopédie* (Paris, 1751–65), 9:511; Mildmay, *Police of France,* p. 91; Delamare, *Traité de la police,* 2:859–60; BN, ms. fr. 21642, passim; La Reynie to Delamare, 12 and 19 November 1694, BN, ms. fr. 21643, fols. 122, 126; Marville to Maurepas, 6 January 1745, in *Lettres de M. de Marville, lieutenant général de police, au ministre Maurepas (1742–47),* ed. A. de Boislisle (Paris, 1896–1905), 2:3; J.-L. Gay, "L'Administration de la capitale entre 1770 et 1789," *Mémoires de la Fédération des Sociétés historiques et archéologiques de Paris et de l'Ile-de-France* 8 (1957): 360ff. and 12 (1961): 173ff.; "Edit du Roy portant règlement pour la jurisdiction du Lieutenant Général de Police et celle des Prévost des Marchands et Eschevins de Paris" (June 1700), BN, ms. fr. 21578, fol. 141ff.

to manage relations between the city and the merchants, Paris-based and itinerant, who shipped by water and sold at the ports. Like the lieutenant general, the prévôt reached far into the supply zone under the banner of the provisioning of Paris. He had permanent subdelegates stationed in many of the entrepôt river towns, and he dispatched his commissaires and *huissiers* to deal with specific problems in the hinterland. The prévôt issued ordinances that had force of law throughout the river system, and he adjudicated quarrels in the municipal court, assisted by the *échevins*. The prévôt and the lieutenant general learned to collaborate on matters of urgent public concern, such as subsistence, often under the mediating aegis of the procurator general.

The lieutenant general and the prévôt des marchands, like the procurator general and the intendants, had to contend with the local police of the regions around the capital from which Paris drew the bulk of its ordinary supply. Authority for the police of provisioning at the local level was widely diffused and fragmented in a crazy quilt of unintegrated, poorly defined, and overlapping jurisdictions. Virtually every public official dealing with administrative and/or judicial affairs, no matter how humble his origin or functions, "held" some sort of grain police. Below or beyond these local authorities, myriad specialized officers—grain measurers, porters, market stewards—and a host of more or less private individuals such as *engagistes* of the royal domain or less mighty seigneurs, lay or ecclesiastical, noble or bourgeois, who owned or farmed market "rights" or related tolls and duties all claimed or exercised some sort of police power. The leading public figures in each town—mayors, lieutenants of police, judges, procurators royal and fiscal—vied for control of provisioning affairs because the political, social and economic stakes involved were so high. In principle they shared the common aim of assuring that their communities enjoyed an adequate supply of grain at a reasonable price. By applying royal legislation, parlementary arrêts, and local statutes, by issuing their own regulations, by promulgating criminal, civil, and police sentences, by monitoring and registering transactions, and by exhorting and menacing the holders of grain and flour, local authorities sought to stabilize the provisioning trade.

The royal government enjoined local officials to cooperate among themselves, to respect the needs and rights of their neighbors and the wishes of their superiors. Disputes frequently arose, however, not only among officials within the same community jousting for supremacy but between different communities and between the local authorities and their hierarchical overlords. Conflicts issued from the competition for subsistence and characteristically took the form of quarrels over rights of jurisdiction, administrative and moral. Did a big community have priority regardless of the circumstances over a small one? Could Paris expropriate supplies that "belonged" to one of the towns in its feeder network when that town found itself inadequately provisioned? Could a community prohibit outsiders (i.e., Parisians) from entering its market and its hinterland? Could it force "exporting" merchants to sell their grain, and to sell it at a fixed price?

The relation of each local community to the capital was by no means the only source of strain, but it was the most significant. Intramunicipal rivalries for power often pitted a pro-Parisian official against an antimetropolitan one. The former wagered upon the intervention of the controller-general, the procurator general, or the Paris lieutenant general; the latter courted *grands seigneurs* with vested local interests or high officials, such as an intendant, who were not part of the Parisian juggernaut. The fiercest intercommunity struggle for subsistence opposed the local market town to the vulturous capital: "the new Rome," "insatiable," "bloodsucking." The Parisian police honored only one imperative: that the capital be fed. In order to mask their own imperialism and to discredit the self-regarding marketplace mentality of the hometown officials, the Paris authorities did not shrink from invoking the cosmopolitan market principle: the liberty of the grain and flour trade had to be respected (provided the traffic flowed uniquely in the direction of the capital). Time after time, especially in moments of subsistence difficulty, Paris "put the knife at the throat of our people," as one of the local officials put it.[25]

Nor did the towns suffer these exactions tamely. Popular uprisings, affirming the intensely felt right of the community to its subsistence, were the most striking and probably the most effective mode of resistance, for they gave local officials (who often condoned these eruptions if they did not actually instigate them) a powerful pretext to take drastic action to marshal supplies. Administrative resistance took the form of legal harassment of Paris suppliers (the publication of local ordinances and sentences barring them from the trade or otherwise crippling them); procedural harassment (long delays at the marketplace, inordinately complex registration and verification stipulations); requisition of Paris-bound merchandise; the elaboration of clandestine circuits of local supply and reserves.

More often than not, however, Parisian and local police found ways to get along—at least in "normal" times. The Parisian authorities overcame their contempt for their local counterparts because they needed their help in managing the metropolitan supply system. And much as Parisian infringement was resented in bad times, an intense Parisian demand was welcomed in other circumstances because it usually contributed powerfully to local prosperity. The Paris police endorsed the practice of the marketplace at the local level, provided the hometown authorities were willing to make certain exceptions for Paris traffic.[26] Such a strategy enabled the local officials to keep control over the behavior of local suppliers and to offer a whole range of commercial

25. Guillemin to procurator general, 4 October 1740, BN, Coll. Joly 1123, fols. 177–78.
26. The fiscal and venal benefits of focusing exchange on the official market site were in some cases considerable. Rarely did these material incentives take priority over political and social concerns in shaping the conduct of the local police.

services to Paris buyers. At the same time it permitted Paris merchants who preferred to operate outside the limits of the local market site (but in the service of the Paris marketplace) to conduct their business. Like their Parisian counterparts, local authorities tried to strike a balance between the requirements of police and those of commerce.

CHAPTER 2

Provisioning Paris: The Goods

*T*he "commodity of first necessity" that mobilized the police and the people of Paris was not just any cereal susceptible to conversion into bread. It was wheat—more or less exclusively. More precisely, it was the *sanior pars* of this noble grain reduced into a rather white flour. Parisians of all ranks expected to eat a loaf of high quality. Provisioning Paris implied a whole range of concerns beyond the crude imperative of achieving "abundance."

The Superiority of Wheat

In eighteenth-century France the use of the word *blé* or *bled* caused considerable confusion. "*Blé,* I mean all the grains," said a priest commenting on the terrible scarcity of 1709. "When one speaks of *blés* in the plural," said Malouin, one of the leading subsistence authorities, "one includes all the grains used to make bread, to wit, the wheats, the ryes, the barleys, etc." Malouin and the jurist Jean-Baptiste Denisart agreed, however, that "the *blé* par excellence" was wheat. "The *blé* in our language," wrote Voltaire, who liked to be taken for a specialist in both subjects, "is devoted to wheat."[1]

1. "L'Hiver de 1709," *Magasin pittoresque,* 24th year (1856): 50; Paul-Jacques Malouin, *Description et détails des arts du meunier, du vermicelier et du boulenger* (Paris, 1779); Jean-Baptiste Denisart, *Collection de décisions nouvelles et de notions relatives à la jurisprudence actuelle* (Paris, 1777): 1:262; Voltaire to Frederick II, 1751 (no. 2238), in François-Marie Arouet de Voltaire, *Oeuvres complètes de Voltaire,* ed. L. Moland (Paris, 1877–85), 5:276.

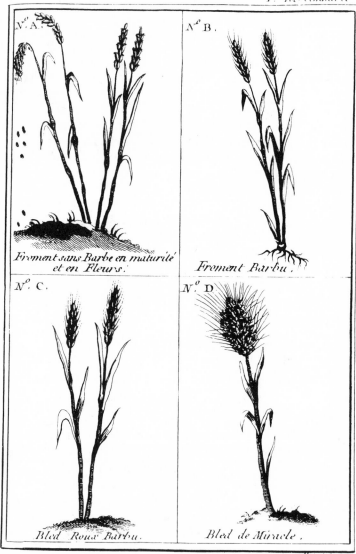

Types of wheat (Louis Joseph Bellepierre de Neuve-Eglise,
*L'Agronomie et l'industrie, ou les principes de l'agriculture, du
commerce et des arts.* Paris, 1761)

Historians quite rightly correlate the extension of the wheat frontier with the dramatic changes of the nineteenth century: modernization, industrialization, democratization, the spread of higher living standards among the poorer sectors of the population. But eighteenth-century Paris was a traditional, preindustrial, royal city filled with vast numbers of poor people who, like their more fortunate compatriots in *hôtels particuliers* and their less fortunate brethren in jails and hospitals, ate wheaten bread.

Nor was Paris singular. The experts, from Arthur Young through Phyllis Deane and W. A. Cole, recount that virtually all Londoners consumed wheat, and by the second half of the century perhaps 70 percent of all Englishmen were on a wheaten diet. Genevans insisted on wheat and so doubtless did the inhabitants of many other European metropolises. As for the rest of France, reported Duhamel du Monceau, a leading agronomist, "the inhabitants of the cities know wheaten bread almost exclusively." "The people here," claimed an official at Toulouse, "know no other food than wheat; it would not be possible to make them adopt another." The situation was the same at Bordeaux, although it is not clear for either city whether the wheat line extended to the lower reaches of the population. On the other hand, it is certain that relatively few people in the rural areas commonly used wheat. Characteristically, the grain-producing regions, Polish as well as French, cultivated wheat for export and survived on secondary cereals or worse.[2]

The abandoning of inferior grain for the grain of the Host, the grain of cleanliness as well as holiness, of opulence as well as nourishment, might fruitfully be viewed as one of the most significant aspects of the experience not of urbanization but of being urbanized.[3] What it meant in psychological, psychosomatic, and physiological terms to change material life-styles, in the short run and across several generations, remains undetermined. On the

2. Arthur Young, *Travels in France during the Years 1787, 1788, & 1789*, ed. Constantia Maxwell (Cambridge, 1929), p. 314; W. J. Ashley, *The Bread of Our Forefathers* (Oxford, 1928), pp. 1–2, 22, 42–44, 47; John Burnett, *Plenty and Want: A Social History of Diet in England* (London, 1966), p. 3; William Alan Cole and Phyllis Deane, *British Economic Growth*, 2d ed. (London, 1967), pp. 62–63; Anne-Marie Piuz, "Alimentation populaire et sous-alimentation au 17e siècle: Le Cas de Genève," in Jean-Jacques Hemardinquer, ed., *Pour une histoire de l'alimentation* (Paris, 1970), p. 139; Henri-Louis Duhamel du Monceau, *Traité de la conservation des grains et en particulier du froment* (Paris, 1753), p. 2; abbé Noël Chomel, *Dictionnaire oeconomique* (Paris, 1767), 2:141; Georges Jorré, "Le Commerce des grains et la minoterie à Toulouse," *Revue géographique des Pyrénées et du Sud-ouest*, p. 42; Joseph Benzacar, *Le Pain à Bordeaux* (Bordeaux, 1905); Joseph Stouff, *Ravitaillement et alimentation en Provence aux XIVe et XVe siècles* (Paris, 1970), pp. 48–50. Cf. Alexander Gerschenkron, *Bread and Democracy in Germany* (Berkeley, 1943), p. 81; Fernand Braudel, *Civilisation matérielle et capitalisme (XVe–XVIIIe siècles)* (Paris, 1967), p. 105; Georges d'Avenel, "Paysans et ouvriers depuis sept siècles: Les Frais de nourriture aux temps modernes," *Revue des deux mondes* 148 (15 July 1898): 425.

3. On the wheaten quality of Eucharist bread, see H.-E. Jacob, *Six Thousand Years of Bread: Its Holy and Unholy History*, trans. R. and C. Winston (Garden City, N.Y., 1944), p. 163; William E. Addis and Thomas Arnold, *A Catholic Dictionary* (London, 1951), p. 328.

popular level wheat was the pendant to the *luxe* denounced by so many moralists as the plague of the cities. One wonders, too, about the impact upon people when wheat privileges were revoked. What happened, for example, to the soldiers of Louis XIV who threatened to mutiny in 1665 because their bread consisted of rye instead of wheat once they left the army? "The people of the big cities," complained a revolutionary official, "unlike those of the countryside, do not know how to shape their tastes to their needs."[4] A group of Parisian workers, lured to Lyon by higher wages in the last third of the century, returned disgusted "saying that they absolutely could not accustom themselves to the usage of the overly dark bread ordinarily made there." Thus, noted Parmentier, "we can see the advantage of procuring for the people a more agreeable and more salubrious aliment" which would "continue more than one can imagine to settling foreigners, preventing emigration, and vivifying industry."[5]

In Paris wheat was taken for granted. The rich hinterland around the capital—the plain of France, the Vexin, the Valois, the Brie, the Beauce and so on—focused on production of wheat for the Paris market. When necessary, the capital drew wheat from the more distant provinces and from abroad. Paris consumed very little rye, maslin, or barley; "Paris wants only pure wheats," reported a memorandum to the controller-general in the early part of the century. Consumers took their delicacy (and vanity) one step further: they demanded not only wheaten bread, but a relatively fine and white loaf. Whiteness was the universal symbol of goodness, wholesomeness, and healthfulness. Already in the first part of the eighteenth century, "the small [Parisian] artisan eats a more beautiful loaf than the best bourgeois of the provinces." The Parisian middling or *bis-blanc* loaf was whiter than the top white elsewhere in the realm. Journeymen and day workers commonly ate the *bis-blanc* and even the white; the market in the capital for dark bread *(bis)* was extremely limited. White bread was not yet "whiter in the popular quarters than in the rich ones," as it would become in the nineteenth century. But already "the worker, who ordinarily eats his bread with little else to accompany it, is more insistent on its quality than the well-off consumer who has delicious morsels to go along with his bread." (Among its virtues, fine white bread sopped up the poor man's broth much better than lesser wheaten loaves.) And the eighteenth-century worker anticipated his nineteenth-century counterpart in his willingness to pay the same price as the bourgeois for a bread of quality: "Am I not as good as he?" asked the worker, in justification of his prodigality and his amour-propre.[6]

---

4. Du Vaucelle, "Offrande civique," ca. 1789, AN, F^{10} 215–16.

5. Antoine-Augustin Parmentier, *Mémoire sur les avantages que la province de Languedoc peut retirer de ses grains* (Paris, 1787), p. 400.

6. "Mémoire sur le prix de bled en la généralité d'Orléans," n.d., AN, G^7 1709. Cf. Abbé Henri-Alexandre Tessier, "Consommation de Paris," *Encyclopédie méthodique, Agriculture* (Paris, 1793), 3:472n; anon., "Mémoire sur le prix du bled en la généralité d'Orléans," AN,

Legrand d'Aussy, perhaps the most modern social historian of the old regime, claimed that rye could make a bread "which is as white as the bread of wheat." In the Auvergne and the Lyonnais it was believed that women were prettier and fresher than elsewhere because they ate only rye. Dr. Le Camus of the Paris Faculty of Medicine praised rye for its vivifying and laxative qualities. A number of fastidious Parisians made it a practice to abandon wheaten bread at regular intervals in favor of rye. "By this means," according to Le Camus, "they refresh their bowels and empty the intestinal tract of the impurities which may have collected there." The mass of Parisians, however, refused to touch rye. "We know the difficulty of getting Parisians to taste rye," remarked the procurator general. In times of dearth Delamare, the police theorist and commissaire, suggested producing rye to take the pressure off wheat, but he acknowledged that it would be necessary to "force the bakers" to accept it. In 1725 the flour merchants refused to buy rye because "this sort of flour is not appropriate for Paris." To counteract the prejudice against it, the commissaire Duplessis tried to arrange a special rye sale day at the Halle, as the capital's inland grain market was called. Contending that "rye is an excellent food," the brilliant Swiss banker Thellusson, who served as victualer to the capital in the dearth of 1738–41, proposed importing considerable quantities from abroad and insinuating it gradually in combination with wheat in the Parisian bread. The procurator general allowed that "there are extremities when anything is good," but he and the controller-general warned that Parisians would resist it stubbornly even in bad times.[7]

Barley, the bread of Christ and of the Roman gladiators, elicited no more favor than rye. It too was said to have certain excellent features. As a grain it never overheated and taken as bread it refreshed and cleansed the body, afforded protection against scurvy, and appeased the gouty without indispos-

---

G[7] 1704; comité des subsistances, 21 December 1816, cited by Armand Husson, *Les Consommations de Paris* (Paris, 1875), p. 146; *Enquête sur la boulangerie du département de la Seine, ou Recueil de dépositions concernant les commerces du blé, de la farine et du pain* (Paris, 1859), pp. 14, 56, 73, 117, 213, 308–9, 357, 426, 500, 533, 642, 654, 768. In the mid-nineteenth century it was generally believed that wheat had not been available to the eighteenth-century working population. See *Enquête de 1859 sur la révision de la législation des céréales* (Paris, 1859), 2:275.

7. Pierre-J.-B. Legrand d'Aussy, *Histoire de la vie privée des françois* (1783), ed. J.-B.-B. de Roquefort (Paris, 1815), 1:150; Le Camus, "Mémoire sur le bled," *Journal économique* (November 1753): 147–48; *Dictionnaire universel françois et latin, vulgairement appelé Dictionnaire de Trévoux . . .* (Paris, 1771), 6:452; procurator general to Marville, 15 September 1740, Bibliothèque de l'Arsenal (hereafter Arsenal), manuscrits de la Bastille (hereafter ms. Bast.) 10277; procurator general to Orry, 15 September 1740, BN, Coll. Joly 1121, fols. 71–72; Nicolas Delamare, "Propositions," BN, ms. fr. 21635, fol. 2; Cleret to Hérault, 1 October 1725, Arsenal, ms. Bast. 10270, fol. 329; Duplessis to procurator general, 17 September 1725, BN, Coll. Joly 1117, fols. 205–6; Thellusson to procurator general, 26 October 1740, BN, Coll. Joly 1109, fols. 50–51. On the role of rye, cf. Marc Bloch, "La Transformation des techniques," *Journal de psychologie normale et pathologique* 41 (January–March 1948): 104–15.

ing them. In eighteenth-century France, however, "only the most unfortunate among the peasants dared to eat it." Frenchmen called barley "the bread of dearth." Even more than rye, barley was not intrinsically conducive to good baking, although the bakers deserved reproach for refusing to apply their cunning to its improvement. The dough dried quickly, crumbled easily, and produced a bread that was generally "very bad" unless dosed with large quantities of wheat. The "little people" of Paris and the environs ate barley grudgingly and in piddling quantities during the crisis of 1725, and Controller-general Orry sternly told Parisians to consider barley "precious" in 1740, but it remained a cereal of desperation. Generally the police did not even include barley in the annual statements of Parisian provisioning, because it was a "small object" which "does not serve ordinarily as food for man."[8]

From the few extant statistics on Paris supply, it is clear that the capital absorbed only small quantities of nonwheaten grain. In the dearth year 1725, the Halle offered 8,232 muids of wheat, 481 muids of rye, and 93 muids of maslin, a mixture of wheat and rye. In 1726, still a crisis year, the Halle marketed 7,877 muids of wheat, 360 muids of rye, 43 muids of maslin, and 1,072 muids of barley. At the port market called the Grève in the same year, there were 13,903 muids of wheat, 155 muids of rye, and 1,644 muids of barley. In 1733, a far better index for "normal" times, the Halle exposed 6,423 muids of wheat, 451 muids of rye, 17 muids of maslin, and no barley. Although bakers and other individuals may have brought in rye and barley directly from the countryside to their shops and homes, in the hundreds of baker after-death inventories and sealings *(scellés),* bankruptcies, and commercial litigations I have examined, I have found only a handful who held cereals other than wheat.[9]

Does one need to appeal to taste and mentality to account for the phenomenon of wheat consumption in Paris and other big cities? It could perhaps be ventured that the choice of wheat is an income effect of higher urban living standards, even of the laboring poor. Income elasticity of demand for wheat, as a substitute for inferior grain, would be considered quite high. Another possible explanation calls attention to the equal bulkiness of wheat and (say) rye. The markups per unit value for transport and transaction costs would be about the same. Since rye is lower priced to begin with, this markup

8. Legrand d'Aussy, *Vie privée,* 1:127–29; Edme Béguillet, *Traité des subsistances et des grains qui servent à la nourriture de l'homme* (Paris, 1780), pp. 91–94; Guéry to Hérault, 5 October 1725, Arsenal, ms. Bast. 10270, fol. 239; Orry to procurator general, 17 September 1740, BN, Coll. Joly 1121, fol. 75; Coll. Joly 1116, fols. 2–3; Le Camus, "Mémoire sur le bled," p. 148.

9. Bibliothèque de l'Institut, mss. 513, 514, 521. A Paris setier consists of 1.56 hectoliters or 4.43 U.S. bushels. A muid, which contains 12 setiers, consists of 18.72 hectoliters or 53.12 U.S. bushels. A setier is the equivalent of 2 mines or 12 (French, eighteenth-century) bushels. See Ronald E. Zupko, *French Weights and Measures before the Revolution: A Dictionary of Provincial and Local Units* (Bloomington, 1978).

equality makes wheat relatively cheaper and could be thought to encourage its substitution for the inferior cereal, apart from taste considerations. We lack the data to test either hypothesis. Neither seems applicable to the tens of thousands of Parisians who were "objectively" and comparatively too poor for wheat. Their claim on wheat had nothing to do with the market. Nor can either argument explain the tenacity of resistance to substitution away from wheat even in calamitous times, when victualers such as Thellusson and philosophes such as Voltaire deplored the "dainty refinement" of urban consumers. Wheat had an institutional anchoring in the capital that only partly reflected economic considerations. Paris invested all Parisians regardless of rank with a sort of cereal franchise. Parisians reckoned the right of wheat-eating and the status it conferred as indefeasible.

Modern authorities ascribe the supremacy of wheat not to its nutritional properties, which are similar to those of the other cereals (wheat holding a certain advantage in quantity and quality of proteins), but to its unique ability to be made into a light, voluminous, finely textured, and savory loaf (owing to the fact that its proteins take the form of gluten, the elastic substance that enables the dough to retain the carbon dioxide generated by yeast fermentation). Rye is the only other grain that contains gluten-forming proteins, but they are incomparably weaker.[10] Eighteenth-century cereals experts emphasized that wheat was not a frill or a delicacy but the most suitable element for the nourishment of man. No other foodstuff was comparable to wheat, claimed the agronomist Poncelet, because none contained "in a more satisfactory proportion all the principles analogous or identical to those which constitute the human body." The significance of this somewhat banal assertion, which could hardly have surprised the simple consumers of the time who knew from instinct and experience the marvels of wheat, is that it was made with scientific authority. "A thing which will always appear astonishing to the eyes of the man accustomed to think and reflect," wrote Parmentier, "is that we have lived centuries without having the curiosity to seek to know the nature of the substance that nourishes us." How ironic and sad, he noted, that savants have devoted volumes to exotic substances like Virginian snakeroot, Peruvian bark, and Brazilian root, while "the simplest and most familiar things . . . whose usage is continually indispensable" remained a mystery. It was only in the past forty years, Parmentier contended, that man had begun to

10. Wheat contains less fat than barley and oats, slightly more than rye; much more niacin than rye and oats, slightly more than barley; less riboflavin than the other cereals; more thiamine than rye, less than oats and barley; more fiber than rye, less than oats and barley. Wheat scores higher in Total Digestible Nutrients, but shares roughly comparable mineral values with the other cereals. On these matters, see W. J. Fance and B. H. Wragg, *Up to Date Breadmaking* (London, 1968), pp. 12–13; Y. Pomeranz, ed., *Wheat: Chemistry and Technology* (St. Paul, 1978), pp. 9–10; F. B. Morrisson, *Feeds and Feeding* (Ithaca, 1956); H. B. Lockart and R. O. Nesheim, "Nutritional Quality of Cereal Grains," in *Cereals '78: Better Nutrition for the Millions* (St. Paul, 1978), p. 217.

study wheat and reconstruct its "natural history."[11] As a result of recent discoveries in botany and food chemistry and the interminable debates on the nature of digestion, Poncelet, Parmentier, and the other subsistence scientists believed that for the first time they could explain why wheat provided the body with all of its necessities in excellent quality and quantity, and why its flour was weightier, better-rising, and more nutritious than that of any other cereal. Once they fathomed its secrets, they believed they could apply this knowledge to the improvement of agricultural, conservation, milling, and baking techniques and thus contribute, even more directly than philosophers and reformers, to the happiness of mankind.[12]

Choosing Grain and Flour

Whether, as Parmentier contended, a baker could not make consistently good bread if he were not familiar with the properties of all the components of the wheat berry is surely debatable. There is no question, however, that neither a baker nor a miller nor a merchant could have successfully operated his business without a thorough knowledge of the criteria of excellence of grain, wheat, and flour.[13] In order to meet his commercial needs, retain his clients, and turn a profit each had to be extremely attentive to the quality of the merchandise he bought and sold. First, he had to be familiar with quality as it varied in space and time. Ideally, according to Béguillet, the buyer should appraise the soil of the peasant farmers (laboureurs) from whom he habitually purchased and visit the wheat while it was still in the ground. Such an examination would reveal the grade of the wheat and its likely yield into flour and enable him to avoid falling prey to fraud. It would also allow him to plan his buying schedule and itinerary ahead of time.[14] Few buyers had the time, the inclination, or the freedom to operate in this manner.

In lieu of direct acquaintance with a given farm or canton, however, all buyers could be expected to know the reputation of wheat and flour produced in a given area or province. The best wheat in France, many experts affirmed, came from the Beauce, followed by the Ile-de-France, the Brie, Picardy, and Champagne. To find the elite of French wheats, Bucquet looked far beyond the Parisian basin to Provence. He also applauded the grain of the Dauphiné

11. Polycarpe Poncelet, *Histoire naturelle du froment* (Paris, 1779), pp. 232–47. The Yale University library now holds this copy. Antoine-Augustin Parmentier, *Le Parfait Boulanger, ou Traité complet sur la fabrication et le commerce du pain* (Paris, 1778), pp. 9–10; Béguillet, *Traité des subsistances,* pp. 16–17. Cf. Feyeux, "Un nouveau livre des métiers," *La Science sociale,* 2d year, 4 (October 1887): 325.

12. Parmentier, *Parfait Boulanger,* pp. 13–14; Poncelet, *Histoire naturelle,* p. xxii; *Journal économique* (April 1751): 3–24. For the debate over the chemical composition of wheat and flour, and over the significance of bran, see below, chap. 11.

13. Parmentier, *Parfait Boulanger,* pp. 24–25.

14. Béguillet, *Traité des subsistances,* pp. 114–47.

(whose bread in the sixteenth century was decried for causing vertigo) and of the Quercy. Bucquet placed the Brie ahead of the Beauce and also spoke highly of the grain of the Valois and the upper Soissonnais.[15] Dr. Malouin called the wheat of Languedoc the best and of the Nantes area the worst, while preferring the Beauce to the Brie because it was higher and drier ground.[16] Dr. Le Camus maintained that the wheats of the Ile-de-France surpassed the finest productions of the Brie and the Beauce.[17]

While almost all of the wheat-producing hinterland enjoyed a solid reputation for quality, there were notable discrepancies. Wheat from the Vitry area, for example, habitually sold for between four and six livres less than that from Brie and "France" (around Dammartin), the result, according to quality tests ordered by the Paris lieutenant general of police, of a striking difference of yield into flour.[18] Evaluation also depended upon vantage point and habit. The Troyes bakers and millers preferred Champagne wheat to the grain from Provins, which they found fatty and difficult to treat under the stone and in the kneading trough; the Paris bakers paid more for Provins wheat than for any other in the region and regarded the Champagne grain as mediocre.[19] Bucquet recommended the flour produced around Châlons-sur-Marne as the finest available. Malouin ranked the flour of Versailles, Senlis, Gonesse, Melun, and Pontoise as the most esteemed and Picardy's as the worst.[20] The Paris bakers had special praise for the flour of Melun. Every trader had his own sense of geographical hierarchy.[21] Certain Gonesse bakers favored Chartrain wheat despite the presence of the rich grain of "France" in their own marketplace. Similarly, a number of Pontoise mealmen often made long forays into the Brie instead of drawing on readily accessible grain from the Vexin and the Soissonnais.

Time was another factor seriously affecting quality. Millers and bakers preferred "old" wheat to "new." New grain required time, as Bucquet put it in the vernacular of the métier, to "faire son effet," to stabilize, and to ripen.[22] Allowed to rest and sweat in the granary at least through the winter or until the following crop year, new wheat improved dramatically in quality.[23] Old

15. Legrand d'Aussy, *Vie privée*, 1:49–50.

16. Malouin, *Description et détails des arts*, pp. 18–19.

17. Le Camus, "Mémoire sur le bled," pp. 124–25.

18. Assembly of police, 22 January 1739, BN, ms. fr. 11356, fols. 382–84.

19. BN, Coll. Joly 1743, fol. 131 and 1314, fol. 50.

20. Malouin, *Description et détails des arts*, pp. 85–86. Cf. Jacques Savary des Bruslons, *Dictionnaire portatif de commerce* (Copenhagen, 1761–62), 2:504.

21. "Mémoire des boulangers de la ville et des fauxbourgs de Paris," BN, Coll. Joly 1314, fol. 73.

22. César Bucquet, *Observations intéressantes et amusantes du Sieur Bucquet, ancien meunier de l'Hôpital Général, à MM. Parmentier et Cadet* (Paris, 1783), p. 46n.

23. Edme Béguillet, *Discours sur la mouture économique* (Lyon, 1773), pp. 50–51; Malouin, *Description et détails des arts*, pp. 20–21. In his edition of Malouin's *Description*, the Swiss writer-agronomist Bertrand scoffed at the notion that wheat improves with age.

wheat had a finer appearance, less humidity and less bran, and was more nourishing. Millers found new grain much more difficult to grind than the old. Moist and fatty, the new tended to mash instead of break, clogging the bolters and leaving a sticky residue on the stones that required that they be dressed every four or five days. A windmiller in the faubourg St.-Marcel claimed he could treat five muids of old wheat in twenty-four hours but only three of the new. Old wheat yielded at least 5 percent more flour than new—in some years, noted Malouin, the difference could be as much as a third.[24] In the early sixties Malisset showed the directors of the General Hospital that the increased productivity and quality of the old wheat would more than compensate for the costs of storage. The results proved somewhat embarrassing for the administration, for the old wheat not only produced more bread but also made it "too white relative to the color prescribed by the rule of the Hospital."[25]

New grain was also widely believed to be the "cause of [certain] epidemic diseases." Parmentier likened the effect of consuming fresh grain to eating fruit before it was ripe. Both the grain and the fruit were still in a state of "movement," emitting a "pernicious gas" and causing the stomach to ache, the bowels to loosen, the blood to inflame, and the body to become feverish. Intestinal ills were especially common in the early fall, when the poorest people, bereft of other resources, devoured freshly cut grain; whole families

"Experience says precisely the contrary," he noted. He is the only writer I have found who contested the conventional wisdom. Paul-Jacques Malouin, *Description des arts du meunier, du vermicellier, et du boulanger,* ed. Jean E. Bertrand (Neufchâtel, 1771), p. 25. Eighteenth-century bakers and millers must have been deeply impressed with the results of aging, for it was by no means risk free. Inadequate storage invited overheating and insect infestation; and it added to overhead.

Today scientists ascribe the superiority of aged wheat or flour to a strengthening of the gluten that results from the slow process of fat hydrolysis. Sweating also seems to improve quality by speeding up the biological process (providing the moisture content is never high enough to induce mold growth). The yellow tinge of freshly ground flour, historically reproved by consumers, tends to fade toward white over time. Dough from new flour is rather sticky and difficult to handle. Today bakers rely increasingly on chemical bleaching and maturing to lighten color and improve baking quality. A growing body of research indicates that biochemical and enzymatic changes occur during storage (or aging) which produce a more desirable crumb structure in the loaf. Other evidence suggests that the chemical and physical changes attendant upon short-time storage (up to two weeks) have little impact on baking procedure. See Natalie P. Kozmin, "The Aging of Wheat Flour and the Nature of the Process," *Cereal Chemistry* 12 (1935): 165–71; Samuel A. Matz, ed., *Bakery Technology and Engineering* (Westport, Conn., 1960), pp. 13–17; C. O. Swanson, *Wheat and Flour Quality* (Minneapolis, 1938), pp. 12, 15, 105; D. B. Pratt, Jr., "Chemical and Baking Changes Which Occur in Bulk Flour during Short-Term Storage," *Cereal Science Today* 2 (1957): 191–95. For their guidance in this domain I am indebted to professors Lamartine Hood and Mark Sorrells of the College of Agriculture and Life Sciences at Cornell University.

24. Cleret to lieutenant of police, 28 September 1725, Arsenal, ms. Bast. 10279; état des Moulins, ca. 1725, BN, Coll. Joly 1116, fol. 228; Béguillet, *Traité des subsistances,* pp. 440–43; César Bucquet, *Manuel du meunier* (Paris, 1790), p. 106; Malouin, *Description et détails des arts,* p. 278.

25. Brillon Duperron, *Considérations sur la mouture,* n.p., n.d.

were said to have died from eating bread made from it. The infamous *soudure* period was not simply the time between the depletion of one year's stores and the harvesting of the new crop, but also between the point when nothing remained and when the new grain became usable. Dearth, of course, upset the normal rhythm and accelerated the clock. Rare and dear as a result of a short crop, grain also suffered in quality because of the haste with which it was processed. The buyer paid much more for much less. Ordinarily, except in years following extremely wet wheat harvests, the *mercuriale,* or market price register, reflected the preference for old over new wheat.[26]

Flour, like wheat, acquired optimal quality only after aging. For best results, according to the eighteenth-century practitioners, flour should repose for a month to six weeks. Under the tremendous pressure and speed of the stones, the flour tended to overheat and the glutinous matter, responsible for giving the dough its tenacity and elasticity, suffered some damage. To be effective in bread making, it needed time to recover. After rest, the flour was drier and weighed less but it drank more water and yielded more bread (Parmentier estimated twelve pounds more bread per 325-pound sack of flour).[27] Freshly ground flour bore the odor of the stones, which it transmitted to the bread, and had less body than older flour. Over time flour became perceptibly whiter and more alluring as the carotin content, which gave it a yellowish tinge, oxidized. The Paris bakers firmly believed that repose perfected the flour but they noted that it was not always commercially feasible. The large number of bakers who struggled to survive day to day obviously could not afford to buy flour in advance and age it. The flour merchants preferred to sell fresh from the stone because they needed money and wanted a rapid turnover and because they tended to lose through evaporation, turning, and cleaning what the bakers gained during repose. The jurors of the baker guild reported in the late sixties that the flours labeled as best at the Halle were fresh.[28] Twentieth-century food scientists developed a chemical process that artificially aged the flour overnight. Lyrically named *agene,* their invention was linked to the occurrence of nervous disorders, ulcers, coronaries, and decreased fertility and after several decades of use was banned in the 1950s in the United States and in Britain.[29]

Wheat and flour had certain characteristics that enabled the perspicacious

26. Bucquet, *Observations intéressantes,* p. 46n; *Journal économique* (March 1772): 97–98; Parmentier, *Parfait Boulanger,* pp. xxvii–xxviii, 137–38; Poncelet, *Histoire naturelle,* pp. 173–78; Malouin, *Description et détails des arts,* pp. 93–94; mémoire, ca. 1725, Arsenal, ms. Bast. 10270, fols. 313–14; mémoire, ca. 1770, BHVP, série 118, cote provisoire 1482; mémoire des marchands de bled, ca. 1737, BN, Coll. Joly 1314, fol. 44.

27. Parmentier, *Mémoire sur les avantages,* pp. 412, 427.

28. "Observations des jurés boulangers," August 1769, AN, Y 12618.

29. Ronald Sheppard and Edward Newton, *The Story of Bread* (London, 1957), pp. 74–75; Thomas Jeeves Horder, Charles Dodds, and T. Moran, *Bread: The Chemistry and Nutrition of Flour and Bread, with an Introduction to Their History and Technology* (London, 1954), pp. 93–97.

buyer to determine their relative quality with some degree of exactitude. Known variously as "the head" and "elite" or, in deference to its most influential judges, "wheat for bakers" and "bakeable wheat," wheat of the first quality was generally light yellow or grayish with an almost translucent appearance, slightly convex with a shallow groove, and thin-shelled but hard, weighty, and dry. Hard wheat was more easily ground than soft because its bran separated more readily from the endosperm (the interior bulk of the berry) and the liberated flour was more readily sifted. As a rule, hard wheats were strong wheats, giving bold, full-bodied loaves of fine texture in comparison with the spiritless, dense bread made from weak wheats. Big berries did not command favor over smaller ones; "big wheat, little bread," the maxim went. Second-quality wheat, called "merchantable" *(marchand)* or "middle," was darker, more opaque, a bit longer, narrower, and thicker-skinned. The third-quality or "common" wheat seemed dirty, was somewhat speckled, lacked vivacity, and was longer, thinner, lighter, and burdened with an extremely thick seedcoat that indicated a superabundance of bran.[30]

Other senses helped the buyer confirm the judgment of his eyes and evaluate the different grades. When chewed, a few grains of good quality wheat formed a small pellet of dough—we would call it gluten—which was tough and elastic like rubber but not sticky. A fruity taste charmed the tongue, and an agreeable odor wafted to the nose testifying to the absence of insect infestation, fermentation, or certain kinds of disease. The wheat was good if it "rang" when one tossed it in one's hand; if a handful of grain spilled out easily and rapidly; if a hand plunged into a sack of wheat reached bottom smoothly. Warmed by the pocket and smoothed by friction in the pouch, wheat sold on sample, even if it was a faithful sample of the batch, often gave a misleading impression.[31]

Sensory examination, however, even when performed by artful and meticulous bakers, was not by itself sufficient guarantee of quality. Although grain was commonly sold by measure, the most reliable test of goodness was weight. Provided it did not fail egregiously on the other counts, the heaviest weight of a given volume was "always the best." Weight could vary sharply from year to year and from grade to grade. Béguillet put the three-quality range at 240-230-220 pounds the setier, measure of Paris, for a normal year, though most experts felt that the elite could reach 250 pounds. At Etampes in early 1769 following a harvest of extremely uneven yield, the head weighed 241 pounds, the middle 236, and the common 233. At the same moment at Pontoise, the head stood at 229, the middle at 223, and the third quality at 220. In that year, wrote the lieutenant general of Provins, "few [wheats] are found which give the setier the weight of 240 pounds." A police official at Etampes claimed that in ordinary years the elite could mount to 260 pounds and that in

30. Béguillet, *Traité des subsistances,* p. 423.
31. Ibid., pp. 148ff.; Parmentier, *Parfait Boulanger,* pp. 119–29, and *Mémoire sur les avantages,* p. 122; Malouin, *Description et détails des arts,* pp. 18–19.

extraordinary times it could rise to 270. In the registers of millers and bakers appear elites fixed at 258, 260, and 262.[32]

To discriminate among different grades of flour was more difficult. The goodness of flour did not depend merely on the quality of the wheat from which it emerged; the milling operation could transform an excellent wheat into a miserable flour or a mediocre wheat into a flour that was quite passable. The different styles of milling produced a confusion of names to characterize the different grades, which were not strictly logical and which varied in meaning from place to place. In one popular classification scheme the "flower of the flour" came first, followed by the "white flour after the flower," the fine middlings, and the gross middlings. But in the milling system called "economic process," the flower was the second grade behind the "flour of the wheat" and it was called "first middlings." The most forthright schedule, and the most widely used in the books of Paris bakers, labeled the first quality "white," the second "mid-white" (or, if one is more cynically inclined, "mid-dark" [*bis-blanc*] or, more tellingly, *blanc-bourgeois,* an in-between flour that, like the social status, partook of two worlds), and the third "dark" *(bis).* This ranking was time- and placebound. There is some evidence to suggest, for example, that the Paris mid-white was whiter and the dark darker at the end of the century than at the beginning, and that the mid-white was often comparable to the elite whites made elsewhere. Nor was the best bread always made of the very finest flour. Middling flour, because of its high gluten content, made a remarkably "savory, light, and agreeable" bread. Although it was difficult to work with, "rough" flour, properly treated by the baker, produced a lustier bread than many of the soft and light flours of top grade. Mixing flour was a far more delicate operation than combining wheats, but a skillful baker could profitably join a rough flour of the Beauce with a Picard flour that had "less body," provided he gave them sufficient time to assimilate before kneading.

The best flour, the one most sought after by bakers regardless of nomenclature, was of a golden white or light lemon color, fine in appearance, dry, weighty, with no perceptible bran, and without any striking odor. The taste test was not always decisive, because a dark flour, given its greater germ content, could be more pleasant than the first grade. As a rule the baker discerned both the piquant taste of salt and the sweet presence of sugar in the best flour. Good flour did not pour out of a hole made in the sack, a test that the mealmen did not appreciate. When a knife was drawn over poorly milled or dirty flour, the surface lacked smoothness and a certain wooliness appeared as the refuse particles came to the top. A buyer with sensitive fingers could

32. Béguillet, *Traité des subsistances,* pp. 331–32; Parmentier, *Parfait Boulanger,* p. 122; Aube's register, Archives Seine-Paris, D5B⁶ 2114; essai, January 1769, AN, Y 12618; Colin to Sartine, 8 January 1769, and Picart to Sartine, 8 January 1769, AN, Y 12618; Duhamel du Monceau, *Traité de la conservation,* p. 275; Nicolas-François Dupré de St.-Maur, *Essai sur les monnaies, ou Réflexions sur le rapport entre l'argent et les denrées* (Paris, 1746), pp. 48–55; "Avis oeconomique sur la boulangerie," *Journal économique* (September 1757): 55, 60–61; Boullemer, lieutenant general of Alençon, mémoire, July 1765, BN, ms. 11347, fol. 198.

distinguish the flour of soft wheat from hard and could identify the kind of grinding process that had been used, thus obtaining crucial information about the baking qualities of the merchandise. A handful of good flour squeezed in the palm formed a sort of pellet instead of sliding out. A "dead" or slippery feel could betray a fungus contamination. Experienced buyers could detect "a little noise" when they rubbed high-grade flour between their fingers.

Bakers had most confidence in the dough or *boulette* test. If a given amount of flour absorbed about one-third of its weight in water and produced a dough that rapidly became firm without separating, it was very likely to be excellent; if the "ball" softened, broke, or stuck to the fingers, caveat emptor! At the Paris market the bakers were assisted in conducting the dough test by the sack holders, women who occupied one of the many marginal employments from which dayworkers tried to eke out a living. Covertly rewarded by flour merchants and brokers for steering business their way, the holders reached into the sacks in behalf of the bakers and made the *boulette* with water from a bottle which they kept behind their aprons. Some of the more enterprising or desperate sack holders, like Marie, colorfully nicknamed "End-of-the-Candle," also kept a large pouch under their aprons in which they stuffed handfuls of flour when no one was looking.

Parmentier felt that the dough test, upon which the bakers relied so heavily, could be extremely misleading, especially if the baker did not take enough time, if he failed to work the dough well, or if he did not compensate for temperature extremes. He proposed a supplementary test, which won the approval of some of the leading bakers of the capital, in which the baker tested for gluten content by washing away the starch of a handful of flour under a gentle stream of water. The tester assessed the quality of gluten by stretching its gray-brown rubbery mass and taking note both of how much resistance it gave to stretching and how far it could be stretched before tearing (extensibility). The gluten required for bread making was supposed to be highly resistant and fairly extensible. A weak gluten impaired the dough's ability to retains the gas generated by fermentation for the purpose of expanding it. The capacity to absorb water was also largely dependent on the quality and quantity of gluten and thus served as an indirect measure of flour strength. Although Parmentier remained skeptical of the nutritional value of glutinous matter, its presence was a sure litmus of high flour quality.

Like wheat, flour was generally sold by volume. Flour dealers and bakers lobbied energetically for conversion to weighing as the standard commercial practice. The careful baker weighed each sack of flour at the time of purchase and, if he did not take immediate possession or if the seller delivered it, again at the moment of reception.[33]

33. Poncelet, *Histoire naturelle*, pp. 154–55; Malouin, *Description et détails des arts*, pp. 81–82; Parmentier, *Parfait Boulanger*, pp. xxix, 203–22; Baudeau, *Avis au peuple sur son premier besoin, ou Petits Traités économiques, par l'auteur des "Ephémérides du citoyen,"* deuxième traité, pp. 66–67; abbé Noël Chomel, *Dictionnaire oeconomique*, 4th ed. (Paris,

In the eighteenth-century society of scarcity and mono-consumption, where grain was the measure of all things, quality, in part because it helped determine quantity, was an obsessive preoccupation. Without the benefit of sophisticated technology, traders developed methods and a vocabulary for gauging the relative goodness of merchandise. The tests described above were not the textbook contrivances of scientific literati—although the Parmentiers tried to explain them scientifically and to perfect them—but the everyday practices of businessmen whose success depended upon meeting the standards of their clients, maintaining their reputations, and satisfying the demands of the police. Self-interest, however, was the source of deceit as well as the best guarantee of quality, or what dealers called "loyalty." In addition to natural defects and human negligence, willful adulteration resulted in low-grade goods. When a merchant suffered loss through improper conservation or freight accident, when he proved unable to "repair" grain and flour that had deteriorated, when the demand was intense and hurried or when he was dealing in markets he did not usually frequent, he was sometimes tempted to commit fraud. The most common artifice, easily detected by the attentive buyer, was "to gild the sack" with a layer of excellent grain on top concealing inferior or corrupt goods below. More imaginative beguilers devised "danger-ous preparations" to give "color" and "hand" to anemic wheat. They heated soft wheat to harden its texture, wet the wheat to increase its volume (another reason for the buyer to demand the scale as well as the measure), and cut good wheat with bad. The grain merchants most often suspected of this chicanery were the *blatiers,* small-scale dealers and fly-by-nighters who packed their grain on a mule or two and roved from market to market.[34]

Flour adulteration was more difficult to mask, and often more threatening to the public well-being. Police regulations strictly and repeatedly forbade millers to add bran, barley, peas, beans, "or any other things whatsoever" to the flour. In the eighteenth century, millers and flour merchants discovered the subtle talents of potato and rice for combining more or less inconspicu-ously with flour and swelling output. The most daring and serious frauds entailed the mixture of inedible, even noxious matter. The presidial of Châlons in Champagne sent the miller Pierre Chaillot to the galleys for in-troducing crushed chalk in his flour in 1727. A riot erupted at Clermont in

1740), 1:1096; Louis de Jaucourt, "Farine," in Diderot et al., *Encyclopédie . . .* (Paris, 1751–65), 17:772; AN, Y 9538, 16 February 1725; Arsenal, ms. Bast. 10141, fol. 310 (2 February 1760); Savary des Bruslons, *Dictionnaire portatif de commerce,* 3:2; Harry Snyder, *Bread* (New York, 1930), pp. 194–95, 210, 241–42; Fance and Wragg, *Breadmaking,* pp. 26–28; Garmont's register, Archives Seine-Paris, D5B⁶ 2682 ("Détaille pour le poids de la marchan-dise").

34. Delamare, *Traité de la police,* 2:638; Duchesne, *Code de la police, ou Analyse des règlements de police,* p. 107; M. Reneaume, "Sur la manière de conserver les grains," *Mémoires de l'Académie des sciences,* 1708 (1709), p. 66; BHVP, Collection E. Thomas, ms. série 114, cote provisoire 4804; Diderot et al., *Encyclopédie,* 2:229; *Encyclopédie méthodique,* Agriculture, 2:286; Parmentier, *Parfait Boulanger,* pp. 128–29, and *Mémoire sur les avantages,* p. 124; Béguillet, *Traité des subsistances,* p. 161.

1771 partly as a result of the charge that two millers had added plaster to the flour. Suspicion about adulterated flour reached a pitch during the Revolution. A pamphlet in 1789 condemned the "homicidal alteration of flour" and crowds at the Halle in the summer of 1791 cried "A la lanterne!" upon the discovery of "corrupted flour." Napoleon demonstrated his sensitivity to popular apprehensions and his flair for public relations when he visited a flour storehouse at Corbeil and ordered its contents to be thrown into the Seine, "saying that he would not have it that such unwholesome flour served for the subsistence of Paris." Ingeniously "sophisticated" flour did not reveal itself until the eating or sometimes until it caused illness; the chemical tests formulated by the subsistence scientists to detect foreign matter were too complicated to be of use to the dealer or baker.[35]

The Preoccupation with Quality

The protection of public well-being and health was one of the primary concerns of the police. They combatted air and water pollution, struggled vainly to keep the city clean, and regulated, with a considerable degree of success, all the branches of the food industry. Fish, for example, traveled long distances and spoiled easily. The police set standards for the sale of different varieties, kept track of arrivals, and inspected the fish frequently. They subjected the butchering, cleaning, preparation, and marketing of meat to detailed regulations to assure proper quality. Authorities took special precautions in checking pork shops because "there is nothing dirtier than the pig" and more likely to cause terrible maladies. Chicken dealers could not sell poultry that died of natural causes and roasters could not keep cooked meat for more than one day. Similarly, dealers in butter, eggs, cheese, fruits, and vegetables had to conform to rules and submit to tests geared to assure freshness and goodness.[36]

The police manifested a special interest in grain, the most common and necessary of all foods. It was kept under surveillance and control from the time it was sown until it was transformed into bread. An ordinance of 1697,

35. Nicolas-Toussaint-L. Des Essarts, *Dictionnaire universel de police,* 7:101; BHVP, n.f. 35 380, tome 141, no. 38; AN, AD XI 38; Gazette à la main, lettres Ossolinski, 10 June 1771, BHVP, ms. 628, fol. 161; Jean-Antoine-Nicolas de Caritat, marquis de Condorcet, *Lettre d'un laboureur de Picardie à M. N.*** auteur prohibitif* (Paris, 1775), in E. Daire and G. de Molinari, eds., *Collection des principaux économistes* (1847; reprint ed., Osnabruck, 1966), 14:487; Ch.-L. Chassin, *Les Elections et les cahiers de Paris en 1789 . . .* (Paris, 1888–89), 2:572; *Révolutions de Paris . . .* (20–27 August 1791), pp. 437–38; Léon de Lanzac de Laborie, *Paris sous Napoléon* (Paris, 1908), 5:158; Béguillet, *Traité des subsistances,* pp. 74–76n. On the folkloric fear of flour adulteration, see "Bone Meal Flour," in Walter Barrett, *More Tales from the Fens* (London, 1954), p. 11.

36. Sartine to Grimperel, 14 September 1763, and notes, AN, Y 11289; Des Essarts, *Dictionnaire universel de police,* 1:271–75, 278–79, 349; Delamare, *Traité de la police,* 2:504.

for example, strictly regulated the use of fecal matter for fertilization of wheat land; Dr. Malouin claimed that the odor ultimately found its way to the consumer's table. An older and more general statute proscribed the sale of any grain or flour that was not "good, honest, and vendible, without any mixture, as good below as above, clean of all refuse and straw."[37] Unwilling to take any risks, if there were questions about the merits of any sort of grain or flour, the police banned its use. Thus, an ordinance of 1546 forbade bakers to add reground middlings to the flour used for bread making, a measure that contributed significantly to long-term technological immobility of the milling industry.[38]

The police had two kinds of concern for grain and flour quality. The first concern, as a matter of public health, construed quality negatively. The police wanted to prevent the use of dubious ingredients that could cause grave illnesses. "Next to the air," declared Malouin, first an eminent physician, then a subsistence specialist, "bread is the most common cause of epidemic maladies."[39] In addition to contaminated water and negligent or fraudulent bread making itself, bad grain and flour were the chief reasons for its potential toxicity. Grain that was rotten, too wet, overheated and fermented, too fresh, too old, or adulterated in some fashion was capable of provoking diseases classified as "epidemic" and/or as "popular" both because they were contagious and because they rarely touched the rich, at least not the first time around.[40] With the exception of episodes involving the ergot fungus (the archenemy of rye, which caused horrible sicknesses and frequent mortalities) and of deaths directly attributable to eating replacement foods, the reports of diagnosis and etiology of grain-related diseases were generally vague and

---

37. "Histoire des boulangers," *Magasin pittoresque*, 25th year (1857): 134; Malouin, *Description et détails des arts*, p. 83; Duchesne, *Code de la police*, p. 103; municipal ordinance, 12 February 1732, AN, F[11] 264; A.-J. Sylvestre, *Histoire des professions alimentaires dans Paris et ses environs* (Paris, 1853), pp. 27–28. For procedures in other cities, see Pierre Lefèvre, *Le Commerce des grains et la question du pain à Lille de 1711 à 1789* (Lille, 1925), pp. 88, 101, and Jean Letaconnoux, *Les Subsistances et le commerce des grains en Bretagne au XVIIIe siècle, essai de monographie économique* (Rennes, 1909), p. 103.

38. Edme Béguillet, *Discours sur la mouture économique*, p. 180, and "Mémoire sur les avantages de la mouture économique," Arsenal, ms. 2891; Malouin, *Description et détails des arts*, p. 40; Parmentier, *Parfait Boulanger*, p. 168; John Beckmann, *A History of Inventions and Discoveries*, trans. William Johnston, 3d ed. (London, 1817), 1:262ff.

39. Paul-Jacques Malouin, *Description des arts du meunier, du vermicelier, et du boulenger* . . . (n.p., 1761), p. 3, and "Histoire des maladies épidémiques de 1750, observées à Paris," *Histoire de l'Académie royale des sciences. Avec les mémoires de Mathématiques et de Physique*, 1750 (Paris, 1754), p. 3n. Cf. Béguillet, who follows Malouin textually without citing him: *Traité des subsistances*, p. 323.

40. BN, Coll. Joly 1743, fol. 157; *Journal économique* (June 1758): 257 and (November 1776): 478; controller-general to Du Cluzel, intendant of Tours, 16 August 1770, AN, F[12] 155; Savary des Bruslons, *Dictionnaire portatif de commerce*, 3:140. Cf. Joyeuse l'aîné to Duhamel du Monceau, 30 August 1756, AN, 127 AP 6; Duchesne, *Code de la police*, p. 72; Maurice Bernard, *La Municipalité de Brest de 1750 à 1790* (Paris, 1915), p. 321.

inconclusive.[41] Lack of scientific verification, however, did not dampen the widely held conviction that consumers were vulnerable to grain- and flour-related disasters. If a Versailles mealman named Maugras were permitted to distribute his flour, which was wet and adulterated with stinking chestnuts to add weight and body, the master baker François Deline warned the authorities, there would be "risk of death" for many Parisians.[42] To my knowledge, Paris never suffered any serious problem with grain-induced illnesses, though there may have been some morbidity and mortality associated with the use of barley in 1709.[43] The fastidiousness of Parisian demand along with police vigilance deserve credit for this record.

The second kind of police concern, in which quality was positively construed, involved precisely this Parisian demand. Parisians insisted not merely that their bread not be defective or noxious; it must be good, even delicious. They often became as splenetic about bread that was mediocre or worse as about bread that was scarce or dear. It was not for rhetorical flourish that the Babouvist slogan went "liberty, bread, and *good bread*."[44] Within certain limits, the police viewed it as their duty to gratify their fellow citizens. Nor did they consider it frivolous to encourage the production of "good" bread; social control and public health were aspects of the same policy. The aims of pleasing and protecting, it is true, sometimes conflicted. Perhaps the most celebrated instance was the great battle in the 1660s over *pain mollet*, which opposed an influential, gourmand segment of Parisian opinion, addicted to this delicate and elegant luxury bread, to the police, who feared that it contained ingredients "not fit to enter the human body" and that "death flew on the wings of pain mollet."[45]

41. *Journal économique* (March 1772): 97–99; *Journal de l'agriculture, du commerce, des arts et des finances* (January 1774): 84–101; *Journal de physique* (July 1774): 41–52; Jean-Pierre Goubert, "Le Phénomène épidémique en Bretagne à la fin du XVIIIe siècle (1770–1787)," *Annales: économies, sociétés, civilisations,* 24th year, no. 6 (November–December 1969): 1562–88. See the reference to a 1951 poisoning by rye ergot in *Le Monde,* 30 April 1968. Ergot provokes, among other things, mental disarray and hallucinations. Its consumption may have played a role in aggravating social unrest in moments of crisis, though it will be extremely difficult for historians to make this case. On the wildness and madness associated with hunger, see the provocative suggestions and intuitions of Piero Camporesi, *Le Pain sauvage: L'Imaginaire de la faim de la Renaissance au XVIIIe siècle,* trans. Monique Aymard (Paris, 1981). Mary Matossian is now giving the ergot issue the serious attention that it deserves. So far, I find her work stimulating but not convincing. See her forthcoming *Ergots, Molds and History.*

42. AN, Y 15601, 6 January 1741.

43. Auguste-Philippe Herlaut, "La Disette de pain à Paris en 1709," *Mémoires de la Société de l'histoire de Paris et de l'Ile-de-France* 45 (1918): 76; Jacques Saint-Germain, *La Vie quotidienne en France à la fin du grand siècle,* p. 179.

44. Cited by R. B. Rose, "The French Revolution and Grain Supply," *Bulletin of the John Rylands Library* 39, no. 1 (1956–57): 171.

45. Des Essarts, *Dictionnaire universal de police,* 1:262ff.; Charles-Marie de La Condamine, "Pain mollet," in *Almanach des Muses* (Paris, 1770), pp. 85–88.

Although it was impossible to examine all the wheat and flour that entered the capital, the police made spot checks and invited the public to register complaints. In order to prevent "our abundance from turning against us," prévôt des marchands Lambert insisted on careful scrutiny of the grain boats and personally toured the ports. Commissaire Machurin of the Halle made surprise visits to brokers to test their flour.[46] The burden of day-to-day responsibility for inspection rested with the measurers and porters, who came into closest contact with the goods and were charged with assuring "good quality" and "loyalty" of exchanges. In October 1725 they confiscated four setiers of flour that were unevenly white in color either as a result of "bad faith" (i.e., adulteration) or careless grinding and bolting. In November 1741 they seized a sack at a broker's place containing a mixture of incompatible wheats. In November 1752 the measurers accused Fourcret, a flour merchant from Villiers, "of having mixed flours of different qualities and prices in order to draw a greater profit." Fourcret vindicated himself on appeal and the lieutenant general affirmed the principle that honest blending was permissible.[47]

Denunciations from individuals alerted the police to illicit practices. A sack holder reported that the wife of a flour merchant selling at the Halle tried to pass off mid-white flour for white upon a buyer who "was not well acquainted" with the trade. At the risk of losing a merchant client but in order to preserve his reputation vis-à-vis the bakers, the broker Chicheret reported that the bottom half of the flour sacks sent for sale by Lavoisier, a mealman based near Pont-Ste.-Maxence, contained flour much inferior to that on the top. Bakers, too, succumbed to the temptation to deceive on wheat and flour quality. In 1699 a commissaire learned that a number of bakers, "in concert with other ill-intentioned persons," were making bread from "infected and corrupt" flour that they purchased in the form of wheat at a large discount. The baker Pasquier was fined 500 livres and had his oven demolished and his business closed for six months, and the lieutenant general ordered "an exact visit" of all the bakers in search of "any bread, wheat or flour of bad quality or capable of damaging health." In 1728 the assembly of police warned a group of faubourg St.-Marcel bakers against using a cheap wheat that "infects."[48]

While they cheated in many other ways, the bakers were more often victims than perpetrators of wheat and flour quality frauds. For most of them, the commercial risk involved in using polluted raw materials was simply too

46. Lambert to procurator general, 25 October 1725, BN, Coll. Joly 1116, fol. 194; Arsenal, ms. Bast. 10141, fol. 266 (6 November 1759).

47. "Mémoire des porteurs" (1736), BN, Coll. Joly 1312, fol. 131; Cleret to Hérault, 23 October 1725, Arsenal, ms. Bast. 10271; AN, Y 9442, 17 November 1741; BN, Coll. Joly 1829, fols. 278–79; AN, Y 9621, 24 November 1752.

48. AN, Y 11223, 24 July 1736, and Y 12607, 27 December 1759; BN, ms. fr. 21636, fol. 294, 21 August 1699; Arsenal, ms. Bast. 10274 (February 1728).

great. Customers tended to frequent the shops and market stalls of those "who have the reputation of making better bread than the others." Once it became known in the quarter that the widow Legrand baked a "defective and bad quality" dark bread, people stopped buying from her. Louis Hiest, a suburban baker, lost his reputation and his clientele and was ultimately forced to establish himself elsewhere because a mealman supplied corrupt flour while he was away on business; his apprentice had accepted it and transformed it into bread not fit to eat. Master baker Nicolas Eloy bitterly assailed two merchants for selling him the "flawed merchandise" from which he made "bad bread" that cost him his best clients, "discredited" him in the neighborhood, and "destroyed" his business. One or two *fournées,* or ovenfuls, of low quality bread was sufficient to ruin a baker's good name and place his commerce in jeopardy.[49]

In order to protect themselves bakers tended to be very cautious in making purchases. Parmentier's exhortation to the bakers to be ceaselessly "suspicious" of the merchants, the millers, the brokers, the transporters, and all other intermediaries was superfluous. The bakers needed no instructions to mistrust the grain and flour dealers not only on the question of quality but also on matters concerning price, amount, delivery date, credit, and sacks due. They expressed their qualms about the probity of the suppliers in collective petitions sponsored by the guild and in innumerable individual court and police actions. Of all the disputes between bakers and suppliers, those regarding quality aroused the deepest passions and resentments, because they involved honor and public standing as well as money. At the end of 1740 four bakers filed a complaint against broker Gaillon for selling flour that produced bread that was "totally defective and unfit to enter the human body and not even good enough for animals." The broker's defense was that the flour was sent by a dealer from the faubourg St.-Antoine "whom she did not know at all." Master baker François Deline made the error of not examining closely all the sacks that he purchased from a flour trader. Later he discovered that several contained either rotten merchandise or flour moistened to augment its weight, "a clear-cut theft and a threat to the public good."[50]

In 1746 master baker Sulpice Garin sued a Montereau flour merchant named Jacques Thuin in the commercial court (*juridiction consulaire)* for selling flour that was overheated and lumpy and not, as promised in their oral contract, "good, honest and vendible." Thuin countersued for nonpayment and rupture of contract, Garin having refused to accept further deliveries. On

49. AN, F[7] 3688[3], 29 September 1693; Gazetins, 10 November 1725, Arsenal, ms. Bast. 10155, fol. 125; Archives Seine-Paris, D4B[6] 42-2307, 16 August 1771 and 20 March 1776; D4B[6] 83-5592, 14 January 1782; and rapport arbitre, 6 November 1783, D6B[6] 11.

50. Parmentier, *Parfait Boulanger,* pp. xxiv–xxv, 522–23; petition of bakers, ca. 1690, BN, ms. fr. 21640, fols. 50–53; "Réponse des marchands de bled aux boulangers," ca. 1738, BN, Coll. Joly 1314, fol. 63; AN, Y 11227, 15 December 1740, and Y 15601, 6 January 1741.

the recommendation of two groups of mediators who found the flour "spoiled and rotten" and "unusable," the judges (or consuls) found in favor of the baker. In a similar case fifteen years later between master baker Caussin and a Versailles broker, the mediators esteemed the flour to be "of a very bad quality" and urged the court to pronounce for the baker. Charles Desauze of the faubourg St.-Antoine was one of a number of bakers who blamed their "indigence" in part on the "bad quality" of wheat and flour that yielded much less bread than promised. In October of 1757, when the conversation of a party of bakers and brokers drinking in the Golden Cross tavern next to the Halle turned to flour trade, Thomas Bontems, a Latin Quarter master baker, remarked that the mealman Pijan [probably Pigeon] did not provide the quality flour agreed upon. Pijan's broker Chicheret rose in defense of his integrity. Bontems called Chicheret a "Jean Foutre," the broker characterized the baker as a "wheedler" and a "damn scoundrel," and the two men almost came to blows. Bontems utilized a device that aroused considerable discussion in the trade to punish the faithless flour merchant without recourse to police or the courts—he unilaterally reduced the price they had agreed upon for the flour in question.[51]

The bakers experienced fewer difficulties in their wheat purchases, perhaps because wheat quality was easier to distinguish. In 1725 the new wheat was humid and spongy and produced a sticky, inferior flour. Two setiers of old wheat were equal in yield to three of the new. Despite the growing pressure of dearth, the "best bakers" refused to buy the new, not only because it was less productive but also because it did not make as good a bread. "The bakers who want to keep their customers," noted a police observer, "seek out the old wheat."

In that same year the bakers boycotted the Ecole port because the wheat there was "very badly conditioned and offensive to the nose." For a while in 1740 bakers scorned the ports in favor of the Halle because the wheat from the ports made a bread that they could not "stomach."[52] In other years they rejected Picardy wheat because of its color, Brittany wheat because it was dirty, Burgundy wheat because it was overheated, Soissonnais wheat because it did not feel right. Generally the Paris bakers were parochial and conservative in their wheat tastes. They preferred the "harvest of the laboureurs" drawn from familiar hinterland, and were reluctant to adapt to new sorts of grain that required different handling, kneading, and baking techniques. Dur-

51. AN, Y 13540, 16 December 1768, and Y 12605, 25 October, 18 November 1757; Archives Seine-Paris, D6B⁶ 800, 8 August 1746; D2B⁶ 813, 11, 20 September 1747; D6B⁶ 3, 13 May, 11, 15 June 1761.

52. Cleret to Hérault, 15 October 1725, Arsenal, ms. Bast. 10270, p. 315; d'Angervilliers to same, 7 November 1725, ms. Bast. 10271; Bourlon to same, 4 October 1725, ms. Bast. 10270, p. 273; Couet de Montbayeux to procurator general, 9 October 1725, ms. Bast. 10270, pp. 211–14; same to same, 5, 14 October 1725, BN, Coll. Joly 1116, fols. 270–71, 285–86; same to same, 24 October 1725, Coll. Joly 1117, fols. 240–43; AN, Y 11227, 1 June 1740.

ing the dearth of 1725–26, the government encouraged the importation of large amounts of hard Barbary wheat. Word spread that it was unproductive and difficult to work with, and the bakers showed extreme reluctance to buy it. To "disabuse" them of their "prejudice" and put the wheat "in vogue," the lieutenant general arranged to bring four Marseilles bakers familiar with the Barbary to Paris to set up a model workshop. For the same purpose, he distributed an "instructive memorandum to all the bakers of Paris to teach them the manner of utilizing and making good bread from the wheats of Sicily, which must be employed differently than those of France." Pressure from the police and lack of alternative supplies, rather than the crash reeducation program, ultimately prompted the bakers to take the foreign grain.[53]

Ironically, the government, guardian of the highest standards in wheat and flour exchanges, acquired a reputation as the purveyor of the lowest quality goods as a result of the purchases it made and sponsored to combat or prevent dearths. Politically the consequences of the government's inability to provide uniformly good merchandise were disastrous. Instead of earning public gratitude for its strenuous efforts to provision the capital (and other places as well), the government aroused suspicion and hostility. Bad quality grain and flour gave credence to the rumors of plots and monopolies involving ministers, courtesans, and financiers and seemed to confirm the charge that the king, or at least his closest counselors, really did not care about the welfare of his subjects. Mercier, writing in the early eighties, claimed that the government of Louis XV had sometimes "forced the people to eat rotten wheat," a notion that gained wide currency during the Revolution.[54] The marquis d'Argenson, prone to exaggeration but a faithful witness of the changing moods of the time, wrote in his journal in September 1740: "There is no more bread in Paris, except the *spoiled flours* that arrive and heat to burning. They are working day and night at Belleville, in the mills, to regrind the old corrupt flour. It is known [that] the people are not unaware of this and cry out everywhere that someone wants to *poison them*."[55]

It is possible that critics of the government, such as merchants and laboureurs who resented the competition of the king's grain and political adversaries who wanted to embarrass the government at any cost, sowed extravagant rumors and distortions in order to discredit both the authorities and the merchandise. "These wheats are very clean, very fresh, and very capable of being converted into bread," wrote a police commissaire charged with inspecting the king's grain stored in makeshift Paris granaries. "It can only be evil-intentioned persons who have propagated the idea that there was

53. "Motifs sur lesquels Chabert . . .," Arsenal, ms. Bast. 10273; Gazetins, 21 January 1726, ms. Bast. 10156, fol. 45.

54. Louis-Sébastien Mercier, *Tableau de Paris,* 2:204.

55. René-Louis de Voyer, marquis d'Argenson, *Journal et mémoires du marquis d'Argenson,* ed. E.-J.-B. Rathery (Paris, 1859–67), 3:169 (19 September 1740). My emphasis.

some defect in this grain because the contrary is very visible." Bakers were among those accused of giving a bad name to government grain. In 1699 a group of bakers allegedly tried to "disgust" the public with foreign grain and thereby maintain the price at a high level. The banker Thellusson correctly predicted, at the outset of his massive grain importation campaign for the government in 1740, that "your bakers would not fail to find defects in them."[56]

Calumny and hyperbole aside, however, the disrepute of the king's grain was largely merited. D'Argenson overdrew the picture when he remarked in the summer of 1752 that the government grains were "half-spoiled . . . so that the people are badly nourished . . . [which] could give rise to maladies." But at about the same time the royal procurator at Beaumont, an important flour market, complained that while an initial batch of some thirty-five hundred setiers of government grain, after having been turned and aired, was "not absolutely bad," a new load almost as large that remained enclosed in sacks gave off "a bad odor" and seemed to be rotten. He feared it would have noxious effects if used by itself or mixed with other grain to mask its decay.[57] If one prefers not to take the lawyer Barbier's word that some of the royal grain serving Paris in 1740 was "a bit spoiled," the administrative correspondence, from Orry in the *contrôle-général* down through the commissaires of the quartiers, provides irrefragable confirmation. Judging by the experience of Jean Laurent, Paris miller and "merchant assigned to the sale of the king's grain," spoiled grain arrived frequently and in substantial quantities.[58]

The police kept an "account of defective grain" and theoretically made sure that irreparable supplies were sold to poultrymen and others for nonhuman consumption. It was widely believed, however, that authorities forced the bakers to take it. Narbonne, a police official at Versailles, charged that the foreign grain purveyed by the influential banker Samuel Bernard "spoiled rapidly" and that portions of it were "so bad that they were offered at 20 sous the setier and no one wanted them." The senior commissaire Duplessis, finding "a flour that belongs to Monsieur le Chevalier Bernard . . . which seemed to have a very bad taste," provisionally suspended its sale and ordered a "baker of confidence" to prepare a bread sample. Meanwhile a lawsuit at the Hôtel de Ville over responsibility for spoilage reinforced popular rumor that the government agents were trafficking in rotten goods. The millers and

56. Pansot to lieutenant of police, 18 June 1739, Arsenal, ms. Bast. 10277; Thellusson to same, 14, 21 February 1739, ms. Bast. 10276; sentence of 21 August 1699, BN, ms. fr. 21636, fol. 294.

57. D'Argenson, *Journal et mémoires,* ed. Rathery, 7:277 (13 August 1752); Pique to procurator general, 15 May 1752, BN, Coll. Joly 1129, fols. 14–15.

58. Edmond-Jean-François Barbier, *Chronique de la régence et du règne de Louis XV (1718–1763), ou Journal de Barbier* (Paris, 1857–66), 3:217; Machurin to lieutenant of police, 5 June 1739, Arsenal, ms. Bast. 10277; Orry to Artaud, 13 March 1741, AN, KK 1005F; same to Buron, 11 February 1742, AN, G⁷ 59; BN, Coll. Joly 1117, fol. 165.

mealmen at Pontoise, another major flour center, refused to buy the king's grain because it was "not nearly as fine a quality as that which is sold here."[59] From Toulouse, Bordeaux, and Rouen came similar complaints during the course of the century.[60] Administrative memoranda and even articles in the press called the king's grain "bad" or "mediocre."[61] A grain expert who followed the king's grain operation from 1740 through the end of the sixties— an adversary, it is true, of government intervention in grain affairs—wrote: "I did not see a single setier that the baker can use pure as a result of the odor that it had or because it badly needed conditioning."[62]

The quality problem occurred characteristically, albeit not exclusively, in times of dearth when Parisians, despite the threat of hunger and the reality of misery, were more rather than less sensitive to quality and when the government commissioned purchases to be made urgently and rapidly under virtually any conditions. Dealing through correspondents and agents of agents, it was impossible to assure the quality of all purchases; indeed, it was often impossible to procure top quality grain, and the buyer, pressed and anxious, was at a serious disadvantage. Even a man as scrupulous and as well connected as Thellusson was "not able to guarantee this perfection [of quality] since the wheat comes from diverse countries, from a thousand different cantons." The geographical origin of the foreign grains was of some significance. Hard, dry, and weighty, the wheat of southern Europe and Africa stood transport well and generally conserved easily, while weaker northern wheat—France drew heavily on the Amsterdam entrepôt and the Dantzig market in times of distress—was much more vulnerable to spoilage. It was during the long sea voyage that the most serious deterioration occurred. The grain and flour were seldom properly prepared for transport; unless it had been kilned and barrel-packed, both of which were time-consuming and costly processes, even with care water and the heat and mephitic air of the

59. Arsenal, ms. Bast. 10273; Gazetins, 15, 30 November 1725, ms. Bast. 10155, fols. 38, 152; Gazetins, 10 March 1726, ms. Bast. 10156, fol. 104; Pierre de Narbonne, *Journal des règnes de Louis XIV et Louis XV de l'année 1701 à l'année 1744 par Pierre Narbonne, premier commissaire de police de la ville de Versailles,* ed. J.-A. Le Roi (Versailles, 1866), p. 138; Duplessis to procurator general, 13 July 1726, BN, Coll. Joly 1118, fol. 174; Cleret to Hérault, 6 October 1725, Arsenal, ms. Bast. 10270, fol. 245.

60. Louis Viala, *La Question des grains et leur commerce à Toulouse au dix-huitième siècle (de 1715 à 1789)* (Toulouse, 1909), p. 49; Guy Lemarchand, "Les Troubles de subsistances dans la généralité de Rouen," *Annales historiques de la Révolution française,* 35th year, no. 174 (October–December 1963): 421; Marcel Marion, "Une Famine en Guyenne (1747–48)," *Revue historique* 46 (May–August 1891): 247–48. Cf., for a later period, Délibérations du comité de salut public du département de Paris, AN, BB³ 81^A, fol. 200.

61. "Mémoire du bureau de l'Hôtel-Dieu," ca. 1739, BN, Coll. Joly 1120, fols. 7, 8; mémoire for Sartine (?), 1761, BN, ms. fr. 11347, fols. 217–18; *Journal de Trévoux* (October 1755): 2600.

62. Daure, "Mémoire," 1772, AN, F¹¹ 264.

hold reached some of the merchandise. In 1738–39, some of Thellusson's ships had been en route for more than two months in foul weather and stormy seas.[63]

In most instances authorities labored to limit the extent of the damage, rehabilitating impaired grain, and keeping the worst-quality merchandise from the public; or at least from the Parisian public. Despite urgent needs, the assembly of police at the end of 1738 was reluctant to draw upon military grain stocks in Flanders and Lorraine for fear that they were not of "good quality." Deteriorated Paris-bound German wheat was sold at Le Havre or Rouen in 1739–40 not only to avoid further decay and economize on the costs of conditioning, storage, and freight, but also because it was judged politically less risky to offer it there than at the capital. Similarly, Orry ordered that Paris-bound southern grains that were "filled with insects" or "rotten" or "of bad quality" or salvaged from sunken boats be sold along the way. Buron, Orry's representative at the canal de Briare, refused grain coming up from Marseilles and Lyon because it was wet or damaged. Throughout the massive provisioning operations of 1738–42, the controller-general tirelessly hounded his agents to give "all the attention required" and "all the care" to the conservation and repair of supplies.[64] Rebuked for sending wheat to the capital that was "not well treated" and "full of dirt," the merchant Savart coaxed his agent to be more diligent: "I know that you are not lazy and [you are] too honest a man to let this grain spoil for lack of attention and vigilance."[65] For the reception of king's grain in 1738–40, the lieutenant general established regenerating and conservation centers in the improvised granaries of the General Hospital and the Halle aux Vins, in which up to sixty workers turned and sifted the grain under the watchful eyes of a team of commissaires who reported daily on the condition of the goods.[66]

The result of these efforts at best was to eliminate the most defective portions of the king's grain. Much of it was still of dubious quality. Often there was simply no time to restore the grain upon its arrival; sometimes storage facilities were not available; frequently, especially in times of dearth when the demand was relentless, merchants were far less sensitive than Savart to quality. Conflicting pressures played upon the government. It was

63. Thellusson to lieutenant of police, 14, 21 February 1739, Arsenal, ms. Bast. 10276. On the quality of foreign grain, see Parmentier, *Parfait Boulanger,* pp. 116–18, and "Rapport au comité de salut public par la commission d'agriculture et des arts," n.d., AN, F[10] 226.

64. Etats des bleds et des farines, 18 April, 2 May 1739, Arsenal, ms. Bast. 10276; Orry to Buron, 23 July 1741, to Pallu, 22 June 1741, and to Artaud, 13 July 1741, AN, G[7] 58; Orry to Buron, 11 February 1742, AN, G[7] 59; Orry to Buron, 10 January 1741, to Artaud, 13 March and 19 April 1741, and to Pallu, 15 December 1740, AN, KK 1005F; assembly of police, 4 December 1738, BN, ms. fr. 11356, fol. 370.

65. Savart to Leduc, 10, 17, 24 January 1741, Arsenal, ms. Bast. 10277.

66. Police reports, 29 May–17 October 1739, Arsenal, ms. Bast. 10277.

imperative to provision the city; it was imperative to waste as little money as possible. In order to save money and grain loss through manipulation, the police decided not to sift the king's grain arriving in 1725, thereby impairing its quality and threatening its conservation.[67] Even when the high-grade commercial supplies that bakers preferred became available, the government could not permit the fragile king's grain to go unsold. To protect its investment—the government never lost money willingly, even in relief operations—it tried in various ways to give priority to the sale of its stocks. In sixteenth-century London and old-regime Lyon the municipalities compelled bakers to buy grain that they regarded as "musty and not holsom for mannes body."[68] Although it is difficult to believe and impossible to verify, it was frequently charged in eighteenth-century Paris that the laboureur was "prohibited from bringing wheat to market because there is spoiled government grain that one wishes to sell."[69] In 1725 and 1740 the bakers bitterly protested that they were "forced to take bad flour and bad grain."[70] When consumers complained about bad bread, the bakers blamed the government. The government contended that the bakers stirred a furor over the king's grain in order to cover their own machinations.

When the government failed to succor the people, it was denounced for cruelty and irresponsibility. When it temporarily went into the victualing business, it found itself accused of cheating and even poisoning the people. The slightest imperfection was sufficient to generate fears, spread rumors, and discredit the most devoted efforts. Unlike a baker, a government that lost its reputation for good-quality subsistence products could neither file voluntary bankruptcy nor move its operations. Royal grain of suspect quality stirred consumers to question the sincerity of the king's commitment to their well-being. It undermined their confidence in the probity as well as the competence of the king and his government and heightened their conviction that the king was accountable to them for his management of subsistence affairs.

Conservation Technology

Ignorance, negligence, and the imperfect state of conservation technology resulted in millions of livres of losses each year, dissuaded merchants from

67. Couet de Montbayeux to procurator general, 24 October 1725, BN, Coll. Joly 1117, fols. 240–43.

68. Béguillet, *Traité des subsistances*, p. 857n; Sylvia Thrupp, *A Short History of the Worshipful Company of Bakers of London* (London, 1933), pp. 77–78.

69. See, for example, Arsenal, ms. Bast. 10027, fol. 391, and Steven L. Kaplan, *The Famine Plot Persuasion in Eighteenth-Century France, Transactions of the American Philosophical Society*, 72, part 3 (1982).

70. Gazetins, 5, 15 November 1725, Arsenal, ms. Bast. 10155, fols. 116, 118; *Journal de Barbier*, 3:217 (September 1740).

undertaking large-scale operations across time and space, contributed to the discrediting of government, and exposed the public to the danger of consuming unwholesome goods. The development and propagation of effective conservation methods, it was believed, would make the grain trade bolder, more profitable, and more reliable. Better conservation would increase the productivity of grain into flour and flour into bread and would also improve both the nutritional value and the taste of bread.[71] It would also help attenuate the risks and the depredations of subsistence crises. According to the physicist Reneaume, the failure to salvage and rehabilitate a large part of the harvest of 1693 was one of the chief causes of the dearth that befell the Parisian area in that year.[72]

The merchants were not the only ones responsible for improper care. The specialists agreed that conservation had to begin well before grain entered commerce. The pharmacist-chemist Parmentier urged cultivators to practice conservation at the very moment of harvest.[73] The Burgundian lawyer-turned-subsistence-expert Edme Béguillet went a step further: "economic" management required the farmer to begin by choosing seed grain heedfully and avoiding the common error of excessive seeding. Béguillet estimated that cultivators and merchants together squandered one-sixth of every harvest by their inattention to conservation.[74] The eighteenth century witnessed a great surge of interest in improving agriculture on the part of administrators, scientists, philosophes, and even some farmers. Some of the ablest activists turned their attention to the problem of conservation. They were primarily concerned with methods of short-term preservation and perfecting in order to draw as much as possible from a crop and protect it for consumption within a year or two, but they also considered longer-term prospects for storage.[75]

Conservationists insisted upon the necessity of preventing and combating the diseases that often ravaged the crop completely or impaired its quality and weakened its resistance. Diderot, who often commented on agricultural questions, claimed that "the *cherté* of the years 1660, 1693, 1698 . . . had no other causes than the blight."[76] According to Tillet, director of the Monnoye at Troyes and later a prominent member of the Academy of Sciences, the malady commonly called blight *(nielle)* was really a *carie,* or rust. For years

71. "Mémoire," AN, F[11] 264; Savary des Bruslons, *Dictionnaire portatif de commerce,* 1:416–22.

72. Reneaume, "Sur la manière de conserver les grains," pp. 76–77, 85n.

73. Parmentier, *Parfait Boulanger,* pp. 54–62.

74. Béguillet, *Traité des subsistances,* pp. 365–66.

75. Abbé Antoine Pluche, *Le Spectacle de la nature . . .* (Paris, 1764–70), 1:494–95; Poncelet, *Histoire naturelle,* pp. 147–52; abbé Henri-Alexandre Tessier, "Conservation," *Encyclopédie méthodique,* Agriculture (Paris, 1793), 3:463–64.

76. Friedrich M. Grimm et al., *Correspondance littéraire, philosophique et critique,* ed. M. Tourneux (Paris, 1877–82), 3:38 (June 1755). On grain disease research, see André J. Bourde, *Agronomie et agronomes en France au dix-huitième siècle* (Paris, 1967), 2: 611–18.

Tillet labored in relative obscurity to discover the nature and cure for the deadliest grain diseases. At the king's request, he repeated his experiments at the Trianon. The Encyclopedist and agronomist Leroy pressed Tillet, through their mutual friend Diderot, "in the name of all the earth," to publicize his "simplest and least expensive procedures for the benefit of cultivators."[77] In the late fifties and early sixties the *Journal économique* and the *Journal de commerce* reported his findings in detail and the government sponsored publication of brochures with instructions for dealing with grain maladies.[78] Even earlier the Academy of Belles-Lettres, Sciences and Arts at Bordeaux sponsored a prize competition for an essay on "the cause that corrupts the grains in the ears and which blackens it, with the means to prevent these accidents," and experts vehemently disputed whether the *nielle* was an internally generated and communicable disease or an exogenous and noncontagious one.[79]

Around mid-century an Italian named Ginanni conducted research paralleling that of Tillet. At the same time Goyon de la Plombanie, a philosophe who wrote extensively on "economic" subjects, devoted a study to "the nature of the wheat grain and that which corrupts it."[80] After his disgrace from the *contrôle-général* in the sixties—largely the result of his inability to resolve the grain crisis on the macro-level—Laverdy attacked the problem on the micro-plane, conducting experiments and publishing essays on rust and blight.[81] In the seventies François Rainville of the Philosophical and Experimental Academy of Rotterdam proposed a number of modifications to Tillet's theses. By then Parmentier and the chemist–subsistence theorist Cadet de Vaux were "the great doers" on questions of grain disease, counselors to the government and authors of widely distributed pamphlets on grain care.[82] Just how effective the new remedies were in dealing with disease remains unknown, but they were widely disseminated through the auspices of the intendants and the societies of agriculture.

"The two greatest enemies" in the battle for conservation, Parmentier contended, were humidity and such insect pests as weevils. The cultivator

77. Mathieu Tillet, *Précis des expériences qui ont été faites par ordre du Roi à Trianon sur la cause de la corruption des bleds et sur les moyens de la prévenir* (Troyes, 1756), p. 16; Diderot to Sophie Volland, 2–8 November 1760, and Leroy to Diderot, 8 August 1756, in Denis Diderot, *Correspondance,* ed. Georges Roth (Paris, 1955–70), 3:243 and 5:13–14; *Journal économique* (June 1757): 36–48.

78. *Journal économique* (June 1755): 59–84; *Journal de commerce* (September 1760): 184–86. Cf. *Journal économique* (March 1755): 72–85.

79. *Journal économique* (September 1751): 11–50. Cf. ibid. (November 1751): 30–51.

80. Ibid. (May 1761): 227–31, and (June 1752): 5–24.

81. Bourde, *Agronomie et agronomes,* 2:1138n.

82. *Journal des sçavans* 83 (September 1775): 464–517; Louis Petit de Bachaumont, *Mémoires secrets pour servir à l'histoire de la République des lettres en France . . .* (London, 1777–89), 29:193 (27 August 1785).

had to guard against the effects of inclement weather. In rainy spells, the grain should be left as long as possible in the ground, he instructed, or cut and left covered with hay. Once in the granary, the grain was easy prey to heat and humidity that spurred fermentation, which spread rapidly until the grain developed an odor so repugnant that even the poultry refused to eat it. To purge the grain, all the experts concurred, it had to be cleaned and aired frequently. Parmentier advised turning fortnightly in the summer and monthly in the winter, and sifting every two months. The physician Malouin warned that wheat, "of all the grains the most difficult to keep," demanded constant "working" if it were not to acquire "nose" and "taste" and begin to rot and invite insects.[83] Laboureurs, merchants, and bakers often lacked the space, the personnel, and the time to work the grain sufficiently; and there is little doubt that the failure to practice this simple precaution was the most common cause of spoilage. To prevent such negligence the police inspector Poussot proposed regular inspection of granaries by "knowledgeable and vigilant persons," a wholly impracticable solution even in the marketplaces.[84] The greatest authority on conservation, and, indeed, on agronomy in general, Duhamel du Monceau, developed a ventilation system similar to one practiced in England, but like many of his devices, it was too expensive to enjoy wide use.[85] A number of inventors developed remarkably effective sieves that cleaned the grain and destroyed insects. Most of them, however, like the cylindrical model awarded a government prize in 1769, were like "a piece of clockwork that required incessantly the hand of the Artist."[86]

The homemade nostrums that Parmentier regarded with such scorn began to reach the public in large doses in the second half of the century.[87] The government paid a modest stipend to an inventor for a "gomme arabique," a fine prophylactic powder to be sprinkled on stored grain. A "dust" invented by a Limousin, which Parmentier surmised was composed of lime and sulphur, produced impressive results in experiments sponsored by lieutenant general of police Sartine. A prominent physician developed another kind of magic powder, while another experimenter proposed an oily potion.[88] The curé of St.-Sulpice concocted a "liquor" of parsley, sage, vinegar, and other

83. Parmentier, *Parfait Boulanger,* pp. 52–62, 81ff.; Malouin, *Description et détails des arts,* p. 24. For an example of an insect "epidemic" in granaries, see BN, Coll. Joly 1428, fols. 170, 172–73.

84. Arsenal, ms. Bast. 10141, fol. 368 (21 August 1760).

85. Parmentier, *Parfait Boulanger,* p. 63. For the English model on which Duhamel drew, see *Journal économique* (October 1753): 174–76, and Bachaumont, *Mémoires secrets,* 1:297 (11 November 1763).

86. Levignen to Hérault, 5 June 1726, Arsenal, ms. Bast. 10273; *Journal économique* (December 1753): 172; Béguillet, *Traité des subsistances,* p. 225.

87. Parmentier, *Parfait Boulanger,* pp. 86–87.

88. AN, F^{11} 1194; Parmentier, *Parfait Boulanger,* pp. 96–103; *Journal économique* (December 1766): 546, and (June 1764): 267.

ingredients whose odor would deliver grain from marauding insects. "It seems that it would be good policy," commented the *Journal économique,* "to order that the grain markets, especially the Halle at Paris, be purified with this drug, at least once a year," and that the rental grain sacks, which were "terribly infected with this troublesome plague [of insects]," be washed from time to time.[89] Promising to "increase the abundance" of the state, a writer in the *Journal économique* suggested a conservation technique involving the removal of the grain from hay.[90] Others, such as Goyon de la Plombanie, Poncelet, and the abbé Tessier, suggested specially constructed granaries or storage cases that required considerable investment and expertise.[91] The proliferation of ideas testified to the interest that the conservation problem aroused, but there is no indication that any of them enjoyed widespread adoption. They were either too exotic, too expensive, or too complex. None could replace labor at the shovel and fussy watchfulness.

The most exciting, controversial, and carefully tested innovation in grain conservation was the *étuve,* or kiln-room, a kind of sauna for grain, heated by a connecting oven that dried the grain and killed the pests that inhabited it. "Le grand Duhamel," as Diderot called him, was largely responsible for its development, though the paternity of the machine was vigorously contested.[92] Galiani accused Duhamel of plagiarizing the system of the Italian mathematician-engineer Intieri, whose work the Neapolitan had publicized in a little-known treatise called *Della Perfetta Conservazione del Grano.*[93] An embittered *commissaire des guerres* and chevalier de Saint Louis named Maréschal made a strong case that an egotistical Duhamel had failed to give proper credit and attention to a simplified and efficient étuve that he perfected in the fifties while working in military provisioning under the auspices of the financier Pâris-Duverney.[94] The principle of the étuve was not a discovery of

89. *Journal économique* (May 1751): 39–47.

90. Ibid. (August 1757): 62–64.

91. Ibid. (November 1752): 5–21; Poncelet, *Histoire naturelle,* pp. 147–52; Tessier, "Conservation," pp. 463–64. Cf. *Journal économique* (November 1758): 490–91, and (May 1761): 225–26.

For other examples of the burgeoning interest in conservation, see Corinne Beutler, "De l'approvisionnement en grains de quelques villes européennes au Moyen Age et à l'époque moderne," in Marceau Gast and François Sigaut, eds., *Les Techniques de conservation des grains à long terme* (Paris, 1979), vol. 1, and Beutler, "Traditions et innovations dans les techniques de conservation des grains à la campagne et à la ville," in ibid., vol. 2.

92. Diderot to Damilaville, late February 1760, *Correspondance,* p. 24.

93. *Mercure de France* (June 1771): 167–68; Galiani to d'Epinay, 13 December 1770, Abbé Ferdinando Galiani, *Correspondance,* eds. Lucien Perey and Gaston Maugras (Paris, 1881), 1:313.

94. Maréschal to editor, *Journal de Paris* (30 April 1781); controller-general to Maréschal, 25 June 1769, AN, F^{12} 153, fol. 38. Duhamel du Monceau, *Traité de la conservation,* pp. 121–22, cited Maréschal's work.

the Enlightenment, however. The Chinese—whose genius lurks everywhere in the shadows of the Lumières—had for centuries used a *kang* to dry and cleanse grain. More important than its origin was the process by which the étuve sprang to public attention.[95] Duhamel built countless versions of the device, improved it through careful experimentation, and made it the keystone of his entire conservation system.[96]

An extraordinarily versatile and productive scientist who has not received the acclaim he deserves, perhaps because too much of his work was artlessly aimed at the "public utility," Duhamel enjoyed enough renown in his own time to serve as the government's most trusted technical counselor on agronomical affairs and to divert the English agronomist Arthur Young to make a pilgrimage to his château-laboratory.[97] His *Traité de la conservation des grains*, published at mid-century, remained the standard guide for many years, though he continued to modify his conclusions until the end of his life. Duhamel worked simultaneously on a wide range of different conservation techniques meant to preserve a large amount of wheat in the smallest possible space and in perfect security for as long as desired.[98] Although exposure in the étuve was the most important stage in the process of preparation for repose, it did not eliminate the need to clean, turn, and air, upon which Duhamel, always cautious, continued to insist. The étuve, a brick-lined chamber of varying size (the one used at the Ecole Militaire measured 12 by 13 feet and had a large capacity), heated a batch of grain for seven to eight hours to extremely high temperatures. The process dissipated any bad odor the grain might have acquired; eliminated all humidity; killed most insects and formed a sort of invisible shield around the hardened grain, protecting it against other insects; checked the disposition of the grain to germinate and ferment; and prepared it to withstand long voyages, even at sea. The étuve

95. Bucquet, *Observations intéressantes*, pp. 130–31; Béguillet, *Traité des subsistances*, pp. 656–70.

96. "Etuve," n.d., AN, 127 AP 6; Duhamel du Monceau, *Traité de la conservation;* Duhamel du Monceau, *A Practical Treatise of Husbandry* (London, 1756), pp. 466–68; Le Roi, "Froment," Diderot et al., *Encyclopédie*, 7:337.

97. For Duhamel's contemporary reputation and accomplishment see Condorcet, cited by Bachaumont, *Mémoires secrets*, 22:249 (30 April 1783), and his rather flat and perfunctory eulogy in G. Cuvier, ed., *Recueil des éloges historiques lus dans les séances publiques de l'Institut de France* (Paris, 1861), 2:233–51; *Journal économique* (May 1770): 205–10; André J. Bourde, *The Influence of England on the French Agronomes, 1750–1789* (Cambridge, 1953), passim, and *Agronomie et agronomes*, 1:253–76. On Duhamel's international resonance, see Arthur Young, *Travels in France during the Years 1787, 1788, 1789*, ed. M. Betham-Edwards (London, 1890), p. 80, and *Revue rétrospective* (January–June 1887), pp. 108–9. On Duhamel's advisory role to the government, see intendant of commerce to Le Nain, 24 April 1750, AN, F[12]* 147, and Duhamel to Marseille municipality (?), 2 April 1757, AN, F[10] 256. See also the excellent discussion of Duhamel's achievements in Charles C. Gillispie, *Science and Polity in France at the End of the Old Regime* (Princeton, 1980).

98. Duhamel, *Traité de la conservation*, pp. 25–43.

Kiln *(étuve)* for drying grain
(Deutsches Brotmuseum)

served as a remedy as well as a preventative; it so thoroughly transformed wheat of bad quality into good that bakers clamored to buy it.[99]

In the sixties, under the impetus of Bertin and Sartine, the government took a direct hand in developing and promoting the étuve. Upon invitation of Pâris-Duverney, commissaire Machurin and inspector Poussot, the grain specialists of the Paris police—assisted by Pierre Malisset and César Bucquet, respectively the most innovative baker and miller of the time—supervised three years of testing. Duhamel himself, even though he had criticized Duverney's design from Italian models, was present intermittently to provide counsel. To incorporate suggestions and profit from the experiments, Duverney altered the design of the étuve several times. On the whole, the results of the tests seem less conclusive than those reported earlier by Duhamel. Never-

99. Ibid., pp. 55–95, 101–75; Parmentier, *Parfait Boulanger,* pp. 71–72; AN, Y 12611, 28 April 1762.

theless, the étuve clearly combated odor and humidity and dramatically curtailed the ravages of insects. The authorities celebrated it as a success.[100]

Malisset brimmed with enthusiasm over the "good effects" of the étuve and the impact it would have on the long-distance trade of grain and flour. He invited Duhamel to set up étuves at the grain storehouses maintained for the government at the St.-Charles monastery in the faubourg St.-Laurent. A few years later Malisset himself built a "hot room" in his huge mill and warehouse installation at Corbeil. Controller-general Bertin urged the municipality of Lyon to establish a kiln in its granaries of abundance. His successor, Laverdy, ordered the Parisian municipality to popularize and demonstrate the merits of the conservation process by building a public étuve under the direction of Duhamel.[101]

Congratulating Duhamel for his achievements in 1769, the deputies of commerce declared that large-scale grain operations were no longer conceivable without the use of an étuve.[102] The international trader and shipper Leray de Chaumont, who knew as much about such operations as any man in France, developed his own kilns on the model of the oriental kang.[103] Pâris-Duverney spread the étuve to Lille, Strasbourg, and Colmar, doubtless as part of the military subsistence system.[104] Bucquet toiled for many years, apparently without striking success, on what might have become the most significant contribution to conservation technology: a cheap, easy-to-install "domestic" kiln.[105] With the same idea in mind a provincial named Guérin presented to his local agricultural bureau in the early seventies an "economical étuve" that doubled as a bread-baking oven.[106] After reading Duhamel's *Traité,* one of the colonial intendants set up a kiln and granary that "responded perfectly to the object of the conservation of grain."[107] In the eighties the School of Baking, founded in Paris by Parmentier and Cadet de Vaux, offered to assist cities, religious and hospital communities, seigneurs, and farmers in the construction of étuves. Science, suggested Cadet, was the new philanthropy: "This establishment of enlightened beneficence would be preferable to the momentary assistance that charity gives the indigent by

100. AN, Y 12611, 28 April 1762–22 March 1765; AN, 127 AP 6, 22 March 1765, 28 April–26 June 1762.

101. Malisset to Duhamel, 5 May 1762 and 3 August 1763, AN, 127 AP 6; "Mémoire," 7 March 1768, AN, F[11] 1194; Adrien Rambaud, *La Chambre d'abondance de la ville de Lyon (1643–1677)* (Lyon, 1911), p. 148; Laverdy (?) to prévôt des marchands, August 1765, AN, 127 AP 6; *Journal de l'agriculture, du commerce et des finances* 2 (September 1765): 143.

102. "Avis des députés de commerce," October 1769, AN, F[12] 715.

103. Béguillet, *Traité des subsistances,* p. 669n.

104. Pâris-Duverney to Duhamel, 3 May 1762, cited by Béguillet, ibid.

105. Antoine-Augustin Parmentier et al., *Traité théorique et pratique sur la culture des grains suivi de l'art de faire le pain* (Paris, 1802); Bucquet, *Observations intéressantes,* p. 124n.

106. *Journal de physique* (October 1773): 340–43.

107. Jacques Maillart du Mesle to editor, *Journal de Paris* (3 January 1781).

assuring a more healthy nourishment, by diminishing the number of sick people or warding off these epidemics whose cause is almost always unknown and which is often none other than the bad quality of the foods."[108]

The étuve drew criticism from many quarters. Parmentier called attention to the "prodigious loss" in weight and measure that the grain suffered in the kiln. The abbé Tessier noted that the city of Geneva had abandoned the use of the étuve because it cost the government too much in grain waste.[109] Partisans of the étuve argued that the increased ability of the flour of kiln-dried grain to absorb water more than compensated for any loss—a given amount of étuve-treated white flour drank eleven ounces of water while the same quantity of nonprocessed flour imbibed only eight, Malisset reported.[110]

Parmentier, however, declared that the intense heat and brusque dehydration blunted the vigor of the grain and prevented it from absorbing as much water as its exponents claimed. He cited evidence that processed grain reacquired humidity after removal from the étuve and that, short of roasting the grain, the heat of the étuve could not kill all the insects and their eggs.[111] Dr. Malouin warned that in their desire to drive out humidity and insects operators sometimes overheated the étuve, thereby drying out the oily quality necessary for perfect grain and making it grind badly.[112] The American master miller Oliver Evans disapproved of kiln-dried grain on the grounds that the berry became so brittle that the stones pulverized the husk, mixing it with the flour and thereby impairing its color and quality.[113] The étuve deprived the grain of *la main,* the smooth and flowing sensation caused by grain passing through the hand, Parmentier complained. Moreover, the flour of this grain lost its "sparkle" and took on a reddish color.[114] "One must . . . agree," Leray de Chaumont wrote Duhamel, "that the flour of the kiln-treated wheat is darker than [nonprocessed] flour."[115] Superfine bolters were necessary to sift the flour of processed grain in order to remove the dried particles that broke off during milling and darkened the color, Duhamel admitted.[116]

Flavor was affected as well. Bread produced by kiln-dried grain lacked the "exquisite" fruity taste and the nutty savor of ordinary bread, Parmentier

108. Antoine-Alexis Cadet de Vaux, *Avis sur les blés germés par le comité de l'école gratuite de boulangerie* (Paris, 1782).

109. Tessier, "Conservation," p. 467.

110. Malisset to procurator general, 5 July 1766, BN, Coll. Joly 1134, fols. 222–23.

111. Parmentier, *Parfait Boulanger,* pp. 78–85.

112. Malouin, *Description et détails des arts,* pp. 23–24.

113. John Storck and Walter D. Teague, *Flour for Man's Bread—A History of Milling* (Minneapolis, 1952), p. 167.

114. Parmentier, *Mémoire sur les avantages,* pp. 108–10; Parmentier, *Parfait Boulanger,* pp. 73–74.

115. Leray to Duhamel, n.d., AN, 127 AP 6.

116. Duhamel, notes, August 1766, ibid.

declared, though it was "good, healthy, and nourishing."[117] The former échevin responsible for the étuve at Lyon wrote Duhamel that the bread fabricated with étuve-grain was "very good, only it had a troublesome little taste which was not, however, the taste bread has when it is made with wheat that is too old or overheated but [a taste] that could not be defined."[118] Bertin, who now held the agricultural portfolio as fifth secretary of state, flatly denied that the étuve made "very bad bread." "I had the contrary verified," he told Duhamel, "by an authentic test which proved that bread made with kiln-dried grain was just as good as that made with non-processed grain."[119] The *Journal économique* reported that Duhamel had obtained tastier and better bread through use of the étuve, but one of Duhamel's own notes calls the bread of the nondried grain "sweeter under the tongue."[120]

Doubts about the feel of the wheat, the color of the flour, and the taste of the bread are perhaps sufficient to explain why the kiln process did not become standard practice in the eighteenth century. Grain merchants had trouble selling wheat that lacked *la main,* mealmen had difficulty selling white flour that was not the right tint, and bakers lost customers when bread flavor was not up to expectations. Dealers preferred to risk the spoilage of part of their top quality merchandise rather than risk alteration of all of it. The étuve seemed ideal for repairing flawed grain, and for preparing grain for long trips and for indefinite storage—but not for conditioning good grain.

But the failure of the kiln to enter into daily use was a matter less of quality than of economy. Malisset estimated that étuvage would more than double the price of a muid of wheat.[121] Even if design improvements could eliminate its defects, Parmentier argued, the étuve was too costly and too complex to achieve wide diffusion. It would not be of great value until a simple, cheap version could be developed.[122]

Grain that survived the field and the granary without deterioration still had to face the perils of transit. Transport by water was especially dangerous for it exposed the grain constantly to moisture. Grain crammed into boats frequently overheated, began to ferment, and acquired bad taste and odor. It was not sufficient to choose only the driest and highest quality wheat for shipment over long distances. A number of precautions were necessary, including cleaning, turning, and drying before the voyage, and turning and perhaps

117. Parmentier, *Mémoire sur les avantages,* pp. 108–10, and *Parfait Boulanger,* pp. 74, 78.

118. Monlong to Duhamel, 13 September 1764, AN, 127 AP 6.

119. Bertin to Duhamel, 4 August 1765, ibid.

120. *Journal économique* (May 1765): 213–15; Duhamel, notes, August 1766, AN, 127 AP 6.

121. Compte, 1766, AN, F^{11} 1194.

122. Parmentier, *Parfait Boulanger,* p. 75; Rollet, *Mémoire sur la meunerie,* pp. 99–101; Baudeau, *Avis au peuple,* troisième traité, pp. 76–79.

drying immediately upon reaching the destination. Packing and loading for river circulation, while much easier than for protracted transit on the turbulent seas, still warranted careful attention.[123]

Merchants, especially those dealing exclusively in the interior, habitually neglected the most elementary conservation measures. "When one wishes to transport grain by means of the navigable rivers," noted a writer in the *Journal économique,* "one ordinarily places it on the boats with as little circumspection as if it were sand."[124] The royal procurator of the Parisian municipality deplored the "little care given to the transport of grain throughout the whole kingdom." Part of the substantial margin of spoilage the merchants experienced was pure loss; "absolutely bad" grain had to be thrown into the river. Some was used for purposes to which the grain was "not naturally destined"—probably for starch making or animal feed—or "to feed the *bas peuple* and the poor . . . which causes disease that can bring death to the subjects of the State." It would not be difficult to cover the grain loaded on riverboats with canvas or tarpaulin to protect it against water and inclement weather, complained the procurator, yet the merchants of Paris refused to follow the instructions of the municipality on this matter. The merchants alleged that it was "almost impossible" to do so, and protested that it would be too costly.[125] One writer suggested that the merchants found negligence profitable, for wet grain swelled sometimes to twice its ordinary volume.[126] In a dearth, observed Monsieur Fromant, merchant irresponsibility rose with prices: "Necessity causes [all the grain regardless of condition] to be taken blindly, and the people are its victim."[127]

The situation was so grave that in 1764 the municipal procurator called upon the king to promulgate a law prescribing exactly the necessary precautions for safe grain freight by land as well as by water and imposing a fine of three thousand livres and confiscation of merchandise for failure to comply.[128] About this time the municipality commissioned the baker and entrepreneur Malisset to conduct tests on various forms of riverboat conservation. In 1765

123. Edme Béguillet, *Traité de la connoissance générale des grains et de la mouture par économie* (Dijon, 1778), pp. 365–66; Turgot to controller-general, October 1770, in Anne-Robert-Jacques Turgot, *Œuvres de Turgot et documents le concernant, avec biographie et notes,* ed. Gustave Schelle (Paris, 1913–23), 3:145; François Lacombe d'Avignon, *Le Mitron de Vaugirard, dialogues sur le bled, la farine et le pain avec un petit traité de la boulangerie* (Amsterdam, 1777), p. 27; Reneaume, "Sur la manière de conserver les grains," p. 75.

124. "Du commerce des grains dans l'intérieur," *Journal économique* (June 1758): 256–57.

125. Jollivet de Vannes, mémoire and letter to St.-Florentin (?), 29 January 1764, AN, O¹ 361.

126. "Du commerce des grains dans l'intérieur," *Journal économique* (June 1758): 257.

127. Lacombe, *Le Mitron de Vaugirard,* p. 28.

128. Jollivet de Vannes, mémoire and letter to St.-Florentin (?), 29 January 1764, AN, O¹ 361.

he reported that covered boats were slowly beginning to come into use.[129] The sixties was a decade of rising prices and, according to liberal theory, should have given the grain owners and merchants incentive to practice careful conservation. They would not make the investment necessary to check spoilage, wrote Turgot, when grain had "little value."[130] Yet more than a decade later, Béguillet and Parmentier both remarked that open transit was still the practice and urged the police to require traders to cover their wagons and boats.[131]

The problem of conserving flour in transit was somewhat different. At the beginning of the century it was viewed as a relatively specialized matter concerning only the export sector of the trade. Flour, in most places in France, was not an object of commerce in the same sense as grain until much later. Most often the process of conversion from grain to flour took place upon demand. The mill was located nearby; the flour did not have to travel a great distance nor was there a long interlude between fabrication and utilization in baking. In the Paris area, where there was an important primary trade in flour, the merchants dealt cautiously in a limited arena, and in sparing quantities, though they became bolder as the century progressed. Convinced that river freight was too dangerous for their delicate product, protected only by cloth sacks, the majority of dealers used land transportation. Authorities never even bothered to establish formal procedures by which flour could be sold at the ports.[132]

The transport of flour abroad was a very different operation. France had a thriving flour traffic with the colonies, based mainly in the southwest triangle formed by Poitiers, La Rochelle, and Bordeaux. A large segment of the milling industry in this region was wholly geared to producing for export. The millers devised extractive methods that they believed made their flour unusually steadfast and resistant. Backed up by research commissioned by the navy, the entrepreneurs developed relatively successful techniques for packing and preserving. The coopers who constructed the barrels in which the flour was more or less hermetically sealed acquired a world-wide reputation for their skill. Spoilage at sea was by no means eliminated, but, within

129. Malisset, "Observations," BN, ms. fr. 14295, fol. 141.

130. Turgot, "Septième lettre sur le commerce des grains," 2 December 1770, in *Œuvres de Turgot,* 3:318. Cf. the similar opinion of Claude Dupin, "Mémoire sur les bleds" (1748), BN, ms. n.a. f., 22777.

131. Béguillet, *Traité des subsistances,* pp. 212–13; Parmentier, *Parfait Boulanger,* p. 134.

132. See, for example, Couet de Montbayeux to procurator general, 24 October 1725, BN, Coll. Joly 1113, fols. 240–43. On flour conservation, see Chomel, *Dictionnaire oeconomique* (1767), 2:6–7 and Abbé François Rozier, *Cours complet d'agriculture théorique, pratique, économique, et de médecine rurale et vétérinaire* (Paris, 1782–96), 7:363–64.

bounds, it was more than counterbalanced by the handsome profits to be made.

Interest in grain conservation naturally extended to flour. Duhamel apparently enjoyed success in sending flour that had been treated in the étuve before and after its transformation from grain from Bordeaux to America. Leray de Chaumont, who conducted an international flour trade, felt that the perfected étuve would eliminate virtually all threats to flour quality during transit. His friend Ben Franklin suggested lining flour casks with strips of pewter for optimal security, a practice he adapted from the Chinese tea-exporting industry.[133]

The example of the export sector, advances in conservation technology, changes in the milling practices of the Paris area, anticipation of a liberalization in the controls governing grain commerce, and the passion for "economical" improvement that had captured the French imagination combined to focus attention on the domestic flour trade during the second half of the century. A growing group of experts and commentators became persuaded that trade in flour was infinitely more advantageous to the public and the state than commerce in grain. They maintained that with modern techniques the conservation of flour in transit was easier, cheaper, and more reliable than that of grain. Once inside the barrel, flour was less vulnerable than the best-conditioned and most carefully loaded grain. Flour merely had to be bolted upon arrival to revivify it. It also took up less space than grain. A cask worth six livres contained as much as three setiers of flour, which made it comparable in volume cost to sacks of grain. At the Corbeil milling factory Malisset worked on developing a cheaper and lighter cask for internal as well as foreign commerce. The royal permission granted in 1763–64 to trade freely in the interior and to export grain and flour abroad stimulated the creation of a number of flour factories that applied the new technology. "Economic milling," a new conversion process, facilitated conservation in transit by separating and bolting the flour at the mill and giving it time for repose and stabilization before packing and shipping. Full of promise for the future, these innovations affected only a relatively small number of merchants in the years before the Revolution.[134]

Conservation science posed a sociopolitical problem. It was clear that truly significant advances in technology would have enormous implications for both private commerce and public authority. Officials responsible for

133. Fougeroux de Bondaroy, ms. note inserted in the copy of Poncelet, *Histoire naturelle*, now held by the Yale University library; Leray to Duhamel, n.d., AN, 127 AP 6; *Journal de Paris* (29 December 1780 and 25 January 1781).

134. Leray et al. to Trudaine de Montigny, 10 May 1768, AN, F[11] 1193; Béguillet, "Mémoire sur les avantages de la mouture économique" (Dijon, 1769), Arsenal, ms. 2891; "Du commerce des grains dans l'intérieur," *Journal économique* (June 1758): pp. 258–59; Savary des Bruslons, *Dictionnaire portatif de commerce*, 3:140–42; Baudeau, *Avis au peuple*, deuxième traité, p. 43; Mathieu Tillet, "Projet d'un tarif," *Histoire de l'Académie royale des sciences. Avec les mémoires de Mathématiques & de Physique, 1781* (1784), pp. 107–68.

provisioning would theoretically be able to contemplate medium- and long-term solutions to the supply problem. But they worried that the capacity to conserve, and thus to withhold and stock, would give profit-seeking grain owners an unfair advantage over consumers. After all, the producers and merchants only came to market during periods of stagnating prices because they had to accept the going rate or lose the crop to predators and rot. Sharing the deeply felt popular anxiety that linked conservation inexorably with hoarding, the authorities looked upon the development of conservation technology with ambivalence.[135]

Nor did this attitude change in the first half of the nineteenth century, despite the radically new landscape featuring railroad, steamship, and telegraph. "The deplorable prejudice, that terrible word 'hoarder' " continued to block the advance of conservation practice. It was not only the psychology of part of the police and much of the consumer-public that remained unchanged. The method of choice for conservation was still *étuvage,* and it was still bedeviled with the same handicaps: high cost and alteration of the merchandise. And rats and worms continued to infest grain stored in barns and granaries at the points of production, while cultivators remained loath to invest in yet another scheme promising their prompt and lasting extirpation.[136]

Parisians took wheat for granted, though for the half of the population comprised of migrants from the provinces the practice of eating wheaten and white must have been at first quite jarring. One of the points on which the police and traders agreed was the existence of a special Parisian grain-flour-bread sensibility. Their perception of this Parisian demand, with its canonical expectations regarding quality as well as price, conditioned both regulatory and commercial practice. The adroit merchant had to be versed in the art of distinguishing good from dubious merchandise even if he did not know the science of it, and he had to be able to repair damaged goods in some fashion even if he could not afford the latest innovations. The government spared no effort to promote new techniques to enhance quality and keepability, but in so doing it learned just how risky it could be to get involved in the provisioning business. Its reputation fared no better than the merchant's when it "deceived" or "betrayed" the consumers. Indeed, since the stakes for the government were political and not merely commercial or financial, the public sanction was immeasurably more significant.

135. Kaplan, *Bread, Politics and Political Economy.*
136. *Enquête sur la boulangerie,* pp. 68, 207, 297, 415, 741–42; *Enquête sur la révision de la législation des céréales* (Paris, 1859), 2:93–94.

CHAPTER 3

Provisioning Paris: The Context

$\mathcal{G}$ rain commerce was not a simple matter, either for the authorities who regulated it or for the merchants. It was framed in a lattice of uncertainties—about the magnitude and quality of the harvest, the weather, the avenues of transportation, the weights and measures, and the attitudes of officials. Nor did the organization of the markets in the primary supply zone of the capital provide steadfast and rational direction. The market "system" was tenuous because it turned on the slippery interplay between local and metropolitan, retail and wholesale, archaism and modernity, marketplace and market principle. Nevertheless, supplies flowed to Paris, by water and by land, arriving for the most part at the markets called the Grève and the Halle. The Halle outstripped the Grève as the primary Parisian market in part because trade in flour superseded trade in wheat and in part because the Paris police favored its development with several audacious modernizing schemes.

Grain Commerce: The Easiest of Trades?

"Of all the types of commerce, the grain trade is the easiest," contended a writer in the second half of the eighteenth century.

> There is neither guild mastership nor reception, a simple registration with the clerks of the Police is the sole formality required. They [the merchants] have the liberty to buy where they please and they have the

facility to summón grain from the most distant Provinces without being subjected to the market *droits,* sometimes they are even exempt from the duties of *péage* and of *travers.* Moreover their merchandise has the singular privilege of not being liable to be seized for whatever reasons, not even for the rights of the King.[1]

This winsome tableau, however, misconstrues and overlooks many aspects of the grain trade that made it a difficult and parlous business. Freedom from guild restrictions also meant the absence of guild solidarities, the want of a countervailing force to oppose to the demands of the authorities and the public, and exposure to ruthless competition. The requirement to register was indeed the only formality imposed on the trader, but not his only obligation. The merchant was not free to purchase anywhere he chose and according to conditions he himself set. Many traders regarded police regulation as their most serious obstacle. The climate of uncertainty and fear generated by the regulations surely dissuaded many talented and wealthy traders from dealing in grain. Nor did police protection always secure the provisioning merchants against interference and harassment. Within the shadow of the capital they enjoyed exemption from many fees and exactions, but their immunity tended to wither away as their commerce became bolder and more extensive.

In his *Dialogues sur le commerce des grains,* the abbé Galiani discussed four broad reasons why the grain trade deterred prospective merchants. First, of all the commodities whose commerce one could undertake, "wheat is absolutely the one which is worth the least in proportion to the weight and space it occupies." A tonneau of wine was worth ten times more than a tonneau of grain and weighed less. Freight costs severely curtailed the grain merchant's profit margin. Second, "nothing is more contrary to commerce" than the nature of grain, which is highly volatile and subject to spoilage in transit and storage. Maintenance was expensive and rarely spared the grain major losses through deterioration. The cost and uncertainty greatly limited the merchant's freedom of action. Third, the harvest calendar increased the risks and cost of the trade by requiring the merchant to move his goods in "the most contrary season" when the weather was "ugly," the days short, the seas stormy, the rivers made perilous by ice or flood waters, and the roads made impassable by snow or mud.

Under the fourth heading Galiani argued that successful speculation in grain depended upon too many incalculables. Unlike, say, the oils of Provence, grain was not the "treasure" of a particular place. Theoretically, it was available everywhere and it was impossible to foresee where and when it might next be lacking. In a given year, region X might be in a position to send grain to region Y—but would Y have need? And could X deliver in time? "It is

1. "Mémoire sur l'établissement d'un poids à la halle," ca. 1760, AN, F[11] 265.

a miracle," remarked Galiani, "if the need and the surplus evenly meet."
When there was concordance of supply and demand, the premium on haste
disjointed the whole commerce. The measure of a merchant's true strength
was his ability to forgo a purchase, or to refuse a sale, if the price was not
acceptable. He wanted to make decisions secretly and execute them discreetly. With grain, however, the trader could not afford to miss an opportunity. He could not conceal his actions, precipitation raised prices and costs,
and once he was engaged he still faced the perils of weather, accident, and
delay. "To call this a commerce," scoffed Galiani, "is to debase the word."

Only a great banker or a merchant prince could undertake this trade on a
grand scale, with its constantly changing loci of surplus and deficit, its need
for a vast network of correspondents, its exorbitant risks, and its enormous
costs. And such men preferred to invest their wealth and energy in other
enterprises. The result was that grain commerce on a truly national or international scale in France was unknown or at best occasional. Even medium-sized
grain trading, which from the local vantage point would appear to be of
considerable magnitude, was relatively uncommon, and the bulk of the grain
trade was "abandoned" to a multitude of petty dealers whose commerce was
inefficient, unreliable, and "too small" to serve the public needs.[2]

The leading authority on commercial affairs, Savary, whose textbook
served Frenchmen from the end of the seventeenth to the beginning of the
nineteenth century, concurred. The grain trade was extremely "dangerous"
and unlikely to be very profitable except in times of dearth, when the risks
and uncertainties were greatest. The trader who desired significant rewards
had to have a "great fund" of capital, a chain of honest and intelligent correspondents, and a "perfect knowledge" of the nature and qualities of grain, the
different regions in which it was available or required, the commercial practices and the weights and measures of those regions, the modalities of
transportation, and the processes of conservation.[3]

Its practitioners' highly unflattering reputation also deterred merchants of
substance and talent from entering the grain trade on a regular basis. Commerce generally was held in low esteem, and the reputation of the grain
merchants, whose commerce concerned the public more than any other, was
particularly execrable (a distinction they shared with millers and mealmen).[4]

    2. Abbé Ferdinando Galiani, *Dialogues sur le commerce des bleds,* ed. Fausto Nicolini
(Milan, 1959), pp. 162–68, and the review of Galiani's thesis in *Année littéraire* (1770),
1:300–302.
    3. Jacques Savary, *Le Parfait Négociant* (Paris, year II), 1:794–96; Savary des Bruslons,
Dictionnaire portatif de commerce, 3:420–22. Cf. the remarks of Séguier, advocate general
of the Paris Parlement, in 1768, in *Recueil des principales lois relatives au commerce des
grains . . .* (Paris, 1769), pp. 115–16.
    4. Raymond de Roover, "The Scholastic Attitude toward Trade and Entrepreneurship,"
Explorations in Entrepreneurial History, n.s. 1 (Fall 1963): 76; R. de Roover, "Scholastic

Merchants blamed the police for fashioning the stereotype of the grain trader-criminal in their statutes and sentences and for teaching the people to view merchants as their born enemies. The police rejoined that the traders' image was the fruit of their own perfidy and that the people required no lessons from the authorities in perceiving villainy in their midst.[5]

As late as the 1850s provisioning merchants still complained bitterly of the obloquy to which they were subjected. Though we are "honorable men," lamented a leading flour merchant, we are treated as "pariahs." This "prejudice" kept the most capable "businessmen and capitalists" from dealing in grain and flour, reported an international grain trader. It was still widely held that grain was not a good like any other and that those who speculated on it were morally tainted. As in the eighteenth century, observers remarked with particular chagrin that this hostile view of the provisioning merchants was not limited to the *bas peuple,* but permeated "to a striking degree into the middling classes of society."[6]

The difficulty and cost of transportation, which retarded growth in all sectors of the economy in the old regime, seriously handicapped the grain trade everywhere in France. Paris, as usual, enjoyed a privileged position: its location placed a half-dozen rivers in its service and the major roads in the kingdom led to and from the capital. Neither route, however, was fully satisfactory. Although the abbé Expilly, well before Arthur Young, described the roadways as the "admiration of foreigners," especially the "beautiful roads" of the Paris circumscription, they were not, as he claimed, "all" well aligned, well maintained, and passable in all seasons.[7]

Complaints about the roads in the Brie, both those leading to Paris and those linking the various parts of the region, persisted throughout the century. The roads in the Beauce inspired similar criticism. Generally the byroads suffered far more from neglect than the major axes, thereby reinforcing local particularisms and inhibiting the development of market relations. The gov-

---

Economics: Survival and Lasting Influence from the Sixteenth Century to Adam Smith," *Quarterly Journal of Economics* 69 (1955): 179–80; Geneviève Bollème, "Littérature populaire et littérature de colportage au 18e siècle," in François Furet, ed., *Livre et société dans la France du 18ᵉ siècle* (Paris, 1965), 1:78–79. Cf. Jacques Le Goff, *La Civilisation de l'occident médiéval* (Paris, 1967), p. 437; Richard Cobb, *Les Armées révolutionnaires: Instrument de la terreur dans les départements* (Paris, 1961–63), 1:188–89.

5. See, for example, prior-consuls of St.-Malo, "Mémoire" (February 1762), AD Ille-et-Vilaine, C 3911; letter of the parlement of Grenoble to the king, 26 April 1769, AD Isère, B 2314, fol. 111. For the physiocratic portrayal of the police, see Kaplan, *Bread, Politics and Political Economy,* chaps. 1, 9, and 10; speech of Creuzé-Latouche, 8 December 1792, *Archives parlementaires,* 54:679; Jean-Baptiste Biot, *Lettres sur l'approvisionnement de Paris et sur le commerce des grains* (Paris, 1835), pp. 58–59.

6. *Enquête sur la boulangerie,* pp. 694 (Darblay the younger), 685 (Bazille), 68 (Gosset), 373–75 (Dailly), 643 (Decauville), 735 (Rabourdin), 389–90 (Aubin).

7. Abbé J.-J. Expilly, *Dictionnaire géographique, historique et politique des Gaules et de la France* (Paris, 1762–70), 5:574.

ernment made considerable efforts to build new roads, but tended to allow existing roads to fall into disrepair and to remain subject to seasonal accidents that made them impassable up to half the year. Road freight was slow and cumbersome. A wagon drawn by four horses pulling four thousand pounds could rarely cover more than twenty miles in a day. Poorly constructed roads often prohibited the use of more than two horses drawing a light cart. As a rule the wagons and carts offered the merchandise indifferent shelter, a situation particularly disastrous for grain and flour traveling in inclement weather.[8]

Overland freight was far more costly than transit by water. It has been estimated that in the second half of the century a hundred leagues' transport by land (about four hundred kilometers) doubled the average price of wheat.[9] It cost one and a half livres in 1760 to transport a setier from Etampes to Paris, ten leagues away. At the end of the sixties Antoine Lelièvre of Arpajon, three leagues closer to the capital on the same road, charged the same price. Many merchants, bakers, and millers could not afford to buy and maintain wagons and horses, and public freight and teamster services were not well organized. A carter in business for himself claimed that he lost seventy-nine horses through attrition in six years, at a cost of three hundred livres per animal.[10]

Although it was more economical, water transport remained highly underdeveloped in the eighteenth century. The government chose to invest what little social overhead capital it earmarked for transportation on the roads, and in many places towpaths were neglected or planted with trees, riverbeds were littered and impassable, and mill sluices and fisheries encumbered navigation.[11] Such obstructions hindered traffic on the lower Seine between Rouen and Paris and upriver around Bar and Méry. Careless maintenance heightened

8. On the state of transportation, see "Mémoire de la généralité de Paris par Phélypeaux," ca. 1700, BN, ms. fr. 32595, fols. 647–48, 651, 653; Louis Bergeron, "Approvisionnement et consommation à Paris sous le premier empire," *Mémoires de la Fédération des Sociétés historiques et archéologiques de Paris et de l'Ile-de-France* 14 (1963): 204. See also Jean Letaconnoux, "La Transformation des moyens de transport," in Camille Bloch et al., *Les Divisions régionales de la France* (Paris, 1913), pp. 42ff.; Jean Letaconnoux, "Les Transports en France au dix-huitième siècle," *Revue d'histoire moderne et contemporaine* 11 (1908–9): 97–114, 269–92; Jean Letaconnoux, "Les Voies de communication en France au dix-huitième siècle," *Vierteljahrschrift für Sozial- und Wirtschaftsgeschichte* 7 (1909): 123–33; Léon Cahen, "L'Economie française à la veille de la Révolution française," *Annales d'histoire sociale* 1 (1939): 24–41; Cobb, *Les Armées révolutionnaires,* 2:376–80; Coucler to Hérault, 4 October 1725, Arsenal, ms. Bast. 10270, fols. 260–62.

9. "Avis des députés de commerce," October 1769, AN, F^{12} 715; Ernest Labrousse, in Fernand Braudel and Ernest Labrousse, eds., *Histoire économique et sociale de la France* (Paris, 1970), 2:415–16, and Labrousse, *Esquisse du mouvement des prix et des revenus en France au dix-huitième siècle* (Paris, 1933), pp. 125–31.

10. Scipion, "Compte des achats faits par ordre de Mr. de Sartine" (1763), Archives Assistance publique, n.s. 47; Archives Seine-Paris, $D5B^6$ 4539 and $D4B^6$ 44-2528, 7 April 1772.

11. Letaconnoux, "Les Voies de communication," 113–14; Letaconnoux, "La Transformation des moyens de transport," pp. 43, 46; Cahen, "L'Economie française," 239–40. Cf. Mercier, *Tableau de Paris,* pp. 248, 252.

the risks of capsizing, a perpetual menace on the rivers. Seasonal impediments such as ice, floods, and low water further limited the utility of the rivers.[12] In some sections the Seine was navigable only four months a year; the Marne functioned well only from May through October; the Loire offered eight good months; the canals of Briare and Orléans closed from the end of July to the end of October and in bad winters barred traffic for an additional five months. In the fall of 1725, during a grave dearth, the government strove to open Briare and prevent the closing of Orléans, both of which provided key channels for provisions arriving from the interior.[13]

Tolls burdened the circulation of goods on the rivers, and the special privileges of pilots and boatmen in certain areas caused delays and arguments and increased costs. Public freight services were not well organized, although the Parisian authorities entertained projects for the introduction of new barge routes in the course of the century.[14] Exposed to humidity and insufficiently ventilated, waterborne grain often suffered damage and loss. Grain boats going downriver usually carried up to sixty muids; upriver capacity was generally less.[15] Downriver freight was relatively cheap; in the mid-thirties it cost ten sous the setier to transport grain from Mary-sur-Marne and less than a denier more per setier to ship from Bray-sur-Seine. Journeys upriver sharply increased the costs. Contemporaries decried the "immense cost" of shipping from Rouen to Paris; a banker in 1725 set the price at three livres the setier.[16]

The most vocal impetus for navigation improvement in the Paris region came from private entrepreneurs interested in canal building. In 1724 the comte de Jumelle presented a plan for the construction of a canal to link the Oise below L'Isle-Adam to the faubourg St.-Martin. The canal, Jumelle claimed, would facilitate the commerce of all sorts of foods, wood, and war materials, reduce the cost of going upriver, ornament the boulevards, and improve water and sewerage service in the faubourgs. In addition, "the bakers of Gonesse and the *fermiers,* able to profit from it to bring their wheat and

12. Petition and remonstrance of the bakers of the faubourgs St.-Jacques and St.-Michel, BN, ms. fr. 21639, fol. 161; arrêté sur les subsistances, conseil de la commune de Paris, 21 September 1791, AN, T 644$^{1-2}$; Pierre Dardel, *Navires et marchandises dans les ports de Rouen et du Havre au XVIIIe siècle* (Paris, 1963), pp. 470, 502–7; Jean Bastié, *La Croissance de la banlieue parisienne* (Paris, 1964), p. 51.

13. Legrand to procurator general, 12 September 1725, and controller-general to procurator general, 17 September 1725, BN, Coll. Joly 1117, fols. 197–99.

14. See, for example, deliberations of the bureau de l'Hôtel de Ville, June 1736, AN, H* 1856, fols. 419–24.

15. BN, Coll. Joly 1117, fol. 101. Considerably larger boats did unload at the ports. See Duplessis to procurator general, 13 March 1726, BN, Coll. Joly 1118, fol. 96. Canal planners envisioned boats with a capacity of 150 muids. Bureau de commerce, 24 May 1727, AN, F^{12} 682.

16. Compte du dépensier, 1735, Archives Assistance publique, no. 2, liasse 3, fol. 465; Pierre Nolasque Couvay to Hérault, 17 October 1725, Arsenal, ms. Bast. 10270, fol. 303; bureau de commerce, 24 May 1727, AN, F^{12} 682. Cf. Georges Afanassiev, *Le Commerce des céréales en France au dix-huitième siècle* (Paris, 1894), pp. 551–56.

bread to Paris, would economize half of their costs and would then be able to offer their bread more cheaply." Rebuffed, Jumelle returned two years later with a project for a canal from the Seine above the Arsenal to the Oise near Pontoise. This scheme offered the additional advantage of creating a captive water space in which mills could be built that would be unaffected by the vagaries of the rivers. The royal council rejected the proposal on the grounds that it was too huge and ambitious. Several powerful seigneurs, fearing that a canal would devalue their lands, passionately opposed the idea.[17]

In 1727, the council examined three new designs, one for a canal between Paris and St.-Denis, another for "a canal around Paris," and a third for a canal from Dieppe to the capital, all of which promised solemnly "to facilitate the transport of the Abundance of commodities necessary to life."[18] In March of 1730 the assembly of police reacted enthusiastically to a new version of the St.-Denis canal idea, but in July it decided that there were "twenty reasons against the Canal for every one that could be made in its favor." Among the twenty negative points was the violent resistance of the millers who would be dispossessed of their present establishments and of the carters who would lose their overland monopoly on freight transfers.[19]

The royal council granted permission for the construction of a canal through Picardy linking the Somme and the Oise. The directors, among whom were several prominent royal accountants and the financiers Crozat and Lenormant, claimed that the new link forged by the canal would enable the capital to draw "at least one-third" of its daily grain consumption from the fertile provinces of Picardy, Artois, and Cambrésis, which hitherto had contributed relatively little.[20] For more than twenty years the family and associates of the duc d'Estrées strove to launch a canal connecting the Yonne and the Loire and serving to complement the already existing Loing and Briare canals. The proprietors of those canals vigorously opposed the plan on the grounds that it "would not procure any utility to the city of Paris" and that "it would cause a very great prejudice to the canals of Orléans and Loing" and would "destroy" that of Briare.[21] Although a lingering case of canal fever continued to generate blueprints and reveries until the end of the century, virtually all the projects for canals that directly affected the provisioning of

17. "Mémoire concernant la construction d'un nouveau canal sous le nom de canal de Bourbon," BN, ms. fr. 21689, fols. 84–87; "Mémoire pour le canal," November 1726, AN, G^7 675.

18. "Nouveau canal projetté de Paris à St.-Denis," BN, ms. fr. 21690, fol. 1; "Canal autour de Paris," BN, ms. fr. 21689, fols. 85–86; deliberations of the bureau of commerce, 1727, AN, F^{12} 682.

19. Assemblies of police, 9, 23 March and 20 July 1730, BN, ms. fr. 11356, fols. 119–21, 128–32.

20. "Instruction générale pour les intéressés au canal de Picardie," BN, ms. fr. 21690, fols. 9–18.

21. BN, Coll. Joly 2025, fols. 58–90.

Paris were forsaken as a result of government apathy or antagonism, the hostility of vested interests, technical imbroglios, and lack of capital.[22]

Weights and Measures

In a commerce where the trader faced acute uncertainties at every turn—uncertainties of weather, of the size and quality of the forthcoming harvest, of the availability of transport, of the speculative climate, of the attitude of the police—not even the system of weights and measures offered an absolute. "The infinite perplexity of the measures exceeds all comprehension," noted Arthur Young acerbically. "They differ not only in every province, but in every district, and almost in every town."[23] Like Voltaire's celebrated post-rider who "changed" legal regimes more often than he changed horses in crossing the realm, the grain merchant had occasion to change measuring customs several times long before his initial mount tired. This multiplicity of systems confused and inconvenienced buyers and sellers, provoked bitter disputes, reinforced insular trading patterns, and confounded the government's efforts to keep track of production and prices.

The Parisian nomenclature—*boisseau, minot, setier, muid*—generally prevailed in the Seine basin, but the content of the measures differed widely from place to place. At Meulan the setier was slightly heavier than in the capital. The setiers of Bray, Vitry, and Châlons were lighter than the Paris standard, and all differed from each other. The Soissons setier weighed only eighty livres. Quite apart from frauds devised to puff volume or augment weight and from differences in measuring "hand" or style that affected measure and weight, the Paris setier itself fluctuated legitimately from 230 pounds or less to upward of 250 pounds, depending on the quality of the crop and the conditions in which it was harvested, the season, and the time elapsed since harvesting.[24] The Paris muid comprised twelve setiers; the Orléans muid consisted of two and a half setiers, measure of Paris. In most places in the Paris region, the setier of oats was not the same measure as the setier used in bread-making grains. In the capital the setier of wheat and flour each con-

22. For an exception that concerned wood rather than grain provisioning, see *Rapport de M. l'abbé Bossut, de M. l'abbé Rochon et de M. le marquis de Condorcet, membres de l'Académie des sciences, sur le canal que le gouvernement fait construire en Nivernais* (Paris, 1786).

23. Arthur Young, *Travels in France during the years 1787, 1788 and 1789*, ed. Jeffry Kaplow (Garden City, N.Y., 1969), p. 258.

24. On the variation in the weight of the Paris setier, see Archives Seine-Paris, D5B⁶ 2114 (miller Aubé) and Dupré de St.-Maur, *Essai sur les monnaies*, pp. 48–55. A seventeenth-century cleric with a curious taste for quantification counted 2,264,000 individual grains of wheat in a Paris setier, while another expert, a century later, found only 2,211,840. Father Mersenne, cited by Delamare, *Traité de la police,* 2:643 and Béguillet, *Traité des subsistances,* p. 171.

tained twelve boisseaux, but the boisseau of wheat weighed twenty pounds while the equivalent flour measure weighed between twelve and thirteen. At Meulan and elsewhere, the size of the measure changed in the course of the old regime, posing vexatious problems of conversion.

Beyond the Paris area the names of measures changed, further complicating transactions. At Dijon one dealt in *bichets* and *émines,* in Lyon in *anées,* in much of the Midi in *charges.* Everyone seemed to agree that an English *quarter* represented about two Paris setiers. If one traded for Dutch grain, however, there was danger of misunderstanding, for two of the most knowledgeable French commentators could not agree if the *last* equaled nineteen or twenty Paris setiers.[25] A glaring reminder of the incomplete sovereignty of the absolute king, the crazy quilt of weights and measures, like other feudal vestiges, continued to find favor with many local and provincial interests. Despite the pleas of scores of writers, including Delamare, for a rational system of uniformity, the government judged the situation too complex and too delicate to reform.[26]

The Provisioning Crowns

Contemporaries spoke of the hinterland that supplied Paris with grain and flour in terms of "crowns," or zones. The primary crown extended slightly beyond the boundaries of the generality of Paris, the largest such administrative district in the kingdom and one in which the grain trade was the chief form of commercial activity. At the center of this crown were the vast and fertile plains of "France," whose chief markets were Gonesse and Dammartin to the northeast of the capital. Further to the northeast lay the Valois; though it had substantial markets at Nanteuil, Crépy, and La Ferté-Milon, most of its grain reached the capital through other channels. The Brie stood to the east, a vast and rich region that stretched into Champagne and boasted many of the most important markets in the zone, on the Seine and Marne rivers and in between.[27] The Beauce, commonly called "the granary of Paris," was situated to the south; Etampes was its most active town in the Paris-bound traffic, but

25. Delamare, *Traité de la police,* 2:641–44; Abbot P. Usher, *The History of the Grain Trade in France, 1400–1710* (Cambridge, 1913), pp. 366–67; Jacques Dupâquier et al., *Mercuriales du pays de France et du Vexin français, 1640–1792* (Paris, 1968), pp. 23–27; Charles Musart, *La Réglementation du commerce des grains en France au XVIIIe siècle: La théorie de Delamare, étude économique* (Paris, 1922), p. 188; Saint-Germain, *Vie quotidienne,* p. 208; Malouin, *Description et détails des arts,* pp. 111–12; Dupré de St.-Maur, *Essai sur les monnaies,* p. 186; Béguillet, *Traité des subsistances,* p. 176; Voltaire, "Bled," *Dictionnaire philosophique,* in *Oeuvres complètes,* 18:14; Baudeau, *Avis au peuple,* premier traité, p. 37.

26. Delamare, *Traité de la police,* 2:926; BN, ms. fr. 21632, fols. 1–31. Cf. Duchesne, *Code de la police,* p. 247.

27. Expilly, *Dictionnaire géographique,* 5:568, 574; "Mémoire sur la fertilité des provinces du royaume pour ce qui concerne les grains, les secours qu'elles peuvent se procurer mutuellement, et particulièrement la ville de Paris," AN, F[11] 227; Arthur de Boislisle, ed.,

much of its wheat went to the capital directly from the countryside or through other markets. The Hurepoix, another wheat-abundant region south and southwest of Paris, served the city through markets at Montlhéry, Dourdan, Houdan, and Montfort. Pontoise, the nerve center of the Vexin français to the northwest of Paris, was an important market for grain, and especially for flour.[28]

The second crown, some of whose markets contributed as significantly as the primary crown towns to the provisioning of Paris, encompassed Picardy to the northwest, the Soissonnais to the northeast, Champagne to the east (Châlons and Vitry regularly supplied Paris), and parts of the Gâtinais and the Orléanais to the south. The third or crisis crown had no definite borders; usually it included Burgundy, Flanders, Lorraine, Alsace, the Bourbonnais, the Poitou, and Auvergne, but it was known to stretch to the Atlantic and Mediterranean provinces. In emergencies Paris also drew upon supplies from northern, southern, and central Europe; in the second half of the century Parisians had occasion to taste American flour as well.[29] Despite the growth of the city, Paris did not seek to draw new areas into its sphere of influence; instead, it sought to make more efficient use of the available supply. The aggressive grain irredentism of the sixteenth and seventeenth centuries gave way to a chary proprietary posture. Parisian hegemony in the first two crowns did not pass unchallenged. Parts of the Beauce and Normandy remained contested, occasionally Rouen siphoned off grain from Soissons and Noyon, Burgundy encroached upon the Brie, and Orléans made forays to Etampes. Still, the eighteenth century witnessed nothing like the bitter confrontations of earlier times, at least not until 1789.[30]

Mémoire de la généralité de Paris (1700), in *Mémoires des intendants sur l'état des généralités dressés pour l'instruction du duc de Bourgogne* (Paris, 1881), 1:341–44. Cf. Le Camus, "Mémoire sur le bled," pp. 124–25, which either served as a model for or more likely pillaged the "Mémoire sur la fertilité" cited above (n. 27). See also Guy Fourquin, *Les Campagnes de la région parisienne à la fin du Moyen Age* (Paris, 1959), p. 500; Bergeron, "Approvisionnement et consommation," p. 206; Bertrand Gille, "Fonctions économiques de Paris," in *Paris: Fonctions d'une capitale,* ed. Guy Michaud (Paris, 1962), p. 131; "La Cherté du pain" (1792), AN, T 644[1–2].

28. Louis Brion de La Tour, *Etat actuel de la France* (Paris, 1774?), p. 57. Cf. Michel Vovelle, "Les Taxations populaires de février–mars et de novembre–décembre 1792 dans la Beauce et sur ses confins," *Actes du 82ᵉ Congrès national des sociétés savantes,* Bordeaux, 1957, *Mémoires et documents, Commission de recherche et de publication des documents relatifs à la vie économique de la Révolution* 13 (1958), p. 110.

29. Bertier de Sauvigny, "Observations sur le commerce des grains" (ca. 1765), BN, ms. fr. 11347, fol. 226; Dardel, *Navires et marchandises,* pp. 226–27; Antoine-Augustin Parmentier, "Expérience," AN, F[10] 257 and "Rapport," n.d., F[10] 226. Cf. David Klingaman, "Food Surpluses and Deficits in the American Colonies, 1768–1772," *Journal of Economic History* 31 (September 1971): 553–69; John G. Clark, *The Grain Trade in the Old Northwest* (Urbana, 1966), p. 177; Thrupp, *Bakers of London,* p. 32. By the mid-1850s, much of the crisis crown had been absorbed into the primary supply zone. *Enquête sur la boulangerie,* p. 481.

30. "Précis sur les moyens d'approvisionner le département de Paris" (ca. 1792), AN, T 644[1–2]. See Usher, *Grain Trade,* for a summary sketch of the grain trade before the eighteenth century.

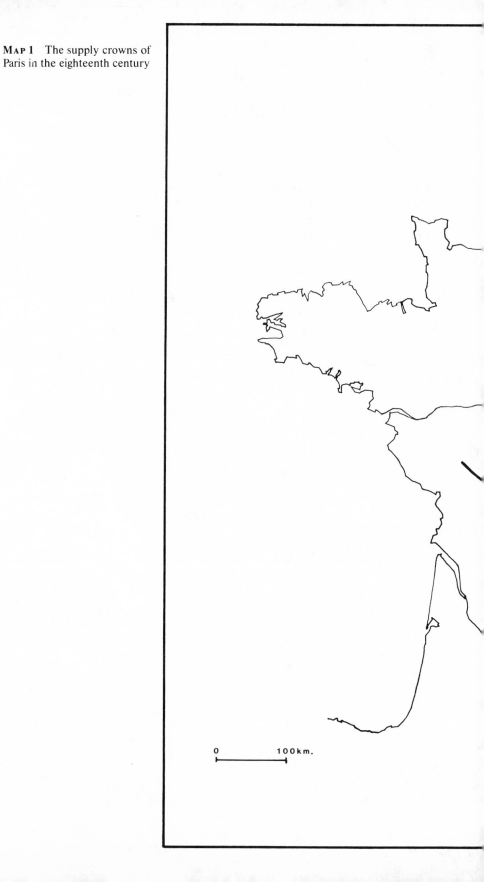

MAP 1 The supply crowns of
Paris in the eighteenth century

0   100km.

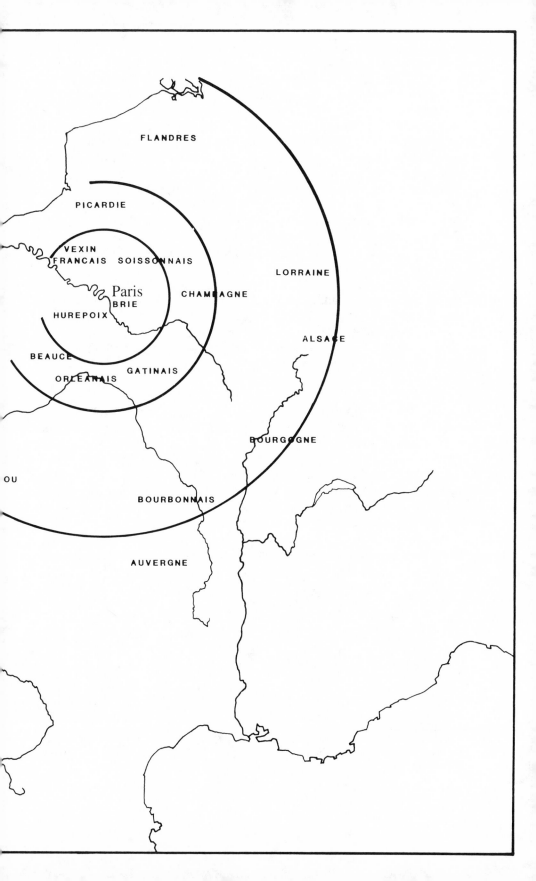

Different soil types, along with variations in microclimate and local adaptation of cereal types, yielded grain of different milling and baking qualities. The soils of the primary crown were marked by a complex alternation of limestones, sandstones, and clays, with a general predominance of limestone subsoil. The limestone plains were to a large extent covered with loam *(limon)*, a finely grained deposit of great fertility. The monotonously flat Beauce lacked rivers and vines and meadows, but its exceptionally thick layer of loam, blanketing a recently constituted limestone base, made it unusually fine cereal-growing land. Lower, wetter, and more undulating than the Beauce, the Brie possessed a variety of soils. The loam-topped stretches were complemented by substantial sections covered with clay-with-flints. The Hurepoix, too, boasted a loam-rich arable, though it was eroding and ceding place to forest-covered clay and sand soils. Less opulently endowed than the Beauce, the limestone of the Gâtinais was frequently associated with clays and sands. The soils of "France" and the Vexin français owed their fertility to the loam-covered limestone, while the Soissonnais and the Valois were divided between limestone plateaus and humid valleys. Developed mainly on chalky soils, the Picardy reserved a substantial part of its loamy arable for Paris-bound cereal production. The Champagne was much less hospitable to cereal production because of its paucity of loam and its surfeit of dry, "dusty" chalk.

The climate, like the topography, was characterized by its overall moderation and by its multiplicity of local nuances. Winters were not bitter, and the coldest season was quite short. Summers were warm, but protracted periods of luminous heat were rare, and oppressive, humid, or stormy spells alternated with more stable and refreshing ones. Despite the frequent summer humidity and the long winter-spring phase of sullen and wet weather, the Paris region enjoyed one of the lowest rates of annual rainfall in France. Excessive humidity was the chief threat to wheat cultivation in the primary crown. During growth it easily tolerated a cold winter, but not a wet one. A warm and sunny spring–summer favored high yields. A very wet summer augured catastrophe, causing the plants to lodge and rot.[31]

One can speak of a market "system" only in a very tenuous way. In political, administrative, and judicial terms, Paris was the kingdom's "central place." In terms of provisioning, however, its central market claims were not rationally institutionalized. Paris had to drain supplies that were widely scat-

31. Margaret R. Shackleton, *Europe: A Regional Geography* (London, 1950), pp. 146–58; Georges Chabot, *Géographie régionale de la France* (Paris, 1966), pp. 373–82; Jacqueline Beaujeu-Garnier, *Le Relief de la France* (Paris, 1972), pp. 125–43; Beaujeu-Garnier, *Atlas et géographie de la région de l'Ile-de-France* (Paris, 1977), 1:24–31; Bastié, *La Croissance de la banlieue parisienne,* pp. 42–51; Jean Jacquart, *La Crise rurale en Ile-de-France, 1550–1670* (Paris, 1974), pp. 7–11; Jean-Marie Constant, *Nobles et paysans en Beauce aux XVIᵉ et XVIIᵉ siècles* (Lille, 1981), pp. 1–4; Pierre George and Pierre Randet, *La Région parisienne* (Paris, 1959), pp. 100–102; Emmanuel Le Roy Ladurie, *Histoire du climat depuis l'an mil* (Paris, 1967), pp. 281–83.

tered in thousands and thousands of small units. In order to concentrate and centralize these supplies most efficiently, the capital needed a chain of hierarchically organized feeder and satellite markets. As a result of a host of ecological, technological, and political factors, including drastically inadequate communications, commercial and administrative rivalries and jealousies, intense grain particularism at the local level, and the ambiguities of the regulatory (or "police") model, this integrated system of circulation and exchange only came fully into being with the information and transportation revolutions of the nineteenth century. Though the welter of local differences impedes generalization—anomalous cases of markets with ostensibly "modern" traits turn up as early as the sixteenth century—it is probably fair to say that until roughly the end of the reign of Louis XIV the provisioning of Paris took place despite rather than because of the supply-zone market system. For a long time the officials of the zone markets continued to think of the grain trade in terms of the preponderance of local interests. This meant that in years of subsistence difficulties provisioning Paris was tantamount to pillaging the provinces.[32]

During the eighteenth century, intermarket trade became highly developed, a number of important distributive centers emerged, and the most important markets concentrated supplies in anticipation of metropolitan demand. But the system was still inefficient and unpredictable, and the markets can be considered wholesale concourses only in an incomplete sense. Much of the supply remained elusive or invisible, only a portion of the exchanges were public and open, the price was not always the product of brisk competition of buyers and sellers, trade on most of the markets was intermittent rather than continuous, there was no rational scheduling in order to remove redundancy and reduce friction, and the proper relationship between wholesale and local needs was still disputed, especially in hard times.

At the end of the seventeenth century, there seems to have been a trend toward concentration of supply in one or two dominant markets in each region, but in the eighteenth century this trend disappears. In fact, the loci of concentration shift, and markets undergo booms and brutal eclipses as a result of harvest conditions, transportation facilities, measuring and market fee management, police enforcement, and administrative fiat. A large part of the provisioning trade took place independent of the market system. Commerce was ubiquitous; it took place wherever there was grain. Traders often bypassed the market because they regarded it, all things considered, as more

32. On central place theory, see G. William Skinner, "Marketing and Social Structure in Rural China," *Journal of Asian Studies* 24 (November 1964): 3–43; R. J. Bromberg and Richard Symanski, "Marketplace Trade in Latin America," *Latin American Research Review* 9 (Fall 1974): 15–17; Brian J. L. Berry, *Geography of Market Centers and Retail Distribution* (Englewood Cliffs, N.J., 1967). On the tension between Paris and its supply provinces, see Kaplan, *Bread, Politics and Political Economy,* 1:29–42.

of a vexation than a convenience. Given the continued expansion of direct baker-operated supply commerce, the growth of the Halle-bound flour trade, and the generous toleration of off-market (country and granary) buying, it is likely that the portion of the provisioning traffic handled by the hinterland markets declined in the course of the eighteenth century.

It is difficult to measure the contribution and determine the precise role of the zone markets in the provisioning process. In a memorandum of 1686 the Paris bakers indicated that they regularly visited thirty-two markets. The average amount of grain that each market displayed per week was 66.2 muids, of which presumably a substantial portion entered the Paris channels. Ten markets offered quantities above 100 muids, including Meaux, Melun, La Ferté-sous-Jouarre, Rebais, Etampes, and Dourdan. The smallest markets were Nogent-le-Roy in the Beauce with 4 muids and Château-Thierry near Champagne with 5.[33]

In a general census compiled by Delamare at the turn of the century, covering merchant and laboureur as well as baker trade, forty-two markets appeared with an average weekly offering of 65 muids each. Montlhéry, with 300 muids the biggest market, which Delamare claimed was frequented by Paris and Gonesse bakers because of the excellence of its wheat, did not even appear on the earlier baker enumeration. The most sluggish markets on the baker lists, Nogent and Château-Thierry, accounted for 40 and 50 muids respectively. La Ferté-sous-Jouarre, where the bakers found upward of 100 muids a week in 1686, exhibited only 6 around 1700.[34] Yet La Ferté, along with Faremoutiers (6 muids) and Nangis (3 muids), figured prominently on the statement of the traditionally favored markets drawn up by the Paris grain merchants in the late 1730s.[35]

Because of its location, the economic interests of its inhabitants, and the great fertility of the soil, Delamare wrote, the Gonesse market "should be one of the most abundant." As a result, however, of the illegal "habit" practiced by the laboureurs of selling outside the public concourse, it offered no more than 50 to 60 muids a week. But if the records for payment of domanial droits due to the Hôtel-Dieu for market sale and storage can be trusted (they would tend to underestimate the amount sold, as a consequence of exemptions and fraud), the average weekly quantity for the years 1742–44, 1746–47, and 1749 was 143.6 muids, a formidable level of sustained transactions. Either Delamare miscalculated or the authorities policed Gonesse with more success than ever before.[36]

33. "Mémoire pour les boulangers" (1686), BN, ms. fr. 21640, fols. 73–76, 82–84.

34. Delamare, Traité de la police, 2:823–27. Cf. BN, ms. fr. 21635, fols. 253–54, and Coll. Joly 1116, fols. 18–19. The "baker" and Delamare averages are implausibly high.

35. BN, Coll. Joly 1314, fols. 20bis–21.

36. Delamare, Traité de la police, 2:823; fonds ancien, Hôtel-Dieu, Archives Assistance publique. Cf. Boislisle, Mémoire de la généralité de Paris, 2:347; Cobb, Armées révolutionnaires, 2:377; Bertier de Sauvigny fils to Necker, 18 May 1789, cited by Gustave Bord, Histoire du blé en France: Le Pacte de famine, histoire, légende (Paris, 1887), p. 51.

On the other hand, Lizy, ideally situated on the Ourcq River near the common frontiers of the Brie, the Mulcien, and the Ile-de-France, seems to have enjoyed no such recovery. Formerly, claimed Delamare, it concentrated three hundred muids of grain a week. Now it had only four or five because the merchants and Paris factors "run the farms" and "buy in the granaries." Seventy years later the fiscal procurator of Lizy mournfully recounted the same story of missed opportunity and a bountiful yet invisible off-market supply.[37] Delamare blamed the modesty of Nogent-sur-Seine's offerings on the same merchant "license," while Missonnet, a special police official assigned to the Brie area in the 1750s who showed no indulgence for off-market activities, ascribed the lack of abundance to the rules of the market that prohibited merchants from buying until after 2:00 P.M. and thus deterred the grain growers from furnishing the town. Delamare described Montereau, at the confluence of the Seine and the Yonne, as a solid market (up to 100 muids) frequented by merchants shipping by water, whereas Missonnet a half-century later intimated that it was a far less well-endowed market serviced by petty traders called blatiers.[38] In the time of Delamare, to afford laboureurs and merchants ample opportunity to furnish, sell, and buy, the authorities at Bray, ninety-two kilometers from the capital, did not enforce the schedule of fixed days and hours, thus enabling the market to become "continual" and wholesale dealers to exchange goods at their convenience. Fifty years later the laboureur supply had dwindled and the failure to fix hours and trading customs produced a chaotic situation in which "an extremely abundant market disappears in an instant without revealing who are the persons who bought."[39]

While grain markets are fluid, the flour markets present a picture of steady growth. As early as 1690, Melun had a thriving flour commerce with the capital. In the 1730s eight large mills functioned primarily for Paris, providing more than five hundred sacks a week *en droiture* to the Paris bakers in addition to the quantities displayed at the Halle.[40] Pontoise and Beaumont, on the Oise, emerged as leading flour centers early in the eighteenth century.[41] Favored by its location, the presence of the court, and the practice of selling

37. Delamare, *Traité de la police,* 2:825; Suart to procurator general, 6 March 1771, BN, Coll. Joly 1158, fols. 223–25.

38. Delamare, *Traité de la police,* 2:825–26; Missonnet report, 17 September 1751, BN, Coll. Joly 1112, fol. 5–7.

39. Delamare, *Traité de la police,* 2:824; mémoire contre la déclaration du 8 septembre 1737, BN, ms. fr. 21635, fols. 166–67.

40. See, for example, police sentence, 1 July 1729, BN, ms. fr. 21636, fol. 338, and Reddeville to procurator general, 20 May 1740, BN, Coll. Joly 1123, fol. 214.

41. Trennin to Moreau, 29 November 1740, AN, F[11] 222; rapport arbitre, 9 June 1769 (Gallien), Archives Seine-Paris, D6B[6] 5; Narbonne, *Louis XIV et Louis XV,* p. 126. Cf. Fernand Evrard, *Versailles, ville du roi (1770–1789). Etude d'économie urbaine* (Paris, 1935), p. 412.

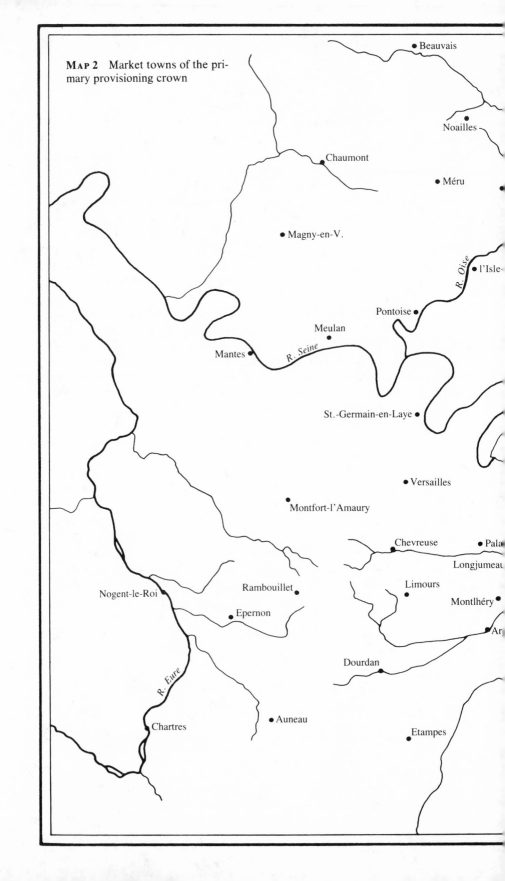

MAP 2 Market towns of the primary provisioning crown

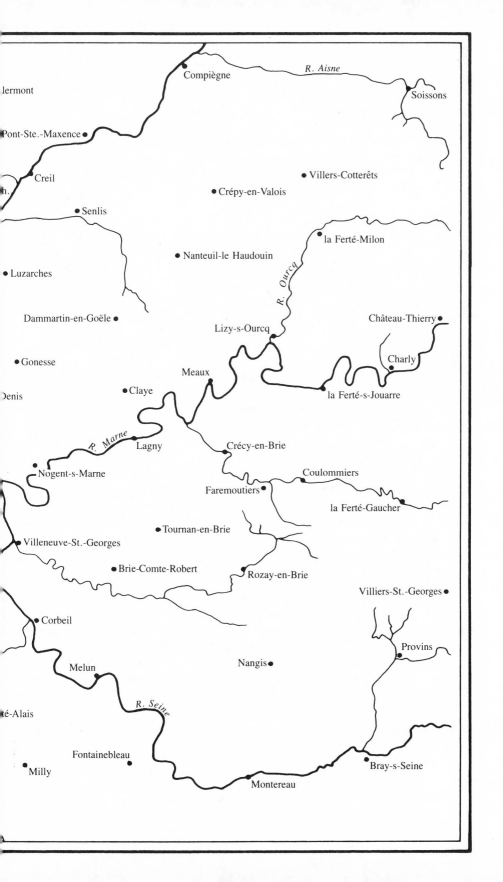

by weight, Versailles developed a major flour market attracting a large number of outside mealmen and Paris bakers. To complement it, a Versailles
official proposed establishing a grain market in the *parc aux cerfs,* a portion of
which Louis XV later devoted to a different sort of commerce.[42]

Sufficient information is available to trace the evolution of a few grain
markets in greater detail. Toward the end of the seventeenth century,
Montlhéry, a town in the Hurepoix, had one of the strongest markets in the
entire hinterland, attracting three hundred muids or more per week.
Laboureurs from the *pays* Chartrain, merchants from Etampes, and blatiers
from all over the Beauce supplied the market regularly, and the high quality of
its wheat attracted bakers and merchants from afar. The market owed its
strength to its location, moderate market fees, and probably an accommodat-
ing police; it was neither better equipped nor more efficiently run than other
markets in the region. In the late 1690s Montlhéry suffered a crisis of erosion
and disorganization of the kind that periodically befell the zone markets,
leading in some cases to renewal and in others to extinction. For reasons that
are not clear but that are probably related to its failure to develop structures
of exchange suitable to handle the heavy trade, the buyers and sellers began
to desert the market, though they continued to use the town as a base of
operations. Paris merchants, jealous perhaps of the independent trade established by the bakers, began to intercept laboureurs on the way to market and
to scour the countryside, despite the fact that Montlhéry lay within the eight-
league area around Paris in which all trade was forbidden in order to force
local growers to supply the capital themselves. The wealthier fermiers (grain-
growing peasants who rented rather than owned the bulk of their holdings)
took to speculating, buying out the laboureurs who went to market. As much
trading occurred in the taverns and inns, based on the display of samples, as
at the public market. Unable to find adequate supplies at reasonable prices,
the bakers of Paris and Gonesse turned to Dourdan and the markets of the
Brie.[43]

Built upon a fragile foundation, the abundance of Montlhéry proved to be
illusory. Yet it is clear that these same flawed foundations, reinforced by a
more attentive police vigilance, could be made to support a flourishing, visible trade once again. In 1725 an officer of the maréchaussée characterized
Montlhéry as a model supply town. The market, he reported, "behaved perfectly well." Dealers exposed all their grain on the market without prodding.
"It would be desirable," the officer concluded, "that things were observed in
the same manner throughout the kingdom." In the thirties the weekly grain

42. Delamare, *Traité de la police,* 2:823–24; BN, ms. fr. 21644, fols. 6–9. Cf. Usher, *Grain Trade,* pp. 89–92.
43. Marchais to Hérault, 26 November, 3 December 1725, Arsenal, ms. Bast. 10271; petition of Montlhéry inhabitants to cardinal Fleury, ca. 1737, BN, Coll. Joly 1314, fol. 30.

offering climbed back to three hundred muids a week. "It is, after a fashion, the center of the other, more distant markets and serves them as a yardstick for the price of grain," the Montlhéry town fathers boasted. The Paris bakers, who found excellent facilities for flour making at thirty mills located on four rivers near the town, were "the prime movers of this market." Although many towns were ambivalent about their attitude toward Paris, especially in times of scarcity, Montlhéry officials saw no conflict between local and metropolitan demand and regarded the town as fully integrated into the wholesale provisioning chain. Indeed, they claimed that Montlhéry and the surrounding villages depended almost completely upon the business of the market and its multiplier effects for their livelihood.[44]

In 1736–37, partly as a result of pressure from the Paris grain merchants and the measurers and porters, all of whom had reasons to want to curtail independent baker grain and flour trade, the police decided to discontinue the tolerance that had permitted bakers to buy more or less freely in the decommercialized zone. Word had reached the capital that the Paris bakers and local dealers were abusing this tacit permission by engaging in "monopoly" practices: buying off-market from speculating middlemen called regraters, forming stocks, buying on sample, and procuring fraudulent certificates to cover their illicit operations. Delegated by lieutenant general of police Hérault to investigate in January of 1737, two porters and a huissier visited Montlhéry, found two faubourg St.-Antoine bakers and a country dealer in violation of trading regulations, and declared their grain seized. Hérault found them guilty and instructed Marchais, the same maréchaussée officer who had hailed Montlhéry as a model market twelve years before, to cry the sentence in the town and sell the seized grain.[45]

Convinced that it meant the ruin of the town, local officials reacted bitterly to the news that their market would be put off limits. Leroy, a cleric who represented the prior of Montlhéry, seigneur of the town, incited a crowd to resist Marchais and his troops, "yelling loudly that one could not deprive the bakers of Paris of the liberty of coming to buy grain in the said market." Brandishing sticks and pitchforks, the crowd drove Marchais and his detachment from the town. While the Paris police investigated the "rebellion," the town notables plaintively petitioned the cardinal Fleury to renew the tolerance. "A grand consternation" seized the whole town because the bakers no longer came, the laboureurs discontinued their supply, and the weekly offering fell from 300 muids to 30. Unlike other markets in the same predicament, such as Brie-Comte-Robert, Montlhéry did not win an explicit exemption

44. Police sentence, 11 January 1737, BN, ms. fr. 21635, fols. 164–66.
45. AN, Y 11224, 4 February 1737; petition of Montlhéry inhabitants to cardinal Fleury, BN, Coll. Joly 1314, fols. 30–33.

from the trading interdiction. Although it is likely that the Paris bakers resumed their purchases, they do not seem to have returned in force. This time
Montlhéry appears to have gone into prolonged eclipse.[46]

Etampes, a Beauce market well beyond the forbidden frontier, stood
ready to profit from Montlhéry's distress.[47] After the river that had permitted
direct water shipment to Paris became unnavigable in the second half of the
seventeenth century, Etampes became a sort of tributary market to
Montlhéry. It continued to display substantial weekly offerings—up to 150
muids—but the bulk of the Paris-bound grain was transferred by merchants
and blatiers for sale to the avid bakers of Paris and Gonesse at Montlhéry, the
real wholesale outlet. Because their market was situated in the midst of one of
the most fertile provinces in the kingdom, Etampes's leaders felt that it should
be a more important commercial center. To make the market more attractive,
they relaxed the police regulations and tolerated illicit trading practices. The
permissive attitude of the Etampes police brought them into conflict with
Parisian authorities, who regarded the Beauce market as a scandal and as a
potential threat to the orderly provisioning of the capital. Widespread regrating occurred at Etampes in the mid-twenties, obfuscating the supply and
driving the price up. Local merchants bought up all the grain at the market,
forcing Paris traders and bakers to buy from them on their terms. Though it is
not clear what action was taken, a police functionary sent to observe denounced the Etampes operation as "a shocking brigandage" and called for a
cleanup campaign.[48]

Backed by a parlementary decree (arrêt), Hérault undertook to purge
Etampes of its "abuses" in 1738 shortly after the closing of Montlhéry had
increased its traffic. He dispatched three men to Etampes to visit the market:
Defacq, a commissaire without extensive experience in grain affairs who
would not be known to the dealers at Etampes; the grain merchant Jean
Gibert, who would serve as a technical adviser on grain matters; and a
mounted huissier. The commander of the local maréchaussée brigade received instructions to join them at the marketplace. They found numerous
violations of the rules: laboureurs bought substantial amounts of wheat and
sold wheat to unauthorized buyers; a miller purchased grain; the wife of a
local measurer conducted a clandestine brokerage; transaction by sample was
a common practice; several merchants and laboureurs maintained granaries
in the town; a gardener offered wheat on sample at 28 livres when the current
head was 25 livres 10 sous. The huissier issued summonses to all the violators

46. Delamare, *Traité de la police*, 2:824. According to one source, Etampes was 12.125
leagues distant from Paris; another fixed the distance at 14 leagues. Because distance had
important political and economic implications, disputes over measurement erupted often.
See BN, Coll. Joly 1314, fols. 26–27, and 1429, fols. 54–55.

47. Lepoupet to Hérault, 2 November 1725, Arsenal, ms. Bast. 10272.

48. Defacq report, 18 October 1738, BN, Coll. Joly 1119, fols. 4–7.

to appear before Hérault at the capital. The following week at the Saturday market the maréchaussée commander again issued summonses, including one to a *cabaretier* who bought large amounts of grain for regrating "to earn a few extra sous." It seems likely that these extraordinary inspections continued for some time.[49]

Furious at this "encroachment on our jurisdiction," Edeline, the police lieutenant of Etampes, who had served the city for thirty-four years, vehemently protested that the lieutenant general of Paris had "no orders to give in the grain market of this city." When he received word from the marketplace that Defacq and his men "were prowling around and haughtily giving orders and thereby interrupting the ordinary course of the market," the Etampes official charged them with spreading fear, harassing buyers and sellers, and driving grain away from the market. He appealed to the procurator general to protect his authority and the prosperity of the market against the inroads of the Paris police and joined with the representative of the *seigneur-engagiste* of Etampes, the prince de Conty, who had a venal interest in the success of the market, in complaining that it was unfair to punish Etampes without applying the same standards to other markets. The procurator general rejected their remonstrance and censured Edeline for negligence.[50]

Indications are that the crackdown of 1738 had no lasting effect on either the size or the habits of the Etampes market. Informed that "there are individuals at Etampes who practice maneuvers prejudicial to the grain trade," the Paris police in 1752 again sent a "man of confidence . . . to investigate surely and secretly." In this instance, the procurator general forewarned the Etampes authorities and they agreed to cooperate. The Paris agent, Bourguignon, holder of a grain porter's office at the Paris Halle, lurked about the marketplace and the cabarets for a few weeks, posing as a buyer and trying to find out where he could make purchases outside the market. On the whole there was less "disorder" in 1752 than there had been fourteen years before. Bourguignon discovered a merchant who bought precipitately without "bargaining" on the price and examining the merchandise, another who maintained hidden storehouses, a third who pretended to buy for Paris while hoarding for other purposes, a fourth who offered to sell off-market, a laboureur who refused to honor his morning price in the afternoon, and other similar suspects, whom the Etampes police promised to prosecute.[51] Etampes, like Montlhéry and the bulk of the zone markets, introduced no innovations in marketing techniques or organization during the eighteenth

49. AN, Y 11225, 25 October 1738.

50. The following correspondence is from BN, Coll. Joly 1129, fols. 59–72: Berryer to procurator general, 9 December 1752; procurator general to Gabaille, 14, 22 December 1752; Gabaille to procurator, 17, 24 December 1752; Bourguignon to same, 16, 19, 22 December 1752. For an example of "abuses" at Etampes later in the century, see BN, Coll. Joly 1111, fol. 236.

51. Delamare, *Traité de la police,* 2:826; BN, ms. fr. 21645, fol. 376.

century. To enhance its competitive position, its officials manipulated the traditional police regulations. The result was to make the market busier at the cost of rendering it less efficient as a wholesale link in the chain of Paris provisioning.

Provins, a "very small" market in the Brie about eighty-five kilometers from Paris, grew substantially in the eighteenth century. Its commerce received an important stimulus at the turn of the century when the Parlement of Paris ordered a religious community, the owner of the marketing and measuring rights called the *minage,* to moderate and simplify the excessively high fees imposed on transactions.[52] In 1725 "disorder reigned in the city." The local officials argued over jurisdiction, insulted each other, and acted at cross-purposes. The police commissaire accused the royal procurator of being "soft," the lieutenant general of being indifferent, and the intendant's sub-delegate of driving away suppliers with his authoritarian manner. An agent of the Paris police found that the market existed in name only; laboureurs and merchants withdrew grain from the public place when they could not obtain a satisfactory price and invited buyers to visit them in their houses and granaries. The Paris purchasing agents hoarded grain instead of shipping it to the capital. The procurator general was apparently successful in arbitrating the disputes among the authorities and enforcing the regulations. The market rebounded dramatically and provided Paris with urgently needed supplies during the dearth.[53]

Despite persistent difficulties with the minage owners, the market continued to expand. By mid-century Provins set "the standard for the price of grain in almost all the markets" of the region. The wholesale Paris demand remained brisk. Problems arose when the feverish competition for supplies induced some of the Paris agents to flee the market for purchases in the countryside. Although Paris buyers were legally authorized to canvass the farms and granaries, Missonnet, the government agent assigned to the area, vigorously lobbied with the Paris authorities to require all merchants to restrict their purchases to the market. Informally, he pressured the laboureurs to spurn offers made outside the public concourse.[54] Toward the end of the century, Parmentier praised Provins as an exemplary market. Bakers and merchants could buy there in confidence and security. Four local notables, Parmentier wrote, "grain connoisseurs," kept a strict vigilance on exchanges and prevented frauds in quality, quantity, and price. The Provins officials, he

---

52. Lobinod to procurator general, 28 July 1725, and Paulfoy to same, 6, 18 August 1725, BN, Coll. Joly 1117, fols. 102–5; Bourlon to Hérault, 4 October 1725, and procurator general to d'Ombreval, [?] August 1725, Arsenal, ms. Bast. 10270.

53. Missonnet to procurator general, 6 June, 17 September 1752, and 22 September 1757, BN, Coll. Joly 1112, fols. 7, 90, and 1130, fol. 195.

54. Parmentier, *Parfait Boulanger,* p. 123.

suggested, understood better than most of their counterparts elsewhere the functions of wholesale commerce.[55]

Reaching Paris by Land and Water

The defects in the Paris-bound freighting system caused inconvenience, raised costs, retarded the development of a national market and of regional wholesale market organization, and discouraged large-scale trading on the national level, but they rarely jeopardized the provisioning of the capital. The dispersion of the Parisian hinterland and the multiplicity of arteries, land and water, that could be used assured a constant flow of supplies as long as they were available. Most of the merchandise arriving by water went to the port markets, especially the Grève, and the preponderance of it was brought in by professional suppliers who intended to offer it for sale at a profit. A small quantity shipped by water was destined for the consumption (or reserves) of well-to-do individuals (habitually denoted in the records as "bourgeois," but including both nobles and commoners) and religious communities and educational and welfare institutions. The bulk of the grain and flour sent overland went to the Halle in the name of the professional sellers (merchants, brokers, and laboureurs), but a substantial portion was brought in by bakers for conversion into bread, and a much more modest amount was destined for the bourgeois homes. Most of the flour came by land and therefore was sold at the Halle (though the Grève marketed as much as a thousand muids in a given year and transferred an even larger dose annually for sale at the Halle), while the ports and the central market both dealt in large amounts of grain.[56]

In an ordinary year, the marketplace suppliers accounted for about 43,300 muids, representing 64 percent of the entire annual provision entering the capital in the form of grain or flour.[57] (This figure surged dramatically in a dearth year—85 percent in 1725—when normal supply lines broke down and when the government intervened on the supply side.) Religious houses and welfare institutions, mobilized by the police in the wake of the crisis of 1725–

55. AN, Y 11219, 24 May 1732; AN, F^{12} 94, fol. 249, 26 April 1747; AN, Z^{1H} 449, 1 October 1765; Bertin to procurator general, 30 May 1759, BN, Coll. Joly 1312, fol. 48. On the sale of flour at the ports, see also AN, MC, VII-375, 19 January 1735 (Ecole), and *Gazette du commerce,* 4 May 1763 (Grève).

56. All the following calculations are based on Bibliothèque de l'Institut, mss. 513–21; BN, LK^7 6789; BN, Coll. Joly 1116, fol. 70; and Arsenal, ms. Bast. 10277. For a critical examination of the entry figures and a revised estimate of annual Parisian consumption, see Kaplan, *The Bakers of Paris and the Bread Question in the Eighteenth Century* (forthcoming).

57. I am arguing here that the proportion of supplies arriving directly by water continued to decline. It must be remembered, however, that much of the Halle-bound, landborne merchandise came part of the way by water.

26 to serve as an emergency granary system for the capital, contributed about 14 percent of the annual grain and flour entries. The bakers of Paris, the most important single nonmarketplace source of grain and flour, furnished most of the remaining 22 percent share of the annual provision. (One should remember that total grain and flour entries cover only about four-fifths of the registered annual Parisian supply of approximately 85,000 muids. The remaining 20 percent is provided in the form of already-baked bread sold twice a week in the Paris bread markets by the itinerant country bakers. For our purposes, however, grain and flour entries constitute a more pertinent point of reference.)

It is certain that a much greater proportion of the grain at the public markets (ports and Halle) came by water, for the most part under the auspices of the major grain traders, than by land in the hands of Paris-based merchants, laboureurs, country dealers (forains), and petty traders (blatiers). Between 1727 and 1733, water-carried grain represented on the average 61 percent of all grain offered at the markets (ranging from a maximum of 65 percent in 1730 to a minimum of 55.6 percent in 1728). The mean figure swelled to 75 percent in the dearth years 1725–26, when foreign or distant provincial suppliers loomed larger in the Paris supply picture. If, however, we take into account grain purchased outside the capital by bakers, institutions, and bourgeois and shipped directly to their granaries, the predominance of waterborne grain evaporates. Unfortunately we have statistics for only two years, neither of which is a flawless example: in the first, October 1737 through September 1738, the harbingers of a crisis become discernible and in the second, October 1738 through September 1739, a subsistence crisis struck. In both years, then, the proportion of water-freighted grain was inflated. In 1737–38, while 79 percent of the grain at the public markets came by water, only 44 percent of total grain arrivals entered Paris by water. Nearly all the flour and 56 percent of the grain came overland. In 1738–39, massive purchases made by government agents manifestly distort the picture: 83 percent of the market grain arrived by water and 58 percent of the total grain supply arrived by water, as laboureurs and blatiers diminished their supply and bakers found it more difficult to canvass grain on their own in the hinterland.

If one takes public market grain and flour together, aggregated by volume, the relative importance of water and land traffic, or port and Halle business, is striking (see Table 1). The pressure of dearth accounted for the strong showing of waterborne commerce in the first two and the last two years. Dearth-provoked recovery was fugitive. Though our data are confined to a few years in the first half of the century, there are strong indications that the trend they show deepened and persisted across time. The proportion of water-conveyed, port-marketed trade declined as the activity of the port-merchant corps stagnated, as flour assumed an increasingly salient role as the supply commodity

TABLE 1

Relative importance of water (port) and land
(Halle) traffic, 1725–39

Year	% water	% land
1725	48.4	51.6
1726	51.0	49.0
1727	33.5	66.5
1728	27.2	72.8
1729	32.6	67.4
1730	35.8	64.2
1731	36.1	63.9
1732	27.8	72.2
1733	27.5	72.5
10/37–9/38	38.4	61.6
10/38–9/39	43.8	56.2

of choice, and as bakers continued to expand their own trading activities.

Another way to make this case is to look at the relative share claimed by the ports and Halle of total Parisian annual supply (a reasonable proxy for consumption that includes the grain and flour used by country bakers who brought their bread to Paris twice a week) and of total annual grain and flour entries (including merchandise that did not pass through the marketplace). See Table 2.

The decline of the ports vis-à-vis the Halle mirrors the political and administrative eclipse of the Parisian municipality, steward of river commerce, by the lieutenance générale de police, responsible for land-based trade and "interior" markets in particular and for provisioning in general. While the ports waned, however, the Halle does not appear to have expanded commensurately. On the contrary, despite the vigorous efforts of the police, the Halle barely held its own. Halle entries in the mid-sixties were in fact slightly lower than in the late twenties or early thirties. It is not clear how significantly the opening of the new Halle at the end of the sixties contributed to the central-market renaissance so ardently sought by the police.

The slack was taken up by the Paris bakers, masters and *faubouriens,* who became increasingly unwilling to pass through the hands of intermediaries. To the chagrin of the market professionals—especially the port merchants, who fought them bitterly—and the police, who tried to force them to pass through the Halle, the bakers expanded their trading activities relentlessly across the century. Again, our data only hint at the developing trend (see Table 3).

In the public markets, flour overtakes grain quite early in the century. Indications are that it increases its lead slowly but steadily across time, save

TABLE 2

Relative shares of port and Halle of total annual Paris
provisioning and of total annual grain and flour entries,
1725–39

	Total annual Paris provisioning		Total annual grain and flour entries	
Year	% ports	% Halle	% ports	% Halle
1725*	32.4	34.7	41.2	44.0
1726*	32.8	31.4	41.1	39.4
1727	18.8	37.3	23.5	46.7
1728	14.2	38.2	17.9	48.1
1729	16.9	34.9	21.2	43.7
1730	18.3	32.7	22.5	40.3
1731	18.4	32.5	22.6	39.9
1732	13.4	34.8	16.4	42.7
1733	12.9	34.2	16.2	42.7
10/37–9/38*	25.9	41.7	—	—
10/38–9/39*	32.6	41.7	—	—

*Dearth years

TABLE 3

Baker share of total annual provisioning and of total
annual grain and flour entries, 1725–38

	Total annual Paris provisioning	Total annual grain and flour entries
Year	% Paris bakers*	% Paris bakers*
1725	9.4	—
1726	11.7	14.7
1727	14.6	18.2
1728	15.4	19.5
1729	17.7	22.3
1730	19.5	24.0
1731	20.3	24.9
1732	18.9	23.5
1733	19.5	24.0
10/37–9/38	32.3	—

*These figures also include an indeterminable but small amount of grain and flour
brought in under bourgeois franchise.

for ephemeral dearth regressions (see Table 4). Flour's proportion of global
grain and flour entries also increases gradually, but it is not likely that it
supersedes grain until mid-century. The locus of the crucial shift seems to be
less the Halle, where the inroads of flour are remorseless but not decisive,
than the baker traffic. Particularly in the second half of the century, the bakers

TABLE 4

Relative shares of grain and flour of total annual grain
and flour entries and of annual public market supply,
1725–39

Year	Total annual grain and flour entries		Public market supply (ports and Halle)	
	% grain	% flour	% grain	% flour
1725	—	—	64.7	35.3
1726	71.9	28.1	67.3	32.7
1727	66.0	34.0	53.9	46.1
1728	65.2	34.8	49.8	50.2
1729	67.9	32.0	53.8	46.1
1730	69.7	30.3	55.1	44.9
1731	69.4	30.6	54.6	45.4
1732	66.4	33.6	47.3	52.7
1733	65.2	34.8	45.2	54.8
10/37–9/38	58.6	41.4	48.5	51.5
10/38–9/39	52.6	47.7	49.5	50.5

increasingly tried to buy flour directly. In response to baker demand and for
other commercial, technological, and administrative ("police") reasons, the
flour trade takes off after mid-century (see Table 5).

The Ports

Grain and flour sent to Paris for sale were not concentrated in a single
market for price-making efficiency, optimal visibility, and administrative convenience. The Halle, located opposite the church of St.-Eustache, received
all grain shipped overland and most flour regardless of its mode of transport,
while the ports marketed almost all the grain arriving by river. Receiving grain
from the upper Seine and Marne, the port of the Grève, situated not far from
the Hôtel de Ville, was by far the most active and largest of the ports.
Although it had regularly assigned measurers and absorbed supplies from the
Aisne, Oise, and lower Seine, the port of the Ecole, established near the
church of St.-Germain-l'Auxerrois, steadily declined in importance. The auxiliary grain ports—St.-Paul, St.-Nicolas, and the Théatins—came into service
only in emergencies (dearths, river accidents, inclement weather) or for the
special needs of the institutional buyers (public assistance and religious organizations).[58] From as early as the twelfth century texts cite the Grève as the

58. Factum pour la communauté des meusniers (1685), BN, ms. fr. 21636, fol. 331; AN, Y
15406, 27 October, 11 November 1735; prevotal ordinance, 1 July 1739, AN, H* 1858, fol.
229; AN, F^{12} 94, fol. 249.

chief market of the capital. Several hundred years later Commines, watching
the port from his jail cell, marveled at the multitude of grain boats arriving.
The Grève did not begin to lose ground to the Halle, it appears, until the
seventeenth century.[59] The ports were among the last showpiece fiefs in the
diminished and declining jurisdiction of the Hôtel de Ville (for lack of extant
municipal records, we know much less about the ports than the Halle).[60]
Though they contrived to find pretexts for encroachment, the police of the
Châtelet never set foot on the ports, at least not officially.[61] A parallel police
responsible solely to the prévôt des marchands, including officials called
commissaires as well as measurers and porters who took oaths before him,
maintained order on the ports and rivers. The lieutenant general of police had
responsibility for the Halle and, he liked to think, for the overall provisioning
of the capital.

The Grève was not exclusively a grain port. It acted as market for a host of
other goods with whose dealers the grain merchants had to compete for
space, priority in unloading, and other services from the port personnel. The
quays, narrow, incompletely paved, and often mired in mud, were habitually
overcrowded. (Acute congestion was one of the traits that the Grève shared
with the Halle.) No one wanted to debark in wet weather. There was little

TABLE 5

Relative shares of grain and flour in Halle trade and in
baker trade, 1725–39

Year	Supply distribution at Halle		Supply distribution in baker trade	
	% grain	% flour	% grain	% flour
1725	31.6	68.5	—	—
1726	33.2	66.8	88.0	11.9
1727	30.7	69.3	91.2	8.8
1728	31.1	68.9	91.2	8.8
1729	31.4	68.6	90.9	9.1
1730	30.0	70.0	91.4	8.6
1731	28.8	71.2	91.3	8.7
1732	27.0	73.0	89.3	10.7
1733	24.4	75.6	89.6	10.4
10/37–9/38	16.4	83.6	80.0	20.0
10/38–9/39	14.8	85.2	61.5	39.5

59. Cherrière, *La Lutte contre l'incendie sur la Seine, les ports, et les quais de Paris sous
l'ancien régime*, in Julien Hayem, ed., *Mémoires et documents pour servir à l'histoire du
commerce et de l'industrie en France*, 3d ser. (Paris, 1913), p. 171; *Magasin pittoresque*, 47th
year (1879): 372.

60. Micheline Baulant and Jean Meuvret, *Prix des céréales, extraits de la mercuriale de
Paris (1520–1698)* (Paris, 1960–62), 1:6. Cf. Meuvret, "Le Commerce des grains et des
farines à Paris et les marchands parisiens à l'époque de Louis XIV," *Revue d'histoire
moderne et contemporaine* 3 (July–September 1956): 169–203.

61. See the prévôt's fury in 1725 over a Châtelet commissaire's incursion on the ports.
Lambert to Hérault, 22 December 1725, Arsenal, ms. Bast. 10270.

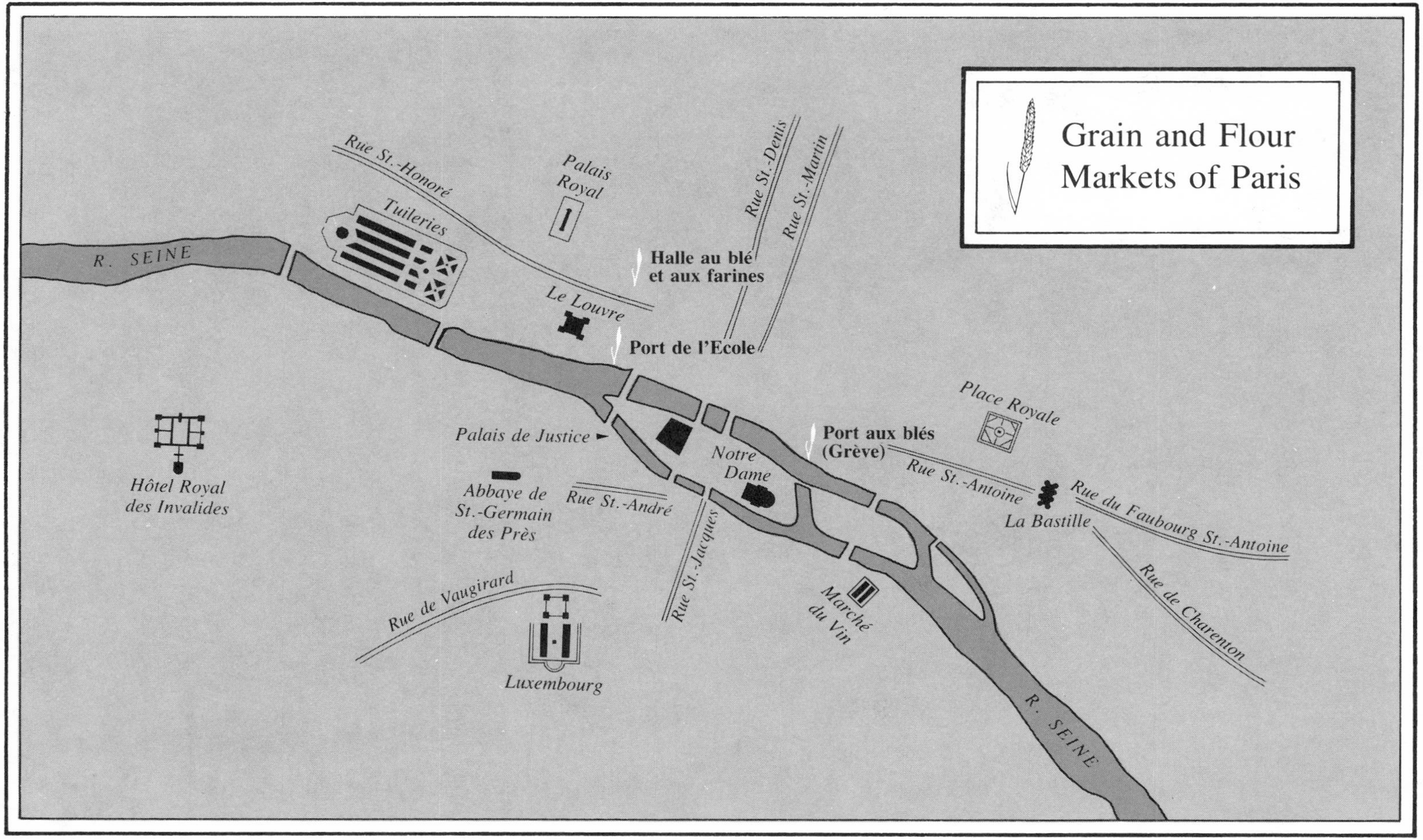
Grain and Flour
Markets of Paris
Rue St.-Honoré
Palais
Royal
Rue St.-Denis
Rue St.-Martin
Tuileries
R. SEINE
Halle au blé
et aux farines
Le Louvre
Port de l'Ecole
Place Royale
Palais de Justice
Port aux blés
(Grève)
Notre
Dame
Rue St.-Antoine
Rue du Faubourg St.-Antoine
La Bastille
Hôtel Royal
des Invalides
Abbaye de
St.-Germain
des Près
Rue St.-André
Rue St.-Jacques
Marché
du Vin
Rue de Charenton
Rue de Vaugirard
Luxembourg
R. SEINE

MAP 3

Les Halles, the central markets: the "Stomach of Paris." Eighteenth century, N. B. Lépicié (private collection, Photo Lauros-Giraudon)

space for the conditioning and repair of humid or damaged grain. Unless the municipality accorded special derogation, grain could be removed from the boat only by the buyer. Exhibition, bargaining, and the formalities of the transaction took place in exiguous quarters on the boats under tight time constraints imposed by the police regulations. Security, for which the independent forces of the prévôt des marchands and the *garde* were responsible, posed a serious problem throughout the century.[62] Fire and theft were major objects of concern. Of the many plans ventilated for the renovation of the grain ports, only one was carried beyond the drafting stage. As a pendant to the project for the construction of a new Halle in the late fifties—as if to keep some sort of rough balance between competing markets and rival jurisdictions—the municipality received permission from the ministry to build a new "station for provisioning" on the waterfront. Work began and was suspended several times, and whether it would ever be finished was still an open question at the end of the reign of Louis XV.[63]

The Halle

Halle, Delamare tells us, is "an old French word which signifies the place where the public market is held."[64] The central market district known as the *Halles* emerged gradually over the course of several centuries in response to the growth of the city. Within an area of several blocks merchants, brokers, hawkers, sharpsters, and peasants sold every imaginable commodity, in special buildings, in stalls, on the streets, and out of wagons and windows. No one has better described the cacophony of sounds and odors, the blend of fragility and brutality, of fertility and sterility, of the fat and the lean, and the confusion of spiritual and material life than Emile Zola, whose nineteenth-century portrait in *Le Ventre de Paris* retains a striking old-regime flavor. Although certain transcendental fidelities united its populace, the Halles was a patchwork of independent principalities rather than a single great market-

62. Cherrière, *Lutte contre l'incendie sur la Seine,* pp. 132–39. For a case of theft, see Arsenal, ms. Bast. 10041, fol. 152 (5 November 1755); for a fire, Marville to Maurepas, 12 June 1743, BHVP, ms. 719 (réserve 21), fol. 156.

63. Deliberations of the bureau of the Hôtel de Ville, 25 November 1762, AN, H* 1870, fols. 60ff.; conseil secret, 23 February and 4 May 1768, AN, X^{1B} 8955; *Journal de l'agriculture, du commerce, des arts et des finances* (November 1772): 143.

64. BN, ms. fr. 21632, fol. 87. On the origins and development of the halles through the nineteenth century, see Ernest Thomas, "L'Approvisionnement de Paris, son histoire et son organisation actuelle" (1879), BHVP, Collection E. Thomas, série 114, cote provisoire 4803; Robert Facque, *Les Halles et marchés alimentaires de Paris* (Paris, 1911), pp. 18–20; A. Jourdan, "La Ville étudiée dans ses quartiers: autour des Halles de Paris au Moyen Age," *Annales d'histoire économique et sociale* 7 (1953): 285–301; Jean Martineau, *Les Halles de Paris, des origines à 1789* (Paris, 1960), passim; Léon Biollay, "Les Anciennes Halles de Paris," *Mémoires de la Société de l'histoire de Paris et de l'Ile-de-France* 3 (1876): 293–355.

state. Different codes of conduct and different police regulations governed each product-defined subdivision. Each had its own jealously guarded territory and rights-of-way, each had economic interests peculiar to its own commerce, each had its own seasonal and daily clock, each had its favorite taverns. Acrimonious commercial rivalries and personal feuds sundered each group but, vis-à-vis its neighbors, each group projected an identity and coherence that were almost corporate in character. Men and women from "grain" and "fish" and "flowers" and "butter, eggs, and cheese" treated each other almost as if they were of different ethnic origin. The insular tendencies toward professional endogamy and hereditary family dynasties did not create inbred merchant-races of termagant-fishmongers, red-cheeked and jowly butchers, and soft and sensuous cheese-women, but they did reinforce the sense of collective distinction. The demands of business forced the service-defined groups such as the *voituriers par terre* (teamsters) to be more cosmopolitan; they had no territorial base of operations, no clear-cut fealties, and although they knew everyone's secrets they enjoyed nobody's confidence.

Despite its primacy in the material life of the capital, grain enjoyed no special facilities in the central markets. The Halle aux Blés was an open-air bazaar surrounded by a belt of buildings used as offices and stalls rather than storehouses. At both the ports and the Halle, grain was sold on Wednesdays and Saturdays. Officially the bell opening the Halle rang at 8:00 A.M. in the summer and 9:00 A.M. in the winter, bakers were excluded until the afternoon to permit individuals to satisfy their retail needs, and the measurers closed the market at 5:00 P.M. The authorities did not rigidly enforce this timetable, however; since the retail trade was generally dull, it seemed pointless to keep out wholesale buyers until the second half of the day. To meet the competition of the ports, where trading hours were more flexible, the police, after mid-century, habitually invited buyers to enter earlier, a decision that delighted the laboureurs and the forain merchants from the country anxious to return home as quickly as possible. To accommodate the large number of marginal bakers who were too poor to obtain credit and who could not marshal the necessary cash until they had sold all their day's bread, the police extended market hours into the early evening. Beginning in the sixties, in order to strengthen further the attractiveness of the Halle, the police added a supplementary market day, Monday, and allowed bakers to purchase flour any afternoon of the week. In practice, however, by this time there was no longer any distinction, either at the Halle or the Grève, between "hot" days (official market days) and "cold" days.[65]

65. "Mémoire sur la création des 150 officiers pour la facture" (1769), Arsenal, ms. 2588; police ordinance, 4 November 1767, BN, Coll. Joly 1111, fol. 178; Arsenal, ms. Bast. 10141, fols. 274 (16 November 1759) and 337 (10 April 1760); Martineau, *Les Halles de Paris*, p. 195; Biollay, "Les Anciennes Halles de Paris," p. 344. On "hot" and "cold" days, see Skinner, "Marketing and Social Structure," p. 21.

The quality of wheat at the Halle was generally slightly higher than at the ports, because it offered the finest produce of the Ile-de-France and the Beauce, cereal centers of high repute, and its grain suffered less deterioration in transit.[66] Bakers protested that the setier at the ports weighed twenty to twenty-five pounds less than the same measure at the Halle.[67] Though the divergences were hardly significant, the price at the Halle tended to be a little higher, primarily on the elite grain.[68] Merchants who shipped by river but packed their grain in sacks had the choice of selling at the ports or the Halle; most preferred the Halle. Psychologically, the supply situation and the price were more important at the Halle than at the ports because the Halle was more nearly at the physical and economic center of Parisian life, amidst a huge market filling a vast panoply of retail as well as wholesale needs and serving as a gathering place for Parisians and visitors. While the Halle price index, called the *mercuriale,* obviously reflected the prices of the hinterland, the authorities believed that the Halle acted as a regulator for the markets of the zone. "All the neighboring markets model themselves on our market," noted Duplessis, the senior commissaire in the Halles district in the first part of the century, "and if the price of wheat rises here, it is to be feared that it would also increase in the neighboring markets."[69]

Properly speaking, there were no *droits de marché* or market dues imposed on grain and flour. Levies on grain and flour entries had disappeared before the seventeenth century.[70] As a rule sellers did not pay for vending space or rights. Measurers collected "rights" or fees from buyers, as did porters from sellers and buyers, theoretically for services rendered. Placers, sweepers, and other service personnel were entitled to demand payment, according to schedules fixed by the authorities, for the performance of their functions. A swarm of casual workers hovered around the Halle and invented ingenious pretexts to extort money from dealers and buyers. Eager to avoid inflating the price of grain and flour as a result of these petty exactions, the police were relatively successful in driving them away from the grain market. To avoid the expense of marketing their goods at the Halle, many peasants sold their vegetables, fruits, and dairy products informally in the faubourgs. The cost of selling grain and flour does not, however, seem to have provoked concern among the laboureurs and merchants.[71]

66. On the deterioration of riverborne grain and its dubious quality in the eyes of the bakers, see César Bucquet, *Traité pratique de la conservation des grains* (Paris, 1783), pp. 47, 50.

67. Petition of forains, ca. March 1738, BN, Coll. Joly 1314, fol. 51.

68. Meuvret, "Le Commerce des grains," pp. 175, 178.

69. Duplessis to Hérault, 30 June 1727, Arsenal, ms. Bast. 10274.

70. Gustave Bienaymé, "La Fiscalité alimentaire et gastronomique à Paris," *Journal de la Société de statistique de Paris,* 31st year (1890): 40–60. Afanassiev's treatment of this question is extremely misleading. *Le Commerce des céréales,* pp. 28–36, 43, 457. For the fees paid by a grain and flour merchant, see Aubert's register, Archives Seine-Paris, D5B⁶ 3282, December 1771.

71. Arsenal, ms. Bast. 10141 (8 July 1756).

Like the ports, the Halle was highly vulnerable to fire, theft, and vandalism. The police required all shops and houses having access to the grain market to be locked after dark and the guard patrolled frequently at night. The prohibition against smoking was universally disobeyed. After a near disaster in 1719, the police prepared elaborate contingency plans for fighting fires.[72]

The most serious cause of dissatisfaction with the Halle stemmed from the stifling congestion of the marketplace and the engorgement of access roads. "The Halle," Delamare reflected at the very beginning of the century, "is surely too small for so great a throng of people who continue to grow in number."[73] During the reign of Louis XV, all the markets of the Halle expanded in volume of business, but most of them did not change in size, creating an increasingly untenable situation. Approaching the Halle on Wednesday or Saturday morning was a nightmare. The streets were narrow, irregular, and far too few to handle the traffic. Besides the vast number of dealers in other commodities and the two hundred and fifty bakers arriving to set up stalls in the bread market, scores of grain and flour dealers leading horses or mules or driving small carts or heavy wagons pressed to reach the Halle. Encumbrances resulted in delays that caused tension that led to outbursts of violence and grave accidents. A flour wagon from Charenton crushed the toes of a seventy-three-year-old woman dayworker; another flour wagon from Senlis speeding at an intersection in the hushed light of dawn overturned a bourgeois carriage; an old baker covered with blood told a commissaire that a flour merchant assaulted him for blocking the road despite the fact that he could not move his cart "because of the bottleneck"; a gang of secondhand-clothes dealers beat up another baker who parked too close to their stands while he stopped to leave his flour sacks at the Halle; two grain merchants fought with whips over the right to enter the Halle first.[74] The police imposed stiff penalties for obstructing the thoroughfares, punished violence, and arranged for immediate cash compensation for victims of accidents, but were helpless to deal with the causes of the problem. Inspector Poussot, himself a near casualty of a grain wagon, blamed the general confusion and the crowded conditions rather than individual traders.[75]

Within the marketplace itself the situation was no less chaotic. Merchants continued to squabble over space to unload, brokers refused to accept consigned merchandise for want of room, measurers and porters could not perform their tasks efficiently, and buyers had difficulty circulating and

72. AN, Y 11228, 9 July 1741; Cherrière, *La Lutte contre l'incendie*, pp. 125, 130–31. Not even the new enclosed Halle prevented thefts. See the complaint of broker Ferret, AN, Y 15389, 13 May 1779.

73. Delamare, "Advis sur la Halle," BN, ms. fr. 21635, fol. 247.

74. AN, Y 11226, 28 August 1739, Y 11225, 11 February 1738; Y 11227, 16 December 1740; Y 13648, 14 August 1752; Y 11237, 10 October 1750; Y 12606, 18 November 1758.

75. Arsenal, ms. Bast. 10141, fol. 303 (21 December 1759); AN, Y 9439, 18 April 1738; Archives Seine-Paris, 6AZ 133 11, 16 May 1727.

inspecting. In times of great abundance, the porters and the menial workers called *forts* piled the sacks of grain and flour pell-mell, causing confusion, provoking quarrels over priority and even ownership, inviting theft, and exposing the merchandise to damage.[76] Perpetual overcrowding created unsanitary conditions, jeopardized the conservation of grain and flour, and encouraged the janitorial service to do a perfunctory job. Mercier, Dussausoy, and other observers of the central markets described them as "disgusting," "filthy," and "infected." Interspersed between the sacks were mud, piles of manure, decayed straw used to cover the sacks, and other detritus. Human beings were hardly more discriminating than horses—tenants in the apartments around the grain market, according to a flour-girl, commonly hurled "pots of urine and fecal matter" on the merchandise and sometimes on the merchants. The air was foul and the noise unbearable. On bad days, the mephitic stench of the nearby cemetery of St.-Jean, tinged with the odor of rotten fish from the neighboring marketplace, wafted over the grain market.[77]

Between 1754 and 1760, Poussot claimed, the territory assigned to the grain and flour market had actually shrunk despite an increase in the amount of merchandise handled. Fruit, vegetable, and egg dealers, candle sellers, pork vendors, and others, by a process akin to squatter's rights, installed themselves on the periphery and gradually encroached upon the terrain of the Halle. Repeatedly expelled, they returned as soon as the porters or the police agents moved on to other business. Poussot, apostle of "good order," argued that it was impossible to operate a proper market in these circumstances. The Halle should be at least three times larger. Tight quarters, he argued, meant unnecessarily high prices: "More space means more arrivals of grain and flour, and a well-furnished market means that the goods will be cheaper."[78]

. The problem of the location and organization of the central markets raised fundamental questions about the function and future of the city and remained an object of heated debate for hundreds of years. It was only a few years ago that the problem was finally solved or, rather, completely redefined. The technocratic planners vanquished the historical urbanists and banished the Halles to Rungis and elsewhere in the infinity of suburbia. Eighteenth-century planners considered many projects for the reform of the central markets, and the issues they raised are not remote from present-day concerns. "Persuaded

76. Arsenal, ms. Bast. 10141 (11 August, 20 September 1754 and 29 May 1758); AN, Y 11224, 2 March 1737; "Lettres sur un nouveau plan de marché des halles," *Journal économique* (September 1765): 393.

77. Mercier, *Tableau de Paris*, 2:128–29; Maille Dussausoy, *Le Citoyen désintéressé, ou Diverses idées patriotiques concernant quelques établissements et embellissements utiles à la ville de Paris* (Paris, 1767–68), p. 79; "Recette pour la conservation des bleds," *Journal économique* (May 1751): 47; AN, Y 11223, 24 July 1736; Arsenal, ms. Bast. 10141, fol. 222 (17 June 1759). Cf. "Lettre d'un bon Parisien," *Journal économique* (July 1769): 308.

78. Arsenal, ms. Bast. 10141, fols. 329–30 (12 March 1760), 333 (22 March 1760), 349 (28 May 1760), 392 (3 November 1760), 356 (1 July 1760); AN, Y 11220, 6 May 1733.

that the [market] places must, as much as possible, occupy the center of a
city," wrote a sympathetic critic of a renovation plan, "and perceiving the
ridiculousness of those who wish to build at the extremities of Paris, as if they
sought to transport this capital outside of itself; he [the author] does not at all
want to place the market of the Halles elsewhere, he leaves it in the spot
where one now sees it; but he proposes to enlarge the place, to give it the
most suitable form, to facilitate the avenues by multiplying, enlarging, [and]
straightening them."[79] The government never seriously considered adopting
any of the global reform projects, for they all required enormous investments
that it plainly could not afford.

On the other hand, the central markets underwent many piecemeal
changes. The proposal to expand the Halle aux blès, made for the first time in
the eighteenth century by Delamare, had a painfully long gestation. In 1717–
18 the assembly of police endorsed it as an "excellent" idea. In 1740 it approved a project for a new covered market building on the condition that the
cost would not be borne by the people in the form of new taxes or fees and
that the new building contain *no* substantial storage facilities, for fear that if
merchants had a place to store their grain and flour they could no longer be
compelled to sell within three market days.[80] This reservation, which suggests
that the police had lost confidence in their ability to enforce the rules and
believed that a new physical structure would somehow undermine the old
way of doing things, was the sort of timid and retrograde argument that
generally appealed more to the politicians than to the police. It was attacked
implicitly by the police agent Foucaud in his plan for the construction of two
new grain halles and explicitly by Poussot, who warned lieutenant general of
police Sartine not "to fall into the error made by the government of believing
that a capacity to store merchandise would cause prices to rise." A new
Halle, Poussot maintained, would bring greater abundance and lower prices;
it would not prevent us from "forcing the merchant to sell" rapidly and in any
event experience convinced him that the police would not have to resort to
constraint "two times in ten years."

Poussot lobbied indefatigably for the construction of a covered Halle with
storage area. He solicited advice from bakers and merchants, worked on
plans with masons and architects, and organized a petition-signing campaign
among the mealmen, millers, and brokers. The flour dealers, unanimously in
favor of the plan, claimed that they suffered major losses from spoilage because their goods could not be adequately protected in the open Halle. Instead of continuing to pay ten sous per load for a makeshift straw covering

---

79. *Journal économique* (September 1765): 393–94. For other reform plans, see Martineau, *Les Halles de Paris.*
80. BN, Coll. Joly 7, fol. 107; BN, ms. fr. 11356, fol. 410.

that afforded little security, they offered to contribute to a fund that would be used to amortize the cost of a new building.[81]

In 1762, the government finally acted to meet the insistent demands for improvement of the grain and flour market. Recognizing that congestion made it impossible "to keep order and enforce the police of goods," to guarantee cleanliness, and to encourage exchanges, royal letters patent instructed the municipality to build a new Halle with "sufficient space and ease of approach" on the vast terrain of the Hôtel de Soissons, a famous mansion not far from the church of St.-Eustache. Despite the objections of the assembly of police, the government decided that the public would indirectly bear the cost of establishing the new market and creating at the same time a new reception facility for boats on the upriver side of the city. For the next twenty years the city was to levy special entry fees on a wide range of consumer goods, which for grain and flour amounted to 1 livre 10 sous per muid. The municipality estimated the total cost of the project, which also included the suppression of a number of minor posts at the markets and the assumption of certain market services by the police, at almost 10 million livres.[82]

Completed after four years' construction, the new grain and flour Halle was a vast circular structure with twenty-five interior arcades and a large open-air central courtyard.[83] Critics found numerous planning and engineering defects in the building, but the users felt that it was an incomparable improvement.[84] The Academy of Architecture eventually gave its "most distinguished approbation" to the Halle in the eighties when the courtyard was covered with a grand cupola, which contemporaries compared in genius to the dome of the Roman Pantheon, to expand storage and foul-weather operating space.[85] While Mercier grumbled that it was too small and inglorious,

81. Foucaud to procurator general, ca. April 1757, BN, Coll. Joly 1113, fols. 240–41; Arsenal, ms. Bast. 10141, fols. 222 (17 June 1759), 247 (5 September 1759), 330–31 (12 March 1760), 358 (2 July 1760), 398–99 (3 November 1760), 463–66 (21 March 1761), 473–74 (12, 17 April 1761).

82. Bernage to royal procurator of the Paris municipality, 17 August 1755, Bibliothèque de l'Institut, ms. Godefroy 551, fol. 324; AN, H* 1870, fol. 60 (25 November 1762); AN, H 2157; arrêt du conseil, 15 December 1771, Archives Seine-Paris, 2AZ 2[76] pièce 3F; Camille Piton, *Comment Paris s'est transformé. Histoire de Paris, topographie, moeurs, usages. Origines de la haute bourgeoisie parisienne: Le quartier des Halles* (Paris, 1891), pp. 128–30.

83. Hardy's Journal, 22 December 1766, BN, ms. fr. 6680, fol. 113; Expilly, *Dictionnaire géographique,* 5:411; Marcel Poète, *Une Vie de cité: Paris de sa naissance à nos jours* (Paris, 1924–31), 1:245–46; Georges Touchard-Lafosse, *Histoire de Paris et de ses environs* (Paris, 1851), 3:524–25; *Cent Ans: La Halle au blé en 1789, La Bourse de commerce en 1889* (Paris, 1889), Collection Marcel Arpin, Bibliothèque de l'Ecole Nationale de la Meunerie, Paris.

84. Bachaumont, *Mémoires secrets,* 18:310 (21 November 1767).

85. *Journal de Paris* (4 November 1783), pp. 1267–69; Maxime de Sars, *Le Noir, lieutenant de police, 1732–1807* (Paris, 1948), p. 98.

Construction of the Halle au blé, 1765 (Musée Carnavelet, Photo Lauros-Giraudon)

suitable at best "for a city of the third order," Arthur Young called the new Halle "by far the finest thing I have yet seen at Paris." Perhaps only a very sober agronomist could gush with such enthusiasm over a corn market:

> It is a vast rotunda, the roof entirely of wood, upon a new principle of carpentry. . . . The gallery is 150 yards round, consequently the diameter is as many feet; it is as light as if suspended by the fairies. In the grand area, wheat, pease, beans, lentils are stored and sold. In the surrounding divisions, flour on wooden stands. You pass by staircases doubly winding within each other to spacious apartments for rye, barley, oats, etc. The whole is so well planned and so admirably executed, that I know of no public building that exceeds it in France or England. And if an appropriation of the parts to the conveniences wanted as an adaptation of every circumstance to the end required, in union with that elegance which is consistent with use, and that magnificence which from stability and duration, be the criteria of public edifices, I know nothing that equals it.[86]

The construction of the new Halle was a landmark step in the ambitious campaign encouraged by Sartine and spearheaded by Poussot to reinvigorate the central grain market. From the moment he assumed responsibility in the halles in the mid-fifties, Poussot's mind swirled with projects for improving the "service" and the "order" of the grain and flour market. Under de Courcy, senior commissaire for almost a quarter century, whose laxity he criticized, Poussot felt that the grain market had been neglected. De Courcy, a man of habit who relished routine and depended on his superiors for all initiatives, had done an able job of repressive police, Poussot suggested, but he had paid little attention to the technical problems of marketing, to the needs of the traders, and to the organization of the service personnel. With the proper care, Poussot believed, the Halle could become a larger, better equipped, more attractive, cleaner, more efficient, and more influential provisioning market. Impatient and resolute, he jarred the regulars at the Halle with his combination of zeal and lordliness. He badgered the lieutenants general of police to take a greater interest in market life. On some issues, Poussot took a hard marketplace (or super-Delamarist) line. For example, he was obsessed with the idea of forcing all bakers to buy flour at the Halle rather than directly from country dealers in order to swell the activity and increase the leverage of the Paris market. Yet he looked beyond the regulations and controls and ignored or defied them when he deemed that they impeded provisioning. He dealt sympathetically with merchants who faithfully supplied the market and preferred to give wide latitude to the market principle in price making rather than pressure merchants to sell under threat of punishment. "There are many things to be done anew in the markets," he liked to say.[87]

86. Mercier, *Tableau de Paris*, 2:129; Young, *Travels in France* (Garden City, N.Y., 1969), p. 71.

87. Arsenal, ms. Bast. 10141 (4 August 1754, 27 January 1758, 17 June 1759, 20 January, 22 March, 4 August 1760).

The most auspicious change in the police of the Halle, from Poussot's perspective, was the appointment of Pierre Vial de Machurin to succeed de Courcy as chief commissaire of the department in 1757. Machurin had been a commissaire since 1739, but he had served most of his time in the Place Maubert and had little competence in provisioning affairs. Poussot established a close working relationship with him and helped to train him in the business of the marketplace. After "much trouble and attention," Poussot reported in 1760 that the commissaire "is without contradiction now familiar with all the matters concerning the Halles," adding: "If he has one fault it is being too indulgent," a fine quality but "detrimental in the Halles."[88]

Like his mentor and adjoint, Machurin was interested in reinvigorating the grain and flour market. "To avoid making mistakes" in their reform plans, they regularly consulted the experts. Master baker Malisset, who Poussot claimed knew the provisioning trade better than anyone, collaborated with them for many months in drawing up a detailed study of the Parisian supply system and determining the relationship of the Halle to the hinterland markets and to the practices of bakers and merchants. Through Malisset, the commissaire and the inspector became acquainted with the new conversion process called economic milling and with new techniques of conservation. They subjected these innovations to rigorous scrutiny in a series of carefully controlled, comparative tests that demonstrated their public utility.[89]

In addition to suppressing, or preventing, flour traffic en droiture, Poussot wanted to substitute weighing for measuring flour, an innovation intensely desired by the flour merchants that was bound to make the flour trade at the Halle brisker, more efficient, and above all more abundant. The weighing system would provide the police with a new source of data meticulously compiled by officials recruited from outside the traditional information network. This would provide Poussot and Machurin with a new lever of power, for the more they knew about supply patterns the better they believed they would be able to deal with mealmen, brokers, and bakers and to anticipate shortages and price fluctuations.[90] The broker corps, which played a crucial role in the sale of grain and flour, was to be purged and reorganized according to new procedures that would guarantee recruitment of cooperative and capable agents. Poussot also expected the brokers to contribute to his data bank by keeping detailed account books.[91] To chasten brokers and flour traders, the inspector obtained authorization for a merchant-protégé of high moral character ("He never goes to the tavern") to establish a small, tactical flour reserve at the Halle itself, to be complemented later by an analogous wheat fund. This

88. Ibid., fol. 316 (17 February 1760); *Almanach royal*, 1739, 1757.

89. Arsenal, ms. Bast. 10141, fols. 333 (22 March 1760), 371 (5 September 1760), and 467 (30 March 1761).

90. Ibid. (9 December 1757). Cf. ibid. (4 August 1754).

91. Ibid. (27 January 1758); Viollet's register, Archives Seine-Paris, D5B[6] 1963.

would enhance the ability of the police "to set the price of the different flours for all merchants" in times of dearth without resorting to brutally authoritarian measures.[92]

Poussot struggled vigorously to subject the willful measurers and porters to police control. He worked to impose new standards of rigor, probity, and consistency in the operation of the everyday police at the Halle. He dismantled the old patronage connections, expelled the incorrigible elements, and offered his protection to those who accepted his terms. He found new ways, institutionally and informally, to extend his own powers of surveillance, verification, and regulation.[93] His idea was not subordination for its own sake, but to improve the public service and render the Halle more attractive.

Poussot's project was doubly audacious: by its sweep and by its coherence. By favoring the efflorescence of the flour trade, by promoting new techniques of milling, conservation, and transportation, by attempting to increase and regularize the supply of grain and flour and to concentrate it at the Halle, by revamping the brokerage institution, by extending and rationalizing the system of information collection, by pressing for major physical renovations that would increase the capacity of the market and facilitate traffic patterns and transactions, and by regulating the functions of the measurers and porters who constituted the ground-level police of the marketplace, Poussot modified the very structure of the Paris provisioning trade.

92. Arsenal, ms. Bast. 10141, fols. 288 (4 December 1759), 317 (17 February 1760), and 382 (2 October 1760).
93. Ibid., fols. 235–36 (23 July 1759), 238 (28 July 1759), 358 (2 July 1760), and 450 (9 March 1761); AN, Y 12612, 3 September 1763.

CHAPTER 4

The Grain Merchants
of the Ports of Paris

*T*he port-based Paris grain merchants were the aristocrats of the provisioning trade. Like other aristocracies, the port corps faced serious problems during the eighteenth century. The merchants' share of total Paris provisioning, like their wealth, was significantly more modest than commonly believed. The bonds that linked them to their protector, the Paris municipality, were strained by their inability to meet their provisioning obligations. The merchants attributed their difficulties to the Paris bakers, once their captive-customers and now their archrivals, who had entered the grain trade directly on their own in precisely those areas traditionally exploited by the port merchants.

Merchant Typology

According to the typology of grain traders fashioned by the philosophe Condillac in the 1770s, there were only two sorts of merchants. The *négociants* he described as extremely wealthy, capable of advancing large sums and taking major risks, backed by a vast network of correspondents, and engaged in dealings across great expanses of space and time, both on the national and the international scene. He characterized the second type as "little merchants" who lacked the capital to buy, store, and wait, whose risk aversion induced them to settle for modest profits, and whose transactions were confined to the regular provisioning of a specific place or area.[1]

1. Abbé Etienne Bonnot de Condillac, *Le Commerce et le gouvernement considérés relativement l'un à l'autre* (1776), in *Collection des principaux économistes,* ed. E. Daire and G. de Molinari (Paris, 1847), 14:332.

On this scale, the Paris professional grain-trading world consisted for the most part of "little merchants." To be sure, some were bigger than others; there was infinitely more diversity than Condillac's crude bipolar model allowed. But one would have trouble discerning any of his négociants, save in times of crisis when a Samuel Bernard or an Isaac Thellusson or a Leray de Chaumont responded to a government appeal to rescue the capital.[2] When compared to the provisioning cohorts of the epoch of Louis XV, Jean Roger, the leading figure on the grain ports at the end of the seventeenth century, and a veritable grain négociant, seems virtually sui generis.[3] Despite its enormous demand, Paris was not integrated into a national or international market system. The city had not placed its provisioning destiny in the hands of the plutocratic elite; on the contrary, supply trade remained largely local and intraregional, and appears to have been even less concentrated during Condillac's time than during Jean Roger's.

The enormous difficulties of communication, transportation, and conservation were certainly decisive reasons why Paris boasted virtually no négociants. Political impediments were also important: the deep-seated hostility to "monopoly" shared by the police and the people and their common insistence, reified into laws and institutions, that grain, as a commodity of "first necessity," could not be treated like any other good.[4]

The Paris-based port merchants, however, can be said to have aspired to quasi-négociant status, viewed not in Condillac's abstract sense, but in terms of their relation to the other grain dealers.[5] At the most general level, their unity and prestige derived from the water. Their command of water transport theoretically gave them greater range than the landbound dealer. The boat evoked a far bolder and nobler undertaking than either the cart or the ass. Nor were the prerogatives of the port accessible to anyone for the taking. The system of admission—a sort of consecration—gave these port merchants an aura and a sense of exclusivity.

The Paris Municipality and the Grain Trade

Historically associated with the promotion of the river trade, the prévôt des marchands, chief of the Parisian municipality, quite fittingly determined whether a grain trader was worthy of receiving a license. Municipal patronage was crucial not merely for symbolical reasons; it conferred very concrete commercial advantages. The Paris license gave the merchant and his commissioned country agents the right to buy outside the marketplaces in the farms

---

2. See Steven L. Kaplan, *Bread, Politics and Political Economy* and *Famine Plot*.
3. Usher, *Grain Trade*, pp. 314–18; Meuvret, "Le Commerce des grains," pp. 200–203.
4. See Kaplan, *Bread, Politics, and Political Economy*, 1:52–71.
5. Cf. Mercier's reflections on the difference between Paris merchants and négociants. *Tableau de Paris*, 1:51.

and granaries. This privilege eddied against the whole tide of police legislation, the aim of which was to concentrate and confront demand and supply publicly and visibly in a given set of places. It gave the Paris merchants access to supplies prior to anyone else and in conditions far more hospitable than those of the supervised transactions. Paris-bound grain also had precedence over other commodities for the use of transport or storage facilities.[6] Moreover, the prévôté vigorously favored "its" merchants, provided they fulfilled what it construed to be their responsibilities. The municipality dispatched its commissaires and huissiers and ordered its subdelegates to assist the merchants with purchases (by providing information and arranging contacts) and to ease their dealings with local authorities.[7] The prévôté did not hesitate to contest and in some cases unilaterally contradict and supersede the decisions of local jurisdictions when they prejudiced Parisian interest.[8]

At the instigation of the prévôt des marchands, the royal council in 1708 promulgated an arrêt forbidding local officials to infringe upon the freedom of Paris merchants to buy wherever it pleased them and to transport their merchandise to the capital.[9] When the merchants filed complaints against local authorities for obstruction of trade, the municipality usually gave them ardent support. In 1740 the police of Crécy in the Brie seized a wagonload of wheat purchased from a laboureur by a self-proclaimed commissioner of a Paris-based grain merchant. Only a relatively small quantity of grain was involved and a face-saving compromise restituting the seized merchandise and saving the expense of litigation could surely have been arranged. But Jean-Baptiste Jauvin the younger, the Paris merchant, whose family had been provisioning the capital for several generations, insisted upon joining the issue for the sake of the "principles at stake." The clash thrust into relief many of the chief points of friction in the unremitting struggle between Paris and the provinces over subsistence and similar issues of politics and patrimony.[10]

The Crécy officials argued, first, that the town stood within the decommercialized zone of ten leagues from which all buyers were banned. Second, and without prejudice to the first argument, they contended that royal legislation required that anyone engaged in Paris-bound trade had to obtain permission from the local police in the area that he frequented and that he regularly had to submit certification from the Paris police that the grain he allegedly supplied the capital was actually marketed there. The "pretended" *commis-*

6. For the absolute priority given to Paris-bound grain, see judgment of the bureau of the Hôtel de Ville, 3 March 1739, AN, H 1939[1] and H* 1858, fol. 131; AN, H* 1858, fol. 65; BN, F 23720, fol. 188 (September 1740).

7. See 19 December 1738, AN, H* 1858, fols. 63–65; 3 January 1739, AN, K 1026; BN, ms. n.a. f. 1032, fol. 93.

8. See Kaplan, *Bread, Politics and Political Economy*, chap. 2; BN, Coll. Joly 1123, fol. 291.

9. BN, Coll. Joly 1123, fol. 279, 16 October 1708.

10. On this struggle, see Kaplan, *Bread, Politics and Political Economy*, 1:28–41.

sionnaire, or buying agent, did not possess "the true character" of a merchant, and he was also known for buying illicitly outside the market and regrating. The person from whom he bought in this instance was suspected of constituting hoards with illegally acquired grain. Behind the formal juridical arguments of the Crécy police lay their real motives. In their view the license claimed by Paris to buy anywhere without control resulted in the desertion of the Crécy marketplace, loss of a substantial amount of ancillary business, a decline in revenue from market tolls, and a grave shortage of grain that sent prices soaring. The "people" were miserable, lacking work and bread, and even the "bourgeoisie" suffered. Significantly, the police had not been solely responsible for the seizure of Jauvin's grain. "The people [had] mixed in," conceded the Crécy authorities.

For Jauvin, the issue was infinitely more simple, turning on two questions, the answers to which he considered imperiously self-evident: whether provisioning operations for the capital had precedence over other grain transactions and whether merchants for the provisioning of Paris had the liberty to operate without hindrance. The Crécy model, which tempted other supply-zone authorities, threatened the whole Paris system. The prévôt des marchands concurred that it was "of infinite consequence" that the Crécy action be repudiated in order to assure the flow of grain to Paris and to chasten the insolence of the hinterland police.

One month after the Jauvin affair the Crécy authorities seized grain belonging to another Paris merchant, Denis Bocquet, who also appealed on the ground that nothing was more important for the supply of the capital than the "liberty" of the merchants. Again denouncing "the vain pretexts alleged" by the Crécy police, the prévôt asked the procurator general to secure release of the grain seized in both cases and to take measures to guarantee "that these officials in the future impose no obstacles to the purchase and shipments of those kinds of grain." Although he discerned some "irregularities" in the trading practices of the merchants, the procurator adopted the recommendations of their official protector. In return the prévôt promised to prevent "our merchants" from buying within the ten-league zone (Jauvin had claimed that the grain his agent purchased actually came from twelve leagues out and was brought to Crécy for the sake of convenience) and to require them to buy firsthand from laboureurs, not from regraters or other intermediaries.

Eight years later Jauvin again squabbled with local officials, this time at Meaux, and naturally he invoked the Crécy precedent. While the details and briefs differed somewhat, the issue remained the same: did the zone police have the right, for whatever legal or political-moral reasons, to abridge the freedom of the Paris merchants to buy? The case underscored the astonishing extent to which usage superseded law, even though the law was constantly reaffirmed. The Meaux police confiscated fourteen muids of wheat that Jauvin's buying agent purchased, and refused to cede to the request of the prévôt des marchands to release it. Their town was only nine leagues from the capital, the Meaux officials maintained, and thus out of bounds to the merchants. There is no question, however, that they would have overlooked this violation had the grain been purchased openly on the market. They feared that clandestine transactions in the granaries would dry up their market and expose residents to *cherté* and want.

Jauvin retorted that "if in fact Meaux is not absolutely situated beyond the ten leagues, the usage has prevailed." Paris merchants had "always" bought at Meaux without impediment, even in the "critical" year of 1740. He frankly avowed that the Paris dealers purchased from samples. The Meaux market was too small to accommodate Paris demand in the open without driving prices up, he explained. Yet it was precisely to avoid price increases that the Meaux officials insisted on public market sales. The new prévôt, Bernage, warmly endorsed Jauvin's petition and accused the Meaux authorities of trying to sabotage the provisioning of the capital. The Meaux police had no right to contravene the royal declaration of 1737 that officially sanctioned off-market transactions for the provisioning of Paris. Indications are that the procurator general, with the advice of the assembly of police, once again decided in favor of Jauvin and the special brand of Parisian liberty.[11]

Another clash occurred in Champagne in 1757, remarkable for the blunt and defiant line of justification adduced by the local authorities and the imputation of corruption made by the merchant. The police of St.-Dizier refused to permit Joachim Pierre Armet, now in his seventh year as a Paris grain merchant, to remove 130 setiers of wheat (200, according to Armet) he purchased for transport to Paris and arbitrarily annulled his contract, with the ownership of the wheat reverting to the seller. They did not charge him with having made his purchases fraudulently or improperly. He bought on the market, he notified the prévôt des marchands that he would soon ship this quantity to the capital, and he informed the prévôt's subdelegate in St.-Dizier that he made the purchase. The local officials appropriated his grain squarely on the grounds that they needed it "in order to prevent dearth" and to parry an incipient price rush. "I shall not," averred the lieutenant of police, let Paris "deprive the city of its own subsistence." No merchant could come to St.-Dizier, even "under the pretext of the provisioning of Paris," and act without regard to local needs. According to an ordinance of 1672 cited by the St.-Dizier police, Paris buyers had to leave places where they bought "sufficiently provided."

Armet did not address himself to the political pretensions of the St.-Dizier officials, but he scoffed at the notion that scarcity threatened. The action against him had nothing to do with the public interest; the local granaries were bursting with grain. Since he had purchased the grain more than six weeks

11. BN, Coll. Joly 1123, fols. 281–87, 290–91, 302, and Coll. Joly 1313, fols. 86–100.

before, "the said wheat has taken a bit of favor and has augmented by three livres the septier." Auger, the man who sold him the grain, wanted to extricate himself from his contract in order to profit from this price increase, Armet suggested, and therefore sought the intervention of the local lieutenant of police, his "relative." Like Jauvin, Armet appealed for vindication in the name of all the Paris merchants, who must not be "troubled" in their purchases. Predictably, the prévôt regarded the St.-Dizier action as a menace to the whole supply system. "It would be quite difficult," he said, "for us to sustain the zeal that we do not cease to inspire in our merchants if they did not have the liberty to buy and to remove" in the provinces. Without reservations, the procurator general decided in favor of Armet, that is to say, in favor of Paris.[12]

Social protectionism and material self-regard were so deeply entangled in the practice of the local police of provisioning that they cannot easily be separated. On some occasions the local authorities acted not to shield their consumers or their town merchants or their relatives, but to defend their own commercial interests. Though the law expressly prohibited them from undertaking grain commerce, they bought and sold surreptitiously. They manipulated the police regulations in order to favor their personal ventures and they drew the veil of public interest across their actions. Early in the eighteenth century commissaire Delamare urged his deputies to be alert to the doings of the officials of the Paris supply zones who "quite commonly engage in a sort of grain trade." Specifically he had in mind the president of the élection of Rozoy, the fiscal procurator of Coulommiers, and the president of the présidial at Melun. Almost two decades later, referring again to Rozoy in the Brie, an officer of the rural constabulary reported that "all the justice of the place, right up to the lieutenant general, is mixed up in regrating." Similarly, "almost all the officials" in the Vitry area, claimed a correspondent of the procurator general, "are in the trade secretly, buying up whole granaries." In 1748 a grain merchant serving the capital filed a formal complaint against the fiscal procurator of Rambouillet for illicit speculations, similar to those for which another trader denounced the royal procurator of Pont-Ste.-Maxence in 1774.[13]

Even when their honesty was not in question, local officials did not enjoy a good name with ministers, intendants, parlementarians, and Paris administrators. Either they were overzealous or negligent, impatient or indifferent; and in any event they were brutish and benighted.[14] Charges of corruption

---

12. Ibid., 1130, fols. 227–37, 247–53.

13. Delamare, *Traité de la police*, 2:925; BN, ms. fr. 21645, fols. 88, 210, 258, 423; Marchais to lieutenant general, 14 December 1725, Arsenal, ms. Bast. 10271, and same to same, 21 June 1726, ms. Bast. 10273; Domballe to procurator general, 25 October 1725, BN, Coll. Joly 1116, fol. 280; AN, Y 11235, 18 October 1748; Archives Seine-Paris, D4B⁶ 52-3196, 23 June 1774.

14. Kaplan, *Bread, Politics and Political Economy,* 2:42–49.

and cupidity further blackened their reputation, and made it easier for Paris officials and merchants to ride roughshod over them. When the Paris merchants refrained from complaining about local officials it may not always have been because they were left unmolested. Sometimes it may have meant that the two parties had arranged a mutually profitable deal. Such complicity was especially plausible in the noncrisis years, when the social and political risks were minimal.

In addition to protecting them against local authorities, the Paris municipality provided the merchants with other safeguards for their commerce. It excused them from the obligation to obtain a notarized certificate attesting to each purchase. On the prévôt's request, the assembly of police interceded in their behalf against owners and operators of market rights called minages who tried to force them onto the markets.[15] Although its decisions were often contested, the bureau of the municipality, sitting as a court, tried to establish the rule that grain destined for Paris, even when it was purchased on the market, was not liable to the payment of "rights" of any kind. Grain bound for Paris could not be seized for recovery of taxes or dues owed to the king or in most instances private debts.[16] In some cases, upon the recommendation of the municipality or the Châtelet, the secretary of state for Paris affairs accorded Paris grain and flour dealers who were "useful" for the provisioning of Paris temporary immunity against any punitive action taken by their creditors while they attempted to set their commerce aright. The grain merchant Lemerge, for example, claimed in his petition for relief "that he was required to contract several debts in order to uphold his commerce, that being obliged to leave immediately following your [the prévôt's] orders to make grain purchases for the provisioning of Paris, he is afraid of being disturbed by his creditors, [and] he begs you to determine whether you believe that there is reason to grant him this safe-conduct that he demands and whether all his debts were not contracted uniquely for the maintenance of his commerce."[17]

When the dayworkers (gagne-deniers) in the port that served Provins tried to win more generous fees for their labor and their good-will by refusing to load Paris-bound grain, sabotaging the boats, and hectoring the Paris agents, the prévôt fixed the wages of the local workers and enjoined them to serve Paris agents faithfully or face "exemplary punishment" and a fine of a thousand livres.[18] The municipality tried to shelter its merchants from compe-

15. BN, Coll. Joly 1123, fols. 288–89; BN, ms. fr. 11356, fols. 137, 30 November 1730, and 193, 18 December 1732.

16. Prevotal sentence, 3 December 1740, BN, F 23720, fol. 207; arrêt of the Paris parlement, 17 January 1742, BN, F 23673, fol. 136; Des Essarts, *Dictionnaire universel de police,* 1:331.

17. Dispatch to Lambert, 25 August 1728, AN, O¹ 375, fol. 283. Cf. Maurepas to Marville, 27 August 1740, O¹ 385, fol. 327, and dispatch to Bertier de Sauvigny, 27 April 1761, O¹ 403, fol. 206.

18. Deliberations of the bureau of the Hôtel de Ville, 14 July 1752, AN, H* 1864, fols. 269–70.

tition not only from outsiders (other towns or provinces, the army) but also from other Paris buyers. A dramatic example of this sort of protectionism occurred in the fifties when Bernage tried to exclude the General Hospital from buying in the Brie and in other areas "in which our merchants habitually make the bulk of their purchases for the very precious supply of the ports of this city."[19] Vis-à-vis other officials charged with responsibility for the provisioning of Paris, the prévôt des marchands frequently took a "liberal" posture. Whereas in difficult moments they tended to favor government buying and requisitioning of supplies, he was more inclined to accord his own merchants the broadest opportunity to respond lustily to speculative incentives on their own.[20] Not surprisingly the port grain merchants made the prévôté their preferred arena of litigation in its capacity as a civil court, a hospitable place in which to confront adversaries.[21] There was nothing unworthy of sacrifice on the altar of "the provisioning of Paris."

The relationship between the prévôté and the "merchants for the provisioning of Paris" turned on a quid pro quo.[22] The municipality labored hard to serve the merchants because it knew that their loyalty depended in large measure on the benefits it afforded them. In return, however, the merchants engaged themselves solemnly to serve the capital faithfully and sedulously. They pledged to obey the established protocols of the hinterland: to respect the ban on all trade in the decommercialized zone that extended for a radius, first of eight and later of ten leagues (roughly between 36 and 45 kilometers), around Paris; while buying outside the markets, to offer prices consonant with market guidelines; to conform to all local rules of behavior when buying on the markets of the provisioning zone; and to abstain from intercepting grain that was en route to market, from reselling grain before it reached Paris,

19. BN, Coll. Joly 1312, fols. 1–30. On hospital provisioning, see also Scipion accounts, Hôpital Général, Archives Assistance publique; deliberations of the Hôtel-Dieu, 7 March 1774, Archives Assistance publique, no. 144; BN, Coll. Joly 1229, fols. 176–81, 208.

20. See, for instance, Lambert to Hérault, 28 September 1725, Arsenal, ms. Bast. 10270.

21. There is considerable evidence that the port merchants favored the municipal court over the Châtelet or even the consular jurisdiction. See, for example: the port consortium led by merchants Greban, Gilbert, and Meusnier against a master baker. Conciergerie, livre d'écrou, AB 96, Archives de la Préfecture de Police; AN, MC, V-375, 19 January 1735 (sentence obtained by Meusnier); Petit v. Rochez, 18 January 1772, Archives Seine-Paris, D4B⁶ 43-2431; widow Guérard v. a broker, 11 September 1726, AN, Z¹ᴴ 239.

22. Every merchant with prevotal sanction was a "grain merchant for the provisioning of Paris" (usually styled *marchand de bled(s)* rather than *grains*), but not every merchant brandishing the "for the provisioning of Paris" label exercised an authentic commission. Coveted for the prestige and power it conferred, the title was often abusively appropriated. See for instance the cases of Claude Theveny, who turned out to be nothing more than a "journalier pour remuer les grains," and Denis Antoine, an unemployed twenty-two-year-old who had done some grain dealing around Chartres. Archives Seine-Paris, D4B⁶ 82-5503, and AN, Y 13518, 5 February 1758. Cf. the complaint by the self-interested owner of the minage of Bray that the provisioning of Paris in grain was a Grand Alibi and invitation for abuse: "the merchants pretend that all the purchases they make are for the provisioning of Paris." Comte de Rochebrune to procurator general, ca. 1730, BN, ms. fr. 21635, fols. 244–53.

and from amassing grain for purposes other than more or less immediate shipment to the capital. In Paris at the Halle as well as on the ports the regulations were geared "to rush" the merchants in order to engage them to sell at "the natural price" and to return to the field for fresh supplies. A merchant was supposed to sell his entire stock within three market days, which meant usually within a calendar week (though bakers could purchase grain and flour between official market days). He had to dispose of his grain at the end of the third market day, regardless of the price, and on the second and third market days he could not ask for more than he had demanded initially. Instead of storing unsold grain, as the merchants would have preferred, the police seized it (but usually not without one day's grace) and arranged for its sale through a broker.[23]

Each merchant made a formal "submission" in which he promised to keep the ports "sufficiently furnished with only good quality grain at all times" and to sell it at the going price.[24] Both the municipality and the merchants clearly understood this task to be a sort of public service rather than an ordinary commercial operation. At the same time that the merchants were given uncommon commercial latitude, they were subjected to more or less rigorous inspection and control, depending upon the provisioning conditions. At the end of each month, merchants were required to submit statements of their projected supply for the coming month. The prévôt imposed precise quotas in times of stress. He asked the intendants and subdelegates of the intendants as well as his own officers to supervise the buying operations of the Paris merchants.[25] If a merchant failed to fulfill his responsibilities he risked a gradation of reprisals beginning with private castigation and ending with public censure, abrogation of commissions for a fixed period or in extreme cases for life, heavy fines, and jail sentences.[26] Commissions automatically expired at the

23. Kaplan, *Bread, Politics and Political Economy,* 1:63–72.

24. Ordinance of the Hôtel de Ville, 12 February 1732, AN, F[11] 264; BN, Coll. Joly 1314, fol. 41.

25. AN, H* 1870, fols. 374–84, February 1764; AN, H* 1859, fols. 204–7, 5 February 1741; Bernage to intendant of Champagne, 29 January, 31 May, 30 June 1768, AD Marne, C 422.

26. See, for example, the sentence striking Bocquet "from the number of grain merchants on the ground that he did not furnish a sufficient amount of grain." BN, Coll. Joly 1312, fol. 29, March 1735. In 1725 the municipality threatened the port merchants with fines of 3,000 livres if they failed to keep the ports adequately supplied and in 1740 it actually imposed a fine of 10,000 livres on the leading dealers. Règlement, 2 October 1725, AN, F[11] 265; AN, H* 1859, fols. 20–22, 17 September 1740; BN, Coll. Joly 1120, fols. 34–40. See also controller-general Dodun's threats to purge the corps of port merchants for their recalcitrance in 1725. Dodun to procurator general, September 1725, BN, Coll. Joly 1117, fols. 182–84. On the practice of fines, see Bignon's remarks to the assembly of police in 1768, AN, H* 1875, fol. 103. The bureau of the Hôtel de Ville also rewarded merchants with bonuses when they performed with special zeal. Witness, for instance, the 1,800 livres' premium paid to Pierre Derain for bringing in grain at "a difficult time" and the 480 livres granted Despreaux for his "special efforts." AN, F[11] 264, 20 September 1740, and K 1056, 4 October 1740.

end of every year. The prévôt conducted a careful evaluation of the contributions and conduct of each merchant and his agents before approving the issuance of new letters.[27]

The municipality developed a keen political interest in the port merchants that had little to do intrinsically with grain police and policy. As it steadily lost ground to the lieutenance of police in the contest for administrative control of Parisian life, the prévôté became increasingly strident in its efforts to retain influence. While the lieutenance claimed to police all provisioning, the municipality insisted upon its hegemony over all river-based commerce. The river was the municipal Rubicon, or, rather, the moat protecting the Fortress Prévôté. From this point of view, the vitality of the waterborne grain trade became as important to the survival of the municipality as it had always been to the sustenance of the capital. Thus, the municipality was doubly motivated to encourage the business and the discipline of the port merchants. During the course of the century, however, it proved unable to prevent the decline of the ports (and the concomitant triumph of the Halle), a failure that further warped its prestige and symbolized its disarray.

The Rue de la Mortellerie

United by a common bond to the municipality, port merchants were also closely linked by neighborhood ties.[28] Most of them inhabited the dense and bustling rue de la Mortellerie, a street near the Hôtel de Ville looking out on the Seine.[29] The Mortellerie merchant lived where he worked: he was at home on the port in a double sense. Living and working side by side, the Mortellerie traders could keep few secrets, professional or personal, from each other. They competed with each other, but their rivalry was structured and tempered by multiple bonds of neighborhood, kinship, and interest—bonds that took on a quasi-çorporate character.[30] They squabbled over prices, sacks, and clients, but they offered one another moral and material support at critical

27. BN, Coll. Joly 1123, fol. 288; AN, H* 1864, fols. 205–6 (16 December 1751); AN, X[1B] 7826, 31 December 1740.

28. Port merchant Edme Forget was tied by another kind of bond to the municipality. His son became one of the principal agents of municipal grain surveillance by acquiring the office of *huissier de l'hôtel de ville-commissaire à la police sur les ports.* AN, MC, CVIII-496, 6 November 1751.

29. On its history, see Jacques Hillairet, *Connaissance du vieux Paris, rive droite* (Paris, 1951), 1:62. The wife of a grain merchant named Rogier lay on her deathbed in a rear ground-floor room on the rue de la Mortellerie "having a view on the grain ports." AN, MC, IV-488, 8 August 1735.

30. The authorities discouraged port dealers from associating for the supply of public markets, but promoted "societies" for institutional provisioning. See, for example, the common enterprise of Jauvin, Despreaux, and Bassery in the forties. Archives Assistance publique, Hôtel-Dieu, n.s. liasse 28, no. 2, fols. 415–17 ("Sommier de l'Hôtel-Dieu").

The grain port at the Grève, looking toward the Pont Marie. Seventeenth-century engraving (Bibliothèque Nationale, Photo Collection Viollet)

junctures.[31] In addition to residence and work place, the rue de la Mortellerie furnished virtually all the other services these merchants and their associates needed. The commissioned brokers and the grain-sack renters also inhabited the street.[32] The Mortellerie inns provided rooms for country merchants or grain correspondents who came to the capital for business or litigation.[33] Dealings too delicate to transact in the open took place in one of the numerous taverns, where traders could discreetly buy and sell on sample or engage in some other illicit exchange.[34] In some cases the Mortellerie inn- or tavern-keeper, like his rural counterpart, played the role of broker and/or banker, and perhaps also that of priest (or, rather antipriest).[35] In a word, the rue de la Mortellerie offered the grain merchants a kind of coherence that they found attractive and reassuring.

Already in the time of Richelieu, when Paris was said to have had "no more than 20 persons engaged in the traffic and merchandise of grain," the leading figures—Sébastien de Paris, Hughes Duclos, Jacques Rousseau, René Lescolle—formed a Mortellerie clan.[36] I have encountered, more or less adventitiously, forty-three Mortellerie grain merchants in the period 1725–40, thirty-eight in 1741–60, and twenty-seven between 1761 and 1775.[37] The Mortellerie grain world may have been somewhat larger, though it is likely that it shrank across the century.

Not every port merchant lived on the rue de la Mortellerie, despite its powerful allure. According to a remonstrance drafted by the Mortellerie inner circle in 1739, there were "more than sixty grain merchants attached to the Grève port," a number of whom certainly lived on other streets in the area.[38] That same year the police hinted that there were some ninety accredited port merchants—twice the number whose Mortellerie residence I have documented—but it is quite likely that a substantial number of these traders were in fact country or forain dealers.[39] Port merchant Estienne Collin lived with his wife in a one-and-a-half-room apartment on the rue Geoffroy Lasnier, a

31. For an example of a violent quarrel between colleagues, see AN, Y 15072, 1 March 1769. In contrast, see the solidarity of Jean-Baptiste Fosseyeux and Pierre Greban before the consular commercial court: Archives Seine-Paris, D4B⁶ 11-526, 3 May 1765.

32. Savard to Leduc, 24 February 1741, Arsenal, ms. Bast. 11494; AN, Y 13741, 11 May 1741 (scellé Leguary). Jean Mahut was at once a grain merchant and a sack renter. AN, Y 12619, 17 February 1770.

33. See, for example, AN, Y 15954, 5 October 1757 (Jean Michin, Fontainebleau grain dealer); AN, MC, CI-448, 29 September 1751 (Nicholas Belly, Provins grain trader).

34. See the case of Jean Lefranc, AN, Z¹ᴴ 239, 25 September 1726.

35. See the claims of Poulain of the Hôtellerie du Barillet d'Or. Archives Seine-Paris, D4B⁶ 49-2956, October 1773.

36. BN, Coll. Joly 1428, fol. 2; BN, ms. fr. 16741, fol. 10; AN, MC, XXIII-264, 15 April 1626. On the role of the street toward the end of the seventeenth century, see AN, MC, LXXXIX-16, 21 February 1673 (Aubert); Meuvret, "Le Commerce des grains," pp. 192–202; Roland Mousnier, *Paris au XVIIᵉ siècle* (Paris, 1961), pp. 214, 254–56.

37. See Appendix A.

38. BN, Coll. Joly 1120, fols. 34–35, and ms. fr. 8089, fols. 521–22.

39. BN, Coll. Joly 1120, fol. 50.

short distance from the Grève. Virtually the only items they possessed beyond the minimum stock of furniture and utensils required for sleeping and
eating were an easy chair, a mirror, and a devotional book. On at least one
occasion, Collin was associated in his purchases with two Mortellerie stal-
warts, Pierre Bayeux and Bernardin Le Sieur.[40] A former furniture dealer
named André Bimuler traded in grain from a comfortable base on the Ile-St.-
Louis. He did not enter the trade, however, until the eighties, by which time
recruitment had undergone a profound change.[41] Still, even if the Grève and
the rue de la Mortellerie were not precisely coextensive, it is not too much to
say that the Mortellerie merchants controlled the life of the grain port.[42]

The vast majority were members of the elite, municipally commissioned
merchants. Yet there were impostors of sorts, lesser merchants who hoped
eventually to insinuate themselves into the port coterie. They assisted the
established merchants or scavenged for business that the port merchants
scorned or neglected.[43] There were seven women in the 1725–40 group (including several who were primarily brokers for country merchants), one in
1741–60, and none in 1761–75. This distribution across time, however, may
merely reflect the caprice of the data.[44] The lack of persistence of individuals
from period to period suggests a considerable turnover rate, but this too may
be a misleading artifact of data collection. At least half of eight "persisting"
merchants are members of Mortellerie family dynasties. Fosseyeux, Jauvin,
Greban, and Denise have either parents or brothers or sons who had or have
or will have port commissions. The Greban *père* and *fils* were linked by
marriage to the Fosseyeux family, which had factor branches in the hinterland
as well as a solid Mortellerie base.[45] Marie-Jeanne Jauvin, daughter of one
Mortellerie baron and sister of two others, married Etienne Pinondel, who
emerged as one of Mortellerie's rising stars in the forties.[46] Michel-Elie Bour-

40. AN, Y 13087, 20 July 1737.

41. Archives Seine-Paris, D4B⁶ 85-5740 and D5B⁶ 3682.

42. The list of ninety appears to be something of an abstraction if one compares it with
the schedule of quotas imposed on the port merchants by the municipality in 1740. Only
twenty-nine merchants were cited, all of them Mortellerie dealers. AN, F¹¹ 264. In the late
fifties and early sixties, according to a prévôt des marchands, there were at times as many as
forty-three Paris-based merchants on the municipal grain-trading roster. AN, H* 1873, fol.
103.

43. See, for example, the case of Françoise Granget, AN, Y 11229, 5 January 1742.

44. Of the 90 names that the authorities placed on the list of port merchants in 1739, 11
were widows and 1 a woman juridically separated from her husband, who also figured on the
list as a grain trader. BN, Coll. Joly 1120, fol. 50. To the 64 names on the list I have added 26
port merchants (all Mortellerie) fined by the municipality in January 1739.

45. AN, MC, LI-972, 2 September 1751; AN, X¹ᴮ 8147, 14 June 1760; AN, MC, CVIII-
492, 10 March 1751.

46. AN, MC, XXVI-698, 30 August 1781. The Jauvins married on the rue de la Mortellerie even when they did not marry into the grain-trading clan. See J.-B. Jauvin's marriage to
the daughter of an *officier porteur de charbon* who had lived his whole life on the street. AN,
MC, IV-576, 18 January 1787.

jot was almost certainly the son of Elie, one of the Mortellerie barons sub-
poenaed by the avenging *chambre des bleds* in the wake of the "famine" of
1709. Bourjot *fils* married Louise Bouillerot, whose family was a Mortellerie
fixture.[47] Neighbors and grain traders on the rue de la Mortellerie, René
Borde and Antoine Lenain became relatives when Lenain married Borde's
widowed mother.[48] The Moussiers, father and son, had independent commissions on the port at the same time, as did Pierre Dumont and his two sons
Jean and Pierre-François.[49] Jean Chevet married his daughter to Moreau, a
Mortellerie comrade.[50] Marie Fortier, niece of a Mortellerie trader, married
César Michel, Mortellerie merchant, and shortly after his death became the
wife of Nicolas Nicole, also a Mortellerie dealer.[51] Aubert and Rousseau may
have belonged to the seventeenth-century grain-trading families of the same
names.[52]

Apart from the dynastic progeny we know little about the origins of the
Mortellerie merchants. René Borde was the son of a butcher.[53] Adrien
Michel's father was a grocer at Bray, a major grain entrepôt upriver on the
Seine.[54] François Letellier followed his father into the wine business at No-
gent, an important grain crossroads on the Oise, before shifting to grain on the
Paris port.[55] These few clues suggest that port merchants came from a wide
range of backgrounds, more often than not of a mercantile character, and that
their families were likely to be reasonably well off.

Mortellerie Fortune

There was also great diversity in the economic status of the port merchants themselves. Their reputation for opulence far outstripped the reality.
They were believed to be affluent and powerful because a few of them were,
more or less. Though it was easier than has been believed for merchants
without significant resources to maneuver on paper in order to obtain and

47. AN, X²ᴮ 1090, 23 January 1710; Archives Seine-Paris, 6AZ 1475. Cf. Archives Seine-
Paris, DC⁶ 23, fol. 156, 18 January 1787.
48. AN, MC, VII-278, 13 April 1751.
49. BN, LK⁷ 6289; AN, MC, XLIX-690, 6 July 1751; AN, MC, LVIII-370, 14 August
1751; AN, MC, XXVI–685, 31 May 1780. The maternal grandfather of Jean Dumont's wife
had been an associate of Mortellerie's most illustrious late seventeenth-century trader, Jean
Roger.
50. AN, Y 11228, 29 July 1741.
51. Archives Seine-Paris, D4B⁶ 51-3601, 24 February 1776.
52. The eighteenth-century Aubert apparently had a Mortellerie son, Archives Seine-
Paris, DC⁶ 19, fols. 41, 121.
53. AN, MC, VII-278, 13 April 1751.
54. AN, MC, VII-390, 28 May 1770.
55. Archives Seine-Paris, D4B⁶ 101-7116, 15 April 1788. Apparently Letellier had also
served for a time as *receveur des coches* at Nogent—an excellent opportunity to become
familiar with the commodity freight system.

extend credit, the merchants with considerable liquidity were obviously in a stronger position to maintain large distribution networks.[56] When the bakers, bitter rivals of the merchants for the control of the grain trade, denounced the Mortellerie barons for amassing prodigious fortunes, their charges surely seemed quite plausible. Jean Delu was said to be worth—apparently in annual income—over 400,000 livres, followed by Derain, Greban, Fosseyeux the elder, and Bourjot at 300,000 livres, Robert at 200,000 livres, Jauvin the elder at 150,000 livres, and three others at over 100,000 livres.[57] We know that Delu was one of the foremost Mortellerie dealers in the mid-twenties and early thirties, with public dealings on the port alone billed at as much as 150,000 livres a year.[58] The governing board of the Hôtel-Dieu, for whom Delu also purchased grain, characterized him as "a rich and honorable man."[59] In 1739 Pierre Greban claimed a fortune of 114,000 livres, including over 46,000 livres in accounts receivable (the bulk of which was for grain furnished), 21,000 livres in the capitalized value of *rentes,* 36,181 livres in real estate, and 5,000 livres in cash. Greban's hard assets were surely undervalued, for he included neither his Paris house nor his rural holdings, on which he may have raised cereals and/or collected rents and dues in kind.[60] Louis Moussier provided his son with a very large dowry of 23,000 livres, enabling him to buy two venal judicial offices and to win the hand of the daughter of a Châtelet *greffier* who brought him 46,500 livres in *rentes* and 2,015 livres in cash.[61] Germain Cormeil, whose wife was the widow of Antoine Blanchet, another Mortellerie merchant, also commanded a considerable fortune.[62]

Nicolas Jauvin senior was not nearly as well off as the bakers allowed. At the time of his death he could boast barely 1,000 livres' worth of furniture and effects, 2,388 livres in silver, and 222 livres in clothing. He and his wife lived rather severely in a three-room apartment adorned by four landscapes, four devotional paintings, an ivory cross, and three mirrors. Still, Jauvin held a middling rank among the Mortellerie merchants, for he owned two houses evaluated at over 23,000 livres and probably some rural holdings as well. A servant tended to their needs. Jauvin's wife gave him a proper bourgeois funeral.[63]

Earlier in his life Jauvin had surely disposed of a larger fortune, for he

56. I believe that Meuvret exaggerated the wealth required to sustain a port enterprise. "Le commerce des grains."

57. "Mémoire des boulangers," ca. 1737, BN, Coll. Joly 1314, fols. 19–20.

58. See Bibliothèque de l'Institut, mss. 513–21.

59. Deliberations of the bureau of the Hôtel-Dieu, 21 November 1730, Archives Assistance publique, no. 99. See also deliberations of 14 January 1727, ibid., no. 96.

60. AN, MC, XCIV-218, 26 August 1739. Greban's inventory underlines how little fixed capital investment grain trading required. He owned 546 livres' worth of grain sacks and a horse assessed at 80 livres.

61. AN, MC, LXXXII-316, 27 December 1751.

62. Archives Seine-Paris, DC[6] 232, fol. 8, 6 March 1746.

63. AN, MC, CVIII-488, 3 March 1750, and CVIII-492, 10 March 1751.

dowered his children with 10,000 livres apiece, and he had at least four, perhaps five. One of his daughters married Etienne Pinondel, who left a more substantial estate upon his death than his father-in-law had. The household and personal effects of the Pinondels were assessed at 5,160 livres, fully a quarter of which represented Marie-Jeanne's elaborate wardrobe. Etienne's passion was Burgundy: he maintained a cellar of both reds and whites. Like the Jauvins, the Pinondels had other resources. Beyond the 16,963 livres in "good" accounts payable that the widow listed (partly nullified by 11,636 in debts), Pinondel owned two farms at La Ferté-Gaucher worth 18,500 livres, other parcels there and at Coulommiers, a large farm in the Champagne, and at least one house. With some help from her mother, Marie-Jeanne continued the grain business after her husband's demise.[64]

Jean Dumont also belongs in this middling category. He and his wife lived simply: their furniture was worth merely 720 livres and their clothing was appraised at 357 livres, to which were added 2,642 livres in silver and 1,001 livres in cash. Dumont's only sign of self-indulgence was a small library of devotional and historical books. He invested in his children's futures rather than in ornamentation, enabling two of them to become architects and a third to enter the royal tax farms. Dumont had channeled the bulk of his assets into his large and costly dwelling on the rue de la Mortellerie.[65] Jean-Baptiste Meusnier's household assets were even more modest than Dumont's: 702 livres in furnishings, 245 livres in clothing, 198 livres in silver, and 316 livres in cash. His only extravagances were two elaborately decorated pistols, a jeweled hunting knife, and six first-quality wigs of different tints. Meusnier had not squandered his earnings, however. He possessed annuities and land worth around 19,000 livres and may also have been the proprietor of a country house.[66]

A number of other Mortellerie merchants were quite badly off. René Borde's widow had reason to be "very upset by the awful state of his business." At his death in 1750, he had large and pressing debts, and was compelled to lodge his wife and children in an exiguous, rather shabby two-room flat.[67] Unlike his brother Jean, Pierre-François Dumont died in heavy debt, with assets, some of which were of questionable solidity, worth barely half the 15,000 livres that his creditors demanded.[68] Jean Chevet, for want of dowry capital, was obliged to see his daughter marry a "gaigne-denier sur le port."[69] Marie-Catherine Foucat sought financial separation from her grain-merchant husband on the grounds that he dissipated their common wealth and

64. AN, MC, XXVI-693, 18 January 1781.
65. AN, MC, XXVI-685, 31 May 1780.
66. AN, MC, V-375, 19 January 1735.
67. AN, Y 15945, 9 October 1750.
68. AN, MC, XLIX-690, 6 July 1751.
69. AN, Y 11228, 29 July 1741.

ruined his business.[70] Charles Carlier was known on the rue de la Mortellerie for his swagger and his elegant appearance, but he filed business failure twice in twenty years, the second time leaving virtually no hard assets and liabilities of over 111,000 livres.[71]

Mortellerie Honor

If Carlier earned a bad reputation because of his repeated failures, it is also true that he foundered in part because of the low esteem in which he was held. Reputation mattered enormously to the Mortellerie merchants. Along with wealth, it was the most significant mark of success. Indeed, they believed that a good reputation would eventually lead to fortune. These merchants fiercely defended their honor as the symbol and guarantor of their standing and regarded the reputation of their adversaries as their most vulnerable point. Typically honor turned on matters of fidelity, either sexual or commercial. Carlier was discredited and dishonorable not because he borrowed money, but because he refused to repay it as he had pledged. In October of 1741, when an ex-concierge, seconded by a lackey friend, demanded the reimbursement of a loan of 384 livres, Carlier's wife called them "atrocious" names, struck them, and expressed her utter contempt by "pulling up her skirts and showing them her behind." The whole neighborhood recoiled at the news of this "ultimate indecency."[72]

The wife of a gagne-denier avenged herself against a Mortellerie merchant named Claude Coppin for having evicted her and her husband from their lodgings by shouting insults. She called his wife "bougre de verrolée" and "cul galeux"—vulgar epithets, to be sure. But more serious was her reiterated charge that Coppin did not pay his debts and that he was a "banqueroutier," a fraudulent bankrupt, one of the gravest assaults one could make upon a businessman's integrity.[73] Similarly, Colmet Lepinay took deep affront when his fellow merchant Moignat claimed in public that "Colmet had been forced to leave his *pays* and could not go back for eighteen or twenty years."[74] No one knew better than Halle-based grain dealer Michel Colat that sullied honor could result in denial of credit, loss of clients, and a certain ostracization in the trading milieux. Colat denounced a Mortellerie conspiracy "to ruin his business" by "tarnishing his good name." Led by Vignard and his wife, the

70. AN, Y 15269, 17 January 1761.
71. Archives Seine-Paris, D4B⁶ 16-763, 1 September 1756. Carlier lived in a Mortellerie house called La Tournelle (a name that became increasingly appropriate as he got more deeply in trouble). He had at least one servant. He did not get on well with his neighbors. See the report of a theft he filed, Arsenal, ms. Bast. 10041, fols. 143–44 (3 November 1755).
72. AN, Y 15337, 6 October 1741.
73. AN, Y 13634, 10 March 1729.
74. AN, Y 15072, 1 March 1769.

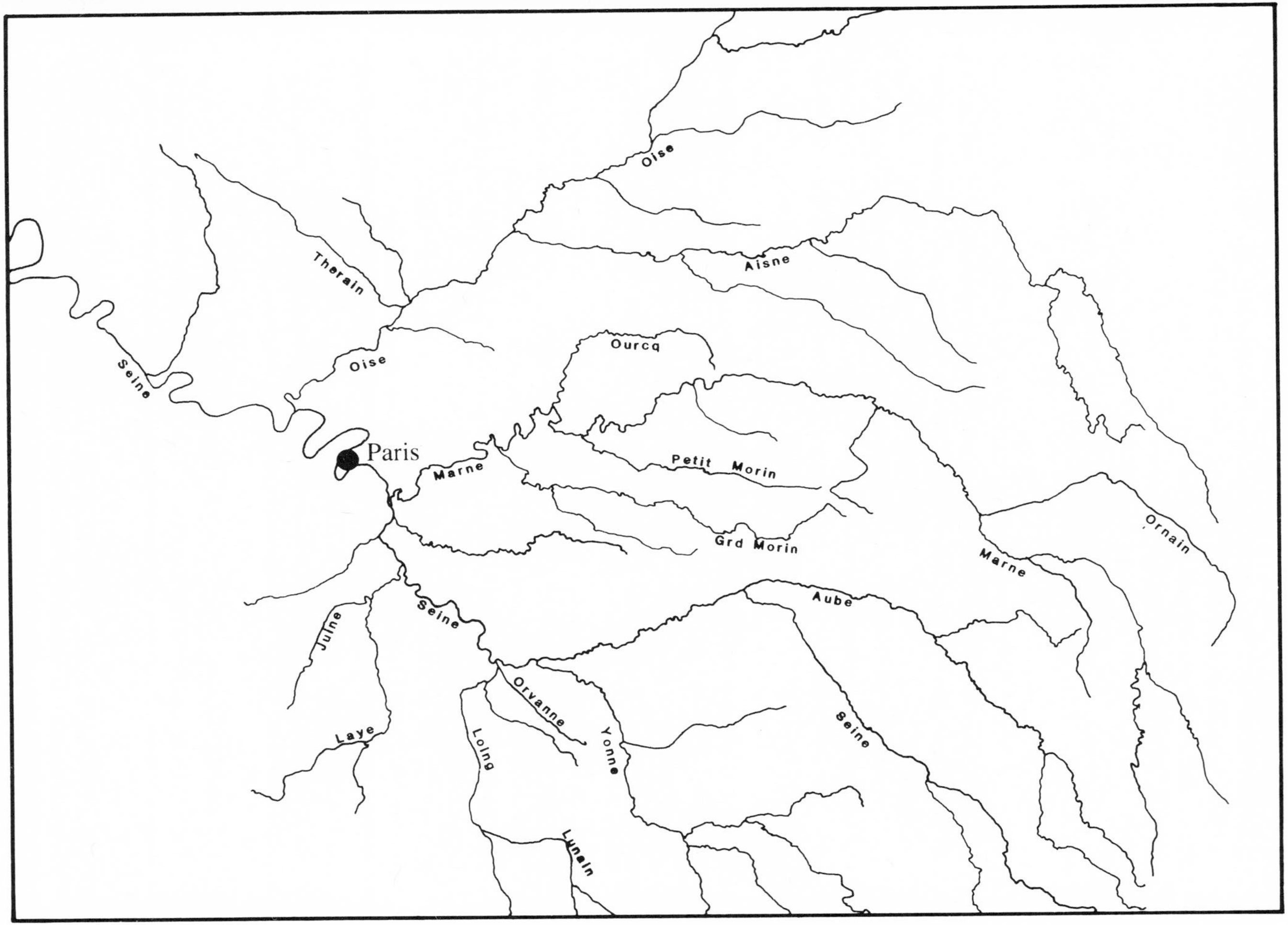

MAP 4   The river system of the Paris supply region

Mortellerie clique "do not stop insulting the plaintiffs [Colat and his wife] everywhere they go . . . in the markets around Paris . . . where they buy grain . . . and in front of all the other merchants."[75]

The Commissionnaires and the Merchants

A good reputation was usually necessary to be successful in business, but never sufficient. One of the most crucial requirements was a dependable connection, or in many cases a network of connections, in the provisioning zones. Despite their own familiarity with the market system and their technical understanding of grain types and qualities, the port merchants would have been far more narrowly confined in range and scale of operations without the local expertise and the firsthand information provided by their agents. (Lack of control over information was probably as important as police regulations and public opinion in limiting firm size in the grain trade.) The port merchants relied on their correspondents for most of the critical field decisions: when, where, what, and how much to buy. And they counted on them for an uninterrupted flow of intelligence on local conditions, weather, rumors, and so on, in order to plan future operations.

The location of the port commissionnaires or agents defined the normal zone of operation of the waterborne Paris grain trade. The agents were most densely concentrated in or near the Marne (Meaux, Trilbardou, Mary, Rebais, La Ferté-Gaucher, Charly, Château-Thierry, Châlons) and the Seine (primarily Bray and Provins). Others operated on or near the junction of these rivers with the Yonne (Montereau, but continuing as far as Sens), the Ourcq (Lizy, but reaching La Ferté-Milon, Neuilly-St.-Front, and Armentières). Connections were less common on the Oise (Pont-Ste.-Maxence and Compiègne), the Aisne (Neufchâtel and Soissons), and the Aube (Arcis).[76]

Characteristically the buying agents were local men with roots in the community. As a rule they dealt only in the immediate area of their home base, though a few covered a second market situated nearby. They exploited their familiarity with local producers, suppliers, and police officials. Generally they were grain traders themselves. In some cases they had even been Parisian suppliers on a regular or occasional basis. A strict construction of the commissions they received from the Paris municipality to serve as agents for the port merchants would have forbidden them to continue trading on their own account even within local confines.[77] This ban was meant to reassure the local authorities, who had a profoundly ambivalent attitude toward the Parisian presence in their provisioning zone and markets and who feared that

75. AN, Y 15934, 19 August 1734.
76. BN, Coll. Joly 1122, fols. 116–20, and Coll. Joly 1117, fol. 181.
77. Controller-general to prévôt des marchands, 7 March 1774, AD Marne, C 419.

Paris agents would use their commissions as a pretext for keeping grain off the home markets, hoarding it, and manipulating the pricing mechanism. In fact the authorities rarely tried to enforce it. In any case it would have proven singularly difficult to separate an agent's putative personal grain enterprise from his commissioned undertakings.[78] It is safe to assume that a good many local dealers solicited Paris commissions precisely in order to enhance their individual trading position. The younger agents construed it as an apprenticeship that would enable them to strike out wholly on their own after they had acquired some capital and experience. Urbain Guillot made the ultimate leap, from simple commissionnaire of Jean Thibault to "grain merchant for the provisioning of Paris, residing at the rue de la Mortellerie."[79]

It is likely that in some instances the agents benefited not merely from the tolerance but from the protection and complicity of hometown police officials, who were ideally placed to organize illicit commerce.[80] Indeed, one even encounters police officials like Bedel, the royal procurator and juror-grain measurer of the market town of Pont-Ste.-Maxence, who himself served as a Paris commissionnaire.[81] Along with venal officials, one finds serving as Paris agents laboureurs, bakers, and innkeepers whose professions formally disqualified them from such activities.[82]

In order to implant themselves throughout the supply crown and thus multiply their sources of grain, and in some cases their sources of credit, the leading port merchants employed several agents at once. Pelletier had at least eight (at Provins, Bray, Vitry, Châlons, Arcis, Montereau, Mousseaux, Rebais). Jauvin the younger maintained at least six (Provins, Vitry, Arcis, Méry, Villenoy, Rebais). Despreaux, Vassery, and Didier Fosseyeux each dealt with at least five agents, while Michel Bourjot and Charles Rousseau utilized at

78. For an example of an independent grain and flour dealer based at Soissons who was also a grain commissionnaire, see Demarre, Archives Seine-Paris, D4B⁶ 100–7066, 8 February 1788.

79. Ibid., D6B⁶, carton 5, October 1769; ibid., D2B⁶ 1078, 27 October 1769.

80. See Kaplan, *Bread, Politics and Political Economy*, 1:42–51.

81. Archives Seine-Paris, D4B⁶ 52-3196, 23 June 1734. This case is vaguely reminiscent of the crucial role played in behalf of Jean Roger in the 1690s by Colmet, receiver of the domain at Bray. See Usher, *Grain Trade*, pp. 77, 306; Kaplan, *Bread, Politics and Political Economy*, 1:45; Mousnier, *Paris au XVIIᵉ siècle*, p. 212. The contemporary portrayal of Roger as a tentacular monster who controlled the entire Seine-Marne supply ground was surely overdrawn. But there is little doubt that Roger "made the law" in a number of key market towns such as Bray, Provins, Méry, and Montereau—thanks to the efficacy of his agents. Mémoire (January 1693), BN, ms. fr. 21642.

82. See, for example, Simonet, a Meaux laboureur who worked for Aubert; Bousset, a Provins baker who served Hémart; and Chauceau, a Montereau *cabaretier* employed by Fosseyeux. Archives Seine-Paris, D5B⁶ 4976; Paulfoy to procurator general, 21 August 1725, BN, Coll. Joly 1117, fol. 109; BN, ms. fr. 21645, fol. 317. Cf. the case of Delille at Lizy, a wool merchant whose profession was not incompatible with simultaneous exercise of a grain commission. Archives Seine-Paris, D4B⁶ 50-3094, 9 March 1774. Also Goier, father and son, wood merchants and grain commissionnaires at Bray. AN, Z¹ᴴ 239, 23 May 1727.

least four apiece.[83] The Moussier and Jauvin dynasties relied on relatives in the hinterland to supervise their buying operations.[84] Instead of investing his hopes in a single buying agent in one town, Nicolas Nicole, another Mortellerie dealer, used three agents simultaneously at Nogent-sur-Seine.[85]

Just as the Paris merchants called on more than one agent, so the agents often served more than one Paris port merchant, not to mention ties with other merchants from Paris or elsewhere. Louis Ledoux at Lizy worked for Jauvin the elder and for Rousseau; Cattet at Provins for Rousseau and Armet; Boyer at Provins for Didier Fosseyeux and the widow Leblanc; Barbier at Châlons for Despreaux and Pelletier; Colmet at Bray for Pelletier and the widow Leblanc. The commercial and political implications of these multiple connections are not clear. They may have acted as de facto associations, dampening competition and violating the spirit if not the letter of police regulations.

Like the port merchants, the agents had links among themselves. The Jolly brothers, employed by Jauvin the younger, were agents based at Méry and Rebais. They were associated with Adam at Varreddes, whose main Mortellerie client was Jean-Baptiste Meusnier. Pierre and Henry Boyer ran commission operations at Provins and Bray. Like the Paris merchants, the most entrepreneurial commissionnaires themselves hired agents to serve their needs, though the local police labored to prevent the multiplication of compacts and contracts.[86] If Missonnet, the royal provisioning monitor at Bray and Provins, had had his way, each Paris merchant would have been limited to one agent in order to alleviate the excessive demand and thus relax the pressure on the price level.[87]

Like the Mortellerie merchants, the commissionnaires of a given market town oscillated between gestures of rivalry and solidarity. Two agents at Vitry came to blows over freight facilities and two others at Rebais quarreled over buying techniques.[88] On the other hand, sixteen commissionnaires at Provins banded together in hard times in order to combat the speculative climate and restore order to the trade.[89]

83. BN, Coll. Joly 1122, fols. 116–20. For other evidence of relations between Mortellerie merchants and agents, see AN, MC, XXVI-459, 22 July 1751 (J. Rousseau), and XXVI-459, 22 July 1751 (Rousseau/Russeau); Bourlon to Hérault, 4 October 1725, Arsenal, ms. Bast. 10270, fol. 272 (Greban). See also BN, Coll. Joly 1117, fols. 119–21, for a list of sixteen Paris port merchants, all Mortellerie residents, and their commissionnaires at Provins in 1725.

84. AN, MC, XV-698, 7 September 1751, and CVIII-492, 10 March 1751.

85. Archives Seine-Paris, D4B[6] 51-3106, 24 February 1776.

86. Controller-general to procurator general, 7 March 1774, AD Marne, C 419; AN, MC, V-375, 19 January 1735.

87. Missonnet to procurator general, 18 December 1752, BN, Coll. Joly 1112, fols. 172–73.

88. Arsenal, ms. Bast. 10275, November 1738, and AN, Y 11224, September 1737.

89. Paulfoy to procurator general, 29 August 1725, BN, Coll. Joly 1117, fol. 118.

The job of the commissionnaires was to buy and transship to Paris. (More rarely they took responsibility for storing grain, but if this was done legally it was always for a relatively brief period and under police surveillance.) Some had standing orders to buy and regular clients who supplied them on a weekly and monthly basis. The latter arrangements were often the fruit of illegal *enarrhement,* the purchasing of a whole crop well in advance of the harvest. Agents also bought on command, in response to changing supply and demand conditions or changing strategic considerations. (Sometimes they also sold on command, another illicit activity, for all grain purchased for Paris was legally bound to be disposed of in the capital.) The agents bought in the market of their home town, where their presence habitually attracted an affluence of blatiers and laboureurs. But much of their buying was "invisible." It took place off the market: in the farms, the granaries (the most promising belonged not to the laboureurs but to "collectors" of rents, droits, fees, and impositions of various sorts: seigneurs, seigneurial fermiers, receveurs, etc.), the inns, even on the roads (forestalling).[90] Undertaken by anyone else such transactions would have been denounced and repressed as monopolistic and dangerous. But it was precisely this derogation from the absolute rule of on-the-market-only that made it so tempting to be a Paris agent and that gave Paris its enormous leverage in the countryside.

Since the port merchants were expected, indeed in a real sense required, to furnish a regular dose of wheat each week, their agents had to maintain a constant flow. As a rule they dispatched modest amounts of as little as 4 to 5 muids in small flat-bottomed boats or barges called *bachots* and *margotas.* Larger vessels, however—carrying up to 400 muids, but more often between 50 and 100—also made the journey downriver. These shipments generally represented the collective efforts of several port merchants.[91] The most common cause of the interruption of shipments was rivers rendered unnavigable as a result of flooding, drought, or ice. Sometimes agents attributed a slackening of deliveries to a lack of liquidity, to local police harassment, or to unwonted competition or other market disruptions.

Like Fosseyeux the younger, the port merchants visited the field occasionally to check up on the agents and keep in touch with distributors and producers.[92] It appears to have been more typical, however, for the agents to come to Paris on a more or less regular basis to discuss tactics and settle accounts. Joseph Desplanques, Colmet Lepinay's agent at Lizy, paid for merchandise by drawing *lettres de change* on Colmet in Paris and by advanc-

90. For an example of seigneurial grain sources, see Gayand's purchase from de Bauville, Archives Seine-Paris, D4B⁶ 52-3196.

91. See shipments discussed in Pillerault to lieutenant general, 29 February 1726, Arsenal, ms. Bast. 10272 and in Carlier's faillite, Archives Seine-Paris, D4B⁶ 16-763, 1 September 1756.

92. See the description of Fosseyeux's visit to Provins, Lobinod to procurator general 25 August 1725, BN, Coll. Joly 1117, fols. 111–12.

ing cash himself. He came to Paris frequently "to count" with Colmet and they were invariably "content with one another."[93] Colmet paid Desplanques 3 livres 5 sous for each muid he purchased in the early seventies, 5 sous less than Halle merchant Nicolas-Louis Martin had paid his agent thirty years earlier.[94] The port merchants appear to have met their obligations regularly in order to keep their agents motivated. The latter usually turned to the consular jurisdiction in case of unpaid commissions or protracted disputes.[95] The port merchants preferred to take their grievances to the municipal court of the capital, where they expected to be favorably treated. Claude Coppin's suit against his Bray buying agent for failing to deliver the stipulated amount of wheat within the time and at the price promised was the most prevalent type of complaint.[96]

The Commissionnaires and the Police

Agents found it considerably easier to please their merchant-employers than to please the police, particularly the local officials. They were repeatedly accused of abusing their off-market prerogatives. They "ran" the laboureurs, they purchased futures, they bought from and sold to each other, they bid prices up, and they exhibited a baleful lack of "restraint and moderation."[97] The commissionnaires had a considerable grip on the grain trade because "they made the price everywhere." Like Billy, Moussier's agent at Provins, they bought large quantities off the market at whatever price the laboureurs asked, and the result was to drive up the market price. Local police denounced them for "causing famine" by choking off the market supply. The lieutenant general of police of Crécy in the Brie reported that "the people were near revolt" in the fall of 1751 because the Paris agents forced the prices up by buying "everywhere," even within the ten-league forbidden zone, without concern for the price asked. A royal agent assigned to Bray and Provins blamed the *cherté* of 1752 on "the avidity" of the Paris commissionnaires and their "rush" to buy everything. At Nogent in December of 1725 local women threatened to throw the Parisian commissionnaires into the Seine if they did

93. Archives Seine-Paris, D5B⁶ 2557. Colmet was less content with his agent Ruelle of Arcis, who drew two letters worth 3,000 livres against him long after they had settled and closed all accounts between them. AN, Y 12618, 5 May 1769.

94. Archives Seine-Paris, D5B⁶ 2557, and D5B⁶ 179.

95. See, for instance, Defontaine, agent at Châlons, against Querot, Mortellerie merchant, 25 October 1743, Archives Seine-Paris, D2B⁶ 766.

96. AN, Z¹ᴴ 239, 23 May 1727.

97. Bourlon to Hérault, 6 October 1725, Arsenal, ms. Bast. 10270, fol. 243; Omballe to procurator general, 25 October 1725, BN, Coll. Joly 1116, fol. 280; Paulfoy to procurator general, 20 August 1725, BN, Coll. Joly 1117, fols. 106–7; BN, Coll. Joly 1126, fols. 13–14. The last-cited source recounts the early morning maneuvers of a Provins baker named Bousset, agent of Hémart of the rue de la Mortellerie.

not leave the market forthwith. In November 1738 the Paris agents, insisting on their "incontrovertible" priority, bought out the entire Provins market by 11:00 A.M., before the local citizenry had access to supplies.[98]

The Paris police reproached the commissionnaires for hoarding, holding back supplies on various pretexts (e.g., lack of sacks or boats), and engaging in other practices geared to drive up prices.[99] Though the port merchants protested their innocence in all this, the authorities strongly suspected that the agents were acting on direct orders from the Grève. City officials vividly remembered the trial of Charles Tournois, a port dealer convicted of "monopoly" during the dearth of 1694 for instructing his agents to withhold shipments until the price rose still higher. In addition to a huge fine of 10,000 livres, Tournois suffered an indefinite ban on any commercial activity on the ports. To counter and expose maneuvers such as his, the Parisian authorities sent undercover agents into the field to spy on the commissionnaires and intercepted correspondence between them and the port merchants. The municipality demanded that the agents document each purchase with local, dated passports and in addition solicited confirmation from local authorities. All delays had to be sanctioned in writing. In order to keep closer control and to trap dissemblers, the authorities required the agents not only to obtain Paris licenses but also to register with the hometown police.[100] Local officials frequently argued that the only permanent solution would be to restrict all commissionnaires to the markets and thus restore a visible, public, governable trade. But the Paris police recoiled from this measure for fear of compromising the capital's supply lines.

Relations with Buyers: Search, Information, and Bargaining

The police expected both the seller and the buyer to bargain (at the Halle as well as on the ports, and in all the hinterland markets as well). Failure to

98. Missonnet to procurator general, 1 October 1753, BN, Coll. Joly 1113, fol. 71, and 24 March 1752, Coll. Joly 1112, fol. 69; BN, Coll. Joly 1112, fol. 220, 2 April 1753; Guillemin to procurator general, 21 September 1740, BN, Coll. Joly 1123, fol. 166; Garnier to same, 22 August 1740, BN, Coll. Joly 1123, fol. 261; Dubois to same, 4 October 1751, BN, Coll. Joly 1129, fols. 47–48; Missonnet to same, 18 September 1752, BN, Coll. Joly 1112, fol. 135; Bourlon to lieutenant general, 16 December 1725, Arsenal, ms. Bast. 10271; Theuny to same, 22 November 1738, Arsenal, ms. Bast. 10275.

99. Paulfoy to procurator general, 20 August 1725, BN, Coll. Joly 1117, fol. 107; Bourlon to Becel, 31 August 1725, Arsenal, ms. Bast. 10270; same to lieutenant general, 1 October 1725, Arsenal, ms. Bast. 10270; same to same, 13 December 1724, Arsenal, ms. Bast. 10271; Vannard to procurator general, 27 October 1741, BN, Coll. Joly 1123, fol. 94.

100. Prevotal sentence, 14 August 1694, AN, AD XI 38; Bourlon to lieutenant general, 1 October 1725, Arsenal, ms. Bast. 10270, fol. 333; Arsenal, ms. Bast. 10270, fols. 49–50; BN, Coll. Joly 1122, fols. 86–87; AN, Z^{1H} 408, 9 April 1726; Guillemin to procurator general, 26 October 1740, BN, Coll. Joly 1123, fol. 289; Couet de Montbayeux to same, 24 October, 13 November 1725, BN, Coll. Joly 1117, fols. 240–43, 249.

bargain constituted prima facie evidence of "monopoly," the gravest market-place crime. The authorities counted on haggling to put downward pressure on prices. In a broader sense than the police envisioned, bargaining helped to bring order into the market. For buyers and sellers who had not yet established privileged trading relations, bargaining was an effective instrument of search. The face-to-face confrontation/negotiation enabled the buyer and seller to feel each other out, decide on each other's trustworthiness, and measure the prospects not only for immediate gratification but for longer-range ties as well. Each party sought an advantage, but they shared a mutual interest in success. Bargaining was an instance and a symbol of the paradoxical relationship of conflictual solidarity that was characteristic of virtually all market contacts. Through bargaining the buyer and seller learned not only about each other but also about the market—how heavy the traffic on the rivers was, how deep supplies were, how brisk demand was. If they did not obtain new information, they were frequently able to test what they already knew about supply and demand conditions, the quality of merchandise, harvest expectations, and so on.[101]

The actual haggling was hedged in by marketplace constraints as well as by a certain etiquette. The grain (or flour) merchant, who usually bid first, had to keep in mind that he would legally not have the right to raise his price beyond that level for the rest of the day (indeed, according to the letter of the law, not until he disposed of all the merchandise in that load). If he opened too high, he could lose his potential customer. The bargaining was not supposed to degenerate into an auction: the buyer engaged in the exchange had primacy over all bystander-rivals. Convention bound both parties to honor accepted bids regardless of what transpired elsewhere or later. There was no tolerance for "cutting," the procedure by which a buyer who purchased on credit compensated himself for losses he later suffered on the merchandise by unilaterally reducing the price that he had agreed to pay the seller.[102]

It was generally expected that the bargaining would move toward a conclusion through more or less symmetrical adjustment. If it were late in the day, however, the buyer might be reluctant to be the one to close the price gap, because he counted on the seller's increasingly ardent desire to get rid of

101. Clifford Geertz, Hildred Geertz, and Lawrence Rosen, *Meaning and Order in Moroccan Society* (New York, 1979), pp. 208, 212, 221–25, 228; Clifford Geertz, *Peddlers and Princes: Social Change and Economic Modernization in Two Indonesian Towns* (Chicago, 1963), pp. 32–33; Fuad I. Khuri, "The Etiquette of Bargaining in the Middle East," *American Anthropologist* 70 (August 1968): 698. On the crucial importance of information search, acquisition, and interpretation, see also George Stigler, "The Economics of Information," *Journal of Political Economy* 69 (June 1961): 213–15, and Michael Rothschild, "Models of Market Organization with Imperfect Information," ibid. 81 (November–December 1973): 1283–1308.

102. See Raymond Firth, *Malay Fishermen: The Peasant Economy* (London, 1946), p. 208.

his goods. Faced with a lethargic customer, the merchant might be tempted to offer him a lower grade of wheat at the price he so stubbornly coveted. While vigorous bidding was not uncommon in the grain and flour markets, especially on the elite qualities, often the "price leadership" exercised more or less discreetly by the authorities and the internalized expectations that governed the behavior of both buyers and sellers reduced the range of maneuver so drastically that the bargaining process lost its vitality.[103]

Relations with Buyers: *Pratik* and Credit

The extension and recovery of credit was a matter of paramount importance not only to the port-oriented grain traders, but to all grain and flour merchants, millers, brokers, and bakers as well. The purpose of credit was not just to capitalize trade, but also to stabilize ties between buyers and sellers.[104] Credit was often an expression of a broader prestatory relationship that aimed to give form and persistence to exchange. This relationship, called *pratik* in Haiti and *suki* in the Philippines, linked a seller and a buyer in a most-favored-client connection. Based on personal engagement on each side, the client bond lowered the costs of search in the trading arena, attenuated the imperfections of the information system, increased the security of transactions (not only by providing guarantees of product quality but also by serving as a sort of social analogue to contract law), and generally helped bring order to the market.[105] In return for a grain or flour buyer's fidelity, the seller granted certain concessions, for example, a price rebate or a bonus in kind (known as *brawta* in Jamaica, *yapa* in the central Andes, *dash* in Africa, and *paaman* in the Philippines, it was called the thirteenth bushel or the "good measure" or the "reward" in the grain and flour markets of the Paris region), or credit.[106]

103. Ralph Cassady, Jr., "Negotiated Price-Making in Mexican Traditional Markets: A Conceptual Analysis," *América Indígena* 28 (1968): 51–78; Victor Uchenda, "Some Principles of Haggling in Peasant Markets," *Economic Development and Cultural Change* 16 (1967): 38–40, 43–44; Geertz et al., *Meaning and Order*, pp. 222, 227–28; William C. Davis, *Social Relations in a Philippine Market: Self-Interest and Subjectivity* (Berkeley, 1973), pp. 161, 244; Sol Tax, *Penny Capitalism: A Guatemalan Economy* (Washington, D.C., 1953), pp. 136–37.

104. Geertz, *Peddlers and Princes,* p. 39. Cf. John Waterbury, *North for the Trade: The Life and Times of a Berber Merchant* (Berkeley, 1972), pp. 179–81.

105. Cyril Belshaw, *Traditional Exchange and Modern Markets* (Englewood Cliffs, N.J., 1965), p. 56; William C. Davis, *Social Relations,* pp. 216–44; Sidney W. Mintz, "The Employment of Capital by Market Women in Haiti," in Raymond Firth and B. S. Yang, eds., *Capital, Savings, and Credit in Peasant Societies* (Chicago, 1964), pp. 261–63; Sidney W. Mintz, "Pratik: Haitian Personal Economic Relations," in Viola E. Garfield, ed., *Symposium: Patterns of Land Utilization and Other Papers,* Proceedings of the 1961 Annual Spring Meeting of the American Ethnological Society (Seattle, 1961), pp. 54–63; Maria C. B. Szanton, *A Right to Survive: Subsistence Marketing in a Lowland Philippines Town* (University Park, 1972), pp. 97–116; Geertz et al., *Meaning and Order,* pp. 218–20.

106. Margaret Katzin, "The Business of Higglering in Jamaica," *Social and Economic*

Nor was the pratik relationship without ambiguity and asymmetry, at least in the context of the eighteenth-century grain and flour trade. At a certain level the parties remained adversaries even as they pledged partnership, each seeking an advantage over the other. Given the intensity of the competition for custom, the sellers had to court the buyers with more fervor than they would have liked. And given the multiplicity of sellers, the buyers felt less constrained to be faithful than they should have been.

Of all the pratik concessions, credit was the most significant and the most problematic. The seller extended credit in the hope of binding the buyer to him. Sometimes the seller even refused cash, as a gesture of trust and an effort to establish a long-term relationship.[107] It was relatively easy, however, for the seller to become snared in his own trap, for the creditor-debtor relationship generated mutual dependence and mutual exploitation. The lender provided the borrower with the wherewithal to do business, but the borrower could threaten to take his custom elsewhere if the lender pressed him too hard or cut him off. The smaller the amount he advanced, the stronger the position of the seller (the safer and more effective his "investment"). Yet if the balance became too small, the debtor might be tempted to turn elsewhere. The debtor had little incentive to make payments unless he received further advances. Thus if he refused further credit, the creditor risked losing not only the debtor's business but also the outstanding accounts receivable. The larger the debt grew, the stronger the position of the debtor (following Keynes's principle that if you owe your banker a thousand dollars you are in his power, but if you owe him a million he is in yours). In this highly personalized system credit was usually based on personal reputation and trust rather than on the provision of direct collateral. The lender had a theoretical mortgage on the borrower's property, but the latter enjoyed full usage and several layers of protection against peremptory seizure. In most cases the chief collateral was the grain and flour that he bought on credit.[108]

Doubtless pratik relationships worked well for many grain and flour trad-

Studies 9 (September 1960): 317; Shephard Foreman and Joyce Riegelhaupt, "Market Place and Marketing System: Toward a Theory of Peasant Economic Integration," *Comparative Studies in Society and History* 12 (April 1970): 197; Ralph L. Beals, *The Peasant Marketing System of Oaxaca, Mexico* (Berkeley, 1975), p. 207; R. J. Bromley and Richard Symanski, "Marketplace Trade in Latin America," *Latin American Research Review* 9 (Fall 1974): 13; Szanton, *A Right to Survive*, pp. 90–93.

107. Khuri, "The Etiquette of Bargaining in the Middle East," p. 702.

108. Geertz et al., *Meaning and Order*, pp. 223, 261n; Geertz, *Peddlers and Princes*, p. 39; Davis, *Social Relations*, p. 215; Burton Benedict, "Capital, Savings, and Credit among Mauritian Indians," in Firth and Yang, eds., *Capital, Savings, and Credit*, pp. 342–43; Ju-K'ang T'ien, *The Chinese of Sarawak: A Study of Social Structure*, London School of Economics and Political Science, Monograph on Social Anthropology, no. 12 (London, n.d.); Barbara Ward, "Cash or Credit Crops? An Examination of Some Implications of Peasant Commercial Production with Specific Reference to the Multiplicity of Traders and Middlemen," *Economic Development and Cultural Change* 8 (January 1960): 154.

ers. The happy instances tend to elude us—we know much more about the problems of debt collection.[109] The focus here is on the baker buyers rather than the institutional customers, who were not necessarily better payers.[110] As a rule bakers do not seem to have been deeply in debt to grain merchants. To judge from the situation of some 120 bakers whose afterdeath inventories (or whose wives' inventories) I have studied, bakers characteristically paid swiftly for their merchandise. Almost three-quarters of these bakers owed nothing to any grain merchant (from the ports, the Halle, or the country). Only 7 percent owed more than 1,000 livres. Mean accounts payable for grain amounted to only 261 livres, less than one week's provisions. Flour debts were more significant. Forty-four percent of the bakers owed millers, meal-men, or brokers something, and almost 10 percent owed over 2,000 livres. Mean accounts payable for flour rose to 711 livres. These were not the bakers who posed problems for the grain traders, though it is plain that if a merchant found himself saddled with a dozen baker-debtors, each of whom was in arrears a week, he could suffer serious cash-flow difficulties. The bakers who threatened the grain merchants were those who failed. Of the bakers in our pool of 144 *faillites,* or business failures, each on the average owed grain merchants of all types 1,186 livres (median = 0) and flour dealers 6,645 livres (median = 4,735). If one focuses exclusively on the bakers who were actually in debt for merchandise, the figures rise. Average grain accounts payable for 43 bakers amounted to 3,972 livres (median = 2,201), while 128 bakers owed an average of 7,251 livres (median = 5,570) for flour. One can see how baker insolvency could jeopardize a merchant's situation.[111]

As far back as the first half of the seventeenth century, the port merchants complained in sharp language that bakers were abusing their terms of exchange. "We buy at great expense and risk, borrowing large sums for this purpose," they claimed, but "instead of meeting their debts as they are obliged to," their baker clients used delaying tactics, especially "letters of respite," which the courts willingly granted them. The public might suffer unless the merchants were seconded in their efforts to recover debts, they

109. Certain port merchants established pratik relationships with their grain suppliers. See, for instance, the loans made to the peasants from whom they bought wheat. BN, ms. fr. 21643, fol. 26, 15 December 1694.

110. See, for example, Jauvin's suit against the Abbaye d'Issy for a grain debt of almost 5,000 livres. AN, MC, LXXII-323, 3 September 1731. Nor am I concerned here with the recovery of sums due for oat sales to carriage drivers and other horse owners. See, for instance, the claims of Guillaume Gratien of the rue de la Mortellerie against a carter for 9,800 livres. Archives Seine-Paris, D4B⁶ 44-2528, 7 April 1772. Nor is there enough data to discuss miscellaneous accounts receivable, some of which were directly related to the merchants' commercial strategies. I am thinking, for instance, of the money advanced by grain merchant Benoist Gouthier to a laboureur near Mary—a loan that implied a whole range of possible future constraints. Archives Seine-Paris, D2B⁶ 1103, 8 November 1771, and D3B⁶ 72, 13 November 1771.

111. For all calculations concerning the bakers, see Kaplan, *Bakers of Paris.*

hinted darkly. In fact the king responded favorably by revoking the baker letters and allowing the merchants to pursue the bakers for collection. Periodically, the merchants asked that the royal arrêt prohibiting respite be renewed.[112]

Some eighty years later the merchants again protested vehemently. This time instead of veiled threats, twenty-seven of them, including all the leading Mortellerie dealers, issued an open warning: the provisioning of the capital would be disrupted and "abundance would be compromised" if they were not given greater facility in debt recovery. They attributed the erosion of the number of port traders in part to the inability of merchants to stay solvent. They did their country buying in cash, they claimed, and they could not go on much longer because "all their capital is scattered about among most of the bakers through the sale of wheat to them on credit." The merchants depicted the bakers as sly and deceitful, remaining at home where they were immune to evade sentences and summonses. They hid away their most valuable possessions, and depended on their wives to buy supplies and to run their businesses "with the money of the grain traders."

The merchants demanded a number of changes in the regulations governing pursuits. They sought the right to have bakers arrested in their homes; they asked that the baker-debtors be declared *banqueroutiers,* making them liable to criminal as well as to more stringent civil action; they sought the power to keep them in jail once they were arrested until they acquitted their entire debt; and they pressed to have their wives, who often were able to siphon off family resources as a result of juridical "separation of property," held jointly responsible for all grain debts. "The security of the grain trade," the merchants esteemed, "is directly contingent on the capacity of the merchants to extend credit to the bakers without risk and with the assurance of getting their money back."[113]

The credit nexus was, according to Delamare, of "great utility" in hard times and for the weaker bakers. Nevertheless, he conceded, the system involved risks, for all bakers were not of equal "solvency," and some schemed to take advantage of the merchants, especially the country merchants.[114] Still, the point was to sustain as many bakers as possible. The assembly of police took the same line in its reply to the merchants' petition in 1733. The assembly had no wish to alienate the merchants, but it regarded their complaints as exaggerated and it bristled at their threatening tone. The assembly denied most of the merchant demands on the grounds that they

112. Arrêt du conseil, 18 December 1642, BN, ms. fr. 21639, fol. 167; BN, ms. fr. 21649, fols. 127–28; BN, ms. fr. 21635, fol. 118.

113. Petition to procurator general, 1733, BN, Coll. Joly 128, fols. 29–31, and Coll. Joly 133, fols. 330–32.

114. Delamare, *Traité de la police,* 2:935. Cf. Breton "usage" not to accord bakers credit on grain purchases. The result was to deter men without substantial resources from becoming bakers. Letaconnoux, *Bretagne au XVIIIe siècle,* p. 96.

contravened time-tested law and custom. Bakers allegedly in hiding could not be declared fraudulent bankrupts unless they had committed and were convicted of fraud. Bakers, like others, had the right to petition for release from debtor's jail once they remitted an initial payment (usually one-fourth) and pledged to pay the rest in installments. Grain dealers in principle could not claim precedence over other creditors, even as "special cases" could not be allowed to supersede "general rules." Nor could creditors obstruct or undo legitimate property separation in marriage. But the assembly made one significant concession: it agreed to recommend that the parlement promulgate an arrêt permitting arrest in the home for debt.[115]

As a rule in the eighteenth century bakers signed private notes rather than notarized obligations for the credit that the merchants extended to them.[116] Bakers were able to renew their indebtedness continuously, provided they amortized the old debts by regular installments. According to one police commissaire, this indebtedness kept many bakers hostage, for if they tried to buy from a new source—from the country traders, for example, who competed with the port establishment—their grain-merchant creditors would threaten to sue them for recovery and even to have them jailed.[117] It should not have been impossible, however, for clever bakers to conceal their recourse to alternative sources of credit.

When bakers clearly failed to meet their obligation and offered neither explanation nor propitiation, the port merchants sued almost always in the court of their protector, the prévôt des marchands. Thus Leger Bourgeot (Bourjot of the rue de la Mortellerie?) had master baker Joseph Boulanger condemned to pay 1,196 livres for grain purchased ten months earlier.[118] Once condemned, the baker could pay up—but it was precisely his inability to pay that brought the suit—or he could seek terms. This was the more common solution, for it enabled the baker to salvage his reputation and to continue his business without harassment. Pursued by César Gibert of the rue de la Mortellerie, baker Claude Tavernier asked installment terms.[119] Master baker Dominique Henry obtained respite confirmed by chancellery letters. In return for a promise to pay one-sixth each year for six years, backed up by his wife's pledge of surety and a mortgage on all his possessions, Henry had his seized possessions returned and the interest on his debt and his court costs forgiven.[120] Adrienne Loisel received similar indulgence in return for a promise

115. Assembly of police, 25 June 1733, BN, ms. fr. 11356, fols. 209–11.
116. Seventeenth-century merchants appeared to have been more cautious and more dependent on the notaries. See, for example, AN, MC, XIII-9, 16 January 1629.
117. Duchesne to lieutenant general, 25 September 1698, BN, ms. fr. 21643, fol. 373.
118. AN, Z^{1H} 239, 12 November 1726. Cf. Lory and Gaultier v. Fremin, Arsenal, ms. Bast. 10150, August 1726, concerning a 53-muid debt dating back to 1724.
119. AN, Z^{1H} 239, 3 September 1726.
120. Archives Seine-Paris, DC^6 17, fol. 207, 20 December 1770.

to repay fourteen installments in eight years.[121] On occasion a cooperative and trusted baker was able to obtain terms without suffering condemnation. Charles Calemet and Louis Troisvalet of the rue de la Mortellerie and several other creditors gave baker Pierre Sacre two years' delay in light of the "misfortunes" and "losses" he suffered.[122] Mortellerie dealer Joachim Armet accepted master baker Antoine Riot's offer to reimburse his 2,000 livres in twenty-seven consecutive weekly payments.[123] Another port merchant accepted a sort of annuity *(rente constituée)* by master baker Nicolas Sauvegrain until he could reimburse a debt of 4,700 livres.[124]

If he failed to reach agreement with his creditors, the baker risked confiscation and sale of his property. Marin Denis of the rue de la Mortellerie had the house of master baker Charles Lelièvre seized; they fought over its disposition for thirty-seven years. Joachim Armet effectively incapacitated master baker Denis Petitfils by securing liens on all his property. The widow of another port merchant, Charles Vassou, won seizure of two houses and some land belonging to the widow of a forain.[125]

Bakers had a third option, which usually implied renunciation of business. In return for the cession of all their goods to their creditors, they were guaranteed against any further pursuit, seizure, or arrest.[126] In most such cases the bakers had precious little to abandon and the merchants resigned themselves to significant losses. A fourth option was more or less violent resistance. An *officier garde du commerce* visited the shop of baker Leveque in order to ask him to pay the 3,309 livres' judgment to which he had been condemned. When Leveque refused, the officer waved his "baguette distinctive" and declared him under arrest. Leveque fled, assisted by his journeymen, who attacked the intruder with bread shovels and oven rakes.[127] Nonviolent resistance, a fifth option, was more common, though it was too costly a path for most bakers to follow, involving counterlitigation and appeal. Condemned by the municipal court to reimburse Vincent Pelletier of the rue de la Mortellerie, baker Antoine Gouffe contested the verdict for three years, all the way to the parlement.[128]

The merchants' aim in these actions was to secure repayment rather than

121. Archives Seine-Paris, DC^6 18, fol. 4, 20 November 1771. This practice varied little across the century. See master Jean Laurent's terms, Archives Seine-Paris, DC^6 3, fol. 219, 1 October 1717.

122. AN, MC, XXVIII-41, 27 October 1698.

123. AN, MC, CXVIII-464, 16 February 1751.

124. AN, MC, V-458, 13 January 1751.

125. AN, Y 11390; AN, MC, VII-279, 20 July 1751; AN, Y 14529, November 1734.

126. Among the bakers who ceded their possessions to port merchants were Dugland, Flechet, Allyot, Auger, Destors, and Lecoq. Archives Seine-Paris, DC^6 18, fol. 249, 21 August 1773; DC^6 19, fol. 21, 12 February 1774; DC^6 19, fol. 20, 5 February 1774; DC^6 19, fol. 290, 30 January 1776; DC^6 22, fol. 4, 5 June 1779; DC^6 22, fol. 159, 1780.

127. BN, Coll. Joly 1416, fol. 126, 19 January 1781.

128. AN, X^{1B} 3489, 10 January 1781.

to punish the debtors. In most cases it was in their interest to see the baker remain in business. But when they were sufficiently exasperated the merchants, like other creditors, were relentless. They turned to punishment as both a sort of moral compensation and as an instrument of leverage. The retribution was jail—a harsh penalty for these unhappy artisans, who were rarely motivated by criminal intent.[129] In some cases the jail cure worked expeditiously. Master baker Lesueur was in prison for barely two days before he raised one-third of his debt to grain merchant Cézard Menessier and won his release with the promise to pay the balance in two installments over four months.[130] Similarly, master baker Nicolas Tousseville was freed after one night in jail when he paid 164 livres.[131] Master baker Gennard was arrested on 22 September 1788 by the same *garde du commerce* who had been beaten up by Leveque's journeymen. He suffered three weeks' incarceration before he raised 70 livres and found a master glassmaker willing to stand surety.[132] Mortellerie merchant Corhu allowed master baker Rateau out of jail after a month in return for a notarized pledge to pay 415 livres.[133] Master Dutocq spent a month in jail at the behest of Mortellerie merchant Jean-Pierre Armet until he paid one-third of a debt of 1,152 livres. But another Mortellerie dealer, Jean-Baptiste Jauvin the younger, had him reimprisoned the same day for a debt of 1,100 livres, and he apparently languished in the Grand Châtelet dungeon for another eleven months.[134] Baker Philibert Bourgeois endured a year of prison.[135] Ex-master baker Charles Gouy managed to get out after a year only because his creditors, including a port merchant, refused to pay for his food any longer.[136]

Business Failures

Grain merchants' inability to collect all their accounts receivable was one of the causes of their failure. Among the other reasons were speculative miscalculations, overextension of buying operations, tight credit, commercial

---

129. For a stringent critique of the "atrocities of debt slavery," see Dupont to Carl Ludwig von Baden, 15 January 1773, in Pierre-Samuel Dupont de Nemours, *Carl Friedrich von Baden Brieflicher Verkehr mit Mirabeau und Dupont,* ed. Carl Knies (Heidelberg, 1892), 2:25–28, and Simon-Nicolas-Henri Linguet, *Théories des loix civiles, ou Principes fondamentaux de la société* (London, 1767), 2:398–410. Cf. Mercier's complaint that "the creditor is always mistreated by the law . . . there is not at all enough severity. . . ." *Tableau de Paris,* 2:329.

130. Archives de la Préfecture de Police, AB 191, 11–13 March 1736.

131. Ibid., AB 185, 24–25 January 1727.

132. Ibid., AB 321, 11 October 1788.

133. Ibid., AB 321, 29 February 1788.

134. Ibid., AB 196, 12 July, 11 August 1742, 7 July 1743.

135. Ibid., AB 193, 10 May 1738.

136. Ibid., AB 185, 15 February 1726.

or familial catastrophe, ineptitude, and inexperience. Legally failure was considered to be *innocent:* the product of accident of one sort or another rather than design or ill will. Filing for failure was very similar to what we call filing for bankruptcy today, but in the old-regime French context bankruptcy necessarily implied fraud and was harshly punished and thus was carefully distinguished from *faillite,* or failure. Grain traders, like bakers or other craftsmen and merchants, had recourse to faillite when they could no longer meet their obligations.[137] It was meant to preempt judicial pursuits and prepare the way for an agreement with creditors that would permit a failing businessman to relaunch his commerce.[138]

We have the faillite record of eight Mortellerie merchants, who failed ignominiously to sustain the image of their street as the home of the barons of the grain trade.[139] Their total assets average 19,680 livres (median = 9,054) substantially higher than those of our entire group of fifty merchant failures, including ten other Paris dealers and thirty-two country merchants (average = 13,615 livres; median = 8,407 livres). But whereas barely over half of the entire group's assets were paper claims, the vast bulk of the Mortellerie assets were accounts receivable. Despite the Mortellerie reputation for solidity, these merchants possessed no real estate in Paris and only a paltry amount in the provinces (167 livres' worth on the average against 3,612 livres for all fifty merchants), no stock (against 667 livres on the average for all fifty merchants), no equipment or tools (against 630 livres for all fifty merchants), a quite modest amount in personal and household effects (1,500 livres against 1,704 for all fifty merchants), and a fistful of *louis d'or* (233 livres). Mean hard (i.e., physical, or nonpaper) assets amounted to 6,850 livres for all fifty merchants and to 5,279 livres for the entire Paris group including the Mortellerie merchants. Average Mortellerie hard assets by themselves were only 44 percent of the mean hard assets of the entire Paris group, even though their average total assets were 3,000 livres greater.

Buyers, mostly bakers (an average of seven per merchant), owed substantial sums to the Mortellerie merchants (about 8,000 livres mean and median).

137. Further indebtedness was the last desperate step that merchants used in the hope of avoiding failure. In 1717 Germain Dumont converted his obligation of 2,770 livres into a loan by constituting an annual and perpetual loan-*rente* of 138 livres backed by a mortgage on his house "at the sign of the three sheep" on the rue de la Mortellerie. AN, MC, LXV-193, 26 June 1717. Towards the end of the century grain merchant Hugot openly borrowed 12,000 livres "à six pour cent d'intérêt" in order to inject some life into his stagnating commerce. Archives Seine-Paris, D5B⁶ 4785, December 1785.

138. As such it might have been included above among the options available to baker-debtors. Failures usually led to *atermoiements,* or formal agreements of respite. See, for example, the ten-year moratorium sought by the associated grain dealers Regnard and Lesourd. Archives Seine-Paris, D4B⁶ 36-1967, 2 January 1770. For a fuller discussion of the mechanism and diplomatics of failure, see Kaplan, *Bakers of Paris.*

139. For the references to Mortellerie and other grain merchant faillites, see Appendix B.

The average grain accounts receivable for all fifty failed merchants were a little more than half that amount, while it was 5,771 for the entire Parisian contingent. Yet while debts due for grain represented the bulk of accounts receivable for all fifty merchants (mean = 58 percent, median = 75 percent), they stood for only about 40 percent of the monies due the Mortellerie dealers. That is to say, the assets column of the Mortellerie merchants was swelled with very sizable paper claims that apparently had nothing to do with the grain business.

Average Mortellerie liabilities were 31,624 livres (median = 16,390), only slightly higher than those of the fifty merchants taken together (but almost 15 percent higher than the liabilities for the entire Paris group). It simply was not true, as the port merchants liked to boast, that they paid for all their purchases on the spot: grain acquisitions account for most of these debts both for the Mortellerie merchants (80 percent) and the fifty (60 percent). Purchases from laboureurs represented under 15 percent of grain liabilities for all fifty and even less for the Mortellerie dealers. It is likely that laboureurs demanded cash for most transactions. Almost two-thirds of the fifty merchants owed 90 percent or more of their grain debt not to laboureurs but to other merchants, including or perhaps primarily commissionnaires. The Mortellerie merchants also owed the majority of their grain accounts payable to other merchants. The Mortellerie dealers had relatively few suppliers (average = 5.8) to whom they could turn and thus disposed of fewer lines of credit than the fifty merchants together (average number of suppliers = 8.4).

The great chain of credit covered the entire distance from the fields (though we have noted that producers, especially petty ones, tended to ask for cash) to the tables of consumers: consumers bought bread on credit in the shops and even in the markets; bakers bought grain (and flour) on credit from merchants; merchants bought grain on credit from other merchants who obtained the grain either on credit or for cash from still other intermediaries or from producers. Indebtedness was rarely so great that the failure of one link could generate a chain reaction of disaster, as, say, in the banking milieu. But given the narrow margin on which many of these artisans and merchants operated, the inability to collect could mean trouble.

The Mortellerie merchants had a significantly greater (or, rather, less catastrophic) net worth (average = minus 11,945 livres, median = minus 4,944 livres) than the entire universe of the fifty merchants (average = minus 16,504, median = minus 8,386).[140] An experienced creditor, however, looking beyond the nominal deficit to the asset and liability components, would have been

140. The Mortellerie range extended from a positive net worth of 7,720 livres claimed by Nicolas Nicole to a recklessly negative balance of minus 51,604 livres filed by Charles Carlier. An outlier of minus 344,758 skewed the distribution of the fifty merchants taken together. Only 18 percent of them had in fact balances below minus 15,000 while another 18 percent had positive net worths.

struck by the surprising precariousness of their commercial position. With rather elusive assets the Mortellerie dealers could not inspire great confidence.[141]

In an effort to justify the gap between assets and liabilities and somehow render it more palatable, 61 percent of all the grain merchants cited losses, almost all over 5,000 livres. Losses were the only entries on the balance sheets that the merchants were not obliged to document *in some way*. Only one Mortellerie dealer, however, Charles Carlier, depended heavily on losses to explain his position. On the surface his claimed losses of 93,898 livres easily bridge the chasm between his liabilities of 111,404 livres and his assets of 59,800 livres (92.4 percent of which were paper; only 20 percent of the paper represented accounts receivable for grain furnished, leaving almost 46,000 livres in more or less obscure paper titles).[142] Some of Carlier's losses seem plausible: 3,700 livres in spoilage, 9,938 in baker insolvency, 15,000 in discounted notes.[143] Another seems rather large for an adroit dealer: 27,880 livres as a result of unfavorable speculations and "price revolutions." Still another seems frankly inflated and perhaps also irrelevant: 36,000 livres as a result of illnesses in the family. To place Carlier's claims in perspective, note that mean total losses for all fifty merchants amounted to 15,250 livres (median = 6,701). Five posited losses of over 45,000; the record individual claim was 105,397 livres. These losses were distributed as follows: 27 percent for commercial and speculative losses; 21 percent for losses of merchandise and matériel; 5 percent for discount losses on bills and notes; 11 percent for unrecoverable accounts receivable; 14 percent for "family" catastrophes; 3 percent for litigation, including court and counsel fees; 19 percent for unspecified losses.[144]

141. It ought to be noted in passing that assets are much less easy to verify than liabilities, which are documented by the creditors and corroborated by the faillis. But assets were often quite difficult to conceal, since the debtors were usually well known to one or more creditors. If the grain merchant were caught trying to cheat, he would face truly severe penalties that could ruin him definitively. Moreover, because the debtor desired to close the breach as much as possible between liabilities and assets in order to make a convincing case that he merited a second chance, i.e., that he was a reasonable risk, he had a certain incentive to overstate rather than obscure his assets. Hard assets were (and are) relatively easy to validate, while paper claims (accounts receivable) often could not be convincingly verified.

142. Carlier had been in serious financial difficulties in the late thirties. He left Paris in 1741, apparently without having satisfied his creditors, to take a post in army provisioning. He made enough money in that enterprise to return to Paris in 1750 to resuscitate his grain business. Understandably—it was a realistic course and a good hedge—his wife was financially "separated" from him. Archives Seine-Paris, D4B⁶ 16-763, 1 September 1756.

143. "Pressé de faire honneur au commerce il a été forcé de faire escompter son papier. . . ," ibid.

144. Carlier was advised by a lawyer. One could appear, however, without representation before the consular jurisdiction. Yet there is no doubt that the judicial system, even in commercial matters, was biased in favor of plaintiffs and defendants assisted by counsel. Many merchants may have miscalculated by trying to protect themselves and pursue others on their own.

The Port-based Merchants and the Provisioning of Paris

Few persons paid closer attention to the Paris provisioning situation than the controller-general, the minister responsible in the broadest sense for social and economic well-being and public order. In 1725, controller-general Dodun wrote that "in all times the supply of the city had been undertaken by merchants using the river; the contribution of the Halle is very little [*très peu de chose*], and the major supply is that which comes [to the ports] by water."[145] Dodun's conviction was doubtless widely shared, for the port merchants traditionally loomed large in the public consciousness. But Dodun was wrong. As we have seen, it was an illusion to impute predominance to the waterborne traffic in terms of total supply and an error to overlook the already important and growing role of flour and ignore the substantial and burgeoning role of nonmarket provisioning. Even in the year in which Dodun wrote—a year that witnessed the massive distorting effects of government supply-side intervention—the Halle already accounted for a larger share of public market (ports plus Halle) business, of total annual combined grain and flour entries, and of total annual Paris provisioning. And in the following years, while the Halle more or less held its own, the ports' share plummeted. If, however, we consider only grain sold at the public markets, then it is true that much more came by water, for the most part under the auspices of the Mortellerie men, than by land in the hands of merchants and cultivators.

Yet Dodun clearly meant more than this. He suggested that the Paris-based port merchants ordinarily supplied about 800 muids a week, or 40,000 muids a year. In fact, in 1724 the ports (Grève and Ecole combined) accounted for 15,370 muids of grain, while the Halle received 32,703 muids in grain and flour.[146] During the dearth years 1725 and 1726 the port figures expanded dramatically as a function of government-sponsored purchases rather than an increased performance within customary supply lines (on the contrary, it was against the miserable failure of the port merchants to meet their "customary" responsibilities that Dodun railed). After the crisis the level receded rapidly: to 14,052 muids in 1727 (vs. 29,078 for the Halle) and to 11,084 muids in 1728 (vs. 31,267 muids for the Halle).[147] "Normally" the combined provisioning of the ports and the Halle in grain and flour barely surpassed the figure posited by the controller-general exclusively for waterborne grain supply.

In 1740, another crisis year, the assembly of police reproached Vatan, the

145. Dodun to procurator general, 25 September 1725, BN, Coll. Joly 1117, fols. 182–84. Writing about the same time, another correspondent told the procurator general that "three-quarters" of the Paris grain merchants used the river. "Mémoire important sur les causes de la cherté des bleds," BN, Coll. Joly 1116, fol. 279.

146. Bibliothèque de l'Institut, ms. 513.

147. Ibid., mss. 515–16.

new prévôt des marchands, for allowing the merchants to decrease the weekly quota "of 500 muids to which they had been committed for a long time" to 300 muids.[148] Five hundred muids a week is more than twice the average weekly amount that was marketed at the ports, if we are to believe the police registers—even if we allow for a "hidden" port supply siphoned off the market by the public assistance, educational, religious, or military institutions and for some reason not recorded. If Vatan succeeded in obtaining 300 muids a week from the merchants, he should have been awarded a municipal medal.

For the six-year period 1728–33—normal subsistence years by contemporary standards—the average weekly amount of grain furnished by the Paris-based port merchants was 155.8 muids, barely half the quota for which Vatan was (reluctantly) willing to settle in 1740.[149] Their combined supply ranged from a low of 113.2 per week in 1728 to a high of 197.5 in 1731. Save for a lapse in 1732 when it fell to 5.06 muids, weekly supply per merchant remained remarkably stable between 1727 and 1733, ranging between 6.7 and 7.8 muids. On the average each merchant was able to supply the needs of four to five bakers each week. To be sure, not all of our merchants had to settle for the equivalent of two margotas a week. Delu averaged 17.4 muids in 1729, Bourjot the elder 16.2 in the same year, Derain (or d'Herain) 15.8 in 1733. On the other hand, the 1.4 muid weekly averages of Simonnet in 1729 and Albert in 1732 were hardly likely to place them in good odor with the Hôtel de Ville.

Prévôt Vatan himself must have realized that his "convention" of 300 muids a week was too high, despite the avid *surenchère* of the assembly of police. The list of "rigorous" or minimal quotas he compiled for September 1740 projects 255 muids supplied by twenty-nine merchants—an average of 8.8 muids per merchant, which was unlikely but not wholly implausible. Almost one-fifth of this burden was to fall on Delu, who was still the master merchant on the ports. The quotas for the following three months were further scaled down, though the single most important factor was the withdrawal of Delu after he was required to pay a 10,000-livre fine for failing to meet his supply obligations. Vatan then counted on a rather streamlined 164.5 muids, or 6.09 muids per merchant. Jauvin the younger and Derain were now the ranking suppliers with 18 muids each, followed by Bourjot the elder with 16 muids.[150]

The number of Paris-based merchants cited in the police register as supplying the capital varied from a low of 16 in 1728 to a high of 27 in 1731 (see Table 6). The average for the period 1725–33 was 24. Virtually all of them lived on the rue de la Mortellerie. A century after Richelieu the scene at the port seems to have changed little: 20 merchants ran the show. The number is

148. Assembly, 1 September 1740, BN, ms. fr. 11356, fols. 425–27.
149. Institut, mss. 513–21.
150. "Taxe à la rigueur" and "état des fournitures," AN, F[11] 264.

TABLE 6

Supply furnished by Paris-based port merchants,
1725–33 (in muids)

Year	Number of merchants	Total annual supply	Average per week all merchants	Average per week per merchant	Average per year per merchant
1725	18	7,760	149.2	8.30	431.0
1726	18	4,666	89.7	4.99	259.2
1727	19	5,347	102.8	5.40	281.4
1728	16	5,888	113.2	7.10	368.0
1729	20	8,068	155.2	7.80	403.4
1730	24	9,160	176.2	7.30	381.7
1731	27	10,271	197.5	7.30	380.4
1732	26	6,837	131.5	5.06	262.9
1733	24	8,390	161.3	6.70	349.6

far below the roster of port merchants cited by the police in 1739 (90) or the number of self-styled Mortellerie dealers whose trace we have unearthed for the period 1725–40 (43). The police figures surely included the country and itinerant merchants who frequented the capital regularly. Certain of the soi-disant dealers were probably in fact brokers rather than direct suppliers. In any case it is significant that the municipality considered fining only 26 merchants for failing to fulfill their responsibilities by sustaining a regular supply in 1739 and established quotas for 29 merchants the following year.[151] As for the Mortellerie roll, it is evident that some of these traders dealt in oats or "little grain" (as *grainiers* or *grenetiers*) rather than in wheat, and that others were inactive or marginal.

Country and *Forain* Merchants

Everyone agreed that Paris-based merchants, for the most part Mortellerie dealers, "made the law" on the ports. They were not, however, the only wheat traders serving the capital by water. An important, albeit declining, proportion of port supply was furnished by the "country merchants" [*marchands de la compagne*] and "itinerant merchants" [*marchands forains*]: a little more than half of total port wheat in 1728, slightly more than two-fifths

151. BN, ms. fr. 8089, fol. 521, 16 January 1739; AN, F[11] 264. It is possible that the police registers failed for some reason to record the provision of the "other" merchants. Such an egregious gap seems extremely unlikely to me. Cf. the "état des bleds," June 1757, which named eighteen traders: J. and A. Armet, Bassery, Denise, Despreaux, D. and J. -B. Fosseyeux, Greban, Hure, N. and J.-B. Jauvin, Lefebvre, Colmet Lepinay, Moussier, Maheu, Pinondel, Pluyette, Sergent. BN, Coll. Joly 1130, fol. 14. Is Maheu the same person who served as a broker at the Halle? See Archives Seine-Paris D5B[6] 3446.

in 1730, and a bit less than a quarter in 1733.[152] There were many more dealers labeled country merchants than forains, though the entry registers do not rigorously separate them (of non-Paris-based merchants supplying the Grève, 19 of 85 dealers enumerated in 1725 and 23 of 99 in 1727 were called forains). Nor is it clear what distinguished the two types. Both came from the "country." Indeed, both came from the same places staked out by the Paris-based merchants: Bray and Mary were the major loci of activity for the Grève suppliers, followed by La Ferté-sous-Jouarre, Vitry, Rebais, Montereau. The merchants supplying the Ecole appeared to have come from the areas around Soissons, Noyon, and Pont-Ste.-Maxence. Contemporaries assumed that the forains were bigger dealers, yet their average weekly supply was barely one and a half setiers more than that of the Grève country merchants.[153]

An intriguing bit of internal evidence suggests that the primary difference between the forains and the country merchants was that the latter embraced the brokerage system run by the Mortellerie barons while the former stubbornly guarded their independence. Connections with a factor spared the country merchant the cost and inconvenience of traveling to Paris every week, selling on the market, and collecting amounts due. Yet dependence on a broker could be a yoke, restricting the dealer's freedom to obtain his price, to expand his clientele, and to act without regard to anyone else. The forains may have had other business to transact in Paris. They may also have built up networks of clients on their own. And they may have detested the brokers.

A number of forains probably resembled Louis Colin of Marcilly-sur-Seine. He bought directly "from the different fermiers in the neighborhood" as well as from other grain merchants. Although he could "neither read nor write," he utilized notes and letters of exchange to make and to receive payment. He kept no written accounts, not because of his illiteracy but because he claimed it was a convention "among forain merchants for the provisioning of Paris that business books are never kept."[154] Unlike Colin, Pierre Gayand of Picardy was educated and relatively well-to-do. He too bought from both laboureurs in the farms and markets and from other dealers, but he seems to have been more interested in local trade around the Pont-Ste.-Maxence area than in furnishing the capital.[155] Louis Charrieu of Bray supplied the port as a country merchant, but he has much in common with Colin (and to a lesser extent with Gayand): he bought from the laboureurs and

152. These figures may be somewhat inflated, because the registers may assimilate "extraordinary supply," often commissioned by the government, to the supply furnished by itinerant and/or country dealers at the Ecole port.

153. In 1725 the forains supplied an average of three times more than the Grève merchants, but the dearth surely distorted the supply situation.

154. Archives Seine-Paris, D4B[6] 97-6766. The laboureurs, as I point out below, alleged a similar convention.

155. Archives Seine-Paris, D4B[6] 52-3196, 23 June 1774.

TABLE 7

Supply furnished by country and *forain* merchants on
the Grève, 1725–33 (in muids)

Year	Number of merchants	Total annual supply	Average per week all merchants	Average per week per merchant	Average per year per merchant
1725	85	8,752	168.3	1.98	102.96
1726	115	9,555	183.8	1.60	83.00
1727	99	4,113	79.0	0.80	41.50
1728	40	2,204	42.4	1.06	55.10
1729	112	4,486	86.3	0.77	40.00
1730	40	4,763	91.6	2.30	119.10
1731	28	1,372	26.4	0.94	49.00
1732	?	2,772	53.3	—	—
1733	?	1,770	34.0	—	—

merchants, he kept no books, he had quite limited resources. What distinguished him from the forains was his dependence on a port broker, whose failure to reimburse him for 2,000 livres of consigned wheat helped drive him into failure.[156]

The bulk of country and forain supply was marketed at the Grève (see Table 7). The Ecole received on the average a little under a third of the country–forain provision between 1729 and 1733. Save in dearth years, when it served as entrepôt for extraordinary supplies, the Ecole was clearly a secondary market. Mean total weekly supply soared in 1725 to 269.5 muids largely as a result of the banker Samuel Bernard's effort to save Paris from famine (see Table 8). By 1728 it had fallen to 71.7, but this figure still reflected "extraordinary" residuals. The average weekly provision from 1729 through 1733 at the Ecole was 36.5 muids, but there was considerable variation from year to year. During these years an average of about fifteen merchants frequented the Ecole, each bringing 2.4 muids each week. Save in crisis years, only one or two brokers operated at the Ecole, but it is not clear how many of the suppliers relied on this factorage service.

Mean total country–forain provision on the Grève amounted to 59 muids a week for the period 1727–33 and it, too, fluctuated a good deal from year to year. The roster of dealers provided in the entry registers is surely incomplete and the average of seventy-four a year for the period 1725–31 understates their number (country merchants and forains combined). We know that turnover in the Grève supply corps was substantial: probably at least 25 percent a year. Instead of indicating the number of suppliers in 1732 and 1733 the

156. Archives Seine-Paris, D4B[6] 72-4725.

registers note that many veteran dealers had "quit the trade because of the quite low price of grain." Much of this supply, then, was circumstantial. It depended on local supply and demand factors and upon the metropolitan price situation. Though most of these dealers (along with the Ecole suppliers) flourished the "for the provisioning of Paris" title, they neither felt obligated nor were they really expected to furnish the ports with the assiduity of the Paris-based merchant. It is quite likely that the number of country and forain suppliers continued to fluctuate substantially throughout the century (within the confines of a secular trend toward contraction of the corps). On the basis of the register figures, seventy-four Grève merchants furnished an average of 1.86 muids a week each, about 6.5 setiers less than their counterparts on the Ecole, or slightly more than the average weekly wheat consumption of the "average" Paris baker.

Between 1725 and 1733, there were an average of fifteen brokers on the Grève. They marketed the bulk of the "outside" traffic, though for lack of certainty over the forains' situation we cannot be precise. In 1727, it appears that fourteen brokers managed the affairs of seventy-six country merchants. While the average number of dealers per broker was 5.4, in fact the distribution was highly uneven: nineteen worked through Rousseau the younger, nine sent their grain to Chevalier, and two each signed up with Moussier the younger and Le Blanc. Each broker handled an average of 218.5 muids for the year, or 4.2 muids a week. But again, there was considerable disparity in the magnitude of factor operations. Le Blanc had the largest supply per merchant (102.5 muids for the year) but Chevalier and Hemard handled the most grain: 9.8 muids a week (510.3 muids for the year) and 7.42 muids a week (386 muids for the year via six merchants) respectively.

TABLE 8

Supply furnished by country and *forain* merchants on
the Ecole, 1725–33 (in muids)

Year	Number of merchants	Total annual supply	Average per week all merchants	Average per week per merchant	Average per year per merchant
1725	19	11,350*	218.20	11.5	574.20
1726	7	14,012*	269.50	38.5	2,001.70
1727	12	5,440*	104.60	8.7	453.30
1728	23	3,729	71.70	3.1	162.10
1729	16	1,951	37.50	2.3	121.90
1730	13	1,811	34.80	2.7	139.30
1731	12	956	18.40	1.5	79.67
1732	17	1,975	37.98	2.2	116.20
1733	7	912	17.50	2.5	130.30

*Includes significant "extraordinary" supply.

Tension between "Itinerant" and Paris-based Merchants

The number of forains was steadily increasing toward the end of the seventeenth century and they were encroaching on the trade traditionally reserved to the port oligarchy. The creation of a body of brokers in the 1690s promised to facilitate forain operations and increase their business. In return for a fee of 3 livres per muid, the brokers took charge of selling the forains' grain and guaranteed the payment of the sale price to them. The Paris-based port merchants resented the increase in the size of the forain contingent and the depressive impact of their expanding provision on prices. Apparently in close concert, under the aegis of Jean Roger, the Paris traders set out to crush this competition. They outbid the forains in the farms and markets, and they made mammoth purchases that became hoards. When the Paris merchants encountered forains with merchandise, they offered them prices that they could not refuse in order to keep them out of the capital. By using their leverage to control much of the river transport system, they tried to isolate or inconvenience the forains. They directly encroached on the factorage functions that belonged to the brokers by marketing in their own names the provision of hinterland suppliers whose favor they courted. In short order the forain provision plunged and the newly created brokers found themselves without sufficient activity to underwrite their venture. In an attempt to expose "this plot," the brokers demanded that all sellers at the ports be enjoined to "justify" their merchandise with *lettres de voiture* that would reveal the provenance of the grain, who sold it to whom and under what conditions, when the transaction occurred, and so on. The city fathers, however, refused to prop up the brokers at the risk of alienating their own merchant corps.[157]

Once the Paris-based merchants drove the new brokers out of business, they took their place. They assumed the role of factor in order to be able to blunt the rivalry of the outsiders and, in a sense, to subject them to their commercial domination.[158] Thus, the brokers in 1725–33 were almost to a man Mortellerie merchants who simultaneously supplied the Grève for their own account.[159] Nor is it surprising, against this background, that a number of the forains refused to be factored by their quondam Mortellerie rivals.[160]

157. "Factum pour la communauté des 70 officiers-commissionnaires-facteurs," 1693, BN, ms. fr. 21635, fols, 316–17; "Factum pour la communauté des 70 officiers-commissionnaires-facteurs contre Jean Roger et al.," BN, F⁰ FM 12919.

158. It should, however, be noted that the Paris-based merchants and the forains had been known to cooperate in the past. The dearth beginning in 1661 was blamed partly on the criminal "intelligence" between them. BN, ms. fr. 21642, fol. 28.

159. Even as the self-anointed Mortellerie brokers acquired de facto legitimacy, so an illicit factorage began to infringe on their terrain. A gagne-denier named Jean Chenu, for instance, pretended to be merely a *placier* for the hinterland suppliers but in fact served as their broker. AN, Z^{1H} 239, 25 September 1726.

160. Antoinette Breffort, widow of a forain, avenged her husband or betrayed him,

Because of the increasingly close association of the Paris-based merchants with the outside traders, it is easy to imagine how contemporaries may have conflated them. It is possible that the authorities assimilated the country and forain provision to the "expected" supply of the licensed Paris-based merchants. Even if that was the case, however, Vatan's proposal was high and Dodun's supposition was exorbitant, for combined (Mortellerie plus country-forain) weekly supply at the ports between 1727 and 1733 averaged only 253.3 muids.

Corporate Tendencies without a Corporation

Politically, it was not always wise for the Paris-based port merchants to insist upon their power and coherence as a group. "They formed neither a corps nor a guild [communauté]," the merchants wrote in reference to themselves in a petition of 1739.[161] Their archrivals in the grain trade, the Paris bakers, made the same point for their own purposes. The fact that the Paris grain merchants "were not even assembled in a guild" was proof, in their view, that grain commerce was "free and open" to all comers.[162] Yet the very necessity of denying the existence of a grain trader guild centered at the Grève suggests that many contemporaries presumed that such a guild existed.[163] Nor was it an unlikely belief in a world replete with corporate structures of all sorts. The merchants were influential, they often spoke with a single voice, and their behavior as well as their discourse bespoke many "corporate" traits. Their enormously important special privileges defined boundaries of quasi-corporate exclusivity.[164] Those privileges, along with the concomitant obligations they implied, constituted a sort of charter, an ana-

---

depending on one's point of view. She moved to the rue de la Mortellerie and became a broker. One wonders if she attracted a theretofore recalcitrant forain clientele. AN, Y 15247, 3 May 1740.

161. BN, Coll. Joly 1120, fols. 34–40.

162. "Sommaire pour les marchands talmeliers maistres boulangers," ca. 1690, BN, ms. fr. 21640, fol. 71.

163. A Swiss banker (Isaac Thellusson?), encouraged by the police to use his international contacts to help supply Paris in grain during the dearth of 1725, claimed that the port merchants leagued against him because he was not "a member of the guild." Anon., "Histoire de ce qui s'est passé au sujet des bleds en 1725," Arsenal, ms. 3308. And if words were not the mere names of things, ponder the significance of the reference to "the guild of grain merchants" in the discourse of the grain porters. "Mémoire des jurés porteurs," 1736, BN, Coll. Joly 1312, fol. 131. Cf. the classification of the grain merchants in a petite société (as opposed to a jurande). Journal économique (October 1766): 436. For a project calling for the incorporation of the Paris grain merchants "in order to know them better," see BN, Coll. Joly 1728, fol. 109.

164. Physiocratic critics of privileged and policed grain trading saw no differences between the "titled merchants" of Paris and the constituted body of 112 privileged merchants at Rouen. Trudaine de Montigny to Miromesnil, 23 February 1768, in Armand-Thomas Hue Miromesnil, Correspondance politique et administrative de Miromesnil, premier président

logue to corporate statutes. The act of enrolling in the municipal register was another symbolic gesture of organization; and the municipal licensing was similar to the homologation of corporate statutes, the official step that consecrated the organization of every guild. Merchants' solidarity in various kinds of litigation, their collective petitions to authorities, and their campaign against common foes like the bakers reinforced the corporate image.[165]

The major reason that the authorities did not encourage grain merchants to articulate their ties and interests into a formal guild structure was probably the anxiety that it would be perceived by the public as an agency of (legitimated) monopoly. Such an image would not only have caused malaise, but would also have deterred outsiders of all sorts from contributing to the Parisian supply. Despite their fears of excessive fragmentation of the trade, the goal of the police was to attract as many suppliers as possible.[166]

Bereft of any formal organization in the eighteenth century, the grain traders had been permitted as recently as the middle of the seventeenth century to establish a surrogate guild in the form of a *confrérie,* or brotherhood, meant in part to counteract "the lack of unity and of friendship" that had marked relations among the grain dealers and had, so they believed, hurt all of them. The confrérie was a pious association devoted to prayer, penitence, and charity. Led by four "master-governors" elected for two-year terms, the Paris-based port merchants and their sons, daughters, and widows who showed proof of "probity and good morals" dedicated themselves to the Virgin and to Saint Nicolas, pledged to celebrate their festivals, to pray for the souls of deceased members, and to offer blessed bread and alms (in the form of wheat) to the poor. On another level, however, the aim of the confrérie was clearly "corporate" in the old-regime sense of the term: to establish bonds that would serve to promote the professional interests of the members and to forestall further public regulation by undertaking to police their trade themselves. In their particulars—concerning such matters as relations with forains (confrérie merchants could not "lend them [the forains] their name" and thus legitimize their speculations), or the incompatibility of

---

du Parlement de Normandie, ed. P. Le Verdier (Paris and Rouen, 1899–1903), 5:93; Georges Weulersse, *La Physiocratie sous les ministères de Turgot et de Necker (1774–1781)* (Paris, 1950), p. 84. Cf. Léon Biollay, who refers squarely to the "corporation des marchands de blé de Paris." *Etudes économiques sur le XVIIIᵉ siècle: Le Pacte de famine; l'administration du commerce* (Paris, 1885).

165. See "Mémoire des marchands de bled," ca. 1735, BN, Coll. Joly 1428, fol. 38; petition of 7 July 1734, BN, Coll. Joly 1312, fol. 123; and the discussions of the dispute with the bakers below.

166. On the fear of splintering the trade into too many hands too difficult to mobilize and police, see A. Gazier, ed., "La Police de Paris en 1770, mémoire inédit, composé par ordre de Marie-Thérèse," *Mémoires de la Société de l'histoire de Paris et de l'Ile-de-France* 5 (1878): 118. Sartine's view, influenced by liberal critics as well as by changes taking place in the organization of production and distribution, would probably not have been shared by La Reynie or Hérault.

exercising certain professions at the same time one was a grain trader (e.g., baker, measurer, porter, etc.), or the disposition of fines levied for violations of selling rules (the confrérie claimed one-third of all fines)—the statutes of the confrérie of grain merchants read like guild statutes.[167] The brotherhood probably ceased to exist sometime toward the end of the seventeenth century, when the government renewed the campaign to eliminate confréries whose piety seemed to be merely a pretext for other enterprises.[168]

"Lack of unity" in the Paris grain trade was most strikingly symbolized by the split between the port and Halle merchants, a division exacerbated by the rivalry between the Hôtel de Ville and the Châtelet. Yet for at least one official purpose, the collection of a tax for the Paris militia maintenance fund, the lieutenant general of police in the sixties perceived the grain trade as a single, organized, corporatelike enterprise. Indeed, in an intriguing phrase, Sartine referred specifically to "the pretentions of the juré-merchants on the ports and Halle," as if all the Paris-based dealers enjoyed a common leadership.[169] In fact the port and Halle merchants together held periodic assemblies to elect collectors of this imposition, and perhaps others as well. It is not known whether these assemblies, convoked at the instigation of the lieutenant general, became the vehicles for discussions of business affairs or police regulations or other matters of common interest. Unlike the mood of the 1650s, there is no sign that the merchants were avid to meet or organize. There seemed to be little corporate nostalgia among the merchants, who saw the trade increasingly in terms of individual initiative.

Yet if nothing else united the Paris merchants, hostility to taxation and to public authority did. Led by Hure, a Mortellerie merchant notorious for his "extreme arrogance" and irreverence toward public officials, they quarreled several times with Sartine.[170] One issue concerned a grain dealer named Hollier. The police considered him to be a forain, since his principal place of residence was the Champagne, where he was also a laboureur. Usually inclined toward exclusiveness, in this instance the Paris merchants insisted that Hollier was one of them (he had a pied-à-terre near the river) because they wanted him to share their militia tax.[171] Another dispute turned on the refusal of the assembly of merchants to name a third collector for 1769.[172]

---

167. BN, ms. fr. 21635, fols. 116–19. There were about fifty-one members of the confrérie at the outset.

168. In reference to confréries, see Steven L. Kaplan, "Réflexions sur la police du monde du travail, 1700–1815," *Revue historique* 261, no. 1 (January–March 1979): 17–77. It is possible on the one hand that the grain merchant confraternity never obtained letters patent validating its existence or on the other that it persisted well into the eighteenth century in very discreet guise.

169. Sartine to Grimperel, 12 October 1768, AN, Y 13397.

170. Grimperel to Sartine, November 1769, ibid.

171. Grimperel to Hure, 15 October 1768, and Sartine to Grimperel, 7 May, 12 October 1768, ibid.

172. Sartine to Grimperel, 15 November 1769, and Grimperel to Sartine, November 1769, ibid.

Collapse under Pressure: The Port Merchants in Times of Dearth

If it is true that the Paris-based port merchants had little affection for public authorities, nevertheless they got along reasonably well with them—by and large. Predictably, antagonisms flared up during times of dearth, that is to say, of great stress and dislocation, when growing public anxiety took the form of heightened suspicion of merchant behavior. This was the time when the police vigorously repressed practices that they normally tolerated, enforced rules that had been ignored by consensus, and expected more from the merchants than usual (in the name of a certain civic duty as well as a quid pro quo for the latitude given them ordinarily) at the very instant when the trade was most disorganized and difficult to conduct rationally. This was the time when the police and the people joined together in what appeared to the merchants to be an inquisitorial, scapegoating crusade against them. This was the time of rumor, speculation, hoarding, the drying up of markets, the multiplication of hands in the grain trade, heavy public sector buying and selling—in a word, of drastic disruption of the usual patterns. Playing the dearth was a high-risk, high-stakes game: there was a lot to be gained (usually by a few) and a lot to be lost (usually by the many).

The dearth falling-out generally began when the authorities accused merchants of not doing enough to parry the shortage. The merchants replied by asserting that, given the difficult conditions, they could not reasonably be expected to do any more. This posture occasioned the rage of controller-general Dodun in the fall of 1725, in the midst of deepening subsistence crisis, when the prévôt des marchands could not obtain a commitment from the Paris-based port traders to provision more than ninety-eight muids a week. Insisting that there was "abundance" in the supply zones, Dodun charged the merchants with "a plot to starve us" by cutting back drastically on their shipments in order to "maintain the high prices."[173] He proposed that each merchant (forain and country as well as Paris-based) be required to justify "with proofs" the erosion in his weekly provision or face perpetual exclusion from the grain trade, plus fines. The controller-general conceded that it was necessary to dose this "firmness" with a bit of "sweetness" in order to mobilize the merchants. But at bottom he was convinced that the merchant corps had to be renewed. "Let us try to find new merchants," he wrote. "The métier is good enough for us to be able to find them."[174] A contemporary

173. Yet another version of the famine plot persuasion—and an official source for the plot rhetoric that looms so large in the eighteenth century. See Kaplan, *Famine Plot.*
174. Dodun to procurator general, 16, 20 September 1765, BN, Coll. Joly 1117, fols. 182–86. One of the reasons that the grain merchants may have cut back, in addition to a desire to sustain high prices, was resentment against the importation of foreign grain by the government. On the former motive, see Bourlon to lieutenant general, 13 December 1725, Arsenal, ms. Bast. 10271. On the latter, see Gazetins, 10 March 1726, Arsenal, ms. Bast. 10056, fol. 103.

police observer had a similar notion—he proposed shifting the burden of responsibility, and thus the mantle of privilege, from the Paris-based merchants to those "at the source," based in the supply crowns.[175] Nothing came of these proposals to purge the corps of port merchants. Nor were the merchants punished, despite the fact that their weekly provision continued to fall and remained well below average through 1726.

Firmness prevailed over sweetness during the next crisis. In January 1738, on the eve of a severe and protracted dearth, the assembly of police investigated an ominous decline in port supply. After hearing police testimony exposing "the maneuvers of the merchants," the assembly interviewed the merchants themselves, "who alleged very long and very bad reasons" for the incipient dearth. The assembly threatened punishment if the merchants did not pledge to increase their provision immediately. As always, the police favored a quasi-contractual formula: they wanted pledges from each merchant to deliver a specific quota.[176]

The merchants continued to protest, and they failed to meet police expectations. The situation threatened to become critical as a result of an extremely bad harvest. The merchants were pleased to see the price rise, according to contemporary reports, and used the shortfall as a further excuse to discontinue supply, while in fact they hoarded and bided their time. Dispatched to investigate in the field, prévôt Turgot's huissiers confirmed the news of the "evil intentions" of the merchants and their agents.[177] "With almost no grain on the ports," in January of 1739 Turgot took the extreme measure of imposing a 10,000 livres' fine on "all the merchants on the ports"—that is, the twenty-six traders who really counted—"for not having kept the ports of this city sufficiently supplied . . . as they are obliged to do."[178]

The prévôt himself worried over the implications of this harsh and symbolically highly charged action. He wondered aloud in the assembly of police whether he should not offer to suspend the sentence in return for a collective promise of supply by the merchants. The assembly felt strongly that hesitation would be fatal: "The merchants would become our masters if we weakened." The assembly did worry about the possibility that the publication of the sentence would "reduce their credit" and thus give them a further pretext to cut back purchases. It decided, however, that the merchants were strong enough to withstand the blow, and would face further penalties if they

175. Couet de Montbayeux to procurator general, 11 November 1725, BN, Coll. Joly 1117, fol. 249, and 9 October 1725, Arsenal, ms. Bast. 10270, fols. 211–14. Couet hoped in part to exploit the old rivalry and jealousy between these forains and the port oligarchs.

176. BN, ms. fr. 11356, fol. 343, January 1738.

177. AN, H* 1358, fols. 63–64, 19 December 1738. See also the assembly of police of 20 February 1738, BN, ms. fr. 11356, fol. 346.

178. Sentence of the prévôt des marchands, 16 January 1739, BN, ms. fr. 8089, fols. 521–22; assembly of police, 22 January 1739, BN, ms. fr. 11356, fol. 380.

did not increase shipments. The assembly recommended a differential strategy: it should strike only "the richest and those who had furnished the least," demanding of them the full amount, but moderating the fine if they were repentant and if they brought in grain.[179]

Infuriated, the merchants expressed their outrage in petitions to the directors of the assembly of police, the first president, and the procurator general of the Paris Parlement. They resented the fact that the prévôt had not given them a hearing before judging them. And they were stung by the publicity given the sentence: they evinced "shame at seeing themselves branded and dishonored by a draconian sentence that tends only to make them odious in the eyes of the public." They suddenly faced not only "hatred and scorn" in the market, but grave difficulties in obtaining credit and in collecting money due for grain furnished. Nor should the authorities console themselves with the notion of recruiting new merchants, for this sort of cruel treatment will dissuade "all persons of honor and probity who might be willing to enter the grain trade."

The merchants insisted on the zeal with which they had always served the public—despite, they remarked mordantly, "the lack of liberty in purchase and the constraints on sales." Wistfully, they evoked the golden age, not long before, "when the greatest magistrates treated the grain merchants with kindness and goodness to encourage them to do well and to increase the provisioning of Paris . . . in time of threatening dearth." Now they were vilified and stigmatized. Ignoring the bad harvest and the adverse navigation and weather conditions, the authorities "ask us to do the impossible" and "oppress us" for failing to do it.

Since the merchants believed that they could only function in an ambience of "liberty and protection"—the best of two worlds—they saw no alternative but to offer their resignations en masse. Yet they emphasized that they would prefer to strike a bargain. If the authorities were willing to spare them from "faults that were not theirs" and to offer them genuine support, they were willing to give "marks of obedience and of zeal," that is, presumably, to augment their provisions.[180]

Buoyed by the arrival of foreign grain marshaled by the Swiss banker Thellusson and vexed at the "mutinous" spirit of the merchants, the assembly remained firm in its resolve that the merchants had to make gestures of "submission." The merchants, too, decided to call their adversary's bluff: "They continued to bring no grain at all."[181] Vatan, the newly appointed prévôt, finally struck the long-awaited and much-postponed exemplary blow

179. BN, ms. fr. 11356, fols. 380–82, 22 January 1739.
180. Petition of merchants, BN, Coll. Joly 1120, fols. 34–40. It was signed by 20 of the 26 condemned merchants and by 62 or 64 other merchants (depending on possible *double emplois*).
181. BN, ms. fr. 11356, fol. 387, 5 February 1739.

at the end of the summer of 1740.[182] He arrested Jean Delu, the richest
member of the Mortellerie clique, and announced that he could purchase his
freedom in return for payment of the 10,000 livres' fine that had been levied
against him and his confreres. Delu protested vainly, spent a miserable night
and day in jail, and finally bought his way out. Perhaps to emphasize that
there would be no negotiated compromise and reduction in the fine, the
prévôt ordered the money to be allocated immediately to the parish priests for
distribution to the poor.[183]

Delu may have provoked this blow by refusing to accept the "convention"
proposed in early September by the new prévôt. He may have esteemed,
quite reasonably, that his assigned quota of 50 muids 10 setiers a week was
exorbitant. Vatan meant to jolt the merchants by making an example of Delu,
but he also sought grounds for compromise by significantly reducing the
official weekly provisioning "expectation" and by offering premiums first of
25, then of 30, then of 48 livres per muid for every muid a merchant supplied
over his weekly quota. The merchants seem to have responded favorably,
despite or perhaps because of the scourging of Delu. Ten merchants, nine of
whom had been among the twenty-six fined in 1739–40, received 3,920 livres
in bonuses in the six weeks following Delu's arrest. The merchants were
surely gratified to learn that Vatan promised three prizes of 3,000, 2,000, and
1,000 livres for the three merchants who exceeded their quotas by the greatest
margins in November and December. Yet they took note that even as he
coaxed with the carrot he brandished a stick, for he announced three booby
prizes: fines for the merchants who failed most egregiously to meet their
quotas.[184]

As far as we can tell, the municipality did not again encounter major
difficulties with the port merchants, and Paris suffered no serious dearth, till
the mid-sixties. Bignon, the prévôt at that time, claimed that the Hôtel de
Ville annually enrolled between twenty-five and forty merchants. Trouble
arose in the wake of the great liberalization law of May 1763 that "freed" the

182. Turgot apparently shied away from executing the sentence against the merchants,
whose ardent protector he had been. According to d'Argenson, who preferred "the good
Turgot," Vatan was a domineering and "sophistic" figure "who took control of the deliberations" of the assembly of police. *Journal et mémoires,* ed. Rathery, 3:223 (14 November
1740). The assembly's minutes hardly suggest that Vatan subjugated its members.

183. AN, H* 1859, fols. 20–22, 17 September 1740. Delu apparently died sometime in the
next few years. After his death his wife applied for "an indemnity"—in fact a retroactive
remission of the fine—and received 7,000 livres. Judgment of 28 July 1742, AN, F[11] 264.
There is a hint elsewhere that one other merchant may have been fined. See "Etat . . . des
fournitures," AN, F[11] 264.

184. AN, F[11] 264; BN, ms. n.a. f. 1032, fol. 93. The assembly of police expressed serious
reservations about Vatan's policy, especially his reduced quotas and his bonus scheme. In
the very first meeting that he attended as prévôt, the assembly warned him that the merchants would demand higher and higher premiums, which seems to have happened in fact,
and that they would try to make them permanent. BN, ms. fr. 11356, fols. 425–27, 1 September 1740.

grain trade, in part by opening it to virtually all comers, eliminating the need to register or seek permission and allowing everyone to trade outside the marketplace.[185] Now that "the declaration of 1763 gave them the same privileges . . . without any subjection," the great majority of Paris merchants renounced their commissions or did not bother to renew them. "We have retained but a small number," lamented Bignon, "and only by showing them the most careful attention."[186] Similarly the municipality lost its dominion over the host of lesser dealers operating in the supply crowns as buying agents, forains, or country merchants.

To some extent, things must have returned to normal after the partial restoration of the police regime by controller-general Terray in the early seventies. Yet it is well to keep in mind that the municipality's patronage was worth less and less and that the center of provisioning gravity had shifted definitively away from the ports. As a result of these phenomena and the lesson learned during the first episode of liberty, it is quite possible that the port merchants seriously modified their manner of doing business. Terray himself took note of the fundamental shifts that had occurred during the previous quarter-century in the Paris provisioning system. He claimed that since five-sixths of the capital's supply now arrived in the form of flour, there was no longer the same overarching need to accommodate grain merchants on whom the population and the authorities were much less dependent. Specifically, Terray saw no reason to perpetuate the special derogation that enabled Parisian merchants to buy outside the market and enjoy other "exceptions."[187] The controller-general did not press his case to make the Paris merchants conform to the general practice, apparently in deference to municipal entreaties. But the very fact that he could imagine such a thing as a function of provisioning realpolitik suggests how distant were the halcyon days of Jean Roger or even Jean Delu.

The Archenemy: The Struggle against the Baker

The Paris merchants had less to fear from the authorities than from their most aggressive commercial rivals, the bakers of Paris, whom they saw as mortal enemies. The merchants felt deeply threatened. They blamed the erosion of their influence on the bakers and denounced them for encroaching upon their enterprise and for using abusive and fraudulent tactics. In this struggle the merchants found strong support from the prévôt des marchands, who wanted to show them that he could be counted on at the critical mo-

---

185. See Kaplan, *Bread, Politics and Political Economy,* 1:90–96.
186. *Recueil des principales loix relatives au commerce des grains* (Paris, 1769), pp. 145–46.
187. Terray to prévôt des marchands, 7 March 1774, AD Marne, C 419.

ments. Indeed, the clash between the merchants and bakers brings to mind the simmering confrontation between the prévôt and the lieutenant general of police. Like the merchants, the prévôt claimed precedence, invoked precedents, felt menaced, suffered status anxieties, erupted in spasms of energetic affirmation, but was unable to sustain a comeback. Like the lieutenant general, the bakers struck into new areas with a pugnacious resolve, felt that the old system had not worked well and was no longer relevant, and believed that the future was on their side. But while the lieutenant general was responsible for the police of the bakery, there is no evidence that he ventured to protect the bakers in the same zealous way that the prévôt supported the merchants.[188]

Alarmed by the diminishing supply on the ports, for which they knew they were held accountable, the Paris-based merchants launched a vehement campaign in the early thirties to show that it was not really their fault. In memorandum after memorandum, addressed to the royal government and the parlement, they denounced the bakers for disrupting the provisioning trade, reducing abundance, and driving up prices. They contended that the bakers violated all the rules: they bid up prices, they bought outside the markets, they plotted with millers and local officials to cover illicit transactions, they regrated and hoarded, and they demonstrated an utter "lack of honesty." As the merchants put it, with unintended irony: the bakers "have openly become bakers and grain traders combined." And that was really the point. The rest of the criticisms were necessary to discredit the bakers by demonstrating that they were criminals who spoliated the public interest. The ire of the merchants was not born of civic-minded scandalization. It grew out of the realization that their functions were being usurped: "The bakers have deprived our role of its usefulness." The merchants claimed that the bakers cheated and infringed upon their rights, but what they avowed implicitly was that the bakers had toiled harder and faster ("They even have more commissionnaires in the field than we do") and outfoxed them. These warm partisans of the freedom of the grain trade suddenly found that freedom to be treacherous

---

188. It must not be presumed, however, that the lieutenant general automatically espoused the baker cause, though in the broadest sense he was the bakers' protector. The attitude of eighteenth-century lieutenants general toward baker grain trade was ambivalent. On the one hand, they acknowledged the contribution that it made to "abundance." On the other hand, they believed it invited many commercial abuses. They desired to see the trade made as visible and public and therefore as countable and accountable as possible. The way to do this, they believed, was to concentrate as much of the Paris supply as possible on the market over which they had supervision, the Halle. Thus they were hostile to baker supply en droiture. Ultimately the only way to eliminate droiture delivery was to keep bakers out of the trade altogether. From this perspective, the prévôt des marchands was perhaps more favorably disposed to baker grain trade than the lieutenants general. If one begins, however, with the proposition that bakers were going to buy in the countryside, the lieutenants general had no incentive to keep them away from or off the rivers. See, for example, the partly divergent *avis* of Hérault and of Turgot in BN, Coll. Joly 1829, fol. 320.

when it was exercised by persons other than their quasi-corporate and officially privileged selves. The merchants wanted to hedge their market principle in the marketplace.

The bakers had moved into their space, a space that they considered sacrosanct, in which they had "always enjoyed the exclusive permission" to do business. This "turf" was defined as all the areas on and near the major rivers.[189] The merchants recalled a golden age that fixed the way things ought to be. It flourished before 1650 when, according to the merchants, they did virtually all the supplying for the capital and the Paris bakers did all their buying intra-muros. Baker grain provisioning was therefore "a novelty" and on that ground alone suspect. The merchants were obliged to acknowledge that the major legislation of the end of the seventeenth century, especially the royal declaration of 1699, neither prohibited the bakers from engaging in the grain trade nor confined them specifically to any given sectors. It was "to the spirit" of that law that they appealed, a spirit informed, they claimed, by the "traditional" attribution of all river traffic to the merchants "to the exclusion of all other merchants, regraters, millers and others."

Their very existence was threatened by baker imperialism, the merchants declared starkly: "We are ruined." According to the merchants, the bakers had already caused the supply to diminish and made it impossible to conduct an orderly police with records of arrival, quantities, and prices. Things would shortly get worse if the clock were not set back. The merchants resorted here to their ultimate weapon: the threat of mass resignation.[190]

In August 1733 prévôt Turgot reported to the assembly of police on "the demoralization of the few merchants who remain on the ports regarding the role of the bakers in the grain trade." One could try to blunt their threat by menacing them with prison, Turgot suggested, but he did not believe there was any point in such an approach, and he intimated that he sympathized with their plight.[191] The assembly, however, did not—not yet. The bakers had a

189. In fact the merchants named names. They demanded exclusive control of the following towns, which were either ports or within a few leagues of the ports: Melun, Montereau, Bray, Provins, Nangis, Nogent-sur-Seine, Villeneuve-sur-Seine, Meaux, Crécy, Faremoutiers, Coulommiers, Rebais, La Ferté-Gaucher, La Ferté-sous-Jouarre, Charly, Château-Thierry, Châlons, Vitry-le-François, Lizy, Neuilly-St.-Front, La Ferté-Milon, Villers-Cotterêts, Mary-sur-Marne, Compiègne, Soissons, Noyon. The following towns the merchants were willing to concede to the bakers: Chartres, Rambouillet, Auneau, St.-Arnoult, Malesherbes, Dourdan, Pithiviers, Etampes, Limours, Houdan, Pont-Ste.-Maxence, Beaumont, Pontoise, St.-Germain-en-Laye, Dammartin, Nanteuil, Tournan-en-Brie, Brie-Comte-Robert, Chevreuse, Montlhéry, Nantouillet, Rozay-en-Brie, Fontenay-en-Brie. BN, Coll. Joly 1314, fols. 20bis–21, 34. This enumeration reflected the historical division of turf according to the merchants. It corresponds imperfectly to the traditional map proposed in 1763 by the intendant of Paris. See "Observations sur le commerce des grains," BN, ms. fr. 11347, fol. 226.

190. "Mémoire," BN, Coll. Joly 1428, fols. 21, 34, 39–45, 51–54, 125.

191. On Turgot's embrace of the merchant cause, see BN, Coll. Joly 1314, fols. 11, 112–13.

right to buy in any market of their choice outside the decommercialized zone, the assembly averred: "If it was indeed true that they had not in the past frequented the markets of places on the rivers, that was not a reason to exclude them, for they had never been restricted from any markets outside the eight leagues [and] the constraints that [the merchants] proposed in this respect would excite protests from the bakers, legitimate protests."

As for the other merchant complaints, since prices had been quite low and supplies copious for some time, the authorities refused to take them seriously.[192] In easy times, the police tolerated a wide range of exceptions to the rules. Thus, the assembly told the merchants that "they merited a punishment" for lamenting the press of buyers in a buyers' market. Nor was it objectionable "in a time of such great abundance" for buyers to purchase large amounts and store them temporarily near the rivers, provided the grain eventually reached Paris. The assembly even suggested that since the Paris grain merchants purchased off market, they were in no position to deny the bakers the right to do the same.[193]

In light of this stringent rebuff, the merchants backed off—temporarily.[194] They returned to the charge a year later and were better received, in part because prices were rising and the police were therefore more sensitive to charges of irregularity or threats of disruption, and in part because they had been lobbying indefatigably since their setback. Turgot blamed the lethargy of the port merchants and the rising prices on unremitting baker infringement on the merchants' municipally licensed prerogatives. The bakers were engaging in grain speculation: not only buying, but selling and stocking. There were too many buyers in the field and not enough buyers on the ports, and the Paris merchants were "disgusted" and angry. Determined to stop the baker "abuses" and yet not drive them entirely from the grain trade, the assembly resolved to give the matter "very serious reflection."[195]

Despite Turgot's pressure the assembly procrastinated, doubtless in large part because its members were divided. Meanwhile merchants had moved around or beyond the assembly and had appealed directly to the ministry and royal council. In December of 1736 they obtained a royal declaration that prohibited bakers from buying "in any of the markets near the rivers" and from shipping any grain by river. (At the same time, as a sop to the bakers, the declaration legitimized baker purchases at Brie-Comte-Robert, one of their

192. On prices, see Micheline Baulant, "Le prix des grains à Paris de 1431 à 1788," *Annales: Economies, sociétés, civilisations,* 23d year, no. 3 (May–June 1968): 520–40.

193. BN, Coll. Joly 1314, fols. 134–35, 27 August 1733 and BN, ms. fr. 11356, fols. 218–19, 27 August 1733.

194. BN, Coll. Joly 1314, fol. 136, 11 March 1734.

195. Ibid., fol. 137, 1 July 1734, and BN, ms. fr. 11356, fol. 243, 1 July 1734. Cf. the rather timid line of attack suggested by Gilbert that would restrict the bakers' freedom of action by requiring them to complete all transactions within two months of receiving the *lettre de voiture* sanctioning a purchase. BN, ms. fr. 11356, fol. 244, 15 July 1734.

favorite markets, which had been off limits legally because it was within the decommercialized zone.)

The news of the declaration stunned and enraged the assembly, which had not been consulted on this far-reaching modification of the police system. The assembly criticized the declaration's excessive vagueness in the formula "near the rivers." To ban the bakers from using the rivers was sufficient; it was gratuitous and even dangerous to suggest that they could not buy *near* those rivers as long as they freighted by land. Because of its ambiguity, the assembly decided to suppress the part of the bill that was dear to the merchants and, ironically, submit for ratification in parlement only the part that awarded the bakers a plum.[196]

So much for the merchants' circuitous triumph. The assembly realized that it could delay no further. Turgot drafted a new version that the assembly finally approved the following summer. The prévôt had convinced himself that the passage of the measure would regenerate the ports overnight. He exhorted his colleagues to act with dispatch: "I believe that the sooner the declaration is registered the better, for the ports are meagerly furnished by the merchants who have been waiting for this with the most vivid impatience and who have promised me to supply the port abundantly as soon as they obtain what they have been demanding for such a long time."[197]

Promulgated on 8 September 1737, the antibaker declaration was immediately registered in the *chambre des vacations* of the Paris Parlement. This declaration excluded the bakers from the rivers not so much because they did not belong there (though it rehearsed in passing the contention that the bakers' recourse to the rivers was "a new usage," as opposed to "the old usage" that gave the merchants exclusive dominion on the rivers) as because they committed "abuses" that somehow were invited by the "facilities" that the rivers afforded. Those abuses amounted to the practice of the grain trade, including selling as well as buying. Bakers had the right only to buy for the purpose of making bread. To restrain the bakers and (presumably it followed) "to increase abundance," the declaration forbade them to engage in the regular grain trade or to ship by water the grain or flour they bought for their usage. Nor was that all. Heretofore the bakers' decommercialized zone was eight leagues in radius and the merchants' ten. The bakers now lost these extra two leagues of reserved buying space. In compensation they were of-

---

196. 20 December 1736, 24 January 1737, BN, ms. fr. 11356, fols. 304–5, 310. The "Brie" declaration had been prepared by the controller-general, but apparently he did not object to the modifications proposed by the assembly. AN, O^1 382, fols. 467–68, 24 December 1736. The parlement registered the revised declaration on 29 December. This incident sheds light on the way legislation took shape in the old regime, a subject much less well known than the historians of institutions and the jurists would have us think.

197. Turgot to procurator general, 30 July 1737, BN, Coll. Joly 1314, fol. 113.

fered the right to buy at the Mennecy market, as well as at Brie-Comte-Robert and Limours, all of which were within the forbidden zone.[198]

In order to document their purchases in these three markets of exception as well as in the areas beyond the ten leagues, the bakers would have to procure certificates from local measurers or other market officials testifying to the quantities bought and the dates of transaction. Bakers who violated the new law risked fines of up to 3,000 livres, confiscation of all grain and flour, and loss of mastership. A further article prohibited millers from buying grain "as commissionnaires of bakers," a common practice that significantly cut costs by sparing the bakers the need to make every field purchase in person, excluding the grain-merchant middleman as superfluous, and shortening the distance to the mills.[199]

The bakers defended themselves and assailed their enemies in a flurry of indignant memoranda. They saw the declaration as the fruit of a sordid and reactionary plot joining together the merchants, jealous of baker autonomy and success, and the measurers, who feared that they would lose income from a decline in Paris port activity.[200] Until now the measurers had always taken the lead in the campaign to hedge the bakers. Back in May 1680 the bakers had obtained a parlementary arrêt that encouraged them to buy beyond eight leagues by assuring them that the measurers had no right to collect duties on this grain.[201] Riposting with the charge, later pressed by the merchants, that the bakers had become "the absolute masters of the grain trade," the measurers avenged themselves with an arrêt in November 1686 that forbade the bakers to buy any merchandise outside Paris.[202] Had that arrêt been enforced, according to the bakers, the result would have been "monopoly" provisioning dominated by a handful of merchants who were indifferent to the public interest, incapable of satisfying the capital's needs, and given to deception on quality and price—all themes that the bakers would echo in 1737. The bakers were vindicated, however, by the royal declaration of September 1699 that reaffirmed the arrêt of 1680 as part of its global codification of existing grain-trade legislation.[203]

The merchants were on no more solid ground today, wrote the bakers in 1737, than their confederates had been in the 1680s. There was nothing new in

198. The bakers rejected Mennecy as "no real compensation," first because it attracted relatively little grain and thus was of little interest and second because it would only be interesting if buyers could profit from the fact that it was along the Seine. BN, Coll. Joly 1314, fol. 71.

199. See the full text in the pages of the municipal registers that seem to exude satisfaction: AN, H* 1857, fols. 201–5. The same text is also in BN, ms. fr. 21640, fol. 63.

200. See BN, Coll. Joly 1829, fols. 342–44, 25 June 1754.

201. BN, ms. fr. 21640, fols. 66–67.

202. BN, ms. fr. 21639, fols. 161–64; Coll. Joly 1829, fol. 334.

203. BN, ms. fr. 21640, fols. 70ff.

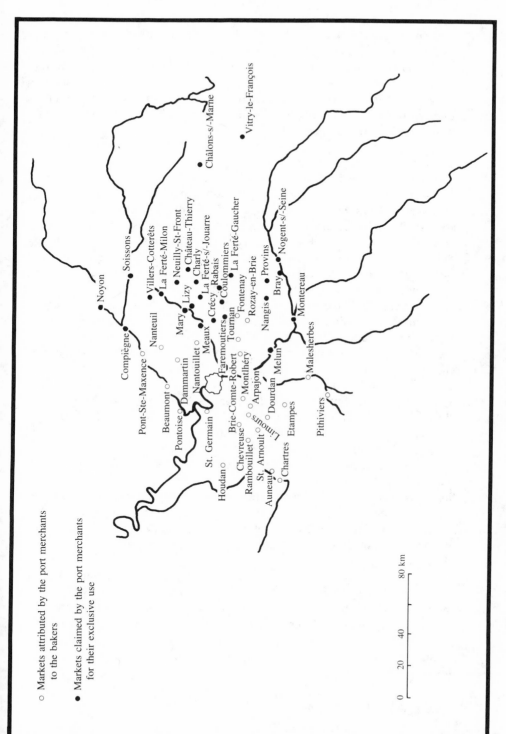

○ Markets attributed by the port merchants to the bakers

● Markets claimed by the port merchants for their exclusive use

MAP 5 Attribution of grain markets in the primary supply zone according to the port merchants

their river traffic, they contended; they had always used water freight. It was irrational and "unnatural" to deny them access. Moreover, a river/road division of labor was inconceivable, for the rivers were the key to successful provisioning. Like the merchants, the bakers hinted that they might be obliged to abandon their profession, because land transport cost at least one-third more than water and was far more difficult.[204] The authorities then would have to decide who was truly responsible for Parisian abundance, a handful of haughty merchants or hundreds of enterprising bakers. These merchants were not men threatened with ruin, the bakers argued, but greedy millionaires who wanted to stifle competition, raise costs by selling second- and thirdhand, cheat on quality, and generally manipulate the market to their advantage. The accusations of fraud especially infuriated the bakers. If they were really guilty, confining them to land trade would resolve nothing. The river ban was merely a ploy, they concluded, to facilitate the maneuvers of the merchants, who were the true hoarders and regraters. The bakers demanded that the merchants be restricted to the markets so that they could be constantly under surveillance.[205]

Nor were these sharp remonstrances limited to the baker corporate elite, as the merchants claimed in an effort to show that the grain-trading issue only interested a smattering of bakers. A group of forain bakers protested even more vehemently against the stifling of "our liberty to trade," declaring that they were among the hardest hit since they did not provision themselves in Paris as the guild bakers could and did. The merchants averred that they wanted "equality," but, complained the forains, "now everything is permitted them and everything is forbidden to us." The forains addressed the question that had caused the assembly to hesitate in the first place: Why are we more harshly treated after a decade of abundance (1727–37) than we had been during the last dearth (1725–26)? The forains assailed the merchants violently. They lacked the capacity to feed Paris, providing no more than 15 percent of its needs. They practiced hoarding in the countryside and instead of bargaining openly on the port they visited bakers with samples. They sold light setiers and they mixed inferior quality wheats. "Paris, which has always eaten the best bread of Europe," the forains dolefully warned, "will henceforth eat the most mediocre."[206]

The bakers received indirect support from a considerable number of persons, a few highly placed, most anonymous and unnoteworthy, who either were from or had interests in the towns where the bakers habitually (though not always legally) bought supplies. They feared that the police crackdown on

204. The forain bakers fixed the difference in a very general way at 24 livres the muid. BN, Coll. Joly 1314, fols. 48–51.

205. Ibid., fols. 13–15, 19–20, 67–74.

206. Ibid., fols. 48–51. On the inferior quality of port merchandise, see also Bucquet, *Traité pratique*, pp. 47, 50.

the bakers would ruin their marketplaces. The flour merchants of Melun composed a sharp "memorandum against the declaration of 8 September 1737" on the grounds that it would force them out of business. They claimed to produce the "best flour in France" and to supply Paris with 500 sacks a week, which they sent by water en droiture. The September declaration would require them to send their flour by land, which would make it prohibitively expensive. Moreover, by redefining the distance in the league measure, the law would relocate Melun within the decommercialized ten league zone and thus theoretically shut off all baker trade.[207]

Even before the promulgation of the declaration, there erupted "a rebellion" at Montlhéry mobilizing scores of citizens to the cry of "Liberty or fight!" against the efforts of the constabulary to prohibit all Paris baker trade because Montlhéry was within the taboo zone.[208] The market there had been "tolerated" since 1699 and in one way or another provided the livelihood of the bulk of the inhabitants. The policy of rigor was the work of "the enemies of the public interest," argued the town fathers, who sought to be assimilated to Brie-Comte-Robert as a market of exception.[209] The town of Arpajon articulated similar protests, powerfully seconded by its patron and seigneur, Madame d'Arpajon, who lobbied directly with the royal council.[210] The duc de Villeroy, "owner" of the Mennecy market, campaigned at a meeting of the assembly of police and later thanked the procurator general for obtaining the legitimation of his market.[211] Presented as a concession to the bakers, the Mennecy exception was in fact a balm to an influential lord. The pressure for most-favored-market status was so intense and the risks of proliferating exceptions so great that the government considered new legislation at the end of 1738 that would revoke all exceptions, including the ones dating from the seventeenth century.[212]

Exuberant and triumphant, the merchants paid little attention to the bakers' counterattack. The bakers, they insisted, had "criminal habits" that somehow flourished on water more than on land. The declaration would stop

207. BN, ms. fr. 21635, fols. 166–67. The Melun dealers volunteered the not insignificant information that the king owned the minage rights and would suffer a serious loss of income if the market became inert.

208. AN, Y 11224, 4 February 1731. The new hard line seems to have been announced in the Paris police sentence of 11 January 1737, BN, ms. fr. 21635, fol. 164. Cf. the rumor that the markets at Montlhéry and Arpajon would soon be closed. Gazetins, 31 August, 7 September 1737, Arsenal, ms. Bast. 10166, fol. 330.

209. BN, Coll. Joly 1314, fols. 30–33.

210. Ibid., fols. 23–24.

211. BN, Coll. Joly 1123, fols. 23–24, and 1314, fols. 78, 117; BN, ms. fr. 11356, fols. 313–17, 14 February 1737.

212. BN, ms. fr. 11356, 18 December 1738. The measurers and porters had always combatted these exceptions. BN, Coll. Joly 1116, fols. 247–48. Cf. the lobbying of the comte de Noailles on behalf of baker trading in Versailles and Arpajon in 1750. BN, Coll. Joly 1314, fols. 160, 162, 177.

the bakers, but even more important, it would save the merchants. Several merchants had allegedly been on the brink of renouncing the trade, and business in general was at a standstill. But "in the wake of the declaration the trade has revived and recovered its pristine vigor."[213]

Toward the end of 1737 the assembly of police rejected the baker remonstrances, though the procurator general did postpone re-registration of the declaration before the whole parlement until the prévôt des marchands heard the bakers out.[214] The tone of the assembly had changed more or less drastically over the past few years. Now it deplored what it labeled "the new tolerance" by which bakers had extended their trade to the rivers. Now it accepted as its rationale the prévôt's dire prediction that unchecked baker trade "would soon have destroyed the merchants and left the city of Paris at the mercy of the bakers."[215] This prospect apparently frightened the assembly into conviction and action. If it hesitated for a moment, it was only to make sure that there was no dearth in the offing, because a supply crisis would obviously give the bakers great short-term leverage.[216] When the bakers hinted in early December that prices were already beginning to rise in the new pro-merchant regime, the assembly scoffed at this "malice."[217] The merchants continued to tease the authorities. Just before Christmas they promised that the ports would be plentifully furnished as soon as the declaration was "fully in vigor."[218]

Was the declaration in fact vigorously executed? The baker guild protested against harassment by the prévôt in the countryside and the forains alleged that he paralyzed them. Both groups may have exaggerated for polemical reasons.[219] There is some evidence that the prévôt tried to enforce the new law energetically. He solicited denunciations of baker turpitude. He dispatched his huissiers (generally accompanied by a measurer—enough to confirm the conspiracy thesis in the eyes of the bakers) to investigate in the hinterland. Huissier Balize was sent to Port Montain to seize the grain that bakers bought along the river and shipped in *margotas* to various towns on the Seine, whence it was freighted by cart to the capital.[220] The prévôt fined the baker named Chevalier for secretly unloading grain at the port de la Rapée and then transporting it to the Halle for sale.[221] He struck Paris port merchant

213. BN, Coll. Joly 1314, fols. 52–66. Unfortunately we lack the data to test the merchants' effervescent claims. It is likely that merchant supply increased—but not for long, as the troubles on the port in 1738–40 testify.

214. Ibid., fol. 4, 28 November 1737.

215. Ibid., fol. 5, 5 December 1737.

216. Ibid., fol. 3, 5 November 1737.

217. Ibid., fol. 5, 5 December 1737.

218. BN, ms. fr. 11356, fol. 340 (19 December 1737).

219. BN, Coll. Joly 1314, fols. 14, 48–49.

220. AN, H* 1857, fols. 319–20, 22 April 1738 (judgment).

221. AN, F[11] 264, 15 July 1738.

Jean Oudard from the list of commissioned dealers and fined him 1,000 livres for an act of apostasy, or rather collaboration: Oudard helped a number of bakers circumvent the declaration's restrictions by serving as their broker.[222]

Yet the merchant victory, like the prévôté's zeal for enforcement, proved to be short-lived. The assembly was again frightened into revising its policy—this time by the specter of shortage. The "malicious" observations of the bakers acquired a prophetic cast in retrospect. The September declaration suffered the taint of legislative incompleteness because it was never formally submitted for registration in the full parlement after the summer–fall recess. The reason, explained the procurator general, was that "we were threatened by a dearth."[223] It turned out that the police needed the bakers more than they had expected. Already in January of 1738 the assembly was tolerating baker river traffic provided the bakers justified their purchases with local certificates.[224] By mid-century, judging by a parlementary arrêt, baker river trade was considered perfectly normal.[225] Even as the municipality vainly called for the rigorous execution of the declaration in the mid-sixties, the intendant of Paris casually noted that the law was wholly moribund.[226]

Nor, apparently, did the merchants help their own cause sufficiently. Though they increased their supply substantially in the year following the promulgation of the September declaration, they still did not furnish enough.[227] As the dearth made itself felt, the assembly of police, including the prévôt des marchands, became increasingly impatient with them. Yet by backing off from the enforcement of the law that it had declared essential to the survival of the merchants, the assembly gave them an alibi for their weak performance.

Off-market Trade

At least one section of the declaration of 8 September 1737 remained in effect for many years to come. This was the unequivocal affirmation of the right of Paris-licensed merchants to buy in the granaries and farms as well as

222. Sentence of 29 November 1737, BN, F 23719 (909).

223. BN, Coll. Joly 1314, fol. 87.

224. BN, ms. fr. 11356, fol. 343, 23 January 1738.

225. Arrêt of March 1750, BN, Coll. Joly 1829, fol. 333. Cf. another parlementary arrêt that confirmed the bakers' right "to buy through factors or commissionnaires," a practice forbidden in the declaration of 8 September 1737. AN, H* 1873, fol. 627.

226. "Mémoire et avis de Mrs. du bureau de la ville," BN, ms. fr. 14296, fol. 34 (ca. 1764); Bertier de Sauvigny, "Observations sur le commerce des grains," BN, ms. fr. 11347, fol. 225.

227. Grain entries at the port for the period October 1737–September 1738 amounted to 17,713 muids, compared to 11,584 for 1732 and 11,071 for 1733. Arsenal, ms. Bast. 10277 and Bibliothèque de l'Institut, mss. 520–21. It is not clear what proportion of the 1733–38 provision was "extraordinary" in provenance.

in the marketplace—the prerogative that controller-general Terray was ready to abolish in the 1770s as superfluous to the public interest. The merchants had sought a clear-cut legislative statement of their right in the thirties with almost as much ardor as they attempted to trammel the bakers.[228] The issue was of consequence to them because the declaration of 19 April 1723, which set the model for most local grain-trade police, prohibited *all* off-market transactions. The Paris merchants enjoyed a toleration to buy anywhere they pleased, but local officials often harassed them on the grounds that they were violating the law of 1723,[229] and they wanted a new declaration explicitly sanctioning their activities. Extremely reluctant to revoke the 1723 law because it was crucial in a dearth and was needed to keep non-Parisian dealers in line, the authorities tried to soothe the merchants by promising to come promptly to their "assistance and protection" whenever they were victimized by local officials.[230]

The merchants persisted and finally the procurator general launched a thoroughgoing inquiry into the question, directed by Leclerc du Brillet, Delamare's collaborator and successor and one of the chief experts on the matter in the realm.[231] It is not certain whether Leclerc ever completed his study. In any event, the assembly decided against revoking the 1723 declaration and opted instead for granting the merchants the written derogation they demanded in clause 4 of the declaration of 8 September 1737. Shortly after its

228. The port merchants not only sent petitions but also gathered outside the house of the first president during assemblies of police that considered this question. BN, ms. fr. 11356, fols. 127, 22 June 1730, and 157–58, 10 May 1731; BN, Coll. Joly 1428, fol. 63, 11 March 1734. The Hôtel-Dieu supported the merchant argument because its suppliers habitually bought "in the granaries of the laboureurs." Deliberations of the bureau of the Hôtel-Dieu, 7 March 1774, Archives Assistance publique, no. 144.

229. Keep in mind that in many instances the local officials were simply trying to protect their own supply from what they regarded as Parisian pillage. See, for instance, Guillemin (Châlons) to procurator general, 4 October 1740, BN, Coll. Joly 1123, fols. 177–78; Lebel (Vitry) to procurator general, 19 December 1694, BN, ms. fr. 21643; Gillet (Lagny) to procurator general, 14 July 1770, BN, Coll. Joly 1150, fol. 37.

230. BN, ms. fr. 11356, fols. 157–58, 10 May 1731. Nor were the local police the only ones who invoked the stringency of 1723. The owners of market rights, such as the abbé de Vilbreuil at Provins, pressed authorities to enforce market sales upon pain of heavy fines and damages in favor of the minage owners or farmers. It goes without saying that at Provins and elsewhere the police and the market seigneurs often had close relations. "Mémoires des marchands de bled pour l'approvisonnement de Paris," ca. 1734–35, BN, Coll. Joly 1428, fols. 38–43. See also the splenetic attack on off-market trading by the comte de Rochebrune, baron of Bray, an important market town. "The king and the seigneurs, owners of the right of minage and of marketing, suffer from the license of the merchants," as did the "little people" who relied on the economic multiplier effects of the market. "The merchants pretend that all their [off-market] purchases are for the provisioning of Paris," wrote the comte, "but would they supply any less if they were buying in the ordinary markets?" "Mémoire to procurator general," BN, ms. fr. 21635, fols. 244–45.

231. BN, Coll. Joly 1428, fol. 65, 30 June 1735; Leclerc to procurator general, 26 April and 16 December 1736, BN, Coll. Joly 1428, fols. 69, 70–73.

promulgation, an anonymous memorialist denounced this dispensation for enabling the merchants to practice "monopoly" with impunity.[232]

The Vengeance of the Marketplace

Such heavy-handed denunciations were increasingly scoffed at in the eighteenth century, by the Paris police themselves as well as by the grain liberals. Occasionally, however, a well-known port merchant committed an act that made those apocalyptic charges sound at least partly credible. In the fall of 1751, in the midst of a *cherté* that caused real consternation, Machault, the controller-general and keeper of the seals, ordered the arrest and imprisonment of Joseph Despreaux, "merchant for the provisioning of Paris," for having used the off-market prerogative as a "cover for criminal acts."[233] Specifically, Despreaux, along with two of his commissionnaires, was charged with buying futures and hoarding grain in various depots for the purpose of causing a dearth.[234] The authorities also wanted to remind Paris suppliers that such practices would lead to a revocation of their off-market permits. One of the most distinguished members of the Mortellerie clan, Despreaux had received civic bonuses in 1740 for exceeding his provisioning quotas. If one is to take his word, he was not only innocent, but he was one of the largest and most faithful Paris suppliers.[235]

Actions such as Despreaux's, according to the police, led to "artificial" dearths. The ministry resolved to punish Despreaux in an "exemplary" manner, but hesitated for fear that such a "sensational" gesture could precipitate a reaction of solidarity among the Mortellerie confreres that would result in a contraction of supply at an extremely inopportune moment. To preempt such an occurrence, the prévôt apparently made discreet demarches among the leading port merchants "to ensure their good will." This was deference paid less to the influence of the Mortellerie group than to the power of the subsistence imperative.

Ennobled by the water, the port merchants were historically the leading figures in the Paris provisioning trade. In return for a blend of freedom and protection (government intervention did not contravene the market principle,

232. "Mémoire contre la déclaration du 8 Septembre 1737," BN, ms. fr. 21635, fols. 168–69.

233. On the *cherté,* see Foucaud to procurator general, 6 October 1751, BN, Coll. Joly 1113, fols. 184–85, and Missonnet's reports, Coll. Joly 1112.

234. On the crime of *enarrhement,* see *Encyclopédie méthodique,* Jurisprudence (Paris, 1783), 1:78–80, and Des Essarts, *Dictionnaire universel de police,* 1:14.

235. Arsenal, ms. Bast. 11743, dossier 339. Despreaux testified that he averaged 25 to 40 muids a week. This is surely an extravagant claim for a man who a decade earlier barely managed 6 muids a week.

in the eyes of the merchants, so long as it favored their commercial interests), the merchants pledged to follow certain rules and to keep the city amply supplied. The rue de la Mortellerie elite were closely linked by ties of neighborhood, kinship, and interest. Reputed to be inordinately wealthy, the Mortellerie merchants in fact had fortunes that varied considerably.

In their purchasing, the port-based merchants depended heavily on a network of local commissionnaires, who not only provided them with critical information but also made day-to-day decisions on their own. The police of the hometown markets complained repeatedly that the commissionnaires jeopardized local well-being by violating the marketplace code "under the sacred banner of the provisioning of Paris." The Mortellerie elite did not furnish nearly as large a percentage of total Parisian consumption as the highest-placed administrators believed. Ironically, the old memories of port hegemony that sustained the prestige of the merchants at the same time undermined their position because they were so incongruent with their real capacity. Predictably, the authorities were most intolerant of the failure of the Mortellerie merchants to meet their obligations in periods of crisis when, in fact, commerce was most parlous. Increasingly sensitive about the erosion of their influence as well as their business, the Mortellerie merchants blamed it on the bakers who aggressively encroached on their preferred buying territory. The merchants obtained a royal declaration that officially barred the bakers from the trade on the river areas, but it was not energetically enforced. Victims of their own lack of initiative, the Mortellerie corps continued to lose ground both commercially and politically. By 1770 certain high officials believed that the capital could largely do without them.

The Mortellerie merchants "made the law" on the ports but they were not the only wheat traders serving the city by water. "Country" and itinerant (forain) merchants operated out of the hinterland. The former tended to use the brokerage services of the Mortellerie elite while the latter seemed to have relished their independence. Their number fluctuated continuously within a secular trend toward contraction. Their supply was largely circumstantial, contingent upon the opportunity costs of the moment. The Paris municipality did not count upon them as it did upon the port-based merchants.

CHAPTER 5

The Grain Merchants
at the Paris Halle

Ecoutez un blasphème: La Bruyère et La Rochefoucauld sont des livres bien communs, bien plats, en comparaison de ce qui se pratique de ruses, de finesses, de politique, de raisonnements profonds, un jour de marché à la halle.[1]

𝒯he Halle bypassed the Grève as the leading Paris market more or less inconspicuously. If contemporaries were slow to perceive the Halle's triumph, it was in large measure because the personnel of the provisioning trade based there were so pedestrian in character. The Halle boasted neither the tradition nor the organization nor the ethos of the rue de la Mortellerie. In a metaphorical sense, it was a more democratic world: more open, more dispersed, more diverse, more *débrouillard,* smaller in scale, newer in origins.

The Halle and the Ports: Differences and Similarities

The organization of the grain trade at the Halle was considerably less elaborate than at the ports. The merchants were not bound by the same sorts

1. "Listen to a blasphemy: La Bruyère and La Rochefoucauld are very ordinary and pedestrian books when one compares them to the wiles, the wit, the politics and the profound reasonings that are practiced in a single market day at the Halle." Denis Diderot, "Principes philosophiques pour servir d'introduction à la connaissance de l'esprit et du coeur humain" (1769), in *Oeuvres complètes* (Paris, 1969), 8:184.

of historical, commercial, social, political, and familial ties. They formed a rather heterogeneous group and had no Mortellerie-type elite to which to aspire or to defer. There was probably more turnover among the Halle merchants than among their port counterparts. Their residences were widely dispersed, and their field operations were scattered throughout the hinterland, unstructured by notorious geographical or traditional imperatives. The Halle did not have the same hold upon them, nor the same significance, as the ports did for the municipally enrolled traders. In no sense, subjective or objective, could the Halle merchants be said to constitute a corps.

The Halle merchants did not have the same sort of relationship to the lieutenant general of police as the port dealers had to the prévôt des marchands. The relationship was not so much looser as more supple, not so much remote as mediated at numerous junctures by lesser authorities. The lieutenant general issued commissions, but as a rule they had to be solicited by the merchants, who had various motives for coveting them. In a narrow sense a merchant did not need the specific permission of the lieutenant general in order to supply Paris. It is not even certain that the Châtelet required registration; the lieutenance seemed to presume that the merchants would in all likelihood be enrolled at the clerk's office (greffe) of some local police jurisdiction in the hinterland, and that in any event they would become quickly known to the measurers and porters if not to the commissaire and inspector of the halles department. Virtually anyone was welcome at the Halle, provided he obeyed the rules governing transactions—basically the same rules that operated at the ports. Competition was promoted in this open concourse, hubris discouraged. Unlike the port merchants, the Halle traders were not taught that they were indispensable. On the contrary, it was hinted that they could easily be replaced. They were required to supply the Halle regularly, but they were not allowed to imagine that they could transform this duty into a bargaining counter.

The Halle merchants were rarely placed under pressure save in periods of shortage. At the outset of a (presumed) crisis, the commissaire canvassed them on their holdings and exhorted them to remain faithful in their deliveries, while the lieutenant general dispatched agents (often exempts from the maréchaussée or the robe courte) to keep the merchants under close surveillance.[2] The lieutenant general tried to coordinate policy with the intendant of Paris and the procurator general, both of whom helped to prod the merchants to perform well.[3] In times of tension the merchants found themselves caught in a struggle for supplies between the metropolitan authorities

2. The merchants regarded the agents as "spies" and resented their presence. Bourlon to Hérault, 4 October 1725, Arsenal, ms. Bast. 10270, p. 273.
3. Secretary of d'Angervilliers to Hérault, 29 October 1725, Arsenal, ms. Bast. 10271, and Cleret to Hérault, 12 October 1725, ms. Bast. 10270.

and the local police. Like the prévôt des marchands, the lieutenant general did not hesitate to usurp local jurisdiction in order to favor the provisioning of Paris and to mobilize Paris-connected merchants.[4] In 1740 Louis Paschot, a flour dealer working out of the Brie, informed lieutenant general of police Marville that he could no longer continue to furnish the Halle because the procurator at Lagny, a major market town, "claiming that all the grain must remain in his country," refused to allow him to buy there. Anxious to prevent Paschot's defection, for his "considerable commerce was of great assistance to us," Marville pledged to have the official disciplined and the anti-Paris policy quashed.[5] Similarly, the Paris police intervened to rescue Halle suppliers at Houdan who were denied access to the market by a group of porters apparently operating in behalf of the local fiscal procurator.[6] Nor did the lieutenant general shy away from administering a lesson to the municipality when its agents got in the way of his in the supply crowns.[7]

Faced with burdens that threatened their ability to furnish the Halle as usual, Paris merchants petitioned the lieutenant general for the same sort of protection that the port merchants expected from the prévôt. In 1738 a miller from Senlis named Baudet wrote lieutenant general of police Hérault that he would be unable to furnish the Halle if he were not excused from contributing the use of his only wagon for the compulsory royal road service *(corvée)*. Once he verified that Baudet was indeed a regular supplier, Hérault imposed upon the reluctant intendant of Paris ("This sets a bad example," he complained) to free the miller from the task.[8]

The Halle-based Merchants

Broadly speaking, the merchants at the Halle formed two categories analogous to those at the ports: the Paris-based dealers and the forains. At the Halle, however, this distinction was far less abrupt and sustained than at the waterfront. The Paris-based merchants did not lord it over the forains. It was not uncommon for a Paris merchant to maintain a home in the countryside as well as a domicile in the capital and to utilize brokers to sell his merchandise instead of marketing it himself. One "forainized" oneself, in this sense, without derogation. Nor was it rare for a soi-disant forain to inhabit Paris and to bypass factorage, or for a forain to rely on commissionnaires and for a Paris-

---

4. Bourlon to Hérault, 15 October 1725, Arsenal, ms. Bast. 10270, pp. 311–12.
5. Marville to Joly de Fleury, 22 August 1740, BN, Coll. Joly 1124, fol. 213.
6. AN, Y 11236, 11 October 1749.
7. See the outrage of the lieutenant general's man in reaction to the efforts of a prevotal official to restrict the purchasing area of land-based merchants. Marion to Hérault, 19 December 1738, Arsenal, ms. Bast. 10275.
8. Harlay to Hérault, 9 November 1738, ibid.

Interior of the Halle au blé. Engraving by Guignet, 1820 (Bibliothèque Nationale, Photo Lauros-Giraudon)

based trader to scour the *plat pays* personally.[9] The Paris-based Halle traders were not necessarily better off than the forains, though it is true that the handful of Hallemen at the summit had a larger business and more alluring perspectives than even the leading forains. The Halle forains, like the country merchants at the ports, were far more numerous than the Paris-based dealers.

Little is known about the recruitment of the Halle suppliers. Louis Rozet's itinerary, from a successful laboureur family in the Mulcien to a grain business centered in Paris, must have been common.[10] Pierre Félix of the rue de Reuilly came from a family of laboureurs and bakers in the Dammartin-Gonesse area.[11] Another common trajectory led from the small grains—the *grainier* or *grenetier*—to the bread-making cereals—a route taken by Paris Halle merchants Nicolas-Louis Martin, Charles Gouay, and Edme Cavrois, among others.[12] Master baker Curieux's daughter was a Halle grain dealer, as was the son of faubourg baker Roch Lepère.[13] In some cases, the affiliation was even closer: Jean-Honoré Aubert's father was also a grain merchant and his mother a sometime broker at the Halle, while François Chevalier established himself at the Halle instead of following his older brother to the Grève.[14] In other cases it was more difficult to discern: it is not clear what drew François Lecocq, son of a wine merchant, to the Halle.[15] The origins of steady suppliers like Charles Gonnet and René Drouet often elude us entirely.[16]

New faces tended to appear in the grain trade during crises in response to the allure of speculative gain. If the authorities did not ordinarily offer these opportunists a warm welcome, they did not usually discourage them either, for a number of their regular merchants were likely to go under and the city would need extraordinary help. Few of these newcomers were "shameless gamblers," to use the anxious words of one police report. Probably a majority were everyday merchants of one sort or another who happened to be in a

9. For an example of the first situation, see Michel Collet, "marchand des grains forain pour l'approvisionnement de Paris," whose permanent residence was in the St.-Paul parish. AN, Y 14946, 8 July 1732.

10. AN, Y 15616, 4 July–30 August 1760.

11. Archives Seine-Paris, DC⁶ 227, fol. 156.

12. Ibid., D5B⁶ 179 and 1902, and D2B⁶ 841 (23 January 1750); grain registration lists, 1770–71, AN, Y 9648. On the profession of *grainier,* see Macquer, *Dictionnaire portatif des arts et métiers* (Paris, 1766), 1:565.

13. AN, Y 12606, 7 January 1758; AN, MC, XX-542, 21 April 1729. Cf. the two sisters of Halle merchant Nicolas-Louis Martin who married master bakers. AN, Y 11231, 18 June 1744; AN, MC, LXIX-320, 10 October 1734, and LXX-303, 7 August 1733.

14. Archives Seine-Paris, DC⁶ 20, fol. 116; DC⁶ 19, fols. 79, 104, 122, 208; D2B⁶ 841, 21 January 1750.

15. AN, MC, XXV-625, 23 March 1741.

16. AN, Y 11236, 7 October 1749; Y 15389, 9 June 1779.

position at that moment to put their hands rapidly on stocks of grain. Their entry did not threaten the social or moral order—the trading floor of the Halle had little in common with the rue Quincampoix—and was even less likely to affect the provisioning system permanently, since most of the newcomers dropped out after the crisis abated and prospects for big returns vanished. The multiplication of hands at the outset of each crisis remained a structural reflex of the Paris trade until the end of the nineteenth century. Experts testifying at a hearing on Paris provisioning in 1859 pointed to the "swarm of [previously unknown] dealers" who descended upon the marketplaces in the hope of "making a killing."[17]

The crisis that influenced merchant recruitment most significantly occurred in the 1760s. It was of a very special nature, for it was triggered by political design. The liberal laws of 1763–64 "freed" the grain trade by dismantling the intricate police apparatus that hitherto had controlled it and inviting anyone with an appetite for risk and gain to join in. The safeguards that were supposed to shield the Paris provisioning system from dislocation did not work. Grain fever raged, and newcomers flocked to get in, especially in the hinterland, but to a surprising extent in the capital as well. The police perceived a direct connection between the proliferation of "abuses" in the grain trade (abuses that the liberal legislation legitimized as beneficent and necessary commercial tactics) and the infiltration of new men into the business: greedy profiteers, merchants lacking equally in skill and probity, men previously excluded from the trade who exploited their wealth and influence unfairly, and above all men who knew and cared nothing for the conventions and responsibilities that had once been an integral part of the provisioning process.[18]

In some ways typical of the new breed was La Place, a miller from Etampes who now sold grain in Paris as well as in his home market area. He bought everywhere he could, outbidding rivals and amassing a huge fund. He sold little because he demanded a price "dearer than [the already high] current." Rebuffing the protests of other merchants, La Place brashly averred that "the trade was now free" and that consequently "he was free to make deals as he wished and . . . feared nothing."[19]

When the police regime was partly restored at the end of 1770, the police required all those who wished to continue or to start in the grain trade to register with local authorities. Though in all likelihood incomplete, the Paris registration list nevertheless tells us something about the new men who thronged to the Halle in the late sixties. Twenty-two of the forty-seven Paris-based merchants who registered in 1770–71 had entered the trade only in the past few years and had no previous experience in grain. Among these new

17. *Enquête sur la boulangerie*, pp. 198, 403, 404.
18. Kaplan, *Bread, Politics and Political Economy*, 1:268–306.
19. AN, X^{1B} 9434, 18 April 1769.

faces were four wine merchants, two other merchants, two artisans, two innkeepers, two clerks, three *bourgeois de Paris,* three bakers, and a soldier's wife.[20] How well they fared and whether they remained or not we do not know. It is unlikely that many followed the erratic path of Antoine Demolle. Born in poverty in Caen, Demolle worked as a servant and served time in prison for assault. On the morrow of liberalization he made a fresh start as a grain trader at the Paris Halle. Later he was arrested again for attempting to rob his ex-master.[21]

The *Forains*

Forain origins are even more obscure. Did the scores of merchants for whom grain trading was only one of two or more occupations begin in grain and then diversify, or did they move into grain more or less by chance as a seasonal or speculative complement to other activities? Unlike a number of more circumspect fellow hotelkeepers who helped to make the cabaret almost as famous a hoarding place as the convent, Pierre Beranger, proprietor of Vert Galant, openly avowed that he was at the same time a grain forain.[22] Pierre Coustard of Crépy-en-Valois combined baking and grain trading, another symbiotic pairing. But the same could hardly be said for Matthias Cabier, a cooper–grain forain at Choisy-le-Roi, or Jean Michin, a wholesale fruit dealer and grain merchant at Fontainebleau.[23] Simon Billot and Jean Gouge traded in horses as well as in grain. Oats provide a plausible connection, but who could have expected to find Picard Jean Fremond's cart filled half with grain and half with "wooden heels"?[24] Jacques Barbant of Mantes contravened the regulations on professional incompatibilities by acquiring a fiscal office *(brigadier des tailles)* with the profits from his substantial grain commerce and afterward continuing to exercise the trade with the help of his wife.[25]

The forain ranks, like the Halle corps, swelled somewhat during crises,

20. AN, Y 9648. Rare before liberalization, the simultaneous exercise of a second profession by a Paris-based Halle dealer seems to have become more common afterward. See, for example, François André, who was a wine merchant, and later a caterer, as well as a grain dealer. Archives Seine-Paris, D5B[6] 22-1133, 13 May 1761, and 82-5503, September 1781.

21. AN, Y 10325, 22 April 1772.

22. Archives Seine-Paris, D4B[6] 49-2956, October 1773.

23. Denisart, *Collection de décisions,* 3:254; Archives Seine-Paris, D4B[6] 49-2956, October 1773; AN, Y 15954, 5 October 1757.

24. AN, Y 18663, 7 February 1767; Archives Seine-Paris, D4B[6] 3873, 10 December 1776, and D5B[6] 6100; AN, Y 9538, 17 December 1726.

25. Archives Seine-Paris, D6B[6], 6 September 1771. Note, however, the *arbitre*'s remarks on the role that wives commonly played in the grain trade: "Dans cette ville où le commerce des grains se fait plus au dedans qu'au dehors, ce sont plutôt les femmes que les hommes qui s'en mêlent."

then contracted, and gradually reached a new equilibrium, as a rule not very far from the old. Newcomers were assimilated throughout the century, though turnover and renewal were rarely brusque and deep. The only episode that seems to have had a jolting impact upon recruitment was the liberalization experience. Scores of "strangers" tried their hand at the Halle in the late sixties—sometimes no more than once or twice, perhaps just for the adventure of testing out the big city. Henry Coquelin, son of a woodworker, was lured into the forain trade by the prospects of laissez-faire. He appreciated the meaning of liberalization and had confidence that the "great freedom of circulation" would enable the provinces of the realm to succor each other effectively. "By embracing the grain trade as an occupation," he thought that he would not only "make do" but also "be useful to the Society of which he is a member." In fact, Coquelin was more ambitious than he avowed. He tried to make a lot of money quickly by artful dealing, and at the end of the decade found himself in jail on suspicion of hoarding. Shrewdly clinging to the letter of the liberal law, Coquelin adamantly denied practicing any "maneuvers or monopolies contrary to the free circulation of this commerce or prejudicial to the public interest."[26]

The newcomers in the late sixties included hairdressers, domestics, priests, and nobles, and yet, judging from the Paris registration list of 1770–71, the forain contingent just after liberalization seems more "professional" than during the first part of the century. More than half of the forains who registered for the grain trade in 1770–71 on the Paris list continued to exercise or had very recently exercised another profession. Most of these occupations, however, were tied to the grain trade (five laboureurs, fourteen millers, one baker, one army supplier). Still, the Paris list touched only a portion of the forain universe. Two-thirds of the 165 traders on the Meaux list were new men, and only about 11 percent of the registrants were habitual Paris-bound forains.[27]

A number of "new" forains in the late sixties were actually veteran grain traders who for various reasons had never provisioned the capital more or less regularly. Fifty-two-year-old Antoine Lelièvre of Etampes belonged to this group. For him, liberalization meant the chance to expand his commercial horizons. Lelièvre was denounced for buying in the farms and markets with the intention of hoarding. Asked by an officer of the constabulary at Arpajon (who no longer had any right to pose such a question) whether he had authorization to buy in the marketplaces, Lelièvre became abusive. Reportedly he expressed delight with the high prices instead of bargaining to resist them and announced with cheerful ghastliness that "it would be necessary to have teeth of gold in order to eat bread this winter."[28]

Forain commerce remained an attractive opportunity long after the end of liberalization; Joseph-Henri Beauregard of Nogent, a café owner, entered the grain trade in 1782 "believing the commerce of grain to be advantageous."[29]

Relations between Halle-based and *Forain* Merchants

Between the forains and the Paris-based dealers at the Halle there was not "the sort of antipathy" that marked relations on the ports at various times— tense relations that the police of the larger cities were expected to promote in order to spur competition and prevent "fraudulent concert" between the two kinds of traders.[30] More often than not, they stayed out of each other's way. Frequently they maintained close business contacts. When forains Edme Besoul and Jean Lefranc visited Paris, they stayed with Paris Halle merchants, and when forain Pierre Garant needed a procurator to press a complaint he too called upon a Halle dealer. Often forains served as buying agents for the Paris merchants. For Louis Rozet, the connection was especially intimate and dependable, for he had three forain sons in the Vitry area. Simonet had two forain sons at Meaux, but he was as often their agent as they were his.[31] Forain Henri Petit was commissionnaire for several Halle dealers. Seven forains on the Parisian register of 1770–71 served as correspondents of Halle merchants and/or bakers, as did two of the Meaux registrants. Paris-based Halle merchants lent money to several forains, and Nicolas-Louis Martin recommended his forain friends as honest and dependable suppliers to the administrators of several Parisian hospitals.[32]

The Business of the Halle-based Merchant

The business portrait of the Paris-based Halle merchant begins with his preference for a one-man (or one-family) operation. Save for occasional,

28. AN, Y 12671, 12 October 1768.

29. Archives Seine-Paris, D4B⁶ 85-5740, 16 October 1786. It is not indicated whether he bothered to register with the local police.

30. Herbert, *Essai sur la police générale des grains,* in *Collection des économistes et des réformateurs sociaux de la France,* ed. E. Depitre (Paris, 1910), p. 22. On the police effort to foster forain trade, see Léon Biollay, *Origines et transformations du factorat dans les marchés de Paris* (Paris, 1880), p. 4. I would suggest that for purposes police the Paris authorities tended to view all the Halle merchants as forains.

31. From the Paris registration list, 1770–71, in Kaplan, *Bread, Politics and Political Economy,* 1:280–88.

32. AN, Z¹ᴴ 239, 23 August 1726; Arsenal, ms. Bast. 10086, 16 June 1774; AN, Y 15616, 30 August 1748; Archives Seine-Paris, D4B⁶ 43–2431, 18 January 1772; Kaplan, *Bread, Politics and Political Economy,* 1:287, 291; AN, MC, XXXVIII-473, 16 April 1779; Archives Seine-Paris, D2B⁶ 849 and D5B⁶ 1902.

specific, short-term undertakings, he did not take advantage of the opportunity the police afforded him to associate with other merchants. In a very limited way, it could be argued that the Halle dealers were associated with their commissionnaires. They had a number of regular correspondents—fewer, it seems, than their port counterparts—and in addition a number of stringers who surfaced with proposals now and then.[33] There was occasional friction between merchants and commissionnaires, generally concerning advances that were unaccounted for, *lettres de change* that either should have been paid but were not or should not have been paid but were, and disputes over quantities of merchandise ordered, shipped, or received.[34] On the whole, however, their relations appear to have been harmonious and mutually profitable. Buying agents tended to stay with Halle merchants longer than with port traders. One merchant in 1784 paid a commission of six livres the muid, but we lack the data to take the measure of such fees across the century.[35]

The faillite dossiers of ten Halle merchants suggest that they relied almost exclusively on agents for their purchases. An average of ten grain middlemen (median = 12) had claims against each of them. The collective debt that each failed merchant owed his agents averaged 14,321 livres (median = 10,600). Only three owed money to laboureurs. Since laboureurs generally refused credit beyond a month (and often demanded cash on delivery or earnest money until full payment), these findings may mean that the Paris merchants were staying home. One vivid exception: Jean-Honoré Aubert, who owed money to ten laboureurs, whom he sought out in their farms (in at least one case within the proscribed decommercialized zone, near Charenton) or met in the markets of Lizy, Rozoy, Mary, and Crécy, among others. Aubert usually made large purchases—between four and eight muids. He paid half immediately and the balance within two weeks.[36]

Perhaps because they were less aggressive and bought in smaller amounts, the Halle agents aroused less intense resentment than those of the port mer-

33. In addition to the forains cited as agents above, see, for example, Tollote of Arcis, Gombault of Troyes, Geoffrion of Nogent-sur-Seine who worked for one merchant, and Lemire of Arcis and Couchat of Meaux who worked for another. Archives Seine-Paris, D4B[6] 85-5740, 16 October 1786, and D4B[6] 50-3057, 3 February 1774. Like many Halle dealers, Gaillard preferred to rely on a relative, a brother-in-law at Vitry, despite the fact that he was a wool merchant with no experience in grain. Paris registration list, 1770–71, in Kaplan, *Bread, Politics and Political Economy*, 1:286–88.

34. See, for example, Raveau (Paris) v. Huette (St.-Florentin) and Lezarre (Provins) v. L. Martin (Paris). Archives Seine-Paris, D2B[6] 1078, 2 October 1769, and D2B[6] 809, 10 May 1747.

35. Ibid., D4B[6] 90–6204, 28 May 1784.

36. Ibid., D5B[6] 3282. Aubert purchased 15 muids from five different laboureurs on a single day in mid-1772 and he paid for them entirely by 12 June. One notation in Aubert's book indicates that he bought 26 muids at the Lizy market in a single day in July 1772—a staggering *enlèvement* likely to have caused consternation if it had been remarked, especially since the early seventies were troubled subsistence times.

chants. Still, the "abuses" denounced are familiar. Take the complaint of the lieutenant general of police of Chartres. He was willing to accord priority to Parisian agents over local buyers provided that they actually fulfilled their mission, but instead of shipping to the capital, these commissionnaires took their grain to Houdan, Gallardon, or Nogent-le-Roy, for regrating or hoarding, causing *cherté* in Chartres without combating it in Paris.[37] Poussot, the police inspector whose passion was the revitalization of the Halle, worried about the proliferation of agents, which he regarded as the major reason for the multiplication of abuses. "Everyone is getting involved in the commissionnaire trade," he lamented in 1760, which resulted in confusion and inefficiency as well as breaches of the law.[38] Their number was to increase further during the next two decades. Poussot's vision of a rationalization of the Halle commissionnaire traffic, wrought by administrative fiat rather than market arbitration, was never realized.

Most of the Halle merchants kept storehouses in the countryside, either in rented rooms of fruit vendors or inns or in the houses of their commissionnaires. Thirty-three of the forty-seven Paris-based merchants in the 1770–71 registry maintained such granaries. Seven dealers had stockrooms in three different market centers.[39] Many of the storehouses were located on the rivers. Despite municipal/Mortellerie pretensions, it seems certain that the Halle merchants transported their grain at least part of the way by water. Nicolas Joullain, commissionnaire of Halle merchants Meillet and Boyer, bought throughout the Champagne and then shipped on his own *margota* to within a few leagues of the capital.[40]

It is virtually impossible to estimate the contribution of the Paris-based Halle merchants to the provisioning of Paris. We have no idea of their number, save for a rapid, partial glance in 1770–71, a time of tremendous instability. Curiously, the Delalande provisioning registers, which supposedly recorded all merchant traffic, made no mention of the Paris-based dealers. According to them, the Halle was furnished exclusively by laboureurs, blatiers, and forains. Though the number of Halle dealers ordinarily residing in the capital may have been small in the twenties and thirties, it seems inconceivable that their supply was too meager to be worth mentioning. Were certain Halle traders ignored because they bypassed brokers and were thus in some way indistinguishable from most laboureurs or blatiers? (Presumably the greater size of their supply would betray them, but their weekly contributions varied considerably, and the range of laboureur–blatier provision was prodigious.) Could a number of Halle dealers have been conflated with the forains because they possessed residences in the country as well as in the

37. Leblanc to Hérault, 4 October 1726, Arsenal, ms. Bast. 10270.
38. Arsenal, ms. Bast. 10141, fol. 326 (10 March 1760).
39. Kaplan, *Bread, Politics and Political Economy,* 1:286.
40. Archives Seine-Paris, D4B⁶ 73-4846, 26 August 1779.

capital? Such confusion might have been compounded by the fact that certain self-styled forains actually had their primary residence in the capital.[41] Were some Paris merchants counted indirectly through their commissionnaires who appeared in the records as country dealers under their own names instead of as purchasing agents? Were some excluded from enumeration because their own provision was mingled with the grain they received in behalf of forains for whom they acted as brokers?[42] Is it possible that until the Paris police launched the campaign to revalorize the Halle the soi-disant Halle dealers preferred to avoid the selling-floor of the marketplace *(carreau)* and to deliver directly to the bakers (en droiture)?

Business Failures of Halle-based Merchants

Because he was both a resounding success and a failure, Nicolas-Louis Martin, one of the foremost Halle dealers in the thirties and forties, stands out from the others. We first encounter him in 1720 at the age of twenty-five, on the eve of his marriage. He lived with his father, a merchant grainier, on the rue Montorgueil, in the shadow of the Halle. Along with his brother Pierre and his sister Marie-Angélique, he followed in his father's professional footsteps, acquiring a mastership as grainier. Two other sisters married Paris master bakers, thereby providing Nicolas with two of his earliest clients when he gravitated from the lesser cereals toward wheat. Nicolas married the eighteen-year-old daughter of another merchant grainier. His father-in-law's connections included a police commissaire who would later sponsor Martin's efforts to win various contracts and places. The couple's marriage fortune was comfortable by artisan and petty merchant standards, but it hardly represented a dramatic forward thrust. The bride's dowry amounted to 3,000 livres; 2,500 was in cash. The groom contributed the same amount, in a mélange of cash, merchandise, and furniture.[43] Because his marriage portion represented an advance on his inheritance, Martin did not receive a great deal when his father died in 1733. The estate was modest in any event, consisting of a house (not evaluated), an annuity worth 8,000 livres in principal, a little over 1,000 livres in jewelry and silver, 1,668 livres in furniture and effects, and 191 livres in cash.[44]

By the mid-thirties, Martin had established a thriving and relatively diversified commerce. Assigning the management of the little cereals to his

---

41. See the case of the forain from the rue St.-Martin. Ibid., D2B⁶ 736, 28 April 1741.

42. In this instance I am thinking specifically of dealers such as Pierre-François Bouchery and Jean-François Aubry, who acted simultaneously as Halle-based grain merchants and factors for grain merchants frequenting the Halle. See the *scellé* of the widow Aubry, 12 November 1777, AN, Y 15387.

43. AN, MC, XCV-69, 8 September 1720.

44. AN, MC, LXX-303, 7 August 1733. By consensus of the five heirs, no inventory was undertaken.

wife, who had learned the business in her father's shop, he focused his energies on the wheat trade at the Halle, serving not only bakers but also the General Hospital, the Hôtel-Dieu, the Incurables, the Pitié, and Bicêtre, as well as several convents.[45]

One of his business registers gives us a fragmentary but vivid look at his trading activities from July 1738 through October 1745. In its columns, 311 transactions are recorded, involving 105 different buyers (all bakers)—a staggeringly large clientele artificially swelled by the exigencies of the dearth of 1739–41, one of the gravest of the century. During this period Martin marketed a large amount of king's grain, emergency provisions purchased more or less directly by the government, most of which arrived at the Ecole, and much of which was sold there as if it were the *carreau* of the Halle.[46] In 1739 alone he served 53 different bakers and his average monthly billings amounted to 11,570 livres, as opposed to 4,093 livres during the tranquil years 1744–45. In 1739 he averaged just under fifty muids of sales a month, whereas he barely disposed of thirty-two in 1744–45. While he had more than twice as many transactions in 1739 as in 1744–45, they were smaller, averaging a bit over three and a half muids against almost five. Not infrequently, both during and after the crisis, he sold bakers more than he was legally permitted in a single market day.[47] During this period Martin had dealings worth over a quarter of a million livres with Dubois of St.-Germain-en-Laye, 223,000 livres with Cleret and Thibault of Noyon, almost 200,000 livres with the Roost brothers of Rouen, and more than 100,000 livres with Lezard of Provins.[48] Between March 1742 and September 1744 Martin had 21,265 livres' worth of business with Jauvin the younger of the rue de la Mortellerie, probably for the provisioning of public assistance institutions.[49]

Martin's horizons expanded dramatically in the early forties. His attention shifted from the Beauce and the Brie to the Orléanais, the Touraine, the Atlantic, and the Mediterranean. He developed relations with prominent international traders and began speculating on occasion in goods other than grain. His accounting was for the most part meticulous: double-entry bookkeeping, supplemented by registers of receipts and orders.

Martin made a great deal of money in the forties and became known for his conspicuous consumption. However, he had little left by 1749 when, apparently as a result of ill-considered speculations and a certain impatience with

45. Archives Seine-Paris, D5B[6] 1902.

46. Exceptionally, during this time, Martin also sold at the Grève and St.-Nicolas port as well as at the Halle.

47. Archives Seine-Paris, D5B[6] 3118. In July 1738 and in December 1744 the average size of a single transaction was over 7 muids. Between July 1738 and October 1745 the price per setier ranged from a maximum of 38 livres to a minimum of 9 livres.

48. Archives Seine-Paris, D5B[6] 179 and 1902. Government-sponsored operations composed a significant part of these transactions.

49. Archives Seine-Paris, D5B[6] 179.

detail that had not handicapped him earlier in his career, he was forced into failure.[50] He showed assets of 32,510 livres, including a home in Paris (12,800 livres), a country residence (6,920 livres) and various furnishings (3,600 livres). He was served by a domestic, to whom he owed back wages. A little less than a third of his assets were paper: accounts receivable for grain furnished, half of them due by eleven bakers. Martin's liabilities rose to 36,148 livres, at least half of which was for grain he purchased from eleven merchants and one laboureur. The character of his other debts remains obscure. Martin attributed his difficulties to whopping losses of 55,200 livres, including 16,000 in unfortunate speculations, 11,600 from insolvent bakers, and 21,600 in litigation to recover other sums. For some reason, Martin's creditors were particularly ferocious. Their unwillingness to trust him impeded his recovery and their intransigence forced him to sell most of his furniture.[51] Yet somehow Martin extricated himself, for he became a grain factor in the early fifties and sought to extend his brokerage to flour at the end of the decade.

On paper Martin's failure seems to have been a relatively mild one. One fellow merchant had a negative net worth of 1,710 livres, but 77 percent of his assets were in paper (all accounts receivable for grain supplied, mostly to bakers). Mean liabilities for ten Halle failures amounted to 21,662 livres (median = 24,122). Almost three-quarters of this sum represented grain purchases; over 90 percent of these grain debts were owed to other grain merchants. Mean assets stood at 14,917 (median = 15,725). Seventy-five percent of these assets were in paper and only about half of the accounts receivable are documented grain debts. Thus, these Halle balance sheets reveal weak enterprises with surprisingly few hard assets. Seven of the merchants claimed losses, averaging 17,988 livres each (median = 10,700). They imputed their heaviest losses to unfavorable speculations.

Most of these merchants won reprieves. Aubert, for example, received approval for a repayment plan on installments.[52] Cession of property to creditors in some cases averted failure and in others accompanied it.[53] Auguste Caron is one of the rare grain merchants, Halle or ports, whom we find in debtor's prison.[54]

Successful Halle merchants did not live like princes, or even *grands bourgeois*. The well-to-do Dubuisson family, for example, on the rue de la

50. See Poussot's occasional remarks on Martin's rise and fall in Arsenal, ms. Bast. 10141.

51. Archives Seine-Paris, D5B⁶ 8403, 30 August 1749.

52. Archives Seine-Paris, DC⁶ 19, fol. 122, 22 September 1774, and AN, MC, LXXCIII-791, 22 September 1774. Eighteen creditors, to whom he owed 35,571 livres, agreed to accept 1,200 livres a month and to renounce interest on the sums due them.

53. For an example of the first sort, see Joseph Lesieur, Archives Seine-Paris, DC⁶ 19, fol. 149, 19 December 1774; for an instance of the second kind, see Aubert, ibid., fols. 79, 104, 208 (August 1774–May 1775).

54. Archives de la Préfecture de Police, La Force, AB 321, livre d'écrou, 27 March 1788.

Huchette, occupied a three-bedroom apartment located over a shop in which they conducted retail small-cereals sales. One bedroom contained a commode, one large and two small wardrobes, three chairs and an armchair, a bed, a carpet, a mirror, and a devotional painting in a gilded frame. The other two bedrooms were similarly furnished (including paintings of the virgin and of a saint). The kitchen was rather summarily equipped with two pantry closets, a sink, table and chairs, and unusually few utensils. Merchandise was stored in a granary above and a stable below.[55]

Business Failures of *Forain* Merchants

Twenty-four forains from throughout the supply crowns are among the grain dealers who failed. They possessed about a third fewer assets than the combined Parisian port and Halle contingent and about a third more than the laboureurs (average = 12,906 livres; median = 7,901 livres). Like the Parisians, the forains extended pratik credit rather liberally—they had to in order to sell. About 44 percent of their assets were in paper, the majority of it in accounts receivable for grain. Like the laboureurs, the forains boasted an average of 7,700 livres in hard assets. They possessed real estate worth on the average more than 4,500 livres. The mean value of their personal household effects was over 2,000 livres. The dealers from the Hurepoix and the Valois had over six muids of stock on hand.

The forains were crippled by heavy liabilities (average = 31,794 livres; median = 16,344 livres). Only a fourth of these debts can unequivocally be attributed to the purchase of grain. Our ignorance of the nature of the other accounts payable severely reduces our ability to pinpoint the forains' difficulties. These dealers invoked losses averaging 14,779 livres (median = 7,473). Over a fifth of the losses were imputed to destruction of matériel and merchandise (Pierre Hugot of Soissons lost 45,200 livres on the sinking of several grain boats). About 40 percent of the alleged losses resulted from speculative disappointments (Claude Martinet of Arcis-sur-Aube suffered losses of 53,597 livres in this rubric). On the average the forains had a deficit of 19,069 livres to make up (median = 7,307). They tried hard, and in almost every case with success, to persuade their creditors to show understanding. "I am not a dissipater," Pierre Gayand of Picardy passionately affirmed. He begged for time to right his situation (a negative net worth of 8,101 livres), and had the courage, despite his vulnerability, to contest the validity of the claims of several creditors.[56] Forain Aubie of Presles asked for a two-year moratorium on all payments, Longpré of Belleville the same moratorium plus seven years to pay, and Regnard-Lesourd of Crécy a ten-

55. AN, Y 15052, 22 April 1748.
56. Archives Seine-Paris, D4B⁶ 52-3196, 23 June 1774.

year moratorium and a 50 percent forgiving of principal, interest, and expenses.[57]

The forains shouldering the heaviest debts came from the Valois (43,481 livres); those bearing the lightest obligations lived in the Beauce (7,398 livres). The Hurepoix dealers marshaled the greatest assets (26,103 livres), while the Beauce forains held the record for the least (6,096 livres). The Briards suffered the greatest misfortunes: losses averaging 12,923 livres. The forains from the Gâtinais (947 livres), the Beauce (1,302 livres), and the Ile-de-France (1,829 livres) had the smallest deficits to bridge, while those from the Valois (18,255 livres) and the Brie (14,060 livres) had the most gaping debit balances.

Forain and *Laboureur* Grain Supply

The Delalande registers are the only sources that offer any clues at all to the magnitude of forain supply. In the tables devoted to the grain trade at the Halle we need to worry not so much about the figures (though they probably underestimate total supply) as the labels. We have already posed the problem of the absence of the Paris-based merchants. In addition, it seems likely that the forains and certain laboureurs, as well as a number of blatiers, were often conflated. The reason is relatively simple: in many ways they resembled each other. The earliest registers extant, covering the dearth years 1725 and 1726, went to considerable lengths to disaggregate them, but failed to follow identical procedures. Nor do we know how the dearth conditions distorted the ordinary pattern of provisioning or the habitual methods of bookkeeping.

In 1725 many laboureurs—we cannot fix their number precisely—marketed their grain through brokers (though that does not necessarily mean that they did not personally assist in the sale at the Halle).[58] They brought a total of 700 muids. Their per capita provision seems to have been significantly below that of the forains (designated as country merchants). The average annual supply of thirty laboureurs who are individually enumerated was 17 muids (as was the mean supply of sixty-nine laboureurs eschewing brokerage), while fifty-four forains shipped 44 muids each. Fifteen laboureurs managed by broker Sevin averaged 16.3 muids; broker Denise's seven laboureurs averaged 14.4 muids; broker Blot's three laboureurs averaged 7 muids. Broker Duchateau's five laboureurs registered a more imposing 31 muids, while his seven country merchants averaged a mammoth 182 muids.

57. Ibid., D4B⁶ 93-6425, 23 March 1775; D4B⁶ 48-2869, 5 July 1773; D4B⁶ 36-1967, 2 January 1770.

58. Why laboureurs paid a brokerage fee when they themselves were present is unclear. Perhaps they did not want to become involved either in the haggling or in the collection of monies due.

Duchateau prided himself on handling the forain elite; in a single month his client Massot of Chartres supplied twice the quantity of grain that a laboureur averaged in a whole year. Broker Martin's eight forains offered far more modest perspectives, but a mean provision of 58 muids a year was still a strong performance. The combined provision of factored and unfactored laboureurs represented 30 percent of the total Halle grain supply in 1725. The forains accounted for a quarter of this supply. An indeterminate number of blatiers contributed 8 percent. The balance was the product of "extraordinary" efforts (requisitions from the convent-hospital-school granary network and from various parishes and generalities).

In the 1726 register the brokers are specialized by type of client: six brokers handled all forty-four forains while thirteen brokers shared 111 "plus" laboureurs.[59] Unlike the 1725 register or the ones that followed, the 1726 recordbook presumes that all laboureurs were factored and that they were nevertheless present at the sale. All nonfactored provision (3,485 muids, or 38 percent) is imputed to blatiers. I have no doubt that this swollen and undifferentiated blatier category embraces laboureurs and perhaps forains. On the average forains supplied twice as much grain in the year as laboureurs: 42.7 versus 22.4 muids (the latter figure somewhat bloated by the uncounted presence of unenumerated laboureurs— the "plus" invoked above). The leading forain dealers were a trio from Chartres, including Massot, the 1725 champion, Puissant, and L'Eveque, each of whom supplied 4 muids a week. Only three laboureurs, from Rungis and Sarclay, averaged as much as a single muid a week. The forains provided in all slightly over a fifth of the total supply; the laboureurs accounted for 27.3 percent.

Beginning in 1727 entry style becomes standardized. There is no longer any enumeration of laboureurs, either by name or number or per capita contribution. There is a combined rubric for laboureurs and "little merchants," presumably blatiers but perhaps also marginal or part-time forains. A small number of laboureurs used brokers, but the great majority did without. The bulk of forains are cited individually under their brokers. An inappreciable number of forains employing brokers are listed as a group, like the laboureurs. Since they are so elusive and never represent more than 5 percent of the Halle provision, they do not figure in our discussion. Nor does grain of "extraordinary" provenance—that is, emanating from sources of supply outside the usual provisioning system (king's grain and local requisitions).

Table 9 shows the relative contribution of forains and laboureurs according to the categories and entries of the register. There is certainly some conflation, but it is impossible to determine how much. We know, for example, that a half-dozen suppliers listed as laboureurs under broker Va in 1726 are identified as merchants in 1727. It is hardly likely that they changed

---

59. "Plus" is used to cover the occasional entries that denote "several different laboureurs" without specifying their number or per capita provision.

TABLE 9

Supply furnished by *forains* and *laboureurs* to the Halle, 1727–33 (in muids)

Year	Provision of forains	Number of forains	Average per forain	Provision of factored laboureurs	Provision of other laboureurs	% forain of total supply	% laboureur of total supply
1727	4,389	131	33.5	702	3,540	48.4	46.7
1728	3,820	93	41.0	596	5,021	38.8	56.9
1729	3,957	99	40.0	936	4,170	42.1	54.3
1730	3,973	67	56.6	574	3,489	47.0	48.0
1731	4,224	79	53.4	875	2,332	51.6	39.0
1732	2,058	67	30.7	495	5,501	25.3	73.5
1733	1,140	27	42.2	918	5,071	16.0	84.0

profession or mode of operation in the course of a year. It is possible that they had always been forains and that they were erroneously amalgamated with the laboureurs. But it is also plausible that they were laboureurs in 1726 and remained so in 1727, despite the change in rubric. The unabated decline in the number of forains and the startling erosion in forain supply following 1731 are puzzles that may reveal themselves as recordkeeping artifacts. Perhaps certain forains lost interest in the grain trade during the easy times following the crisis of 1725–26. They could have turned to other occupations or other markets, whereas in some ways the laboureurs of the decommercialized zone had no choice but to come to Paris. On the other hand it is conceivable that the forain contribution was normally 20 to 25 percent (as the 1725–26 registers suggest—but can one confidently extrapolate "normal" functions in the midst of a profoundly disorganizing dearth?) and that the number rose subsequently as a consequence of category confusion (the "cooptation" of numbers of laboureurs into forain ranks?). Yet if laboureurs were insinuated into the forain camp beginning in 1727, why were they suddenly purged after 1731? Much of this, alas, is likely to remain a mystery. Even if certain of the figures are considered suspect, it is still clear that the Halle depended much more heavily than we have been inclined to imagine on the mass of petty suppliers worth a few setiers a week. Given their importance, it is no wonder that the authorities tried, through a mixture of incentives and constraints, to keep them coming to Paris.

A Profile of *Forain* Business

The forains performed impressively, supplying between 7 and 13 setiers a week, a quantity well above the capacity that contemporaries ascribed to most laboureurs. (If laboureurs infiltrated the merchant category in substantial numbers, they undoubtedly depressed the figure for mean forain provisions.) Of course a handful of forains managed barely 3 setiers a week (perhaps these were the hidden laboureurs). But the strongest merchants more than compensated. In 1730, when Delu vindicated his image as the paramount Mortellerie dealer by furnishing 900 muids at the Grève, two forain merchants from Chartres more or less inconspicuously supplied 832 and 769 muids respectively. For a period of seven years beginning in 1727, Desrues, one of the two Chartrain pillars, sustained a mean provision of 513 muids a year, or over 118 setiers a week.

There were on the average between five and six women among the forains, the majority widows continuing a family business. They supplied almost as much as the men. An unmarried woman from Chartres was among the leading suppliers for several years, averaging almost 58 setiers a week.

The forains appear to have had more habitual sources of supply than the

Paris merchants, judging from the faillite records. On the average each of the forains purchased from five laboureurs and eight grain merchants (as opposed to three and seven respectively for the entire Paris-based contingent). Jean-Louis Lesourd of Rebais reported debts to twenty-one merchants. Louis-Charles Beauvais owed money to sixteen merchants and ten laboureurs. It is impossible to say whether these merchant-sellers were blatiers, forains, or local traders. The large number of (ostensibly nonproducer) intermediaries suggests a highly fragmented commerce, but probably one located more in the marketplaces and less in the interstices of the countryside than often imagined. Yet, since the incidence of failures quickened sharply after 1770, the large number of suppliers may reflect the proliferation of "new men."

The forain trade remained almost exclusively artisanal. Only two of the forains on the Meaux registration list and four *faillis* were associated with other grain dealers in their day-to-day operations. This "individualism" bespoke not merely the long-standing bias of the police against "societies," but also a preference among traders for functioning autonomously. Association appears to be as often the fruit of distress or dislocation as the product of enterprise or vision. The relative lack of association was one of the reasons for the underdevelopment of the grain trade (as it was understood, say, by the physiocrats).[60] The very structure and technology of the trade acted as disincentives to association. The handful of associated traders sport twice the assets of other failed merchants but are also burdened by twice the liabilities, and they adduce three times the losses, almost two-thirds of which resulted from hapless speculations. Most forain operations appear to have been family run and to have been limited in geographical scope and commercial ambition. The opening up of the trade in the sixties may have accentuated (a return to) the familial character of the business, for there is some indication that forains attempted to bypass factorage and entrust sales at the Halle to their wives, children, or servants in the last two decades of the old regime.[61]

I have found only one forward-looking forain who began to trade in flour as well as in grain, though I am sure there were many more. (Diversification in the other direction, from flour to grain, was more common, as we shall see.) A number of forains either invested in or inherited cereal-growing lands and were thus able to market some of their own produce, thereby becoming laboureurs in part and theoretically jeopardizing their merchant status, that is, their right to buy as well as to sell grain.

One reason why forains may have been confused with laboureurs and blatiers is that some of them had rather unsophisticated business habits. Jean Rochery of Montmorency never kept any record of his commerce "since [he]

60. Yet almost 10 percent of the fifty-eight traders enrolled at Maubeuge in 1770–71 were associated with other traders. Kaplan, *Bread, Politics and Political Economy*, 1:292.

61. Still, twenty-three forains on the Meaux register indicated that they were factored. No such data appear on the Parisian list. Ibid., 1:291.

always bought in the markets"—as if that were pertinent.[62] Similarly, Louis Colin of Marcilly-sur-Seine insisted that forains "never keep books." He could not in any case, he added, for he knew neither how to read nor write.[63]

The range of fortune of forains was as sweeping as the variation in their provision. Vinot owned two houses, several parcels of arable and vineyard, and a number of annuities; Louis Antoine of Châteaudun had to share a rooming-house bed with two other clients when business called him to the Halle.[64]

The *Laboureurs* and the Grain Trade

The police counted heavily on the laboureurs to supply the market regularly. Indeed, the authorities drafted the grain-trade regulations specifically in order to mobilize the laboureurs. The decommercialization of the *plat pays* within a day's journey of the capital and the ban on selling or purchasing in the farms and granaries were meant to compel the laboureurs to bring their grain to the Paris market. Anxious to return home quickly, it was argued, they would "relax" on the price more readily than other merchants. The laboureurs, selling without intermediaries, would theoretically show greater flexibility on the price than merchants dependent on brokerage for both buying and selling. As far as the Paris police were concerned, laboureurs living beyond the buffer zone could sell at their homes, provided they sold exclusively to "merchants for the provisioning of Paris," the only dealers empowered to buy off the market. Fearful that such latitude would result in the withering away of their markets, the local authorities looked on the laboureur–Paris connection with less enthusiasm. Regardless of their location, laboureurs were under no circumstances considered grain merchants. In fact, to the extent that such a commerce implied buying and not just selling they were expressly forbidden from engaging in the grain trade.[65]

Laboureur Maneuvers: Buying and Hoarding

The "maneuvers" of the laboureurs differed little from those imputed to other grain suppliers: their paramount aim was a better price, to achieve

62. Archives Seine-Paris, D4B⁶ 43-2431, 18 January 1772.

63. Archives Seine-Paris, D4B⁶ 97-6766, 2 September 1786. Twenty percent of the forains on the Paris register of 1770–71 could not sign. Kaplan, *Bread, Politics and Political Economy,* 1:287.

64. Arsenal, ms. Bast. 10047, pièces 306–8, 15 February 1758. Cf. the case of J.-B. Gauthier of Ruelle, whose flourishing business foundered as a result of wine, women, and gambling. Among his wife's complaints were that he dissipated her dowry and infected her with venereal disease. He ended up in Fort-Lévêque for an unpaid debt of 1,000 livres. AN, Y 11570, 18 November 1754.

65. See BN, Coll. Joly 1312, fol. 117.

which they used many different techniques. The least subtle was to buy for the purpose of more or less immediate reselling or hoarding. A laboureur named Thisaine "buys left and right, even in the markets, it is said that he has 20 muids in his granary," reported the commandant of the Bourg-la-Reine constabulary brigade.[66] On his way home from the Halle, as if to compensate himself for what he had furnished the capital, a laboureur from Villeroy bought grain wherever he could at a price as much as 25 percent above the current. "It is surprising," concluded the Bondy brigade commandant, "that one of the biggest fermiers in this entire region, who has supplied the Halle with prodigious amounts of old wheat in recent times, would now undertake to starve the country."[67]

In 1739 laboureurs at Dourdan, Etampes, Montlhéry, Auneau, Rambouillet, and elsewhere were reported buying on and off the market. Some bought more or less surreptitiously; others claimed that they were buyers for hospitals or colleges or alleged that they had commissions from the lieutenant general of police of Paris.[68] A laboureur from the outskirts of Paris who purchased 5 setiers of wheat on the Grève and then tried to sell it at a profit of 2 livres per setier at the Halle was jailed and fined.[69] Audouin, a laboureur at St.-Maurice, also bought grain in Paris, but for the purpose of reselling it at Montlhéry.[70] A laboureur named Vermois had a miller pick up the grain he purchased at the Halle to cover his illicit purchase.[71]

The most common pretext for laboureur buying was the need for seed. In most places, however, the authorities required laboureurs to replenish the market by replacing the elite seed grain they purchased with an equal amount of grain, or in some cases, with double the quantity. At Etampes in the fall of 1738 a number of laboureurs aroused suspicion not merely because they

66. To Hérault, 8 October 1725, Arsenal, ms. Bast. 10270, fol. 206.

67. Huery to Hérault, 5 October 1725, ibid., fols. 239–40. Note the quasi-famine plot rhetoric. See similar complaints of laboureurs buying at Meaux, Dourdan, and Auneau in 1725–26. Marchais to Hérault, 1 December 1725, ibid., ms. Bast. 10271, and 7 January 1726, ms. Bast. 10272.

68. Lanson to procurator general, 9 December 1738, BN, Coll. Joly 1119, fols. 53–54; Defacq to lieutenant general, 18 October 1738, ibid., fol. 407; Odile to procurator general, 19 October 1738, ibid., fols. 108–9. See also the aspersive attack on grain maneuvers by bourgeois and by market officials as well as by laboureurs in Hubert to Hérault, 27 October 1725, Arsenal, ms. Bast. 10275.

69. Assembly of police, 30 June 1740, BN, ms. fr. 11356, fols. 415–16; AN, Y 11227, 25 May 1740. It is interesting to note that this laboureur was denounced by two bakers who immediately recognized the wheat as port grain. The senior official at the port, a measurer named Buignet, claimed that there had been too many persons on the Grève for him to have picked out the laboureurs. Apparently only the long-festering jurisdictional quarrel between the Hôtel de Ville and the Châtelet saved the laboureur from a criminal trial.

70. AN, Y 9441, 8 July 1740. He was fined 1,000 livres.

71. An ostensibly innocent admission in a commercial suit, arbitre letter, 3 March 1742, Archives Seine-Paris, D6B6, carton 2.

brought no replacement grain but because they bought such large amounts for seed.[72]

It was presumed that the laboureur who purchased grain was either a regrater—(a short-term hoarder)—or a hoarder (a regrater with means and patience for grander speculation). Laboureur hoarding was regarded as particularly insidious. The laboureur could easily mask his illicit holdings as seed or domestic consumption reserve or dues and fees collection or as old grain from his own arable. Less spectacular than merchant hoarding, and therefore more effective, laboureur hoarding was nevertheless the object of incessant police investigation. Many police "visits" were inspired by anonymous denunciations that rarely produced convictions, but that helped to allay consumer anxieties and to keep laboureurs off balance. One fiery letter addressed to the Paris police chief in 1740 inveighed against "these republican fermiers" who "had the audacity to say that their grain would not surface in the markets till the setier reached sixty livres." ("Republican" avarice was indifferent to the imperatives of the moral economy.)[73] In the Brie during the sixties the laboureurs became "as rich as the big financiers" by amassing large hoards, selling clandestinely and in great lots, and replenishing their stocks with purchases made on and off the market.[74] Several years later in Champagne laboureurs sold their crops before the harvest, soliciting earnest money in return for keeping their grain off the market and hoarding for their own speculative account.[75]

The public relished stories of unrequited greed, such as that of the rich Gonesse laboureur who prayed that the bitter cold of the winter of 1739–40 would destroy all the wheat in the ground, "thereby enabling him to make a fortune" on the old grain that his granaries and barns regorged. He was cast into profound despair when he discovered that the wheat was alive and well beneath the frozen soil. To this "punishment of God" the police added the retribution of man by requisitioning all of his stored treasure.[76]

Hoarding created a psychological climate of malaise and disarray, adding indirectly to the upward price pressure generated directly by the reduction of available supplies. Some laboureurs took the psychological assault one step further by openly articulating a pessimistic assessment of things. Another Gonesse laboureur refused to honor a bargain he had made with a baker two weeks earlier, declaring that he would hold the wheat rather than sell, for the

72. AN, Y 11225, 25 October 1738; BN, Coll. Joly 1119, fols. 4–7, October 1738.

73. BN, Coll. Joly 1122, fol. 95, ca. October–November 1740. For examples of the mini-witch-hunts triggered by denunciations of hoarding, see ibid., fols. 69, 71, 74, 76, 78, 80; Guimard to d'Angervilliers, 6 August 1725, and d'Angervilliers to procurator general, 8 August 1725, BN, Coll. Joly 1117, fols. 70–71.

74. Bouquigny to procurator general, 1 April 1769, BN, Coll. Joly 1146, fols. 150–51.

75. Paillot to intendant of Champagne, 23 October 1773, AD Aube, C 1179.

76. Arsenal, ms. Bast. 10167, fol. 58 (15–16 March 1740).

price was high at nearby markets and was bound to force up the local *mer-curiale* imminently. The police indicted him for "seditious discourse . . . tending to alarm the public, cause an uprising and drive up the price of grain and of bread," and fined him 2,000 livres.[77]

For publicly betting a baker that prices would rise by one pistolle each market day in the coming weeks, a laboureur at Dammartin was fined 120 livres. Such talk, reasoned the judge, constituted a self-fulfilling prophecy and could not be allowed to affect both the attitudes of traders and consumers and the making of prices.[78] Two big laboureurs with substantial reserves took advantage of a series of heavy rainstorms on the eve of the 1727 harvest to cut back drastically on their supply. To coax the price up, they went to the Halles empty-handed and began to spread the word among the bakers "that most of the wheat in the ground had lodged and that as a result the harvest would not be favorable." They were fined 1,000 livres and threatened with jail if they allowed further vent to "their evil and sordid interest."[79]

Laboureur Maneuvers: Off-market Transactions

In order to escape detection and obtain the highest possible price, laboureurs often transacted business outside the markets in circumstances permitted by neither regulations nor convention. They made their deals in taverns or in the houses or shops of friends or intermediaries. They spared themselves the cost and onus of transporting the merchandise by selling "on samples" that they kept in leather pouches attached to their belts. They arranged for the buyer to pick up the grain immediately or they agreed to store it indefinitely. These practices dried up markets, drove up prices, and generated anxiety.[80] Off-market dealings culminating in the capital most often took the form of sale and delivery en droiture—declaring at the city gates that

---

77. AN, Y 9499, 22 July 1740. See also Des Essarts, *Dictionnaire universel de police,* 1:234. It was not unusual for laboureurs to insist on a price considerably above the current and to leave the market rather than cede a sou. The laboureurs felt that they fulfilled their responsibilities simply by coming to market, whereas the police regarded their obduracy as a form of monopoly. See Cleret's complaint to Hérault, 7 October 1725, Arsenal, ms. Bast. 10270, p. 197. On the serious penalties that recalcitrant laboureurs could incur, see L.-E.-Alphonse Jobez, *La France sous Louis XV, 1715–1774* (Paris, 1864–73), 3:170–71.

78. Ganneron to lieutenant general, 29 October 1725, Arsenal, ms. Bast. 10271.

79. BN, ms. fr. 21633, fols. 283–84 (28 June 1727).

80. Cleret (Poissy, St.-Germain, Mantes, Meulan) to lieutenant general, 1 December 1725, Arsenal, ms. Bast. 10271; reports, ca. May 1726, ms. Bast. 10273; Ganneron (Dammartin) to lieutenant general, 6 May 1726, ibid.; police sentence, 23 May 1726, BN, ms. fr. 21633, fols. 281–82 (laboureur Pasquier fined 1,000 livres for a sale on sample at Montlhéry); Garnier (Corbeil) to procurator general, 22 August 1740, BN, Coll. Joly 1123, fol. 261; Tappin (Bray) to procurator general, 10 December 1740, BN, Coll. Joly 1119, fols. 88–89; Le Roy (Etampes) to lieutenant general, 26 October 1738, Arsenal, ms. Bast. 10275; BN, Coll. Joly 1119, fols. 4–7 (Etampes, October 1738); Poix (Crécy-en-Brie) to procurator general, 9 December 1738, BN, Coll. Joly 1119, fols. 104–5; Coll. Joly 1111, fol. 236 (Etampes, 1788).

the shipment was destined for sale at the Halle, the laboureur detoured instead to the home or shop of a buyer with whom he had concluded the deal previously in Paris or in the countryside. If he was caught by the patrolling grain measurer or porter, the laboureur risked the loss of his merchandise and/or other penalties.[81]

Laboureur Boycotts

Less brazen than buying up supplies and less cunning than maneuvering in the shadows of the market was the inclination simply to stay at home and wait when the market did not seem sufficiently attractive. In the Crécy-en-Brie area in the late fall of 1738, laboureurs passed up the market "in the hope of stimulating a price rise." The procurator fiscal characterized this boycott as "a monopoly."[82] Similarly, the laboureurs around Beaumont tried to create the impression of shortage in the spring of 1740 by "hiding" on their farms.[83] Authorities marveled and raged at the obstinacy with which the laboureurs shunned the markets.[84] Paris officials were concerned about the domino effect of laboureur boycotts. President Lambert fretted about a "cabal" of Brie laboureurs in June 1726 "because once the prices have risen in the markets around Paris, it will be very difficult to contain the merchants in our ports."[85] The laboureurs' excuse for all seasons when called upon to explain their market absences was the exigencies of cultivation and husbandry: harvest and planting in the summer and fall, spring planting, preparation of lambs for sale at Easter, hay cutting in June, conditioning and redemption of fallow.[86]

In relatively easy times laboureur boycotts had little impact and provoked only occasional repressive action. But in a time of dearth or feared dearth, boycott was no longer a passive caprice but an act of aggression against society, and those who failed to furnish the markets faced stiff penalties. Carefully distinguished from the "merchants" for most purposes, the laboureurs resembled them to the extent that they were "expected" when called upon to meet their "obligations." In the fall of 1738, at the beginning of a protracted period of subsistence difficulties, fourteen laboureurs from the nearby supply crown—Presles, L'Isle-Adam, Massy, Orly, Poissy, Senlis, Gonesse—were indicted for discontinuing their provision. Of the nine con-

81. See, for instance, AN, Y 9538, 15 June 1725; Y 9621, 9 and 16 July 1751.
82. Ozoix to procurator general, 9 December 1738, BN, Coll. Joly 1119, fols. 104–5.
83. Reddeville to procurator general, 30 May 1740, and Pique to procurator general, 8 July 1740, BN, Coll. Joly 1123, fols. 47, 52.
84. Missonnet to procurator general, 24 March 1752, BN, Coll. Joly 1112, fol. 70; Missonnet report, 26 May 1756, Coll. Joly 1113, fol. 23; intendant to controller-general, 6 July 1757, AD Oise, C 316.
85. Lambert to Hérault, 4 June 1725, Arsenal, ms. Bast. 10002.
86. See Duplessis to Hérault, 30 June 1727, ibid., ms. Bast. 10274; Missonnet reports, 15–16, 22–23 October 1751, BN, Coll. Joly 1112, fols. 12, 14–15.

victed, eight faced fines of 500 livres and one a fine of 3,000 livres, payable
within forty-eight hours on pain of incarceration.[87] In February of 1740, with
the shortage worse than ever, eight laboureurs who normally furnished
Gonesse, considered to be an extension of the Paris market, were fined sums
ranging from 100 to 1,500 livres for the same offense.[88] In the course of two
weeks in July the police arraigned thirty-three laboureurs for failing to supply;
most of them paid heavy fines.[89] In cases of "monopoly," warned the police,
laboureurs would face corporal punishment in addition to fines.[90]

Visits, Inventories, Quotas, and Requisitions

During the crises of 1725 and 1740, the Paris police, in cooperation with
the intendants of the surrounding generalities, vigorously sought to expose
the recalcitrant laboureurs by conducting "domiciliary visits," ordering inventories of all stored grain, and rewarding denunciations.[91] On both occasions, the authorities began by trying to "excite" the laboureurs to meet their
responsibilities. Quickly, however, the policy of discretion had to give way to
one of "authority."[92] Nor did the police remain content to punish the
laboureurs who went into hiding. The authorities imposed quotas as well as
fines.[93] Village leaders—syndics and parish officers—were obliged to pledge
in writing to provide a certain number of setiers each week.[94] On 26 August

87. AN, Y 9939, 11 October 1738. As in most such cases, we do not know whether the
fines were in fact collected. Even in symbolic terms it remains very difficult for us to
determine the significance of the fining system.

88. AN, Y 9441, 15 February 1740. The prohibition against discontinued service applied
to the intramural Paris markets and to "nearby markets" as well.

89. Ibid., 8, 15, 22 July 1740. The Farou brothers from La Chapelle and Senlis were
exonerated once they demonstrated that they held no land and were simple blatiers who
could not reasonably be held accountable for regular supply.

90. Ibid., 8 July 1740.

91. See, for example, Arsenal, ms. Bast. 10141, fol. 261 (16 October 1759); ms. Bast.
10167, fols. 136, 146 (19–20, 26–27 September 1725); ms. Bast. 10275 (October 1728); ms.
Bast. 10277 (1738–39); Narbonne, *Louis XIV et Louis XV,* p. 137. Cf. the grain censuses
ordered in the Orléanais, HH 1, Archives communales d'Orléans, in Paul Veyrier du Muraud
et al., eds., *Inventaire sommaire des archives communales antérieures à 1790* (Orléans,
1907).

92. Assembly of police, August and September 1725, BN, Coll. Joly 1117, fols. 28, 53;
AN, O¹ 383, fols. 239, 22 August 1738 and fols. 283–84, 29 September 1738. Cf. the evidence
of "forced" laboureur supply in Bibliothèque de l'Institut, ms. 513.

93. In 1725 many laboureurs apparently complained that they were prevented from
supplying the market on order of lieutenant of police Ombreval, protégé and protector of
Madame de Prie. See Marion to procurator general, 22 September 1725, BN, Coll. Joly 1117,
fol. 239. Similar charges were leveled in 1740. Barbier, *Journal de Barbier,* 3:224 (October
1740). These accusations are manifestations of the famine plot persuasion. See Kaplan,
Famine Plot.

94. During both crises local police in the zone markets urged Parisian and royal officials
to "constrain" the laboureurs to supply. Ganneron (Dammartin) to lieutenant general, 7
February 1726, Arsenal, ms. Bast. 10272; Couvoy (La Ferté-sous-Jouarre) to procurator

1726 the syndics of the parish of Gennevilliers and six laboureurs promised "on behalf of the remainder of the inhabitants" to supply the Halle with 17.5 setiers of grain each week, to be verified by the commissaire "as if it were a royal affair." The fiscal procurator and the parish officers of Clichy-la-Garenne, speaking for the whole parish, guaranteed 30 setiers.[95] In other instances individuals rather than collectivities solemnly engaged themselves.[96] Five villages near Nemours had to be prodded to subscribe by an exempt who combined exhortation with searches and threats.[97]

In September 1740 an ordinance of the intendant enjoined all laboureurs (as well as others "holding" grain as owners, receivers or fermiers) to send one-sixth of all their old grain to market each week (allowance made for a six-week domestic subsistence reserve) along with 2 setiers of new grain for each *charrue* farmed. Syndics were to draw up lists of all those holding grain in the parish, indicating the number of *charrues* involved, "on pain of jail for failure to comply or for inaccuracy."[98] Apparently some effort was made to enforce the quotas, for laboureurs and fermiers, and their protectors, protested vehemently that they could not thresh fast enough or that they had harvested too little. Eleven laboureurs in the election of Nemours—perhaps some of the same cultivators punished in 1725—were fined 300 livres apiece for failing to furnish the required stock.[99] At Montlhéry in 1725 a laboureur named Duvivier made up for the quota he had to supply by commissioning an agent to buy an equal amount secretly and to deliver it to his farm at night.[100] A laboureur at Beaumont went to even less trouble to satisfy (or defy) the quota. He simply bought on the market from other laboureurs and submitted this grain to the authorities as his portion.[101]

The Diversity of *Laboureurs*

There was enormous diversity among the laboureurs in wealth, type of exploitation, and range and style of business. Many were very small cul-

---

general, 1 September 1725, BN, Coll. Joly 1117, fol. 134; Poix (Crécy-en-Brie) to procurator general, 24 May 1740, BN, Coll. Joly 1123, fols. 275–76. The problem with "local" constraint, from the Parisian vantage point, was that it would necessarily encroach upon the business that the laboureurs did with Paris-bound chartered merchants.

95. Arsenal, ms. Bast. 10270, pièces 51–53.

96. See, for instance, the widow of Charenton posting 4 setiers. Ibid. (29 August 1726).

97. BN, Coll. Joly 1116, fol. 70.

98. Narbonne, *Louis XIV et Louis XV*, pp. 470–73; BN, Coll. Joly 1121, fols. 148–49. Cf. the quotas applied locally, informally and rather peremptorily, in the early fifties. Missonnet to procurator general, 4 June 1753, BN, Coll. Joly 1113, fols. 25–26.

99. BN, Coll. Joly 1121, fols. 148–49, 153, 159.

100. David to lieutenant general, 12 September 1725, Arsenal, ms. Bast. 10270. Duvivier was said to be so morbidly preoccupied with his profits that, when the price dipped momentarily right after the harvest of 1725, he tried to hang himself.

101. Doubleau to Hérault, 12 October 1725, ibid., pièce 237.

tivators who elsewhere in France could not have claimed the more or less exalted (and abused and misunderstood) title of laboureurs. Others, possessors of very large holdings, were veritable village notables and could convincingly boast the *qualité* of merchant. There were big fermiers whose manners and milieu were bourgeois and petty fermiers who rented a few parcels that were likely to elude them at the next lease renewal. A substantial number of laboureurs were *receveurs* of some kind or other, which gave them access to large amounts of grain.[102] Some laboureurs exercised several professions at once, like Bullot of Orville, who was also a carter, or like the bakers of the Gonesse-Dammartin area.[103] Some were sheltered by powerful lords, while others could count on neither patronage nor protection.[104] In terms of commercial motivation and constraint and social sphere, these laboureurs had rather little in common.

Aside from a craving to see prices rise, the only commercial trait all laboureurs seemed to share was an unwillingness to keep books. Indeed, this was their prerogative and one of the characteristics that distinguished them from grain merchants proper.[105] The large number of laboureurs who employed brokerage services in 1725 appears aberrant. It is plausible both that a substantial proportion of these suppliers were really forains and that the police required certain laboureurs to pass through brokerage as an extraordinary dearth-control measure. Later in the century one finds an occasional laboureur, such as Guillaume Gouillart, who used a broker.[106] A large majority, however, seem to have sold personally at the Halle, as they were theoretically required to do by the police regulations. Most Paris-bound laboureurs transported their grain by land in carts, but Louis François used a *coche d'eau* that he himself owned.[107] Toussaint Lamoureux of Vuisson conformed more or less to the Delamarist image of the *bon laboureur*. He furnished about a muid a week and he came faithfully.[108]

A growing number of laboureurs across the eighteenth century, however, seem to have followed the model of Langlois of Sonplainville, who shifted his

102. On *laboureur-receveurs,* see "Noms des laboureurs qui ont des greniers" (October 1738), Arsenal, ms. Bast. 10275.

103. Archives Seine-Paris, D4B⁶ 52-3196, 23 June 1774; Kaplan, *Bakers of Paris;* Claude Gindin, "Le Pain de Gonesse à la fin du dix-septième siècle," *Revue d'histoire moderne et contemporaine* 19 (July–September 1972): 414–34.

104. See the relations between président Le Peletier and his laboureurs. Le Peletier to procurator general, ca. 1728, BN, Coll. Joly 1119, fol. 127.

105. "I can submit neither business ledgers nor registers, not having kept any as I am a fermier-laboureur," wrote a cultivator from Villeneuve-St.-Georges. Archives Seine-Paris, D4B⁶ 35-1896, 29 July 1769.

106. AN, Y 12621, 9 November 1771. One of the chief motives for employing a broker was to spare oneself the burden of having to come to Paris. Yet Gouilliart frequently went to the Halle to "help" his broker sell.

107. Archives Seine-Paris, D4B⁶ 35-1896, 29 July 1769.

108. AN, Y 11237, 10 October 1750.

focus away from the land and toward the market, bought from other laboureurs throughout the Beauce, and maintained stocks, "trading, trading, trading."[109] Léon and Etienne Prot, father and son laboureurs from the Corbeil area, tried more or less unsuccessfully to run a farm and a rapidly expanding trading business. Heavily indebted to other laboureurs, grain merchants, and moneylenders, and victimized by bad luck issuing in heavy losses, they were obliged to file for failure.[110] Jean Vermois, a laboureur-entrepreneur at Monjoy, extended his commerce into flour sales.[111]

Laboureur Business Failures

Eight laboureurs are among the fifty merchants in our faillite study. All of them quite consciously appropriated the *qualité* of "marchand." Obviously extremely alert to the play of titles in old-regime society, Charles Simonet from the Brie labeled himself "laboureur et négociant en grains," despite the gaping incongruity between these two callings, as they were commonly understood.[112] Laboureur implied ownership of arable and direct production of grain, a status that gave these dealers certain commercial advantages and at the same time encumbered them as merchants in certain ways. For a few of our faillis, however, laboureur may have merely been a nostalgic evocation on the part of (ex-)peasants whose primary occupation was now trade and who bought as well as sold. Certain laboureurs were actually fermiers, who rented rather than owned land, but who shared the ethos of the laboureur corps and may have been even more acutely business-oriented.

Laboureurs failed for most of the same reasons as other merchants: bad luck (personal or professional), errant speculation, overextension, and faulty day-to-day management. They differed in one important respect: they were untroubled by debt collection problems, probably because they were loath to extend credit. (They did not have the same incentives to be liberal as most grain dealers.) Thus, the laboureurs had no accounts receivable in their assets column, while eighteen Paris merchants (Grève and Halle together) had an average of 5,771 livres (median = 4,530 livres) and twenty-four hinterland-based merchants had an average of 3,777 livres (median = 3,778 livres).[113] Over a quarter of laboureur assets consisted of grain stocks on hand—over six times the amount held by the Paris group and over four times the merchandise kept by the country dealers. The item of greatest value owned by the

---

109. Marchais to Hérault, January 1727, Arsenal, ms. Bast. 10274.

110. Archives Seine-Paris, D4B⁶ 70-4630, 10 February 1779.

111. Rapport arbitre, 3 March 1742, ibid., D6B⁶ carton 2.

112. Ibid., D4B⁶ 86-6089.

113. For an example of a laboureur who did have collection problems, see J. -B. Leduc of Villepinte, to the northeast of the capital (one of whose debtors was the stereotypical hoarder, a grain merchant-innkeeper). Ibid., D2B⁶ 754, 1 October 1742.

laboureurs was, predictably, real estate, 3,216 livres on the average (median = 0, testifying to the presence of land-owning fermiers in the laboureur group?). Mean total laboureur assets were barely half of Paris merchant assets and two-thirds of zone dealer assets. Still, the laboureurs, along with the country traders, boasted more physical assets (over 7,700 livres on the average (5,300 livres) than the Paris merchants (5,300 livres).

Heavy liabilities averaging almost 32,000 livres (median = 22,049 livres) sapped the position of the laboureurs. Whereas 70 percent of the liabilities of the combined Paris group (average = 26,952 livres, median = 22,071 livres) represented debts for grain purchases, only 20 percent of the laboureur accounts payable were for grain. They did not explain their other debts; it is not clear to what extent they were related to grain trading. To some degree they must have reflected the costs of agricultural exploitation and leases.

Commercial relations between laboureurs and grain merchants properly speaking were not strictly one way, as one is inclined to imagine. The balance sheets show that these laboureurs purchased grain not only from other laboureurs (on the average one per failli, amounting to a mean debt of 516 livres) but also from grain merchants (on the average six per failli for a mean debt of 2,540 livres).

If the laboureurs are to be believed, the key to their difficulty is to be found in their disastrous losses, averaging 21,629 livres (median = 19,786 livres), more than half again as great as the losses claimed by Paris- or zone-based dealers. The most important single rubric was material losses, averaging 4,883 livres. But how much credence can we give to Léon Prot of Corbeil, who attested to losses of 33,000 livres on various bad harvests and 10,000 livres as a result of the death of horses and cows? (Beside Prot's claims, Simonet's amounts of 9,000 and 4,000 livres for the same categories appear rather convincing.)[114] Other losses reflected litigation (1,000 livres), discounting (1,667 livres), spoilage (1,500 livres), inopportune grain speculations (1,983 livres), and insolvent baker clients (462 livres, another mark of laboureur credit niggardliness). Mean total losses claimed by the laboureurs were just slightly below their average net worth of minus 23,147 livres (median = minus 18,156 livres).

The *Blatier* and the Grain Trade

The blatier was perhaps the most elusive of the traders furnishing the Halle. Though he seemed to be ubiquitous, part of a protean swarm, he was the most transient, least steady, and ordinarily the paltriest of suppliers. He

---

114. Ibid., D4B[6] 70-4630 and 27-1446.

was both tolerated and mistrusted precisely because he was such a small dealer, a veritable peddlar who appeared to slither through the nooks and crannies of the provisioning structure and showed up more or less unexpectedly at this farm or that market. The socioeconomic function of the blatier was to buy up what others did not want or were unwilling to travel to obtain or were unaware of. One finds the blatier, or a parallel figure, in virtually every developing marketplace society. The "country higglers" play a crucial role in the Jamaican distribution system by transferring goods from remote rural areas to urban centers. In Morocco *arbitragers* perform a blatier-like role, as do the *viajeros* in Mexico.[115]

Information was the blatier's keenest need. If he knew where to go and when, he could succeed. The desire to cultivate reliable sources of information probably induced many Paris-area blatiers to follow several more or less fixed itineraries. Blatiers could not wander at will, for they had to avoid markets run by hostile officials or frequented by uncooperative sellers. An established circuit afforded not only useful social contacts, but also the opportunity for some temporary storage. Despite their reputation for (petty) adventure, most blatiers appear to have been rather risk averse (their perception of risk diminishing in response to the reassuring quality of their information). My guess is that the blatiers were much more regular in their commercial habits than their multiplicity, their incessant movement, and their shifty image led contemporaries to believe.

The blatier was the grain dealer personally most familiar to most Frenchmen. He was a *pauvre voiturier,* in the words of the intendant of Tours; he transported small amounts of grain on horseback or mule.[116] The blatier moved *de proche en proche:* at least this was the rationale invoked by local police here and there in order to justify the blatier role. Everything depended on the vantage point from which one observed the blatiers' movement. For the police to applaud, the blatiers had to be advancing *de proche en proche* in the right direction. Indeed, Parisian officials contemplated formally requiring blatiers to move exclusively *toward* the capital, on pain of corporal punishment, but finally abandoned the idea as unworkable.[117] On the way to Paris, or

115. Margaret Katzin, "The Business of Higglering in Jamaica," *Social and Economic Studies* 9 (September 1960): 299; Mintz, "The Jamaican Internal Market Pattern: Some Notes and Hypotheses," ibid., 4 (March 1955): 95–103; Beals, *The Peasant Marketing System of Oaxaca, Mexico;* Geertz, "Suq: The Bazaar Economy in Sefrou," in Geertz et al., *Meaning and Order in Moroccan Society,* pp. 188–89. See also Usher, *Grain Trade,* pp. 11, 167, whose impatience to view the blatiers as a sign of a kind of modernization I do not share.

116. "Mémoire," ca. 1774, AD Indre-et-Loire, C 94. The royal procurator at Roze in Picardy claimed that they sometimes used horse-drawn wagons, but they were much better known for walking a horse or mule. To procurator general, 18 September 1770, BN, Coll. Joly 1154, fol. 139.

117. BN, Coll. Joly 1116, fol. 279.

to Reims, they might "desolate" the market at Châlons-sur-Marne, or Arcis-sur-Aube.[118] A prudent blatier on the route, say, that crossed Montereau or Villeneuve, or Provins or Bray or Brie-Comte-Robert en route to Paris sold even as he bought, though he was careful to avoid the stigma of the regrater by not reselling in the same market grain that he purchased there.[119]

Market Pimps and Doctors of Adulteration

Writing in the early seventeenth century, the economist Montchrétien violently denounced the blatiers as "market pimps," "dubious maneuverers," "monopolists," and "insects who devoured all the substance and food of the people" and deserved to be "stamped out."[120] Almost a century later Delamare acknowledged that "the question of whether the blatier commerce was useful or dangerous to the public had once been much agitated." His conviction was that on balance the blatiers rendered considerable service: they brought grain to the cities which "would never have arrived otherwise" and they sold at a price below that of the laboureurs.[121] In fact the debate continued to rage. A contemporary of Delamare denounced the blatiers for roving like locusts, "running" the farms and the markets, buying without regard to local needs, regrating, and spreading rumors of *cherté* to enhance their profits.[122] Inspector Poussot called for their suppression in the middle of the eighteenth century on the grounds that they regrated, drove prices up, and depleted instead of enriching the Paris market supply.[123]

The blatiers were best known as doctors of adulteration. The *Code Duchesne* denounced their tactic of "mixing and falsifying grain" in order to make it appear to be of higher quality than it was and of wetting it in order to "repair" or freshen it, "to give it color and touch [*la main*]," and to swell its volume.[124] Blatiers were said to be masters at "capping the sack," that is, covering the mass of merchandise with a layer of first-quality grain to catch the eye and inspire quick confidence. In 1702 police sentences struck down blatiers Lenormand of Belloy and Charpentier of Essuiles for incorporating

118. Guillemin to procurator general, 4 October 1740, BN, Coll. Joly 1123, fol. 178; Missonnet report, 1 June 1753, Coll. Joly 1113, fol. 27.

119. BN, Coll. Joly 1112, fols. 5, 7 (17–18 September 1751), 11 (1–2 October 1751), 47 (21–22 January 1752).

120. Antoyne de Montchrétien, *L'Economie politique patronale, traité de l'oeconomie politique dédié en 1615 au Roy et à la Reyne mère du Roy,* ed. Théodore Funck-Brentano (Paris, 1889), pp. 258–59.

121. Delamare, *Traité de la police,* 2:618.

122. "Mémoire qui marque tous les désordres," BN, ms. fr. 21643, fol. 354. The writer contended that as many as four or five hundred horses and asses descended on a given market in the Paris supply zone.

123. Arsenal, ms. Bast. 10141.

124. Duchesne, *Code de la police,* p. 107.

"cut" and "mixed" wheat into their sacks.[125] So intimately were these practices identified with the blatiers—who were understandably interested in rehabilitating cheap grain—that they were known collectively by the verb *blatier* (or *blastrier* or *blatrer*).[126]

Parmentier turned the prestige of the nascent science of subsistence against the blatiers even as Montchrétien had turned the fire of nascent political economy on them: they were anachronisms and nuisances, they were cheaters, they dealt in inferior goods.[127] The Paris grain measurers inveighed against the blatiers for violating the law by making deliveries directly to the bakers (so-called droiture traffic: another effort on the blatiers' part to steal a march on the competition).[128] For the revolutionaries, blatier was virtually synonymous with hoarder and "remover" of grain.[129]

Despite their dubious reputation, the blatiers were not without defenders. The philosophe Chamousset infinitely preferred the risks of the atomization of the grain trade and of petty fraud to the peril of "capitalist" and "big company" monopoly. He urged protection for the "small men" willing to settle for "a small profit," echoing a view held by the intendant of Amiens in the early seventies.[130] The subdelegate stationed at Troyes did not worry about the maneuvers of the blatiers, because they lacked "the capital" to cause real trouble.[131] Officials in the major hinterland markets tended to share the pragmatism of the lieutenant of police of Etampes: "The blatier trade is not authorized, but neither is it prohibited, [for] it is sometimes quite useful."[132] Though the blatiers frequently purchased grain illicitly off the markets, "the service that they render to this city," wrote a police official from

125. Police ordinance, 22 December 1702, AN, AD XI 38. Of course blatiers had no corner on adulteration. See the sentence rendered against a Sarcelles laboureur for having "coeffé ses sacs." AN, AD XI 39.

126. Diderot et al., eds., *Encyclopédie*, 2:279; police sentences, 22 December 1672 and 23 March 1702, BHVP.

127. Parmentier, *Parfait Boulanger*, pp. 128–29.

128. AN, Y 12607, 28 November 1750, and Y 9538, 6 May 1757. The measurers showed little sympathy for the blatiers even when they sold on the *carreau* according to the rules. They preferred the larger sellers. See the problem recounted by the "blastrier" Faran, Y 11220, 30 May 1733.

129. *Révolutions de Paris*, 7–14 November 1789. Cf. Martin's highly overdrawn picture of the blatier-hoarder. Germain Martin, "Les Famines de 1693 et 1709 et la spéculation sur les blés," *Congrès des Sociétés savantes de 1908 tenu à Paris, Bulletin du Comité des travaux historiques et scientifiques, Section des sciences économiques et sociales* (1908), pp. 160–61. Cf. Charles Desmarest, *Le Commerce des grains dans la généralité de Rouen à la fin de l'ancien régime* (Paris, 1926), p. 66.

130. P. de Chamousset, *Oeuvres complettes de P. de Chamousset* (Paris, 1783), 2:289; réponse, October 1773, AD Somme, C 86.

131. Paillot to intendant, 23 October 1773, AD Aube, C 1179. Cf. the definition of the blatier trade by Leprévost de Beaumont, another fierce enemy of "vulturous" companies and "capitalist" speculators. "L'Arraignée," Arsenal, ms. Bast. 12353.

132. Ms. note, ca. 1738, Arsenal, ms. Bast. 10275.

Reims, "inhibits us from inquiring into the provenance of the grain."[133] The blatiers thus played broker to the laboureurs who were not diverted from the tasks of cultivation in order to market their crops. They also served the Paris-bound grain merchants and commissionnaires by concentrating supplies at strategically placed ports, such as Mary, whence they could immediately be loaded on boats for shipment to Paris.[134]

A Profile of *Blatier* Business

Even when they were tolerated, the blatiers were rarely esteemed. They were "the scum of the earth," in the words of a subdelegate from Alençon.[135] The grain merchants who dealt with them when they found it convenient nevertheless held them in contempt.[136] Most official reports characterized them as illiterate and unable to keep books (thus establishing a rationale for excluding them from the ranks of respectable merchants).[137] Yet they were cunning enough to profit not only from price disparities but also from differences in the measures used in different places—no mean achievement in a field full of nuances and traps.[138] Many blatiers, such as François Laforge, "marchand blastrier de grain et vendeur de fruits," dealt in grain only on a part-time basis and in combination with other peddling, transporting, or service métiers.[139]

Full-time blatiers, like Claude Thirin of Nanteuil, often had a hard time making ends meet. Usually they were quite small tradesmen, dealing in "pichets" [sic] like Billot or selling in retail amounts for cash.[140] Almost two-thirds of the 165 traders who declared that they practiced grain commerce in

133. "Résultat des observations des officiers de police . . . ," ca. 1773, AD Marne, C 417.

134. "Mémoire sur la fertilité des provinces," ca. 1780, AN, F[11] 222. Cf. the similar role played by Meaux area blatiers. Grain trade registration list, 1771, AD Seine-et-Marne, bailliage de Meaux, uncatalogued ms.

135. Bellesuche to intendant, 25 October 1773, AD Orne, C 89.

136. See the testimony of a forain named Pierre Preau. AN, Y 11236, 11 October 1749. Note also that the blatiers are never assimilated to grain merchants properly speaking: they remain a category apart, of ambiguous status. See controller-general to intendant of Montauban, 31 August 1709, in Boislisle, ed., *Correspondance des contrôleurs-généraux*, 3:204 (#532).

137. "Mémoire," ca. 1770, AD Indre-et-Loire, C 94; "Observations sur le commerce des grains," ca. 1770, AN, F[11] 265; Kaplan, *Bread, Politics and Political Economy*, 1:292.

138. Subdelegate report to intendant, August 1761, AD Orne, C 89; Tessier, "Blatier," *Encyclopédie méthodique*, Agriculture (Paris, 1791), 2:286.

139. AN, Y 11221, 16 October 1734. The so-called blatiers who most troubled the police and who gave the whole profession a bad name were those whose main occupation was not the grain trade and who turned to grain occasionally for speculative purposes or in order to take up slack time and space. One thinks, for example, of the *chassemarées* who bought grain on the return trip home from Paris and sold it along the way. Chefdeville to procurator general, 8 July 1740, BN, Coll. Joly 1123, fol. 56.

140. Archives Seine-Paris, D2B[6] 1080, 6 December 1769, D5B[6] 6100, ca. 1770, and D5B[6] 3503.

the Meaux region in 1771 were blatiers of this sort.[141] Symbolic of their situation was the suit that opposed two blatiers over the sum of 39 livres.[142] Yet blatier was no more monolithic than any other *qualité* in old-regime society. One encounters blatiers like La Cour, who sold 2 muids at a time to baker clients; Pierre Lefebvre of Coulommiers, who had a stock of 30 muids; and Brimile, who dealt only in elite wheats in large amounts.[143] The blatiers who were alert enough to turn to flour probably did quite well for themselves.[144]

Four types of suppliers furnished the Halle. Each group was rather heterogeneous in character. They differed from one another in terms of commercial orientation, business practices, and cultural makeup, but they were sufficiently alike to confound contemporary observers.

The members of the first category, the Halle-based merchants, were only the remote analogues of the Mortellerie barons. They were organized less formally than the port merchants, they had a less intimate relationship with the lieutenant general of police than their port counterparts had with the prévôt des marchands (though they were no less required to meet their provisioning obligations), and their ethos and behavior were significantly less corporate. The Halle-based traders were less deeply rooted in grain commerce by familial and generational ties and tradition, though they seem commonly to have come from related occupational spheres, such as farming, baking, and retail trading in small cereals. They preferred to deal by themselves rather than in association with others, though they did have extremely close links with their commissionnaires. The Halle-based merchants built strong pratik relations with their baker customers. Not only did they not bicker with the bakers over grain-trading prerogatives, but there are some indications that they may have had joint buying arrangements with a number of them. In general they seemed more supple and more imaginative in their trading practices than the port merchants, though they failed for the same reasons: uncollected and/or uncollectible accounts receivable and speculative losses.

The second category, the forains, enjoyed much better relations with the Halle-based dealers than their waterborne counterparts did with the Mortellerie corps. The forains served sometimes as purchasing agents for the Halle merchants and the latter occasionally factored the provisions of the former. Forain recruitment was diverse, and it ebbed and flowed with market oppor-

---

141. Grain trade registration list, 1771, AD Seine-et-Marne, bailliage de Meaux, uncatalogued ms.

142. AD Seine-et-Oise, 3B 121 (May 1768), Brogniard v. Chabot.

143. Archives Seine-Paris, D5B⁶ 4420, 16 September 1771; grain trade registration list, 1771, AD Seine-et-Marne, bailliage de Meaux, uncatalogued ms.; Roubquin to Sartine January 1769, AN, Y 12168.

144. Bibliothèque de l'Institut, ms. 521.

tunities. The liberal reforms of 1763–64 brought an infusion of new faces to
the Halle, especially in the forain contingent, and the trade probably experienced more turnover in the next two decades than it ever had before. Forain
"firms" were familial, like those of the Halle-based merchants. If the former
bought directly at the farms more regularly than the latter, nevertheless they
were well known in the markets of the primary supply crown. The magnitude
of their supply was much more substantial than generally believed. A number
of forains furnished virtually as much as the greatest of the Mortellerie barons.

The Halle depended heavily for its provision on the mass of petty suppliers. They included many forains and even a few Halle-based dealers, but
the bulk of them were laboureurs and blatiers. The police contrived to force
the laboureurs within the decommercialized zone to supply Paris personally
on a weekly basis. The laboureurs (who were often in fact fermiers) were
theoretically not merchants: they did not have the legal right to buy for the
purpose of reselling. Yet it is clear that, in increasing numbers, they were
tempted by commerce, and not just coerced by law and necessity, to enter the
market. The laboureurs kept no books, demanded cash as a rule even from
pratik clients, and plowed whatever they earned back into their farms. They
devised a host of tricks to mask their illicit trading practices. Still, in crisis
periods, they were pressured as hard as the Paris merchants to meet their
"obligations."

For all their "maneuvers," the laboureurs had an incomparably better
reputation than the blatiers. At once the most visible and the most elusive of
traders, the blatiers mobilized small quantities of grain from relatively remote
places and moved them in the direction of the central places. Denounced as
debasers and manipulators, they were widely tolerated precisely because
they rendered modest but not negligible services.

CHAPTER 6

The Mill and the Miller

*I*t was not enough for the provisioning trade to assure a regular and ample supply of grain—bread was made from flour, not wheat. It was also necessary to integrate into the trade the process by which the wheat was converted and made ready for the baker, professional or domestic. The mill was one of the fundamental institutions of old-regime life, along with the marketplace, the church, the court of law, and the tavern. Its sociology is as important as its technology, neither of which has received the attention it merits. To some extent the technology determined the kind of social relations the miller could have, yet the social habitus in which he functioned limited his technological options. Before the miller became a notable or a black magician or a money-lender or a speculator, he had to come to terms with his mill.

Types of Mills

The water miller talking about and then to the windmiller:

According to our crafts we may be brothers,
But while we both live we shall never be lovers.
We are of one craft, but not of one kind:
I live by water and he by the wind.

While you, sir, want wind continually
I would like to have rain fall endlessly.
But by experience we may both well see

That seldom together can these two be.
As long as wind howls, it is quite plain,
Ten to one you will get not a drop of rain:
And when the firmament is too oppressed
Down comes the rain and sets the wind to rest.
From this you see we cannot both obtain
For you will have wind while I must have rain.[1]

Poets have found more reason to celebrate the windmill than did most eighteenth-century grain and flour experts. Aside from its imposing stature and the beauty of its movement, what did a windmill have to recommend it? Its paramount advantage was that it was much easier and cheaper to build than a water mill. The wind, being wholly self-renewing and self-sufficient, posed no problem of canalization. Nor did the windmiller have to worry about disputes over wind sovereignty analogous to the bitter quarrels that turned on water rights, although the construction of buildings or the introduction of plantations nearby could threaten a windmill with partial asphyxiation.[2] The wind machine functioned with a lean and straightforward elegance. The sails turned, causing the windshaft on which they were mounted to revolve. A great cogwheel was fixed on the windshaft and as it turned it transmitted its motion, through cogs, to an upright spindle to which the stones were connected. The water mill shared this fundamental simplicity of design.[3]

The most serious grievance against the wind machines was their "lack of certainty," their "fickleness in operation," which menaced the communities that depended upon them.[4] The power source, which tended to deliver in spasms, was also responsible for the uneven quality of the meal, which was alternately "burned," "altered," "too much crushed or too little crushed."[5] When its windmiller died, in 1730, the executive board of the Hôtel-Dieu recommended that the task be henceforth entrusted exclusively to water

1. John Heywood, *The Play of the Weather,* ed. Maurice Hussey and Surendra Agarwala (New York, 1968), pp. 25–26.

2. See Louis Durand-Vaugaron, "Le Moulin à vent en Bretagne," *Annales de Bretagne* 74, no. 2 (June 1967): 313, 327; Lydia Maillard, *Les Moulins de Montmartre et leurs meuniers* (Paris, 1981), pp. 67, 74.

3. For a description of different types of windmills, see Stanley Freese, *Windmills and Millwrighting* (Cambridge, 1957); Rex Wailes, *The English Windmill* (London, 1959); Charles Marcel-Robillard, *La Belle Histoire des moulins à vent* (Chartres, 1960); Henry Picot, *Vieux Moulins de France: moulins à vent* (Paris, n.d.); Bernard Henry, *Des métiers et des hommes à la lisière des bois* (Paris, 1976); R. Geoffroy, *Guide du meunier* (Marseille, 1971); Paul Mandonnet, *Moulins à vent en Anjou* (Paris, 1964); and especially Claude Rivals, *Le Moulin à vent et le meunier* (Ivry, 1976).

4. Couet de Montbayeux, 24 October 1725, BN, Coll. Joly 1117, fol. 241; Béguillet, *Discours sur la mouture* (1775), p. x; Leclerc, cited in Des Essarts, *Dictionnaire universel de police,* 7:110. Cf. the extreme disenchantment with windmills in the Haute-Saône in the year II, AN, F[20] 293.

5. Petition of the mealmen of Melun to procurator general, ca. 1738, BN, Coll. Joly 1314, fols. 36–37.

Windmill, late seventeenth century (Photo Collection Viollet)

machines, "whose flour is more regular and better conditioned."[6] Though the elevation of the windmills generally made for drier and cooler flour that stored better, the air stimulated evaporation and therefore produced greater waste loss.

The success of windmilling was believed to be more aleatory than water grinding because it depended more on skill. The miller had to try to keep the gap between the stones even, whatever the choppiness of the wind. Before the days of the centrifugal governor, this was done by hand. The miller had to study the force of the wind doggedly, determine how much sail to spread, and be ready to stop the mill under sail and either take in or let out more cloth. The sails often seemed to have a will of their own; their enormous size and heavy weight made them hard to control. Before the fantail came into use he had to be alert to the direction of the wind as well and to keep the sails square in the wind's eye. It was immensely difficult to attain the optimal angle of inclination. Failure to do so not only impeded production but placed the entire machine in peril, for it could be badly damaged if surprised by a strong gust.

Longfellow's tranquil "giant" with "granite jaws" was virtually helpless against a fierce storm. Sometimes the brake was of no use at all: the wind that served the mill turned against it in a vengeful jacquerie. Blinded and suffocated by the swirling meal, the miller had trouble working the brake. If his hand were too heavy the brake would generate sparks, which could hardly find a more hospitable environment, given the old dry wood, the grease, and the flour dust. Sudden squalls could also dislodge the caps of tower mills and turn the bucks of post mills over bodily. In the hope of propitiating the gods of storms and lightning, the miller placed a cross on the ridgepiece of his entryway and invoked the protection of the saints.[7] Mistrusted for their inability to tame the wind, windmillers were also reproached for their inability to obtain from it a steady commitment to assure the uninterrupted production of flour in all seasons. Yet they boasted that a well-built machine could grind in a breeze so imperceptible that a lighted candle could be carried outdoors unshielded.[8] Contemporary critics charged not only that no real progress had

6. Deliberations of the bureau of the Hôtel-Dieu, 28 November 1730, Archives Assistance publique, no. 99. Yet Paris windmills were often specialized in regrinding middlings because they ground "more gently" than water mills. Malouin, *Description et détails des arts,* p. 62.

7. Malouin, *Description et détails des arts,* pp. 62–63; Béguillet, *Discours sur la mouture* (1775), pp. 84–88; Wailes, *English Windmill,* p. 160; Freese, *Windmills,* pp. 114–15; William Coles Finch, *Watermills and Windmills* . . . (Sheerness, 1976), pp. 44, 90; Charles Marcel-Robillard, *Le Folklore de la Beauce,* vol. 1, *Moulins et meuniers du pays beauceron* (Paris, 1965), pp. 43–45; Martha and Murray Zimiles, *Early American Mills* (New York, 1973); John Reynolds, *Windmills and Watermills* (New York, 1970), p. 88. See the cross etched over the door of the windmill represented in the Luttrell Psalter, fol. 158r., British Museum, Add. 42130, Index of Christian Art, Princeton University.

8. Edward Pierce Hamilton, *The Village Mill in Early New England* (Sturbridge, Mass., 1964), p. 14.

been made during the eighteenth century to impose greater control upon the operation of the windmill but that, more generally, despite the contributions of scientists such as Belidor and Parent, the basic principles of windmill construction had been "very much neglected" in France, as opposed to other nations, Holland in particular.[9]

The water mill was appreciated for its relative constancy,[10] but it was absurd to hold that water could "turn day and night and in all seasons," for water mills were quite frequently interrupted as a result of high water, drought, and ice. The water current was as a rule even stronger than the wind, but it varied greatly and there was no consensus on the best way to utilize it. The choice of a site was far more complex than for a windmill. Ideally, a stream site offered a maximum concentration of fall and a flow of considerable volume and regularity. The greater the height of the fall, the less the volume and weight of water required to yield a given amount of power, thus reducing the magnitude and the cost of the accessory hydraulic installations. Few millers had the capital either to compensate for site disadvantages or to enhance site capacity by constructing elaborate headraces, penstocks, tailraces, regulatory gates, and wasteways.[11]

Nor could a miller feel wholly secure in his mill seat even after he erected his mill. While the wind was largely free for anyone to harness, a water miller could find his enterprise jeopardized by the installation of another mill above his. Water millers fought bitterly over such issues as encroachment and undue diversion of water. Gerosme, for example, quarreled for years with his fellow millers in Etampes who charged him with "hoarding" water (as one might corner grain—the gravest of social offenses) by draining off huge amounts. In his defense Gerosme cited the praise he received from local and national authorities for his high productivity ("I work for the subsistence of the people") and the efforts he had made to clean up the river.[12] Jean-François de Sailly, owner of a mill near Mantes, won a suit in the court of the Maîtrise des Eaux et Forêts against a nearby miller who "broke down his dam in order to obtain more water for himself."[13] Nicolas Prunelle won a substantial rebate on his mill rent because of the losses he suffered as a result of the reconstruc-

9. *Bulletin de la Société d'encouragement pour l'industrie nationale,* no. 27 (September 1806): 49.

10. "Mémoire sur les moulins," *Journal économique* (September 1760): 399; Roret, *Manuel du boulanger et du meunier . . . par A.-M. Dessables* (Paris, 1825), pp. 195–96.

11. Louis C. Hunter, *A History of Industrial Power in the United States, 1790–1830,* vol. 1, *Waterpower in the Century of Steam* (Charlottesville, 1979), pp. 53–54, 59–60.

12. AD Seine-et-Oise, unclassified series S (usines et moulins). Cf. the admonition of the old windmiller against the perils of the water in the otherwise insipid novel by Germaine Acremant, *Les Ailes d'argent* (Paris, 1933), p. 121. See also Tulliver's anxiety about water rights in George Eliot, *The Mill on the Floss* (Boston, 1961), p. 11.

13. Bibliothèque municipale de Mantes-la-Jolie, papiers de la seigneurie de Sailly (20 January 1756).

Eighteenth-century water mill, from the *Encyclopédie*. (Photo Lauros-Giraudon)

Inside a water mill, vertical wheel (Ronald Sheppard and
Edward Newton, *The Story of Bread.* London: Routledge &
Kegan Paul, Ltd., 1957)

tion of a mill upstream.[14] Where there was no conflict between millers there
was often a constrictive bond of dependence. Like the windmillers who anxiously awaited a breeze, the small-scale water millers on lesser streams had to
be constantly on the alert for the arrival of water in order not to lose the
opportunity to grind faster.

Tensions with fellow millers were not the only source of conflict. Water
millers had to compete for rights of usage with a vast array of shipping and
navigational interests, with lumbering enterprises, with fishermen, miners,
and especially farmers. The mills diverted water not only from the liquid
roads but also from irrigation projects. They caused occasional flooding that
ruined crops or created swampy areas that bred infection in the warm
months.[15]

14. AD Eure-et-Loire, E 469, 31 December 1745. On the "susceptibility" of millers over
water rights, see also Eliot, *Mill on the Floss,* p. 11.

15. For complaints against the depredations of water millers, see Archives municipales
de Pontoise, BB 4, 4 October, 25 November 1764 and 4 September 1766. See also Hunter,
Industrial Power, 1:139–58; rapport au comité de salut publique, AN, F^{10} 226; "Mémoire sur

Boat mill, from the *Encyclopédie*

In addition to more or less peaceful relations with other users, in order to profit optimally from his mill seat the miller needed to choose the most effective type of waterwheel, the mechanism by which he put the stream to work. Mistakes in conception, design, or calculations regarding size, proportions, and speed of rotation imperiled his success. On this crucial matter he was likely to receive contradictory advice, for exponents of undershot and overshot systems argued passionately over the merits of the two technologies.[16] The undershot wheel, in which the force of the current struck the paddles on the upstream side and passed under the wheel, was rudimentary and adaptable enough to work almost anywhere, but wasteful of energy. It was best suited to sites where the water was abundant and the falls rather low. The overshot wheel allied the force of gravity to that of impact. A penstock directed the water to the top of the wheel, where it entered buckets on the downstream side, thus reversing the rotation of the undershot wheel. The breast wheel, a modification of the overshot that began to appear quite early in the century, proved even more efficient by reversing the position of the buckets and the motion of the wheel. This allowed for wheel diameters much larger than the height of the fall, since the water did not need to be carried over the wheel's top, and it thus resulted in much finer adjustment of the revolving speed. The rotation of the lower part of the breast wheel with, rather than against, the current of flow in the tailrace also increased efficiency. This system also enabled the miller to adapt more flexibly to variations in levels of water supply.[17] Most of the mills I have encountered were equipped with undershot wheels.

Building and maintaining the wheel were far easier tasks than conceiving it. The wheel was crafted out of wood with the simplest hand tools—axe, saw, chisel, plane, auger, mallet. The gearing, which furnished the increment of speed required by the stones, was also made almost entirely of wood. Even

---

les moulins," p. 399; Lacombe d'Avignon, *Le Mitron de Vaugirard*, p. 34; Jorré, "Commerce des grains," pp. 35–36; and especially the vitriolic attack on water milling in citoyen François (Ste.-Menehould) to the comité d'agriculture, n.d., AN, F^{10} 266. On the other hand, see the complaint of a Meulan area miller against a neighbor who drained water away from the mill in order to nourish his garden. BN, Coll. Vexin, vol. 69, fol. 61.

16. César Bucquet, *Manuel du meunier et du constructeur de moulins à eau et à grains,* new ed. (Paris, 1790), pp. 16–18; Storck and Teague, *Flour for Man's Bread,* pp. 108–10. See the gaping fissure (60 to 1) that separated Belidor (exponent of the undershot) and Desagulier (champion of the overshot). Andrew Gray, *The Experienced Millwright* (Edinburgh, 1806), p. 25. See also the debate among Parent, Deparcieux, and Smeaton in Donald S. L. Cardwell, *From Watt to Clausius: The Rise of Thermodynamics in the Early Industrial Age* (Ithaca, 1971), pp. 68–69. Cf. the detailed, heavily mathematical text by Jean-Antoine Fabre, an engineer and physicist, *Essai sur la manière la plus avantageuse de construire les machines hydrauliques et en particulier les moulins à bled* (Paris, 1783).

17. Hunter, *Industrial Power,* 1:64–71. On the modest improvements that enabled wheels to perform better in high and low water, see Jean Orsatelli, *Les Moulins* (Marseille, 1979), p. 80.

Boat mills on the Seine. Seventeenth-century engraving (Bibliothèque Nationale, Photo Collection Viollet)

after iron became widely available for other purposes in the mill machinery in the nineteenth century, many millers clung to the wooden construction because of its low cost and ease of repair.[18] When a wooden tooth wore out or broke, the miller had no trouble fashioning a new one and wedging it in place. He was often obliged to turn to outside help when he needed to replace the iron gudgeons that served as axles and the iron hoops and strappings that reinforced the shaft and wheel.

Water mills were situated not only next to the rivers but on or in them as well, mounted on boats. Boat mills had the advantage of being able to change sites as juridical, commercial, and geophysical conditions changed. They were also free of risk from flooding. In medieval Paris there were at least fifty-five between Notre-Dame and the pont aux Meuniers (today known as the pont au Change). Considerably fewer filled the Seine in the eighteenth century, the best of which were of monocoque construction and equipped with two wheels.[19]

The standard complaint about boat mills was that their flour, like wind-ground meal, was extremely unpredictable in quality, as a result of irregularities in water flow and instability in the mill structure. They were also considered a menace to navigation—thirty-four Lyonnais lost their lives in May 1736 when a boat crashed into the Quarantaine mill.[20] Boat mills also became a threat to bridges, often heavily topped with houses, as well as to other boats when ice flows ripped them from their moorings. During the eighteenth century authorities discouraged new installations and attempted to impose strict safety standards on existing boat mills, including obligatory "garaging" in inclement weather.[21]

Building and Maintaining Mills

It is probable that many eighteenth-century mills were built, under the direction of a miller, by carpenters without any millwrighting experience. Although most milling machinery held no secrets that a clever artisan could not unlock upon study of existing models, in variable doses mill construction did call upon the diverse skills of joiner, mason, blacksmith, wheelwright, and surveyor in addition to those of the simple carpenter.[22] The millwright com-

18. Hamilton, *Village Mill*, p. 11. On water mill construction, see also Charles Marcel-Robillard, *Le Folklore de la Beauce*, 1:95.

19. Alain Peyronel, *Moulins bateaux*, in *Les Moulins de France*, nos. 7–8 (1979): 89. Cf. Quixote's encounter with boat mills. Miguel de Cervantes, *Don Quixote* (New York, 1981), part 2, chap. 29, p. 588.

20. Peyronnel, *Moulins bateaux*, p. 101.

21. See the case of the recalcitrant and tight-fisted miller Roussel at the pont de Chatou. Letter to the ingénieur en chef, 4 pluviôse year II, AD Seine-et-Oise, unclassified series S.

22. Hamilton, *Village Mill*, p. 19; Hunter, *Industrial Power*, 1:91.

bined all these talents, along with an acquaintance with a large number of machines, a knowledge of the applications of wind and water power, and an intimate familiarity with grain mills. His prestige as a professional mill builder grew strikingly in the course of the eighteenth century. Increasingly millers called upon the millwright to incorporate all the latest "perfections" into their planned mills or already existing installations.[23] Millwrights commonly seemed to be recruited from the building trades, though others, like Michaux of Paris, began as millers.[24]

Millers turned to millwrights for complicated repairs and modifications as well as for new construction. An alert miller tried to detect wear, decay, and warping and to engage in a constant cycle of preventative maintenance. Characteristically, the millwright was called in after an accident that disabled a major piece of machinery or after it became impossible to rehabilitate radically deteriorated moving parts. The bills they submitted suggest that they addressed difficult problems. To replace rot at the Gournai mill at Oinville, a *charpentier* charged several hundred livres. For work on several mills, the Carmelites of Pontoise paid a millwright 855 livres in 1769, 490 livres in 1775, 1,161 livres in 1781, and 614 livres in 1785. Water mills also required extremely costly foundation and roof repairs, generally undertaken by a mason, who sometimes worked in what appears to have been a quasi-formal partnership with a millwright.[25] Given the high costs of repairs, it is easy to see how a violent storm or comparably destructive floods or icing could put a miller out of business.

The single most important part of the milling machinery common to all types of mills was the stones. The stones had the most critical and delicate task in the milling operation: to obtain from the grain 70–80 percent or more of its content in the pure state by reducing it, under enormous pressure, to tens of thousands of particles, yet without rupturing the cells and damaging the product. The wheat berry's physical characteristics made grinding particularly difficult. It is a small, nutlike seed scarcely a quarter-inch long, deeply folded in on itself along its entire length, with a troublesome beard at one end. As a rule wheat berries are not uniform and therefore respond differently to cleaning and reducing processes. The starchy core is closely covered by a number of fibrous coats. The outer layers are quite brittle; the inner layers adhere tightly to each other and to the rich endosperm. The coarse outer bran

23. Béguillet, *Traité des subsistances,* pp. 131–32; Storck and Teague, *Flour for Man's Bread,* p. 140. For an example of the millwright's expertise, see AN, MC, VII-307, 28 April 1757.

24. Archives Seine-Paris, DQ^{10} 117, no. 2028; AD Eure-et-Loire, G 3005, 31 December 1754.

25. AD Seine-et-Oise: 70 H 7; 70 H 8; E 1855; and notariat de Meulan, tabellion Jambville, 16 November 1710. On repair expenses, cf. G. R. Canton and P. Hainsselin, "Le Moulin de Bus-les-Artois et son exploitation à la fin du 18e siècle," *Bulletin trimestriel de la Société des antiquaires de Picardie* (1967): 120.

coat is easily shattered; when finely dispersed it could not be separated from the flour and adversely affected its color and baking quality. The seedcoat is joined to the endosperm by the heavy-walled aleurone cells that contain substantial doses of protein and if broken sap baking strength from the flour. The seed proper or germ contains an oil which, if pressed into the flour, compromises color, baking quality, and conservability. The starch cells of the nutritious endosperm fragment under too much impact and precipitate chemical reactions that enervate the flour. The stones had to grind sensitively, discriminately—I am tempted to say intelligently—in order to avoid overheating and excessive pressure and to guarantee a maximum yield in quality as well as quantity.[26]

"Smart" stones, as the millers called them, were composed of the highest quality materials, were expertly dressed, mounted, and balanced, and were regularly and vigilantly maintained. "Every [serious] miller is intimately acquainted with his pair of stones," observes Marcel Barbier, a twentieth-century miller deeply rooted in the old traditions. The miller could recognize his stones by their timbre and their tremors. Most millers in the Paris region purchased stones from La Ferté-sous-Jouarre, rich burrstones pocked with a network of quartz cavities that were coveted by millers throughout the world. Several thousand workers labored in the quarries at La Ferté cutting out sections of stone of like hardness and porosity, weighing usually between 75 and 100 pounds each, that were blocked and joined together by plaster and then hooped with iron to form a millstone. A good stone was so even in grit, texture, and color that it resembled a solid piece. It took ten days to two weeks to fabricate and had to dry for six months before use.[27] Prior to the initial dressing, the upper or runner stone had to be "worked" into a slightly

26. Percy A. Amos, *Processes of Flour Manufacture* (London, 1912), p. 14; Storck and Teague, *Flour for Man's Bread,* pp. 197–99.

27. Groupe de Recherches sur les traditions en Beauce, *Marcel Barbier: Meunier à Moutiers en Beauce* (St.-Denis, 1980), p. 231; Storck and Teague, *Flour for Man's Bread,* p. 102; Richard Bennett and John Elton, *History of Corn Milling* (London, 1898–1904), 3:95–100; J.P. Brissot de Warville, *New Travels in the United States of America, 1788,* ed. D. Echeverria (Cambridge, 1964), pp. 163–64 (letter no. 10, 28 August 1788); Auguste Piot, *Traité historique et pratique sur la meulerie et la meunerie* (Paris, 1860), pp. 64, 65, 91; Malouin, *Description et détails des arts,* pp. 65–68; Robert Grimshaw, *The Miller, the Millwright, and the Millfurnisher* (New York, 1882), pp. 289, 318; Georges Darney, *La Ferté-sous-Jouarre* (Paris, 1910), p. 10; Paule Roy, "Moulins à vent de Picardie," *Bulletin trimestriel de la Société des antiquaires de Picardie* (1967), pp. 102–3; Russel H. Anderson, "The Technical Ancestry of Grain-Milling Devices," *Agricultural History* 7, no. 3 (July 1938): 256–70; Emile Eperlding, "Les Pierres à moulins et l'industrie meulière de la Ferté-sous-Jouarre," *Les Moulins,* publication semestrielle de la Fédération française des amis des moulins, no. 7 (1982–83): 83–111. The Russian expert Peter Kozmin wrongly claimed that the French had long ignored the treasures of La Ferté: *Flour Milling,* trans. M. Falkner and T. Fjelstrup (New York, 1917), p. 23. On nineteenth- and twentieth-century stone making, see J. Beauvois, "Quand Epernon produisait des meules à moulin," *Les Moulins* (Fédération française des amis des moulins), premier semestre (1980): 5–13.

concave shape and the lower or bedstone into a less pronounced convex curve. The alert miller sought a runner stone of "ardent" quality, that is, a relatively hard blue-and-white stone with a large number of tiny holes on the surface. A good bedstone was darker in color and less ardent or cutting in texture. Stones that possessed these qualities and that were cut to the same diameter would grind without excessive pressure and thus avoid overheating the meal.[28] Diameter usually measured about 6 feet 2 inches in contemporary reckoning. A new stone was at least 9 inches thick, though stones as thin as 3½ inches could still be used. Millstones were capable of lasting as long as thirty to forty years, though wear depended on productivity and care.[29] New stones were expensive. Paris miller J.-J. Devaux paid a Ferté dealer 360 livres for the runner and 350 livres for the bedstone.[30] Used stones were generally sold by the inch of thickness, the price varying with age and quality.[31]

Before the stones were first mounted, and at regular intervals thereafter, they had to be dressed. Dull stones destroyed "that lively quality of the grain that caused it to ferment" when it was turned into bread. They also made the meal so clammy that it choked up the bolters. "Imperfectly dressed stones," testified a leading Paris miller in the mid-nineteenth century, were still the major cause of poor-quality flour characterized by the commingling of chunks of insufficiently reduced bran and tiny particles of excessively pulverized bran. Dressing permitted the stones to cut, not merely crush and rub, to circulate the grain most effectively across the stone surface, and to aerate and cool the chop as it moved from the eye, or center, to the skirt, or periphery. Well-dressed stones reduced the kernel to a fine powder without overheating and without subjecting the meal to excessive pressure.[32]

The prevalent mode of dressing in old-regime France was by random strokes—à coups perdus.[33] Experts preferred the spokelike row method prac-

---

28. Bucquet, Manuel du meunier, pp. 33–40, 60–64, 71–77. Poncelet wrote that the diameter of the bedstone had to be slightly larger than that of the runner. But Bucquet warned that this would cause friction that would wear "lips" on the stones and thus prevent the ground meal from escaping. Poncelet, Histoire naturelle, p. 159.

29. AD Oise, G 40, 7 January 1771 (moulin de Limaçon); AD Seine-et-Oise, 70 H 7, 29 December 1721 (moulin de Chantereine), and E 2751, 27 March 1729 (moulin de Gency); Bucquet, Manuel du meunier, p. 69; Bernard Forest de Belidor, Architecture hydraulique, ou L'Art de conduire, d'élever, et de ménager les eaux pour les différents besoins de la vie (Paris, 1737–39), 1:281.

30. AN, MC, VII-307, 28 April 1757. Jean Chaveau paid 299 and 300 livres. AN, MC, VII-281, 16 December 1751. See also the debt of Louis Poitou to a Ferté stone dealer. Archives Seine-Paris, D4B⁶ 98-6904, 16 May 1787.

31. AD Seine-et-Oise, E 2751, 21 July 1729; AD Eure-et-Loire, E 469, 27 September 1756, and E 1137, 12 October 1752.

32. Oliver Evans, The Young Millwright and Miller's Guide, 9th ed. (Philadelphia, 1836), p. 247; Grimshaw, Miller, Millwright, and Millfurnisher, p. 322; Enquête sur la boulangerie, p. 720.

33. On the primitive aspect of most eighteenth-century dressing, see N. Chryssochoïdes, Nouveau Manuel complet du meunier, du négociant en grains et du constructeur des moulins (Paris, 1910), 1:154–57.

ticed in the Paris area on the grounds that it produced more and better flour. There was no standard procedure for rational as opposed to random dressing. The approach depended on the "ardor" and diameter of the stones, the force of the mill, the kind of technology used, the type of grain ground, the sort of flour desired, the humidity. The initial dressing involved the cutting of the main grooves, called furrows, complemented by fine grooves called featherings or stitchings in the spaces (called lands) between the furrows. Debate raged over such questions as the width and depth of the furrows, the amount of land to be left between them, the degree of sharpness at the feather edge, their design (a concentric pattern; a system of short grooves of six to eight inches, an inch in width and two inches apart; the creation of as many as forty pairs of shears of varying length, starting off from the center and passing each other at an acute angle that moved continually outward with a cutting effect). Authorities such as the American millwright-miller Oliver Evans argued that when furrows were not deep enough they ground too slowly, were likely to heat the flour, and produced "dirty" bran. Others contended that deep furrows threw out meal particles unground.

Stones had to be redressed periodically by sharpening and recutting grooves. High spots, located by passing a wooden straightedge (called a redstick) coated with moist, red clay on the stone surface, also had to be leveled off. Periodicity of dressing varied from mill to mill; characteristic patterns will be discussed below. A fairly reliable indicator of the state of dressing was the condition of the bran. When the bran was scraped clean in large, flat, thin flakes, the stones were in good shape. They usually needed dressing when the bran was curled and cut, spoiling the color of the flour.[34]

Dressing required, then, a global conception of the milling operation, a strategy that was at once technological and commercial. In addition, it demanded gifted hands, for it was exceedingly difficult to work the curved surface of the millstone. Armed with foot-long bills, chisels, picks, and a proof-staff, the dresser (generally called *rhabilleur,* in some places more colorfully *meulanger*) had the reputation of artist as well as artisan. A dexterous dresser was capable of cutting up to sixteen featherings an inch. The most knowledgeable boasted that they worked "geometrically."

The respect in which professional dressers were held in old-regime European society is revealed in the English phrase "to show one's mettle." Originally the word for *mettle* was *metal,* the name for crushed stone. To show the bits of stone that had become embedded in one's hand after many years of

34. Bucquet, *Manuel du meunier,* pp. 66–70; Malouin, *Description et détails des arts,* pp. 68–69; *Manuel ou Vocabulaire des moulins à pot* (Paris 1786), pp. 89–90; Evans, *Young Millwright,* pp. 248–56; Freese, *Windmills,* pp. 49, 101; Grimshaw, *Miller, Millwright, and Millfurnisher,* p. 329; Maurice Delplanque, *Le Moulin de Frevent: Essai de monographie d'un moulin à eau* (St.-Omer, 1936); J. Russell, "Stone Dressing," in Wailes, *English Windmill,* p. 208; Storck and Teague, *Flour for Man's Bread,* pp. 103–4; Leslie Syson, *British Water-Mills* (London, 1965), pp. 117–26.

Dressing a millstone (Rex Wailes, *The English Windmill*. London: Routledge & Kegan Paul, and Fairfield, N.J.: Augustus M. Kelley, Publishers, 1954)

dressing proved that he was a man of great experience.[35] Far more threatening to the dresser's health than a blue hand was silicone or lead poisoning, which he risked contracting by inhaling the powder that flew into the air as he struck the stone with his bill. Marcel Barbier, who operated a windmill in the Beauce until quite recently, took to wearing protective glasses after steel splinters from the hammer lodged in his eyes on several occasions.[36]

Windmillers used a semaphore signal broadcast by the sweeps of the mill to notify dressers in the region that they were in need of service.[37] Certain millers, such as J.-J. Devaux of Paris and Pierre Bruxelle of Meaux, had

35. Russell, "Stone Dressing," p. 209; Storck and Teague, *Flour for Man's Bread*, p. 105; Alphonse Subtil, "La Fabrication du pain dans le Vexin," *Mémoires de la Société historique et archéologique de l'arrondissement de Pontoise et du Vexin* 56 (1894): 56; Finch, *Water Mills and Windmills*, p. 59; Rex Wailes, "Discussion of H. O. Clark, 'Notes on French Windmills,' " in H. O. Clark, "Notes on French Windmills," *Transactions of the Newcomen Society* 9 (1928–29): 58.

36. J. Delivre and R. C. Plancke, *Les Moulins à vent de la Brie* (n.p., 1976), p. 69; Grimshaw, *Miller, Millwright, and Millfurnisher*, p. 293; *Marcel Barbier: meunier*, p. 232. Cf. the "epidemic of Chartres" in ca. 1880, which left 20 dead and 250 ill as a result of lead poisoning through flour. Marcel-Robillard, *Folklore de la Beauce*, 1:36; Alfred Martinet, *Les Aliments usuels* (Paris, 1910), p. 241.

37. AN, MC, VII-307, 28 April 1757; AD Seine-et-Marne, B 68, pièce non cotée, 29 April 1697. Cf. the inventory of another miller who kept dressing bills, AD Eure-et-Loire, II E 2815, no. 100, 29 June 1809.

sufficient confidence in themselves to do their own dressing.[38] As a rule, however, dressing was undertaken by highly accomplished, itinerant craftsmen like forty-year-old Philippe Vallet of Charenton and fifty-five-year-old Denis Guedée of St. Denis, full-time professionals who went from mill to mill. Barbier affirmed that he "never knew the so-called rhabilleur, I always knew the millers to dress their own stones." Yet he himself boasted a collection of 150 dressing bills and he spent many long days recutting the stones of colleagues who knew of his skill. Belgian "stone furrowers" became prominent in the nineteenth century when they launched a tour de France.

Each time after dressing, the stones had to be mounted and balanced. Badly hung stones guaranteed a wretched, wasteful grinding. If the stones touched during grinding, there was the risk of fire as well as a damaged product. When revolving at a high rate of speed, at no point over the entire stone surface would the runner be separated from its cognate by more than the thickness of a grain of wheat, yet nowhere would the two stones come into actual contact. To suspend the runner, weighing from a thousand pounds to a ton, over the bedstone was an extraordinarily delicate job. Few mills had a crane to ease the operation. Most millers relied upon wooden wedges, blocks and bars, and a tremendous burst of physical energy. Every time the dresser came, the hopper, shoe, damsel, and casing had to be removed and then the runner raised, turned over, and laid on level floor. The lack of space in which to work seriously hampered the dresser's efforts.[39]

Projects for Alternative Kinds of Mills

Considerable energy was invested in mill improvement in the eighteenth century. The most significant innovation was the process called economic milling, discussed below. It focused on increasing the quantity and quality of flour production, a question that most eighteenth-century mill "projectors" addressed only in passing. They attacked what seemed to be an anterior and far more urgent issue: how to shelter the kingdom from the spasmodic ravages of flour crises—shortages of flour caused by mill stoppages. Scores of inventors and entrepreneurs proposed systems that were meant to guarantee a steady, constant flow of production.

The point of departure was a critique of the weaknesses of the conventional wind- and water-milling machines. At issue was not their efficiency, but

38. AN, Y 11583, 18 May 1760; Archives Seine-Paris, D6B⁶, carton 2, 7 July 1743 (Coron v. Desloches); *Marcel Barbier: Meunier,* pp. 82, 230–31; Picot, *Vieux moulins de France,* p. 26.

39. Evans, *Young Millwright,* pp. 256–57; Hamilton, *Village Mill,* pp. 6, 8; Grimshaw, *Miller, Millwright, and Millfurnisher,* p. 295; Freese, *Windmills,* pp. 49ff., 104–5; Suzanne Beedell, *Windmills* (New York, 1975), pp. 64–65; Reynolds, *Windmills and Watermills,* p. 47.

their vulnerability. Neither water nor wind power was immune from meteorological caprice. Time and again Paris and other cities, towns, and hamlets were menaced with disaster because a lack of wind or water or too much water or ice shut down the mills. Encouraged by "the anxiety of the magistrates," for whom flour was the price of social peace, the ambition of the mill innovators was to find a way to manufacture flour without water or wind, or somehow to protect the water or the wind from the vagaries of the weather.[40] Few of these inventions had any practical incidence; many were more or less fanciful. But their inspiration and their variety underscore the intensity of the preoccupation with the flour crisis issue.

One of the oldest alternatives or complements to wind- and water-driven machines was the hand-powered mill. Its promoters were not satisfied to affirm that it was a machine free of any (exogenous) contingencies. Like the entrepreneur seeking a twenty-five-year privilege for his machine in 1650, they contended that the hand mill could be made to run more efficiently and more cheaply than wind or water machines—a claim they never succeeded in proving. The most appealing argument to the authorities was that the mill could "save us in great extremities."[41] Hand mills were put into use in Paris during the subsistence crisis of 1725.[42] Controller-general Orry solicited hand-mill projects in the wake of the grave crisis of 1738–41. The architect Mansart presented a portable hand mill allegedly capable of grinding eight bushels an hour—over seventeen setiers in a day!—to the Academy of Sciences in 1741.[43] That same year a Sieur Delevault received an exclusive royal charter to manufacture a hand mill that he developed under the patronage of the financier and victualer Pâris-Duverney. A conical cylinder constructed of steel, it required two persons to operate and could produce three bushels an hour. Delevault boasted that his mill ground without overheating, and he challenged conventional millers to produce a better-tasting meal. He urged religious communities, seigneurs, fermiers, and bakers to equip themselves with his machine, at least a hundred models of which were already in use in the army.[44]

The next impulse came with the next major subsistence crisis, in the late sixties and early seventies. As controller-general and later as minister for

40. From an application for government support for a new mill conception, in deliberations, bureau de l'Hôtel de Ville, 21 January 1741, AN, H 1859, fols. 159–60.

41. Letters patent, 8 June 1650, BN, ms. fr. 16741, fols. 12–13.

42. Arsenal, ms. Bast. 10155 (24 September 1725). See also the hand-mill project reviewed in 1722. Académie des sciences, *Machines et inventions approuvées par l'Académie royale des sciences* (Paris, 1735–77), 4:37–38.

43. Legrand d'Aussy, *Vie privée,* 1:61–62.

44. AN, F[12] 1299[A]; AD Puy-de-Dôme, C 484. There was an "economic" dimension in Delevault's conception reminiscent of Malisset. He promised that with his mill the army would be able to increase the soldierly ration from 24 to 26 ounces "without costing the king a penny." Louis Dupré d'Aulnay, *Traité général de subsistances militaires* (Paris, 1744), p. 647.

agriculture, Bertin was an active promoter of hand mills.[45] A "mécanicien" from Strasbourg named Reutter came to Versailles with an idea for a portable hand mill.[46] Barthélémy Rostin of Lyon petitioned for support for "a movement" that could grind twelve and one-half setiers in a day. The Academy of Sciences recommended rejecting his request on the grounds that he "lacked sufficient knowledge of motor forces."[47] In 1772 one Berthelot received a twenty-year privilege for the manufacture of a hand mill, probably the same Berthelot whose hand and pedal mills lieutenant general of police Lenoir introduced into the Bicêtre prison and recommended for adoption in the colonies and garrisons and for emergency use in the cities in the late 1770s and early 1780s.[48] An architect named Nicolet also developed a hand mill that aroused official interest in the late seventies.[49] Mustel, well known for his experiments with potato cultivation and potato bread making, developed a "domestic" hand mill that was used in Rouen.[50]

The prerevolutionary crisis and the Revolution itself called forth another wave of ideas, for the most part familiar ones. In the years just before 1789 the royal government ordered the construction of hand mills to help grind large amounts of king's grain that could not be converted as a result of too much ice and too little wind.[51] In 1790 a Paris locksmith presented the dauphin with a working model of a hand mill that he boasted could grind economically as well as by the coarse method.[52] The commission on subsistence dispatched Parmentier to test a new hand mill at Havre-Marat in the year II.[53] A Sieur Gentilliez proposed a method for improving the efficiency of the hand mill in the year IV.[54] The *bureau de consultation des arts et métiers* provided financial support for several hand-mill projects.[55] The Revolution did not

45. Bourde, *Agronomie et agronomes,* 2:910.

46. AN, F^{12} 1299^A, 1766.

47. AN, F^{12} 2198, January–February 1767.

48. AD Doubs, B 2179, fol. 53, 12 August 1772; Jean-Ch.-P. Lenoir, *Détail sur quelques établissements de la ville de Paris . . .* (Paris, 1780), p. 8; Bibliothèque municipale (hereafter BM) Orléans, ms. 1421; Legrand d'Aussy, *Vie privée,* 1:61; Emile Richard, *Histoire de l'hôpital de Bicêtre, 1250–1791* (Paris, 1889), p. 92. Lenoir reported with satisfaction that the yield of these mills proved that millers cheated the public by exaggerating loss through waste. *Quelques établissements,* p. 9.

49. AN, F^{11}* 1, fol. 79, 18 October 1777.

50. *Gazette d'agriculture, commerce, arts, et finances* (11 March 1769): 195.

51. Durand to municipality of Pontoise, 31 August 1793, Archives municipales Pontoise, 5F4; Bord, *Histoire du blé en France,* p. 47n. Cf. Charles Parrain, "Rapports de production et développement des forces productives: l'exemple du moulin à eau," *La Pensée,* n.s. no. 119 (February 1965): 64.

52. *Encyclopédie méthodique,* Jurisprudence (1782–91), 10:148.

53. AN, F^{12} 1299^B. It is possible that a hand mill was developed by Parmentier's sometime associate Ovide, known for his fostering of steam milling in Paris. AN, F^{12} 2379.

54. AN, F^{12} 2379.

55. Commission de recherches et de publications, *Bulletin d'histoire économique de la Révolution, 1913* (1915), pp. 39, 47.

transform the old-regime entrepreneurial mentality of inventors—before making public the details of his "economic mill," a revolutionary clerk and national guard officer from the Var asked for a 300,000 livres' reward and a fifteen-year exclusive privilege.[56]

Miller César Bucquet did not hide his skepticism about these domestic mills that Lenoir and the scientist Cadet de Vaux wished to see ultimately in everyone's home. Bucquet was an unabashed corporatist in his sense of professional solidarity with his fellow millers and his conviction that the division of labor consecrated by the different crafts made sense. By establishing networks of retail flour outlets with storehouses in the cities, Bucquet contended, the miller-merchants would be in an ideal position to prevent flour crises. Milling was too complicated to be understood by unskilled persons. Their machines crushed the grain in the grossest fashion, resulting in great waste. Moreover, the high cost of the mills made their proliferation very unlikely.[57] Yet these mills appear to have penetrated more deeply than Bucquet thought possible—the prefect of the Ille-et-Vilaine reported in 1810 that 250,000 small hand mills ground buckwheat for five-eighths of the rural inhabitants.[58]

The other major alternative to water- and wind-driven machines was also dependent on animate energy: the horse. Similar in design to the hand mills, the horse mill had the advantage of sparing man the hard labor and of producing more flour in the same period of time. Boasting that he had invented an entirely new mill that "defied nature and the seasons," an architect named Claude-François Chapuis sought a twenty-year exclusive charter for the production of his horse-powered machine in 1732. It was less new than he claimed, the Academy of Sciences declared, but it combined known techniques in an original way and would be thus "advantageous to the public."[59] The prévôt des marchands of Paris enthusiastically called the attention of the assembly of police in 1735 to a horse-driven mill capable not only of milling in all conditions, unlike the conventional machines, but also of doing it more economically. Further tests, however, disenchanted him; for the flour was "inferior in quantity and likeness" to the flour of wind or water mills.[60] A few years later a Sieur Fervet implored the royal council for a safe conduct to protect him from the pursuits of creditors. He claimed that he had fallen deeply into debt while trying to perfect a horse mill that would serve the

56. Petition to agricultural committee, AN, F^{12} 1299^B, 1791.

57. Bucquet, *Observations intéressantes,* pp. 74–76.

58. "Etat des moulins," 1 January 1810, AN, F^{20} 295.

59. AN, F^{12}* 79, fols. 126–28, 31 January 1732. For the English use of horse power in milling of various sorts, see Cardwell, *From Watt to Clausius,* p. 71.

60. Assembly of police, 1 December 1735, 22 February, 13 December 1736, BN, ms. fr. 11236, fols. 289–96, 302.

public interest.[61] A "double mill" proposed by a consortium during the terrible dearth of 1740–41 may also have involved horsepower. From a base at St.-Denis, this group of businessmen sought a thirty-year privilege to construct the mill all over France and promised that henceforth flour would be abundant all year long.[62]

The most promising idea resulted from the development of a horse-driven silk mill by the Delavals, merchants near Lyon. They presented their project to Lyon officials in the late 1760s after a year of "near famine in the midst of abundance" as a result of floods and droughts that stopped the Rhône mills. They claimed that a single horse or mule could produce between eighteen and twenty-six setiers in twenty-four hours (it is not clear if this was to be accomplished by one pair of stones or two). The stones turned at fifty rotations per minute, yielding a cooler, more even meal than that produced by the fickle Rhône mills. Supported by the findings of the engineers appointed by the municipality, the Delavals also contended that their machine was cheaper to build and run—including horses, food, interest on capital, maintenance, and so forth—than water mills.[63] In October of 1768 they obtained royal letters patent granting them an exclusive privilege to build their machine throughout the realm for fifteen years.[64] Before registering the letters patent, the Paris Parlement solicited the advice of Sartine, the lieutenant of police, and of the Academy of Sciences. Like his Lyon counterparts, Sartine had experienced the disastrous effects of flour crisis during the previous year, and was keenly interested in promoting the development of machines more reliable than wind or water. The academy, however, evinced contempt for a machine that lacked any originality in design. It pointed to a similar machine submitted by Chapuis in 1732 (the fate of which remains a mystery) and to a text on hydraulic architecture published in 1737 (Belidor's?) that contained a blueprint of the Delaval method. By registering the letters patent, the parlement revealed that it was less worried about paternity of ideas than about the real prospects of application. In any case, the letters patent expressly stated that the privilege could not prejudice machines that had been previously invented or machines yet to be invented that nevertheless showed "marked differences."[65]

61. Dépêche to Hérault, 27 June 1739, AN, O^1 384, fols. 207–8.

62. AN, H 1859, fols. 159–63, 21 January 1741; AN, H 1939^2; conseil secret, 9 January 1741, AN, X^{1A} 8468, fols. 193–94; AN, F^{11} 264.

63. AN, F^{12} 2198. Cf. petition to war minister, Archives des Affaires Etrangères, France, 1371, fol. 29.

64. Letters patent, 29 October 1768, BN, F 23627 (829). Is it possible that the Delevault known for his interest in hand mills in the forties and fifties was the same person as Delaval?

65. AN, Y 9500, 20 January 1769; conseil secret, 4 February 1769, AN, X^{1B} 8957. The parlement seemed deeply impressed that the use of the Delaval machine had "saved the city of St.-Chaumont from a cruel famine" caused by a long drought whose effects were exacerbated by serious freezing in 1767. Cf. Abbé Nicolas Baudeau, *Avis aux honnêtes gens qui veulent bien faire* (Amsterdam and Paris, 1768), p. 97, who noted that these machines could be converted to economic milling.

About the same time Antoine Macary, royal *mécanicien,* received authorization to construct four horse-driven mills, each larger in scale than the Delavals' and allegedly capable of producing enough flour in a year to nourish sixty thousand men. Macary stressed the superior quality of his merchandise as well as the security of his machinery. "The natural inequality and variation" of wind and water propulsion, he argued, not only jeopardized provisioning but also produced exasperatingly inconsistent flour. Macary needed to raise 300,000 livres for his scheme, which simultaneously involved grain speculation and mill construction. Sartine authorized him to advertise for capital and for associates.[66] A mill propelled by a horse-drawn wagon emerged at this time, followed by a similar device in 1813.[67] In 1777 a master locksmith named Durand proposed a horse-driven flour machine "devised to work continuously and independently of the failures of the wind and the water." The Academy of Sciences found the mill "ingenious" because it powered two pairs of stones at a time.[68]

The freshest, most exciting idea for replacing the traditional forms of energy was steam. In 1772, in the midst of the most protracted subsistence crisis of the century, an Englishman named William Blakey sought support in France for his "machine à feu." The Academy of Sciences commended his treatise, which also drew praise from Peronnet of the Royal Academy of Architecture. Twenty-one years later, when subsistence was still very much one of the pressing issues of the day, Blakey was still trying to convince Parisian officials that he had developed "flour mills that are not subject to being interrupted by the accidents of weather." He emphasized his experience, his "scientific approach," and his familiarity with the Paris bread problem. His newest invention was relatively inexpensive to build, required remarkably little combustible, and produced a beautiful flour.[69] In fact, a former agent of the agricultural committee, named Ovide, had just begun to experiment with a steam-fired installation on the Isle des Cygnes, in collaboration with Parmentier and Cadet de Vaux. Though the steam machines broke down frequently, they yielded an excellent meal in much larger amounts than conventional mills. A half-century later, however, steam had still not made significant inroads in the Paris region. It was resisted by some of the largest, most "industrially" inclined millers on the grounds of exorbitant

66. *Gazette d'agriculture, commerce, arts, et finance,* (1 September 1770): 636; Philippe Macquer, *Dictionnaire raisonné universel des arts et métiers* (Paris, 1773), 3:157; controller-general to Sartine, 12 August 1770, AN, F^{12}* 155, fol. 11.

67. Edouard Fournier, *Le Vieux-neuf, histoire ancienne des inventions et découvertes modernes,* 2d ed. (Paris, 1877), pp. 11, 382n; AN, F^{12} 2198.

68. AN, F^{12} 2198. The ex-canon of Semur, "already known for his *poisson aérien,*" appears to have contrived a similar machine in the year III. Ibid.

69. AN, F^{12} 1299^{B}; *Révolutions de Paris* 15 (17–24 October 1789): 25. Bordes and Foure at Lyon and Darnal at Alais had experimented with a "fire-powered" mill earlier in the century. Béguillet, *Discours sur la mouture* (1775), p. 68.

energy costs and recurrent breakdowns requiring costly repairs. Many steam millers apparently failed. The ones who succeeded were millers like Destors of Thillay, scion of one of the best-known eighteenth-century baking and flour families, who built a steam installation adjacent to his water mill and used it only when the waterwheel could not turn.[70]

A number of engineers, such as Dransy, focused on ways to perfect water milling, but within the confines of the traditional power system and its vulnerabilities.[71] Few inventors appear to have addressed the question of somehow redesigning water drives so as to free them from their dependence on the weather. One such project, conceived during the Revolution by a miller from Créteil and an architect, called for the building of small water mills in ordinary domestic wells. Each revolutionary section, the authors suggested, could become flour autarchic by establishing two such all-weather well mills.[72] Various inventors, including Antoine Macary, believed that tidal propulsion could eventually offer more security than river-based mills.[73] The Academy of Sciences examined several projects for a "horizontal mill" that could be driven either by water or by wind, depending on the weather.[74] A considerable number of these machines appear to have been put into operation.[75] A simpler innovation to protect the mill against ice blockage involved the construction of a wooden shelter around the wheel, insulated with hay and heated with carefully enclosed ovens. The Leleu brothers, grain victualers and keepers of the emergency Paris granary during the last decades of the old regime, claimed to have invented this "defrosting cage" during the fierce winter of 1788, when "the frozen waters of the rivers kept the mills motionless, the

70. Report of Ovide to minister of the interior, 21 frimaire year IV and report of bureau of agriculture to minister of the interior, 19 nivôse year IV, AN, F[10] 257; *Enquête sur la boulangerie,* pp. 10, 30, 129, 134. See also Jacques Payen, *Capital et machine à vapeur au XVIIIe siècle* (Paris, 1969). On the use of steam as auxiliary power in water mills, see Cardwell, *From Watt to Clausius,* pp. 71–72.

71. See the prize competition sponsored by the Academy of Sciences that Dransy won. Bachaumont, *Mémoires secrets* (London, 1786), 30:51–52, 12 November 1785, and 25:244, 21 April 1784. See also the project of a *garde-moulin* to increase the productivity of water mills by modifying the wheel design. Pinson (1808), AN, F[12] 2197.

72. AN, F[12] 2197.

73. See, for example, "Projet d'une machine propre à faire mouvoir deux moulins à farine par le flux et reflux de la mer," 1765, AN, F[12] 2198.

74. *Machines et inventions approuvées par l'Académie des sciences,* 1:105, 107; 6:75; 7:117–20. In nineteenth-century Brittany, water- and windmills were often paired in the same lease, though they were not physically integrated. Durand-Vaugaron, "Le Moulin à vent en Bretagne," p. 308.

75. See the "états" of 1810, AN, F[20] 296. "Combined" wind- and water mills were relatively common in certain parts of France, but they usually consisted of two separate mills built next to each other rather than of mechanically integrated operations. See Marcel Gautier, "Un Type d'habitation rurale à fonction 'industrielle': Les Moulins de Bretagne et de Vendée," *Norois: Revue géographique de l'Ouest et des pays de l'Atlantique nord* (1969): 391, and Louis Merle, *La Métairie et l'évolution agraire de la Gâtine poitevine de la fin du Moyen Age à la Révolution* (Paris, 1958), p. 197.

people seemed condemned to the horror of lacking flour despite the ample supply of wheat." From Corbeil, the Leleus' base, this system seems to have spread slowly to a handful of metropolitan localities during the Revolution.[76]

Similarly, inventors proposed no radical ideas about the best way to utilize wind power, but they continued to make suggestions on how best to mount the axle and wings to increase efficiency.[77] A Paris clockmaker proposed an automated folding wing system that would enable the stones to turn more evenly and protect the mill from destruction during storms.[78] The Du Bost brothers, who succeeded in marrying wind and water in their horizontal model, also envisaged a horizontal system strictly for windmills by which all sorts of wind and virtually all weather could be channeled to transmit a smooth movement to the stones.[79] The abbé Rozier announced that a trip through Holland had filled him with interesting ideas about windmill design, but none of his inspirations seems to have been incorporated in a working machine. Nor did the Swedish and Polish ideas of maximizing sail exposure and running in the calm materialize in working models in France.[80]

The Work Place

The miller's world was timeless, for the mill had to function twenty-four hours a day without interruption for as long as possible. Boundaries of night and day meant little. The miller worked long hours—twelve to eighteen hours a day or more—seconded by his wife and usually by at least one journeyman or *garde-moulin*. He took his meals to the rapid beat of the grinding stones. If he were a water miller he may very well have lived with his family in the mill building, though wealthier millers sought some repose by erecting a house a short distance away. In any event, he frequently slept "over the stones," just as baker boys slept "on the oven." The windmiller rarely lived in the mill, but when on duty he too had occasion to sleep near his stones. Often the miller

76. Archives municipales Pontoise, "Compte-rendu au public par les Srs. Leleu sur l'établissement des moulins de Corbeil" (ca. 1789); ministre de l'intérieur to préfet du département de la Seine, 14 December 1815, Archives Seine-Paris, DM^6 2. In 1823 the Société d'encouragement pour l'industrie nationale offered a prize for the best design for a waterwheel that would be free from interruption due to floods or backwater. Marcel Crozet-Fourneyron, *L'Invention de la turbine* (Liège and Paris [1924?]), pp. 21–22.

77. See, for example, "Sur les moulins à vent," in *Histoire de l'Académie royale des sciences. Avec les mémoires de Mathématiques & de Physique, 1711* (1714), pp. 92–100, and Legrand d'Aussy, *Vie privée,* 1:64–65.

78. H. Pigeonneau and A. de Foville, eds., *L'Administration de l'agriculture au contrôle général des finances. Procès-verbaux et rapports* (Paris, 1882), p. 362 (2 February 1787).

79. AN, F^{12} 1299^A, 1741. Cf. letter to Palou, 14 October 1749, AN, F^{12*} 147.

80. Rozier to controller-general, 25 September 1777, AN, F^{12} 1299^A; Béguillet, *Discours sur la mouture* (1775), pp. 93–99; Malouin, *Description des arts* (1771), p. 73n; *Journal économique* (May 1760): 202–4 and (June 1765): 279.

dozed rather than slept, ready to spring with Pavlovian rigor to the bell announcing the need to refill the hopper. When he worked at some distance from the stones, he listened for their "music," which betrayed the imperfections of the grind, just as a master baker listened for the reassuring sighing and groaning of his head journeyman in the cavelike oven room. Neither darkness nor fatigue prevented him from making repairs in the middle of the night. The mill had to be greased at regular intervals, a grueling and sometimes dangerous operation.[81] But in the more opulent mills this was a festive occasion, for it called for the butchering of a pig, half for the machinery, half for a banquet.

The miller was obliged by law to stop work on Christmas, Easter, Pentecost, and·either All-Saints or Assumption. In fact, he rarely stopped for more than twelve hours on Easter and a few hours on Pentecost and Christmas.[82] Floods, ice, or drought may have been catastrophic economically, but the unexpected interlude was a welcome reprieve physically and psychologically.

The miller is most often depicted pouring grain into the hopper or testing the quality of the meal by spreading the flour as it flowed from the spout with his smooth, broad thumb (whence our "rule of thumb," and our admiration for skills "worth a miller's thumb").[83] But he had many other critical and time-consuming tasks, contingent upon the kinds of grinding he did, which in turn depended in part on his clientele and on his ambition and dexterity. Increasingly millers were required to do more than merely receive grain to be transformed "as is" more or less indifferently into meal. The raw material varied from place to place and from season to season, and an alert miller had to adjust constantly to the diversity in order to produce high quality merchandise. Speculative grain trading and flour making imposed more exacting quality standards that required new, complex, and delicate operations such as grain preparation, meal bolting, and flour mixing.[84]

Often grain arrived encrusted with sand, dust, powdered earth, dried manure, weevils, chaff, seeds, cockle, and a hidden mass of microscopic life. The miller who cared about the caliber of flour he produced had to cleanse the

81. Cf. Bernard Henry, *Des métiers et des hommes à la lisière des bois*, p. 22.

82. BN, Coll. Joly 1803, fols. 96–99. See the case of miller Augustin Pichard, operator of a mill under the Pont-Neuf, who was fined 15 livres for working on Pentecost. AN, Z^{1H} 417, 18 December 1744. Millers outside the capital ran the risk of fines of 5 livres for working on the feast day of the parish patron saint, but this did not deter them. See the case of Lecercle from Pontoise. BN, Coll. Joly 1803, fols. 100–101, 1 December 1739. On round-the-clock grinding pressure, see miller Lovejoy's experience: Thomas Hardy, *The Trumpet Major* (London, 1962), p. 95.

83. Bennett and Elton, *Corn Milling*, 3:146; Jacob, *Six Thousand Years*, pp. 129–30. Cf. Chaucer's "Thombe of gold." Jean Harrowven, *The Origins of Rhymes, Songs and Sayings* (London, 1977), p. 99. Snyder maintains that the miller's digital talent resided not in his thumb but in his index finger, which was endowed with an intricate network of highly developed nerves. *Bread*, p. 210.

84. Evans, *Young Millwright*, p. 273.

grain by sieving, blowing, and rubbing. Some millers even washed, scoured, and dried it. The most advanced mills at the end of the century used mechanical suction and aspiration. On the other hand, cleaning necessarily caused some waste and exposed the miller to charges of stealing. Many millers left the refuse in the grain, thus underwriting the self-protective doctrine: "Everything is grist that comes to this mill."[85] The integration of bolting into the milling operation added a whole new cycle of labor. In mills designed toward the end of the century, this process of sifting, separating, and grading the flour sometimes took up two whole floors. Hand bolting was a slow and costly procedure that commercial millers found inefficient. Bolting machinery required a modest capital investment and a new range of expertise, but it did not spare the miller's wife the old-fashioned task of darning the sifting cloths. Bolting, like flour mixing, received its greatest impetus from the new technology called economic milling.[86]

Commercialization, then, meant much more work, yet master millers began to free themselves from the yoke of time precisely as they became more market oriented and shifted from service to speculation. His new business activities required the miller to reorganize and perhaps rationalize the work procedures at the mill. They may have forced him to hire and train new help, or impelled him to introduce labor-saving technologies. As the mill became more like a factory, the miller shifted increasingly from worker to entrepreneur, and a new relation developed between employer and employees. But this evolution affected only a small number of mills before the Revolution.

While the mill was obviously the focus of the miller's energies, he had numerous ancillary tasks that were only indirectly related to milling, other occupations called forth by the mill's "dependencies," and diverse household functions not peculiar to flour making. Numerous confreres must have been as busy as the miller Lucas who "did direct the mill, till his field, hunt, fish, do the work of carpenter, blacksmith and mason, help his wife in all the business of the house, read, write, and keep accounts, etc., etc."[87]

His long hours fatigued the miller, but it was the confined, turbulent space in which he worked that seriously threatened his health. The miller and his aides worked in an atmosphere thick with dust. Mouth, nostrils, eyes, and ears were filled with flying particles. The consequence was eye irritation, infection of the ears, and the miller's wheeze and/or cough, a veritable identification card in the profession. After years of inhaling the dust, the

85. See Snyder, *Bread*, p. 140. Note that certain impurities could damage the machinery. Kozmin, *Flour Milling*, pp. 58–59.

86. Grimshaw, *Miller, Millwright, and Millfurnisher*, p. 254; Amos, *Processes of Flour Manufacture*, p. 65. Yet Philippe Macquer's claim that "the machines do everything" in mills by the 1760s is wildly exaggerated. *Dictionnaire portatif des arts et métiers* (Paris, 1766), 2:226. Cf. Reynolds, *Windmills and Watermills*, p. 53.

87. Pedro A. de Alarcon, *The Three-Cornered Hat*, trans. M. Armstrong (London, 1927), p. 12.

miller often contracted asthma or other lung disorders, sometimes lapsing into dropsy. Cold and humidity further debilitated the respiratory system of water millers, and provoked rheumatisms. The incessant noise of the wheels and millstones and the roar of falling water made millers hard of hearing—another symptom of professional experience. Millers often had lice, commonly known as "miller's white fleas." Contemporary physicians did not know whether millers developed the lice because they were perpetually covered with dirt and hardly ever took off their clothes or whether the flour mixed with sweat and body dirt was irresistible breeding grounds. Finally, millers had to lift sacks of grain and flour that weighed up to 325 pounds. Though they might be as powerful as Chaucer's Simkin or as Thomas Hardy's Loveday, "a bulging fifteen stone man," they suffered chronic back problems and ran a great risk of herniation. Work conditions had improved immeasurably since the pre-Christian days of mill slavery, but the veteran mill worker may still have found the mill as diabolical on the inside as consumers saw it from the outside.[88]

Mill Employees

The miller's assistant was called a miller boy *(garçon meunier)*, a journeyman miller *(compagnon meunier)*, or a miller's aide (garde-moulin).[89] The largest and busiest mills employed more than one aide. Blaise Doudin, age thirty, and Jean-Baptiste Leclerc, age twenty-one, neither of whom could read or write, lived and worked together at the moulin de Trois Cornets (called the Jansenist mill).[90] Miller July of Paris employed a first and a second

88. Geoffrey Chaucer, *The Reeve's Prologue and Tale*, ed. A. C. and J. E. Spearing (Cambridge and New York, 1979), p. 38; Thomas Hardy, *Trumpet Major*, p. 11; "The Miller of Downe," in Katharine M. Briggs, *A Dictionary of British Folktales* (London, 1970), part B, 2:99; Ellen Glasgow, *The Miller of Old Church* (New York, 1911), p. 11. See also the misery of the miller who suffered a hernia while lifting millstones in Turgenev's "Death," *The Hunting Sketches* (New York, 1962), p. 229.

On miller diseases, see Bernardino Ramazzini, *Diseases of Workers*, trans. W. C. Wright (New York, 1964), pp. 231–35, and Philippe Patissier, *Traité des maladies des artisans et celles qui résultent des diverses professions, d'après Ramazzini* (Paris, 1827), pp. 196–97; Finch, *Water Mills and Windmills*, p. 80; Acremant, *Ailes d'argent*, pp. 64–65; Peyronel, *Moulins bateaux*, p. 66; Chris Gibbings, *"Moulins à vent de Bourgogne,"* in *Les Moulins de France* (1978).

In "mill fiction," the noise of the stones and/or wheel is usually portrayed as deafening: e.g., Eliot, *The Mill on the Floss*, pp. 8, 37. Yet in Hardy's *Trumpet-Major* it had a "soothing effect" (p. 164), and for the miller of Petit Cap it became a "lullaby" to which he became drowsily accustomed: Mary Catherwood, *The Chase of Saint-Castin and Other Stories of the French in the New World* (Boston, 1894), p. 85.

89. In the Chartres area, *garde-moulant*. AD Eure-et-Loire, IV E 601, 20 floréal year XII.

90. AN, Y 9649, 29 November 1758.

journeyman who did not get on with one another.[91] The widow Gallorieu at Meaux took on two full-time gardes-moulin, freeing her to devote most of her time to flour sales.[92] In addition to an aide, the widow Laurent engaged a *passeur de bled.*[93] Bolter specialists, commanding twice the wages of aides, began to appear more commonly in the sixties and seventies, probably at the highly commercialized economic mills.[94] In the vast majority of cases, the miller could not afford to employ more than one assistant. Frequently the aide served multiple functions, as in the case of Vassel, called the Picard, who acted both as driver and as garde-moulin.[95] Medard Joselin ran the entire business for his eighty-year-old master miller.[96] The wife of journeyman Jean-Baptiste Godet also worked at the mill, but it is not clear whether she was separately paid or considered a sort of extension of her husband.[97] I have found only one case of a woman who served as a garde-moulin.[98]

Very little is known about the lives of these workers. Recruited almost exclusively from the peasantry, more often than not they appear to have been illiterate. Occasionally they were "fallen" millers who had lost a lease or suffered some sort of disaster.[99] Their relations with their masters do not seem to have been markedly strained. They were bound to the mill, however, by a sort of professional mortmain and they had to be ready to work day and/or night. Characteristically the gardes slept in a garret in the mill itself, like the boy in the famous mill of the Frau. Jean-Baptiste Meignien allocated a small bedroom to his garde in his own house, where he could find genuine repose, but he slept most of the working week on a mattress on the floor of a hut attached to the mill.[100] It goes without saying that the miller boys discharged the most onerous tasks: lifting and loading, greasing, and mounting the wings or descending into the millrace for repairs.

Miller boys started out poor, and it is hard to see how most of them could have avoided remaining poor. They were generally hired by oral contract for three or four months at a time. They were badly paid. A miller at Meaux paid her garde only 10 livres a month in 1776. Jacques Gury earned 15 livres a month in 1750. By the last two decades of the old regime, assistants in the

91. AN, Y 13489, 30 April 1725.
92. AD Seine-et-Marne, 158 E 33, 28 February 1776.
93. AN, Y 11309, 7 July 1748.
94. See, for example, the Daure operation, ca. 1770, AN, F^{12} 1299^A. In the 1850s, a large mill turning four pair of stones required four or five workers in order to operate round the clock. *Enquête sur la boulangerie*, p. 212.
95. Arsenal, ms. Bast. 10080, 15 July 1772.
96. AN, Y 11583, 18 May 1766. Joselin himself was fifty-five years old.
97. AN, Y 13634, 13 March 1739.
98. Widow Plé at Gonesse. AN, Z^{1G} 342^B (1770).
99. See, for instance, *Marcel Barbier: Meunier*, p. 35. Cf. Eugène Le Roy, *Le Moulin du Frau* (Périgord, 1969).
100. AD Seine-et-Oise, 70 H 7, 29 December 1721; AD Seine-et-Marne, 158 E 34, 17 October 1776.

larger mills received one livre a day. In most cases the master nourished them and provided a daily ration of wine, the *pour-boire*.[101] Garde Adrien Diort of Stains, near Gonesse, was so visibly bereft of means that he was assessed a half a sou in *taille*. Fellow villager Jacques Moulu was to pay a livre, as was Michel Graves of nearby Thillay.[102] Antoine Dorget, surely not the only miller aide who suffered chronic misery, lived with his wife, who was gravely ill, in a room described by the police as "extraordinarily small" and foul smelling. They slept on a bed made of "rotten rags."[103] Meignien's boy lived in relative luxury. He slept in a comfortable wooden poster bed fitted with a double mattress, cloth sheets, and woolen blankets. A small mirror, a painting, and a tapestry brightened his walls. He had an armchair, a table, and three straw chairs. These furnishings belonged to his master—the bed was evaluated at 60 livres and all the rest at 7.[104]

Miller boys seem to have been dismissed less often for dishonesty than for lack of alertness.[105] Out-of-work millers' aides, like journeymen *sans condition* in many other trades, easily got into trouble. Desperation born of indigence and frustration or a lust to take vengeance upon a former master commonly led miller boys to break the law: Anselme Thion, a twenty-nine-year-old from the Brie, filched his ex-master's horse, while Pierre Oudin, a twenty-five-year-old native of Dourdan, stole twelve chickens, six geese, and several other items.[106]

The Miller's Other Professions

Given the exigencies of the profession and their paucity of means, the vast majority of millers had to spend all their time at work. Yet a substantial minority engaged simultaneously in other economic activities, usually as a result of family traditions or connections, entrepreneurial ambition, or in a few instances desperation. One miller dealt in hay, an auxiliary form of grain trading. A number doubled as part-time carters, using their wagon(s) and horse(s). Brewing was another grain-linked profession. A miller at Nemours and another at Brueil-en-Vexin had no problems with mill repairs, for each

101. AD Seine-et-Marne, 158 E 33, 28 February 1776; AN, MC, XXXVIII-388, 20 March 1751; AN, F^{12} 1299^A.

102. AN, Z^{1G} 291^B (1740). A number of grades, however, were assessed up to 3 livres. Z^{1G} 397^A, Gonesse and Bonneuil (1781).

103. AN, Y 14946, 19 December 1732.

104. AD Seine-et-Marne, 158 E 34, 17 October 1776.

105. Miller aide Pierre Després was threatened with dismissal not for having impregnated his master's niece, but for having permitted her to distract him while he was in charge of the machinery. BN, Coll. Joly 1802, fols. 112–14, 13 November 1745.

106. AN, Y 10258, 30 May 1764; AN, X^{2B} 1031, 8 June 1764; AN, Y 10370, 26 October 1776. Cf. the case of miller boy Jean Durand, who was executed for murder, rape, and theft: Hardy's Journal, BN, ms. fr. 6681, p. 194 (26 May 1773).

was also a charpentier. Antoine Paran of the Brie was a miller-mason who had collaborated with charpentiers in building mills. Jean Mercier's secondary activity had nothing to do with his Melun flour business; he sold eels that he caught in the Seine to Paris fishmongers. Sieur Devigne, a miller at Vigny, occupied a minor administrative post that was probably grain related. Jean Cochin, a miller on the Bièvre, invested his earnings in a municipal office that required virtually no work: he was a *garde-archer-arquebusier* of Paris. Miller and mealman Jean Foucret had sufficient leisure to serve as an accountant for the *fabrique* of his parish in the capital. Pierre Rousselle, a miller at Chatou, was also a harness maker.[107]

A number of millers on the outskirts of the city had begun to serve wine and offer lodging, even as they continued to grind. One suspects that the fascination with the devil and the sensual allure of the millhouse had less to do with attracting a crowd than the cheap price of extramural wine. Jean-Louis Longpré ran his own cabaret at his moulin de la Couronne at La Courtille, located not far from the Tambour Royal that Ramponneau made the most notorious mill-tavern *(guinguette)*. Pierre Porteman, miller at Grand Gentilly, rented a large room (probably his house next to the mill) as well as a bedroom above it and an adjacent shop to two wine merchants. He retained a granary for his grains and flours.[108]

Farming and baking were the two occupations with which millers most often became involved. Both pointed toward a certain vertical integration and commercial independence. Most water mills and many windmills had some arable land attached to them. In most cases millers used the land for truck gardening and for limited domestic grain produce, but a number of millers, such as Jean François of Rebais, François David of Beaumont, Christophe Marquis of Chambly, Robert Brassard of Crèvecoeur, Etienne Palleau of Dourdan, Philippe Blanche of Blaru, and Jehan Mauvoisin of Jambville, were full-scale laboureurs who grew enough wheat to keep their mills busy for part of the time and to aliment their commercial flour business.[109] François Guibert

107. Archives Seine-Paris, D5B⁶ 4243, 1726; Malouin, *Description et détails des arts,* p. 84; AN, MC, IV-483, 5 April 1734; AN, MC, LXI-601, 26 June 1784; AN, MC, CVIII-492, 26 March 1751; AN, MC, XCI-873, 28 April 1751; AD Seine-et-Oise, Supplément E 322, 3 July 1705; AD Seine-et-Marne, H 559, 1765 (Notre-Dame de la Joye), and H 749, 24 July 1785; AD Seine-et-Oise, unclassified series S (ca. 1790).

108. Archives Seine-Paris, D4B° 16-788; AN, MC, VII-291, 29 April 1754; Sellier, "Moulins," *Bulletin de la Société des amis des monuments parisiens* 7 (1893): 17.

109. Registration list, 29 January 1771, AD Seine-et-Marne, bailliage de Meaux, unclassified; juridiction consulaire, Beaumont, 23 July 1768, AD Seine-et-Oise, 3 B 131; étude Degremont, 22 December 1771, AD Seine-et-Oise; AN, Y 11238, 6 August 1751; AN, MC, CII-363, 20 September 1750; AD Seine-et-Oise, E 3399, ca. 1760 (moulin de Ponceau); notariat de Meulan, tabellion de Jambville, 22 April 1730, AD Seine-et-Oise. For similar cases, see AD Seine-et-Marne: H 38, 7 December 1776; H 559, 10 November 1764; H 730, 23 July 1782. See also Gautier, "Les Moulins de Bretagne et de Vendée," p. 406.

of Meaux had two farms that yielded thirty-five to fifty muids of wheat.[110] André Fouquet, a miller at Beaumont, ran an inn and also borrowed heavily in order to invest in his livestock and grain holdings near Luzarches.[111] François Lefevre of the St.-Denis area was one of several millers who pointed toward the ultimate model of concentration: he was a miller-laboureur-baker.[112] One of the bitterest complaints of the poorest peasants in the Paris region just before the Revolution was that the millers and big laboureurs who were engaged in the flour trade monopolized the land.[113]

Since the fourteenth century, French law had prohibited a miller to exercise the craft of baker, and vice versa. This marriage, it was feared, would result in "frauds" and "manipulations." The miller-baker could become "the master of the price of bread." "Connivance" among miller-bakers could issue in artificial dearths. The incompatibility of the professions was reaffirmed innumerable times in royal, parlementary, and police legislation and sentences.[114]

Yet there were certain arguments in favor of relaxing the prohibition. For classically educated magistrates there was the prestige of the Roman model, in which bakers and millers were one on the grounds that their trades overlapped and indeed were essentially the same.[115] For the sake of efficiency, quality, and economy, a writer in the *Journal économique* in 1757 openly recommended a fusion, at least for rural practitioners.[116] Two decades later Parmentier called for an unconditional merger: "Milling has so much to do with the bakery, that it would be desirable for the same man to exercise both professions."[117] Parmentier remained deeply suspicious of millers who did not have to answer personally for the quality of the bread fabricated with their flour. Since the baker's interest was at stake in the milling process, Parmentier logically contended that he should do it himself. Lieutenant general of police Lenoir shared Parmentier's view and let it be known that "rich bakers" could practice "milling commerce" with his blessing.[118]

---

110. Registration list, 1 February 1771, AD Seine-et-Marne, bailliage de Meaux, unclassified.

111. AN, MC, LXXII-323, 19 October 1751.

112. AN, MC, CXXXVI-285, 21 March 1772. Cf. the miller's boast that he "made more money" than either the farmer or the baker: Grace Fallow Norton, *The Miller's Youngest Daughter* (Boston, 1924), p. 12.

113. I. Loutchisky, "Régime agraire et populations agricoles dans les environs de Paris à la veille de la Révolution," *Revue d'histoire moderne,* n.s. 8 (March–April 1933): 126.

114. BN, ms. fr. 21640, fol. 38ff.; *Encyclopédie méthodique,* Jurisprudence, 2:83; "Histoire des boulangers," p. 132. Cf. Delamare, *Traité de la police,* 2:765, and G. Charlot, "Essai historique sur la meunerie et la boulangerie," *Annales de la Société d'agriculture, sciences, arts et belles-lettres du département d'Indre-et-Loire* 30 (1851): 144.

115. Jacob, *Six Thousand Years,* p. 136.

116. "Avis économique sur la boulangerie," *Journal économique* (October 1757): 48.

117. Parmentier, *Parfait Boulanger,* p. 145.

118. BM Orléans, ms. 1421.

In fact the police position on this question had been ambivalent since the early part of the century. The tension in official thinking is strikingly illustrated in a test case provoked by the widow miller Lubin of St.-Denis,[119] who denounced two forain bakers named Edme and Leger who operated mills in St.-Denis. Other bakers would follow if the government did not enforce the law, she warned; the intensified demand for mills would raise rents, higher rents would compel millers to increase tolls, and this augmentation of fees would raise the price of bread. Moreover, this sort of professional combination would result in the worst "abuses" and "maneuvers." Lubin's crusade, undertaken in the name of the law, was geared to protect her interests and those of other millers who feared competition from integrated miller-baker production units. Her lonely and ultimately vain struggle underlines the price millers paid for not being organized in a guild.

The baker-millers were protected by the prior of St.-Denis (the owner of their mills?), who, for reasons that remain unclear, was counseled by Leclerc du Brillet, Delamare's successor and a leading police theorist. No one was better placed to show them how to circumvent and ultimately obscure the public law position staked out by Lubin and based on four hundred years of precedents. Following Leclerc's line, Edme and Leger argued that their status as forain bakers distinguished them from the faubourg and city bakers, who were the only ones to whom the legislation on incompatibility of professions specifically applied. To support their case, they pointed to other examples of forain baker-millers, particularly in the Gonesse area. Concerning the risk of fraud constituted by the amalgamation of the two professions, the St.-Denis baker-millers observed, not without malice, that one of the reasons they felt obliged to mill for themselves was that they had not been able to find honest millers in the area upon whom they could count. Nor did they hesitate to base their claims on their "natural rights," a logic that proved increasingly attractive in the eighteenth century to those without privileges, though they still subordinated natural law to positive law for the purpose of fixing the rules of social organization. "The public will be much better served," they concluded with reformist zeal, "when the same person [is allowed to] exercise both professions."

The assembly of police decided unequivocally in favor of widow Lubin and the procurator general was instructed to order the fiscal procurator of St.-Denis to enforce the law by shutting down the offending bakers' establishments. Neither the assembly nor the procurator general pressed the decision vigorously, however, and the fiscal procurator was clearly disposed to gratify, if not the baker-millers, then the prior of St.-Denis. Edme and Leger con-

119. BN, ms. fr. 21640, fols. 386ff., and assembly of police, 14 January 1734, ms. fr. 11356, fol. 232.

tinued to operate in peace and others followed in their footsteps, at St.-Denis and elsewhere.[120]

The evidence suggests that the Paris police tolerated mill involvement not only by the forain bakers but by those of the guild and the faubourg St.-Antoine as well.[121] I have encountered fifteen master bakers who owned mills: ten windmills, one water mill, and six mills of unknown type. Michel Fleury and André Leroux each owned two mills; four of these masters operated the mills for their own account. Jean Fleury ground exclusively for his own bakery business and for "that of an associate," probably another master baker. Though it is unlikely that any of the other owner-operators was a commercial miller, it is quite possible that they milled "for the public" (custom milling) once bakery needs were met. Two other master bakers, François Picot and Noël Duval, operated mills that they rented from others. Picot engaged in speculative flour traffic at the same time that he kept a bakeshop. The baker guild administrators (*jurés*) censured Duval for failing to equip his mill with scales and weights, but they did not object to the fact that he exercised a second profession. Master baker Barnabé Grezel owed his prosperous bakery to the commercial leverage that his milling enterprise gave him. And certainly there were others.

Among the nonmaster baker-millers who have surfaced, the forains predominate, but I have no doubt that there were many more baker-millers from the faubourg St.-Antoine than I have found. Fourteen forains rented mills: three at Gonesse, one at Dugny, one at St.-Denis (apart from Edme and Leger), three at Ruelle (sharing the same mill), one at the Haute Borne, one at Courcelles, and two each at La Courtille and the faubourg de Gloire. Forain Charles Gaucher owned a water mill somewhere near Meaux. François Papillon began his career as a miller-forain at Gonesse and like many other forains gravitated to the faubourg St.-Antoine, where, once established, he apparently abandoned milling.[122] Pierre Lepage, an affluent baker from the faubourg St.-Antoine, owned two windmills on the plain of the faubourg St.-Marcel.[123] Two of his neighbors and colleagues, Nicolas Tellier and Charles Leprince, leased mills on the butte de Montmartre and near Fresnes respectively.[124] Louis Lacroix of the faubourg St.-Laurent sold bread twice a week in the bread markets, but consecrated most of his time to selling fellow bakers flour that he manufactured at a mill that he either owned or rented.[125] Outside

---

120. Clément to procurator general, 6 August 1770, BN, Coll. Joly 1152, fols. 6–7.
121. For the sources for the miller-bakers or baker-millers, see Appendix C.
122. AN, Y 11228, 25 October 1741.
123. AN, MC, XXVIII-224, 11 January 1732; BN, Coll. Joly 1116, fols. 226–31, November 1725.
124. AN, MC: LII-37, 14 April 1650; XCII-569, 20 January 1751; VII-283, 3 May 1752.
125. Ibid., XXXIII-58, 15 October 1770. Cf. the case of A.-A. Poucheret, who began as a

the immediate vicinity of Paris, where multiple occupations in all domains were much more common, baking and milling were probably even more entwined. Martin Bordier of Melun, who ran the Mill of the Three Mills, was a baker at the same time. So were millers Jacques Ferre of Lagny and Eustache Lecercle of Pontoise.[126] Moreover, many millers, such as Pierre Bruxelle and J.-B. Ducellier of the Meaux environs, had working ovens in their mill houses and probably baked both for local clients and for the nearby market towns.[127]

The appetite for vertical integration grew in the nineteenth century and reversed the trend, or rather the set of arrangements, characteristic of the eighteenth century. Before the Revolution, it was probably far more common for bakers to seek control of mills than for millers to insinuate themselves into the bakery operation.[128] The bakers had many more incentives to move in this direction than the millers, for whom vast new commercial horizons were just beginning to open. Bakers who became millers wanted to protect themselves against cheating, but above all they desired to secure their independence. "Whoever is attached to the mill wheel," went the adage, "may be turned by the devil." In the nineteenth century, however, as milling became more concentrated and industrialized, the milling companies competed more and more feverishly for Parisian clientele. In part in order to guarantee themselves a piece of the highly fragmented bakery market and in part as a result of defaulted loans made to baker-clients in trouble, more and more millers became owners of bakery businesses—the *fonds* and often the shop-bakeroom-apartment as well. One still encounters miller-bakers at the purely artisanal level in the twentieth century.[129]

Leasing a Mill

Only a few millers owned their own mills. Most of them rented, for periods that ranged usually from three to nine years, though one encounters an occasional emphyteutic lease of ninety-nine years in the greater Paris region. The mean lease time for forty-two water mills in my sample was 7.8 years.

baker, married into a milling business, and later returned to the bakery: Maillard, *Moulins de Montmartre,* pp. 163–65.

126. AD Seine-et-Marne, B 120 (1688), and E 1247, 29 May 1750; AD Seine-et-Oise, 70 H 8, 24 February 1735.

127. AD Seine-et-Marne, B 68, 29 April 1697, and B 411, 17 December 1750.

128. For an exception, see the case of the miller from the Melun area who was the landlord of baker Desrues of the rue de Charenton. AN, Y 13648, 7 September 1752.

129. E. Barrabé, *Le Pain à bon marché: Meuneries-boulangeries, nécessité de leur création* (Paris, 1876), p. 33n; Maurice Bouteloup, *Le Travail de nuit dans la boulangerie,* p. 11; *Marcel Barbier: Meunier,* pp. 36, 52. Cf. Parmentier's warning to bakers not to become indebted to millers. *Parfait Boulanger,* p. 153.

Eleven water-mill owners gave their tenants the option of renewing twice for three-year periods after the first three years. Lease time for windmills was slightly shorter, averaging seven years in nine cases. Four lessees obtained three-year renewal options.[130]

The first and second estates dominated the ranks of the mill owners. Of the sixty-one water mills in the lease series that supply information on proprietorship, thirty-one were owned by ecclesiastical institutions (over half by communities of regular clergy) and twenty-two by nobles, including several princes of the blood. The other proprietors were three millers, two bakers, one laboureur, a merchant, and a *bourgeois-rentier*. Eighteen leases reveal the socio-professional identity of the owners of windmills, a cheaper, less attractive, and less prestigious investment. Nobles and ecclesiastical institutions possessed four windmills each, millers and bakers each owned three, and royal officials and parlementary magistrates two. Other data on owners are extremely ephemeral and inconclusive. On a police listing of mill owners in 1725, we find two master brewers, four lawyers, a parlementary president, two bakers, a surgeon, an abbot, several hospitals, the chapter of St.-Marcel, a Jesuit community, the Hôtel Royal des Invalides, and the prince de Guise.[131] The Hôtel-Dieu owned four mills at Gonesse.[132] The king alienated a considerable number of mills in his domain in the Paris generality.[133] The fabrique of St.-Sulpice, the chapter of Notre-Dame, and the chapter of Ste.-Opportune were among the other religious institutions possessing mills.[134] There were also cases of entrepreneurial millers like the widow Laurent, who owned three valuable mills strategically placed on the Seine.[135]

Parmentier denounced the tendency of owners to rent their mills "at an excessive price, even above the level they could legitimately yield in income were they working day and night and charging the highest tolls." This placed the "honest and intelligent" miller in a terrible bind, for if he faithfully devoted the three-quarters of an hour that a setier of wheat required for a proper grinding he would have trouble paying his rent.[136] The prices of leases of

130. For the list of these contracts and ancillary sources used in this section, see Appendix D.

131. BN, Coll. Joly 1116, fols. 226ff.

132. Archives Assistance publique, no. 110, liasse 632; Adrien-Henri Thery, *Gonesse dans l'histoire: Une vieille bourgade et son passé à travers les siècles* (Persan, Seine-et-Oise, 1960), pp. 97–98.

133. Boislisle, *Mémoire de la généralité de Paris (1700)*, 1:263–66, 270–80. Cf. AN, Y 11583, 18 May 1766 (régie de Charenton).

134. AN, Q^{1*} 1099$^{159-75}$ and F^7 4296.

135. AN, Y 12141, 30 June 1739. Cf. other examples of millers owning as many as four and six mills. AN, F^{20} 293, 12 germinal year II (Mantes district).

136. Parmentier, *Parfait Boulanger*, pp. 153–54. For other hints of high mill prices, see Malisset, "Mémoire," 1770, AN, F^{11} 1194, and Camille Desmoulins, *Les Insignes Meuniers de Corbeil, ou La Compagnie des famines découverte, en présence de M. Necker, accusé par M. Desmoulins* (Paris, 1789), p. 8. Rent gouging by mill owners, usually aristocrats or high-

eighty-one water mills, eight boat mills, and twenty-eight windmills describe a great range. Rental of water mills ranged from 135 to 5,000 livres a year, boat mills from 510 to 1,250 livres, and windmills from 82 to 900 livres. The average price of a water lease was 904 livres (median = 800), of a boat mill 714 livres (median = 600), and of a windmill 369 livres (median = 331). Despite Parmentier's strictures, there was a surprisingly large number of relatively inexpensive mills, not only wind but water driven as well. The most expensive mills tended to be the establishments most deeply involved in the commercial nexus. Given their high volume of activity, much of it to serve Parisian needs, in some cases their propitious location, and more rarely the outstanding quality of their machinery, the dearest mills were not necessarily the most "excessively" priced. In the expensive category would fall the mills called Chantereine (1,700 livres) and de la Fosse (1,415 livres), belonging to the Carmelites at Pontoise; the mill of St.-Sauveur (2,000 livres), owned by the chapter of Notre-Dame at Melun; the mill of St.-Antoine (1,800 livres), at Charenton; and a mill (1,715 livres) let by the grand prieuré de France at Meaux.[137] Parmentier's assessment is probably most applicable to mills priced in the middle and slightly above, which were neither particularly well located nor well equipped and which could not count upon a heavy, steady turnover.

Most transactions called for cash payments. Whereas it was relatively common for owners to demand supplements in kind to rents in cash, leases phrased strictly in kind were rare. The only genuine cluster of leases-in-kind I have found was located in the Chartres area, where ten out of fifteen contracts for water mills stipulated rents in grain, usually in "good grain of maslin," occasionally in wheat. Eight of the ten owners were ecclesiastical institutions. Six of the leases were signed during a period of rising prices (two years of upward movement preceding the signature); four were agreed upon after periods of comparable downward tendency. As far as I can tell, these mills had been customarily let out in kind. In only one case can I show that the owner, the abbey of St.-Père-en-Vallée, switched from a rent in cash to a rent in kind—it so happens, after a phase of at least four years of price stagnation. One would need to establish longitudinal series for each mill before one could venture any kind of useful conjectures about commercial perception and policy. The rewards of leases in kind became increasingly evident in the second half of the century. The cash value of the rent of the mill

---

level clerics, was a staple of folklore and fairytales. See "The Miller of Downe," in Briggs, *Dictionary of British Folk-tales,* part B, 2:100–101; "Bone Meal in the Flour," in Barrett, *More Tales from the Fen,* p. 9.

137. On the other hand, I am less sure about the commercial orientation of the mill rented out by widow Gaston at Noisiel near the Lagny market for 3,600 livres. One must keep in mind that this lease included twenty arpents of rich Briard arable, as well as other dependencies. I came upon Maillard's *Moulins de Montmartre* too late to use her windmill lease figures (ranging from 200 to 500 livres) in my calculations.

owned by the chapter of Chartres in the city hovered around 3,000 livres in 1788, despite the fact that it was no better mechanically equipped or accessorily endowed than nearby mills that rented for a third to a half less.

Price variation reflected a host of concrete matters anterior to landlord greed and intensity of demand. Mills differed in design and construction, condition, power source, efficiency and productivity, location and right of way, character of habitual clientele, and socio-juridical personality. These differences determined the range of costs (e.g., repairs, fees and dues, etc.) and the margins of profit that could reasonably be expected. Moreover, virtually every lease involved "dependencies" of varying importance: houses, barns, stables, arable lands, meadowlands, vineyard, forest, islands, ponds, orchards. In one case, for example, a laboureur paid the comtesse d'Emery 2,250 livres a year for a mill that included a large farm. What really interested him, however, was the land. He sublet the mill to another laboureur for 1,200 livres. Without weighing all of these factors, it is impossible to decide whether a given rent was exorbitant or not.

In addition to money payments, the water leases frequently demanded supplements in kind and/or service that may have had as much to do with the dependencies as with the mills themselves. Seventeen owners required poultry offerings, most commonly ducks and chickens, occasionally turkeys. (The noble owner of the Moulin Neuf d'Auffreville stipulated "four *fat* hens.") Seven leases called for extra payment in grain, in two cases in very substantial amounts of five and three muids (Paris measure), that radically modified the cost of renting, especially in years of high prices. One proprietor received unlimited free grindings; another demanded six and a half muids of conversion to flour a year. The comte d'Antragues asked for two plates of fish a year; the Parisian owner of a Charenton mill settled for one plate worth six livres every Easter. The religious of the abbey of St.-Père-en-Vallée at Chartres had a weakness for eels. Several contracts reserved fishing rights in the mill pond for the owners, and one obliged the tenant to provide a fishing boat. Two proprietors counted on cakes, one on a plump pig (or a cash payment of thirty livres), another on cheese, another on bread, and still another on the planting of certain kinds of trees. In return for the right to lease one of his water mills, the prince de Rohan obtained a *pot de vin* of 400 livres in cash above and beyond the rental price of 1,700 livres. The seminary of Grand Beaulieu at Chartres insisted on a *pot de vin* of 300 livres, but promised to deduct it from the last three years' rent on a nine-year lease. Only two windmill contracts imposed supplementary payments: a royal councillor demanded one roasting pig every year and a master of requests asked for twelve chickens ("good and fat") and twelve setiers of maslin.

There is no doubt that prices tended to rise, especially in the second half of the eighteenth century, though the movement is extremely difficult to document mill by mill and is sometimes less ample than one might have imagined.

The owner of the Green water mill on the western side of the capital more than doubled the rent between 1729 (629 livres) and 1778 (1,300 livres). Yet the proprietor of the Burgundy water mill at Auffreville, located in the same area, increased his price by only 100 livres between 1740 and 1766. The comte d'Antragues added the same premium to his water mill near Chartres between 1746 and 1766. The price of the water mill of Chantereine at Pontoise grew steadily from 1,200 livres in 1728 to 1,400 livres in 1742 to 1,700 livres in 1755, but did not increase for at least the next quarter-century, despite the dizzying surge of prices between 1765 and 1775. Master baker Siméon Delamarre augmented the rent on his Paris windmill by barely 7 percent between 1760 and 1768, despite the cascading price level that resulted in the tripling and even quadrupling of the price of the bread that he sold. In 1770 the marquis de Reverseaux did not inflate the price of 150 livres that he had obtained in 1762 for his windmill in the Beauce, but he shrewdly tripled the amount of grain that was due in kind.

Contracts for water and wind leases were virtually identical. They required the miller to pay a term or sometimes a whole year's rent in advance and to guarantee future payments by stocking the mill with merchandise, equipment, furniture, and effects equal at least to the value of a year's charges. In a few instances the owners demanded a surety bond, either because the rent was very high (as in the case of the widow Gaston's 3,600 livres) or because the lessee did not inspire full confidence (such was the attitude of the royal abbey of St.-Faron toward the miller Candas). A relative, often himself a miller, usually supplied the guarantee.

The tenant pledged to maintain the mill in good condition. He was responsible for all "small" or "current" repairs and more often than not bore the burden of all repairs, regardless of magnitude or genesis.[138] Only two watermill owners agreed to pay for "major" repairs; the chapter of Notre-Dame of Melun paid in all cases and the owner of a large mill in the Brie assumed costs, provided the tenant could show that he had properly regulated the flow of water in the millrace. Two other water-mill proprietors agreed to supply all the wood for repairs, while one windmill owner stood willing to replace the shaft, a considerable outlay, once during the course of the lease. The heavy cost of repairs ruined some millers.[139]

In order to verify whether the miller fulfilled his promise to keep the mill in good condition, an evaluation, called a *prisée,* was conducted, either at the

138. For a particularly rigorous instance of this total tenant responsibility, see AN, MC, LXXXIX-445, 2 July 1737. This concerns a water mill, but wind contracts followed suit, e.g., ibid., VII-325, 12 March 1760.

139. For an example of the impact of these expenses, see Archives Seine-Paris, D4B[6] 75-4975, 12 January 1780. In Brittany windmill owners tried to distinguish between damages caused by "the impetuosity of the wind," for which their tenant millers were not liable, and damages resulting from their "error" in dealing with the wind. Durand-Vaugaron, "Le Moulin à vent en Bretagne," p. 345n.

expiration of the lease (but generally only if the owners had serious doubts about renewing it) or when a tenant was about to leave the mill for good. While the prisée afforded the owner more or less sweeping protection against depreciation as well as damage, it also insured the new miller-tenant against the risk of having to answer for depredations that occurred prior to his occupancy. The prisée could also favor the departing tenant, for if it could be demonstrated that he had made improvements that enhanced the value of the mill beyond the assessment made upon his entry at the beginning of the lease, he was entitled to receive compensation from the owner or, in some circumstances, from his successor. Experts conducted the prisée, either charpentiers, whose business it was to build and repair mills and who were therefore deemed the most authoritative referees, or millers, who were often willing to perform the service without charge for their fellow millers. Very rarely did both parties invest their confidence in the same wise man whose arbitration would be binding. Normally the prisée was a "contradictory" or adversary encounter, in which each expert-advocate bargained for the best possible deal for his party. When differences could not be ironed out, the parties usually turned to another set of experts before considering third-party mediation. Ordinarily, however, the experts managed to reach agreement through discussion and compromise. The prisée was solemnized by the presence of a notary or an analogous legal agent, who gave the agreement a contractual cast.[140] If the "before" appraisal turned out to be the higher, the tenant paid the difference to the owner; if the "after" assessment surpassed the "before," then the owner paid the miller.

The fact that there was no explicit allowance for wear posed the most serious threat to the outgoing miller. The miller was responsible for restituting every inch of thickness of millstone and for replacing wood that had been rotting, metal that had been rusting, and ropes that had been fraying inconspicuously for years. Nor were there standard reference criteria for indemnification, even within the same areas. Everything seemed to be sui generis, dependent on the specific material conditions at a given mill and the particular experiences of the experts. At a water mill near Chartres, a prisée in 1781 set the value of the *pouce*, or inch, of stone at 6 livres, twice the price that had been practiced on a nearby water mill in 1745 and four times the estimation made on another Chartres-area water mill in 1752. Seven years later two charpentiers fixed the stone price at a windmill in Chartres at 50 livres the pouce, an extraordinary discrepancy, even allowing for egregious

---

140. For an example of a classic prisée with charpentiers on each side, see the windmill of Sandeville at Chartres, AD Eure-et-Loir, XVI E 136, 7 May 1788. The same procedure continued to be followed in the nineteenth century. See ibid., II E 2815, no. 100, 29 June 1809 (mill of Chesnay, at Moutiers). Also AN, MC, XXVI-456, 4 January 1751. For instances of a single expert arbitrator, see the windmill at Epiais, AD Seine-et-Oise, E 1852, 29 May 1733 and another at Gency, ibid., E 2751, 27 March 1729.

differences in stone age and quality.[141] In the late twenties, the chapter of
Beauvais accorded an allowance of 4 livres the pouce at its four water mills, a
relatively high price in its view, but justified by its promise to install new
stones at the beginning of the lease. At a nearby water mill a few years later
the owner set the standard at 3 livres.[142] A moderate "erosion" yardstick
might comfort the miller with the knowledge that he would not face exorbitant
departure costs. On the other hand it would serve as a potent disincentive
against improving flour quality and productivity, for the miller would perceive
little interest in replacing the old stones with new, superior ones for which he
would only be very incompletely reimbursed.[143] Certain millers made genuine
improvements that their owners encouraged them to pass on to their successors, that is, to sell to them without imposing any cost on the owners, who
might nevertheless profit from the improvements to raise the rent.[144] A
shrewd miller with a bit of capital hid the deterioration for which he knew he
would be held to account behind "improvements" for which he could legitimately ask the proprietor to indemnify him. Miller Jean-Baptiste Meignien
received 521 livres from his owner in 1776 for improvements that he made on
a mill at Meaux. A miller quitting the Chantereine mill at Pontoise collected
850 livres from his successor.[145] Faced with a bill for almost 200 livres, miller
Jacques L'Enfant attempted to cut his costs by undertaking to make certain
repairs himself. While the owner might have preferred the cash, the *priseurs*
apparently gave the tenant this option.[146]

The leases differed widely in terms of a host of burdens and benefits that
they imposed and/or conferred. One crucial issue concerned compensation
for shut-down time for natural or manmade causes. The Carmelites of Pontoise took the parsimonious posture to which most millers were inured. They
denied their tenants the right to claim any reductions or indemnities for stoppages "on the pretext of war, famine, drought, floods, or other causes." A
number of owners offered compensation due to stoppages caused by the need
for repairs, with a temporal "deductible," calculated cumulatively or case by
case. In the former category was the chapter of Troyes, which promised its
tenant rent adjustments for stoppages totaling more than thirty days during

141. The following are all from AD Eure-et-Loir: II E 84, 21 April 1781; XVI E 309, 7
February 1745; E 1137, 12 October 1752; XVI E 136, 7 May 1788.

142. AD Oise, G 41, 24 November 1728, and H 1460, 20 July 1731.

143. See the explicit disincentive clause regarding stone replacement in the lease offered
by the Carmelites of Pontoise for a highly commercialized Paris-oriented mill whose
operator had to produce attractive flour in order to survive at the Halle. AD Seine-et-Oise,
70 H 7, 9 November 1742.

144. See the encouragement given by the dames de l'abbaye de Faremoutiers to their
miller. AD Seine-et-Marne, H 448 (moulin de Condé).

145. AD Seine-et-Marne, 158 E 34, 17 October 1776, and AD Seine-et-Oise, 70 H 7, 29
December 1721. For another instance of an owner owing money to his tenant, see quittance,
20 April 1751, AN, MC, XLIII-399.

146. AD Eure-et-Loir, XVI E 136, 7 May 1788.

the year. In the latter class were the prince d'Auvergne, who indemnified his miller at Neuville 20 sous a day after four days; the abbey of St.-Séverin, which granted its miller near Châteaubaudon an unspecified rent rebate after a week's stoppage; and the seigneur of Chavigny, who offered the same assurance after two weeks' interruption. The chapter of the Ste.-Chapelle Royale of Vincennes imposed a surprisingly detailed series of conditions on the tenant of its mill in the Brie, including the obligation to remove certain bushes and thorns, to repair fences, to pay local honoraria, and the like. The proprietor of a windmill in the faubourg St.-Marcel forbade his tenant to keep animals of any kind, perhaps partly to deprive him of the temptation to steal from his clients in order to feed his animals. Less ambiguous moralizing issued in clauses of two other leases. A noble proprietor of a water mill near Chartres prohibited his tenant from "chasing" grain or grinding on Sunday or on holidays, a standard of austerity to which the law enjoined all millers but which they could rarely afford to respect. A merchant owner of another Chartrain water mill in the shadow of the cathedral required his tenant "to operate the said mill as would a good family man," as if to combat the image of debauchery that sometimes stigmatized the miller. (Language of this sort of course was not peculiar to mill leases.) Tenants of *banal* mills (mills subject to seigneurial constraints) had to comply with a familiar set of strictures, including the injunction to do everything to prevent "subject-vassals" from taking their grain elsewhere, to collect the grain from them and deliver it to them as flour, and to grind the grain of clients who brought it to the mill themselves within twenty-four hours. It is worth noting, however, that some millers who did not hold leases to banal mills suffered banal-like restrictions. The tenant of the marquis de Reverseaux in the Chartrain, for example, was told exactly where he could "hunt" clients and where not. The duc de Beaumont tried to regulate territorial competition in the region in which he let mills. Finally, the leases differed in the prescriptions for the payment of royal taxes and seigneurial dues, for the performance of various civic duties, for the practice of certain safety precautions, and so forth.

Water mills were of course worth more than windmills. A water mill at Chevreuse toward the end of the century was appraised at 26,000 livres, while Paris bridge mills commanded between 15,000 and 20,000 livres throughout the century.[147] The most expensive windmill I encountered, located at Montmartre, fetched 10,500 livres.[148] More commonly they sold for between 4,000

147. Archives Seine-Paris, D4B⁶ 113-8091, 1 March 1792, and D4B⁶ 68-4428, 1778; Arsenal, ms. Bast. 10152 (September 1727); Cherrière, *La Lutte contre l'incendie dans les halles, les marchés, et les foires de Paris sous l'ancien régime*, in Julien Hayem, ed., *Mémoires et documents pour servir à l'histoire du commerce et de l'industrie en France*, 3d ser. (Paris, 1913), p. 200.
148. AN, MC, VII-307, 28 April 1757.

and 5,000 livres.[149] The lease-mandated evaluation of working parts also reflected the disparity between water and wind. Two water mills were assessed at 1,861 livres and 1,751 livres, while four windmills were appraised at 578, 914, 1,084, and 1,177 livres.[150]

Machines powered by water were the most commonly found mills in the primary Parisian supply crown. Water-driven mills turned more evenly and consequently produced more and often smoother flour than either wind- or boat mills. While the windmiller had more difficulty controlling his machine, the water miller faced a more complex task of harnessing the energy for optimal results. The water miller had to choose his site much more meticulously and he often encountered challenges to his water rights. Both wind- and water millers confronted similar problems of maintenance. The quality of the stones was more important than the type of wheel or wings, and the stones demanded unending attention.

The miller toiled long hours, often dozing near his stones, assisted by one or more *garçons* and by his wife. Notorious for his physical strength, the miller often fell victim to one of several occupational diseases common to the mill. Commercialization, which transformed the milling function during the eighteenth century, imposed new responsibilities such as cleaning grain, bolting meal, and mixing flour. At the same time, it required—and enabled—the miller to abandon more of the physical labor to his aides and to become more of a businessman. It was not unusual for a miller to undertake some farming. Certain millers were also deeply involved in the bakery, despite the official prohibition against combining these trades.

Water mills were worth considerably more than windmills, selling for two to four or five times as much. Nobles and ecclesiastical institutions were the most frequent proprietors in the Paris area. Most working millers rented mills. Water mills commanded about two and a half times more rent than windmills. Prices rose steadily across the century, though perhaps not as sharply as one might have expected. Mill rents reflected a host of factors: owner avidity, intensity of demand, location, design and condition, productivity, clientele, and physical dependencies. The leases passed much of the burden for repair and wear to the tenants.

Millwrights built better and sturdier machines in the eighteenth century than ever before, but they did not fundamentally change the design conception in either water or wind structures. Thus mills remained hostage to the

149. Ibid.: LXIX-316, 20 October 1733; LXIX-317, 16 March 1734. Among the prices of Montmartre mills reported by Maillard are 10,000 livres (1723, Grande Tour); 9,000 livres (1780s, Radet); 8000 livres (1769, Petite Tour); 5,000 livres (1766, Vieille Tour). *Moulins de Montmartre,* pp. 67, 102, 112, 134.

150. AN, MC: CX-377, 11 August 1751; XVII-799, 10 August 1751; III-808, 13 September 1708; V-421, 21 July 1745.

vicissitudes of the weather and the kingdom remained vulnerable to the depredations of flour famines provoked by mill stoppages. A number of innovators tried to find a way to produce flour without relying on wind or water or to shelter the wind and water somehow from meteorological accidents. In the short run, these experiments with hand, horse, and steam mills and with various modifications and combinations of wind and water did not yield practical results.

CHAPTER 7

The Miller and the Public

*T*raditionally the miller stayed at home and waited for his business. During the eighteenth century this "custom" milling gave way to a new sort of enterprise called "merchant" milling. Millers entered the grain trade, made flour on speculation, and competed aggressively for a piece of the metropolitan wholesale market. Commercialization changed a great deal, but not everything, in the relations between the miller and the public: the miller's reputation remained as execrable as ever and nevertheless the robust miller continued to exercise considerable influence in his home community. The police remained less interested in lurid tales of miller roguery than in keeping the stones grinding, especially if the flour was Paris bound.

Custom Milling and Tolls

The vast majority of millers in old-regime France practiced custom milling. This was true even of the large metropolitan areas until the end of the eighteenth century, and in some cases still later. Custom milling meant grinding on command for clients, private (e.g., peasants) or professional (e.g., bakers), who provided the grain. The custom miller was an artisan rather than a merchant. In return for a fee, he performed a service. His role in the provisioning process was more or less passive. Theoretically, he had the liberty to engage in *la chasse,* that is, to seek out clients in neighboring towns and villages.[1] These "encroaching" millers met stiff opposition from fellow

1. L. C. Manesse, *Traité du droit de bâtir moulin et des bannalités en général* (Paris, 1785), pp. 245–52. On the practice of canvassing for clients, see "The Adventure of Cherry of Zennor," in Ernest Rhys, ed., *English Fairy and Other Folktales* (London, 1890), p. 95.

millers who were located or had staked out claims in these places and were prepared to lower fees or to make other concessions in order to retain "their" clients' custom. The juridical and political resistance of seigneurs exercising the monopoly of *banalité* was perhaps more formidable. Backed by his lord, a miller from the Pontoise area had the horses, wagons, and merchandise of "the foreign millers" seized—a staggering blow to their business. Similarly, near Senlis, a seigneur hastened to quell an anti-*banal* revolt fomented by "a town miller" whose challenge to the lord's monopoly was supported by twenty-two household heads. Near Crépy-en-Valois another lord struggled for more than twenty years to prevent "outsiders" from soliciting within his jurisdiction.[2] Local police officials preferred to avoid disorders by dividing the custom terrain among different millers, who were strongly urged to restrict their appetites. More surprising, and profoundly discouraging to enterprising millers, was the decision of the Paris Parlement, reiterated several times, to "forbid millers to seek out and solicit business outside their parishes," an injunction that went against the liberal tide of the late fifties and early sixties that so deeply marked the grain and flour trades.[3]

Of course many millers found it quite comfortable to remain at home. These millers did not even need a mule or a cart. Their customers, mostly private individuals, delivered the grain for grinding and picked up the meal. *Banal* millers were often obliged by their leases to send for the grain of the lord's subjects and to return the flour to them within a relatively limited period of time. By the end of the seventeenth century, millers who hoped to attract baker traffic learned that they were expected to provide transport at least one way and increasingly both ways. Thus Pierre Bruxelle and Nicolas Hemas, millers near Meaux, each kept several horses for the purpose of serving clients. By the middle of the eighteenth century, the strongest millers in the Paris region, such as Louis Lardier of Clichy-la-Garenne, Piedeleu of Valmondois, and Bocquere of Trilbardou, owned their own wagons and horse teams and employed full-time drivers. Middling millers such as Lecercle of Pontoise and widow Dambry of Cramoisy hired drivers and sometimes carts by the day. Smaller millers such as Pierre Bernard of Poissy and Charles Bonnefoy of St.-Maurice picked up and delivered themselves, by small cart and muleback.[4]

Another name for custom milling was toll milling—the miller transformed grain into meal in return for a toll, whose fairness was often questioned.

2. AN, Y 11739, 1776 (Pierre Benoit); AD Seine-et-Oise, E 1216, 1745 (Nesles); AD Oise, G 7208, 1709 (Vincent).

3. Arrêts of 13 June 1758, 9 March 1761, and 8 August 1768, AN, AD XI 39.

4. AD Seine-et-Marne, B 68, 2 March 1683 and 29 April 1697; AN, Y 9539, 26 May 1758 and 1 October 1765; Archives Seine-Paris, D2B⁶ 734, 3 February 1741, and D5B⁶ 4243; BN, Coll. Joly 1829, fols. 293–96; AN, Y 15065, 1 December 1763, and Y 11237, 27 November 1750.

Custom milling. Sixteenth-century
engraving (Deutsches Brotmuseum)

Though "The Miller's Advice to His Three Sons in Taking Off Toll" was an
English tale, the issue it dealt with was of equal concern to the French:

> There was a miller who had three sons,
> And knowing his life was almost run,
> He called them all, and asked their will,
> If that to them he left his mill.
>
> He called first for his eldest son,
> Saying, "My life is almost run,
> If I to you this mill do make,
> What toll do you intend to take?"
>
> "Father," said he, "my name is Jack.
> Out of a bushel I'll take a peck,
> From every bushel that I grind,
> That I may a good living find."
>
> "Thou art a fool," the old man said.
> "Thou hast not well learned thy trade.
> This mill to thee I ne'er will give,
> For by such toll no man can live."

He called for his middlemost son,
Saying, "My life is almost run.
If I to thee the mill do make,
What toll do you intend to take?"

"Father," says he, "my name is Ralph.
Out of a bushel I'll take it half,
From every bushel that I grind,
So that I may a good living find."

"Thou art a fool," the old man said;
"Thou hast not learned well thy trade.
This mill to you I ne'er can give,
For by such toll no man can live."

He called for his youngest son,
Saying, "My life is almost run.
If I to you this mill do make,
What toll do you intend to take?"

"Father," said he, "I am your only boy,
For taking toll is all my joy.
Before I will a good living lack,
I'll take it all, and forswear the sack."

"Thou art my boy," the old man said,
"For thou has well learned thy trade.
This mill to thee I'll give," he cried,
And then he clos'd his eyes, and died.[5]

The same perception of the miller's avid, extortionate, and resourceful comportment was reflected in the adage "prendre d'un sac deux moutures." According to the 1762 edition of the dictionary of the French Academy the saying referred specifically "to the millers who often demand for the grinding of a sack of wheat twice that which is legitimately due them."[6]

But what was "legitimately due them"? Complaints against miller greed pullulated, but there was no general standard against which to weigh (or measure!) them. A multiplicity of different fee systems and schedules coexisted. First, tolls were paid in both money and kind. The Third Estate at the Estates-General of Orléans in 1560 demanded that millers be required to

5. John Ashton, *The History of Bread from Prehistoric to Modern Times* (London, 1901), pp. 116–17. For another version of "The Dishonest Miller," see Duncan Emrich, ed., *American Folk Poetry* (Boston, 1974), p. 761.

6. *Dictionnaire de l'Académie françoise* (Paris, 1762), 2:668. See the similarly greedy and extortionate "mooter-poking" of the Yorkshire miller: "The Miller of Dee," in Harrowven, *Origins of Rhymes*, pp. 101–2. Cf. the disingenuous defense of the miller who claims his "but small" toll is exaggerated by a crotchety public: Heywood, *The Play of the Weather*, p. 23. Note also the way in which the expectation of miller knavery on the toll was built into the law in eighteenth-century North Carolina: Edwin Tunis, *Colonial Craftsmen and the Beginnings of American Industry* (Cleveland, 1965), p. 32.

accept payment only in money (and that they return the grain by weight).[7] Their plea finally received quasi-legislative expression in a Paris Parlement regulatory arrêt of 1719 that restricted tolls to money payments.[8] But the measure was never enforced. Moreover, the coefficient varied enormously. The *juste milieu,* practiced in the eighteenth century in Normandy, Picardy, Flanders, the Hainaut, the Limousin—and Boston—as well as the Paris area was one-sixteenth.[9] Rare was the miller in the Paris region who asked less than one-sixteenth, though one finds tolls as low as one-thirty-second in Auvergne (where there was an "anarchy" of fees), one-twenty-second to one-twentieth in Champagne and the Hainaut, and one-twenty-fourth in parts of Switzerland.[10] On the other hand, tolls of an eighth or a twelfth were quite frequently charged in the Paris area—at Claye, at Etampes, at Gallardon, at Dreux.[11] Almost one hundred years after the abortive parlementary arrêt, a survey of the mills of the Seine-et-Marne conducted by Napoleon's minister of the interior showed that fees in kind were still popular. Fifty-eight percent of the mills for which there was evidence reported tolls in kind, 19 percent collected tolls in money, and 21 percent used both systems. All the tolls in kind were collected on the grain rather than the flour and almost all were taken by volume rather than by weight. The fees in kind were generally quite steep. In the Fontainebleau area, 9 percent were a tenth, 59 percent a twelfth, and 32 percent a thirteenth. In the Meaux region, 6 percent were a tenth, 69 percent a twelfth, 8 percent a thirteenth, and only 17 percent one-sixteenth.

---

7. BN, ms. fr. 21636, fol. 348; Duchesne, *Code de la police,* p. 113.

8. Rozier, *Cours complet,* 7:359. Cf. the contention that by the eighteenth century the law gave consumers a choice—they could claim the right to pay in money or in kind as they pleased. Manesse, *Traité du droit de bâtir moulin,* pp. 234–44.

9. BN, Coll. Joly 1147, fols. 112–19; AD Nord, C 8276, Philippeville (1771) and Landrécy (1771); Turgot, "Septième lettre sur le commerce des grains," 2 December 1770, in *Oeuvres de Turgot,* 3:350; Lefèvre, *Commerce des grains à Lille,* pp. 96–97; E. Villey, "La Taxe du pain et les boulangers de la ville de Caen en 1776. Documents," *Revue d'économie politique* 2 (1888): 187n; Chomel, *Dictionnaire oeconomique,* 1:526; K. J. Friedmann, "Victualling Colonial Boston," *Agricultural History* 47, no. 3 (1973): 192. See also Jackson Main, *Social Structure in Revolutionary America* (Princeton, 1965), p. 82.

10. Abel Poitrineau, *La Vie rurale en Basse-Auvergne au XVIIIᵉ siècle, 1726–1789* (Paris, 1965), p. 209; "Réflexions sur l'édit du mois de juillet 1764," October 1770, AD Nord, C 6690; "Résultat des observations des officiers de police," ca. 1773, AD Marne, C 417; police register, 29 April 1772, AD Aube, C 299; Jean-Louis Muret, *Mémoire sur la mouture des grains, et sur divers objets relatifs* (Bern, 1776), p. 20. Cf. Anne-Marie Dubler, *Müller und Mühlen im alten Staat Luzern* (Lucerne, 1978), pp. 73–78.

11. Rapport arbitre, 3 March 1742, Archives Seine-Paris, D6B⁶, carton 2; Picart to Sartine, 8 January 1769, AN, Y 12618; BN, Coll. Joly 1146, fol. 121, March 1768; BN, Coll. Joly 1117, fol. 258, September 1725; Duchesne, *Code de la police,* p. 114; Parmentier, *Parfait Boulanger,* pp. 152–56. For "abuses" on tolls elsewhere in France, see royal procurator at Cheroy to procurator general, 13 September 1740, BN, Coll. Joly 1123, fol. 292; police register, 29 April 1772, AD Aube, C 299; A. de Francqueville, "Les Vieux Moulins de Picardie," *Bulletin de la Société des antiquaires de Picardie* 23 (1907–1908): 91.

In the Coulommiers vicinity fees ranged from an eighth to a fifteenth.[12]

Money tolls also fluctuated greatly. Ten sous the setier seems to have been the modal rate during the last quarter of the reign of Louis XIV.[13] But several millers at Charenton and Melun were charging 13 sous 4 deniers as early as 1714.[14] In the mid-twenties, the bread victualers to the Invalides paid over 25 sous the setier, while another public assistance institution, the Hôtel-Dieu, was charged only 15 sous, a price it continued to pay for the next twenty-five years.[15] Some bakers paid as much as 20 sous in the late twenties, but miller Perlier of Senlis charged Paris bakers only 13 sous 4 deniers in the early thirties.[16] Miller Paschot of Lagny billed a Paris baker at 32 sous the setier in 1747, but he almost certainly must have been charging for services beyond mere grinding.[17] In 1756 miller Dechais charged some clients 11 sous 8 deniers and others 19 sous. An article in the *Journal économique* of the following year quoted 20 sous as the Paris area price when the miller fetched the grain from the baker and delivered the flour to him and 12 sous when he merely ground it into meal, which may explain the disparity.[18] In 1768, when the going Paris area rate was reportedly 20 sous, an Epernon miller charged 28 sous and an Etampes miller 16 sous—and both appear to have provided transport.[19] Given the capriciousness of the toll rates, it is no wonder that the eighteenth-century writers most familiar with milling could not agree on the going rate in the Paris area. Parmentier suggested 12 sous, apparently excluding transport; Malouin and Béguillet, following Malisset, 20 sous; Baudeau 25 sous.[20]

12. AD Seine-et-Marne, 12M 59. Cf. the miller in the Manche who still took one-sixteenth in 1810: AN, F^{20} 296.

13. "Factum pour la communauté des meuniers," BN, ms. fr. 21636, fol. 332 (1685); AN, G^7 1660–1665.

14. AN, MC, XXVIII-131, 17 September 1714 (inventaire).

15. Archives Seine-Paris, D5B^6 1814, 3 April 1724; Archives Assistance publique, no. 119, 27 April 1750. The Hôtel-Dieu paid a higher toll during the crisis of 1738–41. Archives Assistance publique, n.s. liasse 28, no. 2, Sommier, fol. 421.

16. BN, Coll. Joly 1116, fol. 240; AN, Y 11233, 1 August 1746 (partage).

17. Archives Seine-Paris, D2B^6 809, 5 May 1747.

18. Ibid., D5B^6 1061; "Avis économique sur la boulangerie," *Journal économique* (September 1757): 56. My impression is that millers increasingly assumed the burden of transport and included it in the toll. See, for example, Archives Seine-Paris, D5B^6 4246, 27 July 1769 (Desaubry) and D2B^6 802, 7 October 1746 (Nicolas Noret).

19. Trennin to procurator general and to Sartine, 26 October 1768, BN, Coll. Joly 1142, fols. 153–64; Archives Seine-Paris, D5B^6 5110 (Perineau). Three years later, Thibeau of Compans confirmed Trennin's rule: Archives Seine-Paris, D5B^6 4926.

20. Parmentier, *Parfait Boulanger*, pp. 152–53, and *Mémoire sur les avantages*, p. 407; Pierre-Simon Malisset, "Mouture par économie," *Journal économique* (August 1761): 364; Béguillet, *Traité des subsistances*, p. 301n; Malouin, *Description et détails des arts*, p. 106; Baudeau, *Résultats de la liberté* (1768), p. 25. One reason competition did not even out the toll rate (once one standardizes for differences in quality of services rendered) was the barriers to entry. Access to the milling business was after all governed by water rights, rights of *banalité*, site/seat selection criteria, and so forth. Another reason may have had to do with sheer scale economies in less densely populated regions.

Other factors besides transportation affected tolls. Millers may have sometimes included a commission for purchasing grain or a charge for sack rental. Some millers may have charged less in formal toll in return for the right to claim a higher percentage of waste than usual.[21] Millers and bakers quarreled over the norm of waste, or loss during grinding, throughout the period. Certain millers took whole or part payment in bran—often an extremely attractive proposition because of the middling flour that could be recovered.[22] Millers who performed bolting operations theoretically should have been able to obtain a higher fee (as well as a higher waste allowance). Given the somewhat idiosyncratic nature of the craft, it is not unreasonable to ascribe some variation in tolls to the quality of the grinding. Mill fees sometimes varied with weather conditions, as water mills compensated for their production difficulties by charging more when the water level was excessively low or high.[23] Water millers often demanded a higher rate, on the grounds that they had heavier expenses and a greater and more reliable productive capacity, that there was less loss from evaporation, and that they produced a more evenly ground meal.[24] The Paris bakers bargained for the best price. In return for exclusive dependence on his services, millers such as François de la Cour of Villeroy offered preferential pratik rates to the bakers.[25]

Parmentier spoke for many miller critics when he called for a "general regulation" of the industry. He was no lover of rule by constraint, but he was persuaded that millers would continue "to make the law" abusively—that is, "to take whatever they pleased in kind or money"—unless the law imposed a code. Like Malisset and Malouin, Parmentier wanted the toll to be set in money rather than in kind, because the latter system invited fraud and produced inequities. He also called for the millers to return "weight for weight" with a fixed allowance for waste. Within the confines of a general regulation, local authorities would have the leeway to adjust for their peculiar circumstances.[26]

In the absence of royal initiative, a number of market towns fashioned their own codes in the eighteenth century.[27] The police of Meaux held the

21. Delamare, *Traité de la police,* 2:695.

22. Beauce millers frequently took this sort of payment, but the measure of bran was calibrated on the market price. See the arbiter's report by Malisset, 7 July 1767, Archives Seine-Paris, D6B⁶, carton 5.

23. BN, Coll. Joly 1743, fol. 145.

24. On this highly controversial subject, see the debate between millers in deliberations of the bureau of the Hôtel-Dieu, 15 November 1726, Archives Assistance publique, no. 95. For concessions made to water millers, see these same deliberations, 14 January 1727, no. 96, and Incurables (1754), no. 108.

25. Delamare, *Traité de la police,* 2:695; AN, Y 12589, 7 March 1745.

26. Parmentier, *Parfait Boulanger,* pp. 152–53; Rozier, *Cours complet,* 8:358–59; Malisset, "Mouture par économie," p. 364; Malouin, *Description et détails des arts,* pp. 107–9.

27. An edict of 21 November 1577 called upon police officials to assemble millers and bakers periodically in order to discuss and presumably set guidelines for millers' fees, but

millers directly responsible for the high price of bread, in much the same way as the physiocrats would later. Save for the Paris bakers, who received most-favored-customer treatment, the clients of the Meaux millers had to pay an "exorbitant" toll approaching one-seventh of the value of the merchandise, taken partly in cash and partly in kind on both grain and bran. Fed up with these "arbitrary" practices, the police convoked the millers in 1757 and presented them with a new "regulation." The past was to be marked off from the future by the symbolic burning of all the old measures, a major source of hidden extortion above and beyond the toll. All transactions were now to be conducted by weight and each mill was to be equipped with certified scales. The authorities set up a fee schedule in proportion to the reference price of 9 livres a muid that the millers gave the Paris bakers.[28] The regulation adopted by the city fathers of Soissons was one of the most comprehensive in the realm. Millers had to render weight for weight, with a maximum waste of one fortieth. For this purpose, they had to keep validated scales and weights at the mill. The regulation established a fee schedule in money, varying according to type of milling (coarse, bolted, fine), but an option for payment in kind was retained.[29]

The Paris authorities contemplated such a regulation on several occasions during the eighteenth century, but rejected the idea on the grounds that it was "impracticable." It was felt that a general code for the Paris region—what boundaries?—would be too sweeping and too inflexible.[30] A regulation could not take account of differences in construction and maintenance costs, in sources of power and type of mill, in milling process, in advantage of location, in the vast range of waste depending on mill structure, grain quality, and other factors. "It is no more necessary to sacrifice the miller to the people than the people to the miller," wrote one official. If there were no profit, he added, "there would soon be neither mills nor millers." The liberal policy seemed to many administrators the best: "Let competition bring the low price by itself." Within certain limits the Paris police followed this line. They counted on "public opinion to stigmatize and cause the ruin of the faithless millers and to assure the prosperity of the scrupulous and moderate millers."[31] In ad hoc fashion, however, the police made examples of millers whose demands were considered particularly exorbitant and inopportune.

A debate persisted also on the question of waste allowance. A number of officials felt that even if the toll were left uncontrolled a waste ceiling ought to

this practice does not appear to have been common. Duchesne, *Code de la police,* p. 112; René de Lespinasse and François Bonnardot, *Les Métiers et corporations de la ville de Paris,* vol. 1, *Ordonnances générales, métiers d'alimentation* (Paris, 1886), p. 81.

28. Decau to procurator general, 4 July 1757, BN, Coll. Joly 1130, fols. 148–49.

29. BN, Coll. Joly 1147, fols. 112–19.

30. A sentence of the Châtelet fixed the price for the milling of a setier at 5 sous in April 1578. The Paris police never formally resorted to fee fixing in the eighteenth century.

31. BN, Coll. Joly 1147, fol. 115.

be fixed, in order to close off one of the classic paths of miller fraud. The police of Montereau, less generous than the authorities of Soissons, fixed the maximum loss claim at 4 pounds per Paris setier (240 pounds).[32] Toward the beginning of the century the common allowance in the Paris area had been only 1 pound per 100 pounds of grain for coarse grinding, with a supplement of up to 2.5 pounds if the miller bolted.[33] Around mid-century the General Hospital allowed its millers only 3 pounds and the Hôtel-Dieu gave its millers 4.[34] Yet Malisset, serving as expert arbiter in a case before the consular jurisdiction in the mid-sixties, granted a miller 7 pounds in light of the fact that he sifted and cleaned the grain before he ground it.[35] And lieutenant general of police Lenoir, misled by experiments with hand and pedal mills, considered millers who demanded 3, 4, or 5 pounds dishonest.[36] Bucquet was enraged by the physicist Cadet de Vaux's proclamation of a 3-pound norm. Nothing was more variable than waste, insisted Bucquet. It was contingent upon the weight and quality of the grain and flour, upon temperature and humidity, upon the quality and dressing of the stones, and so on. To create a standard was unrealistic; because it would be impossible for millers to conform systematically, it would be a source of constant conflict between them and the bakers.[37] Malouin, on the other hand, justly contended that the main cause of excessive waste was miller carelessness, which was very much within his power to control—if he decided that discipline was in his interest.[38]

The Beginnings of Merchant Milling

The traditional model of division of labor made the miller the virtual employee of the baker (though in practice this relationship was not at all one of domination-subordination—the baker acquired his grain and charged the miller with the very circumscribed task of transforming it into flour in return for a toll). But in the metropolitan areas, perhaps as early as the fourteenth century, some millers ventured to redefine their role. They were not satisfied with the passive, service function of grinding on command. They began to commercialize flour—that is, to purchase grain, to convert it on speculation, and to offer the flour to those bakers who perceived an advantage in restructuring and rationalizing the ordinary provisioning process. In addition to en-

32. Béguillet, *Traité des subsistances,* p. 361n.
33. "Observations," September 1725, BN, Coll. Joly 1113, fol. 258.
34. Archives Assistance publique, no. 105, liasse 9, and deliberations of the bureau of the Hôtel-Dieu, 29 April 1750, ibid., no. 119. The hospital allowed 5 pounds in 1789, but that was probably in deference to the multiple operations of economic milling. Scipion, 7 December 1789, deliberations of the Hôpital Général, Archives Assistance publique, no. 14.
35. Rapport arbitre, 7 July 1767, Archives Seine-Paris, D6B[6], carton 5.
36. *Détail sur quelques établissements de la ville de Paris* (Paris, 1780), p. 9.
37. Bucquet, *Observations intéressantes,* pp. 63, 115.
38. Malouin, *Description et détails des arts,* pp. 105–6.

trepreneurial ambition, increasing restrictions—seigneurial, municipal, and parlementary—on their "liberté de chasser" may have compelled these millers to rethink their business strategy.[39] Most of these merchant-millers continued to serve baker clients as flour makers even as they expanded their merchant activities. It was not until the eighteenth century that a large number of the most successful began to abandon the service function entirely in favor of speculative provisioning.[40] At the same time custom millers started to lament that they were losing their "professional" clients.[41] This trend prompted circumspect millers like Pierre Bertrand of Poissy to buffer his commerce against "customary" baker defection by launching a speculative side trade in grain and flour.[42] By the end of the century the public authorities in the market centers of the supply zone complained that the current of commercialization had shifted all their local mills exclusively into the service of Paris. "All our millers use their establishments strictly for their own commercial accounts," reported an official at Etampes, thereby obliging "the inhabitants of this city to have recourse to foreign [i.e., unfamiliar and/or remote] mills to have ground the grain necessary for their subsistence."[43]

"Millers must never trade in grain," wrote a Paris police official in 1738. "It is expressly forbidden by all the laws and it would be extremely dangerous to suffer it."[44] This position found wide support in official circles at least until the Revolution, despite the profound changes that were taking place. Millers could not be trusted to engage in the grain trade. Their presence would put heavy upward pressure on the mercuriales. Given their notorious "dishonesty," they would not fail to commit "fraud" and "malversations," to cheat on quality, to concoct noxious mixtures, to manipulate transactions, and so on. Finally, if millers were to involve themselves in grain commerce, the public would suffer, for instead of grinding the grain brought by individuals and bakers, the millers would give priority to their own speculations.[45]

39. See Denisart, *Collection de décisions,* 3:252–53. Cf. John Kirkland, *Three Centuries of Prices of Wheat, Flour and Bread* (London, 1917), p. 17.

40. For a case of a miller who now ground "only for his account," see AN, Y 12141, 3 July 1739.

41. See the case of Louis Creuset, BN, Coll. Joly 1116, fol. 230, ca. November 1725.

42. Archives Seine-Paris, D5B[6] 4243.

43. Greffe, maîtrise des eaux et forêts, July 1791, AD Seine-et-Oise, unclassified series S. It is interesting that already in 1791 officials were calling mills "usines," or factories.

44. Arsenal, ms. Bast. 10275. On the legislation and the sentences prohibiting the millers from engaging in the grain trade, see ordinance of police, 13 February 1699, BN, ms. fr. 21644, fols. 165, 460; royal declaration of 8 September 1737, BN, ms. fr. 21640, fol. 64 (but let us note that the failure of the entire parlement to register this law gave the millers an opportunity to argue that the issue was still open); police sentence, 22 July 1740, AN, Y 9441; *procès-verbaux,* 16, 21 May 1762, AN, Y 9539. The English imposed the same ban. See Donald G. Barnes, *A History of the English Corn Laws from 1600 to 1846* (London, 1930), p. 33 and Bennett and Elton, *Corn Milling,* 3:169.

45. Taboureau to Terray, 27 October 1770, AD Nord, C 6690; intendant of Champagne to Terray, 22 October 1770, AD Marne, C 417; Terray to intendant of Normandy, 25 November

The physiocrats and their friends in the liberal ministries of the sixties were the first to articulate a comprehensive argument in favor of complete commercial freedom for the millers. Controller-general Laverdy welcomed the "salubrious competition" of the millers, which would tend to lower rather than raise grain prices. In order to prevent the trade from becoming increasingly concentrated in the hands of a small number—a goal that in other instances he openly espoused—Laverdy contended that "the little dealers" like the millers had to be allowed a chance. Moreover, the controller-general pointed to the incentives that their expanded business would give to millers to improve the quality and productivity of their operations.[46] The *Ephémérides du citoyen* echoed Laverdy, emphasizing how the desire to maximize profits in the new situation would result in technological modernization that would "increase the [total] subsistence." It did not shy away from the embarrassing matter of miller frauds, though its casuistic reasoning was not likely to convince everyone. Frauds were largely the result of "bad laws," the *Ephémérides* affirmed. Men turned to illicit ways to make money when the "natural" channels were blocked by insipid and unfair laws. Presumably once they had the freedom to do battle for profit on the markets of their choice, the millers would have no further incentive to cheat.[47] Somewhat more cautious, the physiocrat Lemercier de la Rivière stressed the economic reasons for allowing the millers to trade in grain: savings on freight, more rapid and efficient distribution, incentives to produce more and better quality merchandise, and so on.[48]

The appeal in favor of miller grain trade was an indirect plea in favor of the commercialization of milling, although few of the liberals seemed to realize that the flour trade would soon displace and overshadow the grain trade. If Laverdy tolerated a vision of a largely fragmented grain trade, it was because he could not imagine industrial flour production and commercialization. Others like his sometime protégé Malisset could. For Malisset, Bucquet, Béguillet, Parmentier, and other proponents of the modernization of milling, the grain trade was merely a means by which the miller could transform himself into a mealman and a merchant. The cities, they argued, needed flour, not grain. It made sense to encourage the millers to integrate the business in a technologically advanced, rationally managed enterprise that covered all the space from the farmers' barns and granaries to the bakers' flour rooms.

The debate was passionate, but in many ways anachronistic and irrelevant, for the millers had been trading in grain long before anyone had seri-

---

1771, AD Calvados, C 2624; Miromesnil to Laverdy, 18 May 1768, in Miromesnil, *Correspondance politique*, 5:216.

46. Laverdy to Miromesnil, 8 May 1768, in Miromesnil, *Correspondance politique*, 5:179–80.

47. "Objections et réponses sur le commerce des grains et des farines," *Ephémérides du citoyen* 1 (1769): 107–10.

48. Lemercier de la Rivière, *L'Intérêt général de l'état*, p. 324.

ously thought of freedom of the grain trade.[49] As early as 1715 Sieur Navarre of Gressy-en-France and Nicolas Fleury of Breuil-Bois-Robert supplied bakers in both grain and flour.[50] It was quite common for millers such as Jean Laurent, Simon Lecuyer, and Pierre Desloches to style themselves "miller and grain merchant."[51] Jean-François Philippe was one of a number of Paris suppliers who was deeply involved in grain (if not precisely in the grain trade), for he was a laboureur-miller who grew at least part of the grain he ground.[52]

There were three types of miller grain trade. The first involved wheat purchases made directly in the field by the miller on commission for a specific Paris baker. In most instances the miller delivered this grain in the form of flour to the bakeroom. "All the millers are buying agents and factors of the Paris bakers," complained a memorandum concerned with "the disorders that are committed in the environs of Paris" in 1698.[53] "The millers continued to buy on behalf of the bakers despite the fact that I prohibited it," grumbled an officer of the maréchaussée in 1725.[54] At the Dourdan market in 1725 millers Catherine Pachot, Claude Simonneau, and Jules Branchery purchased wheat in amounts ranging from 9 setiers to 2 muids for Paris master and forain bakers.[55] Despite the declaration of 1737 that renewed the ban on miller purchases for themselves or for bakers, miller commissionnaires working for Paris bakers were active at Etampes, Brie-Comte-Robert, and in the Claye area.[56] In July of 1741 a miller named Lamoureux was caught in the Montlhéry market outbidding other buyers and "brazenly" inviting the laboureurs to raise their prices. He was identified as an agent for Paris bakers who had violated the law in several ways by buying not only in the markets but also at the farms.[57] Two baker widows unable to make country buying trips themselves petitioned unsuccessfully for a dispensation to permit them

49. The prohibition was also widely ignored in England. Secrétaire d'ambassade à la cour de Londres to Bertier de Sauvigny, 24 September 1764, BN, ms. fr. 11347, fol. 248; Bennett and Elton, *Corn Milling*, 3:169.

50. AN, MC, XIX-610, 16 February 1715 (Pampelune inventory); AN, MC, XXXIV-388, 31 August 1716 (Larcher).

51. BN, Coll. Joly 1117, fol. 165 (1725); Archives Seine-Paris, D2B⁶ 809, 12 May 1747, and D2B⁶ 762, 28 June 1743.

52. AN, Y 9442, 12 May 1741.

53. BN, ms. fr. 21643, fols. 354, 356.

54. Marchais to Hérault, 15 October 1725, Arsenal, ms. Bast. 10270, fol. 326.

55. Soumissions devant Bouchers, subdélégué, 25 August 1725, ibid., pièce 49.

56. Herbron petition, October 1738, Arsenal, ms. Bast. 10275; rapport arbitre, 3 March 1742, Archives Seine-Paris, D6B⁶, carton 2 (Tilliel-Moncouteau); Archives Seine-Paris, D5B⁶ 3602 (Petit). See the vigorous protest of Etampes area millers against what they considered to be a restriction of "the liberty to buy" that they had enjoyed "in former times." The declaration of 1737, as they construed it, was an innovation rather than a reaffirmation of fundamental principles. De la Potrie to lieutenant general, 10 January 1739, Arsenal, ms. Bast. 10276.

57. AN, Y 9442, 11 August 1741.

to continue to rely on the millers who had served them as agents "with exactitude and honesty" for almost ten years.[58] Most bakers and millers did not bother with authorizations. Nor did an intensive campaign of search and seizure undertaken by the measurers upon millers' shipments entering the gates of the capital deter them.[59] In the fifties and sixties the police seemed to have abandoned the vigorous execution of the September 1737 declaration. There were considerably fewer confiscations, now the fruit of measurer opportunism rather than public policy, and the fines were much lighter.[60]

For every police sentence there are scores of innocent entries in business registers that show that the bulk of millers and bakers persisted tranquilly in a collaboration that served them both.[61] In the business court *(juridiction consulaire)*, the parties openly testified to activities that the police considered crimes. A baker named Boisseau explained how his miller sometimes accompanied him when he (illegally) purchased wheat from laboureurs at their farms and was usually responsible both for picking up the merchandise and transmitting payment to the seller.[62]

Miller Aubry from Meaux sued his baker client Guillemet for payment of grain purchased on his orders, as well as for grinding and freight.[63] In 1760 Claude Robin, a miller at Juilly, denounced his colleague Hublot not so much because the latter "continually violated the ordinances" by buying from the local laboureurs on commission from the Paris bakers, but because he monopolized this lucrative trade and drove rival millers to the point of failure.[64] If the proclamation of the liberty of the grain trade in 1763 did not much affect Paris area millers, nor did its repudiation in 1770. Indeed, the revised system of controls introduced by controller-general Terray was favorable to them, for it permitted them for the first time to register openly as buying agents for bakers and, indeed, as grain traders like any others. Among the millers who registered as agents were Jean-François Touron of Annet-sur-Marne, Jean-Claude Colas of Stains, Louis Dezobry of St.-Denis (who ran three water mills and one windmill), Philippe Thibault (who was a fermier and *receveur* as well as operator of two water mills), Jean François of Rebais, Canda of Meaux and Porvas and Feret of Coulommiers.[65] Fourteen millers of the Paris envi-

58. Utinet and Dubois to Marville, October 1740, Arsenal, ms. Bast. 10275.
59. See the following confiscations: 6 September 1737, 12 August 1737, 31 January 1738 (two), AN, Y 9619. The police sentences were harsh: sale of the confiscated merchandise with proceeds to the measurers and fines of up to 500 livres.
60. See, for example, AN, Y 9538, 10 September 1756, and Y 9539, 1 October 1765.
61. See, for instance, the money owed by bakers Claude Lapareillé, Blain, Thion, Bassy, and T. Lapareillé to millers Cousin, Boulie, and Herbron. Partage, 1 August 1746, AN, Y 11233; partage, 1 August 1753, AN, MC, VII-288; Archives Seine-Paris, registre, D5B⁶ 4575.
62. Rapport arbitre, 21 December 1743, Archives Seine-Paris, D6B⁶, carton 2. The arbiter remarked on the ample opportunity here for miller "friponnerie."
63. Rapport arbitre, 18 December 1767, ibid., D6B⁶, carton 5.
64. Petition, July 1760, BN, Coll. Joly 1130, fols. 160–61.
65. AN, Y 9648, February 1771; registration list, February 1771, AD Seine-et-Marne, bailliage de Meaux, unclassified.

rons and seventeen from the *bailliage* of Meaux were among those who declared that they were grain traders in 1771.[66]

The second type of miller trading was uncommissioned or speculative buying and selling of grain (*without* conversion into flour). Frequently, millers practiced this commerce at the same time that they served as buying agents for bakers. Indeed, one of the reasons police officials were reluctant to authorize baker commissions was that millers were known to use them as pretexts or covers for speculative operations that did not directly serve the provisioning of Paris. Millers Monnery and Gilbert, for example, bought for their own account in the name of Paris bakers whom they sometimes supplied.[67] Under interrogation a miller from Lagny conceded that the wheat he claimed to have bought for a Paris baker named Guiton was in fact his own speculation.[68] Widow miller Brayment showed a certificate from the market of Dourdan for 2 muids purchased by Paris baker Barbier. But when the measurers confronted him with the miller, Barbier swore that he knew nothing about it. Brayment suffered a double indictment, for fraudulent grain acquisition and for the "regrate" of the flour that she made from it.[69] Sieur Vacquere, the collector of minage fees at the Pont-Ste.-Maxence market, facilitated miller grain traffic by selling blank purchase certificates filled out in the names of various Paris bakers with whom they had no dealings. With these passports, the millers could buy their grain anywhere and claim that it was from Pont and destined for the capital. Charged with organizing "a sort of regrate and monopoly" and with abusing his authority, Vacquere was fined 1,500 livres and menaced with loss of his post.[70] A group of flour merchants complained to the police in 1740 against the unfair trading practices of some of their confreres who bought in the name of bakers but used the grain for speculative purposes.[71]

There were, however, a great many cases in which millers simply called themselves grain merchants and bought and sold without any necessary relation to bakers or to flour making. In 1738 a miller near Etampes was accused of hoarding a huge stock of wheat "for the purpose of causing the price to rise."[72] A miller named Fouqueret sold 23 muids of old wheat in two separate transactions to the Hôtel-Dieu in 1740–41.[73] Maurice, a miller from St.-Denis,

66. Kaplan, *Bread, Politics and Political Economy*, 1:287–90. There were also thirty-two grain-dealing millers in the Lille jurisdiction. Ibid., p. 293.

67. AN, Y 9539, 6 May 1751; BN, Coll. Joly 1829, fol. 288. Cf. similar forms of illicit miller grain trade in Brittany: Jean Letaconnoux, *Les Subsistances et le commerce des grains en Bretagne, au XVIIIe siècle . . . ,* p. 124.

68. Gillet to procurator general, 23 January 1771, BN, Coll. Joly 1158, fols. 210–11.

69. Police sentence, 27 June 1744, BN, ms. fr. 21636, fols. 342–43. She was fined 200 livres and her merchandise was confiscated, pending possible appeal.

70. AN, Y 9441, 22 July 1740, and conseil secret, 9 July 1740, X[1A] 8465, fols. 481–83.

71. BN, ms. fr. 11356, fol. 423, 7 July 1740.

72. Hérault to Albront, 22 October 1738, Arsenal, ms. Bast. 10275.

73. Archives Assistance publique, Hôtel-Dieu, n.s. liasse 28, no. 2, Sommier, fols. 404 (November 1740) and 408 (April 1741).

sold 100 setiers of wheat to the highest bidder, a Paris baker who then had *his* miller grind it.[74] Over a period of three years, Charles Orne, a miller in the Rambouillet vicinity, purchased over 100,000 livres' worth of wheat from a single supplier, only one of several with whom he regularly dealt.[75] Millers Lejeune of Pont, Lefoire of Paris, and Lainé of Meaux bought from grain merchants and resold to others, like blatiers, but on a fairly substantial scale.[76] Certain millers had the audacity to purchase grain right under the noses of market officials at the Paris Halle and the Grève, a double offense, for it involved not only illicit miller commerce but also a diversion of supplies away from the capital.[77] Aggressive millers like Claude Aubée of Crécy, J. -F. Tournoud of Rebais, and André Squeville of Gressy scoured the countryside to buy from laboureurs and to intercept grain merchants before they reached market.[78] Firmin Deveaux, a miller at Thieux, owed a total of 1,194 livres to five laboureurs in different villages.[79] The Paris police remained vehemently committed to the repression of speculative grain trading by millers until the early sixties, but even with the assistance of the maréchaussée they did not succeed in apprehending many trader-millers.[80] Finally, a parlementary arrêt in 1763 explicitly authorized miller grain buying on speculation for conversion to flour, provided that the product was ultimately sold at the Paris or Versailles markets.[81]

The third type of miller grain trade concerned the uncommissioned purchase of grain that the miller himself transformed into flour for speculative sale at the markets (or more or less illicitly to bakers en droiture). In terms of the structure of provisioning and probably in terms of sheer value, this was the most significant type of miller grain commerce. It was also the kind that posed the greatest difficulty for the police. How could they reconcile their ardent desire to promote the development of flour provisioning with the aim of repressing miller grain trade? The flour merchants, or mealmen, were more and more often millers capable of handling the entire operation rather than

74. Archives Seine-Paris, D5B⁶ 4926, January 1772 (Longpré).

75. Ibid., D6B⁶, carton 6, 26 April 1773.

76. Ibid., D5B⁶ 4910, 1772 and D2B⁶ 1128, 20 December 1773; statement of A. Picaud, AD Seine-et-Marne, bailliage de Meaux, 16 January 1771, unclassified.

77. Sale by port merchant Meusnier, 19 January 1735, AN, MC, V-375; sale by port merchant Pinondel, 12 November 1777, Archives Seine-Paris, D4B⁶ 65-4227; AN, Y 12607, 13 December 1759 (Jean Duhamel); AN, Y 9539, 11 December 1759. Cf. AN, Y 11225, 20 August 1738.

78. Archives Seine-Paris, D5B⁶ 4216 (1772–75), D4B⁶ 54-3331 (7 January 1775), and D4B⁶ 65-4227 (12 November 1777); registration list, 29 January 1771, AD Seine-et-Marne, bailliage de Meaux, unclassified.

79. Archives Seine-Paris, D2B⁶ 766, 21 October 1743.

80. For examples of a sporadic repression, see Marchais to lieutenant general, 7 June 1726, Arsenal, ms. Bast. 10273; AN, Y 9440, 22 May 1739, and Y 9539, 6 May, 26 May 1758. Cf. similar efforts at Versailles, AD Seine-et-Oise, 3 B 145, July 1740.

81. Arrêt of 3 January 1763, AN, AD XI 39. The evidence suggests strongly that not all of the interested authorities were apprised of this measure or were willing to abide by it.

mere middlemen who had to hire miller service. What was the commissaire of the Halles department to say when the widow miller Bécu contested the seizure of her wheat by the St.-Denis brigade of the maréchaussée on the grounds "that it was permissible [for her to buy grain], being a flour merchant and supplier of the Halle of Paris"?[82] Or when a St.-Germain-en-Laye miller named Fouquet, interrogated by a maréchaussée officer at Montlhéry for buying grain, insisted "that he had to buy, it was his business, he would not be stopped, this was a child's game"?[83] This flour trade seemed to be a maneuver to avoid the rules. In the short run, it resulted in lively upward pressure on grain prices.[84] On the other hand, after a period of adjustment, it became clear to the authorities that these entrepreneurial mealmen would simply force many old-line grain traders out of business and thus eliminate a whole category of intermediaries.

Still, the police remained troubled for a long time by two sorts of practices that shifted the trade outside the market, and thus outside their purview. One was the prerogative arrogated by certain millers and mealmen to buy grain off the market like Paris-licensed grain traders. The Etampes flour dealers went straight to the barns and granaries of the cultivators; miller Donzelle bought on sample from a fermier in an inn near Montlhéry; mealman Lerouge of Gonesse devised a scheme by which he completed a transaction outside the market and then reenacted it on the market as if it were a spontaneous and legal purchase. The other worrisome practice was the sale of flour outside the official space. Miller David Rousset, who made huge grain purchases at Dourdan, aroused suspicion by selling the flour he manufactured almost exclusively off the market. The most common form of this "abuse" was the shipment by the flour merchant—say widow Giboreau, a miller at Maintenon—directly to a Paris baker—say Jacquelin of the rue de Richelieu. This en droiture traffic was considered fraudulent, or quasi-fraudulent, at least until the seventies. The Paris police tried especially hard to curtail it during the fifties and sixties as part of the campaign to make the Halle the unique theater for flour sales to bakers.[85]

The merchant-millers of the eighteenth century embarked upon a trajectory that led to a veritable metamorphosis of their profession. By the middle

---

82. AN, Y 9441, 8 July 1740.

83. BN, ms. fr. 21635, fols. 242–43, 31 January 1738.

84. See the complaints of Brochard at the Versailles market to procurator general, 25 November 1740, BN, Coll. Joly 1123, fol. 215.

85. Leroy to Hérault, 26 October 1738, Arsenal, ms. Bast. 10275; BN, ms. fr. 21635, fols. 242–43, 31 January 1738; AN, Y 9441, 26 August 1740, and Y 9621, 24 November 1752; AD Seine-et-Oise, 4B 1140, 12 March 1741. See also Kaplan, *Bakers of Paris*. By 1771, country millers openly declared that they shipped flour to Paris bakers en droiture, and their traffic was apparently tolerated. See registration list, 29 January 1771, AD Seine-et-Marne, bailliage de Meaux, unclassified. Inspector Poussot, the moving force for the Halle renaissance, must have drafted an angry *procès-verbal* from his grave!

of the nineteenth century, if not before, commercial speculation rather than
the transformation of grain into flour was the major business activity of the
Paris-oriented millers. The "dazzling fortunes" of millers such as the Darblays, insisted an agricultural journalist, were not made by grinding grain into
meal but by buying and selling at the right moment. And when Darblay *fils*
told the Council of State in 1859 that "there is, so to speak, no longer a
commerce in grain," he meant that there were no more grain merchants,
properly speaking, and that the grain trade had been taken over almost wholly
by the millers. "The grain trade is of great importance in the department of
Seine-et-Marne," the secretary of the municipality of Meaux testified at the
same hearing, "[but] it is fully in the hands of the millers."[86]

So completely had the miller displaced the grain merchant in the public
consciousness, at least in the Paris region, that he acquired the merchant's
poisonous old stigma to add to his own already tainted reputation. According
to a leading mid-nineteenth-century miller, during years of dearth "the miller
is paralyzed in his operations" by the "general opinion that he is a promoter of
scarcity and high prices." Unable to make any grain purchases without arousing violent public reaction, the miller was "obliged to hide for fear of these
prejudices." Engrossed by commerce as an end in itself, the miller became
estranged from his mill and lost interest in "the science of milling," an influential economist charged: "The master miller is too much the *grand seigneur:* he
devotes all his time to buying and selling, to his speculations and his wages;
he is rarely at the mill. He knows that he can impose his merchandise, no
matter how it is made."[87]

The spirited development of merchant milling also led to a profound alteration of the relation between miller and baker. An inversion occurred:
whereas in the eighteenth century the bakers took the initiative, defined the
ground rules, forced millers to redirect their energies and change the organization and even the technology of their operations, and in some instances
acquired mills themselves, in the nineteenth century, swelling with
confidence, the millers fixed the terms of exchange, pushed the bakers out of
the grain trade, told them what to bake, and took control of many shops,
either directly and overtly or indirectly and surreptitiously. Once virtually an
employee of the baker, by the mid-nineteenth century the miller had become
master. The baker was nothing more than "the miller's man, the hired hand of
the miller." The chief of military provisioning described the baker as "totally
effaced, purely passive, a simple artisan." In 1859 an economist noted: "The
milling industry runs the bakery, absorbs it, exhausts it." The millers took
advantage of the greater freedom from regulation that they enjoyed, of the
fund of capital that their speculations enabled them to form, and of the disar-

86. *Enquête sur la boulangerie*, pp. 243–45 (Pommier), 509 (Boittelle), and 553 (Lavaux);
Enquête sur les céréales, 2:92–93 (Darblay), 133 (Modeste).
87. *Enquête sur la boulangerie*, pp. 581 (Rabourdin), 71 (Gosset).

ray and torpor that paralyzed the baking community. One of the most effective tools of miller hegemony, besides the pressure of debt foreclosure, was the *marché à cuisson,* a year-long supply contract that locked the baker into dependence and inertness.[88]

The Miller and the Local Community

The miller was more than a key actor in the ongoing subsistence drama. To be sure, his contribution to the provisioning process was his most important role, and the paramount source of his more or less considerable influence. Yet this focus on grain and flour commerce neglects the other ways in which the miller could affect local life in his community. In a number of places he was a *coq du village,* first because he controlled a critical tool upon which everyone depended, but sometimes also because he was an important landowner, because he was a grain or wine producer or a stockraiser, or because he had privileged relations with the seigneur or other investors of wealth and authority. Though often distrusted, feared, or despised, he had or seemed to have power, and villagers turned to him. He was a banker who extended credit for grinding when food was desperately needed, who granted loans in kind for seed or in cash to cover taxes or to buy farm implements, and who could be persuaded to lend or to rent out draft animals. On a modest scale, he served market functions by arranging deals and storing merchandise. He was a maker and disseminator of information about home affairs, since he was in contact with so many villagers, and about outside life, since he might be one of the few villagers with some sort of regular metropolitan connection. For his magical and erotic powers, the miller may have been called upon as healer, soothsayer, or matchmaker. Broadly put, because he was located at such a crucial crossroads in the community, a bit like the priest or the tavernkeeper, he was a social, economic, and political broker for all kinds of exchanges. Of course, not all millers enjoyed this prominence; indeed, a majority were marginal men. Nevertheless, it appears that there were a sufficient number of miller notables, of both customary and commercial orientation, to warrant further inquiry, especially from the vantage point of village and rural history.[89]

Miller Rivalries

If it seems that millers quarreled among themselves less frequently than bakers, it was only because they were scattered and had less occasion to

88. Ibid., pp. 33, 35, 70, 140, 154, 156, 265–66, 544, 641, 789.
89. The point of departure might be to identify the kinds of villages in which millers held a certain sway and their location vis-à-vis the structures of production and distribution.

encounter one another. They bickered and brawled for the same basic reason: professional jealousy. They sought revenge for clients seduced or suborned, for honor sullied, for undertakings violated, for triumphs usurped. Millers Berseville and Albrion both claimed preeminence in the Etampes area, where they were neighbors. They kept each other under surveillance for fear of falling victim to some machination and in hope of discovering some weakness. Each did his best to discredit the other publicly. At an inn in Paris frequented by grain and flour traders and bakers, Albrion erupted against Berseville: "foutu gueux, foutu coquin, foutu misérable, foutu banqueroutier." Berseville, he sneered, "wore the green cap," the traditional symbol of obloquy that marked off the bankrupt businessman. Berseville, to salvage his "honor and reputation," called upon the police to prosecute his rival.[90] Paris mealman Ambroise Delaforge was in the midst of selling flour to a client when the wife of miller Devaux of Montmarte ripped the sack from his client's hand and led him to her place, where she sold him what he wanted. "Unfair practice," cried Delaforge, to which Devaux replied in the only way possible: a discourse meant to justify her commercial "disloyalty" by impugning Delaforge's standing as a worthy partner in exchange. "Bah," she said, "[Delaforge] has been sleeping with his sister-in-law for ten years, he was the father of her child, and he deserves to be hanged." Moreover, she added, with fervor, "his wife is a whore."[91]

Marie-Jeanne Pichard, wife of a miller, gave Jean Joly and his family no peace, apparently because Joly had stolen several Pichard clients. She campaigned against the Jolys all over the capital: at the Halle, the ports, the inns. She denounced Joly's wife as "a whore, a guttersnipe, a pimp, [a woman who] had three children before getting married, a thief . . . who merited a hanging." Fearful that these charges would deter bakers from dealing with them and result "in a considerable blow to our business," the Jolys asked the police to assure them relief and reparation.[92]

The Hallé cousins, both mealmen and sons of millers, denounced each other publicly as "thief" and "scoundrel." After having been briefly associated in a family grain buying business, they became rivals at the Gonesse market as well as on the Paris trading floor. Their professional competition was apparently aggravated by their ardor for the same woman—another lesson in the relentless intersection of personal and professional affairs.[93] The father of Jacques Hallé had a long-standing dispute with his son-in-law, Ambroise Delaforge, the flour dealer, that may also have been the fruit of joint

90. AN, Y 12740, 15 March 1754. Wrote La Fontaine: "Les voilà sans crédit, sans argent, sans ressources, Prêts à porter le bonnet vert," in *Oeuvres complètes* (Paris, 1965), p. 165.

91. AN, Y 12611, 9 July 1762.

92. AN, Y 13634, 11 December 1729.

93. AN, Y 11385, 19 June 1771, and Y 12621, 19 June 1771.

commercial ventures that did not work out. Each man felt cheated and announced to the world that the other could not be trusted in a business relationship.[94]

For the most part, millers struck out at each other through verbal violence, with the aim of demoralizing their rivals or enemies and hurting their standing in the business and social community. Occasionally insults led to blows. Direct violence against property seems to have been rather rare. I have found nothing comparable to the cabal of windmillers at Sergines, near Sens, who resented the installation of a newcomer in 1781 and decided to ruin him by "poisoning" his stones with a noxious substance.[95] The closest case I have encountered concerned miller Jean-Pierre Pannier, incensed by the failure of another miller, Pierre Bourgeois, to live up to an agreement. Assisted by his wife and a group of friends, Pannier laid siege to Bourgeois's mill and began to tear it down with axes and pitchforks.[96]

The Miller's Reputation

The miller's relations with the public, and with public authorities as well, were mediated to some extent by the image that his profession traditionally projected. A corpus of folktales, collective memories, well-traveled rumors, and sententious apothegms portrayed the miller and his mill in a negative and portentous light. Just as "white bread" necessarily meant something good, so the word/name miller evoked something evil, corrupt, shameful. A priori the miller suffered a bad reputation. He did not have to earn it; it seemed to go with the job. Indeed, the futility of resisting this infamy may have led the miller to try to profit from practices for which he was denounced in any case. Millers were suspected all the more because it was so easy for them to cheat on quantity and quality. The universal belief in millers' cheating betrayed a great collective projection of sinfulness—the community discharged itself of guilt by charging the miller.

The very design of the mill was a monument to the miller's perfidy. The miller constructed a square housing around the circular stones in order to catch grain in the corner angles. He siphoned off grain as it fell from the stones in a "blind" trap.[97] What he could not ask the machine to do he did himself. He switched low-quality grain or flour for superior merchandise; he adulterated bad or mediocre flour to make it pass for excellent meal; he

94. AN, Y 12605, 18 June 1757.

95. Chris Gibbings, "Moulins à vent de la Bourgogne occidentale: moulins du centre," *Moulins à vent de Bourgogne*, p. 6.

96. AN, Y 15629, 20 May 1755.

97. On these "structural" tricks, see Delamare, *Traité de la police*, 2:692; Béguillet, *Traité des subsistances*, p. 296; Des Essarts, *Dictionnaire universel de police*, 7:107.

manipulated weight or volume. ("Beside every mill stands a hill of sand.")
Here was "a thief like a miller," and a thief was "as honest as a miller." "You
may change millers, but you will not change crooks," an adage warned.
According to another, "Millers' pigs get fat quickly."[98]

A dying man importuned his family to fetch the two local millers and to
place them within his sight on each side of the deathbed. "Now I take my
leave serenely," he explained. "Like Jesus Christ I die between two thieves."

"What is the boldest thing in the world?" asked the first peasant. "A
miller's shirt, for it clasps a thief by the throat every day," replied the second.[99]

"If you confined in a big sack a sergeant, a miller, a tailor, and a lawyer,"
went the riddle, "which of the four would come out first when you opened it?"
The answer: "The first to come out of the sack would surely be a thief, there is
nothing more certain that can be said."[100]

Children in Somersetshire acted out the common view of the miller's
integrity. They caught a large moth called a miller for its dusty white wings
and chanted: "Millery! Millery! Dousty poll! How many sacks of corn hast
thou stole?" after which they crushed the miller-moth for his misdeeds.[101]

A tale from the Picardy recounts that it was from the top of a windmill that
Christ soared toward heaven. The miller, gazing through a window and seeing
Him climbing up the rungs of the sail-yards, cried out: "Ho, la! Where are you
going?" "I go to heaven," was the reply. "If that is the case," shouted the
miller, rushing out, "wait for me, I'm going with you." "Not so," said the
Christ, "you are going in the other direction."[102]

The festival of Quasimodo was called Millers' Easter because it was presumed that, with a heavy conscience, millers waited until this day—the last
possible moment—to discharge their paschal duty.[103] The curé de Cucugnon

98. Paul Sébillot, *Légendes et curiosités des métiers* (Paris, 1894–95), p. 7; Francqueville, "Les Vieux moulins de Picardie," pp. 91–92; Picot, *Vieux Moulins de France*, p. 28;
R. Gargadennec, "Notice sur nos vieux moulins à eau," *Bulletin de la Société archéologique
du Finistère* 84 (1958): 217.

99. Sébillot, *Légendes des métiers*, p. 5; Bennett and Elton, *Corn Milling*, 3:109. Cf. "On
est toujours sûr de trouver un voleur dans la peau d'un meunier," Paul Lacroix [Jacob],
Recueil de farces (Paris, 1859), p. 236.

100. Sébillot, *Légendes des métiers*, p. 4. Cf. p. 8: "Meunier larron / voleur de blé / c'est
ton métier / la corde au cou / comme un coucou / le fer aux pieds / comme un damné / quat'
diabl' à t'entourner / qui t'emport'ront dans l'fond de l'âme." From the collection of the
Musée de Montmartre: "Meunier larron / Voleur de son / pour son cochon / voleur de blé /
c'est mon métier" and "quand la souris est dans le sac à farine / elle se croit le meunier lui-
même."

101. Ashton, *History of Bread*, p. 117. Cf. the association between the miller and the
fattest pig in the parish. Newton and Sheppard, *Story of Bread*, p. 26.

102. Elton and Bennett, *Corn Milling*, 3:108. Cf. the Normand saying: "No miller can
enter heaven." Jacob, *Six Thousand Years*, p. 129.

103. Francqueville, "Les Vieux Moulins de Picardie," pp. 91–92.

confessed the whole village during the week and reserved all day Saturday just for the miller.[104]

These "popular" suspicions were confirmed by the testimony of the elite: writers, judges, public officials. Chaucer's miller was "a thief outrageously." "Sly", Simkin in *The Reeve's Tale* stole grain before grinding and flour afterward. The miller of the Canterbury pilgrims was "most of sinne and harlotryes" and dishonorable in his dealings. For Rabelais millers were "ordinary thieves." Grindoff, the miller in Pocock's early-nineteenth-century melodrama *The Miller and His Men,* was a vicious, libidinous rogue. Lazarillo's father in Hurtado de Mendoza's novel, *The Life of Lazarillo de Tormes,* was arrested for "certain misdeeds done to the sacks of those who came to have their corn ground." The miller of Abingdon in the British folktale was an insatiable and resourceful pilferer. Even the simple and gentle miller in Paul de Musset's *Monsieur le Vent et Madame la Pluie* was transformed, through his relation to the mill, into a man of avarice and self-regard.[105]

The organization of work in France until well into the nineteenth century was based on the presumption that the master was always right in his relations with his employees. Yet in 1739 in Laval a court refused to believe the master miller's sworn statement concerning his journeyman's wages "on the grounds that his status is too lowly and even too suspect to permit him to take an oath" as other masters did.[106] Turgot, philosophe and administrator, resented the stereotype of avid merchants fostered by the police, yet he depicted millers as both dishonest and stupid.[107] A memorandum from the

---

104. "Ce n'est pas trop d'un jour pour lui tout seul." Alphonse Daudet, *Lettres de mon moulin* (Paris, 1980), p. 135. An epitaph placed on the tomb of a miller named Strange, buried in an Essex, England, churchyard, reads:

> Here lies an honest miller
> And that is Strange.

Cited by Syson, *British Water-mills,* p. 41.

105. Chaucer, *Reeve's Prologue;* Mary E. Whitmore, *Medieval English Domestic Life and Amusement in the Works of Chaucer* (New York, 1972), pp. 228–29; R. A. McCance and E. M. Widdowson, *Breads White and Brown: Their Place in Thought and Social History* (London, 1956), p. 13; François Rabelais, *Pantagruel* (Paris, 1936), book 3, chap. 2. Cf. the similar testimony of a sixteenth-century French royal physician in E. P. Prentice, *Hunger and History: The Influence of Hunger on Human History* (New York, 1939), p. 102; Isaac Pocock, *The Miller and His Men: A Melo-drame, in Two Acts* (London, n.d.); Diego Hurtado de Mendoza, *The Life of Lazarillo de Tormes,* trans. Clements Markham (London, 1908), p. 5; Briggs, *Dictionary of British Folktales,* part A, 2:442–43; Paul Edme de Musset, *Monsieur le Vent et Madame la Pluie* (Paris, 1846).

106. Marcel Marion, *Dictionnaire des institutions de la France aux 17ᵉ et 18ᵉ siècles* (1923; reprint ed., Paris, 1969), p. 35. On the "official" presumption of miller dishonesty, see the intendant of Caen to the controller-general, 26 July 1776, in E. Villey, "La Taxe du pain," p. 190.

107. "Septième lettre sur le commerce des grains," 2 December 1770, in *Oeuvres de Turgot,* 3:349.

The mill as symbol: Christ's flour. Capital, Basilique de Vézelay
(Deutsches Brotmuseum)

intendant of Provence echoed the same image of the miller as a liar and
pillager of the public.[108] Even Parmentier, who claimed to be above these
prejudices, gave the impression that miller dishonesty was a sort of structural
fact of life.[109] The reputation of millers inspired so little public confidence that
bakers—themselves rarely above suspicion—were able to cite the millers'
"lack of honesty" as a pretext for operating their own mills, a practice forbidden by the law but usually tolerated by the authorities.[110]

108. "Objections sur le commerce des grains et farines," ca. 1768, AD Bouches-du-
Rhône, C 2420. Cf. a similar portrayal in Jacob Friedrich von Bielfeld, *Institutions politiques*
(The Hague, 1760–62), 1:126.
109. Antoine-Augustin Parmentier, *Avis aux bonnes ménagères des villes et des campagnes sur la meilleure manière de faire leur pain* (Paris, 1772). Béguillet, doubtless speaking in part for Bucquet, was the only subsistence commentator who sharply denounced the
"vulgar" and "ungrateful" prejudice against millers. But even he avoided giving the issue a
prominent place. "Mémoire," AN, F[10] 256. The rehabilitation of the miller has been a very
slow process. See A. Dugarçon, "Le Blé et le pain: Coopération et intégration," *Revue
d'économie politique* 27 (1914): 299–300.
110. BN, ms. fr. 21640, fols. 389 ff. On the miller reputation, see also Henriette Dussourd, "Les Moulins qui donnèrent leur nom à la ville de Moulins," *Actes du 93ᵉ Congrès
national des sociétés savantes tenu à Tours* (1968), *Bulletin philologique et historique du
Comité des travaux historiques et scientifiques* 2 (1971): 522. In mid-nineteenth-century

The community was hypersensitive about the miller because he mediated its subsistence and thus its survival. Few other social agents were so crucially ensconced in the nexus of social reproduction or so delicately located in the tissue of the collective imagination. His place invested him in the minds of consumers with solemn responsibilities, responsibilities toward which he seemed at best indifferent. He shared the opprobrium of the grain merchant who speculated wantonly on the staff of life as if it were an ordinary commodity. But the miller's involvement was deeper, and more threatening; he did not merely redistribute the raw materials of bread, he also transformed them. He decomposed them and he recombined them. There was something inherently mysterious, even awesome about the process of transforming a substance, especially one that would be assimilated by the human body. This transformation implied enormous power, not only to alter nature (and thus man), but also to denature nature by incorporating extraneous substances, by filtering in impurities instead of filtering them out.[111] This power was frightening because the miller could not be trusted to exercise it properly, honestly, benevolently—in the interest of the community.[112]

There persisted as well something of the classical perception of the miller as a blasphemous magician who compelled the free spirit of the streams and brooks to slave at the mill, who tortured it on the wheel. No wonder the mills occasionally exploded; the water spirits, in league with the realm of fire, avenged themselves. No wonder, too, that nature rebelled against the miller's tyranny by bringing drought or floods that stopped the mill. The appropriation of the wind, primal cosmic force, was a further mark of hubris, of might and cunning.[113]

Even the triumph of Christianity, in which Christ, transformer and trans-

---

France the miller's wealth was still widely presumed to issue from some illegitimate source. *Enquête sur la boulangerie*, p. 495. In mid-nineteenth-century America, if a miller stood the test of trustworthiness, he was quickly given the sobriquet "honest"—perhaps because it was such a memorable phenomenon. Abraham Lincoln allegedly acquired the title "Honest Abe" from working in a mill. Snyder, *Bread*, p. 138.

111. Was it surprising that Carlo Ginzburg's miller knew more than the peasants among whom he lived, and frightened them as a consequence? Carlo Ginzburg, "Cheese and Worms: The Cosmos of a Sixteenth-Century Miller," in *Religion and the People, 1000–1700*, ed. J. Obelkevich (Chapel Hill, 1979), p. 164.

112. One very concrete fear that resulted from the image of the miller as transformer-cheater was that his (adulterated) flour would make those who ate it sick. In this regard, see P. Boiteau, S. Urverg-Ratsimamanga, and R. Ratsimamanga, "Rôle éventuel de la malnutrition dans l'épidémiologie de la lèpre," *Actes du 93ᵉ Congrès national des sociétés savantes tenu à Tours* (1968), *Bulletin philologique et historique du Comité des travaux historiques et scientifiques* 1 (1971): 9–18. Cf. the discussion of quality and adulteration above in chap. 2. On the persistent fear of adulteration by the miller, see *Enquête sur la boulangerie*, p. 588, and Acremant, *Ailes d'argent*, p. 119. Perhaps in part to preempt the instinctive suspicions of manipulation and contamination, a group of American millers founded the Anti-Adulteration League in the late nineteenth century. Snyder, *Bread*, p. 156.

113. On the appropriation of the wind spirits, see Beckmann, *History of Inventions*, p. 269.

formed, became the miller of a new wisdom, failed to vanquish the old mystical ideas.[114] Russians and Serbs went on believing that mill water or mill splinters could cure diseases, and Germans went on believing that millstones could speak oracles. When Dante, in the thirty-fourth canto of the *Inferno,* entered the lowest circle, he saw the arms of a windmill turning in the dusk like a menacing bird. It was the Devil who had transformed himself into a mill and was grinding the souls of sinners.[115] Devils also dwelt in Quixote's mills. The Devil emerged at night, when the miller loved to work, unobserved save by the night birds he kept. Night was a time of occult communication, druidic rites, and black sabbaths. The miller of the Etang de l'Olivette offered his soul to the Devil if he would promise to turn the drought-crippled waterwheel. The Devil kept his word, but the flour that the mill produced dissolved into black coal dust. In a Hungarian folktale, the miller enlisted the aid of devils in order to cast spells on his enemies and to deepen the "extraordinary knowledge" that accounted for his magical powers. The miller was anti-Christ—he transformed blessings into curses and life into death. Aptly, the mill was a gibbet, a monument to infamy and public scorn.[116]

The mill was a frightening place—more or less remote, regardless of its actual location, a place one never visited at night, a machine that seemed always on the brink of running out of control, a spirit that made sounds of lamentation or warning.[117] Its interior was dangerous in another sense. The

114. On the Christian image of the "exegetical" mill see Louis Grodecki, "Les Vitraux allégoriques de Saint-Denis," *Art de France,* no. 1 (1961): 22.

115. This paragraph draws on Jacobs's excellent discussion in *Six Thousand Years,* pp. 124–28. Folk tales and children's stories are replete with allusions to miller magic, as well as miller turpitude. See, for example, the recent tale by Otfried Preussler, *The Satanic Mill,* trans. Anthea Bell (New York, 1973).

116. Delivre and Plancke, *Moulins à vent,* pp. 14–16; Dazelle, "Moulins et meuniers d'autrefois," pp. 366–68; "The Miller and the Rats," in Linda Dégh, ed., *Folktales of Hungary* (Chicago, 1965), pp. 269, 345; Erich Neumann, *The Great Mother: An Analysis of the Archetype,* trans. R. Manheim (Princeton, 1955), p. 234; "The Devil's Mill," in W. B. Yeats, ed., *Fairy and Folktales of Ireland* (Buckinghamshire, 1973), p. 336. Cf. the use of the millstone as a mark of evil. Index of Christian Art, Princeton University: Bibliothèque municipale, Strasbourg, Herrade de Landsberg, *Hortus Delic* (Personification: virtue, temperance), and Nat. Bibliotek, Vienna, 1191, Bible (Dragon imprisoned).

117. On the "strange" and "weird" ambience, see "The Haunted Mill-pool of Trove," in William Bottrell, ed., *Traditions and Hearthside Stories of West Cornwall* (Penzance, 1870), p. 277, and "Mill Valley," in H. G. Dwight, *Stamboul Nights* (New York, 1923), p. 269; "The Miller's Man Who Became an Ass," in Bernard Henderson and C. Calvert, *Wonder Tales of Alsace-Lorraine* (New York, 1925), p. 207.

The voice of the people was the voice of God, it was oft repeated, and that voice was known to cry violently against the devil-miller. But it seems to me that the crowd assaults on mills were much less common than they ought to have been (if, say, we compare their incidence with attacks on bakeries or hoarding convents). It is possible that the lingering fear of the possessed/possessing mill may have contributed toward this (ostensible) reticence. For an example of an attack on a mill see Poitrineau, *Vie rurale,* p. 209. Of course, an attack on a miller *outside* his mill is something quite different and less problematic. See, for example, Gabriel Dumay, ed., *Une émeute à Dijon en 1775* (Dijon, 1886), pp. 6–7, and Germain Martin, *Associations ouvrières au 18e siècle* (Paris, 1900), p. 203.

grinding of the stones, the vibrations that gently agitated the walls and floors, the flow of the flour, and the warm ambiance of mingled spray and dust all conveyed a powerful—transforming, overpowering—sensuality. Thus the miller violates the community in yet another way. From Chaucer to Goethe, literature is replete with testimonies to millstone and miller sexuality.[118] The mill was the trope as well as the place and in some ways the cause of lost virtue.[119] The community had its fill of frivolous bawdy tales, and of horrid sex-linked scandals. Could the citizens of Bussières-en-Brie have been totally surprised when miller Louis Leroy began "criminal commerce" with his deceased wife's daughter?[120] Was it not appropriate that Louis XV, *affameur du peuple,* contracted his fatal smallpox from the daughter of a miller furnished by the royal pimps?[121]

Given the millers' reputation, it is hardly surprising that their honesty was frequently placed in question by their baker clients. Jean Cousin, a master baker, drinking with his business associates in the Inn at the Sign of the Horn, exploded in invective against a prominent Paris miller named Claude Mergery, whom he accused of having cheated a hundred bakers on flour quantity and quality. Mergery was "a thief, a knave, a fucking bastard [foutu coquin]." Stung by this assault on "his reputation and his honesty," before men "with whom he might have occasion to do business," Mergery filed a

---

118. See the two sets of verses cited by E. P. Thompson, "The Moral Economy of the English Crowd in the Eighteenth Century," *Past & Present,* no. 50 (February 1971): 103. First:

> A brisk young lass so brisk and gay
> She went unto the mill one day . . .
> There's a peck of corn for all to grind
> I can but stay a little time.

> Come sit you down my sweet pretty dear
> I cannot grind your corn I fear
> My stones is high and my water low
> I cannot grind for the mill won't go.

> Then she sat down all on a sack
> They talked of this and they talked of that
> They talked of love, of love proved kind
> She soon found out the mill would grind. . . .

Second:

> Then the miller he laid her against the mill hopper
> Merry a soul so wantonly
> He pulled up her cloaths, and he put in the stopper
> For says she I'll have my corn ground small and free.

See also "The Miller's Daughter," in Geoffroy Grigson, ed., *The Penguin Book of Ballads* (Baltimore, 1975), p. 278.

119. Urbain Gibert, "Moulins à vent et meuniers," *Folklore* 21, no. 1 (Spring 1968): 19.

120. AN, O^{1}* 402, p. 268 (2 June 1760). Cf. the statutes of Ethelbert in the sixth century by which a man was to be fined 50 shillings for molesting a servant of the king but only 25 shillings for molesting the miller's servant. Jacob, *Six Thousand Years,* p. 132.

121. [Bon-Louis] Henri Martin, *Histoire de France,* 4th ed. (Paris, 1855–60), 16:308.

complaint with the police.[122] A Porcherons baker named Jean Dumas and his wife publicly took to task miller Jean Devaux of Montmartre on the grounds that "he had cheated and robbed them on the wheat they had sent him."[123] Years later another baker noted in the intimacy of his business register that his miller, Devaux, probably the same, "was a thief."[124]

Clients with powerful cases against millers usually took them to court (an act that did not preclude insulting them as well—both were forms of revenge shaped by very specific goals). Forain baker François Bernier sued miller Louis Lardier of Clichy-la-Garenne to recover two sacks of wheat that Lardier failed to return from a batch that Bernier had sent for grinding.[125] Master baker Antoine Potton sued miller Louis Paschot of the Lagny area for compensation for shortchanging him on several hundred livres' worth of flour.[126] Master baker Dupuis swore that he never received three *voitures* of flour for which he contracted with miller Lamoureux of Etampes.[127] Widow baker Joubert accused widow miller Lecuyer of a similar fraud.[128] According to forain baker Louis Hiest, miller Hallé of Essonnes substituted "inferior flour" for the first-grade wheat that he had purchased for grinding.[129]

The consular court very often sent a disputed case for expert evaluation to the baker guild before judging it—another price the millers paid for lack of corporate organization. In consequence they were found guilty more often than they should have been, according to miller Bucquet. "This is roughly like putting Cartouche in the place of the Chief Judge," he objected, "because, believe me, fairly and without making any accusations (God forbid), the ones [bakers] have no better reputation than the others [millers]."[130]

The Police of the Millers

Because of the absolute primacy of "the subsistence of the people," the authorities subjected milling to a special "police."[131] On the one hand, wrote

122. AN, Y 11235, 13 March 1748.

123. AN, Y 15238, 19 November 1731.

124. Archives Seine-Paris, D5B[6] 4246. Cf. the accusation made by the Meulan municipality that a local miller was a liar for pretending that he had not received 18 setiers of grain. BN, Coll. Vexin, vol. 69, fols. 178–81, 1 January 1790.

125. Archives Seine-Paris, D2B[6] 734, 3 February 1741.

126. Ibid., D2B[6] 809, 12 May 1747. Potton's suit may have been crystallized by one filed against him by Paschot the previous week for mill fees. D2B[6] 809, 5 May 1747.

127. Rapport arbitre, 30 April and 21 May 1767, ibid., D6B[6], carton 5.

128. Ibid., D6B[6], carton 3, 10 March and 22 June 1758.

129. Ibid., D4B[6], 42-2307, 16 August 1771. For an attack on millers who cheated on quality, see Lacombe d'Avignon, *Mitron de Vaugirard*, p. 10.

130. Bucquet, *Observations intéressantes*, pp. 119–20. In fact the baker jurés were not always biased in their judgments. See, for example, Archives Seine-Paris, D6B[6], carton 5, 30 April 1767.

131. On the meaning of police in this sense, see Kaplan, *Bread, Politics and Political Economy*, 1: chaps. 1 and 2.

Delamare, mills were private property no different from other possessions that could be sold, rented, mortgaged, and so forth. On the other hand, "as instruments destined for the preparation of the first and most necessary of foods," mills had to be clearly demarcated from other "things" even as grain had to be distinguished from other goods. As a result of their social function, millers "contract towards the public the obligation of a *service* whose duties they must fulfill exactly and faithfully." Even the "immunities" enjoyed by millers, such as freedom from suffering seizure of equipment for debt, issued from the idea of the priority of public provisioning service. Delamare's conception informed every aspect of eighteenth-century mill police.[132]

The mill police were particularly rigorous because of the notorious propensity of millers to victimize the public. Writing in the early seventeenth century, Montchrétien warned in vehement terms of the need for society to arm itself against the frauds of these artisans whose "conscience was so large." The catalogue of crimes he presented did not vary for the next two centuries.[133] The millers built secret spouts into their machines to divert grain and flour; they changed top quality for bottom; they mixed in stones and dirt; they cheated on weight and volume; they ground indifferently and wastefully; their flour deprived the people of the good bread they merited; they contributed to raise prices artificially. So wily were the miller-rogues that even experienced and alert customers would have trouble detecting their tricks.[134] The only way of dealing with this problem in Montchrétien's view was to subject the millers to tight regulation and to make them liable to severe penalties.[135]

There remained, however, a stark incongruity between the rhetoric of rigor and the actual apparatus of mill control.[136] It was not that the police were indifferent or indulgent, but rather that they were poorly equipped to deal with the mill problem. There were far too many mills; they were too widely dispersed across a host of seigneurial, local, parlementary, and royal jurisdictions as well as across a vast expanse of hinterland. In the absence of

132. Delamare, *Traité de la police,* 2:680–94.
133. See Baudeau's "frightening list of things you have to fear" when you bring your grain to a miller. *Avis au peuple sur son premier besoin,* deuxième traité, pp. 55–60. Frauds at the mill, wrote the principal of the collège of Beauvais in 1756, are "a common evil." BN, Coll. Joly 1428, fol. 198. For other eighteenth-century cases of the frauds cited by Montchrétien, see Religieuses de l'Assomption, "mémoire," 11 March 1738, BN, Coll. Joly 1428, fol. 193; P.-J. Nicodème, "Dissertation économique," *Journal de l'agriculture, commerce, arts, et finances* (February 1773): 42–43; Pierre Marmay, *Guide pratique de meunerie et de boulangerie* (Paris, 1863), p. 84; Parmentier, *Mémoire sur les avantages,* p. 125; Decan to procurator general, 4 July 1757, BN, Coll. Joly 1130, fols. 148–49.
134. On this vulnerability of the experts, see "Avis économique sur la boulangerie," *Journal économique* (July 1757): 99–100.
135. Montchrétien, *L'Economie politique patronale,* pp. 263–64.
136. The lieutenant general asked the assembly of police in September 1739 to discuss a general "regulation" for the mills. The idea, probably inspired by the subsistence crisis of 1738–41, apparently was obscured by the more urgent concerns it generated. There is no evidence that the assembly took up the matter again. Assembly of police, 3 September 1739, BN, ms. fr. 11356, fol. 404.

guilds there was no self-police and in the absence of a specialized service of inspection there was no way to assure the implementation of the rules that the public authorities imposed in place of corporate statutes.[137] The cost and complexity of filing complaints often discouraged individuals from denouncing millers. In rural districts inhabitants had little incentive for quarreling with millers upon whom they were dependent as a result of the strictures of *banalité*. City bakers were less inhibited, but they often preferred to settle their scores with millers outside the system of justice. Intramural millers and those situated close to the towns were the only ones who were truly under surveillance. Without any change in organization or strategy, the Paris mill police became increasingly effective in the eighteenth century as the commercialization of the milling business continued apace. Millers became vulnerable as they were caught in the net of the market. Their flour was subject to a double sanction: that of the buyers and that of the public authorities.

In order to keep millers alert and to repress frauds energetically, it was suggested on several occasions that a core of mill inspectors be created, on either a regional or a national scale.[138] The only such project that came close to realization was a travesty of the original idea: for transparently fiscal motives, a royal edict of 1708 created "officers-controllers-inspectors of weights and measures that are used at wind and water mills." The description of the sweeping range of their authority and the ferocity with which they were charged to act was obviously engineered to frighten millers into rapidly purchasing the posts by which they themselves would become responsible "for preventing our subjects from being exposed to the fraud and the bad faith of the millers."[139]

In place of an official instrument of police specialized in mill affairs there was a de facto core of inspectors constituted by the jurés, the elected leaders of the bakers' guild. The bakers were the "natural" watchdogs of the millers, highly motivated to keep them honest. As Delamare put it, "One could not assign this task to persons more interested in or more capable of uncovering the infidelities of the millers."[140] Usually the jurés were joined in their "visits" by a commissaire and by several huissiers of the Châtelet. The jurés were diligent, but they had too many responsibilities to give the policing of the mills their sustained attention. They conducted several inspection campaigns a year, but it is doubtful that they touched more than 10 to 12 percent of the mills involved in Parisian provisioning. The bulk of this inspection, if it was done at all, was in the hands of the local authorities.

Though the baker jurés were notoriously authoritarian in style and tem-

137. Delamare refers in passing to a Paris miller guild that "has not existed for a long time." *Traité de la police,* 2:694.

138. See, for example, "Mémoire et réflexions," fall 1761, BN, ms. fr. 11347, fol. 220.

139. BN, Coll. Joly 1414, fols. 170–73.

140. "Des Visites des moulins," BN, ms. fr. 21636, fol. 346. An ordinance of Jean II in 1351 presaged the creation of miller inspectors, but it did not generate lasting records. Lespinasse, *Métiers et corporations,* p. 9.

perament, they construed their mill police rather narrowly. They did not conduct a "structural" police in order to denounce millers who built square frames around their stones.[141] Nor did they file reports against millers who kept cows, pigs, or chickens—practices forbidden by law in order to discourage millers from cheating their clients of bran. The law prohibiting millers from keeping stocks of middlings for the purpose of regrinding in order to reduce their temptation to adulterate "the good flour" was recognized as an anachronism by the bakers. They do not even appear to have been concerned by the presence at the mills of bread ovens, whose existence was also prohibited as a further "precaution against cheating."[142] The jurés focused on a single issue, the one that theoretically concerned them most immediately: in order to be in a position to verify the millers' claims, they tried to enforce the requirement—on the books since at least 1350—that all mills be equipped with scales and weights.[143] Even this gesture was partly symbolic, for millers themselves very often transported grain to and from the mill, and bakers rarely accompanied their grain. Still, the principle of accountability was important to the bakers and to the police; and the bakers wanted to insist on their preference for weights over measures, a much surer way of guaranteeing the quality of merchandise and the integrity of the transaction.[144]

One inspection campaign began in Paris at 4:00 A.M. on 30 June 1739. A juré, accompanied by commissaire Cadot, his exempt, and a huissier, visited four mills under the bridges in the city, eight mills located in the Belleville-Courtille area, and one mill at the Petite Pologne. None of them, including one run by a baker's wife, had scales and weights. The refrain they heard was, "We do not keep scales and weights because we mill for the bakers and mealmen"—which presumably meant that these professionals, unlike individual clients, did not request verification.[145] Three days later they visited five mills in the faubourg St.-Laurent, eleven at Montmartre, two at Nouvelle France, and three in unspecified locations. Once again, not a single mill boasted the requisite equipment.[146] Jean Leclerc said that he had no need for scales because he milled for the bakers of Paris "who had their flour weighed

141. This practice was not against the law in all areas. Duchesne, *Code de la police*, p. 13; Cf. André Cochut, "Le Pain à Paris," *Revue des deux mondes*, 33d year, 2d period, 46 (15 August 1863): 977.

142. Duchesne, *Code de la police*, p. 114; Fréminville, *Dictionnaire ou traité de la police générale*, p. 476; arrêt of Paris Parlement, 22 June 1639, BHVP; Musart, *La Réglementation du commerce*, p. 72; Cf. the case of the bread ovens at the two windmills run by Siméon Delamarre, "master baker and dean of the guild." AN, MC, VII-288, 6 July 1771.

143. Delamare, *Traité de la police*, 2:695–97. Scales were installed in the major markets where bakers bought grain and bakers had every reason to keep scales in their shops to weigh merchandise on arrival. See Parmentier, *Parfait Boulanger*, p. 157.

144. See the case of the millers from Clermont en Beauvaisis who used false measures to increase the feed they took in kind. *Gazette d'agriculture, commerce, arts et finances* (26 January 1771): 59. See also Des Essart's *Dictionnaire universel de police*, 7:103.

145. AN, Y 12141, 30 June 1739.

146. For an example of a miller who kept scales and weights, see the after-death inventory of J.-J. Devaux. AN, MC, VII-307, 28 April 1757.

in Paris." Two millers, Antoine Marquet and Philippe Chesneau, reversed the argument commonly used. We have no scales, they declared, because we grind for "le premier venu," the domestic client rather than the baker. A miller in the faubourg St.-Laurent explained that he needed no scales because he was a mealman who ground only for himself and sold his flour at the Halle. A nearby miller intimately familiar with his milieu offered to wager that the visitors would not find a single mill with scales and weights.[147] The inspectors were also supposed to check whether the millers faithfully kept a business register containing the names of clients, the dates of arrival of grain, the amounts of grain, the quantities of flour produced, and so forth. Since fourteen of the millers they visited could neither read nor write, over against eight who could, it is doubtful that many fulfilled this requirement.[148]

All these millers (with the exception of one master baker-miller who claimed that he did not know of the requirement, despite the fact that it was written into the baker corporate statutes) received summonses to stand trial in the chamber of police. Most of them failed to appear; they were fined 5 or 10 livres plus damages to the baker guild of either 30 or 50 livres.[149] A number of the millers who appealed had the penalties, "by grace," significantly reduced to 3 livres in fine and 5 livres in damages.[150] The prévôt des marchands apparently also exercised a mill police concerning volume measures. Denis Thouin, for instance, who was to be condemned in September for failure to keep scales and weights, was fined 200 livres in June by the municipal court for using straw baskets instead of properly verified measures.[151] By 1789 millers were still resisting transactions by weight and the obligation to keep scales, judging by the doléances of the Third Estate extramuros.[152]

Another mill police was concerned with matters of general security. The city fathers heard frequent complaints from shippers that mills were hampering navigation, or that millers held back water in an attempt to extort passage fees. In principle, a miller needed written authorization from the prévôt in order to undertake any repairs or modifications that involved the cage of his mill. The bureau de la ville did not hesitate to deny permission to build mills or to order mills to be dismantled if they blocked traffic.[153] The municipality took precautions—alas, not always successfully—to prevent boat mills from

147. AN, Y 12141, 3 July 1739 (5:00 A.M. and 2:00 P.M.). Parmentier wrongly claimed that the Paris area mills were known to have weights and scales. Mémoire sur les avantages, p. 407.

148. See the rule in the baker statutes of April 1783, AN, AD XI 14.

149. AN, Y 9440, 4 September 1739.

150. Ibid., 11, 18 December 1739.

151. BN, sentence of the Hôtel de Ville, 12 June 1739.

152. Chassin, Elections et cahiers, 4:453.

153. See the sentences of 2 August 1728 and 9 July 1743, AN, Z¹ᴴ 408 and 417; petition of 1 August 1743, AN, Z¹ᴴ 417; investigations of July 1759 (Chevanne) and 10 February 1750, AN, Z¹ᴴ 423 and 449; ordinance of 15 January 1675, AN, F⁷ 4296; sentence of 27 April 1740, BN, F 23720, no. 141.

breaking loose during periods of icing or flooding and imperiling vessels loaded with merchandise.[154] Similarly, the lieutenant general of police took measures to order the demolition of windmills that were dangerously dilapidated or whose location threatened the public good.[155]

The danger of fire preoccupied the authorities, especially in Paris, where the boat mills ignited massive blazes on ports and bridges several times in the eighteenth century.[156] The great quantities of flour dust created an inherent danger of explosion. Dripping oil, damp smut, and the contact between planks of timber and moving parts were other sources of combustion.[157] The slightest spark could detonate an explosion, and the miller and his gardes-moulin had to be unremittingly vigilant.[158] In April 1778 a boat mill burned because two miller boys fell asleep and allowed the stones to turn dry, which produced sparks that set off a huge conflagration.[159] The *bureau de la ville* strictly forbade millers to light fires on their boat mills for any purpose. Municipal police patrolled the mills; millers violating the ban faced not only heavy fines (100 livres) but also the shutting down of their installation.[160] Ultimately the solution was to expel the city mills, in the wake of the cemeteries, to the countryside. There mills continued to burn for many years to come, to judge by the number of sites named Moulin-Brulé, as well as by the collective memory of local disaster.[161]

Another form of mill police had an overtly political character. The aim was to prevent seigneurial privilege, in the form of *banal* rights, from interfering with the provisioning of Paris in flour. In this regard, the Paris police were liberals of the first hour. Long before Boncerf and Turgot, Delamare enunciated the principle that "the liberty of commerce"—that is, the liberty of provisioning the capital—had priority over *banal* claims, in the same way that grain as public property had precedence over grain as private property when the welfare of the commonweal was at stake.[162] It was generally acknowl-

154. For the sinking of a mill, see AN, Z[1H] 423, October 1749. On ice damage, see *Journal historique et politique des principaux événements*, no. 5, pp. 285–86 (20 February 1774), and Cherrière, *La Lutte contre l'incendie*, pp. 198–99.

155. See Lenoir's order to demolish five windmills on the buttes de Chaumont and Belleville, Archives Seine-Paris, 1 AZ 10, pièce 20.

156. See Cherrière, *La Lutte contre l'incendie*, passim.

157. Evans, *Young Millwright*, p. 274; Grimshaw, *Miller, Millwright, and Millfurnisher*, p. 31.

158. Storck and Teague, *Flour for Man's Bread*, p. 219. On other sources of accidents, see Evans, *The Young Millwright*, p. 274.

159. Hardy's Journal, 17 April 1778, BN, ms. fr. 6683, p. 36. Such "negligence" may also have been the cause of a mill fire in 1780. Ibid., 21 July 1780, p. 319.

160. Ordinance of the municipality, 24 January 1728, AN, AD I 25[B].

161. See Delivre and Plancke, *Les Moulins à vent*, p. 13. Catastrophic explosions and fires took enormous tolls in American milling at least until the end of the nineteenth century. See Charles B. Kuhlmann, *The Development of the Flour-Milling Industry in the United States* (Boston, 1929), p. 124, and Grimshaw, *Miller, Millwright, and Millfurnisher*, p. 31.

162. Delamare, *Traité de la police*, 2:691. On the *banal* system, see Manesse, *Traité du droit de bâtir moulin*, and *Les Moulins: Technique, histoire, folklore* (Lille, 1975), pp. 44–49.

edged that the *banal* mills ground poorly, produced a mediocre-to-bad flour, wasted grain, and claimed a toll out of proportion with the service rendered.[163] Given the juridically sound titles on which the *banal* extortions were based, the police felt compelled to respect them to the extent that they victimized domestic clients—"the people of the countryside." But the Paris authorities were adamant that "flour destined to be commercialized"—that is, flour for the provisioning of Paris—could not be subjected "to the avidity and the monopoly" of the *banal* millers and their landlords. Thus they protected Paris bakers and mealmen who used non-*banal* mills even when they were theoretically bound to use the *banal* facility, or who withdrew from *banal* mills because of excessive delay or poor-quality manufacture.[164]

Banal lords aggressively tried to prevent the establishment of new mills in their jurisdiction, even when those mills aimed exclusively at the metropolitan flour trade. One has the impression that the whole royal administration was mobilized when a tanner from Dreux named Leprince requested permission in 1780 to convert his tanning mill into a Paris-directed grist mill. Necker himself examined the petition and referred it to the intendant of Paris and to the intendant of commerce for their recommendations. Though the mill was located on the domain of the marquis de Chatenoy, a royal engagiste, Bertier, the intendant of Paris, envisioned no conflict, since Leprince planned to service the capital exclusively. But Chatenoy was enraged, and bombarded Necker with protests against this "prejudicial" and "illegitimate" competition. As seigneur of the part of the river on which Leprince's mill was implanted, according to the relevant sections of the customary law, only he could authorize a mill, and he adamantly refused. The *bureau du commerce* deferred to this narrow argument and Leprince's petition was rejected.[165] At Beauvais the cardinal de Gesvres blocked every effort to build new mills on the grounds that his authority as *évêque-comte* gave him total sovereignty over the river.[166]

Nor were *banal* lords the only enemies of mill development. Guilds played the same obstructionist role. On the grounds of the benefits it would bestow upon the capital, lieutenant general of police Marville convinced the *bureau du commerce* to override the self-regarding objections of the Corbeil tanners' guild to the conversion of a tanning mill owned by one of its members into a gristmill working for the provisioning of Paris.[167]

163. See the violent denunciations before the comité d'agriculture in Pigeonneau and Foville, *Administration de l'agriculture,* p. 410 (31 July 1787). Cf. Parmentier, *Parfait Boulanger,* p. 153; Béguillet, *Discours sur la mouture* (1775), p. 233; and Alfred Cerne, *Les Moulins à eau de Rouen* (Rouen, 1936). On the tyranny of *banalité,* see also "The Miller of Dee," in Harrowven, *The Origins of Rhymes,* pp. 98–99.

164. Fréminville, *Dictionnaire ou traité de la police générale,* p. 470; Musart, *Réglementation du commerce,* p. 71; Duchesne, *Code de la police,* p. 113.

165. AN, F^{12} 1299^A.

166. AD Seine-et-Oise, G 47 (ca. 1760s).

167. Bureau de commerce, 27 April, 20 July 1741, AN, F^{12} 685.

Traditionally the miller played a more or less passive role in the provisioning nexus as an artisan who converted grain into flour on demand in exchange for a toll. Often denounced as extortionate, the toll varied widely from place to place in type (kind or money) and in rate. It reflected not merely the miller's rapacity but also the sorts of services he included in the price (e.g., bolting, transporting, sacking). In response to calls for rationalization and moralization of toll usages, a number of towns issued regulatory codes that applied to their hinterlands. The Paris authorities preferred to rely on the market principle—policing through competition—which proved increasingly effective as commercialization caught more and more millers in the metropolitan net.

Commercialization—the process by which merchant milling supplanted toll or custom milling—profoundly altered the structure of the provisioning trade. Impelled by ambition and frustrated by a tissue of legal and customary restrictions, more and more millers shifted from a local service routine to an aggressive, independent, and speculative wholesale orientation. Defying the age-old ban on grain commerce by millers, they became buyers as agents for bakers and in their own behalf. The critical innovation was the miller's transformation of this grain into flour for speculative sale, frequently outside the marketplace and en droiture. Commercialization brought millers into a much more intense rivalry than ever before. They fought over clients, impugned each other's honor, and broke agreements governing access to grain. By the early nineteenth century, the millers had become the uncontested masters of the grain trade in the Paris region—in a sense eliminating it as an autonomous commerce by absorbing it into a larger and more rational undertaking. Control over the grain trade helped the millers to take vengeance on the bakers, once their overlords, now their industrial vassals.

If he was prosperous, the miller, customary or merchant, often played an influential role as economic, social, and cultural mediator in his home community. He achieved "notable" status despite (and perhaps in some cases because of) the ignominious reputation that attached to his profession. The word *miller* evoked corruption and evil. The miller's dishonesty was notorious, a kind of structural fact of life. Elite testimony in literature and the law corroborated popular intuition. The miller was also a sort of shaman, a person who trafficked with the Devil, cast spells, and exercised an inexorable sensual allure. The miller's reputation probably served at least one positive social function: it kept his customers alert.

CHAPTER 8

The Parisian Milling Network:
Density and Productivity

> The windmiller to the water miller:
> My windmill can grind more corn in an hour
> Than your watermill can in three or four.
> You may well ask for fountains of rain
> But that would be the worst thing you could gain.
> For in the face of rain or of flood
> Your mills must stand still, they can do no good.
> But when the wind to a tempest will blow
> Our mills work fast and clap to and fro.
> According to the speed the wind can dictate
> We adjust our sails to the very same rate.
> Since our mills grind so much faster than yours
> And since they may work at all times and hours,
> I say we need no water mills at all
> For windmills are sufficient to serve all.[1]

A careful scrutiny of contemporary reports (most of which were highly impressionistic and some of which were tendentious), maps (whose sources of information are impossible to verify), and surveys (often flawed in method, lacking in uniformity, and incomplete) provides a rough measure of mill density and productivity. The texts are subjected to criticism and comparison, their data supplemented through extrapolation and interpolation.

1. Heywood, *The Play of the Weather,* p. 28.

298

Water mills produced approximately two-thirds more than windmills, and were far more numerous in the Paris region. Production figures alone cannot be used to gauge the size of the Parisian mill pool. Given the factors to which mill functioning was hostage, the machines could not operate twenty-four hours a day, three-hundred-sixty-five days a year. Nor did all the mills in the Paris provisioning sphere grind metropolitan white. About two thousand mills worked for Paris at one moment or another. A relatively small number constituted the production nucleus and accounted for 60 percent of the capital's needs. An elastic secondary pool consisting of blatier-type millers and mealmen provided the necessary complement and buffer.

The Debate

Generally observers of the grain and flour trades believed that Paris was served by an insufficient number of mills in the eighteenth century. In the capital and its immediate vicinity, Delamare enumerated eighty windmills and many fewer water mills. Windmills were frequently shut down by fog or by lack of wind; water mills by high and low water and ice. "But [even] when they are all working without interruption they do not satisfy one-twentieth of the conversion needs of the bakers of this city," added Delamare.[2] The Paris bakers, in 1685 and again in 1725, insisted that they had to go deep into the countryside in order to grind three-quarters of the wheat required to feed Paris.[3] Their assessment was not disinterested, for they coveted the freedom to buy on their own throughout the hinterland and to mill on the spot. An article in the *Journal économique* in 1753 confirmed the bakers' analysis and argued that the twelve hundred mills on the rivers and streams of the region were the only guarantee of a steady supply.[4] In the same vein, Foucaud, the Paris police agent most familiar with the provisioning zones, urged the building of more mills "in order to accelerate the grinding" needed for the capital in the late fifties.[5]

There was, however, a minority view that took issue with the mill-penury thesis. The Paris port merchants, inspired in large measure by their desire to

2. Delamare, *Traité de la police,* 1:627. Cf. Guy Fourquin's point linking the development of the vigorous forain baker traffic to the shortage of mills in the late fifteenth and sixteenth centuries. *Les Campagnes de la région parisienne à la fin du Moyen Age* (Paris, 1964), pp. 500–501.

3. "Sommaire pour les marchands talmeliers maîtres boulangers," BN, ms. fr. 21640, fol. 71; "Mémoire des maîtres boulangers," BN, Coll. Joly 1116, fols. 250–51. Cf. Coll. Joly 1314, fol. 67.

4. Le Camus, "Suite du mémoire sur le pain," *Journal économique* (December 1753): 95. But Le Camus drew on both Delamare and the baker factums uncritically and with little allowance for change over time.

5. BN, Coll. Joly 1113, fols. 240–41.

keep the bakers out of their country buying territory, contended that "the mills of Paris and those of the environs are more than sufficient to grind all the wheat necessary for the consumption of the bakers of the city and faubourgs." Poussot, police inspector and subsistence specialist, provided some indirect support for this position by noting that a fourth of the Paris windmills had gone out of business between 1735 and 1760 for lack of work. The reason was that the bakers had shifted the center of commercial gravity deep into the countryside, bypassing both the Paris grain market and the nearby mills. As eager to stifle droiture traffic as the port merchants were to smother baker trading, Poussot may have exaggerated this metropolitan milling overcapacity.[6] Daure, another subsistence specialist, grain trader, and baker, categorically affirmed in 1770 that "for the provisioning of Paris there are many more [mills] than are necessary." He based his case on a personal investigation that revealed an excess in productive capacity marked by "unemployed" mills and by the fact that mill tolls had not followed the sharp upward rise of other goods since the mid-fifties. He claimed that thirty-eight water mills and sixty-one windmills in the greater Paris area covered over two-thirds of Parisian annual consumption needs. But Daure's production figures, as we shall see, were extremely optimistic, and he was motivated in part by his dislike of Malisset and the promoters of the "economic system" who called for royal subsidizing of new mill construction in the Paris area.[7] Writing in 1792, another subsistence commentator found that there were "many more wind and water mills than necessary" in the Paris supply zone. He included in his purview, however, mills located deep in the hinterland toward which the bakers had been moving since about 1730, and as a consequence implicitly impugned Daure's assessment.[8]

The data on mill numbers and production are too sparse and unreliable to enable us to settle this debate. We have no full-scale census until the Revolution, and even then the information on productivity is highly uncertain and there is no guarantee that all the mills in the supply zones were actually covered. For the eighteenth century, Delamare's figure of 80 wind- and 1,500 water mills stood as the point of reference at least until the 1760s, though it was never exactly clear what area was embraced in this estimation.[9] Malouin proposed over 3,000 water mills and fewer than 1,000 windmills in the jurisdiction of the Châtelet, which did not cover all of the traditional hinterland.[10]

6. "Réponse des marchands de bled," BN, Coll. Joly 1314, fol. 65; Arsenal, ms. Bast. 10141, fol. 335 (7 April 1760). Cf. the picture of mills pullulating on the faubourg heights in the eighteenth century as never before in Sellier, "Moulins à vent," p. 13.

7. Daure, "Mémoire," AN, F[11] 264.

8. "La Cherté du pain," AN, T 644[1−2].

9. BN, ms. fr. 21639, fol. 240. Delamare may have borrowed this estimate from the Paris bakers. See BN, ms. fr. 21640, fol. 50.

10. Malouin, Description et détails des arts, p. 62.

The *Encyclopédie* estimated that there were between 500 and 550 water mills and as many windmills in the area "around" Paris.[11] According to a subsistence expert and grain trader named Doumerc, a census by the Paris intendant in the 1780s revealed 600 mills of all sorts working for the capital.[12] The dearth of 1725 impelled the lieutenant general of police to order a mill survey, part of whose results have survived. The exempts counted 77 windmills in Paris, the faubourgs, and such nearby suburbs as Bourg-la-Reine, Arcueil, and Montrouge, and 19 water mills, most of which were outside the city in such nearby towns as Charenton, St.-Denis, and Villejuif.[13] Among the intramural mills not mentioned were several dozen boat mills on the Seine, firetraps and occasional obstructions to navigation, but "indispensable" flour manufacturers in the eyes of the police because they were never halted by high or low water levels.[14]

The Cassini Mills

The splendid "Cassini" maps, drafted largely in the second half of the century, indicate the location of water and windmills in sumptuous detail, distinguishing, for example, between functioning windmills and those that were either partially or wholly destroyed. Their chief weakness is that we do not know precisely how Cassini de Thury's team collected its information, and thus we have no systematic way to test the reliability of the survey. Certain scholars are enthusiastic about the precision of the Cassini count, but they themselves are rarely able to provide independent authentication.[15] I would be inclined to allow for local errors of appreciation of up to one-third. Within these confines, the Cassini map is the best prerevolutionary guide that we have.[16]

11. Cited by Marcel Arpin, *Historique de la meunerie et de la boulangerie depuis les temps préhistoriques jusqu'à l'année 1914* (Paris, 1948), 1:41.

12. Doumerc to procurator general, 19 February 1789, BN, Coll. Joly 1111, fol. 201. Doumerc's criterion of "working for Paris" suggests that Malouin's figures, even if correct, might be largely irrelevant.

13. BN, Coll. Joly 1116, fols. 219, 231. The same survey revealed 72 mills in the 64 parishes of the election of Pontoise, probably the chief flour entrepot for the capital. Cleret to lieutenant general, 28 February 1725, Arsenal, ms. Bast. 10270. In 1809, the arrondissement of Pontoise, which did not correspond exactly to the old election, boasted 165 mills.

14. Assembly of police, 25 February 1734, BN, ms. fr. 11356, fol. 236; Cherrière, *Lutte contre l'incendie dans les halles,* pp. 197–200; *Magasin pittoresque,* 47th year (1879): 372. Apparently there were far fewer boat mills in the eighteenth century than in the fifteenth. See Alfred Franklin, *Dictionnaire historique des arts, métiers et professions exercés dans Paris depuis le XIIIe siècle* (Paris, 1906), p. 487.

15. Marcel-Robillard, *Folklore de la Beauce,* 1:15.

16. I have used several editions, drawing most heavily on the *Tableau des 175 feuilles de la carte de France* (Paris 1768) held in the Lavoisier Collection of the Cornell University Library. For other useful maps, probably based on the Cassini model, see AN, Plans, 3 cl. Oise, no. 168[1] and NN 135, 136.

Detail of Cassini map showing water and windmills

TABLE 10

Cassini Table 1

Map Area	Water mills	Windmills
Paris (Pontoise, St.-Denis)	261	97
Fontainebleau (Corbeil, Etampes)	192	65
Chartres	241	86
Sens (Melun, Provins, Montereau)	150	40
Meaux (Coulommiers, Château-Thierry)	207	41
Evreux (Mantes)	255	35
Compiègne (Beauvais, Lagny, Senlis, Clermont, Dammartin)	294	111
Soissons	401	24
TOTALS	2,001	499 (plus 31 destroyed or partially destroyed)

TABLE 11

Cassini Table 2

Triangle formed by	Water mills	Windmills
1. Pontoise-Chambly-Beaumont	40	1
2. Senlis-Clermont-Compiègne	22	29
3. Provins-Meaux-Ch.-Thierry	86	10
4. Melun-Meaux-Provins	87	37
5. Chartres-Rambouillet-Etampes	30	15
6. Méru-Chaumont-Beauvais	19	9

Table 10 is based upon a visual count of the mill symbols on the eight area maps that embrace the Parisian milling hinterland. The maps are identified by the Cassini geographical labels. I have added in parentheses the major milling centers within that map space.

These figures, which roughly fall between the estimates of Delamare and Malouin, can be broken down in several ways. Focusing on the major milling centers, these localizations are extremely approximate and they produce considerable unintended erosion. First, let us imagine the areas encompassed within six triangles, formed by each of the three town groups associated in Table 11. In the first, second, fifth, and sixth triangles, I find fewer mills than other evidence leads me to believe. For Meaux, Melun, Etampes, Montereau, Dammartin, and perhaps even Pontoise, the results appear understated in Table 12, indicating the incidence of mills roughly within a five-mile radius of each town (with some overlapping).

One final reading suggests the density of water mills on and within one kilometer of the major rivers. It reminds us forcefully that the bulk of the mills are on tributaries or on streams located sometimes at a considerable distance from the main arteries (see Table 13).

The Revolutionary Surveys

The revolutionary government conducted a mill census in the year II. Not all the cantons were covered and not all the information collected has survived. The results for the "department of Paris" are strikingly similar to the findings of the 1725 survey: 71 windmills and 28 water mills (at St.-Denis, Charenton, Gentilly, and Arcueil). In addition, there were 7 boat mills, considerably fewer than at the beginning of the century, and a stream mill in-

TABLE 12

Cassini Table 3

City areas	Water mills	Windmills
Provins	12	0
Ch.-Thierry	14	0
Montereau	3	0
Meaux	8	2
Soissons	21	1
Compiègne	8	3
Pont-Ste.-Maxence	8	3
Senlis	12	0
Dammartin	4	7
Clermont	11	2
Beauvais	17	2
Méru	5	5
Chambly	17	1
Beaumont	14	2
Chaumont	15	0
Pontoise	11	0
Gonesse	14	4
Corbeil	3	0
Melun	6	2
Etampes	7	0
Rambouillet	3	1
Chartres	18	1
Mantes	20	0

TABLE 13
Cassini Table 4

River	From	to	Water mills
Seine	Nogent	Melun	9
(31)	Melun	Corbeil	2
	Corbeil	Paris	5
	Paris	Mantes	15
Marne	Paris	Meaux	19
(58)	Meaux	Ch.-Thierry	16
	Ch.-Thierry	Damery	23
Oise	Pontoise	Beaumont	10
(28)	Beaumont	Pont-Ste.-Maxence	10
	Pont-Ste.-Maxence	Compiègne	8
Aisne	Compiègne	Soissons	5
(18)	Soissons	Condé	13
Yonne	Montereau	Sens	7
(7)			

stalled on the Isle des Cygnes.[17] The 28 water mills are counted a second time in the census for the district of Franciade (ex-St.-Denis). In all, this district reported 37 water mills, 64 windmills, 1 hand mill, and 1 "mechanical" mill, but seven communities had not yet reported. Three of these mills, all wind driven, were in very bad condition. A half-dozen other windmills were in remote or relatively inaccessible locations. The vast majority of the Franciade mills were said to fabricate first-grade flour.[18]

The canton of Claye contained 12 water mills, most of which produced excellent flour. Seven worked exclusively for Paris; the others served both local and metropolitan needs. Three windmills, producing good flour, concentrated on local demand. The canton of Crécy also had 12 water and 3 windmills, most of which served local needs with good to excellent merchandise. Dammartin's 16 windmills and 7 water mills served both Paris and the local area. All 23 mills in the canton of Lizy were waterpowered. Six were Paris directed, 7 strictly local, and the others mixed in commercial orientation. Only 1 of Lagny's 18 water mills and 2 windmills seems to have supplied the capital regularly. Most of the 16 water mills in Meaux produced excellent flour for both Paris and local consumption, whereas its 3 windmills dealt only with local clients. Neither the simple windmill nor any of the 16 water mills of the canton of La Ferté specialized in Paris supply. The 4 water mills of the canton of Crouy also aimed at the home market.[19] Fewer than a quarter of the mills in

17. AN, F[20] 293.
18. Ibid.
19. Ibid.

TABLE 14
Water mill and windmill distribution, year X.

Arrondissement	Number of water mills	Number of windmills
Beauvais	159	67
Clermont	72	175
Corbeil	70	4
Melun	87	20
Coulommiers	109	7
Provins	67	26
Meaux	126	21
Compiègne	116	103

these cantons appear to have concentrated on Paris traffic, but there is a considerable amount of missing data and a substantial number of mills did part-time Paris work.

The surveys for the district of Mantes and Dourdan do not indicate the relation of the mills to Paris provisioning. Mantes had 94 mills, only 6 of which were wind driven. Twelve of the water mills and 1 windmill were in bad physical and/or mechanical state.[20] At least 8 of the mills were of difficult access. The district of Dourdan contained 72 water and 11 windmills that produced flours of a wide range of quality. Many were located on the Paris-Chartres road and would probably have attempted to serve Versailles and/or Paris in addition to local customers. In Chartres and the valleys around it there were 56 mills, mostly water powered. The district of Crécy had 69 water and 11 windmills, the district of Breteuil 5 water and 56 windmills, the district of Senlis 72 water and 6 windmills, and the district of Compiègne 69 water and 11 windmills.[21]

The Imperial Surveys

The censuses of the year II are too fragmented and partial to permit any serious hinterland evaluation. An official estimate in 1806 indicated that Paris drew on 5,200 mills in the region, but we do not know on what data it was based. The major flour centers were Corbeil, Pontoise, Etampes, Chartres, Senlis, Meaux, Creteil, and St.-Denis, and the miller-mealmen were quite rightly perceived as the chief agents in the provisioning system.[22] Table 14

20. Another survey taken at the beginning of the Revolution indicates fifty mills in the Mantes area. BN, Coll. Vexin, vol. 69, fols. 41–42. See also Roger Wolff, *Les Vieux Moulins à eau de la Montcien* (Mantes-la-Jolie, n.d.).
21. AN, F[20] 293.
22. "Réponses aux questions," AN, F[11] 260.

summarizes an inquiry in the year X on the distribution of mills in some of the active flour arrondissements.[23]

The imperial government undertook major censuses between 1809 and 1811. In 1809 the arrondissement of St.-Denis contained 52 windmills and 20 or 21 water mills, fewer than the district of Franciade to which, however, it did not precisely correspond. The bulk of these mills concentrated on local service, but the strongest surely provisioned the capital, and many did both. The arrondissement of Sceaux (which included areas that in 1725 had been called "plain of St.-Marcel and beyond" as well as the Charenton area) counted 24 water and 46 or 48 windmills. Four of the former and 79 of the latter were specifically Paris directed, but others occasionally ground for Paris bakers or marketed meal in the capital.[24]

In 1809 the department of the Seine-et-Oise claimed 766 mills, 92 percent water, distributed as in Table 15.[25]

The *état* failed to indicate which mills dealt particularly with the capital. But we know that Pontoise, Corbeil, Etampes, and to a lesser extent Versailles were the home bases for the leading mealmen as well as the flour markets most attractive to bakers who purchased in the field. This same census, completed in 1810, listed 146 mills for the department of the Seine (45 water, 101 wind) and 548 mills for the department of the Seine-et-Marne (467 water, 81 wind).[26] These three departments encompassed the vast majority of mills that regularly supplied Paris. It must be remembered, however, that other departments contributed in varying degrees to the mill pool on which the capital drew: the Oise, the Aube, the Aisne, the Loiret, the Eure-et-Loir, the Eure, the Seine-Maritime, and the Somme.[27]

Production

In order to determine whether Paris was served by a sufficient number of mills one must know not only how many mills operated in the orbit of the capital, but also how much they were ordinarily capable of producing.[28] Production figures are extremely sparse and equally unreliable. As a rule we do not know the specific source of a figure (administrative estimate, field survey, interpolation of sorts). We do not know to what extent, say, millers underestimated production for fear of fiscal penalties or imposition of quotas, or local

23. AN, F²⁰ 294.

24. "Etat," February 1809, AN, F²⁰ 296.

25. AN, F²⁰ 290.

26. AN, F²⁰ 560.

27. In this perspective, Bergeron's estimate of a 600-mill supply system is too low. "Approvisionnement et consommation," p. 205n. Cf. Jacques-Eugène Armengaud's estimate of 460 to 500 mills for the period 1857–82. *Meunerie et boulangerie* (Paris, 1882), p. 72n. See also, AN, F²⁰ 561.

28. Of course one also needs to know the level of annual consumption, another com-

TABLE 15

Water mill and windmill distribution in the Seine-et-Oise, 1809.

Arrondissement	Number of water mills	Number of windmills
Mantes	122	12
Pontoise	136	29
Versailles	164	18
Corbeil	106	3
Etampes	176	0

officials overestimated it as an expression of local patriotism. We do not know whether mill stoppages—structural, such as dressing the stones, and "conjunctural," such as slack wind, low or high water, or ice—were factored in. We are obliged to assume a twenty-four-hour-a-day operation year round, but we have ample evidence that this cadence was monstrously hard to sustain. We cannot always be certain that the surveyors and respondents shared the same vocabulary or conceptions of the inquiry; thus it is not always clear whether production amounts refer to the grain to be ground or to the ground meal. Nor is there always a consensus on what measures or weights to use, or on what a given measure or weight actually represents. Productivity also depends on the quality or type of flour manufactured, a variable that is rarely articulated. It seems likely that the strongest mills worked for Paris and the weakest for local trade, yet a mill grinding white flour might be less "productive" in a twenty-four-hour period than a mill grinding a whole grain or dark meal. Such a disproportion could invite erroneous inferences and seriously distort the realities of mill production.[29]

The figures I have collected, then, are to be used with great circumspection. Anomalies abound. I have rendered them comparable by transforming them into old-regime Parisian setiers (240 pounds of 489 grams each). My feeling is that bakers and millers "thought" production in terms of wheat to be transformed. Even though several late-eighteenth-century and early-nineteenth-century censuses specifically asked for yield in flour, I believe that in most cases the grain amount is given. If I am wrong, the result is to underestimate production in certain instances by as much as a quarter. Finally, even the "cleanest" figures often have a normative edge. When they are supposed to answer the question "How much do you produce?" many millers (and administrators) tend imperceptibly to address the question "How much

plicated problem that I have addressed elsewhere. See Kaplan, *Bakers of Paris.*

29. See, for instance, the different "settings" of the windmills at Ivry-sur-Seine during the Revolution. District de Franciade, year II, AN, F[20] 293.

can you produce?" in a given period, thus introducing a bias toward overestimation. This tendency is reinforced by the assumption that the wheat is of the most tractable sort. In fact, wheat quality modified productivity, as did the weather and the technology and condition of the mill. Old wheat, for example, because it was dry and hard, tended to grind more rapidly than new wheat, which was fatty and sticky and forced the miller to halt for redressing every four or five days.[30]

First we have the testimony of the experts, which tends to focus on and extrapolate from cases that we would regard as more or less aberrant. Bucquet's Moulin de la Pompe near Notre-Dame transformed 30 to 60 setiers and more a day, but it was an especially strong mill. The average daily yield of the 7 functioning Paris boat mills in 1794 was said to be 25 setiers a day.[31] Bucquet himself set the productivity of a mill of "average power" at 15 to 25 setiers a day. His alter ego Béguillet fixed the lower limit more sagely at 8 or 10 setiers.[32] Malisset's mills at Corbeil, Essonnes, and Robinson, all set for coarse grinding, had a 24-setier average daily output.[33] A police official in 1725 reported that the best mills at Pontoise could do up to a setier an hour in a twenty-four-hour day.[34] According to Malouin, a good mill should be able to do 30 setiers a day and up to 36 setiers in cold weather, which attenuated the risk of overheating.[35] The engineer Belidor was said to have designed a mill in Picardy that produced 38 setiers a day, a figure allegedly approached by the biggest mill in Toulouse.[36] At Caen average production was apparently between 14 and 18 setiers a day.[37]

According to the 1725 police inquiry, 7 windmills at Montreuil and Belleville averaged 8.8 setiers in twenty-four hours (range 8 to 10). But elsewhere the windmill production range was staggering: from 60 setiers at the Moulin des Couronnes at Villejuif to 6 setiers at the mill at the Pointe de Gentilly.

30. See Cleret to lieutenant general of police, 28 September 1725, Arsenal, ms. Bast. 10270. Thus, the two windmills of the Paris General Hospital at Villejuif were able to grind up to 30 setiers each of old wheat but only 18 of new. BN, Coll. Joly 1116, fols. 222–31. Both these figures seem high to me.

31. AN, F[20] 293.

32. Bucquet, *Manuel du meunier,* p. 75, and Béguillet, *Traité des subsistances,* pp. 167–68. Both men referred to traditional or coarse milling technology. Elsewhere, Bucquet proposed 30 to 35 setiers a day as the yield of a mill "of average power." *Mémoire sur les moyens de perfectionner les moulins et la mouture économique* (Paris, 1786), p. 68.

33. Malisset to Courteille, 20 October 1767, AN, F[11] 1194.

34. Cleret to lieutenant general, 28 September 1725, Arsenal, ms. Bast. 10270.

35. Malouin, *Description et détails des arts,* p. 62.

36. Abbé Antoine Pluche, *Le Spectacle de la nature . . .* (Paris, 1755), 5:474; Jorré, "Commerce des grains," p. 37. Belidor wrote that three horses working three-hour shifts could convert 44 setiers in twenty-four hours, while two men could hand-mill 12 setiers in that same period. Belidor, *Architecture hydraulique,* 1:318–19. According to results obtained on a hand mill at Fresnes during the Revolution, Belidor's human energy production figure is greatly exaggerated. District of Franciade, year II, AN, F[20] 293.

37. Villey, "La Taxe du pain," p. 186.

Three water mills at Charenton averaged a little over 10 setiers (11 to 20), while the 5 water mills at St.-Denis produced almost twice as much (13 to 36).[38] These figures seem very reasonable when compared to Daure's 1771 estimate of a maximum of 40.66 setiers and a minimum of 24.4 setiers for 38 water mills in the greater Paris area. Mean production for 61 windmills in times of good wind—47.5 setiers—is not a useful measure of everyday central tendency and is in any case quite exaggerated, in my view.[39]

The *état* for the department of Paris in the year II lists, inter alia, 12 Charenton water mills at 20.8 setiers, 21 St.-Denis area water mills at 16.4, 7 Paris boat mills at 25, and 71 windmills at 10. Total daily production amounted to 1,599 setiers, which the official in charge of the study characterized as considerably below Parisian needs. Yet the striking fact is that the 1,599 setiers a day covered over half of total consumption. I believe that the averages given are too high. While they are not wholly implausible in certain conditions, they do not allow for technical and meteorological interruptions, which were frequent.[40]

Table 16 presents average daily (twenty-four-hour) production in Paris setiers in various parts of the region in the year II. With a few exceptions, these water-mill figures are quite compatible with those from the department of Paris. I believe that they give an excessively optimistic picture of production capacity. The low figure for Mantes is probably due to the poor mechanical condition of many of the mills; perhaps the same is true for Lizy and Dourdan. The windmill figures are very plausible, especially those in the

TABLE 16

Average daily flour production in the Paris area, year II
(in setiers)

District or canton	Water		Wind	
	Number	Average	Number	Average
Franciade (St.-Denis)	30	16.13	9	5.96
Claye	12	17.3	3	7.2
Crécy	12	17.4	3	7.2
Dammartin	7	9.6	16	4.3
Lizy	23	6.4	—	—
Meaux	16	20.2	—	—
Lagny	18	10.7	—	—
Dourdan	52	7.1	4	4.9
Mantes	84	5.46	4	2.8

38. BN, Coll. Joly 1116, fols. 219–31.
39. Daure, "Mémoire," ca. 1771, AN, F[11] 264.
40. AN, F[20] 293. It is also questionable whether the "moulin à feu" at the Isle des Cygnes could have sustained an 80-setier-a-day yield.

TABLE 17

Average daily flour production in the Paris area, year X
(in setiers)

Place	Number water	Number wind	Combined average production
Corbeil	74	—	19.46
Melun	87	20	4.3
Coulommiers	109	7	7.1
Meaux	126	21	8.5
Próvins	67	26	5.83
Clermont	72	125	7.6
Beauvais	159	67	5.07

middle range, around 5 setiers. These windmills should have been able to average 5 setiers a day for much of the year. There is no way to evaluate the proportion of this production that Paris drained.[41]

The set of figures in Table 17, from the year X, do not seem to have been as carefully constructed and they do not distinguish water and wind.[42] Known for their technical advance and commercial energy, the Corbeil millers can reasonably be expected to lead the field.[43] Vis-à-vis the scores of Charenton, Meaux, St.-Denis, Crécy, and Claye, the Corbeil figure is not out of place, though I regard it, like the others, as somewhat inflated. It is hard to know what to make of the other averages. Melun had lost a step on Corbeil since the halcyon days of the early eighteenth century, but it is inconceivable that the disproportion should be so gaping. On the other hand, though I remain very skeptical of the data, a global water/wind average of 6 to 8 setiers seems very possible. If it were true, as the official who gathered the material insisted, that Corbeil produced 1,440 setiers every day and sent two-thirds of this to Paris, then Corbeil alone would have covered 30 percent of Parisian annual needs—an extravagant claim.

The 1809 census yielded several different estimates for the arrondissements of Sceaux and St.-Denis, none of which accords with the figures from the year II. In Table 18, both of the St.-Denis and two of the three Sceaux estimates indicate hypothetical parameters: the amount that the mills "can do" in twenty-four hours. Only the last entry for Sceaux (asterisked) claims to

41. AN, F[20] 293.
42. AN, F[20] 294.
43. On the Corbeil mills, see Archives municipales Corbeil, BB 10 (29 July 1769); Jacques-Amédée-J.-A. Le Paire, *Histoire de la ville de Corbeil* (Lagny, 1901–1902), 2:31 (on the Malisset-Darblay filiation); Léon Combes-Marnes, *Histoire de Corbeil à travers les siècles* (Corbeil, 1950), pp. 240–41; Kaplan, *Bread, Politics and Political Economy*, 1:375–90.

TABLE 18

Normative and actual(*) daily flour production in
St.-Denis and Sceaux, 1809 (in setiers)

	Water		Wind	
Arrondissement	Number	Average daily production	Number	Average daily production
St.-Denis	20	7.95	52	4.88
St.-Denis	21	11.2	52	4.5
Sceaux	24	13.67	46	8.75
Sceaux	24	8.5	48	5.07
Sceaux*	24*	4.5*	48*	2.06*

be actual production.[44] The first St.-Denis figure probably merits more
confidence than the second because the data for it were collected in setiers
rather than metric quintals, and I believe that most of the respondents still
thought in terms of setiers (just as contemporary Frenchmen still talk in
"bricks" of old francs), with which they remained more comfortable. In any
event, both the water figures are below the levels claimed for real production
in 1794 (16) and 1725 (20). The "can do" measure for St.-Denis in 1809 seems
to me the most realistic indicator of what its water mills could actually accomplish. The disparity between St.-Denis windmills in 1794 (5.96) and 1809 is not
huge. In good winds, the former figure is plausible, though it is curious that
the hypothetical estimate is so modest. The first of the two Sceaux hypothetical estimates is too high and should be discarded in favor of the second,
which is quite close to the St.-Denis projections. The "real" figures are star-
tlingly low, and may reflect "conjunctural" difficulties. Remember that
Sceaux embraced, inter alia, the Charenton water mills, which were said to
have produced 20 setiers a day in 1794 and 10 in 1725.

In Table 19 for five arrondissements in the Seine-et-Oise in 1809, production figures signify "can do in twenty-four hours" and water and wind machines are not distinguished. These data, which seem to have been carefully
gathered, argue in favor of a general downward revision of the production
estimates. Corbeil still leads, but at 8.84 rather than 19.46, as in the 1803
appreciation. But Pontoise, the other major pole of Parisian flour supply, is
surprisingly low at 5.4.[45] Mantes, already low in 1794, now stagnates at a level

44. AN, F[20] 296.
45. Ibid. In 1807 the subprefect at Pontoise reported that 150 mills worked in and around
the town and were capable of producing 1,000 to 1,200 sacks (weighing 162 kilograms) in
twenty-four hours. To ministry of the interior, 21 October 1807, Archives municipales Pontoise, F 52. On Pontoise area mills, see also Anatole Devarenne, *Les Moulins de la Vallée de
l'Esches* (Méru, 1943).

that must barely represent the commercial break-even point (and that must represent a form of self-exploitation for the miller family). In terms of a general order of magnitude, I am inclined to invest more confidence in these figures than in any of the preceding ones. On the other hand, I would not be prepared to deflate these hypothetical figures in order to arrive at a measure of "real" production. I do not believe that the real average daily production fell below 5 setiers in the Seine-et-Oise (or below 8 to 9 at Corbeil).

Table 20 shows aggregate departmental production figures ("can do") for 1810.[46] The Seine-et-Oise average is almost a half-setier below the 1809 figure, for reasons that remain obscure. Even with the dragging weight of Mantes, I would have wagered on the Seine-et-Oise for the highest departmental production capacity. The Seine figures are intriguing. On the one hand, the most perfected machines were known to be located in the immediate vicinity of Paris. On the other hand, even allowing for a very high level of water production, one would have imagined that the large number of windmills would have brought down the average. Perhaps there is a greater disparity between "can do" and actual production for wind than for water machines, and as a consequence the wind estimates here are less reliable indicators than the water figures.

Finally, we have data for four arrondissements in the Seine-et-Marne in 1811 (see Table 21).[47] The Provins figure is too high; it so happens that the Provins data are also the least dependable of this group. The Coulommiers and Meaux surveys are the soundest. At least a fifth of all these millers specialized in production for the Paris market. As many as 40 percent of the mills in the four arrondissements were fitted for economic milling.

What was the impact of economic technology on mill production here and in other places in the Paris region? In theory the economic process should

TABLE 19

Normative daily flour production in the Seine-et-Oise, 1809 (in setiers)

Arrondissement	Number of mills	Average daily production
Mantes	134	2.6
Pontoise	165	5.4
Versailles	182	3.3
Corbeil	109	8.8
Etampes	176	7.1
TOTALS	766	5.3

46. AN, F²⁰ 560.
47. AD Seine-et-Marne, 12 M 59.

TABLE 20

Normative daily flour production in four departments in
the Paris region, 1810 (in setiers)

Department	Number of mills		Average daily combined production
	Water	Wind	
Seine	45	101	6.2
Seine-et-Marne	467	81	5.36
Seine-et-Oise	704	62	4.87
Oise	560	422	4.99

TABLE 21

Average daily flour production in the Seine-et-Marne,
1811 (in setiers)

Arrondissement	Number of mills	Average daily production
Provins	83	9.6
Fontainebleau	89	4.65
Coulommiers	118	6.8
Meaux	156	5.5

have decreased the production capacity because it took longer. Yet it must be
remembered that gross meal production in the Paris orbit was less significant
than white flour production. Economic milling was slower, but it produced
considerably more white flour per setier. Moreover, one must be careful to
scrutinize the standard of comparison against which economic productivity is
measured. Coarse-process mills should have been able to grind faster, but
they were often old, more or less decrepit, and mechanically flawed. Economic mills were virtually all substantially renovated or new, equipped with
the most efficient power drives, the best stones, and so forth. Even with their
greater number of tasks, some of them extremely delicate, it is conceivable
that economic mills produced more than many ordinary mills. On the other
hand, it is true that the economic campaign spurred many traditional millers
to perfect their machines, which should have enabled them to turn out more
meal.

The 1811 census contains the only differential production data we have,
but they are far from conclusive. In the Fontainebleau area, where fewer than
a fifth of the mills were economic, the economic mills (water) were twice as
productive as the coarse mills (water). At Meaux, where about two-thirds of

the mills were economic, coarse water production (6.4) was higher than economic water production (5.1), but economic wind production (4) was higher than coarse wind production (1.53). The Meaux data are internally more compelling, and the results theoretically make more sense. If the Meaux data were representative of the economic process, then it might appear on the surface that Paris would have needed to draw upon a larger number of mills after the introduction of the new technology than before. It is likely, however, that the economic mills still produced proportionately more white flour than the ordinary mills, even those that were improved.

What is to be said, then, about mill production in the eighteenth century? Most of the old-regime figures are inflated. The experts naturally gravitated toward the most exciting and least typical operations. Their demarche is useful to the extent that it reminds us of the great range of possible production. But if the outliers were authentic, they were few. The massive mills did not average a setier an hour (and there is no way to tell how many hours per day they ground). The late Napoleonic data—remarkably convergent—are chastening, even if we cannot always guarantee their rigor. Though they are "can do" estimates, they are probably a bit low, perhaps because of confusion over weights and measures, perhaps because some production data were expressed in terms of flour rather than wheat, perhaps because of errors, conscious or involuntary, made by millers and/or officials. In any event, even with the development of economic milling, there is no reason to suppose that productivity was greater in 1725 or 1750 than in 1800 or 1810. Béguillet's low estimate—8 to 10 setiers—constitutes at best the upper ceiling for mean old-regime production. Water mills probably produced on the average 60 to 70 percent more than windmills, though the business of accounting for stoppages is frightfully complex.[48] St.-Denis, Pontoise, Corbeil, Senlis, and a number of other places undoubtedly surpassed the mean rate by a bound. Certain economic mills kept pace with average production or bettered it; others, especially when compared to improved coarse machines, did not. Though it is a parlous enterprise, I would be tempted to fix average daily water production at about 6 setiers and average wind production at about 4 setiers for much of the eighteenth century. Between 500 and 700 mills could theoretically have satisfied Paris needs, if they were capable of milling twenty-four hours a day, three hundred and sixty-five days a year, if they ground more or less exclu-

48. On the limits of windmill productivity, see "état des moulins de l'Oise," December 1808, AN, F[20] 296, and Baudeau, *Avis aux honnêtes gens*, p. 94. Cf. Roy's inflated estimates for windmill production: "Moulins à vent," p. 104. Similarly, Delivre and Plancke, *Les Moulins à vent de la Brie*, p. 18. On the folkloric claims of the superiority of wind productivity over water (in this case by 3 or 4 to 1), see Heywood, *The Play of the Weather*, p. 28.

In the Charente-Inférieure, certain millers possessed wind and water mills but used the former only when the water wheels could not turn. Prefect to minister of the interior, August 1809, AN, F[20] 295. Cf. Claude Dupin, *Forces productrices et commerciales de la France* (Paris, 1827), and *Le Magasin pittoresque*, 43d year (1875): 111.

sively *à blanc,* and if they channeled their entire production to the capital. Since these quasi-industrial conditions obtained in very few cases, it is prudent to imagine the Paris milling pool as two or three times as large. The core producers were relatively few in number, but they probably did not cover much more than 60 percent of the capital's needs. Eighteenth-century Paris remained dependent on a mass of artisans—blatier-type millers and mealmen—to make up the rest. They constituted the part of the pool that expanded and contracted, largely in response to market factors and to changing baker buying practices. The elasticity of this secondary pool gave the city a critical safety margin in times of flour crisis.[49]

Limiting Conditions

Mill productivity depended, as I have indicated, in the first instance on the construction and mechanics of the mill and its power source. Production was hampered by lethargic currents or meager falls, or by mills that enjoyed sufficient drive but were unable to transmit the power to the stones efficiently. Experts and practitioners argued over the best shape and placement of the wings on a windmill, whether overshot waterwheels were superior to breast or undershot wheels, and whether the wheels ought to be endowed with buckets or paddles.[50] Well-mounted and strongly powered mills could risk no more than fifty to sixty rotations a minute for fear of decomposing the wheat berry and overheating the flour.[51] Productivity further depended on the type of technology employed, stone quality and balance, the resistance and friction of moving parts, and the hardness of the grain.[52]

Regardless of power source, construction, and technology, all mills were subject to other variables that sapped their productive capacity. The most important and insolent cause of interruption was the weather. Rare was the mill that, because of its design and location, could boast that it was "sheltered from all the events caused by inclement weather."[53] The windmillers at Argenteuil, Herblay, Sartrouville, Gentilly, Ivry, Montreuil, and Vaugirard complained frequently of "the calm" that ground their machines to a halt.[54] A

49. In 1859 an official at the Halle reported that five hundred millers or their agents regularly came to the Paris market. *Enquête sur la boulangerie,* p. 489.

50. Regarding waterwheels, see the contemporary debate reported by Béguillet, *Traité des subsistances,* pp. 204–7. Cf. Cardwell, *From Watt to Clausius,* pp. 68–69.

51. Béguillet, *Discours sur la mouture* (1775), p. 77; Malouin, *Description et détails des arts,* p. 63. Millers who worked on simple toll had certain incentives to grind as quickly as possible since they were paid the same amount for bad as for good grinding. That was why the mill reformers promoted the development of the flour trade, which frankly made the miller into a merchant and gave him an abiding interest in producing quality merchandise.

52. On these matters, see Bucquet, *Manuel du meunier,* p. 55.

53. See the mills at Montargis, Nantouillet, St.-Amesmes, and Thieux. AN, F^{20} 293.

54. Ibid.

windmill at Aubervilliers had only three months of wind a year, another at La Chapelle six months, and a third at Fresnes eight months. The three windmills in the canton of Rosny near Mantes had adequate wind for only four months' production a year.[55] Icing of wings also cost windmills production losses.[56] Water millers faced multiple threats: drought or low water, floods or high water, and ice all halted production. In the cantons of Claye, Crécy, Dammartin, Lizy, Lagny, and Meaux, 15 of 114 mills were frequently halted by high water, some for as much as three months a year; 14 were regularly stopped by low water; 7 located on tributaries were paralyzed by ice, while virtually all mills on the Marne were subject to freezing. One mill near La Ferté-sous-Jouarre worked well only three months a year, another near Lagny four months, and a third at Meaux six months.[57]

In the district of St.-Denis, in the immediate vicinity of Paris, a mill at St.-Maur functioned only nine months due to ice and low water. Five other mills in the St.-Denis area were subject to catastrophic floods, while 38 percent of the water mills in the subprefecture of Sceaux were stopped by ice.[58] The water mill at Léry in the district of Dourdan produced twice as much in winter as in summer, when low waters hindered operation. At Romville in the same district drought and ice interrupted work for four months. Of the 74 water mills in the district of Dourdan, 15 were frequently subjected to winter freeze and summer drought, 4 to low water, 6 to both low and high water, 3 to ice and high and low water, 1 to floods and ice, and 1 to floods.[59] Of the 74 water mills in the district of Mantes, 19 were habitually hampered by low water, 19 others by ice, and 4 by floods.[60] François Hyaut, a miller near Corbeil, blamed his business failure partly on severe floodings that repeatedly interrupted his work. Another miller estimated his losses directly attributable to low water in 1785 at 1,500 livres.[61] Near Meulan a drought in 1789 reduced mill productivity by half.[62]

The weather indirectly affected production by rendering transport difficult in many places. Only a minority of mills were located on paved roads. Rain,

---

55. Ibid.

56. Cf. the twentieth-century windmiller Barbier, whose wings were no longer made of sailcloth. As a rule, Barbier found the wind much more congenial in the winter than the summer, though he recalled one February when his mill was immobilized for nine days. *Marcel Barbier: Meunier,* pp. 208, 210–11.

57. Malouin wrote that the best grinding season stretched from November to April: *Description et détails des arts,* p. 17. Yet for at least one miller who left a business register, these were his slowest months. Archives Seine-Paris, D5B⁶ 4243.

58. AN, F²⁰ 296. Cf. the destruction of the Dorlcote mill by floodwaters in Eliot, *Mill on the Floss,* p. 455.

59. AN, F²⁰ 293.

60. AN, F²⁰ 296. Cf. the flooding that imperiled the Frau mill. Le Roy, *Moulin du Frau,* p. 75.

61. Archives Seine-Paris, D4B⁶ 53-3245, 3 August 1774, and D4B⁶ 98-6904, 16 May 1781.

62. BN, Coll. Vexin, vol. 69, fol. 61.

TABLE 22
Frequency of mill stoppages for dressing at Gonesse, 1746

Month	Moulin de la Ville	Moulin de la Planche	Moulin du Marais
January	8, 15, 22, 27	7, 19, 29	8, 18, 25, 31
February	5, 12, 19, 26	4, 12, 21	16, [?]
March	5, 13, 21, 28	3, 17, 26	9, 16, 21, 29
April	5, 13, 20, 27	4, 20, 29	6, 13, 26
May	4, 11, 18, [?]	14, 25	2, 9, 16, 23, 31
June	2, 8, 15, 23, 30	13, 22	14, 21
July	7, 14, 27	2, 16, 25	13, 20, 27
August	3, 10, 17, 24, 31	8, 20, 29	9, 18, 29
September	7, 14, 21, 28	23, [?]	14, 20, 28
October	12, 19, 26	1, 10, 17, 27	6, 12
November	2, 9, 18, 23, 30	5, 12, 21, 30	2, 8, 15, 22, 28
December	7, 14, 21, 28	7, 14, 23, 31	5, 13, 20, 27

mud, and snow periodically isolated a windmill at Arcueil, another near St.-Denis, one in a valley near Dourdan, one at Le Pecq, and several in the district of Mantes.[63] Water mills were also halted by sandy build-up around the wheels and the need to drain the millrace or part of the water access.[64] Lack of work—*faute de bled*—occasionally stopped 47 of 73 mills in the Sceaux jurisdiction.[65]

Still other stoppages, independent of the weather but no less inexorable, were preconditions for continued production of good quality merchandise. These were periodic halts for dressing the stones, the miller's most vital task of periodic maintenance. There was no more a standard rhythm of dressing than there was a standard procedure. Oliver Evans advocated two light dressings a week.[66] Béguillet warned, however, that two or more dressings a week resulted in a sandy flour that could cause serious diseases.[67] A Swiss specialist reported that in Saxony a stone was dressed every twenty-four hours if one ground without interruption. The engineer Belidor claimed that a monthly dressing was the rule.[68] Malouin preferred a six-week cadence, but took note of millers who waited six months before renewing the stone surface. I have found not a single case in which a miller kept a spare pair of stones to enable him to avoid shutting down for dressing.[69]

63. AN, F[20] 293.
64. See the "état" for Dourdan, in ibid.
65. AN, F[20] 296.
66. Evans, *Young Millwright*, pp. 254–56.
67. Béguillet, *Traité des subsistances*, pp. 303–4.
68. Belidor, *Architecture hydraulique*, 1:281.
69. Malouin, *Description des arts* (1771), pp. 69–70.

Table 22 sets out the rhythm for dressing halts during 1746 in the water mills of Gonesse owned by the Hôtel-Dieu of Paris. Though it sometimes took two or three days to dress a pair of stones well, here it generally required no more than three or four hours, usually in the early morning. Sometimes the miller profited from the obligatory halt for dressing by calling upon the charpentier to make needed minor repairs. Often the repairs were completed before the dressing; on other occasions, they prolonged the stoppage by as much as half a day.

For the Moulins de la Ville and du Marais, dressings occurred about once a week; for la Planche, there was less regularity: nine or ten day intervals were not uncommon. On the average, the Moulin de la Ville stopped for nineteen hours a month as a result of dressing (the major component), repairs, and high water (only three episodes, one in February from 10:00 A.M to 7:00 P.M., during which time the charpentier was called in, and two in March, from 2:00 P.M. to 6:00 A.M. on the third and from 1:00 A.M. to 10:00 A.M. on the twenty-first). Production at this mill was more often fettered by lack of grain—as many as thirty hours a month. The mill stopped from midnight to noon on Easter and from noon to midnight on Pentecost, but deferred to no other calendar event. The Moulin de la Planche averaged twenty-one hours of stoppage a month, for dressing, repairs, and inclement weather. High water interrupted its production once in each of the months of January, February, and March. This mill stopped all day on Easter and Pentecost as well as twelve hours on Christmas. It averaged over three days a month in nonwork for lack of grain. Dressing, repair, and high water halted the Moulin du Marais an average of seventeen hours a month, following approximately the same pattern as the Moulin de la Ville. Its mean stoppage for lack of grain—over four days a month—resembled more closely the operations of the Moulin de la Planche.

The revolutionary survey presents considerable variation in dressing cadence. In the district of Mantes, 13 mills were dressed weekly, 5 every ten days, 28 every two weeks, 9 every three weeks, 10 every four weeks, 2 every thirty-five days, and 1 every forty days.[70] In the St.-Denis area, the windmills required only a monthly dressing, whereas windmills at Chavenay and Montigny needed weekly treatments.[71] A water mill at Tessancourt interrupted production only twenty days a year for dressing and minor repairs, whereas the four water mills at Charenton shut down four or five days a month for the same purpose.[72] As a result of stoppage imposed by weather, dressing, and repairs, and presuming that there was always work to be done, I do not

---

70. AN, F[20] 293, year II.
71. Ibid. and F[20] 296.
72. AN, F[20] 293.

believe that the average good water mill could produce more than nine and a half months a year and a good windmill more than eight and a half months a year.[73] This is another reason Paris needed a large reserve pool of flour makers.

73. I insist on ordinary repairs, for a major disaster could change the pattern drastically. One miller was out of business for several months because of a broken drive shaft, for example. Archives Seine-Paris, D4B[6] 98-6904, 16 May 1787.

CHAPTER 9

Miller Family, Marriage, and Fortune

𝒯he miller's family was in many ways his richest and most useful capital. Frequently his professional apprenticeship took place within the family, or the family placed him with friends who trained him. The family helped to find the miller a bride and to build his own household branch of the clan. The construction of the new conjugal family often went hand in hand with the miller's establishment as an independent operator. The family was a production force, a commercial firm, and a savings and investment institution as well as a consumption unit, a children's nursery, and a tissue of affective relations.

Marriage and Business: Endogamy

While affective relations were surely significant, more often than not marriage was above all an *affaire*—a business arrangement that had to be carefully prepared before it was formalized by contract. Often it was less an understanding between individuals than a settlement between families. Marriage held the promise of the conquest of money, prestige, and useful contacts. It was a way of setting oneself up, of introducing oneself, of redeeming oneself, of avenging oneself. Sometimes marriage was the most critical single deal of the professional life of the miller.

The few marriage contracts that I have unearthed furnish precious indications on the character of miller marriage. In the strictest sense of the term, it was less endogamous than one might imagine. None of the six flour merchants

321

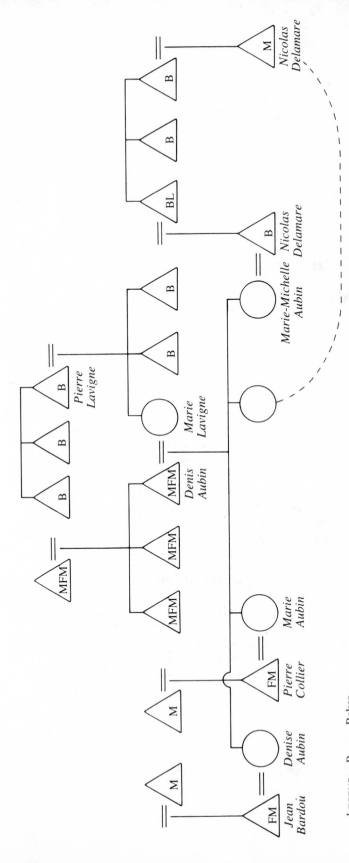

LEGEND: B   Baker
         BL   Baker Laboureur
         M   Miller
         FM   Flour Merchant
         MFM Miller-Flour Merchant

NOTE: The chart reflects only those relationships specifically indicated in the archival documentation. It is very likely that the family was even more extensively involved in the provisioning nexus.

FIGURE 1 The family connection in the grain, flour, and bread business

operating mills, two of whom were sons of flour merchants, married the daughter of a flour merchant or miller. Of twelve millers, ten of whom were sons of millers, only four married daughters of millers or flour merchants. Of four journeymen millers, one of whom was the son of a miller and another the son of a journeyman miller, two took daughters of millers as brides. Yet in order to grasp matrimonial strategy clearly one must situate marriage not in a narrowly and abstractly professional framework but in the practical and commercial context of everyday life, that is to say, in the subsistence or provisioning "complex." Endogamy is fortified from this vantage point, for three of our flour merchants and four of our millers married daughters of bakers.

Drawing on evidence beyond the miller marriage sample, I have found sixteen other cases in which miller sons formed unions with baker daughters.[1] Twelve were the daughters of Paris master bakers, two of faubourg St.-Antoine bakers, and two of forains. The widow of a forain married a Paris mealman. Marie, the daughter of master baker Pierre Lavigne (and sister of two bakers and niece of two others) married miller-mealman Denis Aubin, son of a miller-mealman. One of their daughters, Marie-Michelle, married baker Nicolas Delamare, son of a laboureur-baker at Dugny, a crucial forain-cum-producer connection. Delamare's first cousin, also a Nicolas, was a miller at Gonesse and married the sister of Marie-Michelle Aubin. Two of baker Nicolas's uncles were bakers in the Gonesse area and two of his wife's uncles were miller-mealmen in the same vicinity. Two other daughters of Denis Aubin and Marie Lavigne wed respectively Jean Bardou and Pierre Collier, both of whom were flour merchants and sons of millers (see Figure 1). Master baker Jean Richer married one of his daughters to a Belleville miller and another to a St.-Denis miller, both of whom were from miller families. The Bruslé sisters, daughters and stepdaughters of master bakers, married the Bleziman brothers, miller-merchants and sons of a miller-merchant. Many of the other unions had similarly interconnecting bonds.

I have found ten instances in which millers married their daughters to bakers, seven of whom were Paris masters and three forains. Both daughters of Montmartre miller Pierre Masson married masters. The daughter of mealman Eustache Taboureau married masters twice. Marie Pariset, daughter of a miller, married master baker Jean Piochard, whose mother, a Fleury, was a member of a veritable miller-baker dynasty. Nicolas Gaudet, a miller-flour merchant, whose son was a miller at Beaumont, married one of his daughters to a Gonesse baker and another to a miller-mealman like himself.[2]

---

1. For the sources for the miller marriage sample, see Appendix E. The documentation for the baker-miller marriage connection is listed in Appendix F. Cf. miller Bob Loveday's courtship of a young master baker's daughter in Hardy, *Trumpet Major*, p. 319.

2. On the allure of miller daughters, see the miller in Hans Christian Andersen's "The Ice Maiden," who boasts that his daughter "sits on a heap of grit—gold grit, as you know." *Stories and Fairy Tales*, trans. H. Oskar Sommer (London, 1907), p. 689. Whereas this miller

There were other types of relationships. The brother of master baker Michel Fleury, himself a mill owner, was a miller at Creteil. Master baker François Bonnion's brother Nicolas was a miller at the faubourg de Gloire. The Destors brothers, Nicolas and Antoine of Gonesse, were a baker and a miller respectively. Robert Parquier, a miller near Chartres, supplied flour to his brother, a Paris baker.[3] Noël Duval, the son of a master baker, became a mealman. Jacques Destors of Gonesse, the son of baker Antoine, was a miller-mealman. Jeanne Lesueur, twice the wife of master bakers, was the niece of miller Michel Gosset, who was married to a scion of the Fleurys. Baker Michel Bellot was the nephew of miller Jacques Derancy. Member of a powerful Gonesse baking clan, Pierre Bethmont was the cousin of Jean Robert, whose family furnished the Rambouillet flour market on the other side of the capital. Miller François Gambau was the godfather of Marie-Anne Valtier, daughter and wife of St.-Antoine bakers.[4]

Baker-miller professional interpenetration was the product, and often the strategic aim, of these family alliances. Marriage entailed an intricate pattern of material and moral exchange. Mills passed in dowries from miller and mealmen families to baker families, and more rarely millers received bakeshops from their brides. Even where the union was not consecrated by the transmission of professional goods, the constitution of kinship networks profoundly conditioned the conduct of subsistence business. A marriage allied not merely the bride and groom, but a much larger universe of relations and friends who were bound by ties of patronage, reciprocity, and interest as well as kinship. When a baker married a miller's daughter, more often than not he also "married" the bride's brothers and uncles, who were also millers or flour merchants or perhaps laboureurs or carters or even bakers. Commercial links sometimes led to marriage, but business almost always followed family. Clients, delivery priorities, quality merchandise, credit facilities, and collection forebearance as a rule came in the wake of marriage(s). Crucial market information was communicated on the family wire. Forward and backward linkages and collective resources often gave these millers and bakers a competitive advantage.

Though value in exchange is theoretically independent of the identity of the parties, in reality market transactions are neither perfectly replicable nor

---

warns his daughter's suitor that she is "too far above you," a farmer in an English tale rejects a miller's daughter as too "low born." Bottrell, *Traditions and Hearthside Stories,* p. 190. Cf. Tennyson's "The Miller's Daughter" in Donald J. Gray and G. B. Tennyson, eds., *Victorian Literature: Poetry* (New York, 1976), p. 72.

3. AN, MC, LXXXI-294, 23 June 1742, and LXXXIX-469, 17 July 1740; AN, Y 14535, 28 January 1739, and Y 9539, 16, 21 May 1762; Archives Seine-Paris, DC[6] 150, fol. 55.

4. AN, Y 11219, 23 October 1732; AN, MC, XXVIII-248, 3 July 1737; VII-293, 12 September 1754; LXXXV-528, 18 May 1751; LXXXIX-422, 9 May 1734; XXVII-174, 7 October 1720.

perfectly transferable. Identity matters.[5] Parties can reduce transaction costs significantly when their contract or exchange is embedded in a connection based on identity. Members of a kinship network who deal with one another perceive certain traits in their opposite numbers (e.g., honesty, dependability, astuteness) that reassure them. The cost of arriving at this view of each other is an investment that will facilitate future exchanges. Parties to transactions may devise rules for their exchange relationship and procedures for dispute resolution that can serve them beyond a single transaction. The cost of negotiating these rules will have to be incurred again if the parties change, an unlikely contingency within a family connection. The absence of the sort of trust engendered and symbolized by a family tie can be costly, for it would require the elaboration of exogenous sanctions and guarantees. The identity and community of the parties can reduce uncertainty about the quality of the object of exchange or about the terms of the transaction that arise from imperfect information. The expectation of continued contact will have a favorable influence on the behavior of the parties, discouraging them from cheating to obtain short-run advantage at the expense of ongoing future gains. Investing in and exploiting "specialization by identity," the provisioning-trade family would serve not only as a universe within which orderly, profitable, and predictable exchanges occur, but also as a firm possessed of a collective identity that strengthens it to compete with and do business with outsiders.

Flour Family Dynasties

Apart from the bakery connection, there were still numerous flour family dynasties, the fruit of a certain kind of professional family planning as well as of astute marriages. The four Delaforge brothers, sons of a miller, were all millers, and two of them married millers' daughters.[6] Similarly the four Delamotte brothers, sons and grandsons of millers, were all millers. At least one of them was married to a miller's daughter and at least one of their sisters married a miller.[7] Three of miller Cochois's sons were millers, and two of his daughters were wives of millers.[8] Miller Guillaume Delespine's son and his three stepsons, themselves sons of a miller, were all millers.[9] Jean-Baptiste

---

5. This paragraph is derived from Yoram Ben-Porath, "The F-Connection: Families, Friends, and Firms and the Organization of Exchange," *Population and Development Review* 6 (March 1980): 1–30.

6. AN, MC, LXIX-318, 30 April 1734. On the anxiety of the miller to see his son "follow on at the mill," see Hardy, *Trumpet Major,* p. 14.

7. AN, MC, CV-1238, 28 November 1751.

8. AN, MC, LXV-196, 22 June 1718.

9. AN, MC, LXIX-316, 20 October 1733.

Ducellier was a miller, son of a miller, nephew of a miller, and brother-in-law of two millers. His neighbor and fellow miller, Pierre Bruxelle, was the son and brother of millers and nephew of two millers on his mother's side.[10] At least one of miller Nicolas Lacour's sons was a miller and he married two of his daughters to millers, while miller Sebastien Fourcret was the father of at least one miller and the father-in-law of another.[11]

Miller Jean Clerambault married the daughter of a miller (whose sons, Germain and Jean Fleury, were both millers). Their son Jean became a meal-man and married the daughter of miller Nicolas Noret.[12] Miller Nicolas Gaudet's son, who was a miller, married the daughter of a miller (his daughter also married a miller).[13] Miller Nicolas Ferry was the son and grandson (on both sides) of millers.[14] Among the other dynasties spread across time (at least three generations) and across familial space (more than one member of each generation in the flour business) were the Pigeau of Senlis, famous for their innovative techniques; the Marquis family of Chambly; the Debray and the Menessier of Montmartre; the Giboreau; the Desrue; the Namouy.[15]

Marriage within the subsistence complex was attractive to the young miller (or flour merchant) not only for the familial connections and material benefits, but also for the "professional" experience of his bride. Women raised in mills or bakeries knew the rudiments of the business. They could not only distinguish wheat from rye, but also *revêche* Brie middling meal from the soft firsts of the *pays* Chartrain. Miller daughters knew the daily rhythms; they spoke the language; they were familiar with the inns where their husbands might take refuge or transact deals; they had the right instincts for dealing with competitors, clients, and the police. Their miller-husbands could have confidence in them to represent them at court, to collect money from bakers, to remonstrate with a broker, and even to buy grain or supervise the grinding process.[16] For the sake of their personal relations, it was also helpful for the bride to know that her husband would often not be at her side at night and that he would not be able to leave the mill for long periods.

Marriage Capital

The miller grooms were not rich. The mean male marriage contribution for the entire group amounted to only 2,329 livres (median = 2,063), less than the

10. AD Seine-et-Marne, B 411, pièces 75–77, 17 December 1750, and B 69, pièce 59, 30 April 1725.

11. AN, MC, VII-369, 8 February 1767; AN, Y 12589, 8 June 1745.

12. AN, MC, LXXXIX-469, 3 August 1740.

13. AN, Y 13085, 17 April 1736.

14. AN, Y 12595, 6 October 1751.

15. Archives Seine-Paris, D4B⁶ 52-3199, August 1744 (Aubert failure); D4B⁶ 17-831, 18 October 1757 (Rivière failure); D5B⁶ 5234; Maillard, *Moulins de Montmartre*, pp. 195–97.

16. See, for example, the authority that Daubigny, a Beaumont miller-merchant, delegated to his wife. AN, Y 11045, 9 March 1730.

average level of the bakers of Paris (2,609 livres; median = 1,900). The son of a journeyman made the lowest contribution, 300 livres, while the highest, 6,000 livres, all of it in cash, came from the son of a miller.[17] The mean size of the dowries millers received (1,199 livres) was substantially lower than baker dowries (2,182 livres), though the respective medians converge (1,542 and 1,500 livres).[18] The daughter of a journeyman *charron* accounted for the lowest dowry, 300 livres. The highest bridal portion, 6,590 livres, belonged to the daughter of a master baker who was also the niece of two master bakers and of a miller. The millers are located among the least favored in the category of masters and merchants established by Adeline Daumard and François Furet. Indeed, they are quite near the level of wage earners in commerce and industry.[19]

It is normal for journeymen millers to have had the smallest fortune (husband's dowry of 800 livres, wife's of 900). It is more surprising to note that the average marriage contributions of flour merchant-millers represented only 1,700 livres (median the same), while their wives invested 2,131 livres in the marriage (median = 2,288). Millers boasted a solid contribution of 3,467 livres (median = 3,450), which was greater than the resources of the Paris master bakers (3,169 and 2,413 livres). Curiously, however, they attracted relatively mediocre dowries of 2,218 livres (median = 1,557)—well below the sums registered by the master bakers (2,903 and 1,983 livres). For the group as a whole, the statistical association between the dowries of brides and grooms was quite weak.[20]

Bridal dowries were composed of almost equal portions of cash (52 percent) and of trousseaux (48 percent).[21] All the grooms had some sort of

---

17. Etienne Palleau, a miller-widower, whose first wife was herself the widow of a miller, brought to his second marriage the enormous sum of 24,203 livres. His second wife's dowry amounted to nearly 1,600 livres. I uncovered this contract too late to include it in my calculations. AN, MC, CII-367, 23 September 1751.

18. On the bakers, see Kaplan, *Bakers of Paris*.

19. Adeline Daumard and François Furet, *Structures et relations sociales à Paris au milieu du 18ᵉ siècle* (Paris, 1961), pp. 23–32.

20. The r = 0.23 at 0.308. But the female contribution predicts average *douaire*, which amounted to 853 livres (r = 0.81 at 0.001) and average *préciput* which was 374 livres (r = 0.84 at 0.001).

21. According to folklore, miller brides brought an unquantifiable bonus to their dowries: striking physical beauty. Given the mill's reputation as a place of intense sensuality, it is not surprising that miller wives are portrayed in fiction as especially inviting. For Daudet, they were "as handsome as queens": "Gaffer Corneille's Secret," in *Letters from My Mill*, trans. John MacGregor (New York, 1966), p. 19. Pedro A. de Alarcon's Frasquita had a "luscious," Rubensian body. *The Three-Cornered Hat*, pp. 8, 32–33. The face of the miller's wife in Turgenev's "Ermolai and the Miller's Wife" still "bore traces of a remarkable beauty": *Hunting Sketches*, p. 27. The daughters of millers took after their mothers: "The Miller of Abingdon," in Briggs, *Dictionary of British Folktales*, part A, 2:442; Andersen, *Stories and Folk-Tales*, p. 694. Yet cf. Suzanne, the miller's widow, whose eyes were very black and whose "strange movements with her hands . . . reminded one of a bat": "The Miller's Man Who Became an Ass," in Henderson and Calvert, *Wonder Tales*, p. 206.

commercial element in their contributions (it was in their interest to count as dowry tools, merchandise, and all other forms of working capital), comprising on the average 15 percent of the total. Their clothing and furnishings were less important than those of their brides (29 percent), but they furnished a larger proportion of cash (57 percent). The miller-flour merchants accounted for the largest "domestic" rubric (33 percent), while the millers were the most liquid (65 percent). There was little difference in the composition of the dowries received by the miller-flour merchants and the millers.

The most lucrative union, with a combined mean matrimonial fortune of 6,999 livres, united a miller, who was the son of a miller, to the daughter of a baker. The second and third best marriages, far less opulent than the first, joined first a miller-flour merchant, the son of a flour merchant, to a baker's daughter, and second a miller-flour merchant, the son of an artisan, to another baker's daughter. The bakery constituted such an attractive reservoir of brides in part because the average dowry of a baker's daughter—2,193 livres—was a third greater than that of a miller's daughter and more than twice that of the daughter of a worker. Moreover, whereas the baker daughter's dowry was extraordinarily supple, consisting mostly of cash (80 percent) that could be applied as needed to domestic or commercial ends, the dowry of the miller daughters was dominated (60 percent) by their trousseaux, a reflection perhaps of urban-rural cultural as well as socioeconomic differences. If the groom's contribution had been all that mattered, a woman seeking a husband would have preferred the miller's son (3,604 livres) to the son of a miller-flour merchant (1,850 livres), though the latter supplied slightly more cash.

It would be wrong, however, to rely exclusively on the magnitude of marriage fortune as an indicator of likely success. Though in theory each side had an interest in making manifest and having evaluated its contribution, there were nevertheless hidden elements not subject to evaluation that shaped the future of the new household. One was patronage, which was not rigorously collated with wealth. Protection and support and access to various sorts of commercial *chasses gardées* could prove to be more valuable in launching a business than fancy trousseaux, real estate, or even cash. The connections of miller Jean-Baptiste Laforge's wife, a daughter and sister of master bakers, gave him the inside chance to lease a windmill owned by another master baker.[22] Certain contracts pledged specific business concessions to the couple that were not comprised in the dowries. For example, miller Jean-Jacques Devaux's future mother-in-law promised to allow him and his wife the use of half her windmill and her house.[23] Miller Jean Bleziman's mother-in-law, twice widowed by master bakers, offered the newlyweds a 50 percent silent interest in her bakery, lucrative in itself and also an

22. AN, MC, VII-287, 14 June 1753.
23. AN, MC, VII-307, 28 April 1757 (contract of 15 June 1723).

opportunity to expand his baker clientele.[24] Other millers were able to count on the use of wagons and horses, assistance in mill repairs and maintenance, the use of other mills when their machines were stopped, and the like.

Residence, Education, Age

Three-quarters of the grooms were established in Paris and the nearby suburbs, and most of them recruited their wives in the vicinity of their homes. Two of the millers inhabited the hinterland but married Parisians. The reason was not narrowly material, for the dowry of the country brides was substantially higher than that of the Parisians (2,075 versus 1,168 livres). The urban bridal dowry, however, brought more cash than the rural. In comparison with urban male contributions, the rural contributions were derisory.

The combined fortunes of the thirteen brides and grooms who could sign their names are much higher than the others. The only bride who was illiterate brought a dowry of only 600 livres, all of it in trousseau. Still, the only miller of all categories who could not sign attracted a bridal portion of 2,228 livres, well above the average.[25]

Relative well-being implied a certain rudimentary level of education, but the relationship between wealth and age was less clear. Seventy percent of the grooms had already reached their legal majority, while 80 percent of the brides were minors. Minor grooms contributed substantially more than the "adult" grooms (2,800 against 1,967 livres). But the "adults," projecting a more solid and reassuring image, commanded far larger bridal portions (2,303 versus 1,438 livres). The older brides, despite the overwhelming superiority of their dowries (2,667 versus 1,816 livres), did not lure the best male contributions (1,250 versus 2,670 livres!).

The wealthiest marriage, marked by a fortune of almost 10,000 livres, paired an "adult" groom and a minor bride. In general, marriages between minors were worth more than "older" ones (4,518 versus 2,750 livres). In choosing youth, the grooms opted, inter alia, in favor of liquidity. Cash represented 60 percent of the bridal portions of the minors, as opposed to 20 percent of those of the older women. As might be expected, the older men, who had been in business for a longer while, had a larger proportion of commercial items in their contributions than their minor confreres (38 percent versus 10 percent).

24. AN, MC, VII-297, 31 July 1755.
25. I am struck—but it remains no more than a strong impression—by a very high incidence of inability to sign among millers, far higher than among bakers. See, for example, AN, Y 12141, 30 June and 3 July 1739, and Y 11379, 20 February 1770. Harvey J. Graff cautions that signatures probably underestimate the level of reading literacy. *The Literacy Myth: Literacy and Social Structure in the Nineteenth-Century City* (New York, 1979). See also Turgenev's miller's wife, who "knows how to read and write, in their business, now, that comes in handy": "Ermolai and the Miller's Wife," in *Hunting Sketches*, p. 32.

Widows

Three of the grooms and four of the brides had been married once before. The marriage contributions of the widowers are unknown, but they received larger dowries than millers taking vows for the first time (2,367 versus 1,878 livres). The widows, including one whose first husband had been a miller and another who had been married to a baker, were richer than the virgin brides (3,250 versus 1,790 livres)—a sort of *prime de rachat.* (Unfortunately we do not know the number and ages of the children that these widows brought to their new households.) Their relative affluence did not privilege the widows in the contest for husbands—they drew considerably lower marriage contributions from their new husbands than the virgins (1,700 versus 2,433 livres). Nor could they hope for eventual compensation, for the jointures or widow's pensions *(douaires)* and survivor's portions *(préciputs)* of all the brides were approximately the same.

The widows of millers, like those of bakers, did their best to keep the business going. Widow Chesneau pawned her silverware and clothes in order to raise cash that she needed to avoid liens on her mill.[26] Another widow relied on the substance of relatives who stood surety in order to obtain the extension of a lease.[27] Widows such as Ferri of Persan, Laurent of Paris, Lacquin of Auteuil-en-Vexin, Bertheault of Blaru, and Preot of La Ferté-Alais turned to their grown sons and sons-in-law for assistance.[28] Widow Quandot of Meaux found help in the person of her daughter, herself the widow of a miller.[29] Whenever possible, however, it appears that miller widows sought to remarry—as a rule with a miller. This decision was dictated largely by professional concerns. Even with family help, a widow would have found it quite difficult to run the business on her own. Since living and working space at the mill were practically coextensive, she might have found it uncomfortable, especially if she were relatively young, to share the mill with a celibate journeyman. Censorious, moralizing, and mill-fantasizing gossip could injure her reputation, and her business. The young widow of a Meaux area miller took the risk of living "en pension" with a journeyman miller, but it is not clear whether she attempted to sustain her late husband's business.[30]

One solution, burlesqued in *The Milleress of Gentilly,* was for the widow to marry her late husband's aide. In this comic opera of 1768, the widow covets the aide and plans to give her daughter to the mill owner to assure their renewal of the lease. The aide and the daughter, however, are in love and trick

26. AN, MC, XXXIV-584, 30 December 1751.
27. AN, MC, CIX-581, 9 March 1751.
28. Archives Seine-Paris, D4B⁶ 27-1457, July 1765; AN, Y 11309, 7 July 1748; AN, Y 11220, 29 December 1732 and 3 February 1733; Arsenal, ms. Bast. 10117, 22 January 1774; AD Seine-et-Oise, E 3397, 2 April 1772.
29. AD Seine-et-Marne, 158 E 33, 28 February 1776.
30. AD Seine-et-Marne, B 411, pièces 75–77, 17 December 1750.

the widow into blessing their union.[31] In real life, the internal solution some-times won the day—journeyman Pierre Gallerand married his master's widow and widow Hilaire Picot married her illiterate garde.[32] More commonly, how-ever, widows seem to have looked outside their mills for established millers seeking to extend or transfer their operations or for millers with experience or with strong family support looking to set themselves in business. Widows Potonne, Lagache, Delaforge, Marguerite Casse, Marie Bertout, Marguerite Marchand, Elizabeth Solé, Anne Leloup, and Charlotte Gallorieu all took millers as their second husbands.[33] On 31 May 1747 a miller-flour merchant named Ducler died. His wife buried him the next day and informed De-laroche, his broker at the Paris Halle, that she was taking over the business as of 2 June. Less than four months later, before the end of the conventional mourning period, she married a flour dealer named Rublin.[34] Another widow had no professional problems of adjustment upon the death of her husband, for she had been the miller in the family all along. He had worked as a locksmith and had "lent" her his name in order to obtain the lease to the mill.[35] Certain mill owners were willing to offer leases to experienced widows who chose not to or were unable to remarry.[36] On the assumption that the standard solidarity clause of the contract did not necessarily guarantee his wife the right to succeed him, one husband insisted upon a special clause that stipulated that his wife could assume the lease herself if he should die.[37]

Miller Wealth

It was widely believed during the eighteenth century that millers were affluent.[38] Marcel Barbier, who ran a mill in the Beauce until his retirement a

31. *Journal encyclopédique ou universel* 7 (15 November 1768): 102–4.

32. AN, Y 14941, 9 March 1728 (*scellé* of Pierre Bridault), and AD Eure-et-Loir, G 3005, 3 October 1741. For two other cases of journeyman-widow unions, see AN, MC, XXXV-626, 29 July 1741, and CIX-555, 24 May 1746.

33. AN, MC, CII-363, 20 September 1750, and VII-281, 16 December 1751; AD Aube, G 3410, pièce 99, lease of 18 September 1755; AN, MC, CIX-581, 9 March 1751; AN, MC, XCVIII-516, 10 December 1751, and XXVIII-218, 12 August 1738; Archives Seine-Paris, DC⁶ 258, fol. 166; AN, MC, LXIX-316, 20 October 1733; AD Seine-et-Marne, 158 E 33, 28 February 1776.

34. Archives Seine-Paris, D5B⁶ 5655.

35. AD Seine-et-Oise, 70 H 7, 13 December 1737. I have found a number of cases of unmarried women millers, but they almost invariably come from milling families. See, for instance, Maillard, *Moulins de Montmartre*, pp. 66, 98, 101.

36. Archives municipales Chartres, n.a. 137, 25 February 1788; AD Eure-et-Loir, E 871, 27 October 1754, and E 469, 23 April 1765; AD Seine-et-Marne, H 563, 11 May 1748; AD Seine-et-Oise, E 3397, 2 April 1772, and notariat de Meulan, tabellion de Brueil, 3 July 1731.

37. AD Eure-et-Loir, E 469, 22 September 1756.

38. The widespread belief in miller wealth made them attractive targets for robbery, at

few years ago, has a vivid image, nourished by family memories as well as by folklore, of "the rich millers of yore, lords of the flour, adorned in handsome suits ribbed in white velvet, in the midst of peasants dressed in simple blouses, proud of their mills like a captain of his ship . . . little kings."[39] The eighteenth-century Barbiers may have crossed the path of Menard, a miller from Chartres, who was known in the Maubert market as Milord Marlborough for his ostentatious parade of wealth.[40] In addition to operating four mills in the St.-Denis area, Louis Dezobry also invested heavily in land and houses.[41] Marie-Anne Ponel, the widow of a merchant miller, lent 7,000 livres in cash to a former president of the Paris *cour des aides.* Another miller widow bequeathed 2,000 livres to each of five children.[42]

According to a contemporary memorandum on flour supply, the four millers from Charenton paid "almost all the taille" imposed on their parish.[43] On the 1746 *taille* list, one finds two millers paying respectively 645 and 640 livres out of a total of 5,551, some of which may also have been acquitted by millers enumerated under other professions.[44] At Mours, miller Jacques Brulle's 467 livres' assessment was the second highest in the parish in 1748, after the *receveur* of the seigneur.[45] Millers Germain Fleury (770 livres) and widow Leduc (520 livres) figured among the elite at Creteil in 1740.[46] In 1750 miller Sébastien Poisson was at the summit of the Thillay hierarchy with 1,700 livres.[47] With a prodigious evaluation of 2,724 livres, miller-fermier Philippe Thibault occupied the same position at Bonneuil in 1781.[48] At 1,889 livres for the *taille* and 838 livres for the *capitation,* J.-B. Meusnier, an aptly named miller, was the leading contributor at Stains in 1770. He held a *ferme* of 450 arpents, other lands, and two mills. His flour business was more or less arbitrarily appraised at 10,000 livres. A number of his fellow parishioners

---

the mill or on the road between collections. See, for example, Gazetins (1730), Arsenal, ms. Bast. 10161, fol. 14.

Cf. the remarkable prosperity of eighteenth-century American millers, who were usually large landowners and often farmers as well. Main, *Social Structure of Revolutionary America,* pp. 82–83.

39. *Marcel Barbier: Meunier,* p. 114.

40. Saint-Germain, *Vie quotidienne,* pp. 181–82. Cf. René Bazin's description of the honest but greedy Maître Humeau: "All week long he was the miller, covered with flour from head to feet; but on Sunday, one would surely have taken him for a grand seigneur, for such were his superb clothing, his delicate face, and his air of contentment with life": "Le Moulin qui ne tourne plus," in *Contes de bonne Perrette* (Paris, [1903]).

41. AN, Y 9648, 1771.

42. Archives Seine-Paris, 6 November 1760, étude Lhéritier, unclassified; AN, MC, XCVIII-516, 10 December 1751.

43. *Mémoire important par rapport au bien public et à la provision de farine pour la ville de Paris* (Paris, 1733), p. 3.

44. AN, Z^{1G} 296^A.

45. AN, Z^{1G} 298^A.

46. AN, Z^{1G} 291^B.

47. AN, Z^{1G} 300^B.

48. AN, Z^{1G} 397^A.

complained that Meusnier was in fact undertaxed because "he concealed a part of his productive capacity."[49]

The richest miller about whom I have any precise information is Etienne Palleau, of the Dourdan area. He left an estate of over 60,000 livres, including 10,000 livres in cash, a mill worth 10,000 livres, almost 12,000 livres in other real estate, wine worth 1,000 livres, wheat valued at 3,369 livres (some probably of his own cultivation), and over 7,000 livres in furnishings and effects, including 800 livres' worth of silver.[50] Denis Aubin of La Courtille was also quite well off, though his fortune amounted to only half of Palleau's (depleted in part by the settlement that he accorded his children). It was solidly grounded, however, on real estate worth over 20,000 livres. A speculating flour merchant, Aubin kept a huge stock of 306 setiers of wheat. With under 3,000 livres in household furnishings (including fourteen paintings of mostly religious subjects), only 150 livres in clothing, and merely 150 livres' worth of wine in his cellar, he did not live like a milord. Still, he owned a municipal office *(dizainier)* that conferred prestige at the neighborhood level, and the esteem he enjoyed was reflected by the frequency with which the commercial court asked him to serve as arbiter.[51]

Other millers were quite comfortable without being wealthy. François Chatelin of Tillet earned his security by dint of patience and diligent application. He started to work full time in his father's mill when he was twelve. His apprenticeship lasted sixteen years, until his mother finally ceded him the family mill, to which he added another that he leased. Given his excellent prospects, he attracted a large dowry of 5,000 livres, 80 percent of it in cash, from the daughter of a local fermier—a connection that promised him a chance to acquire land. While he focused on supplying flour to Paris bakers en droiture, during the seventies he became a buying agent and flour manufacturer for a large company whose inopportune and large-scale speculations alarmed the police.[52]

49. AN, Z^{1G} 342^B. Persons indentified as millers in the *taille* rolls as a rule were considered more affluent than those enumerated as flour merchants (fariniers). It may be that the fariniers were millers with few "dependencies" (i.e., arable, vines, forest, etc.), or millers who rented their mills, or millers of small, custom-oriented operations, or mealmen who did not hold mills at all. For fourteen so-called fariniers on the Presles list in 1748, the average *taille* amounted to 36 livres (median = 44.3 livres). For ten fariniers in the same place twelve years later, mean *taille* was 70.3 livres (median = 57.5 livres). The highest assessment on a farinier was 168 livres, on a miller, 400 livres. AN, Z^{1G} 298^A and Z^{1G} 310.

50. AN, MC, CII-363, 20 September 1750. The richest miller on the Paris scene in the mid-nineteenth century was Darblay. Though his immense fortune became a "bench mark" of miller well-being in the public (and to some extent even in the professional) imagination, it was in fact quite exceptional. *Enquête sur la boulangerie*, pp. 392, 394.

51. AN, MC, LXI-422, 30 July 1744; AN, Y 11571, 18 August 1755. Married in 1725, Aubin brought 1,700 livres to the new household and received a dowry of 1,500 livres from his wife.

52. AN, Y 11441, 20 May 1775.

The exact amount of Pierre Delaforge's estate is not known, but it included three windmills worth over 10,000 livres and substantial portions of land.[53] From humble beginnings signified by a combined marriage fortune of a paltry 1,168 livres, Jean-Jacques Devaux amassed a fortune of 18,517 livres. The centerpiece was a windmill atop Montmartre worth 10,500 livres. Devaux operated a second mill that he leased. He kept four horses and a large wagon for transporting grain and flour. Although he set aside a modest cash reserve of 300 livres, he had no grain on hand. His house was spacious and amply furnished. Ten devotional paintings decorated the walls, along with two ivory crucifixes. Devaux's library consisted of fourteen volumes "including an Old Testament and other works of devotion." On special occasions he wore a wig.[54] Jean Clerambault also owned a large house decorated with religious paintings, wall hangings, and mirrors. While he rented a mill, where he kept 51 setiers of wheat, he was the proprietor of a venal office worth 5,200 livres and of annuities worth 2,000 livres. His total fortune at death, including 356 livres in cash, amounted to 13,517 livres.[55]

If one were to examine only the assets that Jean-François François accumulated until his death in 1776, one would have ranked him in this "comfortable" category. He owned a boat mill at Meaux worth 4,485 livres, including the boat, the mill, and the tools of the profession. He was the proprietor of a house that consisted of four bedrooms, a small living room, and a kitchen. Almost half of the total value of his furnishings consisted of five beds worth an average of 74 livres apiece. Household linen and clothing amounted to 616 livres and the fourteen books on diverse subjects in his library commanded 4 livres. His liquid assets were modest: 24 livres in jewelry, 208 livres in silverware, 60 livres in cash, and 500 livres in flour stock. His hard assets totaled 11,895 livres. If one adds his claims for accounts receivable, including a sum of 2,000 livres owed by a Paris baker who obstinately contested this debt, François's fortune appears to be a little over 14,000 livres. Enormous liabilities, however, amounting to over 25,000 livres, utterly obliterated his estate. He owed 276 livres for mill repairs, 415 livres for wood, 293 livres for taxes, and 4,200 livres for a mortgage on his house; and above all he owed 12,830 livres for grain purchased and 7,245 livres for loans to finance, among other things, the acquisition of more grain. It is probable that François's position was undercut by a more or less drastic price change that occurred while he was holding a large stock.[56]

Still other millers, far more numerous, boasted a certain freedom from

53. AN, MC, LXIX-318, 30 April 1734.

54. AN, MC, VII-307. 28 April 1757. Cf. the more sanguine reading of the Devaux fortune in Maillard, *Moulins de Montmartre,* pp. 30–34.

55. AN, MC, LXXXIX-243, 16 February 1713. For other millers in this category, see X-498, 20 October 1751 (André Fouquet), and CX-377, 19 October 1751 (Christophe Fournier).

56. AD Seine-et-Marne, 158 E 34, 2, 4 November 1776.

daily uncertainty, but they were by no means well off. Jacques La France's sole asset was a windmill that he himself helped erect at Gentilly. It was both an instrument of production and a house; assessed at 5,000 livres, it afforded him and his four minor children a semblance of safety.[57] It is not clear whether Charles Cochois owned or rented his windmill. His home was small and rather sparsely furnished. Instead of a horse, he had an old mule worth a few bushels of flour. But he owned five and a half *arpents* of vineyard and one and a half of arable, and he invested in a spiritual pension that would assure that three high masses would be chanted annually for the repose of his soul in the Paris church of Villejuif.[58] Adrien Falentin owned no real property, but he left his wife and two minor children over 1,000 livres in cash, 557 livres in silverware, and 1,124 livres in furnishings and effects, including a superb wall clock, a gold ring and chain, sixteen engravings and paintings, and a gilded crucifix.[59] The shabbiness of most of Pierre Masson's furnishings was more or less obscured by the elegance of the oak commodes and wardrobes and the upholstered *fauteuils de commodité* in each of the bedrooms.[60]

Orphaned by his miller-father when he was twelve, Pierre Bruxelle also died young, leaving five children ranging in age from one to thirteen. He had little to work with, but he lived within his means. If he left no real property, he also left no debts. His household assets, including clothing (303 livres), linens (291 livres), and furniture (352 livres), constituted a very mediocre estate. Somehow he managed to save 2,273 livres in cash. This treasure, along with seven cows, eight pigs, seven horses, and numerous chickens, enabled the widow, the daughter of a laboureur, to face the difficult times immediately following her husband's death without material strain.[61] Miller Quandot left a fortune of the same magnitude, weaker in cash (581 livres) and stronger in silverware (429 livres) and furniture (727 livres), 57 percent of which represented five beds. He appears to have owned at least a part of his water mill, he had one horse, and he was virtually without grain or flour stocks.[62] With a net fortune of 2,273 livres, Jean-Baptiste Meignien was of similar means. He rented his water mill at Meaux (perhaps the same one that his wife's father had operated), he owned one horse, and his assets were composed of almost equal parts of household and commercial items.[63]

All millers appeared to be rich because Milord Marlborough, or his

57. AN, MC, XXVIII-241, 9 November 1735.

58. AN, MC, LXV-196, 22 June 1718.

59. AN, MC, XX-559, 5 October 1736. Falentin's widow, who could not write, was likely to have trouble collecting 800 livres in accounts receivable because her husband kept no written record of sales and deliveries.

60. AN, Y 15257, 17 November 1749. Cf. the *scellé* of Pierre Bridault, AN, Y 14941, 9 March 1728.

61. AD Seine-et-Marne, B 69, pièce 59, 30 April 1725.

62. AD Seine-et-Marne, 158 E 33, 28 February 1776.

63. AD Seine-et-Marne, 158 E 34, 17 October 1776.

equivalent, was obviously very rich. Or all millers appeared to be rich because they speculated and swindled, which was somehow in the nature of their vocation. Or because the acquisition of a lease required a certain initial capital, because choice pastures (or other agricultural exploitations) came with the mill, and because a mill signified a socioeconomic status that was intrinsically superior to that of most rural inhabitants.[64] Whatever the logic behind the stereotype, it was false. Many millers, perhaps most, lived on the margin, poor men who just managed to pay their four quarters' rent. They were highly vulnerable (though surely more so when viewed from the city than from the vantage point of the rural milieu in which they lived). A run of bad weather could ruin them. In any event, they suffered frequent periods of idleness not only because of high or low water or ice or insufficient wind or bad road access, but for lack of grain. They managed in part because they had truck gardens and kept chickens, geese, a few pigs, and perhaps a cow. Even if they had to direct all their fees to paying rent, taxes, and repairs, they could steal enough flour from their clients to keep their families supplied in bread. Without these buffers, many millers would have found it very hard to avoid sinking. Louis Diot, one of these marginal millers, died ten years after his marriage, leaving five children aged from one to eight. His wife brought him a dowry of 600 livres; his own contribution was probably less. He rented a windmill and a small house in the faubourg de Gloire for 450 livres a year. It was summarily appointed with 266 livres' worth of furnishings, including a gilded cross and sixteen devotional paintings. Clothing and linens represented another 176 livres. At his death, Diot had debts of 434 livres, including 60 livres to a part-time aide. In addition, the mill owner was sure to file a claim for an indemnity to cover the difference between the evaluation of the mill and mill tools at the beginning of the lease (2,074 livres) and at the time of Diot's death (1,863 livres).[65]

Jean-Baptiste Ducellier was a miller on the Ourcq near Lizy who started out poor and never had a chance to improve his situation. He died at twenty-two, leaving his wife, the daughter of a servant, with their three-month-old son. Her trousseau represented about 300 livres. Their furniture was worth

64. The rich miller is a common literary figure. Miller Lucas in Pedro de Alarcon's *Three-Cornered Hat* had every comfort in his home (p. 16). Hans Christian Andersen's miller was rich and haughty ("He was accustomed to hear people laugh at his jokes and sayings—for was he not the wealthy miller?"). "The Ice Maiden," in *Stories and Fairy Tales*, pp. 677, 687. The bone miller of the fen, like Tennyson's miller, was affluent. "Bone Meal in the Flour," in Barrett, *More Tales from the Fens*, p. 11, and "The Miller's Daughter," in Gray and Tennyson, eds., *Victorian Literature*, p. 71. George Eliot's Mr. Tulliver may not have been truly wealthy, but he strained to appear so: *The Mill on the Floss*, pp. 69, 310. When the miller is portrayed as poor, it is often because he has "fallen" from a previously comfortable station. See "The Nixie of the Mill-Pond," in James Stern, ed., *Grimm's Fairy Tales*, trans. Margaret Hunt (New York, 1944), pp. 736–37; "The Miller, His Son, and His Ass," in William Godwin, *Fables Ancient and Modern*, ed. David L. Greene (New York, 1976), p. 49.

65. AN, MC, XXXVIII-388, 20 March 1751.

228 livres, and they owned jewelry and silver assessed at 132 livres. A quarter's rent on the mill, 162 livres and ten sous, was overdue.[66] Pierre Bruxelle's miller-parents lived in extreme simplicity in two rooms next to a mill near Meaux. Their sheets and linen constituted their most substantial investment.[67] The widow Preot of La Ferté-Alais, who could not sign her name, was another marginal miller; the theft of her only horse threatened to put her out of business.[68] Mealman Jacques Louvret, for reasons that remain obscure, ended up a *clochard* ("sans azile ni condition") at age thirty-one. He was arrested in the street where he slept. Apparently he subsisted on stolen fruit and on other improvisations of the moment.[69]

Certain millers who should have succeeded, given the solidity of their installations, also hovered on the brink of disaster. Although these millers were better able to manage and mask their difficulties than the structurally miserable ones, they were in a very precarious situation. Augustin Pichard rented a boat mill under the Pont-Neuf for 2,200 livres a year. He owned no real estate and had no other investments. He possessed merely 571 livres in furniture and 261 livres' worth of clothing and linens. Whereas bakers owed him 350 livres at his death, he was obligated to a mass of creditors for almost 4,000 livres. He owed his aide over a year's salary, and he was indebted to two charpentiers for several years' repairs. He was behind a half-year's rent and he owed money for basic supplies to meat, fruit, and wine dealers, to a tailor, and to a shoemaker.[70] His widow married Jean Chauveau, also a miller, who took over the Pont-Neuf operation but failed to improve it in the five years before he died. Although he found two new institutional clients who promised him better days, he could not overcome the debt incubus. At his death, he owed 4,166 livres.[71]

Despite the fact that he held one of the most coveted mill leases in the Paris region, Savart of Gonesse was another victim of excessive indebtedness, and perhaps also of badly planned expansion. His mills, owned by the Paris Hôtel-Dieu, were occupied by soldiers because he was in arrears for several years' *taille*. The Hôtel-Dieu first advanced him 4,000 livres in an effort to bail him out, but it abandoned him and forced him to give up his lease when it realized that he owed substantial sums of money to too many other creditors.[72]

---

66. AD Seine-et-Marne, B 411, pièces 75–77, 17 December 1750.
67. AD Seine-et-Marne, B 68, pièce non cotée, 29 April 1697.
68. Arsenal, ms. Bast. 10117, 22 January 1774.
69. AN, Y 16022¹, 29 July 1774.
70. AN, MC, CIX-554, 21 April 1746.
71. AN, MC, VII-281, 16 December 1751. The widow announced the succession: VII-282, 29 February 1752.
72. Deliberations of the bureau of the Hôtel-Dieu, 2 May 1741, Archives Assistance publique, no. 110.

The choice of a marriage partner was a crucial and often decisive business decision as well as an intimate one. A good marriage launched a young miller into a trajectory toward success. In many cases dowries were less significant than the social and cultural capital the marriage formed. Endogamous alliances within the provisioning complex linked millers to flour merchants and bakers and, less frequently, to sturdy laboureurs as well. An intricate web of kinship relations afforded millers significant advantages in the market. Millers appreciated the professional assistance that brides who grew up in the mill or the bakeshop could render them. As widows these women were competent to continue the business, though they usually sought a second union with another miller.

Reputed as a group to be extremely affluent, the millers in fact varied enormously in resources. Beneath a handful of "lords of the flour," a slightly larger cluster boasted solid but undazzling wealth. Then came a substantial body of millers, including merchant entrepreneurs as well as customary operators, who were free from the contingencies of everyday life but who lived in genuinely modest circumstances. The largest category consisted of the mass of little men, for the most part custom millers, who had not adapted successfully to the new commercial structures.

CHAPTER 10

The Flour Trade

$\mathcal{T}$he emergence of the miller-flour merchant was the single most important change in the structure of the provisioning trade during the old regime. Even as flour superseded wheat as the primary commodity of exchange, so the commercial miller dislodged the grain dealer as its leading agent. The triumph of flour held the promise of an end to chronic flour scarcities that menaced consumers even in the midst of ample supplies of grain. It opened new commercial perspectives on the international and national planes as well as at the local and regional levels. It also presaged fundamental changes in the relations between miller-merchants and bakers and between miller-merchants and public authorities.

Flour Crises

In examining the dislocating impact of subsistence crises, scholars have tended to focus exclusively on the dearth of grain. However, consumers were vulnerable even in the midst of plentiful grain, wrote Parmentier, "because, in the end, it is always flour that we seek to get from wheat, and the abundance of grain is not sufficient to reassure us on subsistence needs."[1] Malouin warned of "the famine that could break out even when grain was abundant, as a result of droughts, floods and freezing weather."[2] During a flour crisis the

1. Parmentier, *Parfait Boulanger*, p. 233.
2. Malouin, *Description et détails des arts*, p. 63. Béguillet used the exact same language in his *Discours sur la mouture* (1775), pp. 64–66. Cf. similar language in mid-nineteenth century. *Enquête sur la boulangerie*, p. 66.

price of flour, and consequently of bread, rose out of all proportion to the price of wheat.[3] Bakers desperately searched for flour or for millers who managed to keep their machines turning. Stalled millers tried to shift their traffic to other mills. The whole system of fabrication and distribution became disjointed. The *soudure* months of late spring–early summer, already perilous because of the exhaustion of the previous year's crop, were the period of greatest risk to the largest number of mills because low water and light wind converged. Nevertheless, acute flour crises often occurred in winter and early spring, when ice or floods impeded transport as well as milling.[4]

Paris suffered serious flour crises in 1649, 1651–52, 1658, 1662, and 1709.[5] In 1725 a flour crisis greatly aggravated the difficulties already caused by a serious dearth of grain. In late October one police official urged the procurator general to refocus attention from grain to flour as rapidly as possible: "otherwise, despite a great abundance of wheat, we could find ourselves in a bread shortage for lack of flour."[6] Within the next several weeks, grain was rotting on the ports and "bakers were killing each other" trying to find flour.[7] The police drew upon the flour stock of the General Hospital and dispatched exempts to induce millers with operating machines to grind more and faster.[8] The controller-general instructed intendants in nearby *généralités* to assign a number of their mills to the grinding of government grain and at the same time had the international banker and victualer Samuel Bernard ship to Paris a large quantity of English flour that he had stored at Rouen.[9] The worst was over by Christmas, though another interruption occurred in mid-January

3. See *Détail sur quelques établissements,* p. 443. Even after steam power had been widely introduced by the end of the nineteenth century, flour prices still tended to rise each summer as a result of low water. Joseph Barberet, *Le Travail en France; monographies professionnelles* (Paris, 1886–90), p. 468. See the gaping incongruity between wheat and flour prices in 1858 triggered by an "extraordinary drought." *Enquête sur la boulangerie,* p. 205.

4. On the calendar/incidence of flour crises, see *Mémoire important par rapport au bien public et à la provision de farine pour la ville de Paris* (Paris, 1733). The flour crisis itself, apart from the inclement weather that caused it, could obstruct river transportation, for in time of low water millers drained off as much water as they could. See BN, Coll. Joly 1742, fols. 30–35, for an example of the flour-transport crisis and of the tension between Paris and the hinterland in 1785.

5. *Gazette d'agriculture, commerce, arts et finances* (1 September 1770): 636; AN, F[7] 4296; François Vincent, *Histoire des famines à Paris* (Paris, 1946), p. 66; Boislisle, "Le Grand hiver et la disette de 1709," 468.

6. Couet de Montbayeux to procurator general, 24 October 1725, BN, Coll. Joly 1117, fols. 240–43.

7. Controller-general to Hérault, 16 November 1725, AN, G[7] 34; Couet de Montbayeux to procurator general, 11 November 1725, BN, Coll. Joly 1117, fols. 248–50; Gazetins, 7 October 1725, Arsenal, ms. Bast. 10155, fol. 91.

8. Gazetins, 23 August 1725, Arsenal, ms. Bast. 10155, fol. 51; Chefdeville to procurator general, 7, 14 September 1725, BN, Coll. Joly 1117, fols. 173, 180.

9. D'Angervilliers to procurator general, 21 September 1725, BN, Coll. Joly 1117, fol. 189; Bernard to Hérault, 27 November 1725, Arsenal, ms. Bast. 10271.

1726.[10] Three years later the assembly of police feared that "the halting of the work of the mills" as a result of ice and cold would result in another flour crisis.[11]

"It is not enough to have a lot of wheat in Paris—we need flour," wrote a morose Barbier at the end of 1740, after a month of flooding followed by freezing. Scores of water mills were stopped, and many major roads as well as a host of minor ones were impassable. A well-informed farmer-general told Barbier that the capital "had been two days from perishing as a result of a lack of flour."[12] The authorities borrowed hand mills from the army and requisitioned others from the convents and hospitals. They forbade pastry makers to bake certain kinds of cakes and tried to borrow flour from other *généralités*.[13] Heavy flooding once again stopped many mills, including some of the largest, in the spring of 1741.[14] Flour crises buffeted Paris again in 1744, 1751, 1762, 1767–68, 1770, 1773, and 1782–83.[15] Ice stopped the mills and snow blocked the roads in the winter of 1784, leaving the capital "teetering on the brink of a flour famine."[16]

Though the flour crises were usually brief and limited, the authorities worried about them on the grounds that even the briefest supply failure could unleash disastrous consequences in the capital.[17] The government promoted the development of alternate methods of milling that would be crisis free.[18] The Paris police quietly began to encourage flour storage by institutions as well as by some bakers and millers.[19] The flour lobby argued that only the development of a vigorous flour trade, replacing the grain trade in all the major markets, would result in the constitution of a sufficient stock and achieve the sort of suppleness necessary to parry flour crises.[20]

10. Procurator general to cardinal Fleury, 19 January 1726, BN, Coll. Joly 1118, fol. 28.

11. Assembly of police, 20 January 1729, BN, ms. fr. 11356, fol. 71.

12. Barbier, *Journal de Barbier*, 3:246, 248 (December 1740).

13. Deliberations of the bureau of the Hôtel de Ville, 5 February 1741, AN, H* 1859; de Breteuil to Marville, 28 December 1740, Arsenal, ms. Bast. 10277; F. de Marville, *Lettres de M. de Marville, lieutenant général de police, au ministre Maurepas (1742–1747)*, ed. Arthur-Michel de Boislisle (Paris, 1896–1905), 1:214.

14. Jean-Michel Desbordes, ed., *La Chronique villageoise de Varreddes (Seine-et-Marne)* (Paris, n.d.), p. 26.

15. See Kaplan, *Bread, Politics and Political Economy* 1: xvi, 310–11; AD Aube, C 1909, pièce 1; BM Orléans, ms. Lenoir 1421; *Gazette du commerce, de l'agriculture et des finances* (26 January 1768): 70.

16. Archives municipales Pontoise, "Compte rendu au public par les Srs. Leleu," p. 11.

17. See *Encyclopédie méthodique*, Jurisprudence, 10:148.

18. See above chap. 6, and controller-general to intendant of Alençon, 19 January 1769, AD Orne, C 90.

19. See the strategy of the Hôtel-Dieu, deliberations of 17 September 1740, Archives Assistance publique, no. 109. In 1809 various prefects called for the imposition of a flour reserve requirement on bakers. Prefect of the Cher to minister of the interior, 10 February 1809, AN, F[20] 295.

20. Parmentier, *Parfait Boulanger*, p. 526.

The Advantages of the Flour Trade

The first and in some ways most powerful argument in favor of the flour trade was that it was easier, more efficient, and·cheaper than the provisioning system articulated by grain commerce. The flour trade simplified and rationalized the process by eliminating superfluous stages. There was no need for bakers and mealmen to buy from grain dealers, who themselves bought from other traders, cultivators, and collectors. This path was tortuous and costly. A flour merchant, usually his own miller, bought grain at the market or closer to the field, cleaned and prepared it, ground and bolted it, mixed it, and delivered it. A considerable amount was saved in trips between the mill and the bakeroom alone, not to mention on buying expeditions, on the commission of intermediaries, and on market and measuring fees. A further substantial saving resulted if the flour merchant used the economic technology. (And while economic milling gave the flour-trade campaign great impetus, it was evident that only a vigorous regional and interregional flour trade could sweep the economic technology into place throughout the kindgom.)[21]

By reducing the number of grain buyers, the flour trade would relax pressure on the mercuriale.[22] With fewer and sharper lines of transmission to inspect, the police would have an easier task of provisioning surveillance. The baker could also relax his police of the miller because the miller was now a merchant with a vested interest in producing the most and best flour from every setier and the baker was free to choose his flour from a host of rival suppliers.[23]

The flour trade also promised broader economic and political benefits. Agriculture would profit, for merchants would buy up the whole crop, even in times of glut, in order to transform it into flour for sale at home or abroad or for stockage. Given the stimulation of the foreign market and the new technology, mills would become factories capable of prodigies of conditioning, conservation, production, and distribution. By a vast multiplier effect, this "new brand of industry," with new establishments all over the realm, especially near the coast, would create jobs in many fields.[24] While the freedom to export grain "would always be dangerous," if only because of "the general anxiety it spreads," the export of flour "could never be deleterious," according to a partisan of the flour trade. A flour export trade would guarantee the nation of a year's supply because the export of crop A would not begin until

21. Ibid., pp. 241–42, and Parmentier, *Mémoire sur les avantages,* p. 153.
22. Bucquet to Fontette, 15 June, 4 July 1769, AD Calvados, C 2653.
23. Louis Cotte, *Leçons élémentaires sur le choix et la conservation des grains . . .* (Paris, year III), p. 26; Baudeau, *Avis au peuple,* deuxième traité, pp. 61–63; Parmentier, *Avis aux bonnes ménagères,* p. 17.
24. Rozier, *Cours complet,* 7:367–69; Parmentier, *Parfait Boulanger,* pp. xxix–xxx; Bucquet, "Mémoire," 2 March 1769, AD Isère, II C 47; Tessier, "Le Commerce des grains," *Encyclopédie méthodique,* Agriculture, 3:379–80.

the state of harvest B was unequivocally known. Moreover, only the "flower" of the meal would be exported; the mid-white and darker meals would never leave the country. Exporting flour rather than grain made the same sense as exporting woolen cloth rather than wool. The price of manufacture, including labor, would be paid by the foreigner and would remain at home to fructify France. The offal, too, would remain in the countryside to provide food for larger numbers of livestock and poultry.[25]

Flour liberalism was (politically) reassuring. Even as the advocates of the flour trade hailed the extension it would give to exportation, so they insisted on the way it would enhance subsistence security. First of all, a highly developed flour trade would spare France entirely from one kind of crisis: the flour dearth. With more and better mills and service and with virtually all the available grain transformed as rapidly as possible into meal, the perils of ice, flood, drought, and calm would be drastically reduced. Second, flour stockage would become commonplace. The mills would become "granaries of abundance." In the big cities, bakers would also keep flour on hand and in the countryside the little people would be able to buy small quantities of good-quality meal cheap at retail flour depots. Third, the large mill factories on the coast would be able to import grain rapidly, restore it to high grade, and turn it into flour. These establishments would also serve the state in time of war for the provisioning of the navy and the colonies.[26]

Flour could be exported and it could be stored more successfully than grain because it could be conserved more effectively, according to the promoters of the flour trade. Malisset, Bucquet, and Béguillet affirmed that the conservation of flour was "easier and surer" than that of grain.[27] Leray de Chaumont, international speculator, innovator, and government subsistence counselor, wrote that "the conservation of flour appears to us to be physically more practicable than that of grain."[28] Flour not only sustained its quality longer, the experts claimed, but it took up less space and was thus cheaper to transport.[29] They made their case in vague and summary terms, doubtless

25. Béguillet, *Traité des subsistances,* pp. xxxvi–xxxvii, 806–7; Béguillet, "Mémoire sur les avantages," AN, F^{10} 256; Leray de Chaumont et al. to Trudaine de Montigny, 10 May 1768, AN, F^{11} 1193. Cf. Etienne-François, duc de Choiseul, *Mémoires de M. le duc de Choiseul . . . ,* ed. Soulavie (Chanteloup and Paris, 1790), p. 52n; *Journal économique* (October 1766): 478–79; *Ephémérides du citoyen* 5 (1769): 5–14, 27.
26. Bucquet, *Observations intéressantes,* pp. 4–5; Bucquet, "Mémoire," 2 March 1769, AD Isère, II C 47; Edme Béguillet, "Mémoire sur les avantages de la mouture économique" (1769), Arsenal, ms. 2891; Béguillet, *Traité des subsistances,* pp. 135n, 218–21; Parmentier, *Mémoire sur les avantages,* p. 153; Tillet, "Projet d'un tarif," pp. 107–68.
27. Malisset, "Observations sur le commerce des bleds et des farines," September 1765, AD Nord, C 9780; Béguillet, "Mémoire sur les avantages de la mouture économique" (1769), Arsenal, ms. 2891.
28. Leray de Chaumont to Trudaine de Montigny, 18 May 1768, AN, F^{11} 1193.
29. Béguillet, "Mémoire," AN, F^{10} 256; Savary des Bruslons, *Dictionnaire portatif de commerce,* 3:140–42.

because they were not entirely sure of it.[30] Neither the problem of conserving grain nor that of conserving flour had been resolved by the end of the eighteenth century. Leray himself had sought the solution in an étuve, but his experiments proved no more conclusive and no more workable than the experiments of Duhamel and Pâris-Duverney with grain.[31] Flour was not, as alarmists believed, fragile and vulnerable in freight or storage.[32] The most promising model for relatively long-term conservation was the *minot* or barrel system of the colonial exporters.[33] The merits of sack versus open flour storage for the short and medium term were still the object of bitter controversy between Bucquet and Parmentier/Cadet in the 1780s.[34]

The flour trade triumphed in Paris well before it conquered the rest of the kingdom. Already at the beginning of the century, at least half of the provisioning of the capital took the form of flour rather than of grain. The figures for the thirties point clearly to the trajectory that flour would take. The bakers, more than anyone else, had been responsible for the dramatic repudiation of grain—assisted, to be sure, by the millers and later by the flour merchants. Writing in 1773, the chief of the subsistence department of the *contrôle-général* observed that the Paris bakers had long abandoned the habit of buying grain, having it milled coarsely, and bolting it themselves. He rightly noted that the transition to a flour-based supply had been accelerated by the introduction of economic milling, though he perhaps underestimated the extent to which the structural change had preceded the technological innovation. The grain business of the ports, he concluded, had fallen by 80 percent (since precisely when he did not say), and the traffic in flour at the Halle had increased commensurately.[35] The following year controller-general

30. For the argument that flour was unstable and difficult to transport or store, see *Gazette du commerce, de l'agriculture et des finances* (11 October 1768): 810. Cf. Roubaud, *Récréations économiques,* p. 222.

31. See Leray de Chaumont to Duhamel, n.d., AN, 127 AP 6. Cf. Fougeroux de Bondy's manuscript note in Poncelet, *Histoire naturelle,* p. 179 of the copy in the Yale University library.

32. See, for instance, Couet de Montbayeux to procurator general, 24 October 1725, BN, Coll. Joly 1113, fols. 240–43. In my view Jean Meuvret exaggerated the difficulty of dealing with flour, perhaps in part because he relied on the more pessimistic sources of the late seventeenth and early eighteenth centuries: "Le Commerce des grains et des farines à Paris et les marchands parisiens à l'époque de Louis XIV," *Revue d'histoire moderne et contemporaine* 3 (July–September 1956), p. 182. Flour could be shipped by water without prohibitive risk. See, for example, "Mémoire pour tirer des farines de Chaslons," BN, Coll. Joly 1117, fol. 244. Cf. the "mémoire" of the merchants of Melun, ca. 1737, BN, Coll. Joly 1314, fols. 36–37.

33. Savary des Bruslons, *Dictionnaire portatif de commerce,* 3:141–42. Cf. the debate over Ben Franklin's Chinese tea-packing system: *Journal de Paris,* no. 364 (29 December 1780) and no. 25 (25 January 1781).

34. Bucquet, *Manuel du meunier,* p. 8, and *Observations intéressantes,* pp. 47–49, 106–12; Parmentier, *Parfait Boulanger,* pp. 226–31, and *Mémoire sur les avantages,* pp. 116–20.

35. St.-Prest, "Mémoire," September 1773, AD Gironde, C 1441. Cf. the early transition to flour in London. John Kirkland, *The Modern Baker, Confectioner, and Caterer* (London, 1934), p. 14.

Terray cited the "états de la Halle" as evidence that five-sixths of the Paris supply was furnished in flour and that as a consequence a ministry could show much less indulgence for grain merchants than it had in former times.[36] The commerce of master baker Gérard confirmed Terray's thesis. Eschewing grain dealings completely, Gérard bought regularly at the Halle from eleven merchant-millers: five from Pontoise and two each from Melun, Chartres, and Etampes.[37] Outside of Paris, the liberal impulse of the sixties that opened up the subsistence trade and stimulated improvements in milling resulted in gains for flour at the expense of grain.[38] There were excellent underlying structural reasons for calling the subsistence riots that buffeted the Paris region in May of 1775 the Flour War rather than the Grain War.

The Emergence of the Flour Merchants

The commercialization of milling was one of the critical structural changes in the trade that provisioned Paris in the eighteenth century. We have seen how millers began to make speculative grain purchases and to manufacture flour for their own account. The millers who broke most decisively with the old custom business became veritable flour merchants: *marchands de farine* or *fariniers* or *meuniers et fariniers* or *marchands meuniers.* The millers who initially opted for the new trade were not always the most dynamic, the most ambitious, and the most richly endowed with capital in machinery, stock, cash, and family connections, though this elite was extremely well represented. It is apparent that certain millers fell into the flour trade more or less accidentally, say, because of their location. Others were virtually forced into it by the bakers, who were the great modernizers of the milling industry in the eighteenth century. Their demands compelled even the most languid custom millers to change their habits or risk eclipse. Still others made the shift defensively, in response to competition.

The use (and even the abuse) of the new titles (or *qualités*) by a growing number of millers was of real moment. It signified a new agenda: new methods, new relations, new horizons. The merchant-miller was the miller

---

36. Controller-general to prévôt des marchands, 7 March 1774, AD Marne, C 419. Contemporary opinion converges strikingly on this issue. See Malisset, "Observations," January 1765, BN, ms. fr. 14295, fol. 161; Parmentier, *Parfait Boulanger,* pp. 232–33; Tillet, "Projet d'un tarif," pp. 146–47 ("If one considers that today very little grain is brought into this city"); Tessier, "Le Commerce des grains," p. 379, and "Consommation de Paris," in *Encyclopédie méthodique,* Agriculture 3 (Paris, 1793):473.

37. Archives Seine-Paris, D5B[6] 5037.

38. See, for example, the victory of the aggressive millers in the Hainaut. Subdelegate of Avesnes, "Réflexions sur l'édit du mois de juillet 1764," ca. 1770, AD Nord, C 6690. On the other hand, there were important trading markets, such as Bar-sur-Aube, that remained virtually immune to the advance of flour. See Trippier to the intendant of Champagne, 19 February 1771, AD Aube, C 299.

Moulin de la Vicomté, "Parisian" merchant mill at Provins (private collection)

and the subsistence distributor of the future. He would become the agent of market rationalization and integration. He would help to change the very notion of market from a physical place, where actual goods were concentrated to confront personified demand, to a set of streamlined transactions that could occur anywhere. Prodded by the bakers, he became the leading commercial and technical innovator in the subsistence business.

The mill was logically the point of departure for the flour trade: most fariniers were millers.[39] But the meal trade was never precisely coterminous with milling.[40] It was this quite limited discontinuity that enabled critics of the flour trade to regard it as a gratuitous multiplication of hands in the provisioning business rather than as the simplification and streamlining that its apolo-

39. For examples of miller-mealmen, see the following references from the Archives Seine-Paris: rapport arbitre, 10 October 1746, D6B[6], carton 2 (Serinan); D5B[6] 2532 (Bonte); D2B[6] 801, 7 September 1746 (Pion); rapport arbitre, 30 April 1767, D6B[6], carton 5 (Lamoureux); D2B[6] 950, 9 February 1759 (Fournier); D2B[6] 1078, 2 October 1769 (Goujon); D2B[6] 1103, 8 November 1771 (Daubigny and Sennève); D4B[6] 71-4710, 5 May 1779 (Colas dit Valentin in Villerot faillite); D4B[6] 106-7518, 4 June 1789 (Picque in Person faillite); D4B[6] 4-183 (Beausse in Mandon faillite). See also AN:Y 12611, 9 June 1762 (Devaux); Y 11220, 29 December 1732 and 3 February 1733 (Lourtier); Y 9474, 29 October 1771 (Bouret); Y 9440, 18 December 1739 (Cheron); and BN, Coll. Joly 1312, fol. 50, 26 May 1759 (Guibon).

40. There are many similarities between the development of the flour trades in the London and Paris areas. See Thrupp, *Bakers of London,* pp. 27, 65–68. There are also parallels with colonial America: Brissot de Warville, *New Travels,* pp. 163–64 (28 August 1788). Afanassiev's claim that fariniers were unknown to Delamare and that they were "a new breed, barely tolerated" under Terray in the 1770s is erroneous: Afanassiev, *Commerce des céréales,* pp. 339–40n.

gists claimed it signified.[41] There emerged a genre of flour trader whose base was not in the mills but in the marketplaces and in the inns. These traders bought grain, farmed it out to be ground (as bakers might do), and then sold it to bakers. I suspect that most of them originally came from mills or milling families, toward which they were inclined to revert. Others came from the grain trade, alert to the changing patterns of commerce, or from agriculture (among the most highly commercialized peasants and fermiers), or from the secondary and tertiary trades in the provisioning nexus. These non-flour-manufacturing merchants found it hard to compete with the strong miller-merchants in the eighteenth century, and for that reason tended to merge with their rivals. Or, as simple intermediaries, they fell into debt to the millers who sold them flour and were more or less absorbed or liquidated by them.[42] The nonmilling flour merchants who prospered were more like brokers than traders. Mabille, Ballet, and Company, for example, obtained the bulk of its flour from other flour merchants and dealers instead of buying grain itself. Ballet was a former farinier who later called himself a banker and Mabille had once been a miller.[43] With the technological improvements introduced by economic milling in the second half of the eighteenth century, the operations of the small nonmilling mealmen who obtained coarse flour and bolted it at home became increasingly anachronistic and costly.[44]

In terms of business practices, types of clients, and style of life, commercially oriented millers and flour merchants supplying the capital were virtually indistinguishable in the eighteenth century.[45] The mill was the lodestone of activity as well as the nursery of recruitment of the flour trade. Yet even as the flour trade eclipsed the grain trade, the two became increasingly blurred. On the one side, flour traders such as Jean-Louis Lebegue of Neuilly, Dumony of Châtillon, Meusnier of Choisy-le-Roy, Gilles of Pontoise, Pierre Chanon of Etampes, and Luc Mergerie of Paris did not hesitate to change their *qualité* to "merchant of flour and grain."[46] On the other side, the flour

41. Wrote the subsistence specialist Daure, an enemy of both the development of the flour trade and the propagation of economic milling: "They are a species of useless persons who established themselves on the negligence of the millers and bakers in doing their work for them." "Mémoire," ca. 1771, AN, F[11] 264. Cf. the similar perspective of a Paris police agent assigned to Beaumont. Doubleau to Hérault, 8 October 1725, Arsenal, ms. Bast. 10270, fol. 203.

42. See the case of Dufoy, miller at the Mill of the Little Calf, v. Lorain, flour dealer at Villejuif. Archives Seine-Paris, D2B[6] 1128, 10 December 1773.

43. AN, Y 12611, 25 May 1762; declarations, 9 February 1771, AD Seine-et-Marne, baillage de Meaux, unclassified.

44. On these bolting mealmen, see AN, MC, XX-559, 5 October 1756 (Falentin), and LXI-422, 30 July 1744 (Aubin).

45. On the interchangeability of "qualities" in notarial code, see, for instance, AN, MC, X-619, 31 May 1770 (Guesnée). See also the discussion of business failure below, where I develop the argument for considering these millers and mealmen as a single group.

46. AN, MC, LXXXV-529, 19 August 1751, and the following references from Archives

trade attracted new recruits as grain traders got the message and began to diversify their dealings.[47] Laurent Leclerc, "raised in the grain trade by his mother, the widow of Charles Leclerc, former grain merchant," gradually shifted to flour and became a regular supplier of the Halle before the end of the sixties.[48] Grain trader Antoine Malisset, revealing the genius his family had for sensing the main chance, switched to flour in the early fifties and bought a mill at Corbeil, where another Malisset built a milling empire in the sixties.[49] Dolivier of Etampes was one of the discrete dealers who continued to list himself as a grain merchant—a shrewd decision that surely facilitated his purchases—even though he clearly specialized in furnishing flour.[50] Another was forain grain dealer Guillaume Grand, who owned two mills near Senlis.[51] Grain dealers Guillaume Desmarre of the Provins area and Nicolas Florantin of Bièvres both announced that they would provide clients with either grain or flour.[52] Michel Beauvallet was one of a number of grain dealers who greatly expanded the waterborne shipment of flour to the Grève (whence it was ordinarily transferred to the Halle for sale).[53]

The flour trade lured men from other professions, many of which were directly connected to the flour and grain business. Some of them became full-time mealmen, but the majority exercised two professions simultaneously. Among the flour merchants drawn from agriculture were laboureurs Pierre Soret and Louis Couturier of Santeuil-en-Vexin; Louis Lameret, owner of 80 arpents planted in wheat near Dampierre; Zachary Bulte of Picardy; Adrien Godard of Mesnil-Aubry.[54] At least a dozen of the mealmen who registered for the grain trade at Pontoise at the end of 1770 were laboureurs.[55] Thomas Devaux used to be a fermier in the St.-Denis area, where the flour traffic was interrupted every year at planting time because most of the mealmen were laboureurs.[56] Following in the footsteps of the Melun baker-traders whose

---

Seine-Paris: D4B[6] 95-6623, 24 January 1786 (Genard-Lebègue); D5B[6] 3883, 1775–77; D6B[6], carton 6, 1 April 1773 (rapport arbitre); D5B[6] 5234 (Tupin-Gilles); D2B[6] 798, 17 June 1746.

47. See the analogies with the English movement from grain to flour. F. J. Fisher, "The Development of the London Food Market, 1540–1640," *Economic History Review* 5, no. 2 (April 1935): 61.

48. Petition to procurator general, ca. October 1770, BN, Coll. Joly 1151, fol. 29.

49. AN, MC, XXXIX-488, 15 June 1751.

50. Rapport arbitre, 14 August 1757, Archives Seine-Paris, D6B[6], carton 3.

51. Petition to procurator general, ca. January 1739, BN, Coll. Joly 1119, fol. 37; Archives Seine-Paris, D2B[6] 736, 28 April 1741.

52. Archives Seine-Paris, D4B[6] 100-7066, 8 February 1788, and D4B[6] 79-5294, 26 January 1781 (Quirot).

53. AN, Z[1H] 449, 1 October 1765.

54. Archives Seine-Paris, D4B[6] 83-5559, 10 December 1781, and D4B[6] 63-4036, 17 May 1777; AN, Y 11220, 29 December 1732, 9 January and 3 February 1733, and Y 13100, 21 March 1747 (*scellé* Hetru).

55. AD Seine-et-Oise, 12 B 720.

56. Archives Seine-Paris, D4B[6] 68-4498, and Benardière to lieutenant general of police, 28 September 1725, Arsenal, ms. Bast. 10270.

"paradoxical" trade fascinated Delamare at the end of the seventeenth century, a number of bakers speculated in flour in between *fournées:* Lerouge of Gonesse; Picot of Versailles; Mathurin Lameret of Dampierre, whose brother Louis was a laboureur-mealman; Claude Jubé of St.-Germain-en-Laye; and Jean-Louis Longpré of Belleville.[57]

In the first half of the century, bran merchants like Jean Dolancourt were as a rule petty traders whose dealings in bread-making flour were sporadic at best.[58] The growth of the middling trade, however, made it possible to mix large-scale bran and flour commerce. Morice of St.-Denis and Dure of Paris dealt in bran, flour, and grain at the same time, serving a staggering range of clients: other flour and grain dealers, bakers, brewers, starch makers, and livestock raisers.[59] Another logical combination was carting and flour trading, since a horse and a wagon were essential for meal dealing. A driver named Bourgeois was probably introduced to the flour trade by his wife, who worked for the brokers at the Halle.[60] Desrues, Doucet, and Jublet took on other freight when their flour business lagged, or speculated in flour when their carting business slackened.[61] François Hyaut was a professional pig raiser as well as a flour merchant, a classic sideline for millers.[62] Quevanne, a flour dealer at Versailles, sold roast pig and other cooked meats, yet the connection here is much less clear.[63] The shift from innkeeping, which often involved a grain brokerage and storage role, to flour dealing was easy for Jean-Marie Mouchy of Bourg-la-Reine.[64] Even certain nobles, skilled grain traders, made the conversion to flour. The marquis of St.-Marc from the Etampes area built his own mill and furnished the Paris Halle in flour.[65]

Self-styled fariniers occupied an ambiguous position in the eyes of the authorities for many years—perhaps until the 1760s—because they did not easily fit the established categories. On the one hand, flour merchants were to be assimilated to millers and thus suffer all the stigmas and restrictions that attached to that craft. Yet one became a flour merchant, at least in part, precisely to escape the stigma of the miller's image and the confines of the police code. His trade required the mealman, if he was a miller, to break the law, for millers were strictly forbidden from buying grain. His interest prompted the flour trader, miller or not, to break the law by serving as buying

57. AN, Y 9441, 26 August 1740, and the following from Archives Seine-Paris: D4B° 82-5476; D4B⁶ 83-5559, 10 December 1781; D4B⁶ 62-3958, February 1777; D4B⁶ 48-2869, 5 July 1773.

58. AN, Y 11219, 2 September 1732.

59. Ibid., D5B⁶ 531 and 3245.

60. Ibid., D2B⁶ 802, 17 October 1746.

61. Archives Seine-Paris, D5B⁶ 5234 (Tupin register), and AN, Y 11220, 5 January 1733, and Y 9539, 6 September 1765.

62. Archives Seine-Paris, D5B⁶ 4385.

63. Ibid., D2B⁶ 841, 28 January 1750.

64. Ibid., D4B⁶ 92-6394, 17 February 1785.

65. Arsenal, ms. Bast. 10141, fol. 262 (16 October 1759).

agents for bakers (a way of cultivating a clientele) or purchasing grain off the market (in order to compete with the grain merchants). The flour merchants met stiff resistance from the Paris-licensed grain dealers and their commissionnaires, who quite rightly saw them as a grave threat to their commerce.[66] The local police in the hinterland favored the claims of the grain merchants, who tried to exclude the mealmen both from the markets and the farms.[67] At Troyes, for instance, flour entrepreneur Belly, encouraged by controller-general Bertin and counseled by expert miller Bucquet, found himself constantly harassed by the town police, "prejudiced against the flour trade in general."[68] The flour merchants based their case on the contribution that they could make to the provisioning of the capital and to the renaissance of the Halle, a matter especially dear to the Paris police. Despite gnawing doubts about their hybrid character, the lieutenant general provided them with "letters of authorization" to facilitate their buying expeditions and improved the conditions for transacting business in the capital.[69] As a mark of their commitment and also as a lever for their commercial dealings, many mealmen adopted the title "flour merchant for the provisioning of Paris."[70]

How the Flour Merchants Provisioned Paris

Flour merchants marketed their meal in three ways. First, they shipped it en droiture directly to their baker clients, bypassing the Halle. The police detested this traffic because it eluded their surveillance and failed to contribute in an orderly fashion to the price-making mechanism of the market. The police also charged, not without some justification, that droiture traffic invited frauds in country grain purchasing. Inspector Poussot campaigned tirelessly to discourage bakers and mealmen from dealing in this direct fashion. So did the measurers and porters, though their motivation was infinitely less disinterested: they set traps for droiture transactions in order to make sure they received their fees. It is impossible to estimate the magnitude of this "commercial" droiture traffic. It was conflated with grain and flour entries

66. Cf. the attack of a Nantes grain trader on Parmentier's brief for the promotion of the flour trade. The merchant reacted with hostility to Parmentier "for fear of seeing his commercial speculations overturned" by the competition from flour. "Mémoire to the Estates of Brittany," 1784, AD Ille-et-Vilaine, C 1710.

67. See, for instance, Arsenal, ms. Bast. 10141, fols. 328, 332 (12, 19 March 1760) and Doubleau to Hérault, 26 November 1725, ms. Bast. 10271. Cf. Narbonne, *Louis XIV et Louis XV,* p. 137.

68. "Mémoire historique de l'émeute arrivée au marché du bled de Troyes le 5 mai 1770," AD Aube, C 1908.

69. Missonnet report, 17 September 1751, BN, Coll. Joly 1112, fol. 5; Arsenal, ms. Bast. 10141, fol. 332 (19 March 1760).

70. Archives Seine-Paris, D2B⁶ 841, 12 January 1750 (Fournier), and AN, Y 9440, 18 December 1739 (Cheron).

undertaken by bakers themselves, and there is a strong likelihood that a significant amount entered the capital clandestinely. Mealman droiture traffic certainly increased markedly between 1730 and 1760. Its growth may have been slowed by the opening in 1759 of a weight station at the Halle, which provided a more hospitable and efficient concourse of exchange.[71]

The two other marketing techniques were quite visible. Some mealmen accompanied their flour to the Halle and sold it personally. Usually they were assigned regular "places" by the measurers, who feared that otherwise they would circulate in search of clients and interrupt the broker market.[72] These freelancers were also known to conduct business in the cafés and taverns around the Halle.[73] A large number of merchants shipped their merchandise to a broker who, for a fee, assumed the responsibility for selling it, collecting the price from the bakers, and fulfilling administrative obligations. Brokerage theoretically spared the merchant the burden of traveling to Paris and worrying about sales. Yet many merchants came to the Halle anyway, either because they did not fully trust their agents or because they wanted "to work" the clientele themselves. Jean Daubigny of Beaumont came to look over the shoulder of his broker Delaroche.[74] Mealmen Foiret and Rimbet, represented by Mabille, visited "their bakers" each week to assure themselves of their fidelity.[75] Flour merchants who could not read or write or who did not know how to keep books often turned to brokers to manage their affairs and spare them difficulties they might encounter in disputes with clients over money due or flour delivered.[76] Certain flour merchants sold directly to the bakers and collected their own accounts receivable, but used the brokers as bankers and as connections for grain purchases.[77] Michel Bethmont of Gonesse hired broker Aubert, but simultaneously sold on his own to bakers at the Halle and by droiture.[78] Merchant-miller François Hyaut signed with broker Viollet,

71. The very incomplete figures we have for registered flour arrivals at the Halle in 1759–60 do not suggest a higher level of supply than that which had been attained three decades earlier—around 20,000 sacks. If this is the case, then droiture traffic must have continued to expand, because we know that the proportion of flour in the total provisioning picture continued to grow. Sartine to procurator general, 4 June 1760, AN, Y 9500. Unless rich new sources are unearthed, we are likely never to be able to follow precisely the curve of flour provisioning.

72. AN, Y 11226, 3 September 1739, and Y 11223, 27 October 1736.

73. AN, Y 11384, 2 March 1771, and Y 12607, 22 January 1759.

74. AN, Y 11226, 3 September 1739.

75. Sandrin to consular jurisdiction, 17 June 1774, Archives Seine-Paris, D6B⁶, carton 7.

76. Archives Seine-Paris, D4B⁶ 43-2415, 22 July 1777 (Chastellain) and measurers to consular jurisdiction, 21 January 1761, D6B⁶, carton 3 (Gassot); AN, MC, XX-559, 5 October 1756 (Falentin); AN, F¹² 716, 24 May 1771 (Ballet, Mabille v. Givry). On their failure to keep books, see also Archives Seine-Paris, D4B⁶ 55-3480, 5 August 1775.

77. Sandrin to consular jurisdiction, 17 June 1774, Archives Seine-Paris, D6B⁶, carton 7.

78. Ibid., D4B⁶ 58-3733, 10 July 1776.

yet continued to handle most of his sales to bakers on his own.[79] There were
flour merchants like Ducler, who stuck faithfully with broker Delaroche for
thirty years, and there were other dealers like Bucquet and Rolland who used
as many as three brokers at once and shipped directly to bakers as well.[80]

Relations between freelance mealmen and the brokers were often marked
by distrust and animosity. The independents charged the brokers with unfair
trading practices, such as bribing bakers to buy from them with pratik bonuses of two or three bushels per delivery.[81] Pierre Chevalier appears to have
been one of several gagne-deniers at the Halle secretly employed by the
brokers to induce bakers to scorn the independents. The wife of flour dealer
La Forest complained that Chevalier and his wife tried to drive away prospective clients by expressing aloud "contempt for her merchandise," charging
maliciously that she was known for trying to pass off dark flour for white. The
pair warned her to expect this sort of abuse every day until "she was forced to
abandon the Paris Halle," and even threatened to harm her physically.[82]

Bitter feelings also erupted between brokers and alienated mealmen-
clients. After fifteen years of close pratik ties with broker Dame Dominer,
widow flour merchant Aubin switched to Dame Ballet. Since that date, Aubin
complained to the police, "the said Dominer has done everything in her power
to destroy the plaintiff's business." She spread defaming rumors against Aubin and dispatched placeboys to talk her clients into switching to Dominer.[83]
According to broker Pierre Girard, his feud with merchant-miller Louitier of
Vallière-en-Vexin began one day when Louitier's wife gratuitously impugned
the quality of the flour belonging to the other mealmen who constituted
Girard's clientele. When in retaliation Girard refused to continue handling the
Louitiers' merchandise, they riposted with a veritable campaign of denigration aimed at persuading his other clients to abandon him. A dozen flour
dealers testified that the Louitiers urged them to boycott Girard on the
grounds that he was "a rogue, a thief, a *cartouchien*, a knave who was marked
on the shoulder [as a convicted felon]." Do not learn the lesson the hard way
as we and other victims of Girard's dishonesty have, the Louitiers exhorted
their colleagues: sell on your own. The Louitiers even refused to grind wheat
belonging to mealmen who continued to use Girard. The Louitiers' reprisal
was brutally effective, for the broker lost a number of his best clients and
expected further defections.[84] On the whole, such spectacular gestures of
solidarity were rather rare among the mealmen—even those of the same

79. Ibid., D5B⁶ 4385.
80. Ibid., D4B⁶ 68-4429, June 1778, and D5B⁶ 5655.
81. See, for example, the Pontoise memorandum, 21 December 1731, Arsenal, ms. Bast.
10271. Their struggle against the brokers persisted well into the nineteenth century: BHVP,
ms. série 114 (ca. 1840).
82. AN, Y 9538, 27 June 1724.
83. AN, Y 11238, 2 April 1751.
84. AN, Y 11220, 29 December 1732 and 3 February 1733.

TABLE 23

Flour supply, Paris Halle (1725–33)

Year	Brokers	Merchants selling through brokers	Total amount of flour (brokered and independent) in muids
1725*	18	257	19,621
1726*	20	204	18,065
1727	21	191	20,492
1728	20	194	21,830
1729	22	195	20,523
1730	31	211	19,741
1731	17	165	20,214
1732	19	159	22,006
1733	17	144	22,067

*dearth years

pays—who relished the opportunity to profit from the tribulations of a rival.

The only aggregate figures we have on flour provisioning cover the period 1725–33 (see Table 23).

The crisis of 1725 marshaled an unusually large number of dealers. The decline in the number of merchants was due to the favorable subsistence "conjuncture" of the early thirties. While the brokered merchants increased their average annual provision from 89.7 muids in 1727 to 126.4 muids in 1733, a burgeoning corps of freelancers—flour forains and blatiers—took charge of marketing their own flour. These independents, whose number is not indicated in the entry registers, accounted for 16 percent of the flour supply in 1727 and 17.5 percent in 1733. Sometimes they sold grain as well as meal, and to retail customers as well as to bakers. They were also much more likely to deal off the market than the merchants using brokers.[85] The range of brokered merchants' supply was sweeping, varying from 12 muids a year (72 sacks) to 520 muids (3,120 sacks). In 1733, 17.4 percent of the brokered merchants came from Paris and the environs, 12.5 percent from Beaumont, 11.8 percent from Presles, 5.6 percent from Pontoise, 4.2 percent from Chambly, 3.4 percent from Persan (43 percent were of unknown domicile). The Pontoise-Beaumont-Chambly-Presles-Persan district dispatched the largest number of brokered merchants to the Halle in 1779.

Flour dealers such as miller Eustache Lecercle of Pontoise, who furnished

85. See Morice of St.-Denis, Archives Seine-Paris, D5B⁶ 3245. For an example of a blatier type bringing six sacks to market on six asses, see Cleret to lieutenant general, 11 December 1725, Arsenal, ms. Bast. 10271.

over 2,500 sacks a year, ranked among the leading suppliers.[86] More common was a merchant like Nicolas Roze, who appears to have lived in Paris and who sold through broker Pilloy. During the four years covered by his business registers, from October 1759 to September 1763, he sold 648 sacks, 803 sacks, 1,055 sacks, and 1,084 sacks respectively, or an average of 75 sacks a month, barely enough to keep two bakers going. During the first two years, the only period for which the names of his clients were listed, Roze conducted 139 separate transactions with thirty-two different bakers. His enterprise was growing: in 1759–60 he averaged 5.4 transactions a month (54 sacks), while in 1762–63 he conducted 8.3 a month (90.3 sacks). Even in 1762–63, however, he did only 33,489 livres' worth of business.[87]

The Flour Merchants and the Bakers

Flour dealers often had close and fruitful pratik-type relationships with the Paris bakers. They met at the Epée de Bois, the Croix Dorée, and other taverns, not only to do business but to gossip and relax.[88] They served as witnesses at the weddings of each other's children or siblings and as god-fathers and tutors for each other's children. While the mealmen extended credit to the bakers in the normal course of events, on occasion the bakers lent the mealmen money to help them out at a difficult juncture.[89] They represented each other in the consular court, even at the risk of alienating colleagues who were parties to the suit.[90] Together they contrived schemes to sneak droiture flour, sometimes made from illicitly acquired wheat, past the market officers.[91]

Contracts were habitually oral, a common practice in commercial exchanges of all sorts. The oral contract seemed to be a guarantee of a sustained mutual relationship, for it was embedded in a sociability that was frequently confirmed and publicly witnessed. It was also a gesture of mutual respect and trust. The moral sanctions for defying the oral contract were far more crushing than the strictly legal ones attendant upon written agreements. If the oral transactions had been reserved for a miller's (or a baker's) preferred partners, as a mark of a special bond, they might have been more powerful welders of reciprocity. The oral contract's ritual content was diluted and cheapened,

86. AN, O*¹ 399, fols. 117–18, 3 March 1757.

87. Archives Seine-Paris, D5B⁶ 5083.

88. AN, Y 13741, 24 December 1740; Y 12605, 18 November 1757; Y 11384, 2 March 1771; Y 12604, 12 August 1756.

89. See, for instance, the widow Leger's relations to Provendier and Chenart in Archives Seine-Paris, D4B⁶ 25-1306, 9 September 1763, and D4B⁶ 24-1249, 1 September 1763.

90. Archives Seine-Paris, D2B⁶ 1103, 8 November 1771 (baker Deschard standing in for flour merchant Mabille).

91. BN, Coll. Joly 1829, fol. 296.

however, by the fact that most millers and bakers used it with virtually everyone with whom they did business. The supreme sign of confidence, often
bitterly regretted by both sides after a falling-out, was the refusal to exchange
receipts for delivery of and payment for goods. My impression is that most
sellers and buyers did ask for receipts, even at the risk of undermining the
deep sense of the oral engagement.[92]

Miller-merchants such as François Hyaut and Nicolas Roze must have
derived great satisfaction from the fidelity of most of "their" bakers. Con-
versely, the merchants sometimes took baker defections very badly. Mealman
Tierce sent his flour boys to beat up a mistress-baker for having left his fold.[93]
The flour dealers worked very hard first to win and then to retain the allegiance of the bakers. We have already noted that mealmen, both freelance
and brokered, courted their clients regularly. To recruit new customers,
Genty of St.-Germain-en-Laye scoured the twelve bread markets on Wednesdays and Saturdays.[94] Some mealmen befriended measurers in the hope that
they could direct bakers their way (while other flour merchants complained
that the measurers favored the bakers in all their transactions).[95] Lejeune of
Gouvieux tried to constitute his personal clientele by inducing bakers whom
he met through his broker, Dame Barbier, to abandon her and deal directly
with him.[96] In order to please his clients, François Cheron of Valmondois
accepted derisory down payments on merchandise delivered.[97] If the merchant pressed too hard for payment, he risked losing the client definitively
and perhaps the sum due as well. When merchant Letellier of Versailles
refused any further flour without earnest money, master baker Rousseau
erupted in a torrent of abuse.[98] Fourcret reserved his best flour for the bakers

92. This casual informality between millers and bakers persisted into the second half of
the nineteenth century. *Enquête sur la boulangerie,* p. 638.

93. Archives Seine-Paris, D5B[6] 4385 and D5B[6] 5083; AN, Y 15929, 20 October 1727. Cf.
Tierce's verbal assault on a former client in AN, Y 11219, 27 June 1732. See also the colorful
fury of twentieth-century miller Marcel Barbier whose client Laure deserted him in favor of
his friend and rival miller Riqui. One day Riqui's mill lost a wing and Laure offered her
custom to Barbier (in extremis):

> Ah non, ah non!
> Pourquoué non?
> Tu m'as changé pour venir chez Riqui, tu vas y rester, qui'i tourne ou
> qu'i tourne pas, je m'en fous.

Finally Barbier agreed to grind her grain, but she abandoned him again once Riqui was back
in action. When Riqui's mill broke down yet again, Laure did not scruple to seek out
Barbier, who exploded: "Tu m'prends tout à fait pour un con . . . tu sais pus ou aller, eh ben,
j'vas t'envoyer chier, allez fout moué l'camp que j'te voye pus!" *Marcel Barbier: Meunier,*
p. 247.

94. Rapport arbitre, 20 August 1774, Archives Seine-Paris, D6B[6], carton 7.

95. Arsenal, ms. Bast. 10271 (21 December 1725).

96. AN, Y 12608, 31 March 1760.

97. AN, Y 9440, 18 December 1739.

98. AN, Y 13516, 13 July 1757.

who were not quite decided on their suppliers.[99] It is likely that the mealmen, like the brokers, also offered extra-measure (or bonus-weight) incentives to favored bakers. Mealmen privileged their regulars with slightly lower than going prices for the same quality merchandise, sometimes in the form of rebates.[100] A standing invitation to drink was not the least of the pratik concessions that they tendered.

Bakers quarreled with their flour suppliers when they felt betrayed on price or quality. Master baker Louy contracted with mealwoman Léger to receive 60 sacks at a set price. After delivering only the first 20 sacks, Léger abjured the bargain—according to Louy, because the market price had suddenly increased and she did not want to sacrifice the increment that she would have made had she not committed herself in advance to a large provision. Louy had made a shrewd deal and did not want to be penalized by having to buy the flour he needed at the higher price.[101] Similarly, merchant Matturin Genty of St.-Germain-en-Laye promised to sell forain baker Jean Pelletier, whose business he had courted with ardor, twelve sacks of white flour at 47 livres the sack. But when the price rose sharply over the next week, Genty denied that the deal had ever been arranged.[102] In both cases, the bakers sued for fulfillment of contract plus damages and costs.

If the bakers felt that they were likely to obtain satisfaction in a dispute over quality of merchandise, they filed suit in the commercial court (juridiction consulaire) as they would for any other "recovery" contest. If, however, they anticipated resistance, they often went to the police, since bad-quality provision was a crime of public interest as well as an act of commercial fraud. They believed that pressure from the police would result in a much prompter settlement. The administrators of the baker guild, convoked by the consular jurisdiction to examine the fourteen sacks of flour that a Versailles dealer sold to a master baker, declared that it was "of very bad quality," that it had "a very bad taste," and that "it was not honest merchandise."[103] Before the same court master baker Sulpice Garin demonstrated, with expert testimony, that twenty sacks of flour that he had purchased from Melun dealer Jacques Thuin were "defective and incapable of being used."[104] Incensed that he had been brazenly "robbed," master baker François Deline filed a complaint with the police against a Versailles merchant named Maugras for having wetted down (and entirely ruined) two sacks of flour in order to increase their weight. Deline's mistake was that he purchased the flour without having inspected it. Maugras allowed that "he didn't give a damn about the justice of Paris or of

99. BN, Coll. Joly 1829, fol. 278 (1752).

100. Archives Seine-Paris, D5B⁶ 5217 and 4385. Brokers may have practiced differential pricing. See the business books of Delaroche, D5B⁶ 5655, 753, 305.

101. Ibid., D4B⁶ 20-985.

102. Rapport arbitre, 20 August 1774, ibid., D6B⁶, carton 7.

103. Rapport arbitre, 11 June 1761, ibid., D6B⁶, carton 3.

104. Ibid., D2B⁶ 813, 11 September 1747, and D6B⁶, carton 2, 8 August 1746.

Versailles."[105] It was not uncommon for bakers on the brink of ruin to blame their fall on "rotten flour" supplied by unscrupulous mealmen.[106] It is impossible to document these often vague charges. But if flour merchants were such easy scapegoats, it was in large part their own fault.

The inability and, in some cases, the unwillingness of bakers to meet their obligations jeopardized the operations of millers and flour merchants. Numerous merchants were driven to file for failure. As part of their everyday business activities, they had to devote an inordinate amount of time, energy, and money to the task of recovering accounts receivable from bakers. As a rule, flour deals were sealed by a down payment that ranged from a quarter to half of the purchase price. Bakers sometimes negotiated longer terms, but generally full payment was due a month after delivery, even in the warmest pratik relationships. After vainly summoning delinquent bakers to pay, miller-merchants usually turned to the consular jurisdiction to sue for condemnation. The consular court was attractive because it was run not by magistrates but by merchants who understood the ways of commerce, and because in theory it cost very little to obtain justice. Yet even if court expenses were modest and ordinarily paid by the loser, the plaintiff had to go to court, often from quite a distance, or delegate a family member or friend, or hire a procurator. Once a sentence was rendered, it had to be served on the condemned baker. In some cases the civil sheriffs (huissiers) hired to serve the sentences also provided their clients with lodging.[107]

Even after a baker was served with a *condamnation à corps* that threatened arrest and seizure of property, he often found ways, legal and extralegal, to delay execution. Miller-merchants on occasion found themselves obliged to hunt down bakers in hiding, fend off infuriated baker-wives whose legal obligation vis-à-vis their husbands' debts was often ambiguous, or hire counsel for confrontation in a court of appeal. The most exasperating cases concern baker-widows who "renounced" their husbands' estates because they were insolvent and yet continued their husbands' businesses without paying off the old debts. Widow-baker Deline denied any responsibility for the 1,331 livres' (80 setiers) worth of wheat her husband had purchased from grain and flour merchant Jean Guibert of Coulommiers.[108] Widow Constant scoffed at mealman Desrues's claim of 392 livres on the same grounds: it regarded her late husband, not her.[109]

---

105. AN, Y 15601, 6 January 1741. Baker Bernier's fury against flour dealer Flabe ("thief, scoundrel") was probably the result of a similar fraud. AN, Y 15067, 22 September 1734.

106. See, for example, AN, Y 13540, 16 December 1768, and Archives Seine-Paris, D4B[6] 83-5592, 23 September 1783.

107. See, for instance, Archives Seine-Paris, D2B[6] 737, 29 May 1741, D2B[6] 736, 17 April 1741, and D7B[6] 337, 16 January 1750.

108. Ibid., D2B[6] 1009, 9 January 1764.

109. Ibid., D2B[6] 841, 15 January 1750. Desrues pursued Constant for over three years. See D7B[6] 337, 16 January 1750.

TABLE 24
Baker debts to millers and flour merchants for
flour (in livres)

	Before 1750	After 1750
Mean	428	782
Median	290	708
N =	33	25

The sums at stake were quite significant. For fifty-eight cases, the average owed by a baker to a miller-merchant was 580 livres.[110] It was not uncommon for a miller or mealman to face three or four delinquent bakers at a time, in addition to brokers representing other bakers and other flour buyers such as pastry makers. Amounts due by bakers after 1750 were significantly larger than debts contracted in the first half of the century (see Table 24). Prices were generally higher in the second half of the century, but it is also possible that bakers were buying in larger lots. Some dealers seem unreasonably precipitate in turning to the court, but they knew more about their clients' character than we do. Etienne Denise of Beaumont waited barely three weeks before suing widow-baker Loriset of Paris for 20,003 livres.[111] Nicolas Noret of Charenton similarly showed less than a month's patience toward his neighbor, baker Guiton of the faubourg St.-Antoine, who owed him almost 1,000 livres.[112]

On the average, however, the miller-merchants gave their clients up to seven and a half months before filing suit. They were sometimes compelled to take rather impetuous action by their own suppliers, who took them to court. Three-way suits were not unusual: miller Augustin Vieuxbled, pursued by laboureur Jacques Lecler for payment of 345 livres in wheat, sued baker Vassou of the faubourg St.-Antoine (and by so doing avowed that he was the baker's buying agent, a commission that was against the law).[113] Sued by a Brie laboureur named Gibert, miller Touroux had baker Claude Ver of Nouvelle France condemned to pay 232 livres remaining on a huge transaction of 64 muids.[114] Aggressive Etienne Denise went a step beyond most of his confreres by filing suit not only against baker widow Loriset but against the consumers who owed her money. He agreed to drop the suit—which caused Loriset considerable embarrassment as a result of her inability to protect her

110. For the sources for baker debts to flour dealers, see Appendix G.
111. Archives Seine-Paris, D2B⁶ 736, 10 April 1741.
112. Ibid., 19 April 1741. In the mid-nineteenth century, millers expected to be paid three to four weeks after delivery. *Enquête sur la boulangerie,* pp. 230, 331.
113. Archives Seine-Paris, D2B⁶ 809, 10 May 1747.
114. Ibid., D2B⁶ 1128, 1 December 1773.

customers from harassment—only after she signed a promise, backed by her son's bond, to reimburse him at the rate of 100 livres a month.[115]

If a baker failed to appear, he was almost invariably condemned *à corps*. Outright default of this sort was not common. Bakers had incentives to be present. If they made a reasonably convincing case, the court might postpone judgment pending clarification (e.g., examination of their books), or send them before an *arbitre*. A master grocer, for example, was able to arrange an out-of-court settlement between a Pontoise mealman and a master baker.[116] When a baker or his representative appeared, he had a good chance of obtaining remission of interest charges that would normally accrue. By agreeing to repay in two installments, widow baker Duclos won forgiveness of penalty from miller Horn.[117] Finally, by arguing his case, a baker had the opportunity to contest the figures presented by his suppliers. Master baker Martin Chantard insisted that he had already paid in full the 192 livres claimed by merchant-miller Jacques Denis of Epernon.[118] He did not convince the court. On the other hand, it supported Vincennes baker Mosny, who contended that he owed miller Noret 237 rather than 318 livres.[119]

Flour by Weight

Transactions at the Halle and ports were mediated by the *officiers mesureurs* and the *officiers porteurs*. They were supposed to facilitate exchanges, and to prevent frauds and manipulations on price, quantity, and quality that were often subsumed under the rubric "monopoly." They were also venal officeholders who had a vested interest in each transaction, for they collected fees for their usually obligatory service. Their utility, as well as their honesty and competence, were sharply questioned by many of the persons whose professional conduct they scrutinized, especially the bakers and the flour merchants. Grain had always been *measured* for sale; the same process of sale by volume was extended to flour, which in the beginning was infinitely less important a commodity. Measurers and porters both had a stake in flour measuring: the latter "broke" the flour from the sack into the measuring receptacle and the former verified the actual measuring procedure. Since they had always handled grain in this fashion, they saw no reason not to continue, despite the fact that flour did not present the same physical characteristics as grain. They hinted that the critics of this system were merely

115. AN, MC, XXXV-626, 18 August 1741.
116. Archives Seine-Paris, D6B[6], carton 3 and D2B[6] 950, 9 February 1759.
117. Ibid., D2B[6] 841, 21 January 1750.
118. Ibid., D2B[6] 801, 7 September 1746.
119. Ibid., D2B[6] 802, 7 October 1746. Cf. the fury of the miller of the Frau when his "jean-foutre de boulanger" renounced his flour debt of 40 pistoles by going out of business. Le Roy, *Moulin du Frau,* p. 483.

seeking an opportunity to elude their inspection in order to cheat the public.[120]

Nearby markets such as Versailles and St.-Germain-en-Laye, however, had begun to sell flour on weight. Bakers were lured to these markets even when flour at the Halle was the same price because, reported a police official, "they get a much better deal by weight than by bushel [volume]."[121] The measurers tried vigorously to prevent Paris bakers from buying at Versailles, on the legally unimpeachable grounds that it was located within the taboo eight-league radius. The police commissaire responsible for the Halle reacted with ambivalence: he understood the baker motivation, but feared that Versailles could grow only at the expense of the Paris central market. So powerful was baker pressure to buy at Versailles that the authorities ended up tolerating such purchases, which were formally permitted in the late thirties.[122]

In 1725, with the idea of taking advantage of a leverage that dearth conditions appeared to give them, a large number of flour merchants and millers joined to petition the lieutenant general of police "to order that their flour be sold on weight at the Halle as it is in Versailles and St.-Germain because of the losses they suffer on the measuring of the flour." They suggested that such an establishment would "enable them to make great efforts for the supplying of Paris."[123] Judging by the success of the Versailles weight system, the predictions of increased supply were not purely demagogic. Farmed out for only 8,000 livres in 1728, the Versailles market drew so many buyers and sellers that ten years later the concession to operate it was worth 20,000 livres.[124]

The Pontoise group continued to agitate for a weight regime and their demands acquired increasing force as the flour trade grew apace in the next thirty years. In 1737 a group of flour merchants based at Melun argued in a petition that "weight is the standard the whole world over" because it was more just and more efficient. The king insisted on trading by weight when he contracted for the army, the merchants reminded the Paris authorities, and the hospitals did the same thing.[125] Encouraged by Poussot, the police inspector determined to breathe new life and order into the Halle, two flour merchants named Coppin and Poilleux prepared a series of memoranda that made a strongly favorable impression on the senior commissaire of the central

120. Apparently King Jean had established a weighing station for grain in the fourteenth century, but it is not clear whether it functioned for long. BN, ms. fr. 21636, fol. 350.

121. Regnier to lieutenant general, 29 August 1725, Arsenal, ms. Bast. 10271. Cf. AD Seine-et-Oise, 2 B 1145.

122. BN, Coll. Joly 62, fols. 252–66 (ca. 1728). Chartres also sold on weight, as of what date we do not know. Police sentence, 2 April 1768, AD Eure-et-Loir, B 3953, fol. 67.

123. Cleret to lieutenant general, 16 October, 9 November 1725, Arsenal, ms. Bast. 10270, and Cleret to lieutenant general, 27 October 1725, ms. Bast. 10272.

124. "Mémoire sur l'établissement d'un poids à la halle de Paris," AN, F[11] 265.

125. BN, Coll. Joly 1314, fol. 38.

market department, Machurin, and on the lieutenant general of police. In March of 1758 thirty-nine flour merchants, supported by the baker guild, formally asked the Paris Parlement to authorize a sweeping reform of the flour sales system to be built around a weight procedure.[126]

The merchants rested their case frankly on the grounds of the losses that measuring unjustly forced them to suffer. The experience of an Essonnes miller named Guibout typified their complaints. Each of the eleven sacks of white flour he brought to the Halle, he insisted, should have yielded 26 bushels. The measurers obtained only 24 bushels, however, thereby causing him a loss of one-thirteenth. In these circumstances, Guibout concluded, "it would be impossible for him to continue to supply the Halle of Paris with flour."[127]

Why did such losses occur? The flour merchants pointed to a number of general principles as well as to certain conditions peculiar to the sales process at the Halle. Weight was a much more constant standard, for it was largely independent of human factors, whereas measuring depended on the skill, strength, and attitude of the measurer. Unlike grain, flour "took all the shapes that one desired to give it." It could be compressed and diminished in volume or it could be made to take double the space by turning and by hand pouring.[128] Poussot contended that evaporation during measuring alone could cost the merchant up to 100 muids a year. Flour could be lost as it was "broken" onto the ground or into a container before it was placed in a measuring receptacle. It spilled on the ground or stuck to the bottom. Or it could be siphoned off by a porter, like the one who left several bushels of merchant Denise Bardou's flour in his scooping pail; a bit of graft she resisted, doubtless because it was her first time at the Halle. The porter set her straight by slapping her violently, calling her a *foutue salope,* and threatening to have her broker "chased from the Halle as a tramp, a skum, a wretch."[129] Flour was also removed by the helpers of the porters and the measurers as a tip for their services, and by the flour *gagne-petits* ("mercenaries who inhabit the Halle") on the pretext of offering "dough tests" to prospective buyers. To these considerations, Poussot added another that directly affected the public interest: measuring, he contended, had a retrograde influence on milling technique. In order to obtain maximum volume for measuring, millers ground "lightly" instead of "roundly"—with the stones low or tight instead of high. Round-ground flour yielded more and better bread.[130]

126. BN, Coll. Joly 1312, fol. 47; Arsenal, ms. Bast. 10141, fols. 331–32 (19 March 1760); AN, X^{1B} 3707, 1 February 1759.

127. AN, Y 12607, 26 May 1759. In arguing in favor of the weight system, lieutenant general of police Bertin called this case to the attention of the procurator general. BN, Coll. Joly 1312, fol. 50.

128. "Mémoire sur l'établissement d'un poids à la halle de Paris," AN, F^{11} 265.

129. AN, Y 11226, 3 February 1739.

130. Arsenal, ms. Bast. 10141, fols. 308–9 (20 January 1760); AN, X^{1B} 3691, 2 March

Before acting on the flour merchants' petition, the parlement called upon the lieutenant general of police and the prévôt des marchands to offer their opinions.[131] Lieutenant general Bertin and his successor Sartine urged the parlement to grant the request. They cited the consensus of merchants, bakers, and brokers.[132] They saw the weight system as the only way to end "the abuses" that tainted flour transactions. Above all—this was almost always the decisive police argument—they contended that the reform would "procure a greater abundance for the city of Paris" and at the same time would save the Halle from drying up, as had the ports, as supply markets. Sartine held that the option to measure had to be retained in order to accommodate those whose habits changed slowly. Yet he tacitly proposed to accelerate their evolution by recommending that all sacks, weighed or measured, be subject to the weight station entry fee. Finally, he called for a triple system of registration of quantities and prices that would provide the police with reliable and comprehensive market information.[133]

More or less predictably, given its festering resentment over the displacement of provisioning traffic from the ports to the Halle and its jealousy of the lieutenant of police, protector of the Halle, the municipality stringently criticized the flour merchants' project. Under the device "All innovation is as a rule dangerous," the prévôté contended that had the weight solution been advisable, it would have been initiated centuries earlier. It found the claims of losses—up to 45 livres a *voie,* or shipment—"greatly exaggerated," for had the merchants been losing that much regularly, many of them would already have failed. It expressed sardonic surprise at the inability of the police to repress the petty criminality that plagued the flour dealers. The enormous advantage of measuring, the city fathers asserted, was that it guaranteed quality control. The flour had to be "broken"—emptied entirely from the sack—and thus "seen" and "breathed," by the market officials and the buyers. In the weight system, the flour remained enclosed in the sack with only the top visible. Tube-drawn samples did not assure the buyer that part of the flour was not humid or overheated or the product of a mixing fraud. Collusion between merchants and bakers would result, warned the prévôté. As for the tacit threat that the flour merchants would abandon the Halle and jeopardize

---

1758. The subsistence specialists later called for the weighing of grain as well as flour. Malouin, *Description et détails des arts,* pp. 109–12; Béguillet, *Traité des subsistances,* pp. 306–8.

131. BN, Coll. Joly 1312, fols. 38–41.

132. Chicheret, soon to be named a broker, vigorously supported the weight project. Arsenal, ms. Bast. 10141 (17 January 1758). In their petition the flour merchants sharply criticized the manner in which the brokers customarily turned the measuring process to their advantage. The brokers had reason to worry about the shift to weighing, for the new system might encourage flour merchants to market for themselves.

133. Bertin, 5 April 1758, and Sartine, 4 June 1760, AN, Y 9500; Bertin to procurator general, 30 May 1759, BN, Coll. Joly 1312, fol. 48; AN, X[1B] 3748, 4 June 1761.

the abundance that Paris needed, the municipality did not take it seriously for a minute. The bakers were not eager to travel afar to buy and the merchants wanted their business. In case the Halle did suffer defection, the municipality did not conceal its interest in taking up the slack on the ports where flour had commonly been sold in the seventeenth century.[134]

The parlement issued an arrêt on 30 May 1759 that authorized the establishment of a weight system but refused to suppress measuring, as the flour merchants had asked. The two procedures would coexist, at the risk of "instituting a confusion of authorities." The parlement left the lieutenant general of police with the freedom to work out the specific modalities of the establishment. Ultimately it came to resemble rather closely the organizational model that Coppin and Poilleux had elaborated with Poussot.[135]

A weighing room was erected in the middle of the flour area of the central markets and fitted with two sets of scales and weights (to which two other sets were added after the center opened and the traffic proved much heavier than expected).[136] On Poussot's initiative, Coppin was named director of the weighing station. Though Coppin was "a bit temperamental" and "nervous," the inspector appreciated his mastery of the flour business.[137] The director was to oversee operations and to report infractions on price or quality as well as other suspect behavior to the lieutenant general. It does not appear that he received the formal charge to attempt to arbitrate disputes between buyers and sellers, with the counsel of baker experts and measurers, as the flour merchants had requested. The municipality had objected strenuously to this de facto court on the grounds that it usurped the functions of the other magistrates and created the impression that the ordinary judges were inaccessible to the public. Nevertheless, it was expected that the director would discreetly try to short-circuit litigation and reconcile disputants. The director was also to keep a register of all exchanges. The process was described by a broker:

> The broker sells to the baker on credit or for cash; either way the baker had to go in person to make his declaration of the quantity purchased and the price at the weight station office; or he had to send a declaration signed by him. The director and controller of the weight station register declarations [which included name, address and profession of buyers and sellers as well as price and quantity]. This register then is the record of

134. Deliberations of the bureau of the Hôtel de Ville, 22 May 1758, AN, H* 1867, fols. 430–53, and 26 October 1758, H* 1868, fols. 71–75. I have been unable to locate the comments—obviously very hostile—of the measurers, who were also asked for their opinion on the flour merchant's project.

135. BN, Coll. Joly 1312, fols. 47ff.; "Mémoire sur l'établissement d'un poids à la halle de Paris," AN, F[11] 265; AN, X[1B] 3693, 14 April 1758, and X[1B] 3691, 2 March 1758.

136. Arsenal, ms. Bast. 10141, fols. 242, 322 (17 August 1759 and 25 February 1760); Sartine to procurator general, 4 June 1760, AN, Y 9500.

137. Arsenal, ms. Bast. 10141, fols. 331–32 (19 March 1760).

daily sales made at the Halle and of their price, and it is submitted every day to M. the lieutenant general of police.[138]

Of course the baker could buy directly from a flour merchant without passing through a broker; and the broker and flour merchants were also supposed to file declarations, providing the director with a means of verification. Convinced that information was the source of power and wisdom—especially serial statistical data—Poussot celebrated the service that the register would render to policy makers: "The register will be most useful because during the crises of dearth we shall know the supply capacity of each baker and merchant, and we can use them to determine how much the bakers have in stock and whether the merchants are furnishing the usual quantities."[139]

While the director ran the daily commercial operations, the controller had overall responsibility for the management of the *régie,* the semipublic corporation that operated the weight station. This official was to remain in the background, whence he audited accounts and kept the police directly informed on all matters of public concern. Not surprisingly, the man chosen for the job, Vigier, had served as clerk to commissaire Machurin for twelve years and was "perfectly familiar with every aspect of the central markets."[140] Mealman Pierre Poilleux, who had hoped to become director as compensation for the major business losses he suffered while he led the flour lobby for four and a half years, was assigned the task, worth around 3,000 livres a year, of recovering empty sacks from baker-buyers.[141] Poussot personally recruited the minor personnel, for he knew that the presence of "knaves" could undermine the entire operation. He chose the *forts* or laborers assigned to the weight station, drawing in part from the flour placeboys who had been let go by the brokers as a result of the new organization of roles and in part from the other "bands" in the central market. As always, he looked for "submission" if not "honesty" and "vigor" if not "intelligence."[142] Poussot's deep personal involvement was the surest guarantee that the weight system would work.

The weight station was to be financed entirely by the flour merchants. They were to pay a fairly substantial fee of 3 sous 6 deniers per sack, which according to Poussot immediately saved them 15 livres per voie on old-style losses. Two sous of this charge went to the amortization of the costs of construction and installation, a burden that would theoretically be liquidated within about five years. The remainder was a permanent duty to cover the maintenance of the station and salaries. In addition, an emergency fund of

138. Rapport arbitre, 29 March 1773, Archives Seine-Paris, D6B⁶, carton 6.

139. Arsenal, ms. Bast. 10141, fol. 222 (17 June 1759).

140. Ibid.

141. Ibid., fols. 308, 331–32 (20 January and 19 March 1760); BN, Coll. Joly 1312, fols 33–34.

142. Arsenal, ms. Bast. 10141, fols. 310, 323 (25 January, 3 March 1760).

3,000 livres would always be on hand for use by the lieutenant general as he saw fit.[143]

Had it been up to Poussot, he would have diverted some of this money to a building fund that would also be nourished by a 10-sous-a-voie imposition on all the mealmen. For Poussot was always thinking ahead, and grandly. Even before the weight station was completed, he called for the construction of a covered halle in which to store the mass of flour that he expected would arrive in ever greater quantities. Such a building would sharply reduce spoilage and maintenance costs, facilitate transactions, and attract new dealers.[144] The central marketplace was chronically filthy: littered with mud and garbage and foul with heavy, mephitic odors. In the current conditions, it was impossible to protect the flour from "corruption." Covered with half-rotten beds of straw (which cost roughly 10 sous a voie, the same amount as Poussot's proposed building-fund tax), the sacks became like "piles of manure" when it rained and especially when it was warm. Though financed somewhat differently, Poussot's dream was to be realized several years later.

With a large audience of enthusiastic *curieux* alongside the buyers and sellers, the weight station opened for business on 27 September 1759. "The bulk of the merchants and bakers," reported Poussot, "expressed complete satisfaction with the station and the system."[145] As the word of the successful opening spread, new faces appeared at the Halle. "I will surely not be the only one to come to Paris," said a mealman from Melun, whose first visit to the Halle delighted him as a result of the ease and rapidity of transactions. A Versailles merchant who had hitherto supplied exclusively by droiture sent a voie to a broker and was so pleased with the sale on weight that he promised to become a regular supplier.[146] "Bakers who had not set foot in the Halle for the last seven or eight years," Poussot observed, returned to use the weight system.[147] In mid-October, despite a reduction in traffic caused by the demands of sowing and by low water levels, the price of flour fell, followed by that of bread.[148] In response to this new competition, the mealmen at Versailles lowered their price, which delighted the police, for it would generate further downward pressure on Paris prices.[149] Nor did the long freezing period

143. Ibid., fol. 308 (20 January 1760); Sartine to procurator general, 4 June 1760, AN, Y 9500.
144. Arsenal, ms. Bast. 10141, fols. 222–23 (17 June 1759).
145. Ibid., fol. 253 (28 September 1759).
146. Ibid., fol. 256 (5 October 1759).
147. Ibid., fol. 261 (16 October 1759).
148. Ibid., fol. 264 (26 October 1759). Based on first weekly entries, the average price per bushel during the year preceding the opening of the station was 32 sous. It never reached that level again until the mid-sixties. During the year following the opening of the weight station, the average price was 28.78 sous. Archives Seine-Paris, D5B⁶ 753, 5655, 3032, and 3681.
149. Arsenal, ms. Bast. 10141, fol. 275 (16 November 1759).

in the early winter that stopped many mills result in the usual increase in price.[150] The weight station attracted an increasingly large mass of flour—total supply grew by a fifth over the previous levels during the first three months of operation.[151] Whereas flour transactions had characteristically been long, arduous, expensive, and exasperating, they were now "a game." The weight system deserved the credit, but Machurin and Poussot helped by creating an ambience in which buyers and sellers *felt* they had more freedom to bargain than ever before.[152] A certain confusion had hitherto clouded transactions as a result of the multiplicity of standards for contents: bushel, setier, voie, and so forth. The weight system clarified the situation by requiring that all prices be quoted in terms of 325-pound sacks.[153] With his usual ebullience, Poussot was ready for the *régie* to assume responsibility for selling butter, eggs, and cheese, and perhaps eventually to undertake the management of the business of the entire central market.[154]

The only shadow over the new system was cast by the measurers and, to a lesser extent, by the porters. Tension between the police and the two corporations of market officers reached a peak when the weight station was opened. Already alarmed by the administrative and commercial innovations and the zeal of the Machurin-Poussot team, measurers and porters quite rightly saw in the weight system the harbinger of an entirely new way of running the Halle and the gravest threat to their authority, despite the short-term consolation that their fees were to be paid even on weighed flour. They had lobbied vigorously against its institution, and now that it was a fait accompli they spared no effort, in Poussot's words, "to trouble its operation." For the first

150. Ibid., fol. 307 (20 January 1760).

151. Ibid., fols. 264, 266 (26 October, 6 November 1759). In the first three months 28,793 sacks were sold, 27,857 in the next three, and 13,942 in the next two. Extrapolated on an annual basis, flour provisioning would be about 17,500 muids a year (allowing 2 setiers to the sack as officials continued to do, which probably exaggerated the total supply). Sartine to procurator general, 4 June 1760, AN, Y 9500.

152. Arsenal, ms. Bast. 10141, fols. 259, 307 (12 October 1759 and 20 January 1760).

153. Archives Seine-Paris, D5B⁶ 753, 5655, 3032, 3681. This standard included the weight of the sack itself, which varied between 5 and 8 pounds. Theoretically the sack contained slightly over 26 bushels. The authorities continued to calculate that it took over 2 setiers of wheat to make one sack of flour. For this 2-setier assumption, see bureau of the Hôtel de Ville, 8 July 1746, AN, F¹¹ 264; report of the measurers, 17 August 1754, AN, Y 11241; "Réponse au Sr. Bucquet," ca. 1769, Arsenal, ms. 7458; AN, Y 12608, 29 January 1760. It is virtually certain, however, that by 1760 most millers were drawing well over a sack from 2 setiers. Malouin reported that 2 setiers yielded 370 pounds of flour in the sixties, though it is not at all clear how common this yield was. See *Journal économique* (March 1768): 117. Bucquet obtained about 367 pounds of economic flour at his bakery in the seventies. This represents 1.77 setiers the sack or an extraction rate of 76.4 percent. The quality was baker's white or just below. Archives Seine-Paris, D4B⁶ 68-4429, June 1778. In 1758 "expert" mealmen testified at the consular jurisdiction that a muid commonly produced 7 sacks of flour. Thus, a sack represented 1.7 setiers. Morel to consular jurisdiction, 4 February 1758, Archives Seine-Paris, D6B⁶, carton 3.

154. Arsenal, ms. Bast. 10141, fol. 261 (16 October 1759).

time in years, there was no lack of measurers and porters in the Halle. Thirty or more milled around the weight station, intruded upon its business, and slowed up the traffic of buyers and sellers. They pressed the bakers to use the measure, vaguely hinting at certain advantages. They spread the word in the bars frequented by the mealmen and bakers that the weight station was to be avoided. A number of bakers ran a public test: after having their flour measured, they weighed it and discovered that on the average it was short by 6 to 12 pounds a sack. "This proof," Poussot noted with satisfaction, "did a great deal to discredit the measurers and almost none of the bakers wants to use the measure now." In fact, during the first eight months that the weight station functioned, only 2.4 percent of the flour sold at the Halle was measured, a resounding repudiation of both measurers and porters.[155] Viewed against the broader landscape of the entire provisioning zone, the triumph of weight in Paris (and even earlier in Versailles) seems quite precocious. For a century later, local reformers were still trying to get markets in the Oise and elsewhere to switch to weight and to make all procedures uniform.[156]

For over a year Machurin and Poussot had discussed the prospects for purging and reforming the measurer and porter corporations. The weight station underscored the superfluousness of maintaining so many officers and the necessity of subjecting them to tighter control. The commissaire and the inspector envisioned their replacement by a *régie* of revocable clerks who could be counted upon to enforce "all the good rules of the police." There was no need to retain more than a dozen of the most tractable measurers and porters for service in the Halle of the future. The others would be compensated for their offices not with jobs at the market but simply with money, upon receipt of which their relationship with the Halle would be severed. "It is not the quantity of men who do the work, it is the quality" was one of Poussot's favorite aphorisms. About the time of the opening of the weight station, an arrêt du conseil suppressed the two corporations for the second time during the reign of Louis XV. From the police point of view, the timing was spectacularly propitious. Though the arrêt invoked lofty political and fiscal motives, it was clearly a manifestation of the interest that Bertin, once the Paris police chief and now the controller-general, took in the reform of the provisioning markets. A lack of funds compelled the government to postpone liquidation and to reestablish the posts within the year, but the passage of the arrêt markedly fortified the hand of the police at the Halle and broke the resistance of many of the measurers and porters. During the tumult following suppression, a score of officers, eager to be considered for appointment as commis-

155. Ibid., fols. 253, 255, 258 (28 September, 3, 12 October 1759). Sartine to procurator general, 4 June 1760, AN, Y 9500. The term *measure* in reference to flour transactions was rarely pronounced in the sixties. See, for example, AN, Y 12613, 30 June 1764.

156. *Enquête sur la boulangerie,* pp. 757, 773. A great diversity of sack weights also persisted. Ibid., p. 774.

sioned agents, made "their submission" to Poussot. He recruited a number of
the least "mutinous" measurers and porters to assist in the operation of the
weight station.[157]

The Flour Police

In easy times, the authorities tended to tolerate a wide range of practices
that, strictly speaking, were illegal. (The toleration did not extend to clandestine droiture traffic, which threatened the future of the Halle as well as the
interests of the market officers.) In crisis periods, however, the police came
alive, placing the trade under close scrutiny and, in some particulars, under
tight control.

During the dearth of 1725, the Paris police worked to mobilize the entire
merchant-milling industry in the region. The lieutenant general dispatched
agents to visit the mills—not only the mills that normally supplied Paris, but
establishments located deeper in the hinterland or integrated into other provisioning systems. Many of them, including the habitual Paris suppliers, were
patently unenthusiastic. They claimed to lack grain or transport facilities or to
have other commitments, yet it appears that their major fear was that they
would lose on the transactions, since prices were still rising even as the police
tried to impose restraint on the sellers. For a brief time the authorities turned
to the carrot, offering the flour dealers bonuses of 24 livres per half voie (six
sacks). It is likely that this measure was taken defensively, in order to prevent
Paris suppliers from being drawn en masse to Versailles, where the king
distributed similar premiums. It apparently did not work: it made the merchants arrogant, wrote an official, "convincing them that we needed them and
that they could therefore take advantage of us." The bonus system seems to
have been discarded in the early fall.[158]

Even as they proffered the carrot, the police applied the stick. The lieutenant general's agents tried to elicit promises from the merchant-millers to
supply the capital regularly. When the agents failed to "excite" the mealmen
to direct their immediate attention to Paris, they resorted to what they themselves called "force."[159] They effected what amounted to requisitions. They
threatened recalcitrant miller-merchants with jail or, what was in many ways
perceived as worse, the obligation to lodge troops. They warned that quotas

157. Arsenal, ms. Bast. 10141, fols. 274, 279 (16, 25 November 1759). On the measurers
and porters, see below, chap. 14.
158. Controller-general to Régnier, 5 September 1725, AN G^7 35; Narbonne, *Louis XIV
et Louis XV,* pp. 127, 137.
159. Cleret to Hérault, 2, 9, 15, 16, 18, 30 October, 6 November 1725, Arsenal, ms. Bast.
10270 and 10271; Doubleau to Hérault, 1, 5, 15 October, 26, 28 November, 17, 26 December
1725, Arsenal, ms. Bast. 10270 and 10271.

would be imposed if the suppliers did not assume their responsibilities.[160] If millers complained that they lacked grain, the police called their bluff by offering them the opportunity to buy the king's grain—an opportunity they did not embrace with relish, given its relatively high price and its reputation for dubious quality.[161] The miller-merchants pressed for authorization to purchase grain at the farms, and although the police staunchly refused to accord this enormous derogation, it appears that the miller-merchants did it anyway.[162] Provided the latter shipped their flour to Paris, the authorities did not ask too many questions about the provenance of their goods. To make sure that the miller-merchants kept their word and hid nothing from the police, the agents paid them frequent rapid visits on horseback.[163] As a control procedure, the Pontoise agent required "his" mealmen to obtain a statement from the Paris measurers indicating how much they supplied, the date, and the kind of merchandise.[164]

Aside from the question of procuring grain (or averting the king's grain), the major crisis issues for the flour dealers concerned transport arrangements, the flour price-setting process, and police harassment. They complained that they could not afford the freight charges, which had more than doubled in many places since the onset of the crisis. Several Beaumont millers stockpiled flour in the fall of 1725 because the old cartage price of 18 livres a wagon had increased to 30 livres. The authorities put pressure on the carters to roll back the prices to the old levels. The millers at Mantes called for the reestablishment of boat traffic to the capital, an idea that had increasing appeal as inclement early winter weather rendered the roads virtually impassable.[165]

While the flour merchants applauded the fixation of freight prices, they bitterly assailed price control of flour at the Halle. Though price fixing was generally discountenanced even in police circles on the grounds that it deterred merchants from supplying the market, the lieutenant general of police considered the situation sufficiently grave to resort to it. Charging that the price schedule forced them to take losses, the miller-merchants of Pontoise and Beaumont boycotted the Halle in November. Supplies were so low by the

160. Cleret to Hérault, 7, 19 October 1725, Arsenal, ms. Bast. 10270, and 11 December 1725, ms. Bast. 10271; "mémoire," August 1725, ms. Bast. 10270.
161. Cleret to Hérault, 28 September, 2, 4, 5 October 1725, Arsenal, ms. Bast. 10270; Doubleau to Hérault, 3 December 1725, ms. Bast. 10271; procurator general to Hérault, 30 October 1725, ms. Bast. 10271.
162. Doubleau to Hérault, 26 November 1725, ibid., ms. Bast. 10271; Narbonne, *Louis XIV et Louis XV,* p. 137.
163. Cleret to Hérault, 5 October 1725, Arsenal, ms. Bast. 10270; Cleret to Hérault, 7 December 1725, ms. Bast. 10271; Doubleau to Hérault, 10 October 1725, ms. Bast. 10270.
164. Cleret to Hérault, 7 December 1725, Arsenal, ms. Bast. 10271. The Pontoise flour dealers complained as bitterly against these "requisitions" in 1793–94 as they had in 1725. Archives municipales Pontoise, 5 F 4, 21 fructidor year II.
165. Cleret to Hérault, 30 October, 11 December 1725, Arsenal, ms. Bast. 10271; "mémoire," August 1725, ms. Bast. 10270.

end of the month that Hérault, the lieutenant general, had to concede a price increase.[166] The pressure eased somewhat as English flour began to arrive around Christmas. The flour dealers felt threatened by this "extraordinary provision" and once again reduced their supply in protest.[167]

Price controls were not the only form of police brutality against which the miller-merchants protested. In a striking gesture of corporate solidarity the Pontoise flour community, acting like an underground guild, boycotted the Halle to protest against the severe sentence issued against a colleague named Etienne Denis—an action viewed by the police as a form of "rebellion." Denis was accused of adulteration and fraud because several of his sacks allegedly contained white flour only on the top layer. He was known as an honest dealer; the lieutenant general's representative at Pontoise defended him and regarded the episode as an accident. But the Pontoise dealers were angry and afraid of harsh, peremptory treatment, and it took a mixed dose of cajolery and threats to get them back into line.[168] They were also deeply unhappy with the treatment that they received at the hands of the Paris measurers. These officers lorded it over them, rarely gave them an honest measure, and favored the bakers with the last "brimming" bushel of measure in the setier. Hérault sought to appease the Pontoise merchants by promising to look into their grievances.[169]

Price fixing was the cause of, or the pretext for, another confrontation in 1729. Hérault again set a price ceiling that the flour merchants found incompatible with the uncontrolled wheat price. Just as hinterland police officials expressed a certain sympathy with the mealmen's predicament, so the commissaire at the Halle detected "a plot among the merchants and millers to bring no flour to the central markets" in order "to occasion a shortage and thereby to raise the prices." The supply had dropped from around 250 muids to under 50. The commissaire drew up a list of all the conspicuous absentees and ordered two porters and the sheriff to visit them to determine why each discontinued his regular provision. Nothing better illustrates how critical the police regarded the very short run than the 1,000-livre fine (payable in forty-eight hours, though the consequences of nonpayment were not spelled out) levied on Jacques Pezan, a mealman from Presles who had missed only a week's supply and who had that very day dispatched a voie to the Halle. A colleague from the same area received the same punishment, though he took

166. Cleret to Hérault, 5, 12, 13, 15 October 1725, Arsenal, ms. Bast. 10270; Doubleau to Hérault, 30 November 1725, ms. Bast. 10271; d'Angervilliers to Hérault, 7 November 1725, ms. Bast. 10271; Chefdeville to Hérault, 9 November 1725, ms. Bast. 10271; Couet de Montbayeux to procurator general, 11 November 1725, BN, Coll. Joly 1117, fols. 248–50.

167. Duplessis to procurator general, 27 March 1726, BN, Coll. Joly 1118, fol. 111.

168. AN, Y 9538, 23 October 1725; Cleret to lieutenant general, 23 October 1725, Arsenal, ms. Bast. 10271.

169. "Mémoire," 21 December 1725, and Cleret to Hérault, 30 October 1725, Arsenal, ms. Bast. 10271.

an insolent posture and, unlike Pezan, failed to attend the court hearing.[170] These "public examples" seem to have induced the others to return to the market. Even in relatively easy subsistence times, the police construed unexplained absence from the market as prima facie evidence of a "criminal plot" to cause scarcity. Thus in October 1735 two merchants who had discontinued supplying for a little more than a month were convicted and fined, "by grace and for this time exceptionally," a mere 50 livres.[171]

During the severe subsistence crisis of 1738–40, the police struck hard at flour dealers who allegedly betrayed the public interest by staying home. In the face of "mutiny," the authorities habitually imputed the existence of "conspiracy," though they rarely bothered to try to prove it. In August of 1738 the lieutenant general fined five flour merchants 500 livres each for "scheming collectively" to force up prices.[172] One of those dealers, Léon of Bournelle, went to great pains to protest his innocence, contending that he had failed to supply the Halle as usual only because he lacked wheat. To buttress his case, he submitted a letter from his priest countersigned by three local notables, all of whom testified that his mill had not turned for lack of grain. His major grain supplier confirmed Léon's story in a letter in which he assumed part of the responsibility for the delays in shipment. While the appeal took shape, Léon himself became a fugitive, for he had failed to pay his fine and was being sought by the constabulary.[173]

A dozen other miller-merchants, along with a few laboureurs, were convicted of a similar plot to create scarcity in October of 1738. Each of them was fined 500 livres, save Guillaume Grand of Senlis, who was given "twice twenty-four hours" to remit the staggering sum of 3,000 livres or face immediate imprisonment.[174] Grand may have suffered a much heavier punishment than the others because he was a far bigger dealer with interests in institutional as well as market victualing and in grain as well as flour. Proclaiming his innocence, Grand presented certificates proving that one of his two mills had broken down and that as a result he was "physically unable" to supply the Halle.[175] In July 1740 five more merchant-millers were condemned for discontinuing their supply. One of them, Gallois of Senlis, won relief by proving that his mill had been halted for major repairs. Another, Ducler of Chambly, was also cleared when he demonstrated that he had in fact never stopped his supply. The other three were fined 500 livres apiece, "by grace," and on the condition that they resume their shipments immediately.[176] Faced

170. Police sentence, 1 July 1729, BN, ms. fr. 21638, fols. 337–38; Regnier to Hérault, 21 June 1729, Arsenal, ms. Bast. 10275.

171. AN, Y 9436, 7 October 1735.

172. Police sentence, 29 August 1738, BN, ms. fr. 21635, fols. 79–80.

173. BN, Coll. Joly 1119, fols. 62–74.

174. Police sentence, 11 October 1738, BN, ms. fr. 21635.

175. BN, Coll. Joly 1119, fols. 37–40.

176. AN, Y 9441, 8 July 1740, and Y 9622, 8 July 1740.

TABLE 25

Monthly flour prices at the Halle, 1731–59 (white flour per boisseau in sous)

	Jan.	Feb.	Mar.	Apr.	May	June	July	Aug.	Sept.	Oct.	Nov.	Dec.
1731	—	29	29	30	34	36	36	35	33	32	30	26
1732	26	24	23	21	22	23	21	19	20	20	21	19
1733	18	18	19	20	19	19	19	20	21	20	20	20
1734	20	20	19	19	19	19	20	20	21	21	21	21.5
1735	21	21	20.5	19	20	21.5	22	23	24	25	25	25
1736	24	24	24	24	24	23.5	22	21.5	23	23	23.5	24
1737	23	23	23	23	23	23	24	25	26	27	28	28
1738	28	28	28	27.5	28	27.5	28	27.5	30	32	34	34
1739	34	34	33.5	33	33	33	33	33	33	33	34	32.5
1740	33	33	32.5	32.5	32.5	33	35	36	40, 48, 62	66	72	72
1741	71	70	60	57	56	55	52	48	47	44	41	39
1742	38	32	31	30	29	28	28	29	28	26	22	21
1743	20	19	19	18	18	17	19	19	19.5	20	19.5	19.5
1744	19	18	17.5	18	17.5	17.5	18	18	17.5	18	18	17.5
1745	17	17	16	16	16	16	18	20	22	23	22	22
1746	21.5	21.5	21.5	23	23	23	23	23	22.5	23	22.5	22.5
1747	22.5	23	23	23	23	23	23.5	23.5	27	30	34	34.5
1748	34	34	33	33	32	32	29	30	32	33.5	33.5	33
1749	33	32.5	31	29	28.5	27.5	29	31	32	32	32	32
1750	31.5	30.5	29	28	28	29	30	30	30	30	30	29.5
1751	28.5	28	28.5	30	31.5	32	33	35	36, 41	42	43	43
1752	43	43	41.5	39	39	39	39	39	39	39	38	38
1753	38	38	37	36	33	30	29	31	31	31	30.5	31
1754	30.5	30	29	28	27.5	26.5	27	27	27	27	26.5	26
1755	25	24	23	21.5	21	21	22	24	25.5	23.5	22	21
1756	21.5	21	20	19	20	20.5	23	26	28.5	32.5	33	35
1757	35	35	35	35	35	40	40	38	35	33	31.5	30
1758	29	28	28	27	27	27	31	32	33	35	34	32.5
1759	32.5	32	31.5	31	29	29.5	30	29	30	—	—	—

Sources: Archives Seine-Paris, D5B⁶ 5655 and 753

with a 1,000-livre fine the following October, miller Mailleser of Essonnes went into hiding.[177]

The police placed great demands on the merchant-millers. Though they were not formally commissioned agents like the port merchants, they were expected to perform virtually as public servants. One could not afford to be either an intermittent or a half-hearted flour supplier. Later in the century lieutenant general Sartine ventured a distinction between commissioned agents and flour traders "who are free to come one market day without being obliged to return the next." His goal was to entice as many traders as possible to the Halle. Genuine casual dealers were able to profit from this prudent liberalism. In practice, however, the police continued to hold the familiar flour merchants responsible for a regular provision, especially during difficult periods.[178]

Paris officials did not resort to flour price fixing after Hérault left the lieutenance in the late thirties. (Table 25 shows monthly flour prices at the Halle from 1731 to 1759.) The general feeling was that such "authoritarian" measures put the flour dealers in an untenable squeeze and ultimately worked against the marshaling of abundance. Even the unofficial ceiling imposed rather rigorously by the measurers, who presided over every transaction on the ground level, came under attack by Poussot. "It is this fixed price," he esteemed, "that has always been the curse of the Halle." It caused the best merchants "to desert" and the market to be "denuded of merchandise." The inspector did not shy away from using force to crush speculative abuses, but provided that good faith reigned he was persuaded "that the greater the liberty between buyer and seller, the more the Halle will be supplied and as a result this abundance of supply will itself bend the prices downward."[179] His relations with the mealmen were sufficiently good that he was able "to engage them" voluntarily to roll back the price when he and commissaire Machurin decided a price reduction was necessary.[180]

The police attitude toward miller grain buying was deeply ambivalent. The crucial thing was to produce and distribute flour, which suggested that the authorities should not look too hard at the millers' purchasing operations. On the other hand, there persisted a strong fear and resentment of miller buying, a sense that it ought never to have been tolerated, a conviction that miller-merchants could not be trusted, especially when the community was vulnerable. Police officials may indeed have been impatient to trap millers in order to show that their suspicions had been well founded. In November 1738 two millers were found "maneuvering" to raise the price of grain in the Meaux market.[181] In July 1740 the widow Bécu, a Senlis miller-merchant, stirred "a

177. AN, Y 9441, 14 October 1740.
178. AN, X^1B 3748, 4 June 1761.
179. Arsenal, ms. Bast. 10141, fols. 253, 262 (28 September, 16 October 1759).
180. Ibid., fol. 323 (25 February 1760).
181. Foucaud to lieutenant general, 25 November 1738, Arsenal, ms. Bast. 10275.

great tumult" in the Gonesse market by failing to bargain and by accepting the highest price for wheat. What alarmed the authorities even more, however, was the panic she allegedly sought to provoke by spreading the word that the country was on the brink of famine and that prices would soon be entirely out of reach. According to the sentence that fined her 2,000 livres and gave her three days to pay or face jail, those were the words of "monopolists and rebels and disturbers of the public peace."[182] With the idea of cornering the market and profiting from public distress, a miller named Lamoureux, the police charged, bid up the price of wheat at the Montlhéry market.[183] The fine of 1,000 livres he received was another message to the merchant-millers, a warning published and posted in all the leading flour centers.

Flour Traffic *en Droiture*

The flour trading "abuse" that most exercised the Paris police was commerce conducted en droiture. Droiture traffic meant direct shipment from the flour dealer to the baker in his bakeroom. The police regarded it as dangerous because it followed a hidden route, because it short-circuited the established system, because it blurred questions of provenance and price. Though the authorities admitted of numerous exceptions in practice, they remained committed to the principle that abundance could not be assured outside the marketplace. Market mediation meant maximum concentration of supply at all points of exchange in order to reassure anxious consumers and to restrain the tendency of prices to rise. A highly visible traffic facilitated the task of police surveillance and reduced the opportunities for "maneuvers." Market-patterned trade provided the police with an information system that enabled them to foresee and perhaps prevent difficulties. Symbolically as well as commercially, the Paris market—the ultimate market of destination—was of special concern to the authorities. As a regulator market for the entire region, as the stomach of a vast city, and as the moral and political core of the entire police machine, the Halle could not be bypassed without serious risk.

Flour droiture was not nearly so pressing an issue in earlier times, when the only flour that bakers could be expected to receive at their shops was meal that came from wheat that had presumably been purchased on the market, ideally at the Halle or on the ports, and that was shipped for grinding to a miller-artisan. Conditions changed as bakers began to engage more aggressively in independent grain buying and as millers began to plunge into frankly commercial or speculative activities. The bakers soon found that it made sense either to have their millers do the grain buying for them or to abandon

182. AN, Y 9441, 15 July 1740.
183. AN, Y 9621, 11 August 1741.

the cumbersome business of grain buying, freighting, and converting in favor of flour purchasing. Once the flour merchant obtained tacit permission to buy grain despite the age-old ban on miller grain trade, it was inevitable that droiture traffic would become a problem. For it was cheaper (even if all the usual marketing fees were paid on entering the city), quicker, and easier for the flour dealer to send his merchandise directly to the baker than for the two to rendezvous at the Halle.[184] From the police perspective, droiture traffic implied illicit, off-market grain purchases in the countryside, often made by illegal agents and covered by fraudulent market certificates, as well as a clandestine transaction in Paris that undermined the influence of the Halle. The official police position was that the flour merchant would be welcomed as a supplier on the condition that he kept rigorously to the market and that the bakers bought flour exclusively on the market.

There is no doubt that droiture traffic was heavy, especially from the thirties onward. It probably abated somewhat in the early sixties after the introduction of the flour weighing station, but it is quite likely that it remained a very important channel of moonlight provisioning. While the authorities looked the other way in regard to many other "abuses," they showed very little indulgence for droiture traffic even in easy times. Because the motives of the police were generally disinterested, it is unfortunate that the major share of the anti-droiture campaign was assigned to the measurers and porters, who had a venal interest in focusing the trade on the market and whose bullying attitude goaded countless mealmen into defying the rules. The porters were theoretically more highly motivated than the measurers to stifle droiture traffic because, unlike the measurers, they were not paid fees at the city gates (*droits*) but only for transactions effected at the marketplace.[185] On the other hand, droiture passers characteristically either tried to enter the city surreptitiously or else they frankly contested the claims of the measurers to collect a fee without reference to service actually performed. Moreover, both measurers and porters had an equal interest in uncovering flour dealers who, though they paid upon entry, still transported loads of dubious origin, for the market officers had an excellent chance of being awarded all or part of the price of the merchandise they seized.[186] As a rule the seller alone bore the entire loss.[187] Working in cooperation with the clerks at the city gates who

184. The brokers claimed that a sack in droiture cost the bakers 50 sous less than a market sack. Arsenal, ms. Bast. 10141, fol. 319 (17 February 1760).

185. Ibid., fol. 468 (4 April 1761).

186. When the police removed this incentive as part of a plan to reform the market police system, they found that the measurers in particular abruptly lost interest in prosecuting the anti-droiture campaign. Ibid., fol. 337 (10 April 1760).

187. Ibid., fol. 327 (12 March 1760). Yet in some cases the baker was the de facto victim, pending litigation that he would have to engage against the flour dealer, because he had already paid. There are cases in which both baker and supplier are fined for the off-market violation. See AN, Y 9621, 11 December 1744 and 12 March 1752.

alerted them when they suspected that the papers of deliverymen were not in order, the measurers and porters prowled the streets day and night in search of suspect shipments.

To avoid trouble upon entering the capital, the flour dealer (or his driver) had to have documentation proving that the baker for whom the meal was destined had purchased it at a given market. In a great many cases, the flour merchants either had no such certificates, or else carried expired or partially invalid documents or forged or altered papers. (In order to promote rapid turnover, certificates of provenance were valid only for two months.) If the supplier's papers were unacceptable, he was arraigned for violating the law (the royal declaration of April 1723 was one of several cited) that forbade off-market transactions. Miller Meunier from Valmondois presented a certificate from the notoriously lax Pont-Ste.-Maxence market for 30 setiers. It was filled out in the name of a mill other than his, however, and had already been used to pass 20 setiers. Convicted of both buying and selling illegally, Meunier suffered confiscation plus a stiff fine of 300 livres.[188] Miller Lacour had seventeen sacks seized along with a wagon and three horses because he could not account for the origin of his flour.[189] Miller Huot tried unsuccessfully to pass 13 setiers of gross flour on a certificate that had already been used.[190] Miller Gailland of Senlis brought in twelve sacks of gross meal on a certificate that had been honestly obtained by his baker upon the purchase of wheat, but was now eight months old. In this instance, the baker absorbed the loss, confirmed on appeal.[191] There was no margin of tolerance: baker Pille suffered the same sanctions for a "good" certificate that was twenty-six days out of date.[192]

In many instances, it was patently clear that the certificates presented by the flour merchants had not been properly obtained. Miller Sorel's driver showed a certificate from the Versailles royal weight station signed by the

188. AN, Y 9441, 15 July 1740. The sentence was probably softened upon appeal. As a rule the fines levied seem excessively modest and wholly out of proportion with the seriousness of the droiture abuse. One must remember, however, that the parties usually suffered a very costly confiscation. Even if the seizure was partly remitted, the "damages" granted to the measurers were never under 100 livres and sometimes much more. For twenty-one cases of fines from all kinds of droiture not including the one cited above, the average fine was 25 livres, the median 20, the range 10 to 100. Fines for falsified certificates were almost twice the amount of fines for partly invalid certificates. The specific magnitude of the fine seems to have depended heavily on the previous record of the merchant as well as on the particular circumstances of the violation.

189. AN, Y 12607, 13 December 1759.

190. AN, Y 9539, 3 September 1761. For other cases of invalid certificates, see AN, Y 9621, 24 November 1752; Y 12608, 29–31 January 1760; Y 9619, 6 September 1737; Y 9621, 11 December 1744; Y 9539, 4 January 1758, 29 August 1758; Y 9621, 17 March 1752.

191. BN, Coll. Joly 1829, fol. 306, 27 March 1733.

192. AN, Y 9434, 27 March 1733. For other examples of expired certificates, see Y 9538, June 1725 (Sauvage-Fournier); Y 9538, 6 May 1757; Y 9539, 26 May 1758; BN, Coll. Joly 1829, fols. 324–25, 1 September 1747.

director but left blank to enable him to use it as he pleased.[193] Another driver, working for miller Robert Parquier of Chartres, had a blank certificate for the Maintenon market, to which was attached the letter by which his wife had solicited it.[194] The Paris porters accused mealman François of filling in the name and amount on the certificate he took out at Pont.[195]

Certain flour merchants took the liberty of filling out certificates in the names of bakers whose permission they had not sought. These bakers rarely made an effort to "cover" the mealman. Faubourg St.-Antoine baker Pierre Lande denounced as false a certificate issued at Etampes in his name to a flour dealer named Hamnis.[196] Widow baker Picard vehemently denied that she had anything to do with the flour that a St.-Germain flour merchant claimed had been manufactured from her wheat.[197] (Of course, she may simply have been trying to protect herself from possible incrimination.)

When they could not obtain blank certificates, determined merchants altered documents that had been issued for other purposes. The driver of miller Rousseau of St.-Denis presented a certificate that had been "retouched and increased [in amount of grain accounted for] by a strange hand."[198] The officers rejected a certificate from another miller because it was written in two different hands, sure sign of "a counterfeit."[199] Miller Briere of Villeneuve-St.-Georges changed the amount of merchandise inscribed on his certificate.[200]

The boldest flour smugglers did not bother with certificates at all. They tried to sneak by, in order to avoid inspection and the payment of fees. When they were caught, they often reacted with violence. The measurers and porters feared these "rebellions" because they mobilized large crowds and served as pretexts for further disorder.[201]

What they lacked in documentation certain flour dealers tried to make up with imagination. The officers seized twelve sacks of flour that miller Brugerin of Valmondois dispatched to baker Garin on the grounds that the certificate presented by the driver did not justify the transaction. In an attempt to recover the merchandise, Brugerin filed an affidavit in the name of his driver that explained that the driver, an illiterate, had innocently presented

---

193. AN, Y 11241, 17 August 1754.
194. AN, Y 9539, 16 May 1762.
195. Ibid., 9 January 1760.
196. AN, Y 12610, 30 July 1761.
197. BN, Coll. Joly 1829, fol. 287.
198. AN, Y 9538, 6 May 1757.
199. Ibid., 1 June 1725.
200. AN, Y 9621, 16 July 1751. For other cases of fraudulent documentation, see Y 9539, 6 May 1765; Y 11225, 30 October 1738; BN, Coll. Joly 1829, fol. 288 (1755).
201. AN, Y 9539, 17 January 1763; Y 12607, 3 December 1759. For nonviolent cases of entry without certificate, see Y 9539, 3 January 1761; Y 9619, 12 August 1737; Y 9618, 20 February 1734; BN, Coll. Joly 1829, fol. 314bis, 30 June 1745.

the wrong certificate, an old one that he happened to have in his pocket. The driver, however, rejected Brugerin's account as a complete falsification.[202] Flour merchant Eustache Lecercle of Pontoise disguised a direct-to-baker shipment as a provision for an educational institution, for which droiture deliveries were customarily authorized.[203] For another occasion he devised a more elaborate ruse: since Paris bakers were permitted to buy at the Versailles flour market, he told his driver to bypass the St.-Denis gate, by which he would normally enter the capital, and to enter instead from Chaillot in the south, as if he were coming from Versailles.[204]

Droiture flour that went directly to bakers was viewed as a diversion and misappropriation of merchandise, but it did have the merit of contributing, albeit circuitously, to the precious fund that the police called "the abundance of Paris." Another sort of flour droiture, however, did not have this redemptive virtue. This was droiture entry for the purpose of the constitution of stocks—hoarding, in the language of subsistence crime. This merchandise was viewed as flour for "maneuvers": it was considered evidence of a sort of monopoly. One driver told the clerk at the barrier of Rambouillet that he was heading for the Halle, but instead he delivered his flour to a mealman's home where the measurers found a veritable "depot of flour," a hoard that could only "cause scarcity and push up prices at the Halle."[205] Measurers found a similar hoard belonging to a Melun flour dealer secreted away in the Inn of the Bon Laboureur at the Grande Pinte de Bercy.[206]

The police official who worked hardest to curtail droiture entries was inspector Poussot. In his view, droiture obstructed the process of rationalization and modernization that could make the Halle a superbly efficient price-making and distribution machine. Not only did droiture have an inflationary impact on market prices, he found, but it also disorganized the trade. The brokers, the Halle's blocks of granite, themselves weakened the structure by channeling flour directly from their mealmen-clients in the hinterlands to their baker-clients in the city. Their rationale: they had no choice but to collaborate in droiture commerce because their best bakers were being drawn away by enticing propositions from flour dealers who promised direct delivery. Poussot met with groups of bakers, mealmen, and brokers to present his case against droiture in terms of their self-interest. He wrested signatures from brokers and flour merchants for a petition demanding the suppression of droiture and the prohibition of baker grain purchases via agents. He elicited public abjurations from notorious offenders in the hope of stirring emulation among the others. Since bakers were increasingly unwilling to bolt at home,

202. BN, Coll. Joly 1829, fols. 271–85.
203. Ibid., fol. 292.
204. Ibid., fols. 293–96.
205. AN, Y 12607, 4 December 1759.
206. AN, Y 9447, 18 November 1746.

Poussot, in the hope of deterring direct shipment, proposed that only un-
bolted flour be allowed to enter en droiture. The inspector suggested a compromise plan for legitimizing droiture by which the buyer would meet the
seller and his merchandise at the Halle for the purpose of registration, after
which delivery could be made to the bakeroom. Indeed, Poussot was even
prepared to allow the bakers to stay home and receive delivery from the flour
dealers once the latter had made their declarations of quantity, quality, price,
origin, and destination at the Halle. In practice this system would have differed little from ordinary on-market purchases that bakers made from freelance mealmen or brokers, but it would have preserved the sellers' and
buyers' sense of freedom of action: "Nothing is better than this liberty,"
Poussot allowed. Nor was his goal merely, or primarily, to tame refractory
bakers and mealmen. The point was to include the full impact of supply in the
price-making calculus of the Halle in order to make the Halle an efficient
instrument of public policy and private exchange, as well as a genuine regulator market.[207]

The inspector urged the lieutenant general of police to take measures
through the royal administration and the parlement to quash the emission of
fraudulent certificates by hinterland authorities that facilitated droiture. He
counted on the allure of the flour weight station (and later the construction of
a covered market building) to diminish market bypass operations. Known as a
stringent critic of the market officers, Poussot nevertheless encouraged them
to pursue droiture violations energetically. He obtained authorization for
them to patrol the *plat pays* as well as the city streets. With the aim of
preventing the officers from overstepping their instructions and of reducing
friction between different units of officers, Poussot assigned one of his men to
each mission and carefully followed its course from beginning to end. He
broadcast the news of each seizure widely, and warned the flour merchants
and the bakers that they risked "severe punishment" as well as confiscation of
goods and equipment. According to Poussot, the results of the anti-droiture
campaign were extremely promising, for by the spring of 1761, supply and
sales were up and prices down.[208]

Business Failures of Millers and Flour Merchants

Millers and flour merchants failed for many of the same reasons as grain
dealers. They were victims of "the conjuncture," like miller Bremant of the
Beauce, who ran aground in 1695 in the midst of "war, misfortune, and rising

207. Arsenal, ms. Bast. 10141, fols. 274–75 (16 November 1759), 326 (10 March 1760),
336 (7 April 1760), 358 (2 July 1760), 468 (4 April 1761), 469 (8 April 1761), 479 (9 May 1761).
208. Ibid., fols. 322 (25 February 1760), 327 (12 March 1760), 434 (27 January 1761), 456
(9 March 1761), 468 (4 April 1761), 479 (9 May 1761).

prices." Unable to collect from bakers, he was compelled to go more deeply into debt in order to meet his obligations. Finally his creditors forced him to seek terms. Crisis failure was perhaps the single most common type. Eighteen millers and flour merchants filed between 1765 and 1777, a period of acute subsistence difficulty and general economic disarray. Others failed ostensibly because of excessive doses of bad luck: accidents resulting in spoilage of merchandise or loss of equipment; epizootics that killed animals; protracted mill shut-downs due to unfavorable weather conditions; shut-downs resulting from damages that required costly repairs; ill health that siphoned off liquidity and prevented the miller from focusing all his attention on the business; a faithless wife who absconded with part of the family's resources.

Bad luck sometimes served to mask bad management, another important cause of failure. Millers made mistakes, lacked aggressiveness, lost clients, overlooked the requirements of maintenance, became embroiled in costly litigation, and so on. Overextension, speculative adventures, and collection or cash-flow problems were causes of failure that were often though not necessarily linked to managerial ineptitude. As he possessed a large water mill worth 26,000 livres, 2,200 livres in annuities, and some land, Louis Lelièvre's problem—4,594 livres in accounts payable—was largely one of temporary liquidity. Overextension in the case of some merchant millers meant offering credit to too many buyers and trying to cover too much commercial space. In the case of others, however, such as Laurent Caron of the Valois, it meant getting bogged down in affairs not immediately related to flour making that forced the stones to grind to a halt. Another genre of failure more common among millers and mealmen than among grain traders seemed to be more an organic or structural development than an accident. It involved relatively small sums of money, but it struck the weak and the poor, those with nothing to fall back upon, those who were always perched on the edge of disaster.

Our sample consists of seventeen self-styled millers or merchant-millers and seventeen mealmen who called themselves *farinier* or flour merchant (*marchand farinier*) or more rarely flour merchant and miller.[209] While to separate them might be desirable for certain purposes, there are several reasons why they should be amalgamated. First, the distinction between these professions tended to disappear in the course of the eighteenth century, especially in the metropolitan provisioning grounds. Second, the majority of our flour merchants ran their own mills, though they were owners less often than were the millers. Third, the choice (or imposition) of a title or *qualité* was sometimes arbitrary and/or adventitious. A miller who in fact went into the commercial flour business may have clung to his old label. A miller with close

209. For the sources for business failures, see Appendix H.

ties to the city may have preferred the urban prestige associated with the title of merchant.

All thirty-four faillis in our sample were men. Though the mill was not circumscribed as male space, I have found few unwidowed women running mills, and the number of unremarried widow-millers was small. The flour business remained artisanal as well as predominantly masculine, despite the modernizing role that it played in the metropolitan provisioning trade. In our faillite sample, one grain dealer in ten in the Paris area worked in association with one or several others, but only one miller-mealman in thirty-four had a partner. Drawing on other data, I have found only one milling company in the Paris area before the time of Malisset.[210] The liberal reforms of the sixties generated a host of speculative "societies," the bulk of which did not survive the decade. From the time of Turgot until the Revolution, I have encountered only two cases of miller or flour merchant association in the private sector.[211]

Most of our miller-flour merchants had been in the flour business since the start of their professional careers. Six had practiced another trade earlier in their lives: a laboureur, two fermiers, an innkeeper, a wine merchant, and a simple merchant. Seven others exercised another occupation simultaneously with their flour business. Three were bakers—another sign of the imbrication of the milling and baking universes—one was a carter, one called himself négociant (one of the most coveted and abused *qualités* in the eighteenth-century business world), one was a military officer, and another claimed the title of bourgeois de Paris, a sort of antiprofession as well as an emblem of vanity and/or esteem. Four inhabited Paris, four the environs, nine the Ile-de-France, four the Hurepoix, three each the Brie, the Beauce, and the Valois, two Picardy, and two the Gâtinais.

The enterprises of our millers and merchants were rather modest. The major exception—a veritable aberration—was the association alluded to earlier linking the renowned miller and advocate of the economic technology, César Bucquet, and his son-in-law, the miller Rolland. For various bakery and milling undertakings, their company spent 700,000 livres on the purchase of wheat in three and a half years. Their debts reflected this grand scale of operations: 245,951 livres, far from offset by assets of 107,488 livres. More typical of the usual range are the balance sheets of Nicolas Roze of Beaumont (liabilities: 6,225 livres; assets: 5,273 livres) and Louis Lameret of Dampierre (61,971 and 70,820 livres). Figure 2 shows the percentage distribution of

210. Called "Henry Houdin et compagnie, entrepreneurs des moulins de mécanique," it was partly an experimental milling enterprise and partly a speculative trading venture. The company never got off the ground. See P. Mandon's faillite, Archives Seine-Paris, D4B⁶ 4-183, 16 April 1742, and D2B⁶ 1743, 20 December 1743.

211. Archives Seine-Paris, rapport arbitre, 17 June 1774, D6B⁶, carton 7 (Rambert and Foiret), and faillite of Louis Meusnier, D4B⁶ 88–6048, 24 November 1783 (Pueche and Tabot).

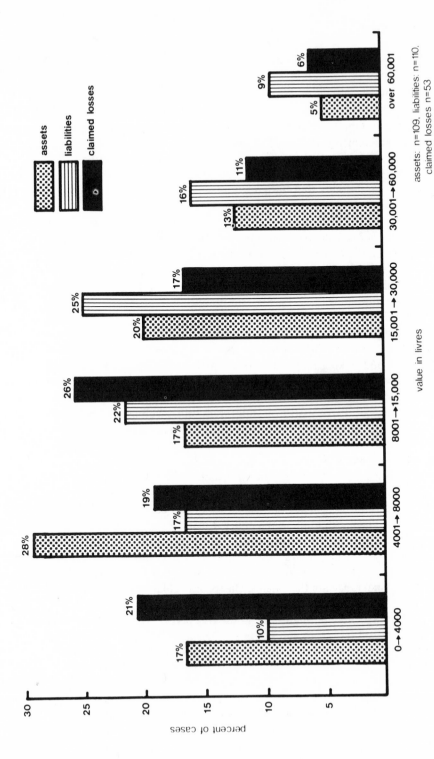

FIGURE 2 Percentage distribution of assets, liabilities, and claimed losses of grain and flour dealers who failed

assets: n=109. liabilities: n=110.
claimed losses n=53
source: *faillités*

assets, liabilities, and claimed losses of flour and grain merchants who failed.

For the group as a whole accounts payable amounted on the average to 21,298 livres and accounts receivable to 18,470 livres, but the medians—9,699 and 7,938—are more useful indicators. Twenty-three percent had debts of less than 5,000 livres, but the debts of another 25 percent surpassed 20,000 livres. Twenty-one percent had assets of less than 4,000 livres, but 26 percent boasted holdings worth over 25,000 livres. Generally the businesses of the "millers" were bigger, if not always healthier, than those of the flour merchants.

Commercial obligations constituted the dominant category of accounts payable. Amounting to more than half of all debts in both mean and median terms, they were doubtless underestimated, because a significant portion of unidentifiable promissory notes were the fruit of business rather than of personal transactions. (Only one-fifth of the group had debts of unequivocal "family" character, yet it is extremely difficult to separate business and domestic accounting.) Almost a third had commercial debts of more than 12,000 livres. Almost 90 percent of these debts reflected grain purchases. The rest concerned mill repair costs and the price of flour that eleven flour merchants purchased from other mealmen and millers. Several faillis owed over 20,000 livres to grain merchants; 15,000 was the highest flour debt.[212] Because they tended to have their own horses and wagons, the millers and merchants owed virtually nothing for transport.

The millers and merchants purchased more than three-quarters of their grain from grain merchants and the balance directly from laboureurs. They avoided becoming hostage to a small number of suppliers. To multiply their lines of credit, the millers and merchants spread out their orders. On the average they dealt with nine laboureurs (but 61 percent contracted with ten or more) who generally provided them with small lots, and with five grain merchants, including several from the rue de la Mortellerie, who furnished larger loads. One flour merchant alone maintained a network of forty grain suppliers and four flour traders. One miller owed money to seventeen grain merchants and four laboureurs.

Assets (Figure 3) consisted of a "soft" rubric—accounts payable and various notes that are difficult to verify—and a "hard" rubric—diverse forms of tangible wealth. Hard assets represented 57 percent on the average (median = 66 percent). There was almost no cash, which is not surprising in business failures. Only two miller-merchants possessed annuities *(rentes constituées)*, and two owned Parisian real estate. Rural property was far more

---

212. For examples of the legal pursuits undertaken by grain merchants against millers and flour merchants, see Archives Seine-Paris, D2B⁶ 1104, 4 December 1771 (Marquet versus Bourgeois for 1,200 livres), and D2B⁶ 1124, 27 August 1773 (Peschot *fils* v. Martin for 1,654 livres). For flour merchants against millers, see Archives Seine-Paris, D2B⁶ 1813, 13 September 1747 (Daubigny v. Courtois for 104 livres).

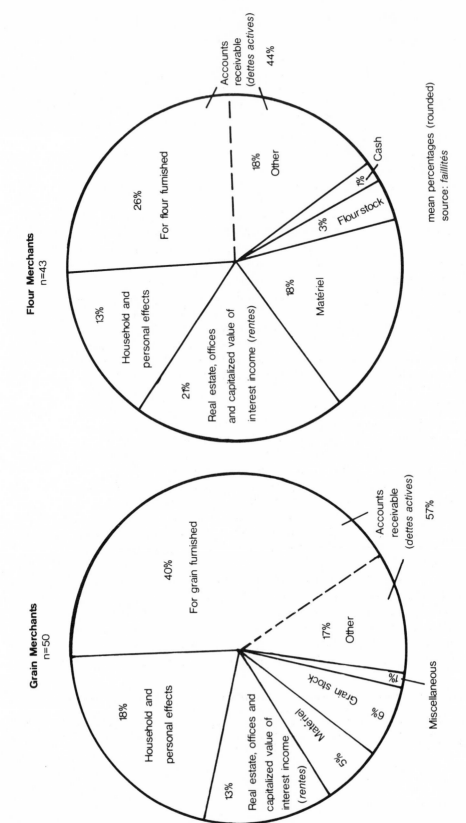

Flour Merchants
n=43

Accounts receivable (*dettes actives*)
44%

For flour furnished
26%

Other
18%

Cash
1%

Flour stock
3%

Matériel
18%

Real estate, offices and capitalized value of interest income (*rentes*)
21%

Household and personal effects
13%

mean percentages (rounded)
source: *faillites*

Grain Merchants
n=50

Accounts receivable (*dettes actives*)
57%

For grain furnished
40%

Other
17%

Miscellaneous
1%

Grain stock
6%

Matériel
5%

Real estate, offices and capitalized value of interest income (*rentes*)
13%

Household and personal effects
18%

FIGURE 3   Kinds of merchant assets

commonly held, worth 3,074 livres on the average per man. The miller merchants owned a total of eight mills whose mean evaluation was 9,376 livres (median = 6,750 livres). Many others leased mills; several exploited two at once. Producer goods represented an average investment of 1,491 livres (the median is reduced to 446 livres because almost one-third had no tools of their own). Household furnishings had an average value of 1,087 livres (median = 638 livres, a quarter of the group reporting none). There was no question of speculative hoarding: 78 percent of the millers and merchants had no stock and only 12 percent had merchandise on hand that was worth over 1,000 livres. The mean holding of the nine millers and merchants who had stock represented almost 120 setiers in real terms (median = 51), enough to supply one Parisian baker for about six weeks (less than three weeks according to the median). Félix's astonishingly large stock of 551 setiers distorted the average.

Almost 60 percent of paper assets resulted from flour sales—accounts receivable claimed by 78 percent of the group. The bulk of these debts, almost 75 percent, were owed by bakers. An average of five bakers, mostly Parisian, appeared on each balance sheet. Collection difficulties ruined a number of millers and merchants. Fifteen bakers owed Piedeleu of L'Isle-Adam a total of 24,740 livres. Since he had virtually no hard assets, his creditors, mostly grain merchants to whom he owed 10,274 livres, were alarmed. Similarly, Nicolas Roze had 4,613 livres coming to him, but he could not make it materialize quickly enough to pay off 6,225 livres' worth of grain debts. Collection efforts were costly in time and money. Millers and merchants who could not chase down bakers personally had to hire civil sheriffs to deliver subpoenas. Those who could not appear personally in court—sometimes more than one court—had to employ procurators to represent them.[213]

The millers and merchants had less trouble collecting the money due them by the brokers, whose role at the Halle developed steadily across the century. They were only cited six times, for an average sum of 792 livres. It was not uncommon for a miller or flour trader to sue his broker for payment even as the broker sued his baker(s). Pierre Charon, a Chartres mealman, obtained a consular sentence against broker Philippe Quevanne for 669 livres. On the same day Quevanne won a condemnation against Paris baker Decant for 669 livres.[214] Smaller amounts had to be recovered from pastry makers, livestock feeders, and bran merchants.[215] Millers and merchants also tried to recover sums for unreturned flour sacks. Worth 5 livres apiece in the 1730s, the sacks represented a substantial capital investment that had a tendency to erode imperceptibly. To assist the owners, the police assigned an employee of the

213. See AN, Y 15263, 7 August 1755, and AD Seine-et-Oise, 3B 121, 5 February 1771.
214. Archives Seine-Paris, D2B⁶ 1034, 3 February 1766, and D3B⁶ 67, 4 March 1766. For a similar case involving the broker Ancelin, see AN, MC, LXI-449, 13 February 1751.
215. Archives Seine-Paris, D2B⁶ 841, 14 January 1750; D2B⁶ 1102, 11 October 1771, and D2B⁶ 1078, 2 October 1769.

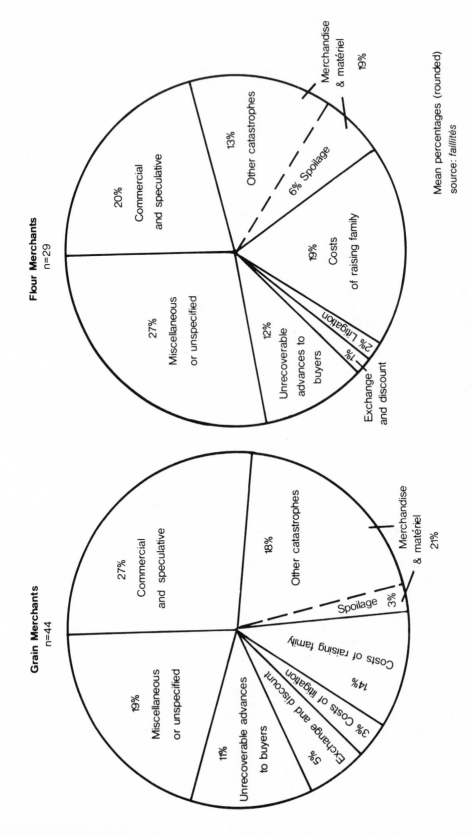

Grain Merchants
n=44

Commercial and speculative 27%

Miscellaneous or unspecified 19%

Other catastrophes 18%

Merchandise & matériel 21%

Spoilage 3%

Costs of raising family 14%

3% Costs of litigation

5% Exchange and discount

Unrecoverable advances to buyers 11%

Flour Merchants
n=29

Commercial and speculative 20%

Miscellaneous or unspecified 27%

Other catastrophes 13%

Merchandise & matériel 19%

6% Spoilage

Costs of raising family 19%

2% Litigation

7% Exchange and discount

Unrecoverable advances to buyers 12%

Mean percentages (rounded)
source: *faillites*

FIGURE 4 Kinds of losses claimed by merchants

flour office at the Halle, a former mealman, to operate a sack-recovery department.[216]

Almost two-thirds of the group listed various noncommercial accounts receivable. A quarter of these claims were for more than 2,000 livres. These paper claims were often suspect, frequently consisting of vague or remote or wished-for funds whose presence was intended to inflate the asset side in order to reduce the disparity between liabilities and assets. One would be inclined to question the "effects" that Laurent Caron of Mesnil-St.-Martin appraised at 16,262 livres or "the estate" of 30,000 livres that Gilles Tiphaine of Presles anxiously awaited (representing almost 70 percent of his total assets).

The balance sheets featuring large doses of hard assets were the ones that most easily persuaded creditors to grant postponements or repayment terms. Despite 30,862 livres in liabilities, the dossier of Antoine Mabine of Andrésy inspired confidence because he possessed "a large bourgeois house" (20,000 livres), a windmill (8,500 livres), four boats (1,200 livres), vineyards (1,600 livres), and other property. Louis Félix of Le Thillay, who was 24,356 livres in debt, made a favorable impression with 4,200 livres' worth of real estate, almost 11,000 livres in grain, 2,400 in vehicles and horses, and so forth. Louis Lelièvre of Chevreuse also resisted successfully, because his accounts payable of 4,594 livres were radically eclipsed by the value of his mill, 26,000 livres, not his only hard asset. The millers and merchants who had the most difficulty in redeeming themselves were those who hovered on the edge of fraud with their swollen paper assets or the genuinely poor, like Etienne Tissier of Corbeil whose assets of 1,936 livres were wholly soft and who languished in prison for a year and a half because he could not pay back 3,036 livres.

In order to justify their difficulties and to give their balance sheets a greater semblance of equilibrium, almost 60 percent of the group claimed losses (figure 4) averaging 13,164 livres (median = 4,680 livres). By adding the losses to the assets, they created a new figure that easily surpassed liabilities in mean (26,918 livres) or median (14,772 livres) terms. The failli hoped to demonstrate by this analysis that, had it not been for a series of accidents or a stroke of misfortune, he would surely have succeeded in his business and that consequently he merited indulgence. Many losses were by their nature "conjunctural." André Squeville of Gressy was victim of one of those "revolutions in the price" that were the most dislocating revolutions up until 1789. "At the time of the death of His Majesty Louis XV," Squeville "lost 2,000 livres in a single grain transaction." Yet there were accidents—that is, losses—of an almost structural character: flooding, drought, the death of horses, the break-

216. Arrêt du parlement, 22 July 1734, BN, Coll. Joly 1829, fol. 307; Archives Seine-Paris, D2B⁶ 766, 2 October 1743; AN, Y 11384, 7 February 1772. The police closely supervised the flour sack-making trade. See Arsenal, ms. Bast. 10141, 20 August 1757.

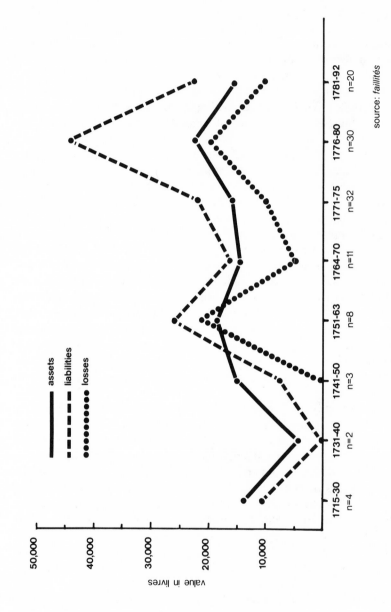

FIGURE 5 Grain and flour merchant failures: mean total assets, liabilities, and claimed losses, 1715–92

ing of a drive shaft. It was precisely because they were quasi-structural and thus suffered by almost everyone that these losses were in the end not very convincing. Equally doubtful were the personal losses that appeared in so many affidavits, such as the 1,000 livres that Hyaut contended that he "lost" on his wife's childbearing. Similarly, by what right did Goriot of Pontoise count as a "loss" eight years of service by four domestics, representing a total of 9,600 livres?

Family crises, often involving illness and medical expenses, accounted for some of the heaviest losses. This category, afflicting three-quarters of the group, represented 19 percent of total losses. Unwise deals that half the millers and merchants acknowledge having made represent 16 percent of total losses. These business reverses did not include commercial or speculative surprises occasioned by sudden price changes, which explain 3.4 percent of losses. The loss of matériel including horses and wagons affected half the group and caused 13 percent of total losses. Louis Poitou of Poissy lost ten horses in fifteen months, a loss he evaluated at 2,850 livres.[217] Merchandise loss, generally due to humidity or overheating, was less common, only 6 percent of the total. Equally rare were "bad debts," or accounts receivable deemed hopelessly unrecoverable. Apparently the failli preferred to put all accounts receivable in the assets column instead of formally burying the most doubtful, thereby deepening the abyss between assets and liabilities. Only two members of the group claimed losses due to recovery litigation and only one suffered losses on discounting paper. Figure 5 charts the mean total assets, liabilities, and claimed losses of merchant failures from 1715 to 1792.

What was the situation of the millers and merchants according to their own calculations? In 63 percent of the cases, their net worth (assets minus liabilities, with losses not taken into account) was negative: $-3,257$ livres on the average for the whole group (median $= -2,037$ livres). While 28 percent had a deficit greater than 5,000 livres, 30 percent had a positive net worth amounting to 3,800 livres on the average. The significance of the deficit (or the positive balance) for each failli depended not only on its raw magnitude but also on the composition of his assets and on their liquidity or convertibility, on the vigor of his business, and on the attitude of his creditors. Many of the creditors were grain merchants of modest means like Pierre Marguerite of Pontoise, who found himself in a untenable situation: "he could not wait any longer [to be paid], since he needed money for the operation of his business."[218] To escape the stigma and pain of failure, some millers and merchants, like Pierre Laforge of the faubourg de Gloire, borrowed money.[219]

217. A half-dozen faillis suffered "horse" losses as a result of disease and old age. But millers were also frequently victims of horse thefts. See Arsenal, ms. Bast. 10055, fol. 159 (5 April 1760); ms. Bast. 10057, fol. 195 (18 October 1760); ms. Bast. 10063, fol. 736 (28 September 1762); ms. Bast. 10083 (3 March 1773).

218. Rapport arbitre, 18 December 1758, Archives Seine-Paris, D6B⁶, carton 3.

219. AN, MC, VII-301, 18 March 1756.

Others, such as Charles Labbé and Etienne Tissier of Corbeil, Guillaume Dumont of Beaumont, and François Picot of St.-Germain-en-Laye, ceded their assets to their creditors, a procedure that usually enabled them to salvage their personal effects but compromised their chances of starting up again.[220] Charles Colas, a Brie mealman, frustrated his creditors by obtaining a year's grace from the royal government, a rare triumph.[221] Because it was not usually in the interest of the creditors to constrain the faillis to abandon their commerce, the bulk of the group obtained a second chance. When they were reasonable—like Aubée, who asked for two years—they usually received the terms they requested.[222] The fate of most of the members of the group is unknown. We can identify positively six who went on to prosper; three retired and two suffered a second failure.

The best results were achieved by the millers and merchants established in the environs of Paris (mean net worth of 6,376 livres) and in the Hurepoix (12,248 livres). The worst results accrued to those from the Valois (− 19,744), the Brie (− 19,114), and Paris (− 9,971 livres). The Hurepoix millers and merchants set the record for assets, averaging 32,178 livres, of which 65 percent were hard. The Parisians and the Valoisiens had resources—mean assets of 26,391 and 32,073 respectively—but they were battered with debts—36,362 and 51,817 respectively. The Valoisiens and Briards were the most heavily burdened with grain liabilities: 15,274 and 14,003 livres respectively. But while the Valoisiens had very few dealings with laboureurs (they owed 14,975 livres to grain merchants), the Briards acquired twice as much grain from laboureurs (who numbered fourteen on the average on each of their balance sheets) as from grain merchants. The Parisians had furniture worth three times that of their most affluent country confreres and they were the only ones to declare cash. The millers and merchants of the Ile-de-France had the most accounts receivable for the sale of flour (6,342 livres); 63 percent of their assets were soft. The Briards and the Beaucerons alleged the largest mean losses, 14,500 and 11,000 livres respectively.

The millers and merchants who owned their own mills appeared to be better off than those who rented. They were far more indebted (38,451 versus 13,804 livres), but their assets were substantially richer (36,982 versus 10,586 livres), leaving a theoretically modest deficit (− 1,469 versus − 3,218 livres). Although they were given a higher evaluation, the assets of the proprietors were not necessarily more robust. Despite their mills, which averaged 9,376 livres in value, and other real estate averaging 4,861 livres, almost half of their

220. Archives Seine-Paris, DC[6] 26, fols. 149–50, 25 June 1783; DC[6] 19, fol. 259, 7 October 1775; DC[6] 20, fol. 182, 27 August 1777; DC[6] 24, fol. 100, 18 August 1781.

221. Ibid., DC[6] 25, fol. 198, 21 December 1782. A Christmas present.

222. Nicolas Roze unsuccessfully tried to avoid failure by offering several of his grain creditors 5 percent interest on his debt. Archives Seine-Paris, D5B[6] 2114, 15 November 1775. Cf. the efforts of Mr. Tulliver to persuade his creditors of his honesty and reliability. Eliot, *The Mill on the Floss,* p. 310.

assets were paper (18,187 livres to recover in accounts receivable). More than three-quarters of the assets of the mill renters were hard, and they had on the average only 2,534 livres in accounts receivable to collect.

In nominal terms, according to the documents, the millers were much more deeply indebted than the flour merchants: 29,008 versus 13,220 livres on the average. Nor was the disparity fully compensated by respective assets: 21,011 livres for the millers versus 15,975 livres for the mealmen. The flour merchants boasted a positive net worth of 1,709 livres, while the millers were in the red by almost 8,000 livres. The millers had more hard assets, but the difference was not significant (53 percent versus 49 percent). More millers owned mills, but the mealmen possessed land and houses worth more (3,819 versus 2,714 livres). Their household effects were of approximately the same value (1,079 and 1,097 livres). Apart from the difference in magnitude, the liabilities of mealmen were distinguished from those of millers by the presence of debts for the purchase of flour (213 livres on the average) from other millers and flour merchants (three on the average). To judge from the losses claimed—27,067 livres by the millers and 3,350 by the flour merchants—the merchants were better managers but more timid businessmen, while the millers were adventuresome and speculative in temperament, ambitious to conquer new commercial space, but less well organized and less prudent. While the flour merchants lost only 694 livres on bad deals and nothing on price fluctuations, the millers complained of large losses in both domains: 10,399 and 4,705 livres.

One cannot characterize business skill merely on the basis of claimed losses. Still, this juxtaposition of millers and flour merchants once again underlines the artificiality of this dichotomy. These flour merchants, who were supposed to be the dynamic, innovating, commercializing force in the provisioning trade, acted more like the risk-averse, rural, service-oriented millers who were legion. And many of the millers in our sample—aggressive, urban and market directed—behaved as if they were first of all flour merchants. In fact the differences between millers and flour merchants were individual and specific rather than generic. We can legitimately envision a single universe dominated by certain millers and flour merchants who in many ways were indistinguishable. The only persons whose place is somewhat anomalous are the mealmen who did not operate mills. Frequently this situation was temporary—a miller fallen on bad times and obliged to retreat or a miller between two leases or a flour dealer recently launched in the business. It was rare for a successful flour merchant not to control the manufacture of his flour.

If the flour trade were encouraged to develop, its promoters contended, Frenchmen would be spared the cruelest of torments: "dying of famine atop a mound of grain." Not only would it provide insurance against flour crises by turning mills into granaries of abundance, but it would also stimulate grain production by offering agriculture new incentives, primarily in the form of a safe and necessarily profitable export trade in flour. It would generate improvements in milling that would result in more and better flour. Every consumer would experience its impact, for it would simplify and rationalize the provisioning process.

These perspectives were a bit remote, but they were not at all quixotic. Indeed, the flour trade revolution had already begun in the Paris region in the early eighteenth century. Milling became increasingly commercialized as millers became merchants (to a considerable extent under the impulsion of the bakers). Flour merchants, most of whom were mill connected, displaced grain merchants in the grain trade, even as the sharpest grain merchants gravitated to the flour trade.

Many flour merchants marketed their merchandise through the brokers at the Halle, while others sold independently to bakers on the trading floor of the Halle or clandestinely at their bakeshops, en droiture. Brokers sought privileged pratik relations with flour merchants even as the latter courted the bakers in the hope of establishing long-term bonds. Both made various concessions (priority services, premiums, price rebates, etc.). Both bitterly resented renegade pratik partners who succumbed to rival blandishments. Breach of promise on price and quality was the major source of baker ire against flour merchants. The difficulty that the merchants had in collecting accounts receivable from the bakers was their chief complaint. Inability to recover credit was one of the leading causes of business failure, along with mill shut-downs, accidents, and crisis dislocation. In order to keep open as many channels of supply and credit as possible, the flour merchants diversified and multiplied their sources of grain.

Though merchant millers were not licensed suppliers like the port merchants, the authorities expected them to perform as if they were public servants. The merchants risked severe penalties if they discontinued their provision (even as they occasionally received rewards for enlarging it). In the hope of attracting more flour dealers and blunting the allure of off-market transactions, the Paris police instituted a weighing station at the Halle at the end of the fifties. Flour supply increased, droiture traffic probably slackened (though it continued to remain quite significant), and the police obtained better information and imposed more efficient order than ever before.

CHAPTER *11*

Economic Milling

*E*conomic milling was the most exciting conceptual and technological innovation in the provisioning system during the old regime. It had the
potential to revolutionize the flour revolution and industrialize the whole
subsistence complex. Born of a number of artisanal initiatives, economic
milling won the support of the royal government, which facilitated its development and diffusion. It also captured the enthusiasm of the "economic"
intelligentsia called the physiocrats, whose patronage turned out to be something of a liability. Economic milling aroused the anxieties and the antagonism
of many millers and bakers because it called into question traditional practices and attitudes. It took root first in the Paris region, and gradually conquered the rest of France during the nineteenth century.

Milling: The State of the Art

The chief identifying characteristic of traditional grain-milling technology
was the single passage of the grain under the stone. Coarse *(grosse)* milling,
as this process was known, implied a relatively rapid grinding, with the stones
close together in order to subject the grain to maximal pulverization. Single-
stroke milling yielded an undifferentiated mixture of torn bran skins, burst
endosperm bag, and vegetable tissue. In commercialized (or "merchant")
coarse milling, mainly found around large towns and cities, the miller rarely
undertook bolting. Bakers performed bolting by hand in their flour rooms.

393

The most skillful and best-equipped practitioners used four different bolters fitted with cloths of varying thicknesses, but the majority probably settled for a more summary operation. They sifted out a white flour known as first or wheaten flour and a mid-white *(bis-blanc)* or second flour. The by-products— middlings and various sorts of bran—were usually destined for animal feed. Outside the commercial circuit, millers commonly employed the "rustic" version of coarse milling wherein a single bolting mechanism powered by the mill worked in parallel with the stones. Fitted with a fine cloth, the rustic bolter yielded an austerely white flour at a very low rate of extraction meant for the wealthy consumer-client. At antipodes from this "rich" grinding was the "poor" grinding meant for the peasantry, in which the sieve was so slack that virtually all the grist save the biggest chunks of bran and offal passed, composing a copious but heavy, dark, and lumpy whole meal. Between these extremes rustic millers also proposed a "bourgeois" meal purged of much of the most offensive bran and waste remnants.[1]

In milling as in law, language, and literacy, there was a north-south discontinuity, though it was neither as brutal nor as widespread as in other domains. "Southern" grinding per se was probably less common below the Loire than various forms of coarse milling. It was widely practiced in the coastal areas, for it was linked in large part with the production of flour for the colonies. Ground even more tightly than merchant coarse, southern grist was sifted neither in the milling process nor immediately afterward at the mill or at the bakeshop. What distinguished the southern technique was the long interval of up to two months between grinding and sifting, during which time the grist reposed, dried out, and began to ferment in great piles called *rames,* after the oarlike shovel used to turn and aerate the grist. Partisans of southern milling contended that the presence of the bran protected the meal and gave it a longer life. Once the grist "cooled," it was easier to separate the bran. The bolters yielded three qualities of flour: the *minot,* used for export and for luxury bread; the *simple* for bakers and bourgeois; and the *grésillon,* analogous to the *gruau* or middling meal of the north, used to make a people's bread.[2]

The basic coarse-milling process had not changed significantly for many generations. This torpor was not peculiar to milling. The history of large sectors of agriculture and the crafts seems to be immobile across the long early-modern run. Such inertia was especially pronounced and predictable within the subsistence nexus, where uncertainty caused such ravages and

1. Malouin, *Description et détails des arts,* pp. 31–34; Parmentier, *Parfait Boulanger,* pp. 165–70; Parmentier, *Mémoire sur les avantages,* pp. 146–51; AN, T 466$^{1-2}$; Cotte, *Leçons élémentaires,* p. 27; Brillon Duperron, *Observations sur la mouture,* p. 3; Antoine-Alexis Cadet de Vaux, *Moyens de prévenir le retour des disettes* (Paris, 1812), p. 13.

2. Malouin, *Description et détails des arts,* pp. 42, 45, 50–52; Louis Ammann, *Meunerie et boulangerie* (Paris, 1925), pp. 264–66.

where risk or novelty was regarded as intolerable. Psychological, regulatory, and commercial rigidities reinforced the timidity of the millers, for most of whom, in any event, technical perfection lay in emulating their fathers and grandfathers. In the eighteenth century, especially at the beginning, millers had no intimation that they were milling badly. The milling industry was extremely fragmented and dispersed, even in the Paris area. Each miller worked for a limited and more or less closed world, even if he had Parisian as well as local clients. For lack of a guild or other pole of attraction, millers had little professional contact among themselves. Turned in upon himself, the miller worked long, hard hours, often alone, sometimes assisted by a journeyman, a servant, and/or a wife. All that mattered for him was to avoid or minimize shut-downs. At least until the process of commercialization changed his view, the miller perceived himself as neither a merchant nor a manufacturer. Rather, he was a sort of mechanic who rented out his services. Quality was not his affair; it depended strictly on the grade of raw material. Nor was he concerned about productivity. That, too, depended on the quality of the grain. Given the regnant conventions, it was reasonable for the miller to presume that other millers would not outdo him.

Another disincentive to change was the miller's dubious reputation. A priori suspect, in legend, song, aphorism, police statutes, and local gossip, the miller could not risk innovations—they were bound to be misread. If he experimented with meal mixes in order to heighten the baking value of the flour or its conservability, he exposed himself to charges of adulteration, fraud, or worse. To introduce strange techniques would appear as a similar provocation. The miller's taste for routine was thus partly imposed by his public. Stagnation was thus a mark of honesty.

Public authorities seconded this tendency. They sought above all to maintain discipline in the chain of provisioning in order to assure social tranquility. Inter alia, that meant to prevent frauds and "maneuvers," to protect public health, to contain the avidity of traders, to promote open and fair transactions. By prohibiting the introduction of certain practices, such as grain purchase on speculation, buying on behalf of bakers, and salvaging and commercializing middling flour, the authorities impeded the modernization of the milling industry and flattered certain consumer prejudices. By enforcing feudal obligations *(banalités)* that manacled the miller, the authorities further reduced the prospects for change.

Finally, the bakers did not encourage technological evolution, at least at the dawn of the eighteenth century. Unwilling to be the tributaries of the millers (as so many would become in the nineteenth century), the bakers preferred not to entrust the whole task of flour making to them. To retain control over quality, to find the best and cheapest grain, and to protect their professional secrets, they were reluctant to abandon the business of acquiring grain, cleaning and preparing it, bolting, working and mixing meal, and stocking flour. The idea of permitting millers to make price and production decisions that would have limited their freedom of action in the bakeroom would have shocked the bakers. From their point of view, too, change was dangerous and gratuitous.

The Critique of Traditional Milling Technology

The conventional milling techniques had serious failings, many of which the millers themselves must have come to diagnose. Most millers did not pay enough attention to the quality of their stones and to the need to mount and balance them carefully and dress and furrow them methodically.[3] Many mills were structurally flawed, especially in the design and building of the drive shaft and gear system, resulting in extraordinary inefficiency.[4] Avid for gain, many millers tried to mill too much, too quickly. Milling was more complicated and delicate than they believed, wrote one baker-miller: "The stones of the mill are like the stomach: overstuff it and it can only produce a bad digestion."[5] Since they were not responsible for cleaning the grain, millers were frequently indifferent to hygienic conditions: dirt, dust, and insects infested the meal, discolored it, and threatened its quality.[6] Coarse milling, northern and southern style, brought the stones too close and turned them too fast. As a result the flour emerged "burning," flecked and reddened with finely powdered shell; diminished in its "drinking" capacity and thus likely to produce less bread; and abruptly "aged" and thus less likely to conserve well. It was argued that the bran in the southern *rame* "corrupted" the flour through fermentation, shortened its life, and imparted a soapy taste.[7] Coarse milling invited miller fraud because all the meal was mixed pell-mell in a sack, making it difficult for the baker to check.[8] Coarse milling without bolting increased final costs significantly by separating and multiplying the necessary operations (transportation, labor, etc.). The jerry-built rustic bolter sifted unevenly and unreliably.

The most telling reproach made against traditional milling technology was that it was extravagantly and needlessly wasteful.[9] Because coarse milling

3. Parmentier, *Parfait Boulanger,* pp. 165–68.
4. Bucquet, *Manuel du meunier,* pp. 119–20. See also *Ephémérides du citoyen* 9 (1769): 107.
5. Malisset, "Observations," June 1763, AD Nord, C 9780.
6. Parmentier, *Mémoire sur les avantages,* pp. 146–51.
7. Ibid.; Béguillet, *Traité des subsistances,* pp. 61–64, 98–99; Parmentier, *Parfait Boulanger,* pp. 170–72; Arsenal, ms. Bast. 10141, fols. 475–76 (26 April 1761). Cf. Grimshaw, *Miller, Millwright, and Millfurnisher,* p. 359 (flour "killed" by overheating).
8. Parmentier, *Mémoire sur les avantages,* pp. 146–51; Charlot, "Essai historique," p. 153.
9. For Malouin, waste in milling was a moral and civic derogation. No one had the right to waste grain, not even rich consumers who relished a very white grist. For in some sense

was inherently crude and ill conceived, wrote one subsistence expert, it engendered "enormous losses." It yielded barely more bread-making flour from three setiers than an improved technology produced from two.[10] Another subsistence commentator pointed to the "latent" abundance that could be tapped in the milling process. Perfected milling could result in huge savings, providing us "with plenty when we believed we had only just enough, and with enough when a dearth threatened." Defective milling, he contended, was "a veritable disaster" in a dearth, "the most onerous tax on the most indigent citizens." Bad milling and bad bread making, to which it was directly connected, he concluded, did more to raise prices than all the accidents of weather.[11] A practitioner with years of experience in baking and milling rose in indignation against "the misuse of one-fifth of the grain which occurs because the finest flour remains attached to the bran due to a vicious manner of milling." The ironic and tragic upshot was that the animals got the finest flour and the people got a large dose of bran.[12]

"The finest flour" to which the bakers referred came from the *gruaux* or middlings (or the *grésillon* of southern grist). The wheat kernel consists of essentially three parts: the bran, made up of several layers including the fruit and seed coats; the scutellum and the germ, which is the embryo of the future plant; and the endosperm, which is composed chiefly of starch, protein, and cellulose cell walls, with small amounts of sugars, lipids, gums, and other matter. Since the wheat kernel is comprised of about 85 percent endosperm, one should theoretically be able to obtain an 85 percent extraction of pure endosperm. This goal cannot be realized, however, even today, because the endosperm separates imperfectly from the bran. Differences in hardness and density of the different components as well as the deep crease that extends into the middle of the kernel on the ventral side further compromise clean separation. Given the inherent intractability of the wheat kernel and the rela-

---

the wasted flour "belongs to all society," not just to its ostensible owner. *Description et détails des arts*, pp. 33–34.

10. Béguillet, *Description historique de Paris*, 1:40n, and "Mémoire" (1778), AN, F[10] 256.

11. "Rapport au comité de salut publique par la commission d'agriculture et des arts," AN, F[10] 226; Parmentier, *Parfait Boulanger*, p. xlv; "Mémoire sur les avantages de la mouture économique," Arsenal, ms. 2891. Cf. the mitron in Lacombe d'Avignon, *Mitron de Vaugirard*, p. 33: "Since economic milling produces more bread than the old method, there will be no longer any reason at all to fear scarcity once this new process is established throughout the kingdom." See also Des Essarts, *Dictionnaire universel de police*, 7:468.

12. Malisset, "Observations," January 1767, AD Nord, C 9780; *Journal économique* (August 1761): 363–64. Middlings were known to make the best "poudre à poudrer" and were therefore much sought by starch makers as well as animal feeders. Narbonne, *Louis XIV et Louis XV*, p.473 A nineteenth-century critic of new process milling complained that one could no longer feed animals the residual meal because the economic technology removed the last iota of tasty and nourishing flour. "Not even the horses want to eat it any more." *Enquête sur la boulangerie*, p. 213.

tively crude and uneven grinding afforded by coarse technology, the meal produced contained, in addition to pure endosperm, middlings, bran of various sorts, and offal. Middlings are richly glutinous particles that adhere closer to the outside than to the interior of the flour bag, or endosperm. Situated immediately beneath the wheat skins, the middlings separate very reluctantly from the bran.[13] The bolter by itself is more or less powerless to salvage these middlings for use by the baker. The cloth is either too fine, in which case the middlings cannot pass, or it is too slack, in which case the bran passes with it. In any event, the few middlings that pass are not ground up and thus cannot drink water and knead into even dough.[14] Because they were generally not understood, the middlings were abandoned by coarse millers for starch or animal feed.[15] The loss of the middlings was not only a quantitative matter, for it impoverished the meal qualitatively. Men of the métier as well as theorists called middling flour "the most beautiful," "prettier than the flower," "superior to the flower," the most nourishing and savory part of the wheat berry. A process that recovered and utilized middlings would yield *more and better* flour, and thus more, better, and cheaper bread.[16]

In place of the traditional technology, the critics espoused a "perfected" milling process that Malisset styled "milling by economy" or "economic milling." The new system was based on the idea that was to remain the central principle of modern milling: gradual reduction of the wheat berry through successive grindings, breaking it down instead of pulverizing it, sifting out the freed particles of endosperm before dispatching the opened grain to the next passage and thus reclaiming the middlings (sometimes referred to as semolina or dunst). "Old process" milling, the late-nineteenth-century term for coarse grinding, sought to have as few middlings as possible. The object of modern milling was precisely the contrary: to produce as large a proportion of them as possible. To put it another way, the goal of the old process was to obtain flour immediately as the chief product, in as large a dose as possible. The aim of the

13. Béguillet and other contemporaries believed that the middlings were composed in part of the germ to which they attributed the fruity taste of middling bread. "Mémoire," AN, F[10] 256; Bucquet, "Mémoire" (1769), AD Isère, II C 47; Société d'Agriculture de Rouen, "Mémoire sur le commerce des blés et des farines," AN, H 1507. Modern flour chemistry tells us that middlings are mostly endosperm and that the germ, because of the oil it contains, is not prized by bakers.

14. Baudeau, *Avis au peuple,* deuxième traité, pp. 7–42.

15. The only consumers to benefit from the *gruaux* were those who ate a "poor" grist dark bread, but this loaf was flawed because of the large amount of bran and offal it contained. In any event, it was wholly unknown in the cities and towns.

16. Béguillet, *Traité des subsistances,* pp. 98–99, 339; Bucquet, "Mémoire" (1769), AD Isère, II C 47; Baudeau, *Avis au peuple,* deuxième traité, pp. 30–42; Malouin, *Description et détails des arts,* p. 84. The famous American millwright Oliver Evans considered that middlings "contain a portion of the best part of the grain." *Young Millwright,* pp. 264–66. But the scientist Tillet disputed the contention of many practitioners that the second middlings were as good as the first, thus lending support to the critics of excessive regrindings. "Projet d'un tarif."

new system, in its most fully developed form, was to produce as little flour as possible during the preparatory or "breaking" stage. Economic millers did not separate the breaking and reduction phases as sharply as their successors, nor did they learn to break and rebreak as delicately as later became standard—in part perhaps because their soft wheats had elastic coverings that resisted reduction and were thus relatively easy to remove through bolting. They lacked the confidence to eschew taking a first flour, though they knew that it was not as good as the middling flour that subsequently emerged. Still, the repeated grinding and coordinated bolting of economic milling opened the way to a host of significant improvements.[17]

To cleaning, grinding, and bolting, the late-nineteenth-century innovators added two more steps: the purification and regrinding of middlings. This "new process milling," as it was proudly baptized in the 1870s, òwed much more to the new economic millers of the eighteenth century than its vaunted Minneapolis practitioners knew. The economic millers lacked the sophisticated purifying machines combining air and sieve separation and the far more efficient iron rolls, but they employed the same basic idea. Economic milling meant above all salvaging the middlings, but it also implied a sweeping array of changes and adjustments in mill construction and operation that moved far beyond the relatively simple exhortation to pass the grain again and again under the stone. The economic system called for a division of the processes into separate stages in which each class of material of approximately the same nature and size received a specific treatment. Nor was grinding the first stage. In order to extract the maximum flour charge from the wheat berry under conditions that would guarantee its excellence, the grain had first to be cleaned. When the wheat arrived at the mill, it often contained chaff, straw, stones, weed seeds, insects, and grains of other cereals. That was especially likely when the baker brought his grain directly to the mill from the market. Even if the baker conditioned the grain before sending it to be ground, it could easily become recontaminated at the mill. As a rule, the miller did not concern himself with the cleanliness of the grain despite the fact that the presence of impurities adversely affected grinding and bolting and damaged the meal

17. On the "new process," see Kuhlmann, *Flour-Milling Industry,* pp. 113ff.; Grimshaw, *Miller, Millwright, and Millfurnisher,* pp. 407–9; Kozmin, *Flour Milling,* pp. 489–90; Douglas W. Kent-Jones and John Price, *The Practice and Science of Bread-Making* (Liverpool, 1951), pp. 23–25. Oblivious to eighteenth-century innovation, many leading twentieth-century experts assimilated everything prior to 1850 to the dark ages of milling. See Amos, *Flour Manufacture,* p. 7. Oliver Evans independently developed many of the "economic" or "new process" techniques, but had difficulty in establishing his exclusive claim to their paternity. In addition to his *Young Millwright,* see Greville and Dorothy Bathe, *Oliver Evans: A Chronicle of Early American Engineering* (Philadelphia, 1935), pp. 12–14, and Thomas Jefferson, *The Writings of Thomas Jefferson,* ed. Andrew A. Lipscomb (Washington, D. C., 1903–1904), 11:200–202 (Jefferson to Evans, 2 May 1807) and 14:63–67 (Jefferson to Evans, 16 January 1816).

product. Before grinding the economic miller thoroughly cleansed his wheat in mechanical, oscillating sifters and winnowers powered by the same force that moved the stones. The operation was rapid, effective, and cheap since it spared the miller any labor. The next logical step was to harness the mill force to drive an elevator, a conveyor, a drill, and a hopper boy. Economic milling in its fullest expression was an integrated, vertical factory of five or six stories run more or less automatically.[18]

The second stage began when the purified wheat, ready to be ground, dropped into the hopper above the stones. Since his goal was to crush all the parts of the berry as fully and as evenly as possible without overheating, the economic miller paid more attention to the preparation and operation of the stones than most coarse millers. He chose stones of firm and durable material and skillful composition unlikely to chip, crack, or sweat. He sought stones that responded well to the dresser's hammer, for the economic miller realized that the proper furrowing of the stones was of decisive importance in successive grindings. Coarse millers tended to groove at random ("à l'aventure" or "à coups perdus"), chiseling sharp and uneven "points" into the stones that cut or "swallowed" grain instead of grinding it and that either reduced it to a dust or left many large particles untouched. Stones grooved in this fashion tended to polish each other and needed very frequent dressing, incapacitating the mill and handicapping the miller until the stones were again broken in. The economic miller inscribed even, circular rows on the stones.

Even well-dressed, high-caliber stones could not give an even grinding if they were not mounted with precision. The economic miller wanted at all costs to avoid overheating, which "fattened" and muddied the best stones, causing the grist to slide without being crushed and flattening the bran without curing it. In addition to rendering a lumpy, coarse flour, the overheated stones imparted a bad odor and taste to the "burnt" meal and made it more volatile and less easy to knead. To prevent overheating, the economic miller ground "round" or "gay" instead of tight. He could afford the "round" approach since he would be regrinding several times. Yet he did not want his final pass merely to caress the wheat berries, and further, he wanted to be able to shift the runner stone easily in order to execute each successive turn à mesure. That required a superbly balanced and reinforced mounting.[19]

The aim of the third stage was to recover the middlings and regrind them separately. This required a far more elaborate and meticulous bolting process than had ever before been envisaged.[20] Like the sifters and winnowers, the

18. See the evocation of Malisset's Corbeil establishment in Kaplan, *Bread, Politics and Political Economy*, 1:351–52, 363–64; Bucquet, *Manuel du meunier*, pp. 78–86; Béguillet, *Traité des subsistances*, pp. 211–25. See also Bennett and Elton, *Corn Milling*, 2:194–97.

19. Bucquet, *Manuel du meunier*, pp. 119–20. He suggested at one point that the chief flaw in traditional milling was structural: a poorly wrought connection between drive shaft and running stone in particular.

20. Though the engineer Belidor wrote as early as 1731 that to be "complete" a mill had to be equipped with a bolting system. *Architecture hydraulique*, 1:295.

bolters were powered by the mill-drive. In the most advanced mills, the bolter consisted of a revolving reel, usually cylindrical, sometimes hexagonal, twenty feet long and thirty inches across. It contained three bolting cloths, often of silk or wool, the finest at the head and the coarsest at the foot. The reel was slightly tilted toward the lower end so that in revolving, the meal was gradually carried through. The flour was sifted through the finest cloth at the head of the reel ("throughs"); from the midsection came the "returns"; the product of the coarsest cloth was called "shorts"; and the bran tailed over the lower end. The returns went right back to the upper end for further separation prior to further reduction. Tailings were sent back to the stones for regrinding. The larger mills had several reels enclosed in a wooden chest to prevent the dispersal of the flour. The most common sifting system was a less elaborate, two-part apparatus, a simple bolter that siphoned off the wheaten or first flour and sent all the middlings and bran to the second machine, usually a cradle-sifter *(dodinage)*, more rarely a cylindrical reel, that divided and separated more rigorously. This second sifting yielded a white middling with barely any trace of shell; a second or gray middling, with some shell and germ, less nourishing than the first but drier and thus able to drink more water; a dark middling, heavily textured with bran; and several different magnitudes and qualities of bran. The practice of grading middlings foreshadowed one of the major nineteenth-century milling innovations.[21]

Dr. Malouin went so far as to argue that economic milling was a misnomer, that the crucial affair was the bolting, and that this in fact could take place away from the mill.[22] The miller Bucquet conceded that the bolting afforded economic milling "the degree of perfection that distinguished it from all other milling," though he vehemently resisted the notion that the bolting stage could be separated from the rest of the economic process and still yield the same results.[23]

Without the fourth stage, which restored the primacy to milling properly speaking, the middling potential would remain untapped. For now each of the middling streams (possibly also the "waste" biproducts called *recoupettes* and *recoupes*) had to pass through the stones and the bolter again. For each stream the stones were set differently. After each bolting, certain streams passed yet again, depending on the production strategy of the miller. The first repassage generated flour called first middling or *blanc bourgeois* to distinguish it from the "flower" or wheaten flour commonly called *blanc*. The *blanc bourgeois* had more body and savor and was no less pretty in appearance.

21. Bucquet, *Manuel du meunier,* pp. 40ff., 91–98; M.B., "Mémoire" (1769), Arsenal, ms. 2891; Cotte, *Leçons élémentaires,* pp. 32–34; Ammann, *Meunerie et boulangerie,* pp. 183–84; Chomel, *Dictionnaire oeconomique,* p. 791; *Journal économique* (August 1761): 363–64; Kozmin, *Flour Milling,* pp. 392–93.

22. Malouin, *Description et détails des arts,* pp. 33–34, 70–71. Malouin remained per-suaded that warm flour bolted badly and that no millwright could successfully incorporate a double bolting system into the mill drive.

23. Bucquet, *Manuel du meunier,* pp. 86–87.

The remaining portions of the white middlings passed twice more, yielding a flour slightly inferior in quality to the first middling but without a trace of bran and with considerable "allure." The head or elite of the gray middlings could be treated with the white; the rest of it produced a dark flour that was largely bran free if it was delicately ground. Grinding on wheat was technically less demanding than grinding on middlings, for the latter were smaller and harder than the wheat berries and they obliged the miller to grind more tightly without, however, burning the meal.[24] Even the *recoupes* could be reground once in order to extract a dark flour that was equal in quality to the second-caliber gray middling meal. Since the different types of flour emerged entirely separate, the baker could verify that he had been honestly served. With this range of qualities, the baker or the miller—the partisans of economic milling insisted that it had to be the venturesome merchant miller—would be in a position to make the most compelling mixtures.[25]

A considerable amount of bran remained, but it was purged of virtually all its endosperm. The first bran, called *fleuret* or *fleurage,* saved the baker several handfuls of flour for each loaf he made by serving to powder or line the oven shovel, the bread molds, and the oven floor (keeping saltpeter out of the bread). The lesser or larger and denser bran went to pigs, cows, sheep, chickens, and horses.[26]

The Advantages of Economic Milling

The specialists contended that it was a simple matter to convert a mill to the economic system, but they had a certain incentive to exaggerate the ease of the transition.[27] The mill had to be structurally stabilized in order to achieve a slow and even grinding rhythm. In some instances, the waterwheel had to be modified to increase the mill's power. It was recommended that the gear system transmitting power from the wheel to the stones be altered for the sake of a smoother, more efficient operation. The runner stone had to be more precisely "suspended" than ever so that it could be adjusted up or down

24. Oliver Evans recommended regrinding middlings with whole wheat berries, "because the grain keeps them from being killed." *Young Millwright,* pp. 208–9.

25. Bucquet, "Mémoire" (1769), AD Isère, C 47. Yet it was precisely this mixing potential of economic milling that aroused fears of fraud and confirmed old suspicions. See "Résultats des observations," 1773, AD Marne, C 417.

26. The exponents of economic milling claimed that while economic milling yielded less bran in weight than coarse processing, it gave just as much in volume, which was the way it was sold. *Nouvelles Ephémérides économiques* 10 (1775): 159–60. This claim strikes me as wholly implausible, given the huge difference in the gross yield of bran in coarse and economic middlings, unless the middlings from the coarse grinding are separated crudely by bolters in the bakeshop and sold separately.

27. *Bulletin de la société d'encouragement pour l'industrie nationale,* ventôse, an XI; Baudeau, *Résultats de la liberté et de l'immunité,* p. 28.

without compromising the evenness of the grinding. More careful attention had to be paid to inscribing the furrows and grooves, and to renewing them regularly. The most delicate change was the incorporation of two bolters, which had to be calibrated with the wheeldrive and the stone rotation. Experts encouraged economic millers to integrate cylindrical sifters and ventilators into the milling process for the purpose of preparing the grain. Enterprising millers could also save on labor by setting up mill-driven elevators, conveyors, and hopper boys.[28] While both wind- and water mills were adaptable, in many instances wind power proved insufficient to drive the bolters, sifters, and pulley systems in addition to the stones.[29]

Malisset and Bucquet concurred that these transformations were "of modest cost," but they had in mind Paris-area mills that were generally "well put together."[30] The minimal investment for conversion to economy ranged from 400 to 800 livres, but many mills must have required substantially more. The bolters were not extremely costly—150 to 200 livres. But if a miller needed new stones (perhaps 1,000 livres), a new mounting chassis (200 livres), and a new drive shaft with trundles and cogwheels (550 livres)—that is, if he had a relatively old and badly crafted machine—he would have to invest a considerable sum. And if he desired to add sifting, ventilating, and pulley systems, he had to allow another 600 to 800 livres.[31] It seems to me that most millers would have needed some help to make the change to the economic way: concessions from the mill owner, lease adjustments, loans with generous terms. The cost factor was surely a serious deterrent, for the mass of millers were relatively poor. One way to resolve the problem of capital accumulation and to maximize the structural and commercial advantages afforded by economic technology was to combine several mills into a large factory on the model of Malisset's Corbeil.[32] A number of such installations emerged, but millers, even those who had no allergy to innovation, overwhelmingly continued to prefer the solitary, artisanal style, until factory competition finally drove them out of business in the nineteenth century.

Advocates of economic milling vehemently denied that it required more time and would thus reduce mill activity and revenue. They called attention to

28. Bucquet, *procès-verbal,* 29 November 1769, AD Côte-d Or, C 421; Parmentier, *Parfait Boulanger,* pp. 181–84, and *Mémoire sur les avantages;* Machurin, *procès-verbal,* 28–29 November 1767, AN, Y 12616; Brillon Duperron, *Considérations sur la mouture,* p. 13. Cf. Elton and Bennett, *Corn Milling,* 2:194–97; Bourde, *Agronomie et agronomes,* 2:913.

29. Réponse du Sr Malisset, 27 June 1763, AD Nord, C 9780; Parmentier, *Parfait Boulanger,* p. 181. Bucquet and Béguillet were more sanguine about using windmills than Parmentier and Dransy. Béguillet, *Traité des subsistances,* p. 338.

30. Réponse du Sr Malisset, 27 June 1763, AD Nord, C 9780; Béguillet, *Traité des subsistances,* pp. 107–8.

31. Bucquet, *Manuel du meunier,* pp. 50–51; Béguillet, *Traité des subsistances,* pp. 107–8, 336–39; Paillot to unknown, 20 April 1769, AD Aube, C 1909.

32. In this regard, see Parmentier's comments on *réunions. Mémoire sur les avantages,* p. 153.

all the labor-saving devices built into the system and to the time and cost that would be spared by on-the-spot bolting and sorting. They argued that coarse milling, because it had to grind tightly in a single movement, slowed up the operation considerably in order to avoid burning the flour. Baudeau claimed that all the economic operations, including cleaning and sifting, grinding without causing heat, and bolting, took only sixteen minutes more than the coarse operation on the same quantity of grain. Malisset reminded Baudeau, however, that even if a given economic passage (including grain preparation and meal processing) took only slightly more time than a coarse grinding, there were nevertheless more passages that had to be accomplished in the economic system. He estimated that milling by economy could take up to twice as long, though he added that an economic mill could run for four and one-half hours on the same magnitude of water power that kept an ordinary mill turning for only three.[33]

Given its multiple advantages, it was "natural," Baudeau maintained, that it cost more to mill economically, usually about 50 percent above the coarse price. In 1761 Malisset reported that the Moulin de St.-Maur charged 20 sous to grind a Parisian setier by the coarse method and 30 sous for economic treatment. Malouin found certain economic millers willing to grind for 24 sous and Baudeau met others who asked 20. In 1771 Malisset's Corbeil mills billed the government only 20 sous the setier, but that may have been a special institutional price. In the eighties the standard economic fee was 30 sous, according to Parmentier, though other observers saw it as high as 40 sous.[34]

There was no consensus on the productivity of economic technology, probably because of enormous variations from mill to mill. Malisset prudently suggested 10 or 11 setiers in twenty-four hours, surely the most plausible estimate. Parmentier set the normative range between 24 and 30 setiers: if the mill produced less, it was grinding "too roundly," leaving too much flour in the bran; if it produced more, then the stones were too close and the flour overheated and became speckled with bran flakes. Bucquet envisaged a minimum of 12 setiers in an undershot mill and a maximum of 31 in an overshot mill, but it appears he considered only the grinding stage in the twenty-four-hour period, allowing for neither preparation nor bolting. For "finished" economic milling, Tillet doubted that a miller could produce more than 16 setiers

33. See Béguillet, *Traité des subsistances,* pp. 30–31; Cochut, "Le Pain à Paris," *Revue des deux mondes,* 33d year, 2d period, 47 (15 September 1863): 420; Baudeau, *Avis au peuple,* deuxième traité, pp. 20–21; "Observations," 16 August 1764, AD Nord, C 9780.

34. Malisset, "Mouture par économie," p. 364; [Louis-] Pierre Manuel, *La Police de Paris dévoilée* (Paris, year II), 1:381; "Etat qui fait connaître l'établissement de Corbeil," 20 February 1771, AN, F[11] 1193; Malouin, *Description et détails des arts,* pp. 107–9; Baudeau, *Avis au peuple,* deuxième traité, p. 41; Parmentier, Mémoire sur les avantages, p. 407; BN, Coll. Joly 1743, fol. 146; députés de commerce, "Premier supplément au premier mémoire," BN, ms. fr. 14295, fol. 41; Tillet, "Projet d'un tarif," p. 158.

in a day. Early nineteenth-century figures suggest that average daily production was much lower than any of the experts had calculated.[35]

Its partisans presented economic milling as a total reform, as a system in which *tout se tenait* in the best enlightened scientific idiom, as a more or less revolutionary achievement (what we would call a breakthrough).[36] It saved labor, time, and money by mechanizing and integrating grain preparation, loading, and bolting. Not only was its yield greater, cheaper, and of higher caliber, but it was also more regular. Its predictability would enable the government to establish a more equitable pricing standard and to plan more effectively to meet subsistence needs.[37] It invited a sweeping rationalization of the subsistence nexus by establishing the scientific basis for a new, invigorated flour trade that would fully eliminate the old-fashioned grain trader, transform the miller-servant into a merchant with a vested interest in high quality and probity, spare the bakers the need to make field purchases, and enable the bakers to offer more, better, and cheaper bread.[38] Flour ground economically would store easily for two years or more because it "was not worn out," thus facilitating both long-distance trade and commercial or public stockage.[39] Economic technology would stimulate the exportation of a finished product, flour, rather than a raw material, grain, thereby inducing foreign countries to subsidize in part a critical French industry.[40] Given the inherent superiority of middling flour (it was sweeter, more absorbent, and lighter and contained more of the "soft mucilage"), the exponents of economic milling pronounced the bread it produced to be of peerless quality: tastier, more nourishing, easier to digest, more appetizing, fruitier and nuttier in odor.[41] Miller Bucquet rightly but vainly reminded consumers that "it is not

35. Députés de commerce, "Premier supplément au premier mémoire," BN, ms. fr. 14295, fol. 44; Parmentier, *Parfait Boulanger*, pp. 194–95; Bucquet, *Manuel du meunier*, pp. 56–60; Tillet, "Project d'un tarif," p. 157.

36. See Parmentier's insistence on this aspect. Parmentier to intendant of Brittany, November 1784, AD Ille-et-Villaine, C 1710; "Mémoire sur les avantages que la province de Languedoc peut retirer de ses grains" (1786), p. 148, AD Haute-Garonne, C 2268.

37. Tillet, "Projet d'un tarif," pp. 107–12.

38. Béguillet and Bucquet emphasized the utility of promoting not only a wholesale flour trade but a retail one as well. They contended rather vaguely that this would somehow "prevent dearths" and "calm popular uprisings in times of high prices and unemployment" by enabling dayworkers to acquire small amounts of flour for a few sous. "Mémoire sur les avantages de la mouture économique et du commerce des farines" (1769), pp. 210–11, Arsenal, ms. 2891. Physiocrats like Dupont insisted upon the salutary impact that economic milling was supposed to have on bread prices. *De l'exportation et de l'importation des grains* (1764), in Edgard Depitre, ed., *Collection des économistes et des réformateurs sociaux de la France* (Paris, 1911), pp. 33–34.

39. Malisset, "Observations," January 1767, AD Nord, C 9780.

40. This argument had powerful appeal in the sixties and seventies, when the debate over the grain trade was the major public issue of the day. See Kaplan, *Bread, Politics and Political Economy*, 1:337–38.

41. *Journal économique* (March 1762): 111; "Mémoire sur les avantages de la mouture

the color that makes good bread."[42] But his fellow crusaders were willing to make no concessions even on this superficial but psychologically crucial matter. Parmentier claimed that a mélange of the yield of a setier of economically ground meal produced a whiter flour than the whitest that could be obtained from the ordinary processes.[43] Béguillet boasted that economic white and dark breads were both whiter than their coarse counterparts.[44]

Still, quality, save to the extent that it meant greater quantity, was considered only a supplementary refinement, a sort of bonus. The most exciting and socially significant news was the striking increase in yield that economic enthusiasts vaunted. The experts did not agree on the exact figure at which to estimate the savings. The theorists as usual were more febrile in their optimism than the practitioners. Mirabeau imagined fully a third more bread and Dupont a fourth, while Malisset talked of a seventh or an eighth and Bucquet prudently posited a range from one-tenth to one-fourth.[45] The new technology will "augment our harvests by a seventh," wrote the liberal Parlement of Provence to Louis XV in 1768.[46] Poussot, the police inspector of the Halles, dreamed of a 20 percent increment in flour productivity.[47] Legrand d'Aussy contemplated an enormous social impact, for while economic milling might not extract more than an eighth more wheat, it would increase the yield of the "popular" cereals—rye and barley—by one-third and one-half respectively.[48] In one place, Béguillet envisioned a savings of between one-sixth and one-fourth, representing one whole harvest extra in four or five years or enough

économique et du commerce des farines," Arsenal, ms. 2891, p. 199; Brillon Duperron, "Observations sur la mouture," p. 9; Roret, *Manuel de la boulangerie et de la meunerie*, p. 192; Baudeau, *Avis aux honnêtes gens*, pp. 88–93; "Mémoire sur l'art . . ." (1777), AN, F[10] 256; Diderot et al., eds., *Encyclopédie*, 10:829; Arsenal, ms. Bast. 10141, fol. 452 (2 March 1761).

42. Bucquet, *Observations intéressantes*, p. 64.

43. Parmentier, *Parfait Boulanger*, pp. xl–xlii. Cf.: "The most expensive bread . . . [now made] is the worst and the least substantial." Ibid., pp. xliii–xliv.

44. Béguillet, *Discours sur la mouture* (1775), p. 191. Cf. Béguillet's claim that Paris owed its bread superiority over the provinces to its use of economic flour. *Traité des subsistances*, pp. 28–29n. Bucquet announced in 1769 that "Lyon is now a Paris for good bread" since it began to adopt the economic technology. "Mémoire," 2 March 1769, AD Isère, II C 47.

45. Georges Weulersse, *Le Mouvement physiocratique en France de 1756 à 1770* (Paris, 1910), part 2, pp. 526–27; *Journal économique* (August 1761): 363; Bucquet, *Manuel du meunier*, p. 117. Moheau, an acute observer and disabused administrator, saw little more than a 5 percent gain. *Recherches et considérations sur la population de la France (1778)* . . . , ed. René Gonnard (Paris, 1912), p. 34.

46. AD Bouches-du-Rhône, C 2420.

47. Arsenal, ms. Bast. 10141, fol. 412 (26 November 1762). This was the figure used thirty years later in the *Encyclopédie méthodique*, Jurisprudence, police et municipalités, 10:32.

48. Legrand d'Aussy, *Vie privée*, 1:75.

Cross-section of an economic mill,
from the *Encyclopédie*

supplementary subsistence to nourish four to five million "more" Frenchmen;
and in another place he foresaw an economy of a good third.[49]

Viewed across the long run and in terms of annual per capita consumption
needs, the results of the new technology seemed even more striking. It was
generally agreed that in Henri IV's time it took four setiers to meet the needs
of an individual in a year. Most observers believe that a century later it
required only three, and by the end of the reign of Louis XV two setiers
sufficed. While some progress had been made during the first half of the
century, economic milling was given most of the credit for the great leap.[50]
For scientists like Parmentier, deeply interested in improving the conditions

49. Béguillet, "Mémoire" (1778), AN, F¹⁰ 256, and *Traité des subsistances*, pp. ix, xlii,
354–55, 399–402. Parmentier contemplated a savings of about 25 percent. *Parfait Boulanger*,
p. xxvii. A mid-nineteenth-century expert estimated that coarse grinding produced 15 to 18
percent less flour than the economic milling of his time. *Enquête sur la boulangerie*, p. 13.

50. Béguillet, *Traité des subsistances*, pp. 354–55; Béguillet, "Mémoire," AN, F¹⁰ 256;
Béguillet, "Mémoire sur les avantages de la mouture économique," Arsenal, ms. 2891;
Malouin, *Description et détails des arts*, p. 59; *Journal économique* (May 1771): 217;
Encyclopédie méthodique, Jurisprudence, police et municipalités, 10:32. Parmentier oscil-
lated between 2.25 setiers and 2 setiers. *Parfait Boulanger*, pp. xliii–xlv and *Avis aux
bonnes ménagères*, p. 105.

of everyday life, no single achievement in the century of Enlightenment was more significant. But it was not enough to celebrate the potential. Following Malouin, Parmentier argued that scientists, like millers and bakers, had a moral and civic obligation to put an end to waste. No one had a right to misuse flour merely on the grounds that he was its owner and could afford to be prodigal, for, Parmentier contended, "it is a question here of a commodity that in some sense belongs to Society."[51]

The Origins of Economic Milling

What were the origins of the new process? Was its discovery as abrupt as some contemporaries seemed to suggest? If the technology was crystallized—conceptualized and realized in its totality—for the first time around 1760, probably by Malisset and his associates, there was nevertheless a relatively long and not so lonely itinerary of preparation, replete with banal and unself-conscious decisions and actions that acquire meaning only in retrospect. No one discovered economic milling, but a considerable number of merchants and craftsmen practiced bits and pieces of it without knowing that they were contributing to a grander enterprise than their own profit margins.[52] We know that certain millers overcame the inertia and ignored the risks in order to experiment with better gear and shaft connections, more efficient wheels or wings, finer stone mountings, and so on; but save in one or two cases we do not know their names. We know that others—bakers as well as millers—reinvented the bolter many times, tempering its jolting movement, nuancing and multiplying its sifting capacity, and so forth.

The least obscure part of the story concerns the gradual rehabilitation of middlings. There were a number of pioneer iconoclasts, as the partisans of economic milling, flattered by a heroic heritage, believed. But the movement was far more widespread than they were aware or cared to acknowledge. The point of departure was a mid-sixteenth-century police statute, renewed a century later, that prohibited grinding grain more than once, on the grounds that repassage facilitated miller frauds and yielded flour that was dangerous to

51. Parmentier, *Parfait Boulanger,* p. 175. Despite their effusive support for economic milling, this is not an argument that the physiocrats would have relished. But it is interesting to see the embryo of an argument from a quasi-scientific imperative that transcends natural law and constrains social obligation by limiting the right of property. For the debate on grain as property, see Kaplan, *Bread, Politics and Political Economy,* 1:181–82; 2:460–61, 596–97.

52. As an experienced, experimenting, lucid miller, Bucquet was enraged at the claim for paternity of economic milling registered by certain savants. He rightly insisted that it was the product of a long evolution, a step-by-step and trial-and-error process. "It is for this reason that the precise date of discovery and the name of the inventor are not known": *Observations intéressantes,* p. 57.

human health.[53] The law was doubtless in large part a consequence of extremely crude milling technology that failed to separate bran and flour and produced a heavy, sticky bread that physicians felt was unfit for human consumption. But the initial promulgation and its reiteration also indicate that bakers and millers had been experimenting with middling potential long before it was forbidden and continued to do so afterward.[54]

Dr. Malouin suggested that the millers of Senlis, led by Pigeault, were the first to practice the systematic separation and regrinding of middlings, beginning in the 1660s.[55] Parmentier gave credit for the innovations to Rousseau, operating out of the Beauce at about the same time.[56] Miller Bucquet, son and grandson of millers, had it from his parents that economic milling took root in the early decades of the reign of Louis XIV in the mills of L'Isle-Adam, Valmondois, Beaumont, Chambly, and Senlis. Bucquet attributed its development to the increasingly insistent Parisian demand for white flour. The only way millers could meet this demand was to break the law and transform the ostensibly inedible into the finest elite flour. These precursors called their technique "grinding for white."[57] An early version of economic milling probably accounted for the "paradox" of Melun that puzzled Delamare. It turned on the decision of the Melun traders to provision Paris in flour rather than in grain, beginning around 1680. They found this business more profitable. After extracting the flower for the capital, they sold their *recoupes* and fatty or mealy bran for use in local bread making. This by-trade is a paradox, wrote

53. Béguillet, *Traité des subsistances,* p. 72; Des Essarts, *Dictionnaire universel de police,* 7:468; Baudeau, *Avis au peuple,* deuxième traité, pp. 34–42; Beckmann, *History of Inventions,* pp. 262ff.; Arpin, *Historique de la meunerie,* 1:117; Béguillet, *Discours sur la mouture* (1775), p. 180. The prohibition figured in the statutes of the baker guild in 1680. Malouin, *Description et détails des arts,* p. 40. Nor was the Paris area the only place where authorities banned the separation and recovery of middlings. "De la récolte dans la partie du Maine qui avoisine la Perche," *Gazette d'agriculture, commerce, arts et finances* (31 October 1769): 860, and Charlot, "Essai historique," p. 145. Cf. the testimony of a mid-nineteenth-century flour merchant who looked back with stupefaction upon the dark ages of the eighteenth century when "middlings, which today give us luxury bread, were banned as unhealthy." Those were the days, observed the merchant, when men starved while animals gorged themselves on the rich middlings. *Enquête sur la boulangerie,* p. 13.

54. See the petulant but not entirely unfounded assertion that economic milling had been known "from time immemorial." *Gazette d'agriculture, commerce, arts et finances* (1 August 1769): 600. Béguillet suggested that the Romans had practiced a sort of economic milling and that technology had regressed since their time. *Discours sur la mouture* (1775), p. 244.

55. Malouin, *Description et détails des arts,* pp. 38–40.

56. Parmentier, *Parfait Boulanger,* pp. 179–80.

57. Bucquet, *Observations intéressantes,* pp. 70–71. Cf. A. Maurizio, *Histoire de l'alimentation végétale depuis la préhistoire jusqu'à nos jours,* trans. F. Gidon (Paris, 1932), p. 555. Mirabeau said that he learned from Bucquet that these vanguard millers tried to keep their discoveries secret in order to protect their self-interest. Arpin, *Historique de la meunerie,* 1:125–26. Yet it was hardly a secret if it was widely practiced in the cantons cited by Bucquet. See also Bord, *Histoire du blé en France,* p. 59.

Delamare, for although the bread that comes out of it is certainly less good it was preferred "even by distinguished persons," and the flour from which it was made commanded a higher price proportionately than the top flour.[58]

By the turn of the century the middling was still wrapped in mystery and misunderstanding. It had not yet entered everyday language invested with the sense that we give it. For Furetière in 1690 *gruau* described primarily a dried oat flour purged of its bran. It also designated a big, coarse, dark loaf made of flour whose bran was not removed.[59] A hundred years later middling bread had come to mean "a bread of superior quality."[60] In 1757 the *Encyclopédie* still stigmatized middling flour as essentially bran laden and inferior to white. Nor is that surprising, since even the promoters of mill reform tended to locate the commercial rehabilitation of middlings in the second half of the century. Malouin maintained that middling flour stagnated in price because bakers remained deeply suspicious of it.[61] Derided as "Champagne flour," a term of disdain in the profession, middling flour, wrote Béguillet, was rejected even in the dearth of 1740.[62] Doubtless this prejudice and hesitation were relatively widespread and lasted for a long time. Yet from the beginning of the century a vigorous middling commerce swam against the tide. While some bakers as late as 1760 may have regarded middling flour as "contraband," others as early as 1719 valued it above all the other types of flour.[63] Some of the impetus to turn inward toward the middlings may have come from the great dearths of the last decades of the seventeenth century and the first quarter of the eighteenth century, which placed great pressure on bakers and millers to increase the productivity of available grain.[64] Wherever the bakers and millers failed to take the initiative they were replaced by bran merchants—superbly resourceful scavengers—who purchased their "leftovers" ostensibly for resale to animal raisers or starch makers, but who increasingly undertook the task not only of recovering the middlings but of having them reground and reselling them to bakers. Retailers of secondary cereals—

---

58. Delamare, *Traité de la police*, 2:824. It is interesting that Delamare, ever alert but sometimes quite consciously indifferent to apparent violations of the law that served the public interest, did not remark on the obvious illegality of the Melun regrinding operation.

59. *Dictionnaire universel françois et latin, vulgairement appelé Dictionnaire de Trévoux* . . . vols. 1 and 2. The *Dictionnaire universel françois et latin*, new ed. (Nancy, 1740), 3:1483, provided exactly the same definition. The word *middling* caused confusion in English milling circles as well. It was used interchangeably for a long time with grits, groats, semolina, and even shorts and sharps. Grimshaw, *Miller, Millwright, and Millfurnisher*, p. 410.

60. *Dictionnaire de l'Académie française*, 7th ed. (Paris, 1884), 1:856. Yet this definition muddles the matter by characterizing middling flour as "the flower."

61. Malouin, *Description et détails des arts*, pp. 84–85.

62. Béguillet, *Traité des subsistances*, p. 670.

63. See master baker Nicolas Bourlon's shop, AN, MC, CXI-96, 20 September 1719.

64. Malouin, *Description et détails des arts*, pp. 38–39; Maurizio, *Alimentation végétale*, p. 551.

grenailleurs or *grainiers* or *grenetiers*—also began to exploit the bran-middling potential.[65] By the late thirties we find men like François Bonnion, son of a master baker, who called himself a "middlings merchant" and was a genuine specialist in this increasingly attractive business.[66] Nor were the mealmen far behind this movement. The wife of flour merchant Michel Gosset of the faubourg Montmartre canvassed bakers in search of mealy bran, for which she offered cash.[67] At one point in the early forties 68 percent of flour merchant Denis Aubin's stock consisted of middling flour.[68] Already by 1725 there were a considerable number of mills in Paris or just outside the walls that specialized exclusively in the repassage of middlings and bran products. Most appear to have been windmills, but a water mill at Charenton called Le Pavillon fabricated twenty sacks of middling flour a day.[69] One of the best-known "proto-economic" millers was Guilleri of Gif, who ministered to the needs of the Missionnaires de St.-Lazare at Versailles. Milling coarse for his clients, he was able to extract almost as much flour for his own profit from the residue as he provided them from the flower or firsts.[70]

Bakers did not remain indifferent to these new commercial prospectives. They called it *grillot, griot, grilleau, gruot,* and *grueau,* but they meant middlings. Forains Jacques Vavasseur of Issy and Pierre Bethemont of the faubourg St.-Antoine and masters Sébastien Lapareillé, Guy Leguay, and Jean Blain were among the bakers who bolted at home and returned their middlings and mealy bran for regrinding.[71] One baker even bought raw bran by the setier from an unenterprising miller in order to mine it for hidden riches.[72]

65. Arsenal, ms. Bast. 10141, fols. 316–18. Cf. the bran sales registers in the Hôtel-Dieu, Archives Assistance publique, liasses 33 and 34.

66. AN, Y 14535, 28 January 1739.

67. AN, Y 11237, 3 September 1750.

68. AN, MC, LXI-422, 30 July 1744.

69. I have counted eleven such specialty mills. BN, Coll. Joly 1116, fols. 219–31. Béguillet called this *reprise* milling and criticized its costliness. *Traité des subsistances,* p. 51.

70. Baudeau, *Avis au peuple.* Other millers cited for practicing around mid-century some form of what later was called economic milling were Pinet of Dugny (who was said to have increased his flour yield by a quarter without overheating) and Halle of Beaumont. *Gazette du commerce, de l'agriculture et des finances* (21 May 1768): 430–31. See also the report that economic-style milling was known at Nantes as early as 1757. Ferdinand Brunot, *Histoire de la langue française des origines à 1900* (Paris, 1905), 6:277.

71. AN, MC, LXVIII-374, 27 April 1729; AN, Y 11233, 1 August 1746; AN, MC, V-524, 22 April 1762; AN, MC, LXXXIV-592, 7 July 1760, and VII-287, 17 May 1753; AN, Y 12607, 13 December 1759. In August 1753 Jean Blain had on hand 36 sacks of first and second white middling flour and 6 sacks of dark third middlings. AN, MC, VII-288, 1 August 1753.

72. Archives Seine-Paris, D5B⁶ 5217 (Laurent Caron). The prices were extremely high during the crisis years of the late sixties. Cf. Archives Assistance publique, Hôpital Général, liasse 21 (Fosseyeux 105). To eliminate this baker "regrating," Béguillet proposed the creation of *halles au son* in the major cities, thereby bringing middling traffic under public scrutiny: *Traité des subsistances,* p. 729.

Middlings received their official rehabilitation in 1739 when the commissaire specializing in subsistence affairs, de Courcy, conducted an "essai," or
trial, to test the yield in quality and quantity of "reground middlings."[73] This
trial marked not only the repudiation of two centuries of statutory hostility to
technological change in the milling industry, but also a fervent commitment
on the part of the Paris police to foster improvements in both the manufacture
and the commerce of flour. Another sign of change was the growing number of
seizures that the grain and flour measurers effected on flour dealers (sometimes conjointly with bakers) for fraud on merchandise involving middlings.
Paschot, a mealman at Lagny, declared the sale of a voie of flour as middling
quality worth 41 sous the bushel. The measurers discovered that it was "only"
wheaten (first) flour, the best of which was worth 39 sous, and denounced the
dealer and his baker-client for a "ruse to force up prices."[74] A mealman
named Fourcret first tried "to pass off ordinary bolted [wheaten] flour as
middling flour" and later "mixed flour of several different qualities and different prices in order to enhance his profit." Fourcret and the official concurred
that the middling flour was "prettier and finer . . . and worth more" than the
other whites.[75]

By the time Malisset arrived on the public scene in the late fifties, then,
the middling traffic was quite brisk. But it was an improvised and inefficient
enterprise. Bolting and grinding were for the most part separated, though
each process had been refined to some extent. Nor was there coordination
and rationalization on the broader phase encompassing the whole nexus from
grain purchasing through bread making. Before it could be technologically
and commercially perfected, economic milling had to be thought up and
thought out as an integrated technology. Then it had to be presented cogently,
first to the authorities and then to the professionals and the public. Simon
Malisset, baker, grain and flour merchant, entrepreneur, innovator, risk taker,
mover and shaker, did all this with considerable success. I have told the
exhilarating and tragic story of this man-in-a-hurry elsewhere.[76] He started
more or less at the bottom, with relatively few resources, and founded a
flourishing bran and middling business alongside his modest bakery operation. He must have been keenly observant and been at pains to study every
aspect of his business, starting with cultivation, harvesting, and conserving,

73. De Courcy to procurator general, 29 January 1739, BN, Coll. Joly 1119, fols. 41–42.

74. Police sentence, 30 June 1752, BN. Later that day another flour merchant named
Fasquerelle, along with a baker named Frise, received summonses for the very same offense. Ibid.

75. BN, Coll. Joly 1829, fols. 278–79 (10 October 1752). Cf. the wonderment of Parmentier, *Parfait Boulanger*, p. 168: "Who would have believed that a discredited and proscribed
substance, once regarded as unworthy of entering the human body, would become one day
the source of the most beautiful flour and the best bread?" See also Parmentier, *Mémoire sur
les avantages*, p. 137.

76. Kaplan, *Bread, Politics and Political Economy*, 1:349–52.

and continuing on to flour and bread fabrication. He must have visited dozens of mills and exchanged ideas with their operators. Though he was disdained and mistrusted by the intellectual and socioeconomic elite because of his lowly origins and lack of formal instruction, Malisset embodied a certain Enlightenment spirit. He believed in the perfectibility of things, if not persons, through technological progress. What we would call capitalism was the tool for applying science to social ends through investment, exchange, and competition. He saw no discontinuity or tension between private and public interest; on the contrary, he was persuaded that the pursuit of the first would necessarily redound to the advantage of the second. Malisset is universally acknowledged to have been the first catalyst in the chain reaction that brought economic milling into the public consciousness and into the countryside. With him begins its modern, documentary history.[77]

It could not have been more fitting, or more cunning, for Malisset to christen the new technology "milling by economy." These were the "economic" years of the Enlightenment, the period that saw the thinkers and doers, in the salons and in the ministries, turn to a whole series of very practical questions that concerned national wealth and well-being. These were the years of agromania, the efflorescence of interest in all aspects of the rural economy—a passion that was easy to caricature but that betrayed a genuine shift in notions of political economy and priorities and values as well as in loftier and more superficial forms of sensibility. Agromania not only focused attention on technology, production, and trade but also mobilized Frenchmen from many different quarters into temporary but powerful coalitions. Along with a call for agricultural renewal came an urgent demand for a whole array of economic reforms in other domains: in internal and foreign commerce, in industry, in the guilds, in tax policy. Implicit in this call for progress through liberalization was a violent critique of traditional police ideology and controls—the same sort of prohibitive system that had put middlings on the index, that harassed grain traders, spied on millers, bullied bakers.[78] There was an intimate although not absolutely essential link between liberalism and the "economic" impulse that was to have serious implications for all reforms, including bread and flour reforms, in the sixties and seventies. There is no doubt that economic/liberal movements created a climate hospitable to the crystallization and dissemination of economic milling (along with the administrative efforts made in Paris to promote and rationalize the flour trade). Economic milling was an idea whose time had come. "Eco-

77. On Malisset's exemplary and critical role, see Béguillet, *Discours sur la mouture* (1775), p. 184, and *Traité des subsistances,* pp. 65–66; Damilaville, in Diderot et al., eds., *Encyclopédie,* 10:828; Brillon Duperron, "Observations sur la mouture," p. 4.

78. On the economic years, the liberal movement, and the critique of the police, see Kaplan, *Bread, Politics and Political Economy,* 1:97–124.

nomic" was a highly charged, combative word and Malisset embraced it in full consciousness of its implications.[79]

The promoters of economic milling came under sharp attack for presenting its history as an entirely French affair. J.-E. Bertrand, a Neuchâtel professor and a member of the Munich Academy of Sciences, contended that French milling was "generally vicious"; even in the Paris area, after Malisset, "one did not mill well." The French could resolve their problems if they were capable "of imitating foreigners in what they do well," a gesture that the French had always found hard to accomplish.[80] Backed by Schreber, a professor at Leipzig, by Muret, a pastor and member of the economic society of Berne, and by the *Journal helvétique,* Bertrand scoffed at the idea, "so much vaunted in all of France," that economic milling was a new discovery. "The milling that the French call economic hardly merits the name," he charged. True economic milling had existed for centuries in Germany and Switzerland. It reached its fullest perfection in Saxony, "unsurpassed by any foreign nation in this domain," whose technology yielded more and better flour.[81]

The French milling reformers paid little attention to this attack. Parmentier, in passing, conceded that the Saxon method might indeed render more, but at the cost of grinding too rapidly and closely and thus producing mediocre quality flour larded with bran and imprinted with the odor and taste of overheating.[82] Béguillet impugned Bertrand's evaluation of French milling on the grounds that he was radically misinformed, in large part because of his dependence on Malouin, who, Béguillet argued, knew little about milling in France and was at bottom hostile to the fundamental principle of economic milling. Though he acknowledged that the Germans had had a technology resembling economic milling as far back as the early seventeenth century, Béguillet insisted that because of the recent "perfecting" of French procedures, the Saxons had more to learn from the French than vice versa. French

79. What an extraordinary irony that Malisset became—involuntarily—one of the agencies of the downfall of the physiocratic and "economic" experiment in the late sixties. See Kaplan, *Bread, Politics and Political Economy,* chaps. 8–11.

80. Malouin, *Description des arts* (1771), pp. 43, 59n, 63. Bertrand was appalled by the arrogance of Malouin's claim that before him the arts of milling and baking had never been seriously treated. Ibid., p. 21.

81. Ibid., pp. 49, 52; Schreber, "Observations," in ibid., p. 451; *Nouveau Journal helvétique* (April 1776): 348–60; Muret, *Mémoire sur la mouture,* pp. 1–5, 23, 80–82. Muret first learned about the French claims in Dupont's edition of Quesnay's *Physiocratie* and began to wonder whether the frequent *chertés* in his area were not the result of backward milling. His investigation convinced him that the Swiss were doing rather well (following the German model) and that the French were rather far behind, despite their boosterist rhetoric. A savant named Sebastien Müller had published a treatise explaining a kind of economic technology as early as 1616 and his work was republished (in Latin) in 1706, and was probably available to the French. Beckmann, *History of Inventions,* pp. 262ff.

82. Parmentier, *Parfait Boulanger,* pp. 188–89.

bolting was superior, the French system of integrated bolting and grinding was more economical, and French flour was whiter, richer, and freer of bran.[83]

Government Patronage and Testing

The decisive step for the future of economic milling was winning the confidence and then the active support of the government. Poussot, the police inspector of the Halles department who had undertaken an energetic campaign to revitalize and modernize the central grain and flour markets, especially the flour trade, seems to have been the first official won over by Malisset. Poussot was impressed with Malisset's sharp, analytical mind and the range of his knowledge about subsistence affairs. Malisset presented Poussot with a series of memoranda that the inspector probably passed directly on—first to Bertin, who served as lieutenant general of police before assuming the controller-generalship (and whose enthusiasm for economic milling never waned), and then to Bertin's successor, Sartine, who became one of Malisset's major patrons (along with the intendant of Paris, Bertier de Sauvigny). As early as the fall of 1760 Poussot lyrically depicted economic milling as a sort of subsistence El Dorado capable of producing fifty more pounds of good (non-*bis*) bread per setier. He proposed dispatching gardes-moulin and other trained instructors to teach "millers of good will" throughout the provinces to convert to the economic technology.[84]

Perhaps because he was vying for the contract to furnish the prisons with bread (and coveted the hospital concessions as well), and/or because he saw the need to give his entrepreneurial innovation a broadly utilitarian cast, Malisset presented his system as the manufacture of "a bread for the poor."[85]

83. Béguillet, *Traité des subsistances,* pp. 497–503, and *Discours sur la mouture* (1775), p. 181. Malouin himself had praised the Germans for their early milling improvements, but he had given credit to Brandenburg rather than Saxony, thereby arousing Bertrand's ire. *Description des arts* (1761), p. 326, and (1771), p. 418. English millers did not turn to bolting until the eighteenth century, when conditions enabled them to amass sufficient capital to develop new procedures. McCance and Widdowson, *Breads White and Brown,* p. 14.

84. Arsenal, ms. Bast. 10141, fol. 412 (26 November 1760).

85. It should be noted, however, that Malisset did not envision the multiple regrinding that Bucquet prescribed for a genuine "popular" or household bread and that became known for a time as Lyonnaise milling. See Trudaine de Montigny to Miromesnil, 22 March 1768, in *Correspondance politique,* p. 130; *Nouvelles Ephémérides économiques* 10 (1775): 161–62; Bosc, "Mouture," *Encyclopédie méthodique,* Agriculture, 5:392; Ammann, *Meunerie et boulangerie,* p. 267. Béguillet called it "la Lyonnaise, dite des pauvres." *Traité des subsistances,* p. 492. Sartine obviously remained very interested in the possibility of developing an attractive popular bread, for he sponsored Bucquet's "Lyonnaise" experiment at the General Hospital later in the sixties. Baudeau, *Avis au peuple,* troisième traité, p. 29. It should also be noted that the provision of prison and hospital bread was a very delicate matter and an issue of public concern, in large part because of occasional violent revolts that were provoked by the distrust of poor quality bread.

Sartine agreed to sponsor a test at the General Hospital. Malisset's goal was "to establish that the milling that he called *economic* has striking advantages and produces a greater quantity of flour than the coarse milling in use in the hospitals and consequently a greater quantity of bread and a bread of much superior quality." Sartine considered this challenge to be of the greatest significance; he himself planned to be there on the day of the baking. In order to guarantee the "fidelity and honesty" of the test, he instructed commissaire de Machurin and inspector Poussot to be present at every stage, to seal and unseal the sacks, to accompany the grain to and from the mill, and so on.[86] The prospect of "frauds" that might discredit Malisset's ideas worried Sartine. He sensed that Malisset would arouse opposition from the hospital staff, fixed in its ways and likely to feel threatened by this outsider-rival. Sartine's legendary intuition proved once again to be on the mark.

Poussot observed that Malisset and the police were "well received [at the hospital], with an air of confidence, even of satisfaction on the part of the personnel." No wonder, reflected Poussot, "since they had prepared maneuvers that would surely have enabled the coarse milling method to outdo the economic approach." First, the head sifter and his aides swept flour from an earlier milling of nontest flour into the crevices of the bolter. When Machurin insisted on weighing this test flour from the hospital's coarse milling after the bolting was terminated, he discovered "an extraordinary and impossible thing": originally weighed in at 471.5 pounds, this flour now weighed over 500 pounds.[87] The milling was no more "faithful" than the bolting, Malisset pointed out, for the miller ground more closely than usual in order to force the extraction of more flour than coarse milling usually afforded and he refused to allow the mill to be examined at the outset to check for the presence of "foreign" (i.e., nontest) wheat. This concerted cheating merely emboldened Malisset: "I shall still have more bread than you . . . and it shall be more beautiful than yours."

The police intervened to demand that the test (or rather the match) be run again under stricter surveillance. Yet despite this vigilance there were signs once again that the hospital staff "wanted to arrange for the failure of Malisset's experiment."[88] The police detected a relatively small dose of naked fraud and a very large dose of extraordinary meticulousness: the reprise miller to whom the bran products were sent for regrinding returned a greater weight than he had received. Ordinarily the hospital's milling resulted in an

86. Sartine to Machurin, 28 December 1760, AN, Y 12610. Baudeau claimed that Sartine advanced his own money to enable Malisset to buy merchandise and material for his initial tests. *Ephémérides du citoyen* 10 (1769): 32. The story that Sartine discovered Malisset as a result of eating an unexpectedly delicious bread made of Malisset flour strikes me as apocryphal. Reported by Des Essarts, *Dictionnaire universel de police*, 7:471.

87. Poussot called the chief sifter to his face "un coquin" and lamented aloud that "the interests of this house are in such very bad hands." Arsenal, ms. Bast. 10141, fols. 430–31.

88. Ibid., fol. 444 (17 February 1761).

average 353 pounds of flour for two setiers; in this test, it attained 397.5 pounds. Its bran was much lighter than usual—74 pounds versus the normal 110.5. In the eyes of Malisset, Poussot, and Machurin, this departure from everyday practice constituted fraud. Yet what the disparity really seems to underline is, on the one hand, the artificiality and unreliability of such head-to-head, hothouse trials and, on the other, the impressive potential of a perfected, semieconomic (because of the recovery and regrinding of middlings) form of traditional milling. The hospital's test results were so stunning because its everyday operations were so slovenly. What was true in this encounter proved true on a much grander scale in many places in the kingdom during the ensuing decade; even where economic milling was resisted, its presence and its competition induced coarse millers to improve their procedures. Thus, to judge the impact of economic milling merely in terms of the number of establishments that fully adopted the new technology does not give a true picture.

The police decided to pursue the test anyway, Poussot consoling himself with the thought that even if the hospital produced as much bread as Malisset it could not attain his "superior" level of quality.[89] The hospital administrator in charge made a concession by establishing a second hospital entry drawn from current flour reserves in the amount of 353 pounds, the quantity that he himself conceded the hospital normally counted on from two setiers of wheat. Beginning at 5:00 P.M. on 23 February 1761, Machurin and Poussot spent nineteen consecutive hours in the oven room of the Scipion annex to the hospital overseeing the bread-making operations (including sealing the three kneading troughs after each renewal of the yeast). The test required that the bakers make 17 five-pound loaves of white bread for the officers of the hospital and the rest in five-pound dark loaves for the inmates.[90] The hospital's original test entry, using 397.5 pounds of flour, yielded 530 pounds of bread, 17 white loaves and 89 dark. Its second entry, using its standard 353 pounds of flour, generated 475 pounds (17 plus 78), which was 47 pounds above its average everyday production, once again provoking suspicions about the integrity of the process (and perhaps causing some embarrassment to the bakers, highlighting their everyday lack of zealousness). Despite still another act of petty subversion—the hospital aides overheated Malisset's oven, causing his breads to suffer excessive weight loss in the cooking—Malisset made 505 pounds (17 plus 84).[91] Machurin and Poussot proclaimed the test a clear-

89. Ibid., fol. 445. Poussot would have preferred a wholly new and even more carefully controlled test based on 6 muids.

90. According to Poussot, the bakers observing the operations agreed that Malisset's manner of preparing the yeasts, kneading, etc. was better than their own. Ibid., fols. 446–50 (23 February 1761).

91. Malisset had 27 pounds less flour than the original hospital entry. The latter had 21 pounds less bran and 6 pounds less mill waste than Malisset. The hospital flour drank 22 pounds, or 11 *pintes*, more water. AN, Y 12610. According to Béguillet and Bucquet, Malis-

cut victory for Malisset, first because he produced more bread than the hospital *ordinarily* did (by either 30 or 77 pounds, depending on the point of reference) and second because it was judged by experts to be "more beautiful" than either of the hospital entries. The "dark" economic bread was "infinitely superior" to the hospital dark and it differed little in whiteness from either the economic bread or the hospital bread destined for the officers.[92]

The leading subsistence writers assailed the "test" method of evaluation. Conducted in artificial conditions that could not be expected to obtain in "reality," the trials, as the Malisset test seemed to prove, yielded extremely misleading and highly variable results, hardly the basis for founding a policy.[93] Yet economic milling continued to be called upon to prove itself and there seemed to be no better way to demonstrate its advantages to a more or less skeptical public, especially the public of professionals comfortable with their routine. Some of the tests were veritable triumphs for the exponents of economy. Bucquet, styling himself "engineer in milling," represented the reformers in the tests conducted before the combined hospital administrations of Troyes. The local setier produced seventy-nine pounds more bread when treated economically than when processed coarsely. The judges found the economic bread to be "infinitely superior in taste, in quality, and in whiteness" to the ordinary bread. The experts esteemed that the economic bread was worth 6 deniers more the pound. The savings or extra profit resulting from the seventy-nine pounds and the superior quality amounted to a staggering 25 livres per setier.[94] Earlier, at Bordeaux, Bucquet had similarly good results, producing more, whiter, and finer bread than his adversary.[95] Malisset conducted a trial in November of 1767, again under Sartine's spon-

---

set conducted a test in 1760 that yielded 392 pounds of bread from 2 setiers. This was almost 25 percent more than Delamare reported on the test that he supervised in 1700. And whereas 41 percent of the Delamare bread was white, 40 percent mid-dark (or mid-white), and 19 percent dark, more than 90 percent of Malisset's economic bread was white. *Nouvelles Ephémérides économiques* 10 (1775): 156–57; Delamare, *Traité de la police,* 2:1071–78.

92. AN, Y 12610. There was a final scandal. Shortly after the bread was removed from the ovens, it was discovered that 5 of the Malisset loaves were missing. Exasperated, Machurin and Poussot walked out on a dinner that the hospital officials had organized in their honor. Arsenal, ms. Bast. 10141, fol. 450 (23 February 1761).

93. Parmentier, *Parfait Boulanger,* pp. 597–98; Malouin, *Description des arts* (1761), pp. 247, 276–80. See also the skepticism evinced by the author of "Réflexions sur le commerce du pain," *Journal économique* (July 1761): 318–20. So difficult was it for the lieutenant general of police of Provins to effect a successful test—he claimed that he was "tricked" every time in either the milling or baking parts—that he still used the standard set in a trial conducted in 1686. Colin des Murs to Sartine, 8 January 1769, AN, Y 12618.

94. "Procès-verbal qui constate les avantages de la mouture économique," 30 April 1769, AN, F¹¹ 264; *Journal économique* (June 1769): 262; Béguillet, *Traité des subsistances,* pp. 81–82; "Les avantages des moulins à bled montés à mouture économique sur les moulins à mouture ordinaire," ca. 1770, BHVP, série 118, cote provisoire 1482.

95. Four hundred and nine pounds of white and 96 pounds of dark bread from two Bordeaux setiers that yielded 404 pounds of flour. Baudeau, *Avis au peuple,* troisième traité, pp. 17–18.

sorship, but apparently it was designed as a demonstration of the merits of economic milling rather than as a comparative showdown. Two light Parisian setiers (235 and 228 pounds) produced 348 pounds of flour (154 pounds wheaten, 70 pounds first middling, 61 pounds second middling, and 63 pounds third and fourth middling combined) which in turn rendered 446 pounds of bread (240 white, 102 middle-white, 104 dark).[96]

Other trials yielded results that were either ambiguous or unfavorable. Bucquet visited Caen in 1769 after the municipality reported that it had tried "the new milling" several times "without convincing itself that it was advantageous." Despite his exuberant discourse, he failed to change local opinion. From 325 pounds of wheat, Bucquet obtained more total bread than the local artisans did using ordinary methods (342 pounds versus 328), but less white bread (193 pounds versus 210). Bucquet insisted that his bread was "more nourishing," but the judges deemed his white loaves "much darker and less pretty" than the ordinary ones and his dark bread "as dark as the darkest country bread and very badly baked, which makes for a very bad food." The promoters of economic milling were never without an alibi: Bucquet asserted that the stones on the new mill he used were not broken in and that in addition his bread had been overcooked. The city fathers, although extremely cool to economic milling, obliquely paid homage to its salutary impact in forcing traditional millers to do better than they normally did: "Our local millers give the same quality and as good a quality with the old-style milling when they take the trouble to do so."[97] At Amiens in the same year Bucquet again obtained more total bread but less white, and there was disagreement as to its relative quality.[98]

A test conducted a year later at Châlons-sur-Marne rendered another

96. AN, Y 12616, November 1767. It is interesting to compare the results achieved at about the same time *outside* the testing arena. The following figures come from commercial production conducted by Malisset for the provisioning of Paris at the Moulin de la Justice in May 1768. A heavy Parisian setier (250 pounds) yielded 181 pounds of flour (81 pounds of wheaten, 37 pounds of first middling, 25 pounds of seconds, 38 pounds of thirds and fourths). On the surface these "ordinary" economic results are about as good as Malisset's trial results. AN, F[11] 1194. Compare these real, unselfconscious results with Parmentier's claims for the yield of a 240-pound setier treated economically: a total of 180 pounds of flour comprised of 92 pounds wheaten, 46 pounds first middling, 23 pounds seconds, 12 pounds thirds, and 7 pounds fourths. *Parfait Boulanger,* p. 197. In another place Parmentier characterized a procedure that wrought these results as "perfect milling." "Mémoire sur les avantages que la province de Languedoc peut retirer de ses grains" (1786), p. 150, AD Haute-Garonne, C 2268. Parmentier is not far from what Malisset actually produced for Paris. And remember that Malisset was producing in dearth, primarily for quantity and under stringent pressures of time. Parmentier's setier yielded between 202 and 234 pounds of bread, depending largely upon the type of kneading. *Parfait Boulanger,* p. 595.

97. Procès-verbal and "Observations et réflexions," 1769, AD Calvados, C 2653. Bucquet was not all bravado: he offered to run an economic flour commerce at his own financial risk if the city was not ready to undertake the task.

98. *Emphémérides du citoyen* 6 (1769): 269–71.

equivocal verdict. The economic flour produced a richer, more consistent dough and a larger amount of bread, but the economic bread betrayed "a certain taste" that might offend "a sensitive palate." This unpleasant taste allegedly resulted from the large bran residue that critics maintained could not be avoided in a technology of gradual reduction.[99] Bucquet claimed a landslide victory in Dijon, where the economic system not only produced almost 20 percent more bread (349 pounds versus 292), but also more than twice as much white bread (230 pounds versus 105). The judgment, however, was not untainted, for the arbiters pronounced both the white and dark economic bread "inferior in beauty and quality to that of ordinary milling." Ever buoyant and resolute, Bucquet exonerated the milling and blamed the uneven results on the failure of the baker to refresh the second yeast on time.[100]

On the whole it is fair to say that the royal government and the Paris police paid attention only to the successes. Disappointments or weaknesses of the economic process were either the fruit of accidents or were subject to rectification with more experience. The government committed itself firmly to the development of the new technology. In the winter and spring of 1761 Malisset, assisted by Bucquet, conducted a series of experiments at the General Hospital, converting the Scipion pantry into a subsistence laboratory.[101] In August he published the first essay on economic milling—a simple, straightforward, and rather modest exposition of its principal features and advantages.[102] He obtained the concession for the provision of bread to the prisons of Paris, another official consecration of the new system. Shortly afterward he received a politically crucial royal commission to maintain a substantial emergency granary system for Paris on the Seine at Corbeil. There Malisset built a monument to his teaching: an economic flour factory located in a multistory building (with water-powered elevators) containing several mills and an elaborate bolting system.[103]

The New Political Economy and Technological Innovation

Economic milling enjoyed the enthusiastic patronage of the physiocrats, which turned out to be a mixed blessing. It was no accident that the new political economy and the new subsistence technology both crystallized at the

99. Farachon (apothicaire), procès-verbal, AD Marne, C 416.

100. Procès-verbal, 29 November 1767, AD Côte-d'Or, C 421. Cf. Béguillet, Discours sur la mouture (1775), pp. 279–81.

101. Arsenal, ms. Bast. 10141, fols. 474–75 (20, 26 April 1761). Malisset insisted on the global implications of economic milling. He contended, for example, that the hospital's flour stock would conserve far better were it economically milled, for the presence of bran tended to overheat the flour and give it a bad odor.

102. Journal économique (August 1761): 363–64. For Malisset's other efforts at propaganda, see Béguillet, Traité des subsistances, p. 666.

103. On Malisset's relations with the government in the early sixties and the fate of the Corbeil establishment, see Kaplan, Bread, Politics and Political Economy, 1:197–98, 325–26, 351–52, 375–89, and 2:646–47, 674–75.

same time. They were responses to problems that were closely associated. The very name "economic" milling evoked the physiocratic school, whose members were known to contemporaries as *the* "economists."[104]

The physiocrats tried their best to appropriate economic milling and to present it as an integral part of their sweeping reform program. However sectarian their motivation, it cannot be gainsaid that they invested enormous energy in publicizing the economic system. The key figure in this campaign was the abbé Baudeau, indefatigable promoter, teacher, defender. Often reproached for an excessive taste for theory and abstraction and an estrangement from the real world that had nothing to do with his tonsure, in this instance Baudeau revealed a very different side of his personality. He consulted numerous bakers and millers, especially Malisset and Bucquet. He participated in tests at the General Hospital and at Corbeil. Toward the end of the sixties, moved in part by the grave dearth that jeopardized well-being in the capital, he established a bakeshop that made "domestic" loaves from (Malisset's) economic flour that sold more cheaply than other bread available.[105] More significant, his brochures and articles reached across the entire kingdom.[106] The city fathers of Caen were surely not the only persons who first learned of the economic process through the columns of the *Ephémérides du citoyen*.[107] Baudeau criticized the shortcomings of the traditional method and explained in straightforward terms the advantages of the economic way. He urged millers and bakers to take the initiative and he counseled them on how to find assistance. He called upon the government to accord "franchises and distinctions" to economic millers (as well as to dynamic grain and flour traders), which included giving exemptions from burdens such as the *taille* and militia and *corvée* service and awarding titles "assimilating them to the most notable bourgeois of the cities."[108]

Their enemies testified to the success of the physiocrats in identifying economic milling with their project. Linguet, Galiani, and others remained suspicious of the new technology precisely because it loomed as "a system of milling extolled by the *économistes*."[109] The physiocrats claimed to be de-

---

104. It is not at all clear that Malisset overtly sought to capitalize on a certain philosophical prestige by soliciting the physiocratic cachet, as Cochut suggests. "Le Pain à Paris," p. 985.

105. "Etats," July–December 1768, AN, F^{11} 1194.

106. Indeed, they reached beyond. See Muret, *Mémoire sur la mouture*, pp. 10, 11n.

107. "Observations et réflexions" (1769), AD Calvados, C 2653. Cf. Mirabeau's claim that without Baudeau's contribution economic milling would have remained an esoteric affair. Béguillet, *Traité des subsistances*, pp. 126n, 128. *Avis au peuple* was Baudeau's most influential pamphlet.

108. Baudeau, *Avis au peuple,* deuxième traité, pp. 61–67.

109. Simon-Nicolas-Henri Linguet, *Réponse aux docteurs modernes* . . . (London and Paris, 1771), 1, and 2:9, 122; Galiani to Morellet, 26 May 1770, Abbé Ferdinando Galiani, *Lettres de l'abbé Galiani à Madame d'Epinay,* ed. Eugène Asse (Paris, 1881–1903), 1: 84; Bachaumont, *Mémoires secrets* (London, 1783), 21:9 (4 July 1782); Henri Curmond, *Le Commerce des grains et l'école physiocratique* (Paris, 1900), p. 242.

lighted by this *amalgame,* for it enabled them to argue that those who opposed the freeing of the grain trade also opposed progress in general.[110]
Baudeau and Dupont were very troubled by Brillon Duperron, military victualer, administrator of the General Hospital, and subsistence specialist, because he showed that physiocratic ideology and "economic" technology had
nothing inherently to do with each other. Brillon Duperron opposed the radical grain reform of 1763–64 at the same time that he vigorously espoused
economic milling. To emphasize the discontinuity between the two projects,
Brillon Duperron suggested that the economic technology described by
Baudeau was larded with errors and misconceptions and that the genuine
economic recipe was untainted with political economy.[111] Despite such efforts, the link between liberalization and economic milling—the politicization
of the technology—deterred a number of communities from adopting the new
way.

Why was economic milling so important to the physiocrats and to the
others in the liberal camp? The liberals understood that the grain trade reforms would be dangerous, at least in the short run, because prices would rise
and grain would move toward the ports and frontiers. Economic milling offered them an unexpected form of insurance that would guarantee safe and
easy transition to free trade. If it were properly tapped, the liberals contended, economic milling would become a source "of overabundance." This
supplemental supply would tend to blunt the bread price increase and satisfy
consumers at the same time that it made a larger disposable surplus available
to exporters and offered flour exporters a sharp competitive advantage in
price and quality on the international market.[112] Technological innovation
would thus make possible and at the same time mercifully obscure the impact
of radical political innovation, in the eyes of many liberals.[113] The new tech-

110. Baudeau, *Avis aux honnêtes gens,* pp. 113–14.

111. Brillon Duperron, *Observations sur la mouture des bleds;* Pierre-Samuel Dupont de
Nemours, "Observations sur la mouture," *Ephémérides du citoyen* 9 (1769): 149–58;
Baudeau, "Suite des avis au peuple," *Ephémérides du citoyen* 10 (1769): 17–42.

112. *Gazette du commerce, de l'agriculture et des finances* (4 October 1768): 789; Parlement of Provence to king, 21 November 1768, AD Bouches-du-Rhône, B 3677; "Résultats de
la liberté parfaite et de l'immunité absolue du commerce des grains," *Ephémérides du
citoyen* 9 (1768): 90–95; Bachaumont, *Mémoires secrets,* 4:137–38 (23 October 1768); Grivel,
"Boulangerie," *Encyclopédie méthodique, Economie politique,* 1:380–84.

113. See the "Premier supplément au premier mémoire" of the deputies of commerce for
a striking example of this argument. BN, ms. fr. 14295, fols. 25–45 (ca. late 1763). Implicitly
the deputies made Malisset into the father of liberalization. Thus, Malisset was in a sense
responsible for the abundance that made exportation imperative, profitable, and safe. A few
years later, according to the believers in the famine plot, Malisset was responsible for
starving France by exporting grain massively and clandestinely under the cover of "economic" legislation. It is no surprise that the denunciator of the famine plot, Leprévost de
Beaumont, regarded economic milling as a diabolical and manipulative technology in the
service of monopoly. See Kaplan, *Bread, Politics and Political Economy,* 1:389–400, and
Arsenal, ms. Bast. 12353.

nology would compensate the consumers for what the new political economy did to indemnify, or privilege, the producer. Economic milling became the key element, then, in the equilibrium that liberal theory promised and that the liberal ministry coveted.

On the eve of the grain reforms of 1763–64, the liberals optimistically looked to economic technology to smooth the way. Their argument changed, however, once the liberal experiment began to turn sour in the late sixties, in part because of inherent flaws in the program and in part because of a series of bad harvests. Now the liberals were on the defensive. At all costs they had to demonstrate that the grave socioeconomic crisis was not the fruit of the liberalization itself. In part they did this by arguing the reciprocal of the economic technology line. Economic milling had not had sufficient time to make itself widely and tellingly felt.[114] Prices were excessively high not because of the freedom of the grain trade but because of the crude and wasteful state of the arts of milling and baking. Because millers did not know how to mill or bakers to bake, society registered a loss of "twenty to twenty-five percent on the Subsistence of the People."[115] Even as the liberals maintained that economic technology *could* (and would) have made the world safe for liberty, so they asserted that technological stagnation had first delayed and finally undermined the liberal regime.

Diffusion of the Economic Way

Even in the Paris area, where it was best known, it is impossible to measure with any precision the diffusion of economic technology. Much of the testimony comes from more-or-less interested parties and in any case the appreciations are highly impressionistic. As early as 1763 Malisset estimated that two-thirds of the flour entering Paris was of economic provenance.[116] Writing at about the same time for the *Encyclopédie,* Damilaville, who admired Malisset and depended on him for most of his information, put the figure at only one-third.[117] The deputies of commerce marveled at the spread of the new technology in Paris and its hinterland. In a memorandum drafted in

114. This did not prevent the liberals from arguing later that the reform laws had spurred the perfecting of milling and baking. Parlement of Toulouse, arrêt of 14 November 1772, AN, AD XI 39.

115. Lemercier de la Rivière, *Intérêt général,* p. 404; *Lettre d'un gentilhomme des états de Languedoc à un magistrat du parlement de Rouen,* pp. 36–44, AD Loire-Atlantique, C 774. The latter reads on page 41: "Bread is expensive no doubt about it, it is too expensive. But that is not the fault of the wheat nor of the harvest nor of the grain trade nor of the government. It is the fault of the milling and baking arts."

116. "Réponse du Sr. Malisset au mémoire concernant les boulangers de Valenciennes," 27 June 1763, AD Nord, C 9780. Cf. Malisset to Trudaine de Montigny, 1769, AN, F[11] 1194.

117. Diderot et al., eds., *Encyclopédie,* 10:828.

early 1764, they claimed that over three-quarters of the bakers were now integrated into the economic system and noted that sixty new mills, economically designed, had been built in the past three years on the Seine and on the Marne.[118] Brillon Duperron observed at about the same time "that the millers who engage in the flour trade [that is, the most dynamic and entrepreneurial] have abandoned the old milling in order to practice the new and that none of them had gone back to the old."[119] Indeed, in his *Dictionnaire des arts et métiers,* Macquer defined a miller in implicitly economic fashion as the artisan who transforms grain and flour "and who also bolts it."[120] Writing at the beginning of the seventies, the chief of the controller-general's subsistence bureau, St.-Prest, noted that economic milling had not only captured the Parisian flour trade but had given it a second wind.[121] Malisset's enemy Daure, himself a baker and a grain and flour trader, conceded that the economic war had been won in Paris by 1770.[122] Hinting that the change had in fact occurred in the sixties, Béguillet wrote at the end of the seventies that "most" Paris-area millers had gone economic.[123] With his usual élan, Bucquet affirmed that by the early eighties virtually all the millers in Paris and the environs had adopted economic technology.[124] When Dominique Lanet petitioned the royal council in 1771 for permission to install a boat mill at Meaux, he emphasized his intention "to mill according to the new economic method," in the hope that this information would impel the councillors to overrule the objections of the five millers already established there.[125] According to the council of agriculture in the year II, economic milling was the only technology practiced in the Paris area.[126] On the other hand, in 1782 the *Mémoires secrets* characterized economic milling as "the least known and the least used." Several years later Dupont echoed this evaluation almost word for word. Another perspicacious observer who liked to count, Moheau, esteemed that

118. "Premier supplément au premier mémoire," BN, ms. fr. 14295, p. 43. Legrand d'Aussy was also struck by the "surprising rapidity" with which the new technology was adopted in Paris and the Ile-de-France. Legrand d'Aussy, *Vie privée,* 1:71. Cf. similar observations by Baudeau, *Avis au peuple,* troisième traité, p. 3.

119. Brillon Duperron, *Considérations sur la mouture,* p. 8.

120. Macquer, *Dictionnaire portatif des arts,* 2:225.

121. Saint-Prest, "Mémoire," September 1773, AD Gironde, C 1441. Cf. the police report suggesting that if millers were not economically equipped they could not grind for Paris, AN, F²⁰ 293.

122. Daure, "Mémoire," ca. 1771, AN, F¹¹ 264.

123. Béguillet, *Traité des subsistances,* pp. 75–76. He used Malisset's two-thirds flour figure. Cf. his claim that by the end of the seventies, there were a multitude of economically trained millers and journeymen millers who could not find work in the Paris area and who could be mobilized into an expeditionary corps to convert the provinces. Ibid., p. 862. Cf. Rozier, *Cours complet,* 7:367, and Bucquet, *Manuel du meunier,* p. 86.

124. Bucquet, *Traité pratique,* pp. vi, 10.

125. AD Seine-et-Marne, B 726, 29 January 1771.

126. "Rapport à la commission d'agriculture et des arts par son conseil," 21 floréal year II, AN, F¹⁰ 226.

"economic mills, like skilled millers, are even harder to find than excellent wheat."[127]

"Private" sector conversion to economic technology was paralleled by its adoption in certain "public" sector establishments about which we have a little more concrete data. After carefully weighing the test results, accompanying Malisset on visits to the unsung economic pioneers of Beaumont and Pontoise, and conducting his own investigation, Brillon Duperron began to put the General Hospital on an economic diet in 1761. Lambert, recruited from Pontoise, took over direction of the hospital's boat mill and its two windmills. Flour and bread production increased substantially, and the quality of the product was strikingly improved. In 1763 1,964 muids of wheat were ground coarsely as opposed to 398 economically. During the next year, however, almost 1,300 muids were ground economically against 683 by the coarse method. By 1764 three-quarters of the hospital's flour was economically treated, enabling the institution to save considerable money (though probably less than the 80,000 livres a year trumpeted by Malisset and Béguillet) and to satisfy its consumers.[128] The Hospital of the Incurables also switched to economic technology, and was quite likely emulated by others.[129] In 1761 Malisset converted a convent and it is possible that other religious communities followed.[130] Given the demand of the bakers and the public-assistance, religious, and educational institutions, it seems plausible that resistance to economic milling became increasingly difficult for Paris-oriented merchant-millers and mealmen to sustain.

Committed to a policy of agricultural renewal that was explicitly destined to raise grain prices, the government of the early sixties was especially interested in ways to increase abundance or "economize" on flour and bread. From the ministry's vantage point, Malisset could not have emerged at a more propitious moment. Bertin, the controller-general, believed that economic milling could transform the whole process of commercial distribution, bread fabrication, and price making. Economic milling would modernize the structures of the trade, make them more supple and responsive and efficient. It would represent the beginning of the industrialization of both agriculture and

127. Bachaumont, *Mémoires secrets,* 21:9 (4 July 1782); Pigeonneau and Foville, eds., *Administration de l'agriculture,* p. 141; Moheau, "De l'étendue de la France et de son revenu territorial " AN, F²⁰ 403.

128. Archives Assistance publique, Hôpital Général 105, liasse 9, no. 2, registre concernant la recette et dépence; Arsenal, ms. Bast. 10141, fol. 477 (3 May 1761); Béguillet, "Mémoire sur l'art," ca. 1777, AN, F¹⁰ 256; Béguillet, *Traité des subsistances,* pp. 573–75; *Nouvelles Ephémérides économiques* 10 (1775): 160–61; Brillon Duperron, *Considérations sur la mouture,* passim. The economic technology yielded a surfeit of beautiful white flour, enabling Brillon Duperron to market some of it at the Halle, to the consternation of the flour merchants, and to envision the possibility of large-scale commercialization by the general hospital. *Considérations,* pp. 16–18.

129. Archives Assistance publique, Incurables, nos. 134, 152.

130. Arsenal, ms. Bast. 10141, fols. 482–83 (17 May 1761).

of subsistence. It would help to generate a veritable national market, indeed even an international market, in which flour would play the decisive role. It would help to equalize prices throughout France and it would make flour dearth extremely unlikely. It would have beneficial micro- as well as macro-functions, for it would offer consumers everywhere a cheaper, better range of breads. In a word, for the government, as for the physiocrats, economic milling was the logical technological pendant to liberalization, with significant political and social as well as economic implications.

Bertin took a keen personal interest in the propagation of economic milling. He received Malisset, listened to him, questioned him, and then offered him several government commissions to illustrate his confidence in the economic projects. He provided funds for publishing economic propaganda written by Malisset, Béguillet, and Baudeau, among others. He dispatched Malisset and Bucquet and a handful of other specialists on veritable *tours de France,* not merely to spread the word but to set up economic operations.[131] He believed in the tonic effects of competition and emulation; he felt that a working mill was the best laboratory and the best classroom. In many ways Bertin had a sounder strategy of dissemination than the second generation of enthusiasts, led by Parmentier and Cadet de Vaux, perhaps because he had a better understanding of the miller-baker milieu and mentality. Even after he left the *contrôle-général* at the end of 1763, as secretary of state for agriculture he remained the most vigorous promoter of economic milling in the government, seconded by Trudaine de Montigny. To set a personal example and to enable his own dependents to profit from technological progress, Bertin had Bucquet introduce economic milling on his lands at Bourdeilles in Périgord.[132]

Malisset and members of his family and enterprise visited Lille several times during the sixties. Convinced of the advantages of economic milling, the intendant warmly supported his efforts. Malisset urged the Lille municipality to construct six water mills, whose cost, roughly 100,000 livres, would be amortized in only a few years by profits from milling and flour sales. He envisioned a link between this economic milling factory and the already

131. The Malisset and Bucquet technologies differed in certain details of construction and operation, but were inspired by the same fundamental conception. Turgot's anxiety—"I do not know which of the two methods is better"—was superfluous. Turgot to Dupont, 26 December 1769, *Oeuvres de Turgot,* 3:76–77. It appears that Malisset and Bucquet made a conscious effort to avoid a political and commercial rivalry that would have hurt them both seriously. Bucquet began as Malisset's employee—in Poussot's eyes, he lacked Malisset's leadership qualities—and may have harbored a lingering resentment or jealousy toward his superior. In his publications, however, which were often polemical, Bucquet treated Malisset with respect. See Arsenal, ms. Bast. 10141, fol. 476 (26 April 1761).

132. Bertin to élus des états de Bourgogne, 7 November 1769, AD Côte-d'Or, C 3355, fol. 75; Béguillet, "Mémoire sur l'art," ca. 1777, AN, F[10] 256; Béguillet, *Traité des subsistances,* pp. 89–90, 104; Béguillet, "Mémoire sur les avantages de la mouture économique" (1769), Arsenal, ms. 2891, fol. 192; Weulersse, *Mouvement physiocratique,* 1:225.

existing Lille granary of abundance, which he promised would provide better and cheaper subsistence insurance.[133]

It is not clear what resulted from his efforts at Lille. Malisset claimed to have established several operations in the intendancies of Hainaut and Flanders, with the support of the influential minister Choiseul. We know that he had a business at Valenciennes. In an almost theatrical trial staged for the Valenciennes city fathers, Malisset transformed 2,500 pounds of "offal bran destined for animals" into 1,900 pounds of bread "of a better quality than that made by the city hospital with the whole product of the wheat." Apparently lack of capital and cooperation prevented him from expanding his business at Valenciennes. He sketched vistas of "an immense commerce" in flour with orders from Dunkirk and from abroad. Here, too, he suggested converting the municipal storehouses to flour and paying for them by means of a city-run retail and wholesale flour business.[134] In the early seventies, after Malisset passed from the scene, the "compagnie bourgeoise" that acquired the farming contract for collecting certain indirect taxes *(octrois)* proposed setting up an economic granary of abundance along the lines laid out by Malisset a decade earlier.[135]

At the request of the intendant, the government sent Bucquet on a mission to Picardy "in order to assess the state of imperfection of the crude milling processes of this province and to substitute for them the new perfected procedures." Bucquet claimed that he convinced town council after town council to establish economic mills and even to open depots for the retail sale of economic flour.[136] Nevertheless, when Parmentier and Cadet went on a similar mission fourteen years later, they claimed that "the bakery and especially the milling industry [are] still in their infancy, as they were two hundred years ago" and that the rustic form of coarse milling was the only technology known. (In order to enhance the intensity of the light they spread, Parmentier and Cadet had a tendency to exaggerate the darkness they encountered.) They gave a series of lectures before an audience of several hundred—"a brilliant assembly"—presided over by the intendant and the bishop. According to the *Mémoires secrets*, "the luminous teachings" of the two savants convinced "the stupid and vulgar artisans" of the superiority of the economic

133. AD Nord, C 9780; Lefèvre, *Le Commerce des grains à Lille,* p. 88n.

134. Malisset, "Mémoire concernant les moutures par économie" (20 June 1765), "Mémoires pour Msgr. l'archévêque duc de Cambray" (ca. 1764), and "Observations" (September 1768), all AD Nord, C 9780; Béguillet, *Traité des subsistances,* pp. 548–62; Béguillet, "Mémoire sur l'art," AN, F[10] 256.

135. AD Nord, C 5977.

136. Bucquet, *Observations intéressantes,* pp. 121–22; *Ephémérides du citoyen* 6 (1768): 268–71. We know that economic mills were set up at Montdidier and Amiens, but we lack the information to take the measure of Bucquet's sweeping claims, inspired in part by polemical ardor. Cf. Calonne, "La Vie agricole," *Mémoires de la Société des antiquaires de Picardie* 9 (1920): 454–55.

way. Whether or not this mission had practical consequences we do not know.[137]

The intendant of Normandy invited Bucquet to visit Caen in order to inspect local milling operations. Bucquet started an economic mill there that boasted all the most advanced techniques, including cylindrical bolters and mechanical ventilators. Apparently because the art of milling was less flawed in the Caen area than elsewhere in France, Bucquet's innovations did not have enormous impact.[138] While in Normandy, Bucquet arranged for the establishment of an economic mill at Rouen, where other millers soon followed suit, and he demonstrated economic techniques at Lisieux upon the request of a parlementary president.[139]

The Provincial Estates of Brittany encouraged technological innovation by awarding an entrepreneur named Robert Grandville a lease on public land and an unspecified award of money in order to enable him to operate an economic mill in the late sixties. They honored him and his ideas further by naming him to the Société d'Agriculture, de Commerce, et des Arts.[140] In the early 1780s Parmentier was invited by the intendant of Brittany in collaboration with the Provincial Estates—an economic entente—to find the "cause of the bad quality of flour and bread that are fabricated in almost all the cantons of Brittany despite the excellence of the grain and the water." After a field survey that took him to many granaries, mills, and bakerooms, Parmentier recommended the introduction of the universal economic process, including mechanical cleaning, economic grinding and sifting, sack storage, and encouragement of the flour trade.[141] Perhaps as a result of Parmentier's study, a company formed to provide naval provisions indicated that it would manufacture flour according to the economic method.[142] The comte de Montausier, assisted by Bucquet, set up an economic milling factory on his estates in the Poitou in order to produce flour for the navy and the colonies. Millers at Nantes were said to have followed his example.[143]

Without the lucrative business prospects and status enhancement that economic milling seemed to promise, Malisset and Bucquet would perhaps

137. Bachaumont, *Mémoires secrets,* 21:147–49 (21 October 1782).

138. AD Calvados, C 2651; Bucquet to Fontette, 12, 30 April 1768, Fontette to Bertin, 2 May 1768, and Duperron to Trudaine de Montigny, 7 May 1768, AD Calvados, C 2652; Bertin to Fontette, 4 July 1769, AD Calvados, C 2653; Béguillet, *Traité des subsistances,* pp. 130–35, 198–201; controller-general to municipality of Caen, 2 July 1769, AN, F^{12*} 153. On his visits to Caen, Bucquet received 24 livres a day for honorarium and expenses. Receipt, 19 October 1768, AD Calvados, C 2652.

139. Bucquet to unknown, June 1768, and same to Fontette, 2 June 1768, AD Calvados, C 2652.

140. AD Ille-et-Villaine, C 1710; *Ephémérides du citoyen* 4 (1769): 213–19; Béguillet, *Traité des subsistances,* p. 79.

141. Parmentier, "Mémoire" to the estates, November 1784, AD Ille-et-Vilaine, C 1710.

142. Parmentier, "Observations relatives à l'agriculture," November 1784, ibid.

143. Arpin, *Historique de la meunerie,* 1:126–27.

have been less ardent in their dissemination of the new technology. From simple "miller to the General Hospital," Bucquet swelled into "milling engineer" and négociant. It was clear to Bucquet, paid 24 livres a day as a government consultant, that to make his fortune he must capitalize more significantly upon his expertise. The contract he signed at Troyes satisfied his ambitions as well as those of his associates and of the government. The cathedral chapter of Troyes, spurred by "its patriotic love of the public interest" as well as by its desire to profit from the new commercial conditions created by liberalization and by technological progress, contracted to form a "company" with Bucquet for the manufacture and sale of economic flour. The chapter agreed to advance him 30,000 livres and to divide profits as well as losses evenly. Bucquet promised to convert the chapter's three mills to the economic mode, to commercialize the flour operation as he saw fit on both retail and wholesale levels, and to maintain a constant granary of six thousand sacks of flour "for [emergency] public needs." Based in Paris, Bucquet would make periodic visits to the economic installation, whose books would be kept by the chapter. Unable to raise funds from local entrepreneurs, the chapter had to borrow the 30,000 livres; ultimately, it claimed to have spent 100,000 livres on conversion and construction. The chapter was unable to interest local merchants in associating themselves with local flour sales. Nevertheless the business flourished, though it was the object of considerable controversy (whose characteristics are examined later).[144] Independently of Bucquet, a merchant-investor named Milleville built three economic mills on his lands in the nearby generality of Châlons, whence he developed a thriving flour traffic to the Paris Halle with entrepôts at Château-Thierry and in Picardy.[145]

It is not clear who financed Bucquet's economic flour enterprise in Dijon. From the point of view of the police, his operation was a success. His relatively cheap high-quality flour forced both millers and bakers to reexamine and renew their techniques. The provincial estates of Burgundy, which had encouraged him to set up in Dijon, awarded him a pension. In addition, the estates subsidized the efforts he and Béguillet made to retrain millers and to publish economic do-it-yourself manuals.[146] At Lyon Bucquet failed to win local support, perhaps in part because he was overconfident and did not spend enough time preparing the ground. He visited Grenoble filled with

144. "Mémoire du Chapitre de l'église de Troyes" and "Mémoire to the intendant," AD Aube, C 3410, pièces 20–22, 61–62; Paillet to controller-general, 29 April 1769, and controller-general to Rouillé, 1 April 1769, AD Aube, C 1909; *Ephémérides du citoyen* 4 (1769): 220–26 and 9 (1769): 199–206.

145. Milleville to intendant, 8 March 1771, AD Marne, C 416.

146. Deliberations of the élus-généraux, 18 December 1769, AD Côte-d'Or, C 3220, fols. 347–48; "Mémoire du Sr. Bucquet," 2 March 1769, AD Isère, II C 47; Béguillet, "Mémoire sur les avantages de la mouture économique," Arsenal, ms. 2891, fol. 214; P.-E. Girod, "Les Subsistances en Bourgogne et particulièrement à Dijon à la fin du XVIIIᵉ siècle, 1774–1789," *Revue bourguignonne de l'enseignement supérieur* 16, no. 4 (1906): 25n.

enthusiasm, but we do not know what he achieved there.[147] Malisset was equally sanguine when he first dispatched his agents to Languedoc in the early sixties, but nothing seems to have come of these early demarches. The hospital of Montpellier conducted tests and the Estates of Languedoc sponsored a long sojourn by a *cordelier* brother who was supposed to build a "regrinding mill" on the Parisian model.[148] With the hope of overcoming the torpor of the local millers, the Estates launched a new series of public trials in the 1780s. They also commissioned Parmentier to undertake a detailed study of wheat, flour, and bread production in the province. In his long report published by the Estates, Parmentier urgently recommended the dissemination of the economic technology.[149]

Economic milling was better received at Bordeaux, where Bucquet set up a model mill in 1766. The intendant offered millers who converted a reduction in their *taille*. Assisted by one of Bucquet's pupils, an army supplier turned merchant named Labat mounted a huge six-mill factory with a totally integrated and mechanized economic operation from cleaning to bolting and cooling. A merchant of initiative and imagination, even before he learned to apply Bucquet's techniques Labat had been buying up the middlings disdained by other millers, who retained only the flower for export to the colonies. Labat bolted and reground them and obtained a flour of first quality, equal to the *minot* flour manufactured by his rivals. Labat's factory became the showpiece of the southwest and he made a fortune in both domestic and overseas flour trade.[150] In the eighties Sclalch and Company, an international trading establishment based in the same region, offered stock for sale in an enterprise organized to construct a vast economic flour factory.[151] On his way back to Paris from the Bordelais, Bucquet helped to set up several other mills on the Dordogne River.[152] In the nearby generality of the Limousin, the intendant Turgot encouraged owners to transform their mills. He arranged for Bucquet

---

147. Béguillet, *Discours sur la mouture* (1775), pp. 186–90; Bucquet to Fontette, 8 August 1768, AD Calvados, C 2652; "Mémoire du Sr. Bucquet," 2 March 1769, AD Isère, II C 47. Bucquet insisted that economic milling was adopted at Lyon and enjoyed success. *Traité pratique de la conservation des grains et des farines et des étuves domestiques* (Paris, 1783), p. vi.

148. Arsenal, ms. Bast. 10141, fol. 482 (17 May 1761); "Réponse du Sr. Malisset," 27 June 1763, AD Nord, C 9780; Béguillet, *Traité des subsistances,* pp. 372–75.

149. Antoine-Augustin Parmentier, *Mémoire sur les avantages que la province de Languedoc peut retirer de ses grains* (Paris, 1786). See also Parmentier to the estates of Brittany, November 1784, AD Ille-et-Vilaine, C 1710.

150. Bucquet, *Traité pratique,* p. 36.

151. The *actions* were worth 3,000 livres apiece and were put on sale in September 1785. Prospectus, Burt Franklin Collection, New York City.

152. Béguillet, *Discours sur la mouture* (1775), pp. 190–91, and *Traité des subsistances,* pp. 89, 95, 106–9, 112–15, 120.

to construct a model at Limoges, as he had already done at Clermont, and as Malisset had done in the Angoumois.[153]

Emulating Bertin, a number of prominent individuals sponsored economic mill installations in order to encourage the dissemination of the new technology. The marquis de Puiségur, agronomist and improver, had Bucquet build a mill on his land near Soissons in 1764.[154] Bucquet did the same for Bertier de Sauvigny, intendant of Paris, on his Burgundian estates.[155] Robert de St.-Vincent, a magistrate in the Paris Parlement, erected a Bucquet mill on his property in the Gâtinais.[156] The physiocrat Mirabeau had several economic mills constructed on his properties, near Nemours and Montargis, where he "personally" conducted experiments proving that the new technology offered a 20 percent savings.[157]

Finally, we must not neglect the incidental impact of the efforts to spread the new technology. The economic campaign benefited milling in general, not just those establishments that adopted it. The public trials and experiments, the lectures and courses, the visits, the quarrels, the brochures and the books, the articles in the periodical press, and the information diffused by central, regional, and local government officials alerted practitioners all over the kingdom to the new perspectives. More telling perhaps were the contacts that thousands of millers were able to have with the millers in their communities who made the conversion and with the bakers who sent them middlings. Better informed, more self-conscious about their work, and in some cases subjected to competition and to client pressure (possibly reflecting official pressure through revised price schedules), many millers made an effort to improve. They remounted and rebalanced their stones, they dressed them differently, they experimented with stone speed and distance, they paid more attention to grain preparation, they learned how to bolt more effectively.[158] By incorporating certain features of the new technology, they modified the coarse process. Béguillet himself, not known for attachment to the old ways, conceded that the claims for the comparative advantage of economic milling based on confrontations in the sixties were now exaggerated in light of the revitalization of the coarse method.[159]

---

153. Turgot to Dupont, 26 December 1769 and 2 March 1770, *Oeuvres de Turgot*, 3:76–77, 380. Cf. Weulersse, *Mouvement physiocratique*, 1:199.

154. Bucquet, *Observations intéressantes*, p. 77n.

155. Béguillet, *Traité des subsistances*, pp. 46–47.

156. Ibid., p. 215.

157. Bucquet to Fontette, 4 July 1769, AD Calvados, C 2653; Mirabeau to Béguillet, 19 October 1769, in *Traité des subsistances*, pp. 124–27n. Cf. Mirabeau to Margrave of Baden, 21 October 1770, in Weulersse, *Mouvement physiocratique*, 1:240.

158. Parmentier, *Parfait Boulanger*, p. 167; Tillet, "Projet d'un tarif," pp. 112, 145–46; Béguillet, *Traité des subsistances*, p. 120.

159. Béguillet, *Traité des subsistances*, p. 121.

The machine was crucial; Belidor, Bucquet, and Dransy never tired of emphasizing how important it was to perfect "the mechanics."[160] But in the end the machine was less important than the miller. Success depended on "the intelligence" of the miller, through which he was rehabilitating himself morally as well as professionally.[161] "Perhaps millers have [had] the reputation of being scoundrels only as a consequence of their ignorance," suggested one observer.[162] Enlightened and zealous in the pursuit of his own interests, the new miller would have healthier relations with the community because he would win its esteem. Economic milling gave millers not only a treasury of instruction but also a cachet of prestige and an enhanced sense of self-worth and of public utility.[163]

Béguillet urged that the Flour Enlightenment be institutionalized in milling schools—subsistence seminaries—that would spread the gospel to the profane and impart the latest findings to the veteran improvers.[164] The idea had already been aired in cruder form by Lacombe d'Avignon, who imagined a thirty-mill factory school that would train miller-missionaries (recruited among the sons of millers: a corporate reflex that the savants might have found archaic) who would be sent to teach millers throughout the provinces.[165] Parmentier and Cadet de Vaux, who founded a school for baking in the eighties that addressed many issues relevant to milling, lobbied for years for the creation of schools for economic milling in all the major cities. These schools would cost the government nothing, for they would be established by miller-entrepreneurs who would be recompensed by exemptions from troop lodging and by civic medals. The Parmentier-Cadet plan was part of a far more sweeping reform project that called for loans to millers from regional and local institutions for conversion to economic milling, official pressure on all religious communities and public-assistance establishments to adopt the economic technology, authorization for proprietors to increase rents before lease expiration in return for converting their mills, a requirement that all engagistes of the royal domain transform their mills, and the abolition of the

160. Belidor, *Architecture hydraulique,* 1:278; Bucquet, *Observations intéressantes,* p. 87n; Dransy, in Parmentier, *Mémoire sur les avantages* (1787). Dransy won the prize competition sponsored by the Academy of Sciences for the perfection of milling.

161. Poncelet, *Histoire naturelle,* p. 154; Parmentier, *Parfait Boulanger,* p. 145.

162. Muret, *Mémoire sur la mouture,* p. 5.

163. Béguillet, "Mémoire sur les avantages de la mouture économique," Arsenal, ms. 2891, fols. 193–94.

164. Béguillet, *Traité des subsistances,* pp. 375–79. Turgot evinced keen interest in miller education. "Septième lettre sur le commerce des grains," 2 December 1770, *Oeuvres de Turgot,* 3:349–51. On the vast array of things that millers had to know, see Bucquet, *Manuel de meunerie,* pp. 14–16.

165. Lacombe d'Avignon, *Mitron de Vaugirard,* p. 33. He suggested that Bucquet's son-in-law, Rolland, might be able to develop this idea.

droit de banalité that hampered technological and commercial (not to mention social) modernization.[166]

Mill reform did not have a high priority in the turbulent revolutionary years. Not all revolutionary authorities understood that economic milling could serve their major goal of increasing available supply. Indeed, on a number of occasions, officials proscribed the economic technology (and persecuted Parmentier, among others) on the erroneous grounds that the economic system necessarily meant "white extraction"; that is, in the revolutionary purview, an aristocratic technology associated with old-regime privileges. Knowledgeable officials, such as Doumerc, understood that the economic process yielded the most and best-quality "equality bread," a domestic loaf composed of all the flour. The elaborate process of economic bolting, however, appeared to reproduce the hated hierarchical structure of the old regime, and it remained suspect at least until the ascension of Napoleon. Late in the 1790s, the government again began to show interest in miller education and the propagation of economic technology. Even as the ministry of the interior distributed circulars hailing the economic process, the indefatigable Cadet de Vaux appealed to the Society of Encouragement for National Industry in 1804 to found a school for economic milling.[167]

Resistance to Economic Milling

Along the itinerary of diffusion, the promoters encountered not only indifference and skepticism but also deep-seated hostility. Much of it appears to have been the product of the sort of jealousy, anxiety, and avarice that Malisset faced from the very beginning. The pantry workers at the General Hospital of Paris, according to inspector Poussot, "fear economic milling because it

166. *Encyclopédie méthodique,* Jurisprudence, police et municipalités, 10:33–34, and Antoine-Alexis Cadet de Vaux, *Traités divers d'économie rurale, alimentaire, et domestique* (Paris, 1821), pp. 39–41. Cadet de Vaux claimed that from his chair in the School of Baking he personally "provoked" the perfecting of economic milling throughout France. One of his ideas was to require real seminarians to take a course in economic milling so that when they took up their responsibilities as rural priests they would be able to convert local millers to the new technology. On the program for material incentives including tax and militia exemption and subsidies for converting to economy, see also Béguillet, *Traité des subsistances,* p. 683.

167. Arpin, *Historique de la meunerie,* p. 244, and Arthur Birembaut, "L'Ecole gratuite de boulangerie," in René Taton, ed., *Enseignement et diffusion des sciences en France au 18ᵉ siècle* (Paris, 1964), p. 506. Both Parmentier and Cadet de Vaux served on the "Commission pour les arts économiques" of the Society. *Bulletin de la Société d'encouragement pour l'industrie nationale* no. 2 (vendémiaire year XI): 27. A catechistic presentation of the advantages of economic milling appeared in the year III. Cotte, *Leçons élémentaires,* especially pp. 27–31.

would cast too much light on their activities."[168] They were joined in the anti-economic resistance by the hospital millers, who felt threatened by the new technique, resented the encroachment on their territory, and evinced "bad will" and "stubbornness" in order to subvert "the innovations."[169] Similarly, at Lyon, a baker-miller *fronde* at the General Hospital of Charity undermined the economic system established by Bucquet in 1764. New tests conducted in Bucquet's absence proved "entirely favorable to the old milling and contrary to economic milling." The hospital "totally abandoned" the new technology. Nothing if not combative, Bucquet returned and set up a private economic enterprise in association with two local bakers. Economic flour won warm approval at the marketplace but the Lyonnais milling-baking establishment remained resolutely hostile.[170] At Valenciennes, Malisset found himself immediately detested as "an innovator." Convinced that they would make less money, not so much because of direct "economic" competition as because of the way in which the terms of exchange would be modified, the millers and the bakers joined hands in a sort of boycott. Malisset was willing to settle the issue in the marketplace, provided the subsistence professionals gave him a reasonable chance. He found it difficult to function, even with the support of public authorities, as long as the bakers and millers refused to do business with him and circulated vicious rumors about his merchandise and his character.[171]

At Dijon, Bucquet confronted another coalition of millers and bakers who, like the hospital resistants, were mobilized "to keep the light out of their activities." The millers hoped to discredit the economic system by spreading the word that Bucquet's handpicked successor adulterated his flour with minerals, plaster, and chalk, and committed other perfidies.[172] The baker resistance was a well-founded, highly rational movement rather than a more or less tropismatic reaction to innovation. The Dijon bakers, like those in many other cities, fought against the economic system in order to preserve an exorbitant *rente de situation*. They realized that the economic process would enable the police to rewrite the price parameters and impose a more-or-less invariable set of production expectations. Indeed, this point was made again and again by the advocates of economic milling when they addressed the

168. Arsenal, ms. Bast. 10141, fols. 449–50 (23 February 1761).

169. Ibid., fol. 482 (17 April 1761); Béguillet, *Traité des subsistances,* pp. 577–79; *Nouvelles Ephémérides économiques* 10 (1775): 100–101.

170. Béguillet, *Discours sur la mouture* (1775), pp. 186–91. Cf. miller-baker hostility to the introduction of cylindrical grinding in the nineteenth century. Chryssochoïdes, *Nouveau manuel complet du meunier,* pp. 140–42.

171. "Réponse du Sr. Malisset," 27 June 1763, and "Mémoire," 20 June 1765, AD Nord, C 9780. Cf. Béguillet, *Traité des subsistances,* p. 555.

172. Béguillet, *Traité des subsistances,* pp. 72–74. Béguillet conceded that this miller was less able than Bucquet, but an investigation by the Academy of Dijon in January 1771 cleared him fully. Millers at Clermont-Ferrand spread strikingly similar rumors against a

public and the authorities on the advantages of the new system.[173] Economic milling would enable the police to institute a just bread price (or maximum), suggested the deputies of commerce in 1764, and in turn this rigorous schedule would oblige recalcitrant bakers (and millers) to adopt the new system.[174]

Even if they secretly used the perfected method of extraction, these bakers had every reason to hide the true yield of wheat into bread. The Dijon bakers were furious when Bucquet, at the request of the Dijon Parlement, sent several wagonloads of economic flour to the capital of Burgundy when famine meanced in 1770. His economic flour cost only 3 sous 6 deniers a pound and could make one and a half pounds of bread of shop quality, while bread at Dijon was selling at 5 sous a pound. This experience impelled the parlement to order a series of tests to determine "the veritable product of grain into flour and into bread in order to have a sure base from which to fix the rate of the price of bread relative to the price of grain."[175] Bucquet represented a direct threat to the bakers, as he fully realized: "The [price] regulation for the bakers of Dijon allows them 39 pounds of bread per measure of wheat weighing 45 to 48 pounds, while I clearly prove that economic milling can do 47 to 48 pounds of bread at least as good and even better."[176]

Bucquet had a rough time at Caen for much the same reasons. "You doubtless are aware of the *tapage* I suffered at Caen at the hands of the millers and bakers who were afraid that I would unmask them," he wrote the intendant, who had invited him to set up his establishment on his lands.[177]

---

colleague who dared introduce economic milling. Partly because of these suspicions, a crowd tried to raze the mill. Turgot to Condorcet, n.d., *Oeuvres de Turgot,* 2:54.

173. "Observations relatives à l'agriculture," November 1784, AD Ille-et-Vilaine, C 1710; Malisset, "Observations," January 1767, AD Nord, C 9780; Parmentier, *Parfait Boulanger,* pp. xxxiv–xl; Parmentier, "Mémoire sur les avantages que la province de Languedoc peut retirer de ses grains" (1786), AD Haute-Garonne, C 2268; Béguillet, *Traité des subsistances,* p. 292. Just as the greedy bakers of Montpellier, La Rochelle, and Dijon were about to ask for an upward revision of the official price schedule, noted with satisfaction the *Journal de l'agriculture, du commerce, des arts et des finances,* the economic system would enable the police to revise it downward (September 1772): 182ff. This possibility was of particular interest to the physiocrats in the late sixties and early seventies, for they were obliged to show somehow that higher grain prices need not necessarily result in higher bread prices. The irony was that the bakers were soon obliged to defend *taxation* schedules that they had hitherto reviled as unjust.

174. "Premier supplément au premier mémoire," 1764, BN, ms. fr. 14295, fol. 43.

175. Béguillet, *Traité des subsistances,* pp. 84–85n.

176. "Mémoire du Sr. Bucquet," 24 March 1769, AD Isère, II C 47. Béguillet claimed that the economic system could produce as much as 50 pounds per Dijon measure and that scrupulous bakers using "ordinary" methods could get as much as 44 pounds if they really wanted to. *Discours sur la mouture* (1775), pp. 227–28. Still, Bucquet apparently succeeded in forcing the Dijon bakers to improve the quality of their bread in order to compete successfully with his retail flour operation. Béguillet, *Traité des subsistances,* pp. 55–60.

177. Bucquet to Fontette, 8 October 1768, AD Calvados, C 2652. For a moment, Bucquet ceded to a certain demoralization, but he vowed to try again.

Bucquet clearly upset the local subsistence complex by publicly criticizing wasteful practices, excessive mill fees and dough tithes, and bread supply contracts based on anachronistic extraction rates.[178] An economic miller named Lambert from Pontoise was similarly·"repulsed" when he tried to set up elsewhere in Normandy.[179]

At Troyes wall posters denounced Bucquet as a vicious profiteer and threatened to burn his installation.[180] Bucquet claimed that "the people of Troyes [were] excited [against him] by the millers and bakers."[181] In fact, the situation was more complex than he allowed. To be sure, he threatened the interests of the millers and bakers, but in addition he loomed as an enemy of the local consumers.[182] For even as he offered them high quality, cheap retail flour, he siphoned off a large amount of the local grain supply for the provisioning of Paris. Bucquet defended himself on the impeccably liberal grounds—*économiste* rather than economic—that the grain trade was free and a dealer had a right to move grain wherever he desired.[183] But the local consumers were always uneasy about the outbound movement of grain, all the more so when it was undertaken by a stranger and in a period of severe protracted dearth.[184] To say the least, Bucquet's stand was impolitic and perversely stubborn. The Troyes police unequivocally supported the people and, indirectly, the local bakers and millers against the innovator and interloper. The local lieutenant general of police accused Bucquet of illicit grain traffic and gave a certain credence to the charges of flour adulteration by ordering an official investigation.[185] Though the town fathers of Troyes officially recognized economic milling as "a great resource for the city and the countryside," it continued to cause malaise well after Bucquet's departure.[186]

178. Béguillet, *Traité des subsistances,* pp. 144–48, 150–51. Practicing a Kissengerian sort of linkage, the physiocrat Baudeau characterized the adversaries of economic milling at Caen as "the enemies of liberty." *Avis aux honnêtes gens,* p. 115.

179. Béguillet reports Lambert in Caen. *Traité des subsistances,* p. 178. But another subsistence writer placed him at Rouen. "Lettre d'un gentilhomme des états de Languedoc à un magistrat du parlement de Rouen," pp. 36–40, AD Loire-Atlantique, C 774. Cf. Legrand d'Aussy, *Vie privée,* p. 72. One wonders whether the seigneurs of the *banal* mills around Rouen were as hostile to the new technique as their millers. See also the antieconomic milling publicity emanating from Nantes. *Désavantages de la mouture économique,* cited by *Enquête sur la boulangerie,* p. 788.

180. Paillot to unknown, 13 July 1770, AD Aube, C 1909.

181. Terray to Rouillé, 1 July 1770, ibid.

182. Beyond the usual fears and resentments aroused by economic milling, the Troyes millers held Bucquet responsible for driving up the price of mill leases and the bakers complained that he outbid them for control of local grain supplies. Paillot to intendant, 15 April, 13 July 1770, ibid.

183. Terray to Rouillé, 8 April 1770, ibid.

184. Paillot to intendant, 15 April 1770, ibid.

185. Terray to Rouillé, 1 July 1770, and Paillot to unknown, 13 July 1770, ibid. Ricommard saw the episode too narrowly in terms of traditional webs of influence, patronage, and privilege. Jean Ricommard, *La Lieutenance générale de police à Troyes au XVIIIe siècle* (Troyes, 1934), pp. 254–56.

186. Municipality to intendant, 1 July 1771, AD Aube, C 1909.

On the eve of the Flour War in the spring of 1775 the owners of the economic establishment at Troyes feared "a popular riot."[187]

This episode at Troyes calls attention to the double connection (embodied by Bucquet and especially by Malisset) between economic milling and politics and between economic milling and ideology. Without the ardent support of the liberalizing ministry and its ideological mentors, whose needs and ambitions it brilliantly served, it is possible that the introduction of economic milling would have been delayed. Yet it is clear that the double association hurt as much as it helped, or more. Under the impact of the scarcity and market disarray wrought by the combination of harvest failures and radical grain-trade reforms, a great many consumers were in a state of extreme uneasiness, hypersusceptibility, and near panic in the decade between 1765 and 1775.[188] There was an air of carnivalesque inversion, as the world was stood on its head not by the people, but, inexplicably and ominously, by their leaders. The old covenant, based on the primacy of subsistence, was replaced by a new one based on the primacy of self-interest. The producers and the traders rather than the consumers were the favored sons of the new regime. Commercial practices that had been considered crimes under the police regime were now viewed as salutary expressions of liberty. Strange faces proliferated in the grain trade, but the most threatening newcomers were not individuals but companies, monsters with tentacular reach and more-or-less official sanction. Consumers blamed the long (although in their view "artificial") dearth, continued high prices, burgeoning unemployment, and growing misery on "all these novelties."

These were not propitious conditions for the propagation of economic milling. In the minds of many Frenchmen, the new technology, just like the new grain-trade laws of 1763–64, was merely "a cover" for heinous antisocial speculative operations. Since the same men who lauded the one lauded the other, there was no reason to expect the one to be any less inimical to the interests of the people than the other. Regrinding, like off-market trading, had been against the law when the law still served the commonweal. The new political economy and the new milling by economy both transgressed the moral economy. Moreover, aside from the "economic" link between physiocratic liberty and the new technology, it was not hard to mobilize suspicion against millers, proverbial thieves, sorcerers, manipulators. Troyes was no aberration; Bucquet risked a lynching or at least a tarring wherever he went. His own testimony, written in the third person, was hardly an exaggeration:

187. Paillot to intendant of Champagne, 1 May 1775, Turgot to same, 29 April 1775, and Paillot to same, 10 May 1775, ibid., C 1908. Unlike Bucquet, Turgot did not perceive the bakers and millers united in a block against progress, but instead denounced the reactionary, selfish bakers for foiling the attempts of the millers to extract more flour per measure of grain.

188. For a more nuanced and detailed view of this situation, see Kaplan, *Bread, Politics and Political Economy,* chaps. 4, 5, 7, 10, 12.

"Crisscrossing the provinces of the realm, at the government's command, in order to reform mills and milling, Sieur Bucquet met only with challenges and persecutions; he even risked his life several times, because he was looked upon as the instrument of a horrible Monopoly."[189]

Far more than Bucquet, Malisset represented monopoly.[190] Cosigner of the infamous Famine Pact, which was in fact a contract to provide Paris with a grain reserve in order to facilitate the transition to liberalism, he was living proof of the intimate and sordid link between liberalization and the new technology. Malisset headed a "company" that made large grain purchases, often indiscreetly, in the name of the king and in many parts of the kingdom regardless of the local subsistence situation. He operated from a heavily guarded mill-citadel at Corbeil, which several times came under assault by citizens suspecting hoarding and adulteration. It was charged that he manufactured an inferior, trafficked flour for consumers, reserving his best flour for exports, now freely permitted. Rumors spread that Malisset flour afflicted whole villages with horrible maladies, in some cases fatal. Economic flour, liberty's porridge, was poisoned! These stories were false, but it was true that under the pressure of severe dearth and of an unfavorable contract that threatened to ruin him, Malisset did not agonize over the quality of his flour or the reputation of his technology. His major concern was to extract as much flour per setier as possible. Moreover, increasingly he had to work with mediocre wheat or with overheated, partly rotten foreign grain that the government imported.[191]

It is not surprising that the image of economic milling was tarnished—what is amazing is that, unlike liberty, it managed to survive at all. Gradually the economic process was depoliticized. The new ministry repudiated liberalization without renouncing its patronage of economic milling. The return of (relative) abundance took the pressure off. The "miller-economist-merchants" of yesterday became simple miller-merchants again. Yet for many persons economic flour continued to have a strange and disturbing aftertaste. And it can be argued that the economic debacle of the sixties made it possible to defend (improved!) coarse milling without suffering rebuke as a reactionary.[192]

There were concrete, reasoned complaints against economic milling that implied that some critics had been willing to give it a hearing. Many millers

189. Bucquet, *Manuel du meunier,* pp. 6–7.

190. For the Malisset story, see Kaplan, *Bread, Politics and Political Economy,* chap. 8, and *Famine Plot.*

191. "Mémoire sur les désavantages de la mouture économique," cited by Brunot, *Langue française,* 6:277.

192. See the question asked by Condorcet: "Do you believe, Sir, that it will be impossible to persuade the people that . . . economic millers do not put chalk in their bread . . . ? Condorcet, *Lettre d'un laboureur,* p. 487. Cf. similar prejudices in England. Bennett and Elton, *Corn Milling,* 3:288–89.

complained that it was too difficult, despite the assurance of Malisset and Bucquet. Dransy, an engineer, agreed. The economic system, he claimed, made milling "extremely complicated" instead of "simplifying" it. The new process "subordinated" the miller to the mill instead of making it dependent on him. Bucquet's needlessly labyrinthine gear systems would be costly to install and to maintain.[193] Now Dransy, convinced that Bucquet had erred both in his instructions for mounting the stones and wheels and in his conception of the grinding and bolting processes, proposed several structural modifications that would result in a more even, cooler grinding, a more discriminating bolting, and a higher quality flour.[194] He made greater technical demands than Bucquet on the millers; but he articulated certain reservations entertained by many practitioners. Economic milling was more work than ordinary milling, no matter how one tried to streamline it. Though it saved in some ways, Dransy charged, it "caused waste, delays, and expenses" in others. Moreover, economic milling required a "delicacy" of skill of which all millers, however diligent, were not capable.[195]

At bottom Dransy was less worried about the difficulty of Bucquet's system than about its "exaggeration."[196] In far more stringent terms, he echoed the fear expressed by Malouin almost two decades earlier that repeated regrindings would "destroy or weaken" the quality of the flour.[197] Bucquet's avidity for extracting more and more, he suggested, would have "returned" milling "to its first state of imperfection."[198] Taking up the call for moderation, Parmentier called for "restricting rather than increasing the number of regrindings, for each time that the grain and its products pass under the stones there is always a more or less palpable alteration."[199] Dransy, like Parmentier, considered Bucquet's Lyonnaise grinding "an abuse" or perversion "rather than a refinement."[200] Yet the Lyonnaise technique, which involved multiple regrindings in order to extract over 80 percent and to obtain over 190 pounds

193. In vaguer terms, Malouin made similar reproaches. *Description et détails des arts,* p. 52.

194. Cf. the reproach of a fellow miller that Bucquet "lost a ninth of the price" on elite wheat because he ground too fast and thus produced "choked" flour with a poor capacity for water absorption. "Résponse au mémoire du Sr. Bucquet," Arsenal, ms. 7458.

195. "Mémoire sur la construction des moulins," AD Haute-Garonne, C 2268. Malisset and Bucquet were not in favor of slowing down the stones as Dransy proposed, but they were sympathetic with his ideas for dressing the stones and for bolting.

196. Ibid., p. 158.

197. Cf. Malouin, *Description et détails des arts,* p. 59.

198. "Mémoire sur la construction des moulins," pp. 156–60, AD Haute-Garonne, C 2268.

199. "Mémoire sur les avantages que la province de Languedoc peut retirer de ses grains," pp. 154–55, AD Haute-Garonne, C 2268. Cf. Rozier's attack on "the extravagant partisans of economic milling," clearly inspired by Parmentier. *Cours complet,* 7:359.

200. Parmentier, *Parfait Boulanger,* pp. 175–78, and Dransy, "Mémoire sur la construction des moulins," p. 158, AD Haute-Garonne, C 2268.

of bread per Parisian setier, was not envisioned by Bucquet as a universal model for France. He meant it for the public-assistance institutions, for the masses of very poor who needed a cheap and nutritious "household" bread, and for times of dearth. Bucquet himself counseled against "an excessive" processing of middlings and knew very well that the Lyonnaise method was only a very special and limited kind of refinement.[201]

The Demon Bran

The Lyonnaise quarrel pointed to a more fundamental debate about the quality of the bread made economically. This debate on quality was not dispassionate, but it was for the most part devoid of the suspicion and the hysteria of ill-willed bakers and millers or frightened consumers. On the other hand, implicitly, it took the story of economic milling full circle, back to the Dark Ages when the authorities banned middling recovery on the grounds of public safety.

To the extent that it failed to purge the bran—the alleged master contaminator—economic milling was open to criticism. Estienne and Liébault had put the case succinctly in their famous household treatise at the end of the seventeenth century: bran should be left for the dogs.[202] The scientific community was divided on the issue. The minority opinion, represented by doctors Le Camus and Malouin, presaged a viewpoint that has recently become fashionable again: that some bran (but how much?) facilitated digestion, served as a gentle laxative, purified the system, and fortified the strength. Both physicians had in mind primarily the mass of poor rural consumers, and were in fact justifying a fait accompli rather than envisioning a new way to perfect bread making.[203] The majority opinion, which had not changed in several centuries, was that bran was at best difficult for many stomachs to

201. Bucquet, *Manuel du meunier*, p. 58. Bucquet contended that his Lyonnaise method was not a refinement of economic milling but a different approach that involved mixing all the flours to satisfy the needs of "a certain class of men more efficiently than economic milling can do." He insisted that he allowed virtually no bran to enter the flour but rather removed every bit of flour from the shell. *Traité pratique*, p. xiii. Cf. Arpin's harsh strictures against Bucquet. *Historique de la meunerie*, 1:120–34.

202. Jean Liébault, *L'Agriculture et maison rustique de MM. Charles Estienne et Jean Liébault* (Lyon, 1689), p. 498.

203. Malouin, *Description des arts* (1761), p. 261, and Le Camus, "Suite du mémoire sur le pain," *Journal économique* (December 1753): p. 98. Athanaeus, a third-century Egyptian philosopher, saw bran as the most nutritious part of the wheat berry. Kirkland, ed., *Modern Baker*, 1:6. Certain British experts looked upon bran favorably in the eighteenth century. Newton and Sheppard, *Story of Bread*, p. 72. The Prussian savant Frederick Hoffman, promoter of *bonpernickel*, called for retaining all the bran, but he focused on rye rather than wheat. Parmentier et al., *Rapport sur le pain des troupes* (1796), published by A. Balland, *La Chimie alimentaire dans l'oeuvre de Parmentier* (Paris, 1902), p. 249.

digest and at worst seriously damaged them, and therefore ought to be avoided whenever possible.[204]

Firmly rooted in scientific as well as in folkloric tradition and in everyday household experience, this appreciation could not be rigorously tested so long as the inner structure of the wheat berry remained a mystery.[205] Beccari launched the process of demystification in the forties with his convincing demonstration of the existence of a "glutinous" agent in wheaten flour. This substance, known to us as gluten and prized for its rich protein lode, had a tough, tenacious, and elastic quality that gave the dough its cohesiveness and its ability to retain gas. Beccari contended that the glutinous matter rather than starch, which was merely its bulkiest constituent, comprised the principal nutritive part of wheat. Presented as a Latin dissertation at Strasbourg in 1759, Kesselmayer's study corroborated Beccari's conclusion on the nutritive charge of the glutinous substance. Touvenol announced the same finding at Montpellier in 1770, asserting that wheat was extraordinary precisely because it contained such an abundance of glutinous matter. Two years later, in still another thesis, Portal de Bellefond obtained similar results; though he claimed, in a controversial addendum, that other cereals shared the glutinous treasure of wheat in smaller dosages.[206]

After the successful repetition of experiments in the Faculty of Medicine, the Royal Botanical Gardens, and the Cours de Chymie, Beccari's conclusions seemed unassailable. Beginning in the late sixties, however, Parmentier, himself an army pharmacist, encountered the work of Model, chief of the Russian military pharmacy. While Model substantiated Beccari's discovery, he found that the glutinous matter was a product of the bran, or shell of the wheat berry; that as such it was significantly less nutritious than the starch; and that in the last analysis this gluten, like bran, was of marginal importance. Parmentier concurred; he conceived the glutinous matter as "a small bran" and bran as a rather pernicious substance that "damaged the alimentary effect" of the wheat or flour. If the glutinous matter accounted for the nutritional properties of bread, then white bread, which had significantly less bran, would be less nourishing than dark; yet the contrary was universally acknowledged. No matter how finely fragmented, Parmentier charged in a celebrated aphorism that food scientists still like to cite, bran "makes weight and not bread." A pound of bread without any bran nourished better than a pound and a quarter with it. Parmentier urged enterprises that had to feed large numbers

---

204. J.-J. Expilly, *Tableau de la population de France* (n.p., 1780), p. 12.

205. See the twelfth-century verse celebrating "the true bread without bran," the bran having been expertly purged by the miller pall. Grodecki, "Vitraux allégoriques," p. 22. For a harsh scientific condemnation of bran from a nonchemical perspective, see Joyeuse l'aîné to Duhamel, 20 August 1756, and "Essay sur les bleds de froment pour en déterminer le choix dans les boulangeries du roy," AN, 127 AP 6. See also Baudeau, *Avis au peuple,* deuxième traité, p. 15.

206. Béguillet, *Traité des subsistances,* pp. 549–54n, 564–74.

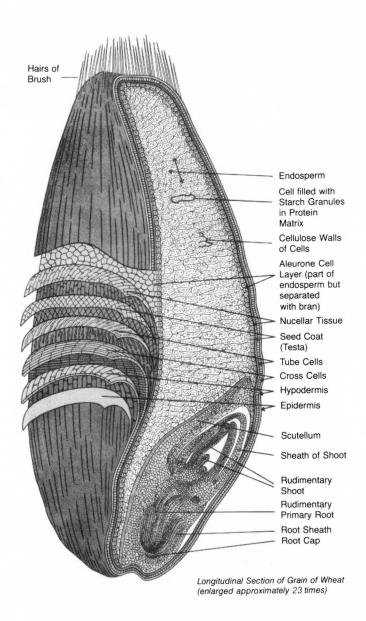

Hairs of Brush

Endosperm

Cell filled with Starch Granules in Protein Matrix

Cellulose Walls of Cells

Aleurone Cell Layer (part of endosperm but separated with bran)

Nucellar Tissue

Seed Coat (Testa)

Tube Cells

Cross Cells

Hypodermis

Epidermis

Scutellum

Sheath of Shoot

Rudimentary Shoot

Rudimentary Primary Root

Root Sheath

Root Cap

Longitudinal Section of Grain of Wheat (enlarged approximately 23 times)

The composition of a kernel of wheat (Wheat Flour Institute, Washington, D.C.)

of people to provide their workers with a smaller quantity of bread of a higher quality ("less dark" and thus less contaminated with bran).[207]

For a number of reasons Parmentier's thesis alarmed the government as well as his fellow subsistence specialists. The army, where the bread question stirred strong feelings, fed the troops a bread with a relatively high bran content. Parmentier described the bran-laden military *pain de munition* as "putrid, dysenteric, and scorbutic." Supported by the government, Malouin, among others, encouraged the dissemination of an economical household bread *(pain de ménage)* made for the working population from a flour of a high extraction.[208] He did not construe the use of bran as a way to perfect bread, but rather as a means of resolving a social issue. In other contexts, the physician was not the friend of middling recovery and multiple grindings. Finally, as a staunch advocate of the virtues of the new milling technology, the ministry was worried about Parmentier's implication that efforts to achieve economy through middling redemption were ill conceived and baleful.

Given its political and social implications, it is not surprising that the government, probably the war ministry, commissioned the academician Sage to refute Parmentier's chemical analysis. Vigorously sustaining Beccari's findings, Sage "demonstrated" that half the weight of bran consists of "an alimentary matter" and that the rest was "analogous to the glutinous substance." The quality of wheat, he maintained, depended largely on the glutinous matter. Sage consulted with other chemists in the academy who assured him that bran was "nourishing"; he cited Malouin and other physicians who found that it was not deleterious to health, and he queried soldiers who insisted that their bread was "good."[209]

In a scathing pamphlet published the same year Parmentier depicted Sage as a bilious, narrow-minded, hopelessly self-regarding man and an unprincipled and incompetent scientist. Unfamiliar with the literature, Sage misunderstood the rudimentary phenomena of grain and flour chemistry. A

207. Johann Georg Model, *Récréations physiques, économiques et chimiques,* trans. and ed. Antoine-Augustin Parmentier (Paris, 1774), 1:xiii and 2:441ff.; Antoine-Augustin Parmentier, *Eloge de M. Model* (Paris, 1775); Parmentier in *Journal de physique* (February 1773): 158–59; Parmentier in Rozier, *Cours complet,* 7:374, 378. Cf. Poncelet, who considered the debate over "the alimentary properties" of wheat to be utterly "futile." *Histoire naturelle.* The government appointed Parmentier to act as censor for this book. Jealous and vain, Parmentier inserted footnotes to indicate that he had demonstrated this or that point before Poncelet—see, for instance, p. 57. Fougeroux de Bondaroy, academician and nephew of Duhamel du Monceau, once owned the edition that I used in the Yale University Library. He caviled in the margins with Poncelet's findings, insisting that the seminal work in the field had been done by his uncle.

208. Malouin, *Description des arts* (1761), p. 261.

209. Balthasar-Georges Sage, *Analyse des blés* (Paris, 1776). On Sage's utter mediocrity as a chemist, ("the verdict on Sage as a chemist is almost universally negative"), see Henry Guerlac, "Balthazar-Georges Sage," in Charles C. Gillispie, ed., *Dictionary of Scientific Biography* (New York, 1970–80), 12: 64.

shameless plagiarist, he copied Parmentier's experiments and utilized his findings without attribution; but at the same time he did not shrink from "mutilating" the sense of Parmentier's writings in order to discredit him.[210]

This essay afforded Parmentier the occasion to moderate his substantive positions on the pretext of restating them in order to correct Sage's misrepresentations. In fact, even before Sage's attack Parmentier had begun to retreat, though it is unclear whether he did so for properly scientific reasons or for fear of jeopardizing his career.[211] Even if large amounts of bran ruined bread, he argued, small amounts were probably inevitable and were often beneficial. An insignificant dose of bran pleasantly seasoned the loaf and facilitated digestion. Food had to be conceived in socially or occupationally differential terms. A bread containing some bran was especially appropriate for manual laborers, because it was extremely filling and preserved the feeling of satiety for a long time.[212] In his major work on bread and baking, *Le Parfait Boulanger,* published two years later, he continued to describe starch as "the most essential part" of the wheat berry invested with "the greatest nutritive faculty." He conceded, however, that the glutinous matter accounted for "the superiority" of wheat even if it was less remarkable for its "alimentary virtue." He characterized it as a gum resin rather than as "a little bran" and he treated bran judiciously as a substance that in certain circumstances offered real advantages.[213]

In chastening Parmentier, Sage also posed problems for the partisans of economic milling. In defense of bran, he risked giving the new technology a bad name, for he declared that "this [economic] discovery is nothing other than the art of introducing as much bran as possible into the bread"—that is, doing exactly what the police, counseled by the Faculty of Medicine, had striven to prevent since the sixteenth century.[214] Now, it was one thing to argue that bran was not noxious and quite another to suggest that it was the

210. Antoine-Augustin Parmentier, *Expériences et réflexions relatives à l'analyse du bled et des farines* (Paris, 1776), passim.

211. See Antoine-Augustin Parmentier, *Examen Chymique des pommes de terre: dans lequel on traite des parties constituantes du bled* (Paris, 1773), pp. 128–31.

212. Parmentier, *Expériences et réflexions,* pp. 115ff. Based on different assumptions about flour chemistry, Poncelet came to strikingly similar practical conclusions in a work published in Paris in the same year. *Mémoire sur la farine* (Paris, 1776), pp. 77–80. He found a real "nutritive" element in the mucus substance of the bran, though he contended that it was largely negated by the dominant presence of the woodlike fibrous substance.

213. Parmentier, *Parfait Boulanger,* pp. 23, 24, 27, 222–23, 549–50. But cf. his chariness in *Expériences et réflexions,* p. 190, and *Mémoire sur les avantages,* p. 148. Commissioned to assess the quality of the troops' bread in 1796, Parmentier reverted to his more strident antibran position. Bran had no scientifically verifiable advantages; it lacked any nutritional properties, its presence accelerated the deterioration of flour, it obstructed kneading and fermentation, and it caused or helped to cause constipation, dysentery, and scurvy. *Rapport sur le pain des troupes,* published by Balland, *La Chimie alimentaire,* pp. 238–62.

214. Sage, *Analyse des blés,* pp. 30, 31, 52. Cf. Malouin, *Description et détails des arts,* pp. 55–56.

secret principle of a sweeping reform program that promised to make not only more but also whiter and better flour and bread. If Sage was right, then economic bread was merely adulteration sanctioned and obfuscated by the double authority of government and science.[215] If economic milling was to win widespread adoption, its supporters would have to show that the "economy" was in flour rather than in bran.

Parmentier avoided the trap by vigorously denying the validity of Sage's assertion. He, too, had once held this mistaken view; and now Sage was perpetuating his error. Intensive scrutiny had convinced Parmentier that the economic process, properly applied, offered compromise no purchase. Optimistically and severely, he defined economic milling as the production of "the greatest quantity possible" of "the most beautiful flour," with almost no trace of bran, whole or pulverized. Led astray by their "enthusiasm," Bucquet and Béguillet had committed unjustifiable excesses that aroused suspicions of bran abuse. They jeopardized the new technology by pushing too far with their Lyonnaise version, seeking more or less furtively to valorize bran and sacrificing quality to quantity. "Everything has its limits." Parmentier exaggerated the extent to which the two economic promoters had transgressed reasonable limits and had given primacy to the Lyonnaise style. By portraying the Lyonnaise way as a caricature of authentic economic milling, by identifying Bucquet and Béguillet exclusively with the Lyonnaise extreme, and by projecting a conservative image for his less aggressive rendition of the new technology, he hoped to deflect criticism and suspicion from the economic process.[216]

Bucquet and Béguillet regarded the critique of both Sage and Parmentier as distortions and calumnies. "In flour ground economically, there remained no bran"; economic milling was devised precisely to rescue all the flour particles "without any admixture of bran." Flour blemished with bran could result only from a maladroit, "overly round" bolting. In any event, they did not consider the Lyonnaise version the best and most perfect form of economic milling—it was only one of many options, appropriate in certain well-

215. Cf. the warning that the rehabilitation of bran opened the floodgates to miller and baker frauds. Comité du salut public, 20 frimaire year III, Archives municipales Pontoise.

216. Parmentier, *Expériences et réflexions*, pp. 85ff.; *Parfait Boulanger*, pp. 185–90; and *Mémoire sur les avantages*, p. 148. Would Parmentier have dared to inveigh against what he styled "a deleterious abundance" in a time of dearth? Malouin wondered about what no physiocrat, however enthusiastic, would have dared to consider openly: given the need to reinvigorate agriculture, he worried that economic milling might prove counterproductive by generating "an overabundance" and thus depressing prices. Malouin, *Description des arts* (1761), p. 59. A writer in the *Journal économique* made the case that economic milling was more or less exclusively suited for dearth. The grounds he invoked, however, were that in other times it would deprive horses, pigs, and chickens of food, since it removed all the fatty meal from the bran (May 1771): 216–17. In another context, Nicolas-Edme Restif de la Bretonne made this same argument, insisting on placing animal consumption in the economic equation. *La Vie de mon père,* ed. Gilbert Rouger (Paris, 1970), p. 130.

defined circumstances. Finally, they reminded all the adversaries of innovation that while the economic technology guaranteed scrupulous separation and removal of bran, in coarse milling the bran was always mixed in with the white meal in varying proportions.[217]

According to Bucquet and Béguillet, economic flour owed its superlative quality to the high concentration of glutinous matter in the recovered middlings. This glutinous matter was not a bran but a resinous mixture formed in the vessels of the berry by mucilage, starch, and oil. Bran by itself, they agreed, had nothing to recommend it: it had no nutritive properties, it was acidic and indigestible, and it hindered the conservation of flour. Nevertheless, they noted, even when present in fairly large amounts, as in military rations and in many country breads, bran seemed not to do any damage. So long as "the Troops and the People are in the habit of eating bread in which everything entered without any visible harm resulting," it was pointless to use scientific arguments to embarrass the government and to create needless difficulties.[218]

Neither Sage's chemistry nor the image of hearty peasants or grinning soldiers succeeded in dissipating the prejudice against bran. Ironically, during the Revolution an expert named by the Commission on Subsistence and Provisioning assailed Parmentier for creating a new sort of bread made of "flours mixed with much bran." The addition of bran, he claimed in language Parmentier must have found hauntingly familiar, "will increase the weight" but will add nothing to the nutritive substance.[219] An article published in the *Encyclopédie méthodique* shortly after the Revolution described bran as a nuisance substance containing empty calories that gave the stomach a misleading sense of repletion.[220] A modern authority, writing in the 1930s, suggested that bran contained a substance called *céréaline* that impeded kneading and inhibited the rising or proofing process by attacking the gluten. It followed that the gray color of dark bread was not caused by bran fragments per se but by the *céréaline* that oxidized the flour. Contemporary medical opinion, the author remarked, was divided over the importance of the vitamins, minerals, and proteins lodged in the bran and over the possibility of digesting bran, whatever the value of the elements it contained.[221] In 1941 the

217. Béguillet, *Traité des subsistances*, pp. 332–34; *Nouvelles Ephémérides économiques* 10 (1775): 157–58.

218. Béguillet, *Traité des subsistances*, pp. 81, 324–27n, 555–71, 628–32. Cf. Ammann, *Meunerie et boulangerie*, p. 53. See also a late-nineteenth-century writer who claimed that the presence of bran enabled bread to last longer. A. Feyeux, "Un Nouveau Livre des métiers," *La Science sociale* 4 (1887): 328.

219. AN, F^{12} 1299^B (pluviôse year II). "Bran does not make bread," an arrêt of the Committee of Public Safety reminded Frenchmen a year later. Archives municipales Pontoise (20 frimaire year III).

220. *Encyclopédie méthodique*, Agriculture, 6:344.

221. Alfred Gottschalk, *Le Blé, la farine et le pain* (Paris, 1935), pp. 22, 23, 49. Cf. the eighteenth-century administrator-savant who contended that the presence of bran dimin-

French Academy of Medicine, in a harsh condemnation of flour extracted at a rate above 80 percent, invoked the authority of Parmentier—the *old* Parmentier—staunch adversary of bran, whose conclusions, the Academy claimed, had not lost their validity despite the enormous advances made in the biochemistry of bread and bread making.[222] In a recent study on food shortage two French physicians, again citing Parmentier and also referring to American studies, denounced bran, save in very slight doses, as "an anti-aliment," and thus vindicated the historical obsession with white bread—not a simple matter of snobbery.[223] Research in Britain and the United States has tended to show that whole-meal flour is no more nutritious than 70 percent extract commercial flour.[224]

Against this tide of opinion eddied a sort of pro-bran counterculture and counterscience. Its most emphatic spokesman in nineteenth-century America was Sylvester Graham, who argued that bran was a positive good. It cured both constipation and diarrhea, conditioned the teeth and gums as well as the alimentary canal, and helped fortify consumers morally by teaching them to reject the "wanton and luxurious" ways of the eaters of superfine wheaten bread. There was a wonderful and purposive coherence in the way grain was composed. "To put asunder what God has joined together" by expelling the bran from grain was "in direct violation of the laws of constitution and relation which the Creator has established in the nature of man." A mid-nineteenth-century French chemist, Mège-Mouriès, reported that it was more than risky to disturb this ideal natural equilibrium: domestic animals nourished on flour devoid of bran died in short order. Flour must contain "a certain proportion of bran in order not to be dangerous," Mège-Mouriès concluded. About the same time the Bread Reform League in England also advocated the incorporation of bran in a "whole" loaf. In the past few years, new medical evidence has suggested that the regular consumption of foods rich in cellulose and fiber can prevent and alleviate a wide range of intestinal maladies. Bran bread has conquered a major place on the "dietetic" and "health-food" market. Ironically, however, it appears that Paris-area bakers now find a genuine bran bread too costly and complicated to make. Recent inspections revealed that virtually none of the whole-grain or bran breads sold contained the

ished the drinking capacity of the meal and thus rendered a heavy, languid dough. L. de Boullemer, "Traité sur les bleds," *Journal économique* (May 1772): 149. Parmentier's collaborator, Cadet de Vaux, made a similar point. *Traités divers d'économie,* p. 57.

222. *Bulletin de l'Académie de médecine* 124, 3d ser. (25 February 1941): 223–24.

223. Charles Richet and Antonin Mans, *La Famine* (Paris, 1965), p. 108. Cf. the recent line that a substance like bran, which is used industrially for polishing steel, could certainly do no good to the human intestines. Colin Clark and Margaret Haswell, *The Economics of Subsistence Agriculture,* 3d ed. (New York, 1967), p. 53. Grimshaw had made the same point in 1882. *Miller, Millwright, and Millfurnisher,* pp. 379, 427.

224. Richet and Mans, *Famine,* p. 108, and Horder, Dodds, and Moran, *Bread,* p. 149. Cf. F.L. Dunlap, *White Versus Brown Flour* (Newark, 1945).

minimal portion of cellulose required, despite the advertised assurances. Imagine what an eighteenth-century consumer would have thought of the idea of a so-called bran bread *adulterated* by high-quality white flour![225]

Another related criticism of the economic method was that, in exchange for a much greater extraction of white meal, it yielded a depleted dark meal in diminished quantity. Since there were more poor people than rich, argued Malouin, and since dark bread was the principal food of the poor, "it is thus more humane and more politically wise" to gear production toward the dark and to leave "the most nutritious elements" in the dark meal.[226] A practicing farmer named Cretté de Palluel complained that the multiple grindings left a dessicated, "insipid" dark flour, lacking savor and nutritiousness.[227] The agronomist Poncelet echoed these concerns, but in terms more poetic than scientific. He worried that the rigorous segregation of qualities practiced in economic milling would destroy the natural harmony—"ce bel accord"—of the constituent parts of the meal and that as a result the poorer consumers of the lower-grade flours would suffer more than the others.[228] These reproaches merely betrayed a lack of understanding of the operation and uses of economic milling, its partisans replied. By expelling the bran and recovering the middling flour, the economic process improved and enriched the dark meal as well as the white. Moreover, the economic range allowed millers to target any socio-nutritional universe desired: they could make as much middle-dark and dark bread as they wanted. Part of the long-term allure of economic milling, however, was that it could make a better (whiter, more savory, more nourishing) bread available to the laboring poor at a price equal or close to what they had previously paid for a coarse, heavy, dark loaf.

Another line of criticism took its inspiration from the old prejudice against mixing flour of wheats of different provenance. Public authorities had always been inclined to regard a mélange as a form of adulteration, as an effort to conceal inferior quality. The champions of economy, on the other hand, contended that expert mixing could dramatically improve quality. They pointed out that the economic method facilitated such mixing.[229] Precisely since eco-

---

225. Sylvester Graham, *A Treatise on Bread, and Breadmaking* (Boston, 1837), pp. 40–42, 53–62, 68; *Enquête sur la boulangerie,* p. 370; Snyder, *Bread: A Collection of Popular Papers on Wheat, Flour and Bread* (New York, 1930), pp. 124–25; "Pain au son ou pain trompeur," *Le Monde* (15 October 1980): 15.

226. Malouin, *Description et détails des arts,* pp. 54–55. Malouin was pleading for a perfected coarse style of milling. Cf. *Journal économique* (March 1768): 115.

227. François Cretté de Palluel, "Mémoire sur les moyens d'économiser la mouture des grains et de diminuer le prix de pain," *Mémoires d'agriculture, d'économie rurale et domestique publiés par la Société royale d'agriculture* (Fall 1788): 20–27. This flour was of poor nutritional value because the multiple grindings had partly destroyed the glutinous matter.

228. Poncelet, *Histoire naturelle,* pp. 172–73. Poncelet's solution, with which many writers and administrators were sympathetic, was to reconstitute and revalorize the flour by mixing together all the meal after multiple grindings and boltings in order to make a household bread.

229. See, for example, "Mémoire du Sr. Bucquet," March 1769, AD Isère, II C 47.

nomic technology made mixing easier and more attractive to the millers, its critics regarded it as a menace to the well-being of consumers. "Since the establishment of economic mills," noted the police of Troyes, "[flour] frauds have become far more frequent throughout the realm."[230]

Inevitably, questions about the quality of economic flour concerned not only its conversion into bread but also its conservability. The issue was of capital importance to the exponents of economic milling, for they contended that the new technology would give greater impetus to both national and international trade in flour. Despite Malisset's extremely promising early experiments with barrel-packed economic flour, Malouin remained skeptical. He maintained that the southern *rame* and *minot* style, which demanded a respite after grinding and escaped regrinding, produced the most stable flour, capable of the longest storage and/or travel. Not surprisingly, he was seconded in his thinking by Leclerc, the director of naval provisioning at Bordeaux, who had a lifetime of experience with the southern method.[231] Bucquet and Béguillet pointed to the enormous success of the Labat enterprise at Bordeaux, which shipped flour to the colonies and elsewhere abroad. Comparison proved, they wrote, that *minot* flour was more vulnerable to humidity and therefore to spoilage than economic meal, because its particles were less hard, less firm, and less dry at the time of packing.

Economic Milling after the French Revolution: Density and Production

An article in the *Encyclopédie méthodique* published in 1791 estimated that there were no more than 700 to 800 economic mills in all of France.[232] As late as 1804 Cadet de Vaux allowed that economic milling was still unknown in nine-tenths of France.[233] Bosc, writing for the 1813 *Encyclopédie méthodique,* acknowledged that cost and ignorance still inhibited diffusion, but took heart in the fact that economic mills were now numerous in and around big cities and ports.[234]

Several milling surveys conducted by the ministry of the interior under

---

230. "Résultat des observations des officiers de police" (1773), AD Marne, C 417.

231. "Précis d'observations sur l'objet des moulins," cited by Des Essarts, *Dictionnaire universel de police,* 7: 108.

232. *Encyclopédie méthodique,* Jurisprudence, police et municipalités, 10:34. The towns and cities where economic milling was most perfected, according to this article, were Pontoise, Corbeil, Etampes, Chartres, and Melun, all in the Paris area, and Rouen, Amiens, and Nantes.

233. *Bulletin de la Société d'encouragement pour l'industrie nationale,* no. 7 (ventôse year XI), cited by A. Birembaut, "L'Ecole gratuite de boulangerie," p. 506; Arpin, *Historique de la meunerie,* 1:244. Eight years later Cadet de Vaux wrote that a sixth of all the flour produced in France was economic. *Retour des disettes.*

234. *Encyclopédie méthodique,* Agriculture, 5:376.

Napoléon sought to determine the state of the art throughout the nation. The results are at best fragile and incomplete, and ought ideally to be verified independently by and used in conjunction with local sources. In many instances, however, those local sources are widely scattered or stubbornly parsimonious. The surveys are honeycombed with methodological flaws, of which the most serious is the lack of uniformity in language and collection procedures. Several of the prefects noted a confusion in "denominations." It was apparent that not everyone understood the question: Is milling done according to the economic method (also called Parisienne) or the coarse method (also called Lyonnaise)? "I have not found anyone," wrote the prefect of the Charente, "who could explain the difference between economic or Parisienne milling and the coarse or Lyonnaise method."[235] The prefect of Léman found that "the difference between the two was perhaps not always perfectly grasped, and some mayors may have taken the one for the other in their answers."[236] In the Creuse, all these distinctions were foreign; they were regarded as Parisianisms—light years away.[237] "The denominations economic or Parisienne milling and coarse or Lyonnaise milling are unknown in the Hautes-Alpes," wrote the prefect, echoing his colleague in the Basses-Alpes.[238] Bewildered by these terms, the prefect of the Gers asked for and received from the ministry a simple, trenchant definition: "Economic milling means passing the grain several times under the stone in order to separate the flour entirely from the bran," while the coarse process was "a one-stroke operation that gives a much less perfected flour."[239]

The issue was further complicated by the fact that "Parisienne" was used as a synonym for "economic" and "Lyonnaise" as a synonym for coarse. "Parisienne" may have evoked many different reactions. Certain millers (or

235. Prefect of Charente to minister of the interior, 20 July 1809, AN, F^{20} 296. The prefect described the local technology as *minot*, which he explained meant removing the bran at the mill. Yet the *minot* in the Atlantic and Mediterranean regions usually meant leaving the bran in the *rame* and bolting several weeks after grinding, frequently away from the mill. This was how the prefect of the Lot described his area's milling and he subsumed it under the coarse rubric. To the ministry of the interior, 27 March 1809, ibid.

236. This may help account for the prodigious number of economic mills—557—claimed by this Genevan department. The prefect also noted that the economic technology was used primarily for the largely urban, well-off consumers while the coarse method was used for the military and for the rural inhabitants. If economic milling had been properly understood, however, it would have been used for both purposes. Prefect to the minister of the interior, 16 February 1810 [*sic*], ibid.

237. Prefect of the Hautes-Alpes to minister of the interior, 10 February 1809, and prefect of the Basses-Alpes to minister of the interior, 23 February 1809, AN, F^{20} 295.

238. Prefect to minister of the interior, 3 February 1809, ibid.

239. Ministry of the interior to prefect of Gers, 29 July 1809, ibid. The prefect of the Pas-de-Calais also asked for a definition of the terms, but in the same breath he estimated that 20 percent of the mills in his jurisdiction were economic, thus placing the reliability of his survey in question (218 versus 816 coarse mills). Prefect to ministry of the interior, 5 April 1809, AN, F^{20} 296.

The Vieux Moulins of Meaux, converted to the economic process (private collection)

administrators) may not have wished to think of themselves as imitating the mode of the capital. Others may have reacted with strong hostility to Paris for wholly irrelevant reasons. Still others may have read Parisienne milling as white milling, which was not at all perfectly synonymous with economic milling.[240] How coarse milling acquired the Lyonnaise imprimatur is even more curious. Lyon rejected economic milling rather spectacularly in the wake of Bucquet's first visit, but it is unlikely that this fact enjoyed nation-wide notoriety. What is especially ironic and confusing is that "Lyonnaise" in the "economic" vocabulary was the description of the most radical form of the new technology, rather than of the most traditional manifestation of the old.

How the surveys were taken is unclear; whether local officials actually went into the field, whether they had any knowledge of the industry, whether they tried to check on the testimony of the millers.[241] They did not follow the metrological system of the ministry, making it difficult to compare reports from different places. Indeed, some surveys used two or three different measures simultaneously. Nor was there a consensus on what those measures signified—St.-Denis production reports were given in setiers rather than hec-

240. By the 1870s, "economic milling" was equated with "French milling" (as opposed to "American milling") and was taken to be the common technology throughout the country. Pierre Larousse, ed., *Grand dictionnaire universel du 19ᵉ siècle* (Paris, 1866–[90]), 11:632. See also Armengaud, *Meunerie et boulangerie,* p. 72.

241. The "observations" on some of the tables—some printed and others entirely manu-script—suggest that some officials were far more aggressive and better informed than others.

toliters or metric quintals, but the ministry of the interior asked whether the setier invoked was the old (presumably Parisian) setier or the new one, equal to a hectoliter according to recent legislation.[242] Finally, the ministry suspected—quite rightly, I think—that instead of reporting the amount of flour that they could manufacture in twenty-four hours many millers indicated the amount of wheat that they could transform in that time.

For all these reasons, we must use the survey data with extreme caution, as rough indicators rather than as proofs. Eighty-eight departments responded to the survey of 1809. In thirty-eight departments there was apparently no economic milling at all.[243] In nine others the situation is unclear. Among the forty-one departments that seem to have adopted economic milling there are some troublesome elements. All 974 mills in the Vosges are listed as economic, as are 689 of the 695 in the Landes, 458 of 656 in the Forêts, 577 of 1,413 in Léman, and 636 of 2,531 in the Finistère. Even if one is on the side of progress, one feels more comfortable with the reports that label as economic 4 of 1,554 mills in the Nord, 1 of 1,000 in the Haute-Savoie, 1 of 681 in the Drôme, 3 "factories" out of 1,331 mills in the Loire-Inférieure, 23 of 462 in the Indre-et-Loire (all situated in towns), and 3 of 1,543 in the Haute-Garonne (all at Toulouse).

A number of prefects expressed frustration at the failure of the new methods to penetrate. In the year XI a group of Besançon city improvers, led by an entrepreneur prepared to invest in the new milling technology, asked the Society of Encouragement for National Industry to place and train two local millers with specialists in Paris, "where this art is carried to a very high degree of perfection."[244] Yet five years later the prefect deplored the triumph of "routine over the spirit of perfection."[245] The prefect of the Orne observed: "Despite the teaching of experience and reason, only a handful of millers use the economic way and then only during dearths."[246] Wrote the prefect of the Maine-et-Loire: "I am told that a single miller [in the entire department] has established a bolter at his mill and that another regrinds his grain several times; but such is the empire of prejudice and habit that these two millers are ridiculed by everyone, and their practices have no imitators."[247] "Milling here is reduced to a single operation," the prefect of the Nord reported, "and one

242. Minister of the interior to prefect of the Seine, 30 November 1809, AN, F[20] 296.

243. See, for example, the statement of the prefect of the Pyrénées Orientales: "Economic milling is not used in this region; one passes the grain only once under the stone, which gives a flour mixed with bran." To minister of the interior, 21 May 1810 [sic], AN, F[20] 295.

244. Bulletin de la Société d'encouragement pour l'industrie nationale, no. 7 (ventôse year XI).

245. Prefect to minister of the interior, 15 June 1809, AN, F[20] 295.

246. Prefect to ministry of the interior, 4 September 1809, AN, F[20] 296.

247. Prefect to minister of the interior, 4 January 1811 [sic], AN, F[20] 295.

can evaluate at more than a fourth the amount of flour that is lost by this ridiculous manner of milling."[248]

Back in the 1760s, Malisset regarded Languedoc as one of the areas most ripe for conquest by the new technology. The miller and baker whom he dispatched there, however, made very little headway.[249] The next major innovation effort did not occur for almost forty years until Ovide, the former director of the steam mills on the Isle des Cygnes in Paris, arrived in Toulouse. Using "all the movements to be found in Philadelphia," where Oliver Evans had been perfecting his own version of economic milling, Ovide constructed a massive, five-story mill-factory with twenty sets of stones capable of transforming twelve hundred sacks of wheat per day. "Everyone in this city is talking about our establishment," boasted Ovide. "It is without doubt the most beautiful operation of its type in all of Europe."[250] A leading local miller declared that "the introduction of this sort of industry [was] one of the most decisive steps that could be made in the region [toward perfecting] the art of milling."[251] Elated by this installation, the minister of the interior effusively praised Ovide and his associates as pioneer modernizers of the Midi whose example "will be widely followed."[252] Despite the government's high hopes and its vigorous promotional efforts, the Toulouse enterprise does not appear to have stirred much emulation. The preference for coarse milling in the Haute-Garonne may have been due in part to the desire to preserve a rich food for the animals.[253] In the Touraine, serious dissemination of the new milling technology did not really begin until the Restoration.[254]

A total of 8,593 economic mills are enumerated in the survey—ten times the estimate of the *Encyclopédie méthodique* at the outset of the Revolution. A little over three-quarters of the economic mills for which we have data (only 3,065 reported this information) were water mills. Almost 72 percent of the 18,768 coarse mills for which we have data were water mills. The economic mills represented 20.85 percent of all the mills in the departments where they existed—8,593 of 41,209—but only 9.4 percent of all the mills reported in France (which numbered 91,134, a much higher total than anyone had previously estimated, even allowing for imperial annexations). In the

248. Prefect to minister of the interior, 11 July 1809, AN, F^{20} 296.

249. "Réponse du Sr. Malisset," 27 June 1763, AD Nord, C 9780. See also Béguillet, *Traité des subsistances,* pp. 372–73.

250. Ovide to Molard, 27 June 1804, Bibliothèque du Conservatoire des Arts et Métiers, ms. 358.

251. Proprietors of the mill of Bazacle to minister of the interior, 30 fructidor year XIII, AN, F^{12} 2197. See also *Encyclopédie méthodique,* Agriculture, 4:408.

252. Minister of the interior to régence des moulins de Bazacle, 25 brumaire year XIII and 12 vendémiaire year XIV, AN, F^{12} 2197.

253. Prefect to minister of the interior, 27 September 1809, AN, F^{20} 295.

254. Charlot, "Essai historique," pp. 147–52.

grande nation, then, nine of ten mills, as Cadet de Vaux had suggested, were more or less untouched by economy.

The departments with the heaviest implantation of economic mills were for the most part in the Paris region: the Eure-et-Loir with 661 (and no coarse mills); the Oise with 926 mills (and no coarse mills); the Seine-et-Oise with 667 (and 99 coarse mills); the Marne with 402 (and 542 coarse mills); the Seine-et-Marne with 386 (and 162 coarse mills); the Seine-Inférieure with 377 (and 329 coarse mills); and the Seine with 145 (and no coarse mills).[255]

In the Seine-et-Oise, 87 percent of all the mills were economically mounted. All 165 mills in the arrondissement of Pontoise, perhaps the foremost flour-trading area in the Paris region, were economic. Pontoise is the only locality in this department of which we can compute economic production, and even here at best we can establish a range. Each of the economic mills at Pontoise was able on the average to manufacture 1,285 pounds of flour (which would imply approximately 6.9 setiers of wheat) in twenty-four hours or to convert 5.4 setiers of wheat into flour, depending on how the respondents interpreted the question.[256]

A little over 70 percent of the mills in the Seine-et-Marne were economic. Three of the five arrondissements—Coulommiers, Provins, and Melun—reported 100 percent economic technology. In these three localities, 85 percent of the mills were waterpowered. The mills of Melun, whose renown for flour rivaled Pontoise's, produced on the average almost exactly as much as the Pontoise mills: 1,289 pounds of flour, which meant a transformation of roughly 5.4 to 6.9 setiers a day. The Coulommiers mills were less active, working on 4.3 to 5.5 setiers (1,030 pounds of flour), while the mills of Provins achieved the best score, 6.8 to 8.7 setiers (1,632 pounds).[257]

Our most detailed information concerns the Seine-et-Marne, but it comes from another survey conducted in 1811 whose results in many ways, alas, contradict those of 1809.[258] My impression is that the second survey was conducted with greater care. It is clear that officials had profited from their previous experience. Economic milling appears in 1811 to be far more modestly implanted than we have believed.[259] Almost two-thirds of the mills of Meaux were now listed as economic, whereas Meaux boasted only 46 percent

255. Anomalies: Forêts with 458 mills capable of economic milling; Finistère with 636; Landes with 689; Vosges with 974; Léman with 577; and Loiret with 314.

256. Certified report by prefect of Seine-et-Oise, 17 May 1809, AN, F^{20} 290.

257. Because millers habitually talked in terms of quantities of wheat to be ground, my belief is that the production figures refer to metric quintals (or hectoliters or myriagrammes or setiers) of wheat before transformation and *not* (as the ministry desired) to real yield in flour. One must also question the authenticity of the figures volunteered by the millers (when they were not simply estimated by the data collector on the basis of size and type of mill, reputation, hearsay, etc.). Were the millers inclined, for fear of fiscal or political consequences, to underestimate their capacity? Did they implicitly factor in an allowance for *chômage* in their estimations?

258. AD Seine-et-Marne, 12 M 59.

259. In the 1811 survey, the term *Lyonnaise* is not used at all to describe a type of

economic mills in 1809. In the other three arrondissements for which we have data, there were only a total of thirty-one economic mills: 7.2 percent of the mills in Provins (over against 100 percent in 1809), 11 percent in Coulommiers (100 percent in 1809), and 16.4 percent in Fontainebleau (18 percent in 1809, the only near convergence). In addition, a number of mills—a little over 10 percent of all the mills in the arrondissements of Provins, Coulommiers, and Meaux—allegedly employed both economic and coarse technologies. Malisset and Bucquet would surely have scoffed at this sort of androgyny, for economic technology implied fundamental structural changes as well as procedural ones. Once a mill was economically mounted, it could not mill coarsely, unless the miller either decided not to repass his middlings (conceivable, but unlikely) or to disconnect his bolters. On these grounds it is probably reasonable to count the androgynous mills as economic installations. In this case, 40 percent of the mills in these four arrondissements would be economic and 60 percent would be coarse.[260]

We can calculate differential production over a twenty-four-hour period per pair of stones, expressed in Parisian setiers of wheat for two of the four arrondissements. In Meaux, average production for all mills was 5.5 setiers (if the respondents answered the question: How much grain do you transform?) or 1,330 pounds of flour which would represent the conversion of about 7.5 setiers of wheat (if the respondents answered the question: How much flour do you manufacture?). Mean production for water-driven economic mills amounted to either 5.1 or 6.5 setiers (1,223.4 pounds), while water-driven coarse mills handled between 6.4 and 8.2 setiers (1,541.4 pounds). With a daily production of 4 to 5 setiers (952 pounds), economic windmills outdid coarse mills (1.53 to 2 setiers, or 367 pounds), but the total number of windmills was quite small.

The figures for Fontainebleau are far more precarious. Mean production varied between 4.65 and 5.9 setiers of grain (or 1,115 pounds of flour). Coarse (water) production seems implausibly low: 3.6 to 4.3 setiers (or 859 pounds), while economic (water) yield seems too high (7.9 to 10 setiers, or 1,895 pounds). Theoretically coarse mills should ordinarily have handled more than economic mills, because they were burdened with fewer procedures and could thus turn over grain at a faster pace. Everything depended, however, on how well mounted the economic mills were, how many times they reground, how poorly the coarse mills were constructed, and how efficient and stable the power source was. Thus, the Fontainebleau figures are unlikely but not impossible, while the Meaux figures are reassuring but do not constitute a standard.

---

milling. The arrondissement of Coulommiers reported three categories: Parisian (economic), coarse, and *au petit sac* or *à la monnée* (for individuals). The other three arrondissements used the binary Parisian/coarse.

260. There were only eight fewer total mills listed in 1811 than in 1809.

If the Coulommiers data are to be believed, not only had coarse milling improved since the 1760s, but it was able to match economic milling in flour yield per setier. (About quality we have no information of any sort.) On the average the mills in Coulommiers, 70 percent of which were coarse, produced 190 pounds of flour for each setier of wheat. One-quarter of the economic mills generated 223 pounds apiece, but half yielded only 181 pounds and one-quarter only 175. While over one-third of the coarse mills produced 175 pounds or less, 60 percent produced over 184 pounds. Of the latter, 31 percent yielded over 206 pounds—a remarkable performance.[261]

If we judge by waste *(déchet)* or loss in milling, as well as by fees charged, the gap between milling labeled economic and coarse milling seems to have been diminishing. At the outset Malouin had warned that economic milling caused more waste than the coarse method (because it increased the number of manipulations to which the grain and flour had to be subjected) and that this fact had to be reckoned with in calculating the "economy" of the new technology.[262] Parmentier and Tillet both reported that the waste in the economic process should be 6 pounds the setier, a figure confirmed by the Moulin de la Justice during its ordinary (albeit somewhat hurried) operations in 1768.[263] At Caen in 1769, however, the waste rose to 7.4 pounds, and in a trial held elsewhere in 1770 average economic waste climbed to 9.5 while the coarse loss amounted to 7.25 pounds. A contract to supply Paris in 1789 allowed a Meulan miller 8 pounds.[264] In the Fontainebleau survey of 1811 there is still a significant hiatus: whereas half of the economic mills wasted 6.4 pounds, 83 percent of the coarse mills wasted under 4.8 pounds. But in Meaux, 86 percent of the coarse millers joined 93 percent of the economic millers in the 6.4 pound category.[265] Expressed in terms of old-regime setiers, the standard waste allowance toward the middle of the nineteenth century was between 6 and 7.2 pounds.[266]

Based on milling fees taken in kind, which were still the most common, coarse milling was on the whole more expensive than economic, despite the higher costs and greater refinement of operation normally associated with the latter. Over 30 percent of the economic fees were one-fifteenth or one-sixteenth, while only 1.3 percent of the coarse fees were this low; 28.2 percent of the coarse mills took one-thirteenth as opposed to 3.9 percent of the

261. In the Meaux survey all the mills were listed as rendering 180 pounds per setier, which suggests that the question was never really posed.

262. Malouin, *Description des arts* (1771), p. 392.

263. Parmentier, *Parfait Boulanger*, p. 197; Tillet, "Projet d'un tarif," p. 127; AN, F[11] 1194.

264. AD Calvados, C 2653; BHVP, série 118, cote provisoire 1482; BN, Coll. Vexin, vol. 69, fol. 43.

265. *Enquête sur la boulangerie*, p. 213.

266. In all four arrondissements, about an equal percentage of economic and coarse mills were in the highest waste category—8 to 9.5 pounds.

economic mills; one-twelfth was the most common fee taken by nearly 60 percent of both the coarse and the economic mills (60 and 58 percent respectively); 10.3 percent of the coarse mills took one-tenth—a rate considered extortionate on the eve of the Revolution—as opposed to 3.9 percent of the economic installations. The sparse data on differential cash fees, confined to Meaux, show relatively little difference: 56 percent of the economic mills and 66 percent of the coarse mills charged either 1 franc 30 centimes or 1 franc 40 centimes.

Despite the apparent leveling of differences between economic and coarse milling, the two types of mills remained far apart in their commercial orientation (though here, too, the survey appreciations are impossible to validate). Virtually all of the coarse mills were primarily integrated into local economic life. Many worked for small clients or individuals and others for local bakers. They converted on demand in the traditional custom fashion. Almost half of the economic mills, however, were clearly involved in more-or-less speculative flour traffic and most of these mills were part of the Parisian supply circuit. These millers were merchants with an urban rather than a rural orientation. When the Coulommiers surveyor noted that economic milling was the business of "the strongest mills," he was referring to their commercial horizons rather than their motor power.

Bucquet's Story: Practice and Theory

Thanks to economic milling, César Bucquet moved into a new world. From obscure Senlis miller he rose to national entrepreneur, international flour trader, government advisor, technical expert, and zealous propagandist. Though less spectacular, in many ways his career paralleled Malisset's. Both men began as humble artisans, without capital or connections. Both recognized the extraordinary opportunity offered by economic technology for commercial development. Both had an instinctive sense of the utilitarian ethos, embodied in projects that derived their power from self-interest and their legitimation from the public interest they incidentally but significantly served. Both started in the hospitals and then shuttled between the public and private sectors, whose frontier remained blurred in the old regime. Each tried to profit from the new climate of liberty that seemed to fit so well with the economic technology and each discovered that large parts of the population turned furiously against him as a result. Each suffered serious commercial reverses. Each became involved in bitter polemics that jeopardized his reputation.

Very little is known about Bucquet's early career. He came from a long line of millers and he married a miller's daughter. He ground for Paris bakers, but does not seem to have been among the early core of aggressive millers who became speculative mealmen. The Hôtel-Dieu of Paris retained a Sieur Bucquet during the subsistence crisis of 1738–41 to handle the arrival and conditioning of foreign grains, but it is not certain that he was our miller.[267] Twenty years later César Bucquet was to be found working in another public-assistance institution, the General Hospital, where he assisted Malisset in the early tests of the economic technology.[268] He impressed the hospital administrators sufficiently to win the lease for their Paris boat mill. Later he rented another hospital mill at Corbeil, where he probably also collaborated with Malisset on the latter's monumental economic installation.[269] Calling himself "milling engineer" and "négociant," by the end of the sixties Bucquet had interests in milling and flour-trading operations in several cities.[270] In some cases, it appears that he invested only his skill and his partners provided the capital. In others, such as his flour export commerce to the colonies or his milling operations at Etampes, he seems to have invested his own funds or money he borrowed.[271] Rolland, his son-in-law, joined him in a grain- and flour-trading venture with the marquis de Feuquières that ended in disaster, and probably also succeeded him as "director of economic milling" at the General Hospital.[272] Twice the English government is said to have coaxed Bucquet with incentives to migrate and twice he is said to have "patriotically" refused.[273] As we have seen, Bucquet combined private and public undertakings, devoting a great deal of time in the sixties to traveling throughout the kingdom at the government's behest to diffuse the good economic news. His office on the quai Pelletier was a sort of workingman's salon and laboratory, where he received visits from millers, officials, and writers who wanted to learn about his method.[274]

Bucquet's business empire collapsed in the late seventies. He filed for faillite, a form of "innocent" bankruptcy meant to buy time and goodwill in the hope that the enterprise could be salvaged. Perhaps his biggest disappointment was his inability to make a success of the huge Vaugirard bakery, supplied in large part by his own flour, that he established in 1774 in a Paris suburb for both military and civilian provisioning. He baked a white bread,

267. Vigneron to procurator general, 5 May 1739, BN, Coll. Joly 1120, fol. 17.

268. Arsenal, ms. Bast. 10141, fol. 476 (29 April 1761).

269. Brillon Duperron, *Considérations sur la mouture;* Archives Assistance publique, journal de l'économe (1768–70), Fosseyeux, Hôpital Général 105, liasse 7.

270. "Procès-verbal qui constate les avantages de la mouture économique," 30 April 1769, AN, F[11] 264; *Journal économique* (June 1769): p. 262.

271. Controller-general to intendant of Provence, de la Tour, 25 June 1769, AN, F[12]* 153; Archives Seine-Paris, D4B[6] 4429, 1778.

272. AN, Y 9648, 19 March 1771; AN, MC, LXII-534, 15 November 1770, and XVIII-759, 23 October 1773. Rolland owed Feuquières at least 49,000 livres when the marquis took steps to dissolve the relationship.

273. Bucquet, *Traité pratique,* p. viii. Cf. Arpin, *Historique de la meunerie,* p. 136.

274. See Baudeau, *Avis au peuple,* deuxième traité, p. 18; Malouin, *Description et détails des arts,* p. 45; abbé Para du Phanjas, "Le Commerce des grains," AN, T 466[12].

but the loaf on which he staked everything was a cheap and nourishing domestic bread made from the radical economic technology called Lyonnaise. The bakery functioned for twenty-eight months, running up a deficit of almost 80,000 livres (398,655 livres in expenses against 320,258 livres in receipts). Undoubtedly the operation was hurt by the price fluctuations and the turbulence of the Flour War crisis in the spring and summer of 1775. There appears, however, to have been a structural flaw as well as a "conjunctural" hardship: consumers manifested insufficient interest in the (almost) whole grain domestic bread, despite the fact that it cost no more per pound than a pound of raw wheat.[275]

Bucquet also failed to profit from his extensive grain and flour traffic—purchases of over 680,000 livres between April 1773 and November 1776—apparently as a result of unforeseen "revolutions in the prices." His debts totaled almost a quarter of a million livres. He had 39,495 livres in assets, the most substantial part of which was a boat mill worth 15,000 livres under the Notre-Dame bridge in Paris. He exhorted his creditors to take account of his "enormous misfortunes and losses," but was obliged to cede them his possessions in order to avoid further pursuits.[276] We lose track of Bucquet's dealings after this episode.[277] In 1794 a citoyenne Bucquet, who may have been his wife or widow, petitioned for an indemnity for the projected displacement of her two mills at the pont au Change and the pont de la Raison.[278]

A mover and doer par excellence, Bucquet also became a writer through the pen of Edme Béguillet. Parlementary lawyer and notary of the Burgundian Estates, Edme Béguillet was also a man of letters and a savant, correspondent of the Academies of Science and of Inscriptions and Belles-Lettres and honorary member of a host of academies in Italy, Switzerland, and France. He was Voltaire's friend and fellow academician (Lyon); the patriarch followed his writings on economic milling with interest.[279] Béguillet discovered Bucquet in the late sixties when the miller set up a model economic installation at

275. Archives Seine-Paris, D4B⁶ 68-4429. Cf. Béguillet's effort to remain optimistic. *Traité des subsistances,* p. 651n.

276. Archives Seine-Paris, D4B⁶ 68-4429 and DC⁶ 23, fol. 115. To protect her financial interests, his wife obtained a juridical "separation" of finances shortly afterward. DC⁶ 24, fol. 117.

277. His son-in-law Rolland, who filed for failure with him, apparently continued to counsel and work for the General Hospital. Cochin to Julien, 7 February 1780, Archives Assistance publique, Hôpital Général 105, Fosseyeux, liasse 18.

278. Comité de salut publique to the commission des armes et poudres, 22 fructidor year II, Archives Seine-Paris, 3 AZ 146, pièce 5.

279. Mémoire de Béguillet, ca. 1778, AN, F¹⁰ 256; Bertin to élus des états de Bourgogne, 7 November 1769, AD Côte-d'Or, C 3355, fol. 75; Voltaire to Bucquet, 16 April 1777, in François-Marie Arouet de Voltaire, *Correspondence,* ed. Theodore Besterman (Geneva, 1953–65), 96:149–50; Voltaire to Béguillet, 14 October 1775, ibid., 92:82; Voltaire to Germain G.R. de Ruffey, 26 January 1770, ibid., 74:61. Cf. Lublinsky, "Voltaire et la guerre des farines," *Annales historiques de la Révolution française,* 31st year, no. 156 (April–June 1959): 139.

Dijon.[280] Deeply impressed by his knowledge and utterly convinced of the boundless public utility of the economic way, Béguillet accepted an invitation from the ministry to collaborate with the miller on a series of textbooks and brochures designed to diffuse the new system.[281] Béguillet ghostwrote a number of "economic" works signed by Bucquet, cosigned several, and published others under his own name. Though they focused on milling, both Béguillet and Bucquet, along with Malisset, conceived of the economic system as a total, vertically integrated project that began with the harvest and the conditioning and preparation of grain for sale and continued through to the stage of bread making and distribution, with a special emphasis on the local, regional, and international flour trade.

One cannot speak of a genuine solidarity of spirit among the apostles of the economic gospel. Malisset was perhaps the only economizer to whom all the reformers deferred, an ironic fate for a man who was vilified by almost everyone else for his central part in the so-called famine plot. Malouin drew criticism from all sides. Parmentier gently reproached him for the superficiality of his investigation and the unevenness of his judgments.[282] Béguillet was more severe. Malouin's book was "full of errors" and of "contradictions." Moreover, it was dangerous, for it cast discredit on the economic system by falsely claiming that economic stones ground hot, that the economic process resulted in heavy evaporation losses, and that bolting could not be effectively integrated into the milling process and ought to be undertaken by the bakers.[283]

The bitterest and most passionate quarrel opposed Bucquet and Béguillet to Parmentier and Cadet de Vaux. Temperamentally, the moving force in this confrontation was Bucquet, whose polemic was not only a plea for personal recognition but also a brief for the worth of a certain kind of popular culture and against the arrogance of a certain kind of elite culture. The least interesting part of the quarrel concerned Bucquet's defense of his "honor" and his "status." He angrily resented Parmentier's and Cadet's efforts to claim paternity for "the new art." They usurped discoveries that he had made "before these Mssrs. had left college." They not only failed to cite him but went so far as to plagiarize.[284] They overlooked the great sacrifices he made during two

280. Béguillet, *Discours sur la mouture* (1775), p. xiii. Béguillet also seems to have known Malisset and to have inspected Corbeil. *Traité des subsistances*, p. 263n.

281. Béguillet, *Discours sur la mouture* (1775), p. xiii. Cf. Bucquet's request for an indemnity for the data he provided Béguillet for the immense, government-sponsored *Traité des subsistances*. De Montaran to Parent, 1 February 1778, AN, F[11]* 1, fol. 219.

282. Parmentier, *Parfait Boulanger,* pp. xviii–xix. Cf. Condorcet's *éloge* to Malouin, *Histoire de l'Académie des sciences,* 1778 (1781), p. 64.

283. Béguillet, *Traité des subsistances,* pp. 54–55, 61, 280–85.

284. Bucquet, *Observations intéressantes,* pp. v–vi, 3–9, 56–57, 71–72, 98, 99n. Baudeau supported Bucquet warmly. Baudeau to editor, *Journal de Paris* (12 August 1782): 916–17. Béguillet claimed that Parmentier had been "very much set against economic milling before reading our works." *Traité des subsistances,* p. 852n.

decades of public service. Not even satisfied to deny him credit, they tried to discredit him. Bucquet was outraged and wounded by "stealthy and shadowy insinuations"—in fact grave accusations—that he and his son-in-law had produced inferior quality flour resulting in bad bread for the General Hospital and the prisons, and that this situation had persisted until Parmentier and Cadet introduced "perfection." Making beautiful flour was his life and his business, Bucquet protested, and these charges were "vile calumnies." They not only wounded his pride but probably also damaged his chances of recovering from his commercial setbacks.[285]

These calumnies cárried so much weight because they represented the dominant culture, the culture of prestige and power, an elite culture of literature and of science, bent since the conception of the *Encyclopédie* on imposing its brand of Reason on the world of work. Despite certain propitiatory gestures, that elite culture had little use for the popular culture of artisanry and traditional work, a physical rather than an intellectual culture, a practical rather than a theoretical one, an oral rather than a written one. If there was a *rien* of demagogy in the juxtaposition of "a poor miller, white by his craft" and the blackguard intellectuals, there was also a well-justified cry of indignation: Parmentier and Cadet held "the simple, unlettered miller" in "contempt."[286]

The "doctors in milling and baking" toiled to show the millers and bakers how benighted and feckless and devoid of real understanding they were; how vicious were their instincts which, unwittingly but treacherously, led them to fool themselves and then to dupe and cheat society; and how desperately they needed help.[287] The "professors" (Parmentier and Cadet had founded the School of Baking in Paris) offered the craftsmen a Manichean reading of history. Before Parmentier and Cadet there was darkness; after their arrival on the scene, there was light. Baking and milling had been practiced for thousands of years, yet it was not until the savants scrutinized them that they began to improve.[288] The "blind routine" that Cadet reviled for impeding progress in milling was nothing other than the accumulated experience of

285. Bucquet, *Observations intéressantes,* pp. 84–85 and passim; *Journal de Paris* (6 August 1782): 892.

286. Bucquet, *Observations intéressantes,* pp. v, vi, 3–4, 55–57.

287. See Parmentier's memorandum to the Estates of Brittany, ca. November 1784, AD Ille-et-Vilaine, C 1710. Cf. Simon Linguet's scorn for "the abbots, the gentlemen, the provincial judges, etc. who all of a sudden came to teach the millers that they did not know how to grind, the people that they had excessive appetites, and the bakers that they left too many middlings in their bran." *Réponse aux docteurs modernes,* 1:9. Also the attack on "les docteurs de l'école panaire" in the "Mémoire sur les désavantages de la mouture économique," cited by Brunot, *Langue française,* 6:277.

288. See *Journal de Paris* (9 August 1782): 905. Cf. Frederick W. Taylor's testimony before Congress in the early years of the twentieth century: "It is next to impossible for the workman to develop a science." Cited by Harry Braverman, *Labor and Monopoly Capital* (New York, 1974).

generations of more or less skilled millers.[289] The "popular errors" that Parmentier wanted science to extirpate were by and large the *secrets du métier* passed from father to son, the miller's patrimony and reservoir of self-esteem.[290]

The scientific discourse, Bucquet recognized, was one of the chief vehicles used by the savants to displace and dominate the men of the crafts. The savants set about studying and classifying the crafts in order to translate them into the scientific language as part of a project of rationalization and control. Bucquet avowed that he had always preferred "the science of things" to "the science of words." But he had had little choice. For him and his confreres, the language of "systematic chemistry" practiced by Parmentier and Cadet was "a foreign language," in a double sense: it was not "accessible to . . . ordinary and common minds" and it was a language that threatened those on and about whom it was used.[291]

For Bucquet, the scientific language was a discourse of technical mystification meant less to enlighten the miller and bakers than to help the savants to extend their empire. It was also a discourse that reeked of vanity even as it "smelled of the pharmacy." What were the millers and bakers and their garçons to make of Parmentier "mounted on his Pegasus" traversing the globe in space and time? Wasn't this pomposity yet another expression of condescension and another form of domination?[292] Parmentier and Cadet vowed "to enlighten [us] by the torchlight of theory." But what good was this theory devoid of experience with dressing and mounting stones, with feeding the stones, with bolting, with mixing: "Theorists without practice, learn to be skeptical sometimes of grandiose speculations and vain promises; and do not always turn your noses up at ignoramuses like me who are not capable of taking charge of things by making fancy speeches, but who at least can offer concrete, verified facts."[293]

Bucquet affirmed that only men of the métier could have developed economic milling and that there was no need for chemistry in order to make the finest bread in the world.[294] On occasion he succumbed to a vulgar macho-

289. The phrase belongs to Cadet de Vaux (1780) and is inscribed, in context, on the wall of the entrance foyer of the Ecole nationale supérieure de la meunerie in Paris.

290. See Parmentier, *Mémoire sur les avantages*, p. 416.

291. Bucquet, *Observations intéressantes*, pp. 7, 15, 121.

292. Ibid., pp. 18–21.

293. Des Essarts, *Dictionnaire universel de police*, 7:473; Bucquet, *Traité pratique*, p. 42.

294. Bucquet, *Observations intéressantes*, pp. 16–17, 57. Cf. Béguillet's remark on "chemistry, this obscure and overbearing science that pretends to extend its domain everywhere, that claims for itself all discoveries." *Traité des subsistances*, pp. 398–99n. The professional trade journal *The Miller* editorialized in 1930: "What high hopes were raised when the chemist first started to appear in our mills, and yet, except in the study of such things as improvers and bleachers (things really added to the flour), what has chemistry done for us?" Cited by Coles-Finch, *Water Mills and Windmills*, p. 118.

métier impulse: thus he challenged Cadet to "mettre lui-même la main à l'oeuvre"—to put his practical skill to the test by grinding to perfection a freshly harvested muid of wet wheat.[295] Despite the derision he expressed for "the useless reasonings" of "the comic-chemical theory," Bucquet was by no means hostile to ideas or to learning per se. And he himself was acutely critical of the philistinism and inertia in the ranks of the milling and baking industries. He knew that "good and solid experience" was not the unique source of useful knowledge. He recounted how, in some ways, he had outgrown his own milieu. In words that could have been Cadet's, Bucquet described his own dissatisfaction with "a blind practice and routine, without reasoning and without principles."[296] Yet he felt a deep cultural solidarity with his confreres. He rightly pointed out that in many ways the savants' contemptuousness and remoteness constituted a greater obstacle to modernization in milling and baking than the stubborn habits of the men of the métier. Bucquet resented not the science of the savants but their aggressive and arrogant posture, their refusal to learn his language, to inform their theory with his experience, and to honor his kind of knowledge and practice and creativity, that is, his culture.

It is very likely that Bucquet's sentiments were shared by some of his fellow millers and that the second wave of economic diffusion was less successful than the first precisely because it was confiscated by Science.

The "economic" process was the most significant innovation in milling methodology and technology in hundreds of years. The principle of gradual reduction on which it was based remains the basic concept of modern milling. In the traditional or coarse grinding, the grain made a single passage between the stones, and the middlings were abandoned to the animal raisers and the starch makers. Indeed, the law specifically prohibited middling usage on the grounds that its product would contaminate the flour. By recovering and rehabilitating the middlings, economic milling achieved a kind of alchemical miracle (or the squaring of the subsistence circle): it made excellent white bread from neither wheat nor (what was officially defined as) flour. It incorporated not only bolting (which permitted middling grading) into the opera-

295. Bucquet, *Observations intéressantes*, pp. 56–57. Even here Bucquet insisted on the complexity of the craft and argued not that it could be done by anyone with a little experience, but that on the contrary it was extremely difficult even for those with great experience.

296. Ibid., pp. 7 and 68, and Bucquet, *Traité pratique*, pp. iv, 52. Cf. the cautious defense of "experience and tradition" and the critique of superficial "cabinet" inventors who were either ignorant or contemptuous of local conditions and customs (with specific reference to economic milling and milling practices at Metz). "Discours sur la lenteur des arts," *Journal de l'agriculture, des arts et des finances* (December 1773): 135–37. See also the story of the French academicians who concluded after laborious calculations that the windmillers had been setting their sails precisely as science would have had them set the sails. Legrand d'Aussy, *Vie privée*, 1:64–65; *Histoire de l'Académie des sciences* (Amsterdam, 1765), pp. 120–30; Bennett and Elton, *Corn Milling*, 2:262.

tion of the mill, but also grain conditioning and cleaning and the mechanization of many costly, time-consuming, and cumbersome tasks.

The chief contribution of economic milling lay in the enormous savings that it promised: between a quarter and an eighth more flour could be extracted from a given unit of wheat. Since a person could now be fed with two setiers (instead of three at the end of the reign of Louis XIV), a significantly larger population could be supported without any improvement in agricultural production—a potential bounty of extraordinary importance in a period of rapid demographic expansion. Economic milling promised not only more bread but a better-quality bread—tastier, more nourishing, whiter. Indeed, economic milling implied a sweeping modernization and rationalization—ultimately an industrialization—of the whole subsistence complex. It was marvelously consonant with the ambitions of the flour trade. It was bound to accelerate the commercialization process by which the miller became a merchant and the flour trade absorbed the grain trade, and bakers were spared a host of onerous tasks.

Tested initially under the auspices of the Paris police, economic milling quickly obtained the enthusiastic endorsement of the royal government. Malisset and Bucquet (representing the work culture of the crafts), followed a number of years later by Parmentier and Cadet de Vaux (representing the high culture of science), traversed the kingdom to spread the good news. Intendants, provincial estates, parlements, public-assistance institutions, ecclesiastical organizations, and "improving" lords welcomed the emissaries. The jealousy, anxiety, and avarice of the provisioning professionals, especially the bakers and millers, slowed diffusion. Quite rightly, they felt threatened by new techniques that would not only require them to change the way they practiced their trade but in so doing also deprive them of the substantial material advantages that the old mill fees and bread price schedules, based on anachronistic and misleading production assumptions, guaranteed them.

In a more general sense, the climate of the late sixties and early seventies was not wholly conducive to innovation in the subsistence domain. On the one hand, rising prices and the laissez-faire policies adopted by the government, including freedom to export, surely stimulated investment in and conversion to economic milling. On the other hand, it was a time of scarcity, of economic and social disarray, and of malaise provoked by a combination of several harvest failures and the radical grain-trade reforms of 1763–64. Extremely worried, consumers and local officials were loath to take risks. It was as easy to see economic milling as it was to see the freeing of the grain and flour trade as a cover for heinous manipulations. After all, the regrinding of middlings, like off-market speculations, had been illegal until very recently; and Malisset, the champion of economic milling, was also the signatory of the *pacte de famine.* Nor did the patronage of physiocracy help: the stigma of the new political economy further tarnished the image of the new milling technology. There were other, more banal obstacles to the propagation and adoption of economic milling: it was a complex affair (more so than its exponents allowed), it was relatively costly to convert to it, and no matter how appealing it might be, news of it could not possibly reach 80,000 millers overnight.

It is extremely difficult to assess the real impact of economic milling. Contemporaries believed that it quickly took root throughout the Paris region. It is possible that the "economic" surplus helped to temper prices there during the last decade and a half of the old regime. The Napoleonic surveys suggest that 90 percent of the French milling pool remained outside the economic sphere of influence. Yet it is vital not to overlook the indirect or incidental benefits of the economic campaigns. Hundreds, perhaps thousands, of millers heard about ways in which to improve their operations without necessarily adopting the new process. Competition and client pressure probably forced many recalcitrant millers to make changes. There is no doubt that in many places in France coarse milling was less coarse and more economical in 1811 than it had been in 1750.

CHAPTER 12

The Bakers and the Grain
and Flour Trade

$\mathcal{T}$he bakers were not permitted to undertake the grain or flour trade, that is to say, to buy for the purpose of resale. All that the bakers had a right to do was to purchase grain and flour necessary for their own bread making. The authorities feared that if bakers were allowed to trade in grain and flour they would be in a position "to make themselves masters of the whole supply," to hoard, "and therefore to set whatever price they wished" first on grain and then on bread.[1] It was also felt that bread making was such a complicated and delicate operation that bakers ought not to allow themselves to be diverted from the bakeroom. Thus the police favored a division of labor that served to prevent "monopoly" and to promote efficiency. Let the baker bake and let the commercial specialists and professional suppliers take care of furnishing the raw materials. Not only were the bakers supposed to limit their grain and flour dealings to purchases for their baking needs, but they were also encouraged, and on a few occasions legally enjoined, to address themselves to the merchants and brokers on the ports and at the Halle instead of doing their own buying in the hinterland. In the course of the eighteenth century, however, bakers took to the country to make their purchases in increasingly large numbers.

1. *Journal économique* (January 1754): 103–4, and Des Essarts, *Dictionnaire universel de police*, 2:251.

Buying at Home

Virtually all the city and many faubourg bakers did at least some of their buying at the Halle and at the Grève. Intramural buying was alluring because it was convenient. With the supply so close at hand, bakers did not have to plan expeditions in advance, nor did they have to budget money for traveling expenses. (If they sealed the deal in a tavern, the seller habitually paid for the collation.) Courted by a host of sellers, bakers had the impression that they could command relatively favorable terms. They haggled over price (it was considered a sign of collusion with the seller if they did not), they discussed provenance and quality, they moved from place to place to compare goods and to make themselves visible.[2] Bakers took pride in their ability to judge merchandise and to obtain what they considered the fair price.[3] In the flour area, they were offered dough samples and lured with promises of bonuses on the measure. Generally they could obtain credit without great difficulty.[4] Their purchases were "clean" from the police and administrative vantage points. The bakers were not responsible for any of the market fees that had to be paid nor did they have to answer for the legitimacy of the acquisition of the merchandise. The bakers knew most of the regular suppliers, personally or by reputation; the market "wire" kept them informed on new developments. As we have seen, their relations with suppliers were sometimes quite stormy when they felt betrayed or cheated on price or quality or timing of delivery. We should not lose sight, however, of the bonds forged among them by marriage, family, friendship, and pratik reciprocity.

Master baker Garmont had a buying strategy that involved, in addition to intramural purchases, country buying (more than thirty different merchants and laboureurs supplied him, but it is not clear whether these transactions took place on or off-market) and droiture shipments. In the course of the first three weeks of November 1771, he made the following purchases:

4 November 1771—26 setiers of wheat at Gonesse [a market in which he did not have authorization to buy because it was located within the ten-league decommercialized zone around Paris] at 22 livres 10 sous the setier, paid cash.

6 November—8 sacks of flour (325 pounds) at the Paris Halle at 55 livres the sack, paid cash.

2. See the haggling of bakers M. Fleury and J. Ferret. AN, Y 11243, 1 April 1756, and Y 11227, 1 June 1740.

3. See the scorn baker witnesses expressed for their colleague master Lecoq, who ruined his business in large part because he did not know how to buy grain. AN, Y 15053, 23 August 1749.

4. When bakers could no longer find credit in Paris, they had a difficult time staying in business. See Trudon to Sartine, 12 September 1772, AN, Y 15114.

14 November—32 setiers of wheat at the Grève at 25 livres 10 sous, on credit.

16 November—10 sacks of flour at the Paris Halle at 55 livres, on credit.

18 November—25 setiers of wheat at Gonesse at 24 livres, on credit.[5]

Garmont rarely took longer than six weeks to pay his suppliers. His contemporary, baker Jardin, made all of his purchases in flour, simultaneously from broker-widow Barbier (approximately one transaction a month) and from freelance mealmen.[6]

Master Toupin consciously sought to spread out his flour purchases to avoid becoming excessively dependent on or indebted to a single supplier. He shopped around at the Halle, usually eschewing the brokers in favor of direct contact with the mealmen. In a little over four years, he used twenty-nine different suppliers, with whom he had an average of about three transactions worth a little over twenty sacks each. On five occasions he purchased from two different merchants on the same day. Only twice did he buy from the same dealer on two consecutive occasions. Habitually he paid slowly and in installments, taking up to three months and sometimes longer. Now and again he was charged for unreturned sacks. He kept thoroughly reliable records that he periodically revised and corrected. He always sought receipts from his merchants, though they were often imprecise ("quite de toute choze").[7] In the eighties master baker Andriot turned to the Halle when he judged that the country price was too high in relation to the Paris price to afford him an advantage.[8]

Theoretically grain and flour sales took place only on regular market days, Wednesday and Saturday. In practice, however, bakers were able to buy on most days of the week, though they usually found more choice and price flexibility on market days. Poussot was especially concerned to accommodate the really marginal bakers, "numerous" in his calculation, who were too poor to obtain credit and could only buy flour on a day-to-day basis as they sold their bread. The inspector ordered the measurers to delay the ringing of the market's end in order to give these bakers time to get to the Halle from their bread-selling stations.[9] Paris purchasing was officially reserved to city and

5. Archives Seine-Paris, D5B[6] 4420.
6. Ibid., D5B[6] 3546.
7. Ibid., D5B[6] 5234.
8. AN, Y 12826.
9. Arsenal, ms. Bast. 10141, fol. 337 (10 April 1760).

faubourg bakers. Yet the forains insinuated themselves more or less conspicuously in good times and petitioned for derogation in bad times. As Etienne Faron of Passy learned, the Paris bakers often resented their intrusion.[10]

Bakers could not buy as much merchandise as they pleased on a given day at the Halle or Grève. The ceiling—two muids of grain or one of flour per market day—was more than ample to meet the baking needs of most bakers. The rationale for this limitation was to prevent "monopoly" and hoarding, especially on the part of the big bakers who could thereby crush the little ones. It could also be read as an incentive to the stronger bakers, who could look at the supply situation in speculative terms, to supplement their intramural provisioning by searching for grain beyond the decommercialized frontier (first eight leagues, later ten).[11]

In practice the authorities paid very little attention to this ceiling, at least in periods of relative abundance, as the senior commissaire of the Halles department himself noted after the crisis of 1725–26.[12] I have found only one instance of a condemnation for violating this ceiling, in 1719. A baker named Sens bought over three muids of flour from broker Lecoq and refused to permit his neighbor and rival, baker Leroy, to purchase two and a half setiers until his own lot was fully broken, measured, and loaded. Leroy complained to the senior measurer, Leroux, who reprimanded Sens for buying more than one muid. In response to Sens's manifest "contempt" for his warning, the measurer issued a summons. Sens was permitted to make the purchase, however, and Leroux did not dare to confiscate it. The lieutenant general of police must not have hoped to teach the bakers much of a lesson, for he fined Sens only 30 livres and did not even order the posting of the sentence.[13] The Hôtel de Ville annulled a number of large transactions—for example, the deal by which ·Mortellerie merchant Armet promised master baker Payen twenty muids of wheat in 1756—but it changed its thinking on the matter several times during the century.[14] The prevotal court said nothing in 1726 when Mortellerie dealer César Gibert sued baker Claude Tavernier for payment for seven muids that he purchased on 15 February 1726.[15] Baker Tourney bought

---

10. AN, Y 12619, 17, 21 February and 1 March 1770; and Y 9539, 20 June 1759; and Y 11227, 30 May 1740; Archives Seine-Paris, D4B⁶ 27-1457, June 1765 (Vaugirard and Nanterre bakers); Gazier, ed., "La Police de Paris en 1770," pp. 124–25.

11. Delamare, *Traité de la police,* 2:758; BN, Coll. Joly 1111, fol. 174 (30 March 1735); Duchesne, *Code de la police,* p. 115. The eighteenth-century ceiling was set in 1672. Earlier in the seventeenth century it had been one muid of grain.

12. Duplessis to procurator general, 24 April 1726, BN, Coll. Joly 1118, fols. 135–36.

13. AN, Y 9538, 10 November 1719.

14. Sentence of 25 September 1756, AN, F¹¹ 264. Cf. the sentence of 27 July 1725, ibid.

15. AN, Z¹ᴴ 239, 3 September 1726.

five muids at the Ecole port from a forain merchant in 1727. Another baker purchased fifteen muids and two setiers on credit on 8 January 1735.[16] In the late thirties and forties, Nicolas-Louis Martin commonly sold as much as six muids at a time, both on the ports and on the Halle. (Master baker Louis Suire bought ten muids on 23 July 1738, just when the news of a harvest disaster was beginning to spread.)[17] In the fifties broker Jean Maheu was noted for his gargantuan transactions, among them the sale of eighteen muids of wheat on Christmas Day 1755 to baker Pierre Deschamps the elder.[18] In the second half of the century flour transactions ordinarily involved well over a muid.[19] Moreover, buyers could circumvent the regulation by making purchases on nonmarket days.

The baker guild repeatedly denounced the ceiling and warned that it could "substantially" reduce bread production.[20] In the thirties, port merchants demanded a formal end to buying quotas, though they acknowledged that the quotas were rarely enforced. They contended that without a wholly open market they could not be expected to risk large shipments, especially since the ports lacked proper storage facilities.[21] Both the parlement and the municipality seemed favorably disposed to the merchants' request, but no action was taken. In 1759, when the merchants petitioned for permission to sell up to six muids a day, the city fathers pronounced categorically against the proposal on the extremely unlikely grounds that the ports would quickly be stripped bare (but would not the port merchants, who desperately needed a stimulus, significantly expand their provision if necessary?), "a general and public alarm provoked by the fear of want" would spread, and the price would rise despite an abundance of supply.[22]

The measurers endorsed the ceiling as a wise and necessary check: "There is danger in giving the bakers too much liberty." The strong bakers, according to the measurers, would use the freedom to build up hoards. They cited the picturesque and doubtless atypical case in the fifties of master baker Lefèvre, who had so much flour stored in a room over his shop that the floor caved in.[23]

Country Buying

There were a number of reasons why certain bakers were not content to furnish their needs within the capital. In their view, intramural purchases

16. Archives Seine-Paris, D5B⁶ 4243; AN, MC, V-375, 19 January 1735.
17. Archives Seine-Paris, D5B⁶ 3118.
18. Ibid., D5B⁶ 3446.
19. See, for example, Piochard's purchases, ibid., D5B⁶ 1963.
20. BN, Coll. Joly 1116, fol. 249.
21. BN, Coll. Joly 1314, fol. 43.
22. AN, F¹¹ 264, 20 September 1759 and 3 July 1736; BN, Coll. Joly 1829, fol. 321; deliberations, 20 September 1759, AN, H* 1868, pp. 311–16.
23. BN, Coll. Joly 1314, fol. 12 (4 March 1760).

were not nearly as easy to make as they should have been. Conditions were extremely crowded at the Halle. Bakers literally fought to get served once they fixed on a seller. Numerous bakers lamented that without "recommendations to the measurers," it was impossible to get flour the same day. Others complained that the measurers expected gifts rather than letters. It is hard not to feel a certain sympathy for the Graizel brothers, master bakers and bullies, who got waited on by grabbing a measurer, whom they greeted as "Monsieur Foutre," and physically forcing him to measure their sacks. Bakers Beauquigny and Bleau and baker wife Marie-Louise Blot did not lose their composure after four hours of waiting for a measurer, because they were inured.[24] Even if one succeeded in getting served, there was no guarantee that one could call in a wagon and horses to remove the merchandise the same day. The Grève was only slightly more inhospitable; in inclement weather, it was probably even less attractive. And in any case it offered no flour for sale. (Still, it must be noted that the situation at the Halle improved significantly with the introduction of the weight station, which displaced the measurers and accelerated transactions, and the construction of the new grain and flour building, which made business far easier to conduct even if it did not resolve the problem of congestion.)

Bakers contended that intramural purchases were more costly as well as more cumbersome. Grain bought from merchants or brokers had frequently passed through three pairs of hands, if not more. The price had to reflect their remunerations, as well as the cost of moving the merchandise into the capital. In the case of wheat, it was neither rational nor economic to take this same merchandise and return it to the countryside for milling, only to make the trip to Paris again.

Finally, the moral (and political) atmosphere of the Halle and ports did not please these bakers. Beyond the matter of the favoritism of measurers and porters, the bakers resented the general climate of surveillance and intimidation. They detested the petty vexations that seemed so pointless, such as the imposing on a baker of a fine of 20 livres plus the confiscation of a setier of wheat because he had delegated a neighbor, a fruit vendor, to pick up some badly needed supplies.[25] They found the larger conception of the police of the market no more congenial. They craved greater freedom to make deals with merchants, they did not want to have to account for every step they took, and they coveted the opportunity to exercise their cunning.

Convinced that they could do better and feel better outside Paris, bitten by a speculative bug, sometimes encouraged by a network of country relatives, these bakers turned to the hinterland to make at least part of their purchases. It is impossible to measure the magnitude of country buying or to plot its movement across time with any precision. We know that a substantial number

24. Regnard the elder to Hérault, ca. May 1726, Arsenal, ms. Bast. 10273; AN, Y 11226 and Y 9440, 7 August 1739.
25. AN, Y 9621, 24 November 1752.

of bakers were already frequenting the *plat pays* by the end of the seventeenth century. The late 1670s and the early 1680s seem to have marked the
beginning of this first wave. A second and far more powerful wave swept
scores of bakers into the field between 1730 and 1760. Even as the Halle
triumphed over the ports, the steady growth of baker droiture traffic
threatened to undermine the Halle. This wave of country buying appears to
have slowed down as a result of several convergent factors. First were the
reforms that improved the service in the Halle, especially the creation of the
weight station, the disciplining of the measurers and porters, the new rules for
the brokerage, and the construction of the new building. Yet it was not Poussot's war against droiture that drove the bakers out of the countryside.
Rather, they retreated voluntarily for reasons of self-interest as the very
structure of the provisioning trade was gradually transformed. The commercialization of the flour trade made country buying increasingly less enticing.
Meticulous bakers still wanted to feel and bite the wheat before they bought
it. Now that they had a wide choice of flours and mealmen, however, the trip
became harder to justify. The development of economic milling in the sixties
and seventies reinforced the tendency to focus on flour. Even among bakers
who continued to buy grain, there was a strong temptation to leave the buying
operations in the hands of the millers once the initial contacts with laboureurs
or country merchants had been established.[26]

François Deline, one of the jurés of the baker guild, argued in 1726 that "it
would be a good thing if all the bakers . . . were in a position to supply
themselves in the far-off country markets, for this could only make the provision of Paris more abundant."[27] Not all the bakers were able to envisage this
strategy—far from it. On the eve of the French Revolution a journalist who
knew the bakers well reported that only "a very circumscribed number" of
more or less wealthy bakers could buy at Pont-Ste.-Maxence, Noyon, Soissons, Senlis, Nanteuil, Coulommiers, Rebais, Provins, Châteaudun, Dourdan, Chartres, and other country locations. (Yet at that very moment one
picks up the trail of Paris bakers buying as far away as Noyers, in Restif's
Burgundy.)[28] Commissaire Lemaire observed in 1770 that it was "the
strongest bakers" who went ten, twenty, or twenty-five leagues into the countryside to buy.[29] Yet country buying was not so elitist as these observers
suggested, even if the biggest buyers—like the baker Paillet, who offered to

26. On the decline of baker field operations, see Saint-Prest, "Mémoire," September
1773, AD Gironde, C 1441.

27. Deline, *Mémoire* (Paris, 1726), p. 1, BN (factum).

28. Jean-Jacques Rutledge, *Second Mémoire pour les maîtres boulangers* . . . (Paris,
[1789]), p. 24; municipal deliberations, 13 April 1789, AD Yonne, dépôt 5, BB[9].

29. Gazier, ed., "La Police de Paris en 1770," p. 123. Cf. the claim by the bakers in the
1680s that they went as far as forty leagues into the countryside. "Sommaire pour les
maistres boulangers," BN, ms. fr. 21640, fol. 71.

procure four thousand muids for the city during the subsistence crisis of 1725, or Pierre Brot, a rue Mouffetard master who registered at Meaux as a grain and flour merchant in 1771 in the wake of the great grain-trade reforms—were quite well off.[30] A "middle class" of country buyers, represented by bakers such as Garin, Gouillard, and Mouchy, operated in a fairly wide expanse as far as twenty-five leagues out.[31] Juré Deline himself was a middling baker who tended to buy relatively close by at Versailles, Tournan-en-Brie, and Etampes.[32] Then there were the genuinely modest bakers, such as the widow Chaudron and Gilbert Paris *fils* of the faubourg St.-Antoine or master Etienne Huin and widow-mistress Françoise Constant, who made periodic forays to specific places in the country with which they were familiar, such as Claye or Dourdan or Versailles or Etampes.[33]

Country buying did not require substantial fixed investment. Few bakers owned their own means of transportation. They hired professional transporters or arranged for their millers to pick up their purchases (the seller infrequently undertook shipment). Most traffic took place by land transport, though beginning about 1730 more and more bakers turned to river freight for at least part of the distance because it was considerably cheaper. Bakers with liquid capital had a decided advantage, because credit was not as readily available as in Paris and in any case cash meant an economy, for sellers almost always charged a premium for credit transactions.[34] Country purchases were habitually larger than Paris transactions: the case of Sulpice Garin's purchase of thirty-two muids is not at all atypical.[35]

Country buying was not without risk. It could endanger the businesses of the middling bakers, who had no speculative margin in their treasuries. Pierre Garmont lost 2,800 livres on country grain whose price suddenly bottomed out. Pierre Dufour lost 2,400 livres in six months on grain for which he overpaid.[36] So abrupt were price fluctuations at times that Louis Hiest lost 660 livres on 66 setiers of country wheat before he got them back from the mill.[37] Bad luck or bad judgment contributed to the failure of these three

30. BN, Coll. Joly 1117, fol. 162, and AD Seine-et-Marne, baillage de Meaux, unclassified, 9 February 1771.

31. BN, Coll. Joly 1829, fol. 297, and petition, February 1728, Arsenal, ms. Bast. 10274.

32. Deline, *Mémoire*, pp. 2–5, BN (factum), and AN, Y 15601, 6 January 1741.

33. Procès-verbal de l'émeute, 9 July 1725, AN, Y 10033; Archives Seine-Paris, D4Bᵒ 43-2468, 17 February 1772; AN, MC, VII-291, 28 May 1754, and XLIV-310, 22 May 1762. On the Etampes and Dourdan traffic more generally, see BN, Coll. Joly 1111, fol. 237, and Boucher to Hérault, 4 October 1725, Arsenal, ms. Bast. 10270, pièces 260–62.

34. On the problem of obtaining credit, see the case of Largy in rapport arbitre, 27 March 1782, Archives Seine-Paris, D6B⁶, carton 11. On credit surcharges, see the losses column of Meusnier's failure, D4B⁶ 88-6048, 24 November 1783.

35. BN, Coll. Joly 1829, fol. 297.

36. Archives Seine-Paris, D4B⁶ 47-2825, 24 April 1773; D4B⁶ 104-7356, 31 December 1788.

37. Ibid., 42-2307 (16 August 1771).

bakers. Some bakers tried to spread out the risk of country buying by forming "coalitions," as joint purchasing ventures were later called.[38]

There were two categories of baker trade in the hinterland: legal and illegal. Legal purchases were made exclusively in any market beyond the eight-league (after 1737, ten) radius and in several expressly named markets within the decommercialized zone: Limours, Brie-Comte-Robert, Mennecy, Dammartin, and Versailles, to which Choisy was later added.[39] The illegal category embraced all purchases made off the market, at the farms, granaries, taverns, and on the road, and those effected in unauthorized markets within the decommercialized sector. In order to demonstrate the legality of their country purchases, bakers were required to get a certificate of provenance indicating date, place, and amount of transaction, signed by the local market official or, in his absence, by a local notary. If a baker, or his deliveryman, could not produce such a certificate, or if it was judged to be invalid, the police inferred that the baker had conducted illicit operations.

For many bakers, buying in the country did not necessarily mean going personally to the country. Indeed, the baker guild contended that implicit in the permission to buy beyond the decommercialized zone was the authorization to call upon agents to make purchases, for it would be "ridiculous" to imagine that the overworked bakers could otherwise profit from this disposition.[40] François Deline traveled to the nearby markets, but relied upon "commissioners" for the faraway ones because "his profession rarely allowed him [the time] to leave his shop without jeopardizing the bread-making process."[41] While the original rationale for country buying turned on the baker's exercise of his own skills in a vast arena, the bakers insisted that they could find the same advantage by proxy. Yet such purchases remained formally against the law, as reiterated by the royal declaration of September 1737 and the arrêts du conseil of 1754 and 1761, because the authorities feared that they would serve as covers for illegal trading, hoarding, and price manipulation.[42]

The law, however, had little bearing in practice. Bakers bought on commission on a more or less massive scale. Neither condemnations nor fines nor threats daunted them. In his passion to halt droiture traffic, Poussot envisaged an ordinance requiring the bakers to sign the market certificate testifying to the validity of the purchase at the market before witnesses. This last-gasp effort to stem the tide was never implemented. In 1762 the measurers still seized putative contraband on the grounds that the police regulations "enjoin the bakers to go personally to make their purchases." In 1764 the city fathers

38. *Enquête sur la boulangerie,* p. 755.
39. BN, Coll. Joly 1111, fol. 173.
40. BN, Coll. Joly 1829, fol. 343.
41. Ibid., fol. 317.
42. BN, Coll. Joly 1111, fol. 174.

renewed the prohibition against purchases by baker agents.[43] Yet by 1770 the parlement unequivocally declared in an arrêt that it *"maintains* the bakers of Paris in the right to buy by themselves or via grain and flour brokers or commissionnaires in the markets located ten leagues beyond [the capital]." That same year commissaire Machurin asserted that a baker must have a market certificate for grain or flour entering the capital signed "by himself or by his commissionnaire."[44]

Miller-Commissionnaires

The millers, as we have seen, were the "natural" commissionnaires of the bakers, for they were rooted in the countryside, they knew grain, they had means of transport, and they wanted the baker business. As early as 1698, a memorandum on "the disorders committed in the environs of Paris" claimed that the millers were "all agents and commissionnaires of the bakers of Paris."[45] An officer of the maréchaussée noted with resignation in 1725 that "the millers are still buying in behalf of the bakers despite the fact that I forbade them to do so."[46] Master baker Petit's miller not only picked up the grain that the baker bought on the Grève, but also purchased grain on his order at Brie-Comte-Robert.[47]

In the candid ambiance of the commercial court, miller Aubry from Meaux openly avowed that he bought in behalf of a faubourg St.-Antoine baker and that he purchased in the farms, a "double violation of the law," as the measurers put it.[48] Aubry's neighbor Hublot did not even have to leave his mill to purchase grain: the laboureurs came to him, and he supplied at least a half-dozen Paris bakers in flour.[49] Millers Pachot, Simonneau, and Branchery bought for Paris bakers in the Dourdan market.[50] Millers Herbron, Conty, and

43. AN, Y 9539, 16 May 1762; deliberations, February 1764, AN, H* 1870, fols. 374–84.

44. Arrêt, 1 June 1770, BN; police sentence, 16 November 1770, AN, AD I 23^A.

45. "Mémoire qui marque tous les désordres," BN, ms. fr. 21643, fol. 354. It cited the case of Couvart, a miller from Juvisy, who was known to buy as much as 50 muids in a single day for the Paris bakers. Ibid., fol. 356.

46. Marchais to Hérault, 15 October 1725, Arsenal, ms. Bast. 10270, fol. 326. Certain bakers, surely few in number, accompanied the millers to the farms and markets, selected and bargained for the grain they desired, and then left arrangements for transportation and payment up to the millers. See rapport arbitre, 21 December 1743, Archives Seine-Paris, D6B⁶, carton 2, and 30 December 1743, D2B² 768. In regard to baker-miller relations, note also the extraordinary instance of an agreement on the amount of flour that a given setier should yield. D2B⁶ 809, 12 May 1747.

47. Archives Seine-Paris, D5B⁶ 3602.

48. Rapport arbitre, 18 December 1767, ibid., D6B⁶, carton 5.

49. BN, Coll. Joly 1130, fols. 160–61, ca. July 1760.

50. Soumission, 25 August 1725, Arsenal, ms. Bast. 10270, pièce 49.

N°. ~ *Officiers Mesureurs, Controlleurs &*
Visiteurs de Grains & Farines.
P A S S E' par la Barriere de
le
la quantité de
à la conduite de
reçû

MARCHÉ DE SENLIS.

JE soussigné, Receveur du Boisselet & Minage de Senlis, certifie
que le nommé   Voiturier,
demeurant à   conduit sur sa Voiture la
quantité de   Bled ou Farine, ou domicile
de   Marchand Boulanger, demeurant à
Paris, rue   provenant des
Sacs de Bled par lui achetés le   sur le Carreau
du Marché de Senlis, conformément à la Déclaration du Roi,
du 19 Avril 1723, suivant sa Déclaration enregistrée N°.
de lui   signée, ayant déclaré ne savoir signer. Fait à Senlis
ce   jour d   mil sept cent soixante &

Wheat or flour passport, Senlis market with visa of Paris entry, 1771 (Archives de Paris)

Cordard of Etampes and d'Ansell, Forquet, and Lamoureux of Montlhéry supplied the Paris bakers from their home marketplaces.[51] Millers Canda, Lemaire, Bocquere, and Tilliel of the Meaux area and Feret and Poras of Coulommiers performed the same services.[52] When the police began to crack down on miller buying during the crisis of 1740, miller Cousin of Blancmesnil warned his clients that he would not be able to assure their provisioning. Two of them, widow bakers Utinet and Dubois, appealed to the lieutenant general of police for dispensation: "Not being able themselves to go to the markets to buy wheat, they have always used various commissionnaires to make their purchases." Among them was Cousin, who "had served them with precision and honesty for the past ten years." As if the ports and the Halle did not exist, the baker widows announced that unless Cousin were authorized to supply them, "they would be reduced to the harsh necessity of shutting down their bakeries." Marville denied the request, and it is not clear what happened to the widows. Cousin, however, stayed in the business of buying for various Paris bakers.[53]

Baker country buying gave powerful impetus to the commercialization of milling. Millers who began as baker agents became impatient with contract buying in behalf of individual baker clients. They made themselves into merchants: they started manufacturing flour on speculation. To "cover" themselves, millers such as Jean-Claude Colas of Stains and Jean-François Touron of Annet-sur-Marne had or claimed to have what they called "verbal commissions" or open standing orders from "numerous Paris bakers" to buy virtually unlimited quantities. Even when they purchased at the farms, they obtained certificates from the markets made out in the names of the Paris bakers. They then had the option of offering the flour to the baker named on the certificate, even if he did not order it, or to another baker, for delivery en droiture, or of sending it to the Halle for public sale.[54]

Millers were not the only commissionnaires employed by the Paris bakers. A former Paris baker named Girault purchased grain in the countryside for a number of his ex-confreres. Local bakers in market towns such as Etampes, Melun, Dourdan, and Coulommiers served as agents for the Parisians. A tough, shrewd twenty-five-year-old porter at the marketplace of Houdan ran a buying brokerage for Paris bakers and did not hesitate to use strong-arm

51. Petition, October 1738, Arsenal, ms. Bast., 10275; Archives Seine-Paris, D5B⁶ 4575; AN, Y 9539, 1 October 1765; AN, MC, VII-288, 1 August 1753; AN, Y 9619, 31 January 1738.

52. Registration list, February 1771, AD Seine-et-Marne, bailliage de Meaux, unclassified; Archives Seine-Paris, D6B⁶, carton 2, 3 March 1742, and AN, Y 9442, 11 August 1741.

53. Utinet and Dubois to Marville, October 1740, Arsenal, ms. Bast. 10275. See Cousin's purchases for master Sébastien Lapareillé, AN, Y 11233, 1 August 1746.

54. AN, Y 9648, February 1771. The concerted ploys of millers and bakers to boost the mercuriale remained a problem a century later. *Enquête sur la boulangerie*, p. 88.

tactics to eliminate competitors. Dourdan grain dealers Besnard and Jacques
Lefebvre bought in behalf of the Paris bakers. Grain merchant Mallard bought
for master baker Tupin and delivered directly to his miller at Persan.[55] Since
he operated in an area twenty-five leagues distant from Paris, grain merchant
Adrien de La Forge contended that his purchases for Paris bakers should not
be considered as violations of the law.[56] Other grain merchant-baker commissionnaires worked the Beauce, the Brie, and the Valois.[57] Poussot blamed the
proliferation of baker commissionnaires among the hinterland grain traders
on the laxity of the local police.[58] Paris-based suppliers also took on baker
commissions. Harboux and Billy, who furnished the Halle, operated on the
side for baker widows Lapareillé and Richer respectively.[59] In a harsh sentence that was meant as a warning to all traders on the ports, the prévôt des
marchands expelled Grève dealer Jean Oudard from the ranks of the city
merchants and fined him 1,000 livres for "exercising the function of buying
broker for various [Paris] bakers."[60] This sentence was issued less than two
months after the promulgation of the royal declaration that severely circumscribed baker buying rights.

Opposition to Baker Country Buying

From the outset the bakers had to fight for the right to go into the countryside. Certain members of the police establishment, clustered around a bloc of
parlementaires, were openly suspicious of baker motives and anxious about
the imbalance in relationships that country buying might cause among the
agents in the subsistence nexus. According to this view, the bakers were
irresponsible buyers who purchased from anyone (thus encouraging regrating), anywhere (thus depleting the markets), at any price (thus setting "a fire
of rising prices"), and then did not hurry to put their grain to use (thus
building hoards that pushed prices up). To prevent disorder, one had only "to
prevent all those who are not Paris merchants from mixing in the trade and [to
oblige] bakers to get supplies only at the port or the Halle."[61]
    Another antibaker argument anticipated Poussot's campaign to focus all

55. AN, Y 9621, 16 July 1751; BN, ms. fr. 21644, fols. 128, 436, 493; AN, Y 11236,
11 October 1749; arrêt du conseil, 25 June 1754, BN, Coll. Joly 1829, fol. 345; Arsenal, ms.
Bast. 10270, 25 August 1725; Archives Seine-Paris, D5B⁶ 5234.
    56. "A mon seigneur Ayrault [Hérault]," February 1728, Arsenal, ms. Bast. 10274.
    57. Archives Seine-Paris, D5B⁶ 4119, July 1766; BN, Coll. Joly 1112, fol. 5 (17–18 Sep-
tember 1751); Couet de Montbayeux to procurator general, 5 October 1725, Coll. Joly 1116,
fols. 285–86.
    58. Arsenal, ms. Bast. 10141, fols. 274–75 (16 November 1759).
    59. AN, Y 11233, 1 August 1746, and Archives Seine-Paris, D2B⁶ 809, 10 May 1747.
    60. Sentence of 29 November 1737, BN, F 23719 (909).
    61. Couet de Montbayeux to procurator general, 5 October 1725, BN, Coll. Joly 1116,
fols. 285–86.

trade on the public markets by a half-century. It held that the "only way to reduce prices and fill the markets with abundance" was to prohibit bakers from buying outside the capital. Such a concentration would have the secondary advantage of making inspection infinitely easier.[62] Yet there was another, more moderate police view best represented by Delamare. He argued that only a small number of bakers could be expected to go beyond the eight leagues, that they would complement the merchants, that they would add to the abundance of the capital, and that they would bring a large part of their purchases in the form of flour, which would give Paris extra protection against mill stoppages.[63] Had the police authorities not been divided in their attitude, it is virtually certain that baker country buying would not have gotten off the ground.

The most strenuous opposition to baker country buying came from the measurers, seconded by the porters and by the city-licensed port merchants. The measurers and porters feared that their revenues would be seriously diminished by the decline of market-located commerce in favor of droiture traffic. The merchants worried that the baker competition would ruin their business.

After two arrêts in 1680 and 1683 that opened the way for an expansion of baker field operations, the measurers obtained an arrêt in 1686 that confined all baker buying to the Paris Halle and ports. The bakers lobbied intensely against this measure, though it seems doubtful that their country buying was seriously curtailed, and were vindicated by a crucial royal declaration of September 1699 that reiterated the basic principles of the police of provisioning and incidentally authorized baker purchases beyond the eight-league line provided that the bakers showed market certificates to justify those purchases. Neither the measurers nor the porters ever accepted this law as the final word. They continued to challenge country-buying bakers throughout the first half of the century, on the grounds that the bakers committed one abuse or another. Their aim was to break baker morale by confiscating their merchandise, subpoenaing them, delaying them, harrying them. Supported by the guild, many bakers fought back in the courts. Several epic battles lasted up to twenty years, a telling indication of what each side felt was at stake.

Even as they faced the threat of abolition, so the measurers and porters clung more and more tenaciously to their supposed prerogatives (much in the manner of the Hôtel de Ville in its struggle against the Châtelet). They felt obliged, however, to change their line significantly. By mid-century they gave up hope of keeping the bakers out of the country entirely. Rather, they insisted that they should receive certain fees on *all* country merchandise,

---

62. "Mémoire qui marque tous les désordres," BN, ms. fr. 21643, fol. 354.
63. Delamare, *Traité de la police,* 1:627–28.

whether or not they performed services for the bakers, that bakers should be rigorously kept out of the decommercialized zone and confined to the market-places beyond ten leagues, and that the bakers should not be allowed to use purchasing agents. The royal council supported the measurers in all of these matters, but the bakers, as we have seen, successfully evaded some of them all of the time and all of them some of the time. The porters were not success-ful in prosecuting their claims to collect fees on legal droiture merchandise. The bakers exploited the jealousies between the measurers and porters, using the measurers' testimony to discredit the porters' efforts to justify their fees as remuneration for the exercise of "police functions"—functions that the measurers would have liked to reserve strictly for themselves.[64]

The chief argument employed by the measurers against baker country buying was that it would reduce abundance—the reverse of Delamare's rea-soning in favor of it. The bakers would communicate disorder by stepping outside the traditional supply lines. The laboureurs, followed by the mer-chants, would go to the mills to sell to the bakers. Off-market transactions, masked by false certificates, would prompt maneuvers on price and quality. The hinterland markets would die of inanition and the Paris markets would stagnate and decline. Bakers would themselves begin to trade in grain and flour, in association with their commissionnaires, who would amass hoards in secret country depots. Such was the stark scenario of the measurers, who preferred to be perceived "in our quality of police officers" rather than as the rapacious toll collectors that the bakers disrespectfully made them out to be.[65]

In the thirties, the port merchants took over for the measurers on the front line against the bakers. (According to the bakers, the two groups had always been in league and continued to support each other's positions.)[66] We have already had occasion to discuss the merchant campaign, orchestrated by the prévôt des marchands. The merchants had reason to be alarmed. Their busi-nesses were in trouble, and country buying of the bakers was surely one of the major reasons.[67] Unable to compete—horrified by the specter of liberty that they claimed was so dear to them—the merchants invoked a hodgepodge of precedents, conventions, and concessions to support their exclusivist pre-tensions. In case the argument from custom failed, however, the merchants fashioned another, more powerful one. The bakers were not merely transgres-sing merchant space, but they were also doing violence to the public interest, as the measurers had suggested: they abused the faculty of water traffic for

64. AN, F[11] 94, 26 April 1747 (Plet), and H* 1873, fols. 608–27, June 1770 (Noblet).
65. "Factum pour les mesureurs," ca. 1686, BN, ms. fr. 21640, fols. 65–97; BN, Coll. Joly 1313, fols. 148–49 (ca. 1750) and 1829, fols. 325–43.
66. They were always united because they had "the same interests." BN, Coll. Joly 1314, fols. 13, 67–68.
67. For a hint that the bakers had not been deeply involved in river traffic until the late 1720s and early 1730s, see their memorandum, ca. 1725, BN, Coll. Joly 1116, fols. 445–52.

the purpose of hoarding and regrating, they established dubious associations with miller commissionnaires and with their fellow bakers, they siphoned all the grain off the local markets, they plotted shortages for the purpose of driving up prices. They also reduced aggregate abundance by abandoning their usual country buying areas away from the rivers.[68]

The merchants, as we have seen, obtained a royal declaration in September 1737 that banned the bakers from the rivers, pushed back the decommercialized zone from eight to ten leagues, and required them to buy in person and only on the markets.[69] This law was never seriously enforced. Within weeks of its promulgation, the police "tolerated" baker river traffic.[70] The procurator general never submitted the declaration for ratification by the full parlement, thus depriving it of the judicial blessing it needed in order to be executed. His reason was the imminence of a subsistence crisis, whose baleful effects he feared would be aggravated by forcing the bakers to change their ways.[71] Beyond this circumstantial hesitation, however, it was clear that the authorities were no longer convinced that baker buying should be curtailed. The prévôt des marchands spasmodically struck a blow against bakers by confiscating their riverborne merchandise and fining them.[72] His colleagues in the assembly of police, however, were not willing to declare war on the bakers, perhaps in part because they realized that the bakers were more aggressive suppliers than the port merchants.

The Baker Defense

The bakers defended themselves vigorously against the accusations of the measurers, the porters, and the merchants. They argued first for the utility of country buying as they practiced it and then they assailed the motives and the machinations of their adversaries. Paris could not get by without their contribution to its daily provisioning, they contended. The merchants brought too little and their shipments were too irregular as a result of inclement weather or speculative decision—the bakers increased the amount of grain available

68. BN, Coll. Joly 1314, fols. 11, 34; assembly of police, 27 August 1733, BN, ms. fr. 11356, fols. 218–19.Cf. assembly of police, 5 December 1737, Coll. Joly 1314, fol. 5.

69. BN, ms. fr. 21640, fol. 63.

70. Assembly of police, 18 December 1737, 23 January 1738, BN, ms. fr. 11356; Bertier de Sauvigny, "Observations sur le commerce des grains," BN, ms. fr. 11347, fol. 225. For baker-bought grain arriving at the ports, see Arsenal, ms. Bast. 10277. For the evidence of baker river traffic, see BN, Coll. Joly 1829, fol. 333.

71. BN, Coll. Joly 1314, fol. 87.

72. See, for example, Lefebvre's case in the fifties, BN, Coll. Joly 1829, fol. 343. As late as 1764, the Hôtel de Ville was still calling for the enforcement of the prohibition of baker river traffic. "Mémoire et avis de Mrs. de la Ville," BN, ms. fr. 14296, p. 34.

and thus helped to moderate prices.[73] Some bakers could not obtain all the merchandise they needed as a result of the purchasing limits.[74]

Since there was an insufficient number of mills in the immediate Paris area, the bakers maintained, they had to go deep into the countryside anyway with the grain they bought intramurally, which needlessly increased both costs and the price of bread. Many bakers lacked the horse and wagon necessary for hauling merchandise, while many of the faubourg bakers who had to have vehicles and animals for transporting bread to the markets could not amortize their costs unless they were able to use them for country buying as well. Bakers who made country purchases could drop off their grain for grinding on the spot or have the miller pick it up for them.[75]

Nor were the bakers satisfied with the quality of Paris-marketed grain, especially the merchandise sold on the ports. It was often wet and "altered" because the complacent merchants did not bother to take proper "precautions." A setier of wheat at the port commonly weighed as much as twenty to twenty-five pounds less than a setier of country-bought wheat.[76]

The bakers affirmed that the charges leveled against them by the merchants were "absurdities and lies" meant to conceal the merchant "monopoly." With exclusive control of the rivers and the right to buy on the farms, the merchants would be in a position to control the whole provisioning machine, to hoard, to ruin the markets that the bakers frequented, and to set prices at their guise. The bakers insisted that river trade was "a right" they had always exercised rather than "a tolerance" and that they could not afford to renounce river freight because of the exorbitant cost of land transport. To protect the merchants from competition was to subsidize inefficiency. To entrust the fate of Paris to a handful of "greedy" merchants was folly. In order to assure order and abundance the power of the merchants had "to be counterbalanced by this great number of bakers."[77]

Like the merchants, the measurers and porters were motivated by "sordid avarice." These market officials practiced a sort of "monopoly" by placing a claim on all the merchandise that entered the capital, regardless of provenance. They wanted to collect fees on all goods, even those that they neither measured, nor "broke," nor loaded. The bakers maintained that they deserved to be remunerated only for services actually performed and that the measurers and porters were never invested with a *droit d'entrée*. Their fees

73. BN, ms. fr. 21639, fols. 161–64, and 21640, fols. 50, 68–69, 161–64; BN, Coll. Joly 1116, fols. 245–52. Cf. Deline, *Mémoire* (1726), p. 5, BN (factum).

74. BN, ms. fr. 21640, fol. 73.

75. Ibid., fols. 50, 79. Delamare put the case more cogently, *Traité de la police*, 1:627. Cf. *Journal économique* (December 1753): 95.

76. BN, ms. fr. 21640, fols. 70–71; *Journal économique* (June 1751): p. 257; Savary des Bruslons, *Dictionnaire portatif de commerce*, 3:139–40. The bakers also lamented the uneven quality of flour at the Halle. Arsenal, ms. Bast. 10160, fol. 140 (28 November 1729).

77. BN, Coll. Joly 1829, fol. 347, and 1116, fols. 245–52. Cf. "Mémoire sur l'établissement d'un poids à la halle," AN, F^{11} 265.

created a "double duty" when added to those paid by the bakers (or the sellers) in the local markets. The result was "a tax on necessity," an extra cost burden on the poor consumers. Some measurers tried to extort supplementary fees in return for vague assurances of future indulgence or on other pretexts.[78]

The measurers and porters were perfectly right to complain that the bakers did not "honor" their position. The bakers deeply resented their bullying and peremptory manner, and refused to regard them as representatives of "the public ministry." They were "wig-heads," empty and pretentious, with no real knowledge or authority[79]—they were "the little tyrants of the city and suburbs" who carried swords with which to intimidate bakers and did not hesitate to destroy evidence unfavorable to them by tearing up baker certificates.[80] The bakers were willing to submit to inspection at the gates and barriers, but they detested street ambushes and harassment. (The bakers often rallied their neighbors, clients, and passers-by to repulse the measurers and porters, who were obliged to call upon the guard to deal with "public riots provoked by mutinous and incorrigible bakers.")[81] The bakers called for strict limitations to be placed on the power of the measurers and porters because they abused it by setting themselves up as judges in cases in which they were parties and by denying the bakers due process (violating their "natural rights"). In particular, the bakers denounced "verbal confiscations" and the failure to notify the bakers of the *procès-verbaux* they drafted.[82] By "troubling our commerce," the bakers concluded, the measurers and porters not only committed flagrant injustices but also compromised the provisioning of the capital.

In practice the baker position vis-à-vis the market officers was not inflexible. The bakers wanted the legitimacy of country droiture and purchasing by commission to be admitted. They wanted market certificates, signed by the buying agent, to be valid for four months rather than for two. They had no use for the porters, but they were willing to pay a reduced quasi-entry-fee to the measurers (18 sous the muid on flour, 12 sous on grain) if they had to, provided they were only challenged at the city gates (which left them home free if they were able to sneak into the city).

Baker Allies in Country Buying

The bakers had allies in their struggle to continue country purchasing. They were warmly supported by a number of market towns located within or

78. BN, Coll. Joly 1829, fols. 333ff.; BN, ms. fr. 21640, fol. 71; Trudaine de Montigny to Sartine, 10 June 1769, AN, F^{12} 153.
79. AN, Y 9474, 22 November 1771.
80. Deline, *Mémoire* (1726), pp. 2–4, 6, BN (factum).
81. See, for example, AN, Y 12609, 5 December 1760, and Y 11240, 4 August 1753.
82. BN, Coll. Joly 1829, fols. 317ff.

just at the limit of the decommercialized zone. Whereas certain hinterland communities protested bitterly against spoliation by Paris suppliers who were indifferent to local needs, these market towns, surrounded by rich wheat-producing arable, welcomed the link with the metropolis. The town of Montlhéry depended for its economic survival on "the prodigious concourse of buyers and sellers" that the grain market attracted. As a result of this activity, "everyone, no matter what his condition, found a sure resource." The prosperity of the market, which drew meat, poultry, dairy products, cloth, and hardware, depended totally on the presence of the Paris bakers, who were its "prime movers." If the bakers stayed away so did everyone else, and the market simply disintegrated. Mobilizing sometimes as much as 500 muids a week from the fertile Beauce, Montlhéry was an extremely large market.[83] It lured the Paris bakers because they could visit it and return in less than a day, and they could save time and money by leaving grain they bought in the hands of the thirty millers set up on the four rivers that surrounded the town. Yet the existence of the market was precarious, for Montlhéry was located six leagues from Paris and survived as a baker preserve after the declaration of 1699 only "on tolerance [of the police]."[84]

Only once between 1699 and 1737 did the Paris police try to shut down the Montlhéry bakers' market.[85] During the subsistence crisis of 1725, whose acuity the authorities attributed in large measure to "maneuvers" and "monopolies," lieutenant general of police Hérault "judged it necessary to take this liberty [of buying at Montlhéry] away from the bakers because they were abusing it." He drew a harsh picture of baker egotism: "they burned up the market by their number," in complicity with the local laboureurs and merchants they drove the price up, and they did everything they could "to perpetuate the dearth" in the expectation of profiting from it. The fate of Montlhéry did not interest Hérault. On the contrary, he rejoiced at the prospect that the suppliers who abandoned that market now that it no longer attracted clients from the capital would ship their merchandise for sale at the Paris Halle.[86] Six weeks after Hérault's crackdown, Paris bakers were again at the Montlhéry market, and they continued to buy there without incident until the beginning of 1737.[87]

In years of plentiful supply the Paris police tended to avert its eyes and *laisser faire.* In the case of the country trading of the bakers, however, they

83. Delamare, *Traité de la police,* 2:824.

84. Petition of the inhabitants of Montlhéry to cardinal Fleury, 1737, BN, Coll. Joly 1314, fols. 30–33.

85. Despite the efforts of the prévôt des marchands to persuade the assembly of police to prosecute the law on the forbidden zone. BN, ms. fr. 11356, fol. 162 (24 May 1731).

86. Cornellyer to intendant of Paris, 30 October 1725, Arsenal, ms. Bast. 10271; Chatautillard to Hérault, 31 October 1725, ibid.; Hérault to intendant of Paris, 1 November 1725, ibid.; Marchais to Hérault, 29 October 1725, ibid.

87. Marchais to Hérault, 11 December 1725, ibid.

chose to enforce the law with an unwonted rigor in 1737, a year of relative serenity and low prices. The issue had been high on the agenda of the assembly of police for over a year; the campaign against the bakers seemed to be the harbinger of its new hard-line policy. On January 5, in response to reports of hoarding, transactions on sample, and the sale of official certificates meant to launder off-market purchases, the lieutenant general of police dispatched—of all persons!—two porters to Montlhéry "in order to take note of the monopoly of the said Paris bakers." The porters seized the grain of several bakers and sent a paroxysm of anxiety through the marketplace.[88]

Several weeks later another porter delegation, backed this time by a constabulary detachment, visited Montlhéry to seize the grain purchased by bakers in violation of the eight-league taboo. Led by Leroy, the representative of the seigneur of the town, a large, angry crowd composed of "all sorts of persons," including millers, grain merchants, bakers, and townsmen, blocked their passage to the marketplace and then chased them out of the town with sticks, pitchforks, and rocks. Leroy aroused the crowd with a passionate harangue on the city's inalienable liberty to buy and sell, and especially on "the liberty of Paris bakers and millers to come to buy wheat in the said marketplace." The talk of a royal declaration banning baker trade at Montlhéry could not possibly be true, he assured the crowd, because the king would never have approved a law that traduced this liberty. This appeal to a higher, quasi-sacred right had great allure when the more-or-less remote central government transgressed local norms and expectations.[89]

The inhabitants of Montlhéry petitioned cardinal Fleury for a derogation in deference to the forty-year-old custom of baker buying in their market and to the dependence of the town on this traffic. The town faced "desolation" and the population was "in a state of great consternation," for since the bakers were banned the market attracted less than a tenth of its usual supply. The petitioners traced the campaign against baker buying to "certain enemies of the public interest who had only their self-interest in view," a composite portrait of the Paris measurers and port merchants.[90]

While police pressure kept the bakers away for a short period, there is no doubt that they returned. Paradoxically, it may have been the grave crisis of 1738–40 that opened the way to a renewed laxity. On 8, 11, and 14 October 1740, the constabulary conducted raids on Montlhéry to enforce the declaration of 8 September 1737. They found numerous bakers in the taverns along the marketplace drinking with grain dealers, including master baker Vincent Segond, who "declared with effrontery that he had indeed come to Montlhéry to do business," and a guild juré named Petitot "who engaged the other bakers to come to the said market of Montlhéry." Nine bakers received summonses,

88. Police sentence, 11 January 1737, BN, ms. fr. 21635, fols. 164–66.
89. AN, Y 11224, 4 February 1737.
90. Petition, BN, Coll. Joly 1314, fols. 32–33.

but the lieutenant general of police discharged them all in his weekly audience.[91]

Was this meant to be a signal that Montlhéry could return to the old system of "tolerance"? The town of Montlhéry would have preferred a legal written dispensation rather than a fragile tolerance. It had a specific model to which to refer. Brie-Comte-Robert, which also boasted a large market, a rich cereal hinterland, and a burgeoning water-mill industry, and was situated six leagues from the capital, had profited from tacit authorization to sell to the Paris bakers since the declaration of 1699. When faubourg St.-Antoine baker Jacques Paris told the measurers who stopped his wagon in 1725 that "he did not know that it was forbidden to buy wheat in the town of Brie," he was in all likelihood telling the truth, for Brie drew scores of bakers every week.[92] In 1729 the town sought to regularize its situation with a petition. The engagiste of the domain of Brie—daughter of a distinguished parlementary magistrate, the first president de Mesmes—strongly endorsed the request. The assembly of police, however, rejected out of hand its plea for an exemption.[93] The town and its benefactor/seigneur continued to press the government. In December 1736, on the recommendation of the controller-general, the king issued a declaration allowing bakers access to Brie. Apparently the controller-general did not bother to consult the assembly of police, despite the fact that it had been studying the baker-trade question intensively for the past year.[94]

Similarly, the farmer of the Versailles market, located only four leagues from the capital, lobbied for an arrêt du conseil authorizing bakers to buy there freely. In the meantime, he renegotiated a "tolerance" every time that the lieutenance of police changed hands.[95] Duplessis, the senior commissaire of the central market department in the twenties, deplored the Versailles connection and encouraged the measurers and porters to seize Versailles merchandise, grain or flour, on the grounds that the market was off limits. Like Poussot a quarter-century later, Duplessis anguished over the decline of Paris as a market: "I am very fearful of seeing our Halle denuded of grain and flour if the [Versailles] farmer gets what he wants."[96] Hérault was willing, however, to honor the Versailles request on the same grounds of "customary usage" that he found unacceptable in the Montlhéry case. He seemed convinced that Paris profited from the Versailles market, especially from the flour

91. AN, Y 11227, 3 October 1740, and Y 9441, 14 October 1740.
92. AN, Y 9538, 15 June 1725. On the presence of Paris bakers, see also Marchais to Hérault, 7 February, 25 July 1727, Arsenal, ms. Bast. 10274.
93. BN, ms. fr. 11356, fol. 88.
94. AN, O¹ 382, fols. 467–68, 24 December 1736. Cf. BN, Coll. Joly 1314, fol. 11.
95. Regnier to Hérault, 16 February 1728, Arsenal, ms. Bast. 10274. On the baker presence at Versailles, see also Regnier to Hérault, 19 October, 24, 31 December 1725, ms. Bast. 10171.
96. AN, Y 9538, 1 June 1725; Duplessis to Hérault, 11 March 1728, Arsenal, ms. Bast. 10274.

traffic.[97] The assembly of police reported that the royal council promulgated an arrêt in December 1738 exempting Versailles from the ban of the decommercialized zone. Yet twelve years later, the comte de Noailles courted the procurator general in an effort to obtain permission for Paris bakers to buy grain at Versailles. At least until then, only flour seems to have enjoyed immunity from seizure.[98]

A war of influence waged behind the scenes as protectors of different markets competed for favor. The Hôtel-Dieu, engagiste of the domain of Gonesse, supported that town's bid for exceptional open-market status within the forbidden zone. The resuscitation of their market, the town fathers of Gonesse contended, would relieve the "misery" of the inhabitants and enable them to meet their fiscal obligations.[99] The duc de Villeroy, owner of the market of Mennecy, located almost on the eight-league line, personally attended a meeting of the assembly of police to argue in favor of opening his market to the bakers. Somehow Villeroy managed to obtain for Mennecy what other patrons could not win for Arpajon, Bruyères-le-Châtel, and Montlhéry. One of the reasons that the authorities may have been willing to offer the bakers Mennecy as compensation for everything they lost in the royal declaration of September 1737 was that Mennecy was a minor market that had never interested the bakers. Its strong point was that it was located on the Seine, an advantage, alas, that the bakers would not be able to exploit, for they were authorized to use Mennecy only by land traffic.[100]

Frustrated in 1737, the patrons of Arpajon—the marquise d'Arpajon and the comte de Noailles—continued to campaign for their market with all the zealous boosterism of a modern American town seeking to become the seat of a state fair. Located nine leagues from Paris, almost far enough away to qualify, Arpajon stood at the crossroads of the cereal-rich Orléanais, Gâtinais, and Beauce. It vaunted spacious, newly renovated market facilities, plus twenty hotels and taverns to accommodate buyers and sellers. Until the declaration of 1737, the market was allegedly so busy that twenty measurers worked till nightfall. Arpajon merited better treatment, its supporters argued, for it had faithfully contributed to the provisioning of Paris for generations. Moreover, the exclusion of Arpajon compelled bakers to buy clandestinely in the farms and villages—"the fleeting markets of the night"—because they

97. Hérault notes, 11 March 1728, Arsenal, ms. Bast. 10274. Behind the anti-Versailles movement, Hérault discerned a cabal of measurers and porters who wanted to ban these droiture entries in order to preserve their revenues.

98. BN, ms. fr. 11356, fols. 340–41 (19 December 1737); Noailles to procurator general, 27 April, 4 May 1750, BN, Coll. Joly 1313, fols. 160, 162.

99. The assembly of police denied the request. BN, ms. fr. 11356, fols. 190–91, 31 July 1732.

100. BN, ms. fr. 11356, fols. 313–14, 14 February 1737; BN, Coll. Joly 1314, fols. 78, 117; "Mémoire des boulangers," December 1737, BN, Coll. Joly 1314, fol. 71.

could not find enough grain to satisfy them on the few conveniently placed markets that were not off limits.[101]

The declaration of 1737 also threatened the existence of the mealmen of Melun, whose market was owned by the king. The flour dealers claimed to produce "the purest" and "the finest" flour consumed in Paris on eight of the most modern and productive mills in the realm. They had supplied "the best bakers of Paris" for over thirty years with as much as 500 sacks a week, which they shipped by river. Unless they procured an exemption, their operation could not continue, for two reasons. First, according to the new measuring system (2,400 toises to the league instead of 2,000), Melun was now within the decommercialized zone. Second, the obligation to ship by land would triple their freight expenses and make their merchandise prohibitively costly.[102]

The lack of coherence in the policy toward supplicant markets located in the forbidden zone had troubled the assembly of police. On the one hand, the royal council seemed to have been much more susceptible to lobby pressure. The assembly does not appear to have been consulted on the Brie-Comte-Robert declaration at the end of 1737. And it learned of the arrêt du conseil opening Dammartin and Versailles only after they were printed, a legal anomaly in the view of the procurator general, for an arrêt could not contravene a royal declaration.[103] On the other hand, the assembly itself appears to have written the Mennecy exception into the declaration of September 1737. By the end of 1738, the assembly seems to have been ready to reexamine from the beginning not only the market-exemption issue but the question of baker river traffic. Cardinal Fleury let it be known that he favored new legislation that barred bakers from *all* the markets within either an eight- or a ten-league radius, without any exemptions, not even Limours. The lieutenant general of police seemed inclined to tolerate baker use of water transport. As a result of the worsening dearth, however, none of these questions was fully discussed. Nor did the assembly or the government ever consider them again in a systematic way. Instead, the authorities and the bakers improvised a series of shifting arrangements, contingent upon short-run provisioning and political needs, that bore only the most casual relationship to the laws of the land.

Abusive Buying Practices

In the end, the police tolerated baker country buying because it facilitated the task of provisioning Paris. Certain baker practices, however, were judged

101. BN, Coll. Joly 1313, fols. 175–77; "Mémoire pour le marché au bled de la ville d'Arpajon," BN, Coll. Joly 1123, fols. 23–24; gazetins, 31 August–7 September 1737, Arsenal, ms. Bast. 10166, fol. 330.

102. "Mémoire contre la déclaration du 8 septembre 1737," BN, ms. fr. 21635, fols. 166–67. The *presence* of the Paris bakers was crucial for the life of the market and the town. Otherwise the mealmen could have adjusted easily to the new constraints by selling the flour at the Paris Halle through brokerage.

103. Assembly of police, 19 December 1737, BN, ms. fr. 11356, fols. 340–41.

to be dangerous and contrary to the interests of the capital. Throughout the century, the Paris police labored to prevent or repress these "abuses." The most frequent complaint against the bakers was that they acted or conspired to push up the posted price of wheat in the expectation that the adjusted bread price would favor them, especially if they managed to find less expensive wheat with which to do the bulk of their baking.[104] This desire to raise prices was "a natural inclination" among the bakers, save for the poorest among them, observed commissaire Duplessis.[105] The first lieutenant general of police, La Reynie, had a name for this inclination: "malevolence." The bakers shrunk from no maneuver in their quest for "pretexts to sell their bread at a higher price."[106] According to the measurers, the bakers were responsible for provoking *cherté* time and again, for they were preoccupied exclusively with "the goal of making wheat *appear to be* expensive." Those same measurers were themselves accused of "plotting with bakers" to increase the current price at the ports and the Halle.[107]

"Unable to earn enough on his bread if wheat is not dear, the baker does not bother to bargain on the price," noted the author of a memorandum on "the disorders in the environs of Paris" in 1698. A Paris baker named Moncouteau was arrested for failing to haggle: "This baker, present in the market of Montlhéry, had the sellers close their sacks right away [signifying sale] in order to nourish the upward price movement." So grave was this affair considered that it was discussed in the assembly of police and a lettre de cachet was obtained to dramatize Moncouteau's imprisonment. Reports continued to reach the capital in 1725 and 1726 that Paris bakers not only failed to bargain but actually refused to buy wheat when the sellers did not insist on a sufficiently high price! Elsewhere bakers and merchants made "conventions" to raise the price level. At Dammartin a Paris baker fumed when the market official refused to document the excessively high price that he paid. At Crécy in 1738 and at Bray in 1740, Paris bakers were guilty of "monopolies" aimed at driving prices up. A faubourg St.-Antoine baker caused a riot in Montereau in

104. See Turgot's classic statement of this accusation, to the intendant of Bordeaux, 24 May 1775, AD Gironde, C 1448. Cf. Labrousse, *Esquisse du mouvement*, p. 29; Benzacar, *Pain à Bordeaux*, p. 119n; BN, Coll. Joly 1111, fol. 226; 2322, fol. 211; and 1743, fol. 1; Lemarchand, "Troubles de subsistances," p. 411; Masson to intendant of Champagne, 29 May 1770, AD Aube, C 299; Cypierre to controller-general, 11 September 1768, in Camille Bloch, *Le Commerce des grains dans la généralité d'Orléans (1786)* . . . (Orléans, 1898), p. 76. In Brittany, the merchants surreptitiously compensated the bakers for the high price by giving extra weight. Letaconnoux, *Commerce des grains en Bretagne*, p. 112. Nineteenth-century Paris bakers had the same interest in raising the mercuriale. Biot, *Lettres sur l'approvisionnement de Paris*, p. 83; *Enquête sur la boulangerie*, p. 724.

105. Duplessis to Hérault, 23 August 1727, Arsenal, ms. Bast. 10274.

106. La Reynie to Delamare, 15 January 1694, BN, ms. fr. 21643, fol. 58. Cf. same to same, 12 July 1693, ms. fr. 21638, fol. 396.

107. "Factum pour les jurez mesureurs," ca. 1686, BN, ms. fr. 21640, fol. 85; BN, ms. fr. 21642, fols. 25–27.

1768 by "buying up as much as he could at the price asked" and even "offering more than asked."[108] He was arrested.

The Paris bakers were more audacious in the country than at home because the police surveillance was generally less rigorous. Yet in 1729, under the very nose of the lieutenant general of police, a baker named Gagne "had the temerity during three successive market days [at the Halle] to take the merchant's first price and have the sacks immediately closed." The result was a general rise of 30 sous that was not warranted by legitimate supply or demand factors. The baker planned to sell bread made from other, cheaper wheat that he had previously bought and put aside, and not from wheat selling at the higher price provoked by his own purchases. Gagne's shop was walled up for six months, which gave him time to raise the 1,000 livres' fine that he also suffered.[109]

The second major "abuse" in baker country buying which was also believed to increase prices, was off-market transactions. The temptation was almost irresistible. Why bother to go to the crowded market? Moreover, the bakers considered it unfair that the licensed Paris grain merchants were authorized to do business wherever they liked while their own freedom of action suffered multiple restrictions. Off-market buying was extraordinarily widespread; some bakers procured most of their country grain in the farms.[110] On commission from the bakers, the millers also purchased outside the markets. Much of this off-market buying was doubly illegal, conducted in the forbidden zone.[111] It was impossible to police the farms and the granaries. All the authorities could do was to try to trap the baker on his way into the capital. If the baker was resourceful, however, he could obtain documentation to "cover" the illicit purchase. The market for the sale of false certificates remained brisk throughout the century. In 1698 Houssu, the senior measurer of Dourdan, sold Paris baker Duval a certificate, antedated by two weeks, to cover the off-market purchase of four muids. Commissaire de Courcy complained bitterly in 1740 that the Meaux market officials "issue their certificates in blank to the Paris bakers," enabling them to fill them out as they pleased and thus encouraging them to make their purchases in the farms. In 1749

---

108. BN, ms. fr. 21643, fol. 354; Arsenal, ms. Bast. 10875; Lepoupet to Hérault, 10 October 1725, ms. Bast. 10270; Marchais to same, 26 March 1726, ms. Bast. 10272; Couet de Montbayeux to procurator general, 14 October 1725, BN, Coll. Joly 1116, fol. 270; Ganneron to Hérault, 18 October 1725, Arsenal, ms. Bast. 10270; Poix to procurator general, 9 December 1738, BN, Coll. Joly 1119, fols. 104–5, and Barbe to same, 17 September 1740, Coll. Joly 1123, fol. 88; AN, Y 14095, 28 October 1768.

109. Assembly of police, 12 May 1729, BN, ms. fr. 11356, fols. 97–98; BN, Coll. Joly 1111, fol. 176.

110. See, for example, master Garin, BN, Coll. Joly 1829, fol. 326; Jean Blain, AN, MC, VII-288, 1 August 1753; and Denis Pillée, Archives Seine-Paris, D2B⁶ 986, 15 February 1762. Cf. Bertier de Sauvigny, "Observations sur le commerce des grains," 1763, BN, ms. fr. 11347, fol. 225.

111. See, for instance, AN, Y 9539, 6 May 1758.

baker Bontemps was caught with just such a certificate, filled out in part by the indulgent Meaux *minager* and in part by the baker. Twenty-two years later Meaux was still a haven for bakers in search of papers. For a fee, master baker Bernier received a "bulletin" to cover the sixty-eight setiers that he had bought at the farm of laboureur Hanoteau.[112]

In September of 1711, the measurers stopped a driver transporting seventeen setiers of wheat to baker Leduc. The driver innocently reported that he had picked up the grain at a Malmaison farm and then proceeded to Rambouillet, where he was instructed to obtain a certificate. The market officers refused to issue one, however, since the grain was not bought there. When Leduc was questioned, he expressed astonishment. "Every time that he bought wheat in the farms near Rambouillet or on the Dammartin side or elsewhere," he testified with candor, "he was in the habit of getting a certificate from the market closest to the place where he made his purchases."[113]

Bakers who could not obtain made-to-order false papers doctored old certificates or papers belonging to others, presented expired certificates or papers dealing with other transactions, or tried to sneak by without any papers. Baker Pierre Bire and widow Amand attempted to use duplicate copies of other certificates to get by the measurers and porters. Widow baker Henriette presented a Meaux certificate that had expired ten months earlier. Since master baker Chartié took the trouble to alter the amounts specified on his two-month-old Meaux certificate, one wonders why he did not change the date at the same time. Baker Davercy's driver tried to get his country grain by with a certificate made out to baker Longpré for purchases made at the Grève. Master Boulanger declared his flour to be from Versailles, but his certificate was issued at Maintenon. Master Brocq vainly sought to substitute a written statement of authorization to buy grain that he himself issued to his miller in place of an official market certificate. Baker Leduc claimed that he had lost his papers, while his colleague Bonhommet "made a great show of taking out his certificate" but refused to let the measurers scrutinize it. Bakers Ballery and Legrand "scoffed" at the request to present papers, as if the measurers had no right to demand an accounting.[114]

The police feared that once bakers made their purchases they would be tempted to hoard the merchandise, again with the hope of seeing prices rise. In 1697, an innkeeper in the faubourg St.-Jacques served as a custodian of several baker hoards, as did another at La Villette in 1752. In 1725 two bakers

---

112. Police sentence of 14 November 1698, BN, ms. fr. 21643, fol. 298; AN, Y 9441, 12 February 1740; Y 9622, 28 November 1749; Y 9474, 24 May 1771.

113. AN, Y 9539, 11 September 1761.

114. AN, Y 9539, 6, 17 May 1758; Y 9441, 12 February 1740; Y 9440, 12 June 1739; Y 9633, 14 November 1766; Y 9539, 12 December 1759; Y 9474, 1 June 1774; Archives Seine-Paris, 6 AZ 472, 7 February 1766; AN, Y 9474, 16 November, 17 December 1771.

from the faubourg St.-Antoine made a huge purchase of 34 muids, which they apparently stored with a local hotelkeeper before going on to make further "removals" at other markets. The police expected two forain bakers from St.-Denis who filled a boat with grain at Pont-Ste.-Maxence to put it in an inn on the Oise.[115] The authorities worried that the innkeepers would gradually shift from a passive stocking role into an active buying role as baker accomplices.[116]

Monasteries, convents, and colleges were even more attractive granaries for the bakers, because they conferred an aura of legitimacy on the hoards—these institutions were required by the royal government to keep on stock an amount of grain equal to two or three years' consumption. Master Leroux, a juré and pillar of the baker community, used several "borrowed" names to constitute a huge stock at the collège de Montaigu. The collège could claim the stock as its own if the police ever made an inspection, giving Leroux superb cover for speculative operations. Though the assembly of police prohibited bakers to store in behalf of these institutions, the practice continued because of the service rendered both parties.[117] In the second half of the century the lieutenant general adopted a more permissive stance on stocking that must have encouraged country buying, a tacit admission that the police had not been able to prevent baker hoarding and that it made more sense to try to put it in the service of the provisioning of Paris than to persist in vain efforts to repress it. He authorized bakers to maintain stocks outside their shops provided that they solicited permission from him.[118]

Stockage was frequently a prelude to regrating, an abuse that the police never tolerated under any circumstances. Regrating was prohibited because bakers did not have the right to buy for the sake of resale or speculation. This practice, like the other abuses, meant a less visible supply and higher prices. Though baker regrating was not uncommon, it was usually a petty operation rather than a veritable commerce in grain or flour. The baker sellers one encounters most often were those who discreetly built up clienteles among colleagues who did not go to the country to buy. All kinds of bakers were involved in this subspecialty: masters Devaux and Cauchois, faubourg St.-Antoine baker Deshayes, forains Garmont (who may also have been a miller) and Thirouin.[119] A number of bakers tried to conceal their sales by using the names and sacks of grain or flour brokers at the Halle. Master Brocq used the

115. BN, ms. fr. 21710, fol. 219, 13 December 1697; AN, Y 9621, 10 March 1752; Laurent to lieutenant general, 11 December 1725, Arsenal, ms. Bast. 10271; Bourlon to lieutenant general, 25 October 1725, ms. Bast. 10271.

116. Gabaille to procurator general, 16 January 1739, BN, Coll. Joly 1119, fol. 121.

117. Moreau to procurator general, 17, 24 April 1736, ibid., 1120, fols. 321–25; assembly of police, 19 December 1737, BN, ms. fr. 11356, fol. 341; AN, Y 11238, 19 July 1751.

118. BN, Coll. Joly 1111, fol. 174.

119. AN, Y 12729, 1 March 1735; Archives Seine-Paris, D5B⁶ 4246, 2707, and 2682 and D4B⁶ 79–5287, 6 December 1780.

large bakery operation he ran at the Ecole Militaire as a cover for the sale of wheat to other bakers. Master Aubry supplied a hospital in grain, while his colleague Lemerle sold in wholesale quantities to various individuals. A forain from Choisy-le-Roi dealt in oats and other fodder grains. Michel Fleury, a master and juré who also ran a mill, claimed that he regrated only occasionally when he "had need of cash."[120] Sometimes what appeared to be regrating was in fact an effort to get rid of undesirable merchandise.[121]

Beginning in the late seventeenth century, large numbers of Paris bakers began to purchase grain in the hinterland. The bakers felt cramped by the marketplace of the Halle and the Grève, physically and morally. The countryside attracted them because it offered them the open and unwatched spaces where the market principle prevailed. Moreover, the bakers contended that country buying was both necessary and rational. Paris merchandise was more expensive because it passed through many more hands and multiplied transfer costs. The bakers alleged that the supplies at the Paris markets were neither sufficiently abundant nor of sufficiently high grade to meet their needs.

Country buying expanded dramatically between 1730 and 1760. It was not limited to an elite of powerful bakers. Bakers who did not scour the provisioning zone themselves purchased through intermediaries, most commonly millers. Commissioned buying, like off-market purchasing, was strictly forbidden but massively practiced (and frequently "justified" with fraudulent documentation). Even as the Halle triumphed over the ports, the steady growth of baker droiture traffic threatened to undermine its foundations.

The Paris police were of at least two minds about baker country buying. On the one hand, they were alarmed about the loss of control it implied and by the proliferation of trading abuses (hoarding, regrating, monopoly) it seemed to facilitate, if not encourage. On the other hand, country buying palpably increased the capital's total provision (especially in flour, a precious form of crisis insurance), and it multiplied the lines of supply (another useful type of crisis protection). Inspector Poussot was less preoccupied with country buying per se than with the impact it had upon the Halle. He would have endorsed it had the bakers been willing to pass through the Halle on their way home. He pressed the anti-droiture campaign energetically, but if droiture traffic lost some momentum by the early sixties, it was less because of this repression than as a consequence of improvements in service at the Halle (the opening of the weight station, the disciplining of the measurers and the por-

120. BN, Coll. Joly 1111, fol. 174, 11 August 1751; police sentence, 29 January 1768, AN, AD XI 39; Archives Seine-Paris, D5B⁶ 2169; Archives Assistance publique, Incurables, no. 79, 1722–23; Archives Seine-Paris, D5B⁶ 3833, November 1770, and D5B⁶ 3327; BN, ms. fr. 21640, fols. 182–83, 12 April 1737.

121. See, for example, AN, Y 9621, 7 July 1751, and Y 9538, 20 May 1757.

ters, the reform of the brokerage, and the construction of a new trading building) and the commercialization of the flour trade that made direct country buying less inviting.

The most stringent opposition to baker country buying came from two interested bodies. The port merchants strenuously resisted it because baker competition menaced their businesses. The measurers and the porters denounced and actively sought to stifle droiture traffic because it threatened their revenue as well as their authority by bypassing the marketplace. The bakers rebuffed the first as pretentious monopolists and the second as venal tyrants. The bakers found strong support for their position from the officials and protectors of the market towns of the hinterland that they most frequented.

CHAPTER 13

The Brokers

*I*n order for a transaction to occur, a seller had to meet a buyer. This encounter did not always take place in person. For various reasons, one or both parties may have preferred to rely on intermediaries. The agents who represented sellers in the capital were called brokers *(facteurs)*. As a result of the commercialization of milling, the flour brokers at the Halle played a critical mediating role. They relieved merchants and millers of a number of burdensome tasks, and established relations with buyers that facilitated transactions. As the brokerage function grew in importance during the course of the century, it came under increasing criticism. The authorities were loath to permit the brokers to operate as if they were merely private middlemen governed exclusively by the market principle.

The Origins of the Brokerage

Little is known about the brokerage function in Paris before the 1690s. On the one hand there was repeated legislation reminding the merchants that they were forbidden to become part of a broker network and enjoining them to handle all the transactions personally or through a family member. On the other hand, there were brokers who assisted in the sale of goods in many of the sectors of the central markets as early as the fourteenth century. In 1569, 1633, 1634, 1644, and 1648, the royal council created titled broker posts in a number of nonsubsistence trades. In 1623 a group of flour merchants and laboureurs petitioned the government for permission to rely on brokers to facilitate marketing, claiming that their nearly universal illiteracy handicapped them in keeping registers, dealing with credit, and conducting litigation.[1] By the 1660s a number of brokers, without any official commission, provided factorage services.

In 1690 the government established sixty posts of titled brokers for grain and flour and several other commodities worth 10,000 livres apiece.[2] This measure has been called a "purely fiscal" device, a judgment that strikes me as overdrawn. To be sure, the royal government raised a nice sum (supplemented by another dose in 1692, when ten more broker charges were created).[3] But the edict also addressed the crucial issue of the organization of the subsistence trade in the central market. In some ways it made good sense to make the brokers dependent on royal authority and subject to close scrutiny before being allowed to acquire the post and to steady surveillance afterward. The brokers were instructed to sell for merchants and cultivators, to arrange for advances of up to 25 percent of the price to sellers, to extend credit to bakers and stand as guarantors of their solvency, to record all transactions, and to receive for their trouble 3 livres a muid.

Parisians, regardless of profession, were forbidden to sell merchandise in behalf of grain and flour dealers in what would have amounted to a parallel brokerage system. Similarly, upon risk of heavy penalties, the former "unestablished" brokers were prohibited from interfering with those who purchased the new charges. Supply merchants could still sell in person for their own account, but they could not entrust the task to anyone outside their immediate family. The titled brokers were organized as a corporation with elected officers accountable to the membership. To reduce the friction caused by rivalry for clients, it was agreed that all revenue would be equally shared through a "collected treasury." All the new posts were rapidly subscribed.[4]

The new brokerage structure did not last long. The parlement had been divided on the utility of the project; it was also criticized by a number of merchants, by the measurers, and of course by the ex-broker *politique-de-pire* lobby. It was the dearth of 1692, however, that turned the tide. It gave the enemies of the new system the opportunity to blame the price rise partly on the "excessive commissions" exacted by the titled brokers. (In fact they were exactly the same as the fees the untitled brokers had collected.) As a result of these complaints, in 1694 the government suspended the collection of broker fees, after the brokers themselves had made a partial renunciation in an

---

1. Ordinance of 1577, BN, Coll. Joly 1312, fol. 117; BHVP, série 114, cote provisoire 4802; Bertin and Dambraine, "Mémoire," Arsenal, ms. 2588.
2. Edict of September 1690, BN.
3. Edict of June 1692, BN; Biollay, *Origines du factorat,* p. 11.
4. BHVP, série 114, cote provisoire 4800; Bertin and Dambraine, "Mémoire," Arsenal, ms. 2588; statuts et règlements des 70 commissionnaires facteurs (1692), BN, F 22337.

attempt to steal a march on their adversaries. This step was tantamount to disestablishment, which did not occur officially until the end of the decade. The former brokers interpreted the measure as authorizing them once again to set up business.[5] Apparently unable to compete successfully with the old brokers, who had retained close ties with the supply merchants, most of the titled brokers vanished from the scene. Though it had no formal legitimate existence, the self-propelled brokerage thrived and multiplied. According to one of their critics, by around 1730 the untitled brokers had made themselves "masters of the Halle."[6]

Much later in the century, a group of veteran brokers argued that they had never been "created" in any official sense, that they owed their existence not to administrative fiat but to the decision of merchants, pursuing their own interests, to invest confidence in them.[7] By and large this version of their genesis appears to be correct. The merchants themselves assigned the broker they chose to the "place" where they usually camped on market days, then presented him or her to the commissaire for his approval, which was perceived as a simple formality. It seems true that, at least before mid-century, the police did not question the merchants' preference. Later, the brokers themselves sought official recognition in the form of *brevets,* or licenses, perhaps with a view toward enhancing their security and strengthening their competitive position. This thirst for legitimation, however, offered the authorities a standing invitation to intervene more actively in the organization and operation of the brokerage. For inspector Poussot, a *brevet* implied no less a public trust than any official commission. Perpetually revocable, its possession and use were contingent upon good behavior.

Broker Recruitment

In the first half of the eighteenth century, only a minority of first-generation brokers appear to have been drawn from the subsistence nexus. More important than familiarity with grain and flour seemed to be experience in commerce, in middleman organization, in market relations, in collecting and handling money. Thus it is not surprising to find grocers prominent among the early brokers, despite repeated prohibitions against their undertaking

5. Royal declaration, 1 March 1694, BN, ms. fr. 21643, fols. 3–4; arrêt du conseil, 17 November 1693, BN, ms. fr. 21642, fols. 247–48; édit du roy portant suppression des commissionnaires de la ville de Paris, August 1700, BHVP; Bertin and Dambraine, "Mémoire," Arsenal, ms. 2588.

6. "Mémoire des malversations, exactions, et prévarications," BN, Coll. Joly 1429, fol. 205. Polemical exaggeration, to be sure, but the brokers nevertheless played a crucial role in the daily business of provisioning, infinitely more important than Léon Cahen believed. "A propos du livre d'Afanassiev," 164.

7. See *Mémoire pour les marchands de farines et leurs facteurs* (1779), BN, 4 FM 25012.

grain and flour factorage.[8] The authorities worried that the grocers would integrate their two businesses and thus make the subsistence-provisioning side partly dependent on extraneous factors. Indeed, a number of early grocer-brokers apparently suffered business failure, their grocery operations bringing down their brokerage affairs and hurting numerous grain and flour dealers. In the fifties Poussot cited the case of one grocer-broker whose placegirls, to whom he abandoned virtually all of his factorage duties, distinguished themselves by their substantial thefts of merchant flour. Poussot thought highly of one young grocer who solicited a broker's post in 1758, especially since he was the son of a flour dealer and thus knew the trade, but wondered aloud "whether he could fulfill the obligations of the two professions."[9] By this time the police were clearly moving toward the professionalization of the brokerage through a more rigorous recruitment and regulation, as well as by phasing out the practice of exercising the brokerage as a sideline.

Beyond the grocery, brokers came from a crazy quilt of métiers that for the most part suggest no natural link with the subsistence business: a stocking maker, a cloth maker, a master coppersmith, a fish dealer, a mercer, several fruit and orange merchants.[10] The small-grains and dried-vegetable trade was the only source of brokers who had some familiarity with the subsistence world. Ancelin, Dame Sergent, Nicolas Martin, Jeanne Bigot, Jean Boulanger, and Jean Delaistre were all *marchands greniers* before they became brokers.[11] Rivals over other commercial issues, the *greniers* (sometimes called grainiers or grenetiers) and the grocers tried to have each other disqualified from grain and flour factorage. Later in the century, when the fruit-seller and *grenier* guilds merged, the new corporation sought to prevent any of its members from simultaneously practicing Halle factorage, on the grounds that it was not possible for one person to exercise both professions properly.[12] Compared to later brokerage enterprises, the pioneer generation in the eighteenth century seems to have operated on a decidedly modest scale. If they were more than the clerk-watchmen that the later brokers made them out to be, it is nevertheless true that they were extremely reluctant to undertake commercial risk.[13]

Recruitment in the first half of the century appears to have operated on two tiers. The first and probably dominant sphere was private and commer-

8. Bertin and Dambraine, "Mémoire," Arsenal, ms. 2588.

9. Arsenal, ms. Bast. 10141, 29 January, 31 July 1758.

10. Archives Seine-Paris, D4B⁶ 102-7168, 17 June 1788 (Auger); D4B⁶ 13-589, 1 September 1753 (Merlin); D2B⁶ 736, 28 April 1741 (Laroche); Arsenal, ms. Bast. 10141, 21 April 1756 (Paris); AN, Y 12613, 30 June 1764 (Charpentier); Y 11232, 26 May 1745; Y 11235, 21 June 1748.

11. AN: F¹² 76, fol. 76, 2 June 1729; Y 11238, 14 December 1751; Y 11228, 10 July 1741; Y 12608, 19 March 1760; Y 11235, 24 July 1748; Y 15389, 26 February 1779.

12. Chassin, *Elections et cahiers*, 4: 543–44.

13. "Mémoire pour les marchands de farines et leurs facteurs" (1779), BN, 4 FM 25012.

cial. Brokers assumed a prescriptive right to their posts despite their lack of titles and disposed of them as if they were private property. Cosme Delaistre passed his brokerage on to his son Nicolas. Indeed, by a sort of mitosis, the one post actually became two for a long period.[14] Frémont, a city drum major, and his sister each inherited one-half of their father's brokerage.[15] The police respected the hereditary imperative, even when it threatened to compromise the public interest, as in the case of the broker Delorme, whose children "were brought up in the grocery business and knew nothing at all about flour."[16]

The brokers not only bequeathed their posts without permission, but also modified their character by taking associates to operate them, in some cases as a prelude to selling them. This unregulated commercialization also posed problems that would ultimately lead to the end of broker autonomy. The "society" between André Rivière and Dame Aumont, established by notarial contract, worked quite well.[17] Aumont ran the floor operations and Rivière served as business manager-accountant. (Unlike many brokers, Rivière kept a daily register, based on the "tablettes" submitted to him by Aumont and by his saleswomen, containing the names of flour dealers and baker buyers, the quality sold, and the amount of money received.) Aumont died, however, after less than two years of partnership, and her successor, Louise Guiot, apparently felt that she did not need Rivière. Without informing him in advance, she took legal steps to dissolve the association de jure and assumed control of it de facto by persuading the merchants to deal exclusively with her. Rivière vowed to fight "this usurpation," even at the cost of disrupting the provisioning of the Halle.[18]

The other tier of recruitment was located in what we can call the public sector. By this I mean that it was directly controlled by public authorities, who implicitly considered the brokerage places as quasi-public charges. Yet this public vocation was quite limited in both space and time. It was limited in space because it only covered nomination to newly created posts or to posts that, by a very rare accident, devolved to or were repossessed by the police. It was limited in time because it appears that once the post was assigned, after a brief probationary period, it slipped into the private sphere. Theoretically the lieutenant general of police himself named a broker to a vacant post, but in practice it seems to have been part of the patronage controlled by the

14. Archives Seine-Paris, DE[1], carton 6, dossier 6, 7 May 1784, and DC[6] 260, fol. 162 (1774).
15. Arsenal, ms. Bast. 10141, 27 January 1758.
16. Ibid., 20 January 1758. Authorities in the grain markets of North China in the early twentieth century felt that hereditary brokerage would serve as a guarantee of the transmission of knowledge and dexterity. Y. Li and J.B. Tayler, "Grain Marketing in Hopei Province," *Chinese Social and Political Science Review* 17 (April 1933): 123.
17. I could not locate the notarial act, signed before Delamarche on 8 October 1742.
18. AN, Y 11232, 17 August 1745.

senior commissaire of the central market quarter. In March of 1736 commissaire de Courcy appointed Marie Carré, the wife of one Charles Fournier,
whose profession was not mentioned. She was given a space nine feet long by
seven feet wide on the row on the left side of the selling floor as one entered
by the gate of the Pointe St.-Eustache. Curiously, it was stipulated that Dame
Fournier was to receive the merchandise of her "ordinary" merchants and "to
help them to sell the said flour," the assumption being that the merchants
would be there with her, despite the fact that the point of the brokerage
system was to spare them the trip to Paris. The commission also enjoined her
not to obstruct the public thoroughfare with her wagons, encroach on her
colleagues' terrain, or dispose of her place without the commissaire's explicit
consent. Dame Fournier, like most of her fellow brokers, ignored all these
stipulations. In May 1739, de Courcy assigned a place to Catherine Lazure,
despite the fact that neither she nor her husband had any experience in grain
or flour affairs. Sieur Payen, whom de Courcy named in 1742, must have
enjoyed his special favor, for he received a place twelve feet in length, about
25 percent larger than most places—a veritable boon in this world of exi-
guity.[19]

Women and Widow Brokers

Women abounded in the marketplaces of old-regime France. Usually they
were limited to petty exchanges which, though often critical to the survival of
the individuals in question, collectively did not have much raw commercial
significance.[20] The brokerage, in which women were present in substantial
number, was a glaring exception. Factoring was a complex responsibility that
required the broker to do things that women usually did not do, such as
perform collection and banking functions with large sums of money and engage in relatively frequent civil litigation. It is not clear why women were
permitted to assume these functions. They may have been considered temperamentally better suited to be vendors than men, as in antiquity.[21] It may
also be that women did not really exercise their responsibilities as independent agents. We know that in many cases they acted morally (if not always

19. AN, Y 11223, 24 March 1736; Y 11226, 27 May 1739; Y 11223, n.d. (Payen might
have been a *marchand grainier*).
20. The women who proliferate in the marketplaces of Africa and Latin America appear
to have similar functions. B. H. Hidden, "The Yoruba Rural Market," in Paul Bohannan and
George Dalton, eds., *Markets in Africa* (Evanston, 1962), pp. 103–17; Beverly Chinas,
"Zapotec Viajeras," in Scott Cook and Martin Diskin, eds., *Markets in Oaxaca* (Austin,
1976). Yet as Sidney Mintz has shown, the role of these women was by no means always
marginal. "Men, Women and Trade," *Comparative Studies in Society and History* 13 (July
1971): 247–69.
21. Polanyi, *Livelihood of Man*, p. 191.

legally) for their husbands, who had other occupations, or they took over the brokerage after a husband's death. Françoise Bazin (Girard), Denise Copin (Prévost), Laurence Prévost (Villain), and Anne Chabin (Boulanger) were among the wives/widows who served as brokers. Some women appear to have had more or less autonomous brokerage enterprises, though it is possible that they would have been unable to operate without the moral and material guarantees provided by their husbands. Jacquelan Delahaye was the wife of a cavalier in the Regiment du Lac. Marie Olive's husband was a stocking maker. Catherine Legrand was married to a wine merchant. Jeanne Delaistre's husband, Louis Pellerin, was a miller, which gave her direct access to the flour milieu as well as to baker contacts. Margueritte Petit's first husband was a bourgeois de Paris, her second a mercer. Madeleine Sevin was the wife of a master clock maker.[22]

Still, whatever the hidden dynamics of female participation, women came to play *in public* a cardinal role in the brokerage very different from the role they were expected and allowed to play in other domains. They acted with initiative and authority and made important business decisions on their own. By no means did they always have a man behind them. Widowhood did not divest women brokers of their freedom of action. And Jeanne Bigot may not have been the only broker who infiltrated the profession as a single woman and remained unmarried. I suspect that this ambiguous and more or less accidental itinerary was one of the ways by which women began to surmount some of the professional barriers of old-regime society. The marketplace, a circumscribed and partly female space, provided the path.

Critics of the broker wives contended that this system served as a cover for the husbands to undertake illegal grain and flour commerce. While their wives prepared paper alibis for them, it was alleged, the husbands made purchases in the farms and off the markets, amassed hoards, and diverted the supply from the capital.[23] There was some clandestine trading by brokers, though it is not clear that the husbands did it, but these charges were surely exaggerated. More serious, because it was more concrete, was the reproach that broker widows manipulated their husbands' estates so as to avoid responsibility for paying their debts, but at the same time continued their husbands' brokerage business. This issue was joined with considerable éclat by Claude Lemèze, a prominent grain trader who had distinguished himself by his civic zeal during the dearth of 1725–26. Lemèze won a judgment against his broker, Louis Sergent, for the payment of 4,000 livres for grain sold at the Halle. Before Lemèze could compel collection, Sergent died, and shortly after that his widow remarried. She and her new husband refused to honor

22. AN, Y 11229, 10 May 1742; Y 11237, 10 October 1750; Y 11226, 27 May 1739; Y 12608, 19 March 1760; AN, X^{2B} 991, 14 August 1742; Archives Seine-Paris, DC^6 18, fol. 273, 23 October 1773, and DC^6 21, fol. 172, 13 April 1779.
23. Bertin and Dambraine, "Mémoire," Arsenal, ms. 2588.

Sergent's debts, though Lemèze had no trouble proving that Sergent's wife had sold grain at his place and therefore had collaborated in the brokerage all along. The parlement decided the case strictly in terms of customary law, without regard for the public interest. Lemèze was rebuffed: the widow Sergent was known for operating her own small-grain business and was not considered "a recognized public merchant in the brokerage." Lemèze could only pursue Sergent's estate, not his widow, since she had renounced the succession precisely on the grounds that it was too onerous to assume.[24]

Angry and frustrated, Lemèze put the government on notice that if the courts denied him elementary justice on these narrow grounds, they could not afford to neglect the implications for the provisioning of Paris. The merchant announced "that he cannot without ruining himself continue this trade if the brokers of the Halle . . . can with impunity use their wives to siphon off the price of grain and if their wives . . . though themselves transacting sales and purchases and receiving payment are discharged from all pursuits once they renounce their [late] husbands' estates." In support of Lemèze's appeal to the royal council to quash the parlementary arrêt, twelve well-known Paris suppliers stated that they, too, "would be forced to abandon their provisioning" if they did not receive proper legal guarantees. The council rejected the appeal more or less reluctantly on the grounds that the civil jurisprudence favored the defendant. Sensitive, however, to the "police implications" of the affair, the council decided to propose a royal declaration making wives "responsible for the price of goods absolutely necessary for sustenance" that were entrusted to their husbands.[25] I have found no trace of this declaration, but the fact that the issue did not arise again suggests that the desired modifications in either law or practice were made.

The Functions of the Broker

The primary function of a broker was to serve the itinerant merchants, especially the flour dealers, who regularly supplied the capital. These merchants chose brokers who they believed would turn their merchandise over rapidly at the best price, who would remit payment most expeditiously, who would extend credit prudently, and who would recover accounts receivable energetically. Mealmen, unlike bakers, tended to deal through one broker; they felt that this was the best way to maximize their commercial leverage. If a pratik relationship developed, it would usually last for many years. Ducler

24. But compare the case of Dame Raoult, another small-grains dealer whose husband was a grain broker. It would have been unfair to hold her responsible for his business, for, as she clearly demonstrated, "he had plunged into all sorts of debauchery, especially that of wine," to the neglect of his affairs. AN, Y 11219, 10 February, 13 March 1732.

25. AN, F[12] 76, 2 June 1729.

stuck with the same broker for thirty years, Chapon for eighteen, Daubigny for seventeen, and Dezobry for twelve.[26]

Prior to selling merchandise, the broker graded it to facilitate sales (reserving certain grades for his pratik bakers). In addition to having a sound knowledge of the origins, types, qualities, and weights and measures of grain and flour, the broker had to be able to predict how much merchandise was likely to arrive the next day, how much of it could be absorbed, and so on. He stored unsold goods and looked after their keep. Upon instructions from his merchants, he transferred grain and flour to any local address and throughout the region as well, despite police prohibitions against removing "subsistence merchandise" once it had come on the market site. Like the powerful brokers who dominated the grain markets of North China in the first half of the twentieth century and like the landlord brokers who still run the cattle markets of West Africa, a number of eighteenth-century French brokers provided personal accommodations for their merchants and fed and entertained them as part of the eternal client courtship.[27]

The brokers also provided a number of valuable banking services. Brokers Fleury, Guillin, Barbier, Pilloy, Lagache, and Jubin "advanced" money to their merchants, ranging from small sums to cover their expenses while visiting Paris (12 livres, 72 livres, etc.) to quite large amounts that might have been destined to finance wheat purchases (3,500 livres). The brokers considered these advances loans, for the money passed hands before the merchandise that served as collateral was sold. Critics charged that these advances should not be called loans, for they really represented sums due to the mealmen for the sale of their flour. According to this view, the brokers called them loans in order to extort interest from the mealmen and to make them feel dependent. As far as I can tell, the advances in question seem to have been free customer services, undertaken to create goodwill to sustain commercial activity.[28] Brokers also helped to arrange transactions between mealmen and their suppliers, as well as transfers of money. Broker Guillaume de La Salle served as intermediary between his mealman Pierre de Ricq and Ricq's miller at Etampes. Flour dealer Berthault asked his broker to forward 15,000 livres that he had left on deposit with him to Aubert senior, a Paris grain merchant.[29] The brokers kept accounts for merchants who were uncomfortable with books.

26. Archives Seine-Paris, D5B⁶ 5655.

27. See Li and Tayler, "Grain Marketing in Hopei Province," p. 142, and Abner Cohen, "The Social Organization of Credit in a West African Cattle Market," *Africa* 35 (January 1965): 10–11. Madame de Laguet, the sister of a broker, ran a boarding house (the Cheval Noir) reserved for flour merchants. *Tableau universel et raisonné de la ville de Paris* (Paris, 1760), p. 37.

28. Archives Seine-Paris: D4B⁶ 49-2956, October 1773; D4B⁶ 83-5559, 10 December 1781; D5B⁶ 753; D4B⁶ 61-3909; D5B⁶ 3681.

29. AN, X¹ᴮ 9435, 25 May and 28 June 1770.

The brokers did not have the same autonomy with all of their mealmen. When the flour merchants were present on the trading floor they made the final decisions on price bargaining. Nevertheless, they depended on their brokers for crucial market information, which saved them considerable time and helped reduce their risks. Other dealers sent specific instructions that circumscribed broker freedom of action. "Madame," wrote Perot, a miller from Crosne, "here are the twelve sacks of flour that I ship without having had the honor to discuss this deal with you. You can go ahead and sell the lot, but I beg you not for less than 50 livres the sack. I shall have the honor of seeing you next week."[30] Probably a majority of suppliers left all negotiations up to the brokers, but the latter could expect to be obliged to explain the prices obtained item by item.

The brokers received a commission from their mealmen in return for sales and attendant services. It is likely that the rate varied from broker to broker as a result of special arrangements, supplementary charges, bonuses, and so on. Information on fees is extremely sparse and it is never absolutely certain whether data drawn from different sources are comparable. Widow Rivière received about 12 livres the voie (presumably of twelve sacks, but certain brokers received voies of eleven or less) in 1757. This amount is plausible, although somewhat precociously high. It may also include noncommission market costs borne by the broker.[31] Pierre Chicheret, Rivière's contemporary, charged only 4.5 to 5 livres, but he was a new, "reform" broker and may have been under pressure from inspector Poussot to moderate his commission.[32] Several years later, representatives of the measurers and porters testified in a consular court hearing that "the usage of the merchants was to give 12 livres to the broker for each voie of flour they sold."[33] This rate was confirmed a few years later by two of the most stringent critics of the brokerage system, who would not have missed the chance to cite a higher figure had they deemed it plausible.[34] Widow Delaistre only charged 17 sous 6 deniers the sack (or 10.5 livres the voie) in 1768, but the client in question was the king, whose emergency flour was marketed in the midst of a crisis, and there is little doubt that the broker was expected to make a civic-minded concession.[35] Given the fact that the commission had been close to the 1 livre per sack level since the late fifties, the government's decision to fix the ceiling at 1 livre 1.5 sous the sack in 1779 seems quite reasonable. We cannot determine how much of this

30. Notes in the binding of business register D5B⁶ 4307, September–December 1772, in Archives Seine-Paris.

31. Archives Seine-Paris, D4B⁶ 17-831, 18 October 1757. Cf. the ambiguous evaluation in AN, H* 1867, fol. 432, 22 May 1758.

32. Arsenal, ms. Bast. 10141, 7 June 1758.

33. [De] Vanne to consular jurisdiction, 4 March 1762, Archives Seine-Paris, D6B⁶, carton 4.

34. Bertin and Dambraine, "Mémoire," Arsenal, ms. 2588.

35. "Etat général des ventes des farines," 1 April–10 December 1768, AN, F¹¹ 1194.

fee covered real costs sustained by the broker and how much could be considered profit. The measurers and porters suggested that at least half the commission was pure compensation, but there is no way to verify this claim. If this were true, it would mean that in order to earn 7,000 livres net—the highest range of income made by the brokers, according to Poussot; barely a fraction of what the top brokers earned according to Bertin and Dambraine—a broker would have to sell 1,167 voies in a year, more than two and a half times what Chicheret sold in 1773, one of his better years.[36]

Brokers supplemented their income in a number of ways. Those like Lagache, who invested heavily in transport matériel, rented out their horses and wagons with or without drivers to mealmen and bakers.[37] Virtually all of the brokers did some retail selling of flour and small grains. The truly substantial profits, however, were to be made in a wholesale speculative trade in grain and/or flour. Though such traffic was expressly forbidden by the police, it was relatively common at a moderate level of activity. In his business failure deposition, broker Viollet acknowledged the loss of 5,333 livres on "merchandise that I had [manufactured] by different millers and that I sold at the Halle."[38] Nor did Viollet hesitate to enter purchases he made from various mealmen in his business register, which was supposed to be examined each month by the senior commissaire of the central markets department.[39] Broker Aubert bought widely in the farms and markets of the hinterland and on the Halle, and he had most of this grain converted into flour that he sold at his own place.[40] One of the complaints that the other brokers had against their colleague Mabille was that, under the cover of police patronage, he smuggled his illegal flour into the capital illegally, en droiture.[41]

Brokered Flour Supply at the Halle

The Delalande registers provide us with the only available data on "brokered" supply (see Table 26). The average number of brokers for the nine-year period was 19, each of whom handled on the average 10 merchants. Five brokers from the 1725 list, probably victims of the crisis, left the business by the end of the year. They were replaced by 7 new brokers in 1726. Virtually no new faces appeared during the next seven years for which we have data. The mean number of merchants who marketed their merchandise through brokerage was 191 a year, 180 if one eliminates the crisis years 1725 and 1726.

36. Archives Seine-Paris, D5B⁶ 1870. In the year XI, brokers took a commission varying between 2 and 3 percent. D5B⁶ 5656.
37. Ibid., D4B⁶ 61-3909, especially the losses column.
38. Ibid., D4B⁶ 25-1269, 1 July 1773.
39. Ibid., D5B⁶ 4385.
40. Ibid., D5B⁶ 3282.
41. Arsenal, ms. Bast. 10141 (4 December 1759).

TABLE 26
Brokered flour supply at the Halle, 1725–33

Year	Number of brokers	Number of merchants	Average number of merchants per broker
1725	18	257	14.3
1726	20	204	10.2
1727	21	191	9.1
1728	20	194	9.7
1729	22	195	8.9
1730	19	211(?)	11.1
1731	17	165	9.7
1732	19	159	8.4
1733	17	142	8.4

The averages must not be allowed to conceal significant differences in broker strength. In 1732 broker Delaistre had only 2 clients and broker Mastrait 1, while Laroche *fils* and Beranger had respectively 21 and 27. The range in 1733 was from 1 to 21 clients, in 1739 from 3 to 37 merchants. Nor was one client as good as another. In 1727 the mean supply per brokered flour dealer was 89.7 muids (538.2 sacks), but in real terms it ranged from 12 muids (72 sacks) to 520 muids (3,120 sacks). In that same year mean provision per broker amounted to 816 muids (4,896 sacks). But whereas Delaistre sponsored only 2.1 percent of the total flour supply (345 muids or 2,070 sacks), Beranger commanded 21.7 percent of the flour traffic (3,568 muids, or a staggering 21,408 sacks). Beranger, however, could not claim the largest mean provision per merchant. While his clients averaged 111.5 muids (or 669 sacks) per merchant, broker Vieille's 11 merchants averaged 152 muids (or 912 sacks).

The aggregate flour supply data in the Delalande registers is not entirely satisfactory. For the years 1727, 1728, 1732, and 1733 it indicates a non-brokered blatier flour supply comprising between 13.2 and 17.5 percent of the total flour supply at the Halle. Yet for the years 1729 through 1731 the blatier figure mysteriously falls to an average of 1.7 percent. Moreover, I am inclined to believe that the nonbrokered merchants contributed a significantly larger amount than Delalande allows for. Nor were nonbrokered dealers necessarily of the extremely modest blatier category. I suspect that a number of them rivaled the factored merchants in their annual provision.

The Business of the Brokers

The business records of several brokers give us a closer glimpse of everyday flour provisioning. On 19 December 1778 Dame Bokain had 515 sacks available for purchase. They were supplied by twenty-four different merchants based in nineteen different hinterland locations, embracing the entire provisioning zone from Chartres in the southwest to Soissons in the northeast and from the Vexin in the west to the edge of Champagne in the east. The average size of stock per merchant amounted to 21.46 sacks, but the real range went from 3 sacks to 71. The latter belonged to a merchant from Noyon, who rebuked his broker for not turning it over rapidly enough.[42]

Chicheret had substantial dealings in 1773: he sold 5,156 sacks in 317 separate transactions, for a monthly average of 430 sacks and 32 transactions. He probably had no more than twenty regular merchant clients. In the month of April, sixteen merchants shipped him 792 sacks, for an average of almost a voie per week, a cadence of remarkable assiduity. Chicheret's sales were worth over a quarter of a million livres in 1773, high prices swelling the billing level. As far as one can tell, there seems to be at least a six-week lag between the time the broker received the merchandise and the time that he acquitted payment. For reasons that are not clear—I suspect that Chicheret had trouble collecting from bakers and paying dealers, who began as a result to turn elsewhere—the broker's business abruptly disintegrated. In 1774 he handled less than half as many sales. In 1775 he averaged only 81 sacks a month in fewer than 7 transactions. Still, there are some indications that Chicheret had tried to spread the risk faced by each merchant supplier by breaking up his shipment and selling each piece to a different baker. Then, if one of the baker buyers defaulted, the loss would not fall entirely on one of the broker's merchants.[43]

Broker Charles Viollet ran a more modest operation than Chicheret. He averaged under 90 sacks a month. His sales were rather small in magnitude, averaging 5.5 sacks per transaction. During a seventeen-month period beginning in October 1759, he sold to twenty-one different bakers. Three bakers made purchases more than once a week and three others were frequent buyers. The bulk of the bakers, however, were rather casual customers most of whom visited Viollet's place only once or twice during this interval. The broker always asked for a down payment, and as a rule was paid promptly. Let us follow the buying and remitting rhythm of one of his best customers, a relatively small forain baker named Delaubray (see Table 27).[44]

Day-to-day data on payments by brokers to their suppliers are extremely rare. Broker Aubert received 10 sacks from miller Desachet on 3 August 1774

42. AN, Y 15388, 19 December 1778.
43. Archives Seine-Paris, D5B[6] 1870. A series of figures in the Delaroche register for the period 1728 through 1735 indicate a mean annual supply of 11,248 sacks—937 a month, representing the reception of 2 to 3 voies every day. These figures are implausibly high even for a leading broker. I suspect that they refer to activities that transcended Delaroche's own brokerage. D5B[6] 3681.
44. Ibid., D5B[6] 1963. Widow Rivière also ran a small brokerage comprising about a dozen suppliers, but she had at least sixty-nine baker customers, mostly casual buyers. D4B[6] 17–831, 18 October 1757.

TABLE 27

Purchases of flour and payments by baker to broker, 1759–60

Date of purchase	Number of sacks	Date of full payment
31 October 1759	3	5 November 1759
8 November	2	12 November
14 November	5	26 November
3 December	2	?
5 December	2	26 December
20 December	2	22 December
22 December	2	26 December
24 December	1	26 December
26 December	5	10 January 1760
2 January 1760	8	28 January
11 January	1	28 January
21 January	6	7 February
28 January	6	11 February
7 February	6	20 February
11 February	2	19 February

and paid him exactly one week later. In six earlier transactions involving the same client, Aubert remitted on the average eighteen days after receipt of the merchandise. The quickest payment was the very same day in one instance; the longest delay was thirty-four days.[45] Broker Lagache was perpetually behind in his payments to flour merchant Cassin (see Table 28). After several months, Lagache had covered only a little more than three-quarters of the price due his client. Indeed, after the first four months, he had paid only a little more than half the sum due to Cassin, which may explain why the latter reduced his shipments.[46]

The Brokers and the Bakers

The brokers wooed the bakers in a number of ways. Almost invariably, they offered a line of credit, the magnitude of which depended on the baker's consumption and his reputation. Often the broker was caught in a double pratik bind, torn between the fear of alienating a baker client by pressing too hard for payment and the need to appease his merchant clients. The plaintive note sent by one broker to master baker Albert bears witness to this dilemma: "Monsieur, here are the twelve sacks of flour that we settled on at the price of

45. Ibid., D5B⁶ 4307.
46. Ibid., D5B⁶ 2638. In the financial statement Lagache filed in 1773, he acknowledged a debt to Cassin of only 1,100 livres. D4B⁶ 61-3909.

40 livres the sack. I beg you to give as much money on account as you possibly can to my driver, as well as your empty sacks."[47]

The brokers tried to furnish the types and qualities of flour favored by the bakers. Brokers handling many different mealmen could generally offer a richer array of flours and in some instances a more generous line of credit. Certain brokers were known for flour made of Beauce wheat or for a middling meal rich in gluten or for a mid-white flour that was yellower than the competitor's. In any case, each broker assured each of his baker clients that he was favoring him in terms of quality over all the others. Although the brokers were eager to please the bakers, disputes over flour quality were one of the main sources of contention between them. Four bakers complained that broker Gaillon had sold them flour that produced bread "totally defective and unworthy of entering the human body and not even good enough for animals." Revealing a curiously narrow conception of her function, Gaillon denied responsibility on the grounds that the flour was sent by "an individual from the faubourg St.-Antoine whom she did not know at all." Master baker Caussin sued his factor for selling him flour "with a very bad taste." Caussin felt betrayed because he had counted on *his* broker to protect him against such risks. Master baker Bontems and broker Chicheret came to blows in a tavern when the former censured the latter for passing off mediocre flour belonging to one of the broker's preferred mealmen as first-rate merchandise.[48]

To their pratik partners brokers promised priority deliveries or rapid measuring (through more-or-less corrupt arrangement with the measurers). A

TABLE 28

Sale of flour by broker and payment to merchants, 1771–72

Time period	Number of sacks	Price obtained for flour sold in livres	Payment by broker in livres
December 1771	40	2,005	1,783
January 1772	60	3,106	1,127
February	50	2,545	1,518
March	50	2,010	1,158
April	30	1,631	2,794
May	60	2,510	1,268
June	30	1,187	1,874
	320	14,994	11,522

47. Ibid., D5B[6] 733, 21 March 1788.
48. AN, Y 11227, 15 December 1740; Archives Seine-Paris, D6B[6], carton 3, 11 June 1761; AN, Y 12605, 18 November 1757.

number of brokers undertook to provide the transportation to the shop free of charge.[49] The brokers lured the bakers with various kinds of rebates, bonuses, and price differentials. Most common was the "good measure" premium, from 3 to 10 bushels per voie, that each baker was supposed to believe was reserved especially for him. Broker Gaillon charged different bakers different prices for the same quality of flour in approximately the same amounts. Broker Delaroche appears to have offered price incentives for cash payments.[50] Brokers such as Chicheret and Pilloy urged their bakers to visit them in the taverns that served as their offices so that their deals could be properly sealed.[51] Brokers Delaistre and Gosset were related to bakers, upon whom they counted to favor their conquests in the baker milieu.[52]

Shrewd bakers shopped around carefully to play one broker off against another in order to obtain a larger bonus or better price or quality. One or two doses of *brawta,* however, did not suffice to draw the baker into a pratik commitment. Many bakers stubbornly resisted pressure to buy exclusively from a given broker. Master baker Larcher, who made all his Paris purchases for a twenty-year period from broker Delaroche, was an exception—most bakers opted for a more eclectic buying strategy. Unable to find satisfaction at the place of broker Dame Frémont, Marie-Anne Nerodeaux, wife of a master baker, bargained with two other brokers before finally making a deal with a fourth, de La Salle, for two voies. Similarly, Françoise Picard, wife of a Porcherons baker, announced aloud to a handful of brokers that they could bid for her business.[53] I have the impression that bakers frequently dispatched their wives to the Halle to buy because they stood a better chance of fending off the *vendeuses* and *tendeuses* competing for sales commissions from the brokers.[54] When a more-or-less "regular" client abandoned his broker, the event made news throughout the marketplace and was almost invariably marked by anger and recrimination.[55]

Next to the unfaithful baker, the baker whom the broker most resented was the one who failed to return the empty flour sacks. Usually the flour merchants owned the sacks, though in some cases the brokers themselves rented sacks out to their mealmen, or arranged for rental.[56] The merchants

49. AN, Y 12625, 30 March 1775.

50. AN, H 1867, fol. 432 (22 May 1758); AN, Y 12606, 24 April 1758 and Y 11227, 15 December 1740; Archives Seine-Paris, D5B[6] 5655.

51. AN, Y 12604, 12 August 1756, and Y 12605, 18 November 1757. The Croix d'Or right opposite the Halle was a favorite meeting place of brokers, mealmen, and bakers.

52. AN, Y 12605, 25 October 1757; Archives Seine-Paris, DC[6] 13, fol. 169, 29 October 1754.

53. AN, Y 12615, 3 October 1766, and Y 12608, 31 March 1760.

54. On the *vendeuses,* see AN, Y 11232, 17 August 1745, and Archives Seine-Paris, D2B[6] 802, 17 October 1746.

55. See, for instance, the confrontation between Dame Jubin and master baker Gombault. AN, Y 11219, 4, 7 July 1732.

56. AN, Y 12622, 7 March 1772, and Archives Seine-Paris, D2B[6] 1109, 15 May 1772.

usually expected their factors to assure the return of the sacks, marked with their names or the names of the renters, from their baker customers. The brokers complained that a shortage of sacks often delayed flour shipments. Moreover, at 3 to 5 or sometimes even 7 livres apiece, the sum in question represented a significant investment. A large number of bakers were delinquent in returning the sacks, through indifference or indolence or because they found them useful for storing grain or charcoal. They also cut them up to make cloths for proofing the bread or aprons and shorts for their journeymen, or used them as insulation or as windows to keep pigeons out of granaries. The sacks that they finally returned were often "spoiled," "torn," "burned," and "no longer in service."[57] Even after the parlementary arrêt of 4 June 1761 that required bakers to return the sacks within a month of delivery or face both a fine of 50 livres and a levy equal to the cost of a replacement of the missing sacks, the bakers showed little enthusiasm for meeting their responsibility.[58] At one point, for example, in February 1762, twelve bakers owed broker Jacques de Monnery an average of almost 5 sacks apiece. One baker owed broker Frémont 17 sacks, another owed broker Mabille 16, a third owed broker Barbier 15. Baker Matry refused to return 109 sacks to various mealmen, while his colleagues Bernier and Lafosse withheld 84 each.[59]

Recovery was a process of gradual escalation. First the broker summoned the baker to pay up, presumably in amicable terms. Then he sent his placeboys to request or demand collection. Not infrequently, they got into brawls with the baker or his journeymen.[60] The next step was to file suit in the consular court, but after 1760 the brokers were able to request direct police action, which they preferred to sometimes protracted civil pursuit. The commissaire of the central markets ordered negligent bakers to return their sacks or face jail; he had their bake and storage rooms searched; he threatened to ban them from the Halle. The task of recovery was immensely simplified by the creation of a sack-recovery bureau. First proposed at the time of the introduction of the weight station, this bureau did not function effectively until the opening of the new Halle. Vigier, an experienced police official trained by Machurin, oversaw the bureau for a number of years, assisted by Poilleux and Pierre Mousset, a veteran of fifteen years as a broker placeboy. This office had considerable success in accelerating the turnover of sacks and reducing vandalism and dereliction.[61]

57. AN, Y 9539, 22 August 1763; Y 12611, 25 February 1762; and Y 12613, 8 June 1764.

58. AN, X^{1B} 3748. The sense of this arrêt was twice reiterated in police ordinances of 27 June 1764 and 16 May 1771. AN, Y 9499.

59. AN, Y 12611, 25 February 1762; Y 12613, 31 January 1764; Y 12611, 24 February 1762; Y 12612, 22 August 1763; Y 9474, October 1771. See also Y 12611, 29 July 1762 and 20 October 1762.

60. AN, Y 12612, 25 August 1763. Cf. the case of Barbier's placegirl, beaten up by baker Marois. Ibid., 22 August 1763.

61. AN, Y 11386, 4 November 1772; Y 9474, 21 June 1771 and 15 November 1771; Y 9632, 9 February 1770.

Broker Feuds

The major source of tension among the brokers, as among the merchants we have met, was the competition for clients. This struggle for success, or survival, was particularly acute among the brokers because it took place simultaneously on two different fields: they had to worry not only about pleasing the buyers (the bakers), but also about winning the favor of the sellers (the mealmen). Animosities were intensified by the extremely confined professional, physical, and psychological space in which they functioned. The brokers were relatively few in number, they worked literally elbow to elbow every day, and whether they wanted to or not became a part of each other's lives. The occasions for the quarrels that envenomed the ambience at the Halle are familiar: alleged efforts to steal another's clients in one manner or another; attempts to sully the reputation of a rival; intimidation, moral and physical; subversion of business through lack of cooperation and bad-faith gestures.

The very first on-the-job lesson that Catherine Legrand, wife of a wine merchant and caterer and a newly named broker, learned was that "peace [with the others] is a difficult thing to obtain in a market like this." A number of colleagues were nice to her, and she depended on them "for she had not been raised in this profession" and needed their advice. But her immediate neighbor, Dame Bazin-Girard, wife of a fruit seller, was relentlessly hostile. "Violent" and "fiery" in character, Bazin-Girard resented the newcomer's successful debut. This "commercial jealousy" led her to "interrupt" Legrand's dealings in numerous ways. She spread the word that Legrand could only have risen so fast by letting others—specifically the measurers and porters—mount her. Not yet inured to this harsh and vulgar transactional discourse, Legrand was concerned about the repercussions these insults would have on her business and on her family life.[62]

It is no surprise to learn that beneath the rough and hot-tempered exterior of Dame Bazin-Girard lurked a businesswoman who did not blush to pose as a victim of just the sort of abuse that she meted out. She filed charges against Pierre Ancelin, a broker located on the other side of Catherine Legrand's place. Bazin-Girard complained that Ancelin's placeboy whipped and insulted one of her merchant clients and publicly called her a "bitch" and a "beggar" and the widow of a "thief." The broker felt that these "calumnies" recited "in the Halle in the presence of several merchants" could jeopardize her business.[63]

Ancelin had been vexed with Bazin-Girard at least since 1745, when he accused her of luring away one of his women sellers who scoured the market

62. AN, Y 11226, 27 May 1739.
63. AN, Y 11236, 24 June 1749.

floor, the taverns, and the bread markets in search of baker buyers. The seller had a different explanation for her defection: Ancelin beat and insulted her. Ancelin was also charged with assaulting Dame Bazin-Girard's chief helper, a woman named Marie-Jeanne Hervieux, whose husband also worked in the flour sector. The victim blamed the attack on a long-festering "animosity" inspired by Ancelin's "professional jealousy and the pain it caused him to see her take so seriously the interests of the person for whom she works."[64]

An erstwhile flour placeboy himself, Pierre Ancelin, like Dame Bazin-Girard, had a reputation as "a violent, hot-tempered person," yet like her he also became quickly indignant when he was the object of aggression.[65] Six years after Marie-Jeanne Hervieux denounced him to the police, Ancelin filed charges against her. While her punches, claws, and kicks did not hurt him, her words seared him deeply—she had impugned his integrity in the midst of a busy market by calling him "the bankrupter of the flour merchants" and "a fucking pimp [Jean Foutre de maquereau], devourer of the wealth of the merchants." With a slight variation, the theme was rehearsed in another encounter that mortified Ancelin, who was portrayed not only as a thief-embezzler but also as a man incapable of managing his own affairs. In front of several of his merchants, the widow Etape, placegirl for the broker widow Frémont, called him "a tricky bankrupter who had eaten up 150,000 livres belonging to the flour merchants." Ancelin discerned in these words "a blow to destroy him and to cause him to lose his credit." Still another time Ancelin was vilified in the same manner, this time by Flaquet, broker Pilloy's placeboy. In a tavern frequented by flour merchants, Flaquet called him "the bankrupter, the robber who had ruined all the merchants."[66]

It is not easy to imagine how "the public," especially the flour merchants, reacted to such accusations. They were stock epithets, echoed a hundred times a day in confrontations in all the different market trades. On the other hand, the focus on a more-or-less specific kind of dishonesty and on the chronic strain between the broker and his clients may have raised damaging doubts about Ancelin, whether or not they were founded in commercial reality. Ancelin had every reason to be alarmed by this confluence of insinuations.

Justice at the Halle meant that virtually everybody had his turn on the pillory. Broker Michel Pilloy, whose placeboy helped to stigmatize Ancelin, found himself the target of widow Barbier, an infuriated broker. One of Barbier's merchants, Lejeune of Senlis, was unhappy with the relatively low price that she obtained for his flour and intimated that he was considering

64. AN, Y 10559, 29 April 1745, and Y 13640, 3 April 1745.

65. According to one report, Ancelin began as a domestic servant. His sense of honor must have been sharpened by his keen awareness of his own upward ascension. AN, Y 10559, 13 April 1745.

66. AN, Y 11238, 13 February and 14 December 1751; Y 11241, 15 July 1754.

switching allegiance to Pilloy, whose reputation he understood to be excellent. Barbier hurried to disabuse him. Pilloy, she announced, had been in jail and was so afraid of being imprisoned again that he was reluctant to leave his house. Moreover, his affairs were in terrible disorder. This rumor spread rapidly from the Cabaret de la Fortune in front of the Halle to the entire market community. Pilloy was horrified to learn that at least one of his flour dealers had made inquiries into his standing with the concierge of the porters and with a master baker.[67] This was not the first time that Pilloy's stature and capacity had been questioned. A porter's helper scoffed aloud at a flour delivery addressed to Pilloy: "It's not for this bugger Pilloy, it should be for brokers who pay [their merchants]." Pilloy, he added, was "a spy" and an operator "who tried to draw away the merchants of other brokers."[68] Now it is true that Pilloy had close relations with inspector Poussot, whom he kept informed on the attitude and behavior of the Halle personnel, and that he became a sort of police auxiliary, a huissier, or sheriff, just at about the time that he was obliged to file for business failure (as Dame Barbier had obliquely foretold).

Broker Dame Morisset, an aggressive tradeswoman, openly avowed that her goal was to outdo her neighbor and sister broker Jeanne Bigot. The method she chose was "to destroy her [rival's] reputation" by depicting her as an unreliable person of no means and lowly status and thus unfit as a commercial partner. She told Bigot's merchants that their broker "does not have a penny, that she borrows from everyone right and left, that she lives in a garret." In addition to presenting herself as a more solid agent, she offered an almost irresistible incentive, but one that was generally decried in the corporate ambience of the Halle: "to take a lower commission from the merchants." Morisset worked the other side of the fence as well by warning prospective baker buyers that Bigot would "trick" and "cheat" them. With a good sense of the psychology of demoralization, Morisset did not fail to bombard the obese Bigot with tender sobriquets such as "fat pig" and "fat horrid creature."[69] To demonstrate the worthlessness of her rival widow broker Lory and put a taboo on her place, widow broker Boulanger denounced her for bearing four bastards in her *pays,* spending time in the hospital (either as a whore or as a beggar), and employing "rotten" women helpers who were "tramps known in the brothels and on the Pont-Neuf."[70]

67. AN, Y 12607, 22 January 1759; Arsenal, ms. Bast. 10141 (26 February 1759).

68. AN, Y 12604, 16 October 1756. Just a week earlier, another porter helper publicly insulted Pilloy and raised questions about his integrity vis-à-vis his flour dealers. It should be noted, however, that the porter helpers were enraged that they had just lost a 10-sous perquisite on each voie of flour, perhaps in part because of Pilloy's opposition to it. Y 12604, 5 October 1756.

69. AN, Y 12617, 30 April 1765. Cf. the acrimonious disputes among West African cattle brokers over the "stealing of dealers." Cohen, "Social Organization of Credit," pp. 11–12.

70. AN, Y 11235, 24 July 1748.

Cramped business space impelled the brokers to practice a sort of territorial imperative despite the manifestly blurred boundaries of the market. Brokers Delaroche and widow Rivière clashed through their intermediary place aides. François Ducormier, Rivière's boy, stepped into Delaroche's area in order to talk to a baker who had in the past bought from Rivière but who was now dealing with Delaroche. Outraged by this encroachment, Delaroche's helper Dame Flaquet (the wife of Ancelin's scourge) berated Ducormier "for going after buyers on another's place." As the verbal exchange became heated, Ducormier gallantly allowed that "if you were not a woman, Manon, I would apply my hand to you and teach you how to speak to me." To which she replied, "Then I'll give you a lesson," and "delivered a great blow beneath his left eye."[71]

The rights of space and the obligations of collegiality caused bickering. Unable to store all her merchandise, Jeanne Bigot temporarily put some across the line in Pierre Chicheret's place. Chicheret indemnified himself by selling it, keeping the money, and treating himself to the pleasure of calling her "a fucking thief," apparently an allusion to previous friction between them. The helpers of broker Beranger and widow Delaistre brawled over the extra space that the former appropriated in order to receive a big delivery.[72]

A similar confrontation enabled broker Bazin-Girard to demonstrate once again that she knew how to protect her interests. Marguerite, the placegirl of broker widow Villain, refused to permit Dame Bazin-Girard to store a large shipment on her space. Bazin-Girard turned on her violently, all the more so because Marguerite had once worked for her (the turnover and circulation of subaltern personnel created a web of intimate and grating links among the brokers). Bazin-Girard struck her and reviled her as a woman who "hid her [bastard] daughters in a convent" and who came "from a family of canaille."[73]

"Professional jealousy" snapped even family bonds. Jacques Frémont shared a broker's place with his sister, who apparently agreed to run the business that they inherited from their father for their mutal benefit. Under the influence of her husband, Pâris, however, she excluded Frémont entirely, reducing his wife to the status of placegirl and inviting him to start his own business if he was discontent. Frémont did not bother, it seems, to heap public discredit on his sister and brother-in-law, perhaps because he did not want to damage the business, which he still claimed was partly his. Instead, he denounced them to Poussot and Machurin, who controlled broker recruitment and were in a position to remove brokers unworthy of the responsibility. His

71. AN, Y 11237, 22 December 1750.

72. AN, Y 12608, 19 March 1760, and Y 11223, 11 September 1736.

73. AN, Y 11235, 21 June 1748. Cf. an episode several years earlier in which broker Villain and her husband were attacked by a *fripier*, perhaps at Bazin-Girard's instigation, as "thieves, robbers of flour . . . who deserved to be chased from the grounds of the Halle." Y 11232, 21 September 1745.

sister and her husband committed "thefts and abuses" on the flour merchants, Frémont charged, and should not be allowed to continue as brokers.[74]

There were no specialized mediators at the Halle to resolve conflict like those in Moroccan tribal markets, who held court in open air and decided on the spot.[75] Practice or usage was supposed to socialize all participants in inner-market life and to govern their relations. When the violation of the norm was unequivocal, the transgressor came under intense, often effective community pressure to back off or make some sort of amends. Often, however, the issue was cloudy and the consensus never crystallized as neighbors and associates calculated the opportunity costs of espousing one cause or the other. Mutual friends, trying to mediate disputes, frequently got burned by both sides. Perhaps because the police were so deeply involved in the grain and flour marketplace, parties to a quarrel turned to the official institutions more rapidly and more frequently than seems to have been the case in other facets of eighteenth-century society. Inspector Poussot appears to have been unable to convince many local plaintiffs, including brokers, to opt for his vernacular mediation in lieu of filing formal complaints.

Grain Brokers

The flour brokerage was the most important factor service in the Paris provisioning trade. It should not be forgotten, however, that the grain brokerage was still quite active, especially in the small grains, and a number of prominent flour brokers, such as Dame Barbier, widow Delaistre, Guillaume de La Salle, and Pierre Chicheret, simultaneously dealt in grain, albeit on a rather small scale.[76] According to Poussot, in 1760 there were thirty-two brokers in grain and small grains, as opposed to fourteen brokers in flour. It is likely, however, that a number of the flour brokers handled grain on the side and a number of the grain dealers, several of whom, like Nicolas-Louis Martin, aspired to a flour brokerage, sold flour at retail, and perhaps covertly undertook some wholesale selling as well.[77]

The Delalande registers report that the number of grain brokers at the

74. Arsenal, ms. Bast. 10141 (21 April 1758).

75. See Walter Fogg, "The Organization of a Moroccan Tribal Market," *American Anthropologist* 44 (January–March 1942): 51–53.

76. See, for example, Barbier's sales to Pointeau in 1772, Archives Seine-Paris, D5B6 2532; Delaistre's work for the Hôtel-Dieu, Archives Assistance publique, deliberations of the bureau of the Hôtel-Dieu, 8 October 1751, no. 120. De la Salle, who called himself a *grainier* and a grain merchant as well as a broker, was highly praised by Malisset and by the Hôtel-Dieu for his factoring services. "Estimation de Corbeil," August 1768, AN, F[11] 1194; Archives Assistance publique, deliberations of the bureau of the Hôtel-Dieu, 14 December 1768, no. 137, fol. 366; AN, Y 12619, 17, 21 February and 1 March 1770, and Y 10351, 1774; St-Florentin to Bignon, 9 June 1769, AN, O[1] 411.

77. Arsenal, ms. Bast. 10141, fol. 400.

Halle ranged from seven to nineteen in the period 1725 through 1733. We have already met the brokers on the ports. Some, such as widows Leblanc and Chevet and Dame Picard, all of whom lived on the rue de la Mortellerie, were strictly brokers.[78] Many of the brokers on the Grève, including Gibert, Bassery, Denise, Rousseau, Paillard, Fosseyeux, and the Moussiers, were also members of the Mortellerie merchant clan, despite the prohibition against exercising brokerage functions at the same time that one engaged in the grain trade. The Delalande registers indicate that the number of brokers on the Grève fluctuated between seven and twenty-three during the period 1725–33, while usually only one or two operated on the Ecole port. The magnitude of activity of the grain brokers on the ports and at the Halle varied as widely from broker to broker as it did in the flour business. Rousseau, Vicquet, and Hemard on the Grève and Va, Furet, Martin, and de La Salle (father of Guillaume?) of the Halle were among the leading grain brokers in the late twenties and early thirties.[79] A price-control project drafted for the police around 1740 allowed a payment of 6 livres the muid for brokerage. In the fifties and sixties, however, the standard grain brokerage fee appears to have been 4.5 livres the muid, substantially less than the flour commission.[80]

In the mid-fifties, Jean Maheu was one of the busiest grain brokers in the capital. In 1755, he handled 816 muids (the equivalent of about 4,896 sacks of flour), worth almost 135,000 livres. Between March 1754 and June 1757, seventy-three different bakers purchased at his place, many of them returning repeatedly. Bakers bought in astonishingly large lots, as a rule well over the statutory limit of two muids per market day. Maheu recorded single transactions worth 18.16, 16.16, 13.83, 12.5, and 12.4 muids each. The mean size of a baker purchase in 1755 was 6.2 muids. During the month of December, an "average" buyer purchased enough in a single transaction—10.3 muids—to keep his oven full for a month and a half. In 1757 it dropped to 3.6 muids, perhaps because the significant increase in prices during the year spurred more rigorous police surveillance. In 1760, bakers bought an average of 4.3 muids per transaction. In subsequent years, Maheu's business declined steeply for reasons that are not clear. In 1760 he sold 486 muids and in 1763 only 186. For the next seventeen years, sales stabilized between 180 and 210 muids. Maheu retained about the same number of clients, who bought in more modest lots than they had previously. In the sixties his total annual billings were barely a quarter of what they had been in 1755, despite the fact that

78. AN, Y 15247, 3 May 1740, and Y 11228, 29 July 1741; Savart to Leduc, 24 January 1741, Arsenal, ms. Bast. 10277.

79. Bibliothèque de l'Institut, mss. 513–21, and BN, LK[7] 6289.

80. BN, Coll. Joly 1143, fol. 107; état général, St.-Charles, February–November 1768, AN, F[11] 1194; Archives Assistance publique, deliberations of the bureau of the Hôtel-Dieu, 8 October 1751, no. 120.

prices had risen. He appears to have turned increasingly toward the small grains, perhaps because baker demand focused increasingly on flour.[81]

Broker Business Failures

The business failures of the brokers, more than those of any of the other agents in the subsistence orbit, engaged the public interest because they affected such a significant part of the supply structure.[82] Profoundly disruptive, these failures were denounced by critics of the brokerage system as symptoms not merely of defective organization and inept management but also of corruption. They were particularly reprehensible in a quasi-public service whose task was so delicate and whose success depended on the confidence it inspired.[83]

The official record of broker failure is almost certainly incomplete. It enumerates eight cases in Paris (plus two in Versailles with similar consequences), all of which occurred between 1757 and 1779. The extraordinary incidence of failure in the seventies—seven of the ten cases—surely contributed to lieutenant of police Lenoir's tough ordinance that required the brokers to offer financial guarantees in return for accreditation. It is quite likely that other brokers filed for failure in the first half of the century. It is certain that still others, such as widow Maitre, failed with éclat but without initiating the legal procedures that signified the desire and presumably the capacity to refloat the business.[84]

If we exclude the two Versailles brokers who had considerable assets and the grain broker at the Halle whose debts were quite modest, we find that mean liabilities of the Paris flour brokers amounted to 35,521 livres (median = 30,062). They owed almost all of these accounts payable to an average of twenty different flour dealers (median = eighteen). Many of the individual obligations were quite large. Broker Rivière owed over 11,000 livres to Pigeau father and son, millers at Beaumont, and over 8,000 livres to Marquis father and son, millers at Chambly. Pilloy owed 8,818 livres to a Paris flour dealer, 4,444 livres to a Pontoise mealman, and 3,397 livres to a Persan miller. Where relations were good, the broker indulged the supplier as long as he could.

81. Archives Seine-Paris, D5B⁶ 3446.

82. All the following are in the D4B⁶ series of Archives Seine-Paris: 71-4665 (10 March 1779); 52-3199 (27 August 1774 and 16 June 1775); 63-4098 (4 July 1777); 47-2845 (26 May 1773); 41-2177 (5 December 1770 and 5 May 1772); 25-1269 (6 April 1763 and 1 July 1773); 17-831 (18 October 1757); 37-2013 (31 March 1770 and 30 June 1781); 27-1457 (July 1765 and October 1771); and 61-3909 (14 January 1777).

83. Bertin and Dambraine, "Mémoire," Arsenal, ms. 2588.

84. On 29 April 1759 Poussot called attention to Desgland, "one of our flour brokers who has just filed for failure." Arsenal, ms. Bast. 10141. Yet I find no trace of him in the faillite archives.

Such was the case of Languedin of Pontoise, who finally pressed the widow Pellerin for the 6,000 livres she owed him only because he was desperate himself.

The usual procedure of recovery began with court action in the consular jurisdiction. Thus, for example, laboureur Charles Demries of Villiers had Viollet condemned to pay 339 livres due for flour he sold and miller Daubigny of Beaumont obtained a similar sentence for 2,670 livres against Pilloy. The broker could seek terms, contest the sentence or appeal it, or seek other ways to delay and/or evade, including legal tactics such as the filing of failure and illegal ones such as flight. When flour dealers approached Poussot for help in winning payment, the inspector did not hesitate to pressure the brokers, regardless of the state of litigation between them. Not even Poussot, however, could remedy a situation in which a broker "was owed a great deal and had no cash on hand."[85] In theory, the brokers were supposed to answer for the solvency of their clients. In practice, they lacked the will and the means to assume this responsibility.

The mean assets of this same group of brokers, the vast bulk of which were paper, totaled 26,570 livres (median = 25,736). Virtually all of this sum represented accounts receivable from an average of thirty-seven bakers per broker (median = thirty-one) for flour they purchased on credit. The brokers could not pay their flour dealers because they could not compel their baker clients to make good on their obligations. On the one side the flour dealers were probably being pressed by their grain suppliers, and on the other the bakers had difficulty calling in debts from their customers. Poussot regarded this precarious structure with horror and vowed to combat this willingness to extend "unlimited credit on demand," which he regarded as the primary cause of failures.[86] The brokers used the lure of credit to blandish bakers into pratik relationships, or at least regular patronage. Rivalry was too keen among brokers to permit them to exchange information about bad risks or unkept promises in the manner, say, of the Ibadan cattle brokers, who blacklisted severely delinquent butchers.[87] In some instances, a threat to go to court was sufficient to bring a baker to terms. One broker offered to forgive interest and costs in return for prompt payment. Frustrated and wrathful, another broker physically assaulted a baker debtor and reviled him as "a bankrupt, a thief, a bugger."[88]

In most cases the brokers had to sue. The court almost invariably ruled in their favor, but not even judicial action enabled the widow Pellerin to recover

85. Archives Seine-Paris, D2B⁶ 1109, 6 May 1772, and D2B⁶ 1012, 13 April 1764; Arsenal, ms. Bast. 10141, fol. 409 (19 November 1760).
86. Arsenal, ms. Bast. 10141 (29, 30 April 1759).
87. Cohen, "Social Organization of Credit," p. 15.
88. Hamot v. Albert, Archives Seine-Paris, D5B⁶ 733; AN, MC, XV-690, 24 January 1751; AN, Y 11221, 2 August 1734.

debts as large as 4,017; 3,091; and 2,237 livres. Poussot would have castigated her for renewing the credit line of these delinquent bakers time and again. Eight of broker Viollet's bakers died before he could collect, including two in a state of destitution at the Hôtel-Dieu (with debts of 3,406 livres, not including penalties); eight others fled (2,118 livres); and three languished in Bicêtre prison, probably for indebtedness (1,551 livres). For fear of hurting his "baker-side" reputation, Viollet allowed some of his clients five and six years' grace. Bakers who were able to pay often contested the amount of the claim. The knowledge that the broker was in a financially weak position sometimes emboldened bakers to delay and resist in the hope that the brokerage would go under and abandon its accounts receivable.[89]

The brokers' paucity of hard assets was striking: no real estate, no cash, a few sacks of flour worth on the average 250 livres, and only 900 livres (median = 450) in furniture and personal effects. Critics of the brokerage system hinted that these faillis actually possessed considerable resources that they had siphoned off and hidden in various ways. It seems to me unlikely, however, that persons who had been virtually on public display in the marketplace for years could have managed to hide substantial wealth. On the contrary, they seem to have been relatively poor to begin with and to have failed in part because they had nothing on which to fall back. None of her creditors contested widow Pellerin's statement that her fortune, apart from 52,342 livres in accounts receivable, consisted in nothing more than a bed ("garny"), clothes, and household linen worth a total of 600 livres (items which, incidentally, she tried to transfer secretly to a daughter in order to shelter them from seizure by her creditors).[90] On the other hand, Chicheret's failure to enumerate any hard assets in his balance sheet appears very suspect. Lagache was the only Parisian broker with substantial nonpaper resources: 3,000 livres in furniture, 1,500 livres in clothes and linen, 2,750 livres in grain, and 15,000 livres in four large freight wagons and a dozen horses. The only authentically well-to-do broker was Louis Leroy of Versailles, who owned two houses worth 32,000 livres, furniture and effects valued at 4,000 livres, and an office that sold for 10,000 livres. Mean net worth of the group of Paris flour brokers was −8,951 livres (median = −5,088). It is hard to reconcile these figures with the often reiterated claims of the brokers that they were businessmen of considerable substance and solidity.[91]

To explain and in a sense bridge the gap between liabilities and assets, the brokers cited losses averaging 5,760 livres. Unfortunate commercial speculations in which the brokers were not supposed to have engaged accounted for 1,191 livres. Legal fees for debt recovery were a serious drain at 1,231 livres.

89. Archives Seine-Paris, D2B⁶ 801, 19 September 1746.

90. AN, Y 15389, 26 February 1779.

91. See "Mémoire pour les marchands de farines et leurs facteurs" (1779), BN, 4 FM 25012.

Charles Viollet claimed 4,754 livres in court costs plus another 3,865 livres disbursed to lawyers and huissiers who obtained and served sentences. Using Viollet's standard, one wonders what the widow Pellerin would have felt entitled to "deduct" as a loss for over fifty sentences that she won against delinquent baker debtors. Louis Leroy of Versailles spent so much time in various courts that he inscribed 5,000 livres as a loss for time compensation (in addition to 2,500 livres that he lost as a result of litigation that went against him). Unrecoverable debts from bakers resulted in losses of 1,024 livres. Losses of matériel were of little significance: 260 livres. The single largest rubric subsumed under losses actually reflected domestic expenses for child-birth and child raising and illness: 1,662 livres. In addition to the 150 livres he cited for the birth of a child and 2,500 for family sickness, grain broker Jean Maheu had the temerity to invoke the aggregate sum of 18,000 livres for "the food and upkeep" of his wife and himself during an unspecified number of years.

What happened to the failed brokers? Widow Rivière could hardly wait to extricate herself from the business in order to retire. She sought neither reductions in amount nor moratoriums. She wanted to transfer for collection all of her accounts receivable, amounting to 27,920 livres divided among sixty-nine bakers, to the ten mealmen to whom she owed almost 30,000 livres. That is to say, she wanted to saddle them with the broker's burden of collec-tion. Her creditors had no choice but to accept, since she apparently had no hard assets.[92] Widow Pellerin ceded all her possessions in order to escape further pursuits from her creditors in April 1779, just about the time that Lenoir elaborated the new rules that would in any event have made it virtually impossible for her to relaunch her brokerage.[93] Chicheret had great staying power, even after he no longer benefited from police patronage. He and his associate André Lauvernier—Poussot had argued that association would strengthen the financial base and managerial rigor of the brokerage and thus diminish the probability of failure—ceded their belongings to creditors in 1777. In 1780, however, Chicheret still appears to have been acting as a broker, though I am inclined to believe that he could not have met Lenoir's criteria of selection.[94]

Three Paris flour brokers, one Paris grain broker, and a Versailles flour broker recovered from the trauma of a first failure and later suffered a second. Maheu, the grain broker, survived only two years after resuscitation, during which time he neither fell more deeply in debt nor improved his situation. During the eleven-year interval that separated her failures, widow Quevanne of Versailles did not stagnate. Though her net worth in 1770 was over 4,000 livres, she owed her suppliers almost 37,000 livres. By 1781, while her net

92. Arsenal, ms. Bast. 10141 (20 August 1757).
93. Archives Seine-Paris, DC⁶ 21, fol. 172, 13 April 1779.
94. Ibid., DC⁶ 20, fol. 163, 8 July 1777, and DC⁶ 22, fol. 164, 10 March 1780.

worth was about zero, she had reduced her debts to 5,928 livres. Paris flour broker Charles Viollet was driven under in 1773 by 10,835 livres in flour debts. His eleven creditors gave him terms, but during the next ten years he succeeded only in increasing his flour indebtedness almost twofold, acquiring fourteen more mealmen creditors in the process, without making serious progress in the collection of accounts receivable.[95]

Jean-Honoré Aubert, another Paris flour broker, obtained terms from eleven creditors to whom he owed about 35,000 livres. He seemed to be a reasonable risk, for he had 50,183 livres in accounts receivable from bakers and, more important, he appeared to have a coherent collection strategy. Aubert agreed to pay 1,200 livres a month until he liquidated his debts. In return his creditors abandoned further legal action and renounced claims to interest.[96] In less than a year, however, Aubert failed again. His debt had increased by 23.9 percent; imprudently, perhaps as a gesture of good faith, his old suppliers continued to send him flour for marketing before he had cleared away his old obligations to them. Meanwhile, Aubert's collections advanced much more slowly than he had projected and at the same time he continued to offer credit to some of his regular clients and extended credit to fourteen new ones.

The last of the double failures was complicated by the ambiguity of the relationship between husband and wife. Michel Pilloy gave his wife more and more responsibility in managing the brokerage as he concentrated increasingly on exercising his huissier's post. In fact, Pilloy had contracted heavy debts and managed to keep the business going only by creating the fiction of a separate brokerage run by Dame Delaroche, his wife, using her maiden name. Together, they filed for failure in 1764 under the weight of 30,316 livres in obligations, most of which was owed to nine mealmen. Somehow Pilloy persuaded the creditors to grant them eight years in which to pay, despite the fact that they had less than 3,000 livres in hard assets, including the price of the huissier's office.[97]

Six years later they failed once more. The balance sheet that Pilloy first submitted resembled the 1765 dossier, as if time had stood still since the first failure. But Pilloy soon had to make a major rectification that he explained in a story of questionable credibility, given what we know about his character, his relations with his wife, and the eye that he always kept on the trading floor as he rode by on his sheriff's horse. Corrected liabilities now amounted to over twice what they had been in 1765 and there were more than twice as many mealman creditors. Assets had increased by less than a third, but they were still overwhelmingly in baker paper. Pilloy recounted that he was aston-

95. See his cession to creditors, ibid., DC^6 18, fol. 222 (5 July 1783).
96. AN, MC, LXXVIII-791, 22 September 1774.
97. Archives Seine-Paris, DC^6 15, fol. 273, 1 September 1764.

ished to discover, after he had prepared the first statement, that his wife had suffered "considerable losses," that "to cover the hole" in her treasury she had turned to desperate expedients "that further precipitated her [toward ruin]." She borrowed money at usurious rates and she sold her flour at a loss in order to raise as much cash as possible on a higher volume turnover ("100 to 200 sacks a day"). This confession proved to be neither convincing nor reassuring, and the Pilloy-Delaroche brokerage went out of business after ceding its assets to a host of glowering creditors.[98]

Broker Wealth

Two preliminary afterdeath inventories *(scellés)* give us a rapid glimpse of the living standards of two brokers who did not fail. Widow Jubin was living in a small three-room apartment overlooking the Halle when she died in 1738. Her bedroom was comfortably furnished with a large bed, a rug, a commode, a wardrobe, a wall clock, several chairs, four mirrors, and several paintings. A second bedroom, serving as salon and guestroom, was similarly appointed. A closet-sized kitchen had all the proper utensils. Jubin had relatively few clothes. Two and a half muids of red Burgundy aged in the cellar. She left a very large amount of cash, 4,106 livres, which suggests that she was still actively trading at the Halle. Perhaps even more surprising, she had no debts. One of her daughters was married to a master baker, which points to yet another line of subsistence intermarriage.[99]

Almost a half-century later Antoine Pontois and his wife lived in a slightly larger apartment in the same area. More candid than the Pilloy-Delaroche couple, they described themselves as serving "conjointly" as brokers.[100] They kept their business register exactly as Lenoir had requested in the ordinance of 1779. It is probably safe to assume that they found a person or persons to stand as financial guarantor. They themselves do not appear to have been well off, though they lived comfortably and were served by a cook, who could find red and white Burgundy in the cellar to complement her meals. Several mirrors, paintings, and engravings decorated the bedroom, while the salon contained a library of thirty devotional works. Pontois and his wife each had a considerable array of clothing. They kept no cash at home and do not seem to have been in debt.[101]

98. Archives Seine-Paris, DC[6] 17, fol. 264, 21 July 1771.

99. AN, Y 11225, 10 April 1738.

100. The Revolution opened a new option. See the case of Dame Marie-Anne Pinsard, "épouse divorcée de Pierre Garin, factrice à la Halle." Archives Seine-Paris, D11 U[3] 19-1364, 29 April 1803.

101. AN, Y 15397, 30 September 1785. Cf. his will, which suggests that he had some wealth to bequeath. AN, MC, XXII-45, 3 September 1785.

The Critique of Broker Abuses

Though the brokers were "tolerated" for the putative services they rendered to the mealmen, many flour dealers denounced their practices as abusive, and as the century advanced a growing number of officials began to share this view. The brokers "hurt the provisioning trade," wrote the *mitron* of Vaugirard, "[because they] robbed the merchant-suppliers and caused the price to rise and fall at their whim."[102] Together as a group, it was charged, the brokers made life difficult for the independent dealers who did not want their assistance. In league with the *tendeuses,* the chorus of vengeful sack holders and baker-procurers, to whom the brokers paid a fee called *ratro* for steering clients in their direction, the brokers worked to ruin the standing of the freelancers. The *tendeuses* "denigrated their merchandise and turned away buyers." The brokers spread the word that the independents could not give credit and could not be relied upon for regular deliveries. Nor were the mealmen who signed up with them spared their tyranny. The brokers invariably passed on the cost of their *ratro* to their merchants. The *tendeuses* were expected to "kick back" a part of the *ratro* to their brokers. Some brokers tried to extort a supplementary commission in return for pushing the sales of a given merchant. To please their bakers, the brokers offered "good measure" bonuses, again absorbed by the merchants. On the other hand, buyers who were not pratik clients were often "fooled and cheated." The brokers kept for themselves the flour that "remained" at the bottom of the sacks—often a curiously large residue. Another racket, which victimized alternately the merchants and the bakers, turned on the removal of apronfuls of flour for dough tests that in fact never took place. "Usurious" brokers pretended that the money they paid to their needy and importunate merchants was not the money received for their flour, which was allegedly not yet sold, but a friendly bridge loan—at interest. The old charges resurfaced that brokers secretly sold their own flour and/or formed clandestine "societies" with one or two merchants to the detriment of the other dealers. Causes célèbres, such as the conviction of broker Madeleine Sevin in 1742 for having defrauded her merchants by misappropriating their flour and embezzling their money, gave credence to the idea that brokers could not be trusted.[103]

Certain efforts that the brokers made ostensibly in behalf of their clients were regarded with alarm by the authorities. A number of brokers were said

102. Lacombe d'Avignon, *Mitron de Vaugirard,* p. 10.
103. "Mémoire des malversations, exactions, et prévarications," ca. 1730, BN, Coll. Joly 1429, fols. 205–7; AN, X²ᴮ 991, 14 August 1742; Bertin and Dambraine, "Mémoire," Arsenal, ms. 2588; Arsenal, ms. Bast. 10141, fols. 310–11 (2 February 1760); AN, Y 11223, 24 July 1736. In the mid-nineteenth century flour brokers were still being accused of engaging in illicit personal speculations. *Enquête sur la boulangerie,* p. 529. On *ratro,* see BN, ms. fr. 21558, fol. 245, 11 February 1698.

to encourage their suppliers to stay away when the trading was dull. They advanced money to their merchants in order to encourage them to hold out on price. Time and again brokers tried to raise the price of grain and flour either overtly, with the idea of raising the whole price level, or covertly, with the aim of siphoning off the difference between the price officially declared and the higher price actually demanded. In the first category falls the case of broker Madelon, called Aunt Ollive, who urged her suppliers to set a price above the current and "to hold firm, because today there is not much arriving at the Halle and you will get what you ask for [if you are patient]." Aunt Ollive might have contended that she was merely forecasting a new equilibrium price, but in the view of the police she was orchestrating a maneuver to raise prices "unduly." The second category is represented by broker Dame Callion, who declared her merchants' flour at 30 sous the bushel but sold it for 31 sous, 32 sous, or more, depending on what she could get her clients to pay.[104] Brokers sometimes arranged with "their" bakers to bid the price up in return for a sub rosa rebate. As a rule the brokers gave preference to the highest offers and neglected the more moderately priced goods.

Poussot's New Rule

Poussot was the first official to attempt to reform the brokerage system. He had no doubt about the need for such intermediaries, a need that he believed would increase with the growth and rationalization of the flour trade. It was clear to him, however, that many of the brokers were "elements of disorder" who stood in the way of his market modernization project. He envisioned two remedies: first, to impose new standards and methods of recruitment and to establish a new set of business procedures—"the rule"— that all brokers would be required to honor. No broker should be allowed to serve who did not hold, directly from the lieutenant general of police, a revocable commission that would remain contingent on continued good behavior. He had in mind a gradual renewal rather than a sudden purge, for he feared the deleterious impact that a violent jolt would have on provisioning. But henceforth a candidate would have to win Poussot's approval; to do that he would have to be "disposed to obey all the regulations that are presented to him."[105]

104. Bertin and Dambraine, "Mémoire," Arsenal, ms. 2588; BN, ms. fr. 21640, fol. 335, 8 August 1727; AN, Y 12607, 3 December 1759. Cf. the false declarations of price by brokers Ayzerlet, who declared it higher than he actually sold the merchandise "in order to sustain the high price level," and Pâris, who declared it lower than he actually sold in order to pocket the difference. AN, Y 9474, 15 May and 24 August 1771. The measurers were the officials best placed to expose "these prevarications," and this was one of their most useful functions.

105. Arsenal, ms. Bast. 10141 (30 April 1759 and 29 January 1758).

The "new rule" meant first of all close cooperation with the police. Brokers would have to conceal nothing, reveal everything. They would have to embrace the ethic of public service, based upon the goal of maximizing abundance. Poussot was willing to give the brokers a greater liberty in making prices than they had hitherto enjoyed, but he required that they be prudent, sensible, and sensitive to public opinion and the needs of the market. He expected them to keep books scrupulously and make them available to the merchants as well as to the police. He would not tolerate "disorder" in their relations with their clients. If they did not know how to manage their businesses, they should not be brokers, though he did not press for the sort of concrete guarantees that many mealmen would have liked. Poussot relied heavily, perhaps excessively, on his own judgment and influence, and on the honest disposition he discerned in a candidate for brokerage.

Poussot refused to cede to the usual pressures in the selection process for vacant or new broker places. One woman "applied a great deal of favor [from above]" and tried to bribe Poussot by offering him money, gifts, and the promise of one-half her post to his brother and sister-in-law. "These demarches were not to my taste," the inspector allowed, and her candidacy was rejected. Nevertheless, she challenged Poussot directly by setting up as a broker, without authorization, to compete for the merchants who had signed up with the handful of brokers that Poussot had recently named. She was quietly but strongly supported by the old-time brokers, who felt threatened by the new regime, and by the porters, who feared that Poussot would soon strike a blow against them. Poussot had this "turbulent" and "dangerous" woman removed from the *carreau*. But he did not underestimate the depth of malaise and hostility that his "new rule" provoked, not only in the grain and flour sectors but throughout the central market: "I am sure that it is to the liking of no one in the Halles that the Magistrate takes the trouble and care to make appointments to each place, however that is very necessary for good order."[106]

Nor did Poussot automatically honor the hereditary/proprietary claims of the broker families. He rigorously examined and eliminated the family pretenders to the brokerage of the widow Villain. Her daughter Perrette, age twenty-one, was "the most well behaved" of her children, but she worked as a laundress, "has little knowledge of this commerce" and thus would "not be in a position to fulfill the duties of the place." A son-in-law, Marc Maurice, could barely read and write; "it would thus be impossible for him to obey the regulations and to keep the books demanded of brokers." A master shoemaker named Pierre Mozard sought Villain's place on the grounds that he had been associated with her for almost three years. Poussot argued, however, that Mozard had disqualified himself because he had formed a "soci-

106. Ibid. (27 January 1758).

ety" with Villain despite the fact that the lieutenant general had prohibited such an association. The inspector was determined to put an end to all wildcat partnerships, which he regarded as a ploy to escape police control and public responsibility. The last candidate for Villain's place, Nicolas-Louis Martin, had no link with her and enjoyed the inspector's esteem as "an honest man," a man "of good sense . . . disposed to obey the orders of the Magistrate." The problem was that Martin, who had already made and lost a fortune as a grain trader, was currently a grain and small-grain broker. Poussot felt that it would be wise to separate these tasks, each of which was onerous. In the end, the lieutenant general followed Poussot's recommendation by suppressing Villain's place, on the grounds that there were more brokers on the *carreau* than necessary.[107]

It would be wrong to imagine that Poussot was wholly indifferent to "the protection" or influence that candidates marshaled, or that his judgment was unerring. He enthusiastically welcomed Sieur Gosset, who had no commercial experience but was "a man of right conduct" and, more important, a former head clerk of a police commissaire. Yet Gosset proved to be "a stubborn and narrow-minded man" who was unwilling to take advice from the grain and flour specialists with whom Poussot had associated him. Indeed, Gosset joined the enemy camp, throwing in his lot with "the [established] placemen of the Halle who have always been opposed to good order," a veritable apostasy for a former police official.[108]

Michel Pilloy, an old-time broker who courted Pousset's favor by providing intelligence on the attitudes and actions of the other brokers, tried to profit from their relationship by obtaining a larger place. Poussot rejected this greedy request—"bien gourmand"—on the grounds that Pilloy already operated "one of the best places." Without looking into his business, however, Poussot helped the broker, who called himself bourgeois de Paris, to become a huissier at the Châtelet at the very moment that his brokerage was falling to pieces. Pilloy doubtless hoped to use the quasi-judicial authority attached to the huissier's office to protect the brokerage that was now operated by his wife and to fend off the claims of his merchant clients. To his great embarrassment, Poussot found himself closely linked with a broker whose reputation was badly tarnished.[109] Shortly afterward, Pilloy's wife filed for failure.

From a candidate he considered serious, Poussot first demanded a sort of curriculum vitae. He then scrutinized his or her family background, commercial experience, fortune, and, above all, moral character and temperament. The inspector urged the lieutenant general to appoint Sieur Viollet because he

107. Ibid., fols. 239, 241 (6, 16 August 1759).
108. Ibid. (21 April 1756 and 27 March 1758).
109. Ibid. (20 August 1757 and 5, 6 August 1760); AN, Y 11243, 22 March 1756; Archives Seine-Paris, D2B⁶ 986, 26 February 1762.

knew the subsistence nexus, was "a docile man willing to follow the counsels we give him," and boasted a wife "who writes very well." He supported Sieur Danet because he came from a successful merchant family with flour connections and because he embraced "the new rule" with zeal.[110]

Poussot's Protégé

Poussot hoped to build the new broker system around his protégé, Pierre-Martin Chicheret, a grain dealer whose mother had been a small-time grain broker and whose father had been a humble gagne-denier.[111] Poussot apparently discovered him in about 1757, helped him to launch a small-grain brokerage, and encouraged him to seek formal recognition as the first flour broker in the new regime.[112] The inspector wanted Chicheret because he was experienced, he shared Poussot's reformist ardor, and he was "the enemy" of the established brokers and of their "disorder." Poussot delighted in the idea that Chicheret's appointment "will please no one in the Halle because he [and his associate] will preach an example that will worry the other placemen not only in the flour sector but in the grain and small grains sectors as well." Chicheret would embody "the new rule"; his brokerage would become the model to which all the others would gradually be compelled to conform. He would keep books indicating names and addresses of sellers and buyers, the amount of merchandise received, the amount sold, and the price. These registers would enable the police to assess the status of supply in a moment of crisis (exposing diffident flour dealers and hoarding bakers) and they would help to establish confidence between mealmen and brokers. If the other brokers resisted subjecting themselves to the light of the written word, it was because they feared it would place into relief "their wicked maneuvers." Chicheret promised to set a new standard for honesty by not siphoning off flour in the bottom of sacks and measuring containers and by prohibiting dough tests, *ratro* collection, and other forms of extortion. Poussot also aspired to a more fundamental reform that would have modified the banking and commercial functions of the brokers—he wanted Chicheret to refuse to grant credit to the bakers unless the flour suppliers themselves personally assumed the financial responsibility.[113]

It is hard to judge the extent to which Chicheret succeeded in practicing "the new rule." We know that he kept books, but if the one that survived is any indication, they contained much less data than Poussot desired and in

110. Arsenal, ms. Bast. 10141 (20 August 1757).
111. AN, Y 11218, 10 December 1731, and Y 12605, 31 July 1757.
112. At about this time Chicheret took the "quality" of bourgeois de Paris. AN, Y 12605, 18 November 1757.
113. Arsenal, ms. Bast. 10141 (20 August, 9 December 1757, and 31 May 1758).

some respects were less rigorous than the registers kept by certain of the "old-regime" brokers.[114] Chicheret may well have been able to eliminate some of the abuses on the *carreau,* but he must have been tormented by the flour furies—the *tendeuses* and the *forts* and *plumets* who assisted the porters and measurers—thereby losing potential buyers.[115] Surely he did not succeed, if he dared even try, in shifting the credit burden onto the flour dealers. If he had, he would have deprived them of their chief incentive for selling through brokers. Chicheret's inability to get along with a series of associates did not enhance his prestige in the marketplace.[116] His standing as a model suffered further when he was suspected of grain speculation and hoarding in the midst of the terrible crisis of 1768.[117] He recovered sufficiently in status to be called upon as an arbiter by the consular court, but in the end he suffered the worst ignominy that could befall a broker: he filed for failure in 1777.[118] Chicheret's institutional "example" may have induced some brokers to modify their practices, but it did not snowball into the sort of universal reform that Poussot had in mind.

Chicheret and Poussot had a brief but serious falling-out in 1760 as a result of the favor that the inspector accorded to another broker, Mabille, a twenty-six-year-old of high moral character from a well-known flour-trading family. At Poussot's bidding, commissaire Machurin commissioned Mabille to invest 20,000 livres, with the expectation that he would put in more later, in a flour business that would serve as an emergency public reserve that the police could deploy at short notice in an attempt to influence supply and price patterns. Mabille would constantly rotate the stock by selling at both retail and wholesale. The other brokers, including Chicheret, bitterly resented the privileged status that they feared this position gave Mabille. The brokers imagined that the police would pressure bakers to buy from him to keep him afloat and the rumor spread that he would soon be given a monopoly on retail flour sales. The brokers protested (somewhat disingenuously in light of some of their clandestine activities) that a broker "is not allowed to be a [flour] merchant at the same time." Poussot resolved this matter equally disingenuously by announcing that Mabille's mother was now the operating broker at the Mabille place and that Mabille himself was a simple mealman. The other brokers met on a number of occasions and considered various tactics that might force the police to disestablish the Mabille enterprise. Poussot got wind

114. Archives Seine-Paris, D5B⁶ 1870. This register mentions only the supplier, the amount of merchandise, and the remittance of funds upon sale.

115. See Chicheret's high-minded refusal to accord a "good measure" bonus or rebate to a baker-buyer because "this usage is contrary to the good order [*bonne règle*] of the carreau." AN, Y 12606, 24 April 1758.

116. Arsenal, ms. Bast. 10141 (27 March 1758 and 30 April, 29 May 1759).

117. Bertin and Dambraine, "Mémoire," Arsenal, ms. 2588. I have found no evidence that Chicheret was actually indicted or punished.

118. Archives Seine-Paris, D6B⁶, carton 7, and D4B⁶ 63-4098.

of "the cabal" and convoked its "leaders," including Chicheret, who was quickly repentant. The brokers pledged that they would obey, but Poussot remained skeptical of their good will.[119]

Like Sartine and Lenoir and other reformist police officials, Poussot clung to the corporate model of organization. He did not perceive the corporation as inimical to modernization and rationalization. On the contrary, by organically bridging and reconciling public and private interests, it was capable of facilitating the necessary adjustments. Thus, had the Chicheret example taken hold, Poussot would have liked to organize the reborn brokers into a corporation that would take "the new rule" as its charter. The corporation would speak with a single voice, police itself, and command the respect of the buyers and sellers as an impartial, quasi-public agency. Eventually it might be able to assume banking and recovery functions and serve to insure the funds of the mealmen. In the short run, the brokers would establish a collective treasury in which they would deposit all their earnings for equal distribution among all the brokers at the end of each month. This drastic restructuring of internal broker relations, in Poussot's view, "would put an end to jealous rivalries, thus preventing the maneuvers of the brokers to win the business of the merchants and the bakers."[120]

Other Reform Projects

Poussot's egregious lack of enthusiasm for the one systemic reform plan presented to the government during his tenure was a reaction less to the sweeping changes it projected than to the "private" nature of the enterprise. In return for 1,200,000 livres, a self-styled "company" asked the king to constitute in its name twelve broker offices for the conduct of transactions in the central market and the ports. It is interesting that the inspector did not reject out of hand the idea of transforming nearly one hundred posts into a dozen, though he must have worried about the coverage that the twelve could provide. What troubled him most was the fact that the brokerage would be entirely independent of police control and could as a result become "onerous" and even "abusive" to the suppliers and to the public. A realist and a fervent monarchist, Poussot did not disdain "the great resource" that the brokerage system, implemented first in Paris and imitated throughout the provinces, would offer the crown. On balance, however, the political costs struck him as prohibitive. A safer scheme, he suggested, might be to levy a sort of graduated legitimation fee on each broker in every significant market in the realm in return for a royal commission. This device would raise money

119. Arsenal, ms. Bast. 10141 (20 August 1757 and 17, 21, 25 February 1760).
120. Ibid. (31 July 1758).

rapidly, but it would also allow the police to cleanse the ranks of the brokers, for commissions would only be sold on recommendation of local authorities and would expire every ten years.[121]

The only other serious project for a wholesale brokerage reform was submitted to the controller-general in the late sixties and early seventies by a small-grain merchant named Bertin or Batin and a former lieutenant general of the Duché de Guise named Dambraine de Berlise. Nostalgic for the system of official brokers fleetingly installed in the 1690s, these petitioners contended that the de facto brokerage had proven a disaster. They assailed the brokers for their incessant "maneuvers," "malversations," and "monopolies." Avid and dishonest, the brokers "started from nothing and became rich" at the expense of the flour suppliers, whom they "ruined," and the public, whom they "starved." In order to eliminate corruption and fraud, making the policing of the market easier and more effective, and guarantee a greater abundance and regularity of supply, Bertin and Dambraine called for the creation of royal factor offices—60 in an early draft of their scheme, 150 in a later version—organized in a corporation administered by four syndics (themselves and two of their relatives), under the administrative aegis of a *régie* governed by a controller-general and assisted by receivers assigned to each part of the marketplace. These 150 brokers would replace the swollen ranks of the 802 brokers who were said to operate in all the markets of the Halles. Of these 802, the petitioners claimed, 96 operated in the grain and flour Halle (a figure not too far off from Poussot's estimates), and 34 on the grain ports. They would be replaced by 36 broker-officers at the Halle and 10 at the ports.

Everyone would benefit from this restructuring, Bertin and Dambraine boasted. The crown would gain a windfall, for each office would sell for 22,000 livres. The allure was meant to be reformist as well as fiscal by inserting the broker-officer in the context of a more comprehensive reorganization of market administration that had been envisioned from the early part of the century. With this ample treasury generated by the sale of the new offices, the king would be able to realize the long-promised suppression of the posts of the measurers, some of whose police functions could be assumed by the broker-officers. (If the government wanted to extinguish the porter corps in the same blow, the authors recommended increasing the number of broker-officers to 172 and the price to 27,000 livres for each.) The public and the buyers and sellers would applaud the disappearance of these officers, whom they considered vexatious, authoritarian, and corrupt. The king could choose to continue to collect their fees or to abolish them and thereby reduce prices. In any event, prices would be reduced by the abolition of brokerage fees on grain and flour. Only tolls on the other goods would persist, and these would be halved. Out of the fee fund the crown would pay the *gages* of the brokers,

121. Ibid., fol. 363 (4 August 1760).

who would operate collectively as Poussot had desired in order to inspire the confidence of the merchants, no longer "prey to usurious" agents. The security of transactions, the guarantee against bankruptcy, and the mediation of the *régie*'s central bureau would attract a much larger number of suppliers. The police would have access to complete records on the circulation and storage of supplies. Assisted by the syndics, the police would set the rules for the broker corps, which would have great incentives to discipline itself. The public would enjoy a steadier and cheaper supply all year round.

The project's breadth and complexity were probably its chief drawbacks. The idea of displacing eight hundred brokers and the thousands of auxiliary personnel in a single stroke would have made any government tremble. By the time Bertin and Dambraine submitted their plan, venality as a fiscal and institutional device was under sharp attack. (The authors themselves seemed to realize this, for they preferred to talk of "préposés en titre" rather than of hereditary officeholders.) Moreover, Bertin and Dambraine combined the ponderous and sometimes intractable venal office model, tempered by corporate socialization that was supposed to produce a public service ethos, with a *régie* management system whose purpose was to make administration as supple and responsive as possible—a curious and not wholly persuasive hybrid. Finally, after assailing the old brokers and measurers, Bertin and Dambraine suggested that they would be welcomed as purchasers of the new posts.

Lenoir's Coup de Force

Although the government rejected this project, it acknowledged that something had to be done about the disarray in the central markets, especially at the grain and flour Halle. In an effort to stamp out many of the abuses highlighted by Bertin and Dambraine, lieutenant general of police Lenoir promulgated a draconian ordinance in June 1779 that was meant to shake up the brokerage world. It began with a stinging bill of indictment against the brokers, who were reminded that their existence had no legal grounding, that it was merely "tolerated" because they facilitated the provisioning of the capital. Lenoir castigated them for "deceiving and cheating" the merchants, jeopardizing their financial situation and driving them into failure, extorting supplementary fees or kickbacks on the price of flour, and associating themselves secretly with merchants in the grain and flour trade. The first task of the police was to intervene immediately in the business relations between brokers and suppliers in a brutally direct fashion never before attempted. Lenoir gave the brokers two weeks to submit detailed financial statements to him concerning both their commerce and their personal holdings, in order to put him in a position to constrain them to meet their obligations to the merchants. The second clause of the ordinance radically modified the conditions for the recruitment of brokers. To instill confidence in the suppliers and to reduce, if not eliminate, the possibility of chain-reaction business failures, henceforth no broker would be allowed to operate who could not either prove that he or she owned 50,000 livres' worth of real or liquid property or nominate a person approved by the lieutenant general who possessed this wealth and was prepared to stand surety. The third article required the brokers to pay the merchant on the very day his flour was sold, which implied either that the broker could extend no credit to the bakers or, more likely, that he had to extend the credit strictly at his own risk.[122] Lenoir's contention that this was merely a "recall to order," since the brokers had "always" been supposed to remit immediately, was manifestly false.

The lieutenant general took the first step toward the professionalization of the brokerage by explicitly forbidding any broker to exercise a second occupation simultaneously and ordering all current brokers with more than one occupation to opt for one or the other within two weeks. It followed that brokers would henceforth be expected to pay closer attention to their floor-level business transactions instead of entrusting them to subordinate personnel, whose behavior often enraged buyers and sellers and violated the law. Specifically, article 8 enjoined the broker or an immediate member of his or her family to take personal charge of sales. Another article menaced brokers with immediate loss of their places and a fine of 500 livres if they engaged in the flour or grain trade, leased mills, or bought flour alone or in association with merchants. For the first time the police expressly imposed a ceiling on broker commissions: they would no longer have the right to demand more than 21 sous 6 deniers per sack.

The remaining clauses of the ordinance dealt with registration and documentation. The institution of the weight station in 1759 had obviously not resolved this problem, despite the emphasis placed on data collection by the director and controller. The lieutenant general was to name a clerk to establish separate account records for each supplier who would present a running inventory of his shipments, sales, the price, and the remittances made to him. This clerk would operate independent of, and in part to serve as a check upon, the brokers, who were required as before to declare every day at the bureau of the Halle the amount of flour they received, the amounts they sold, the prices, and the payments made to the merchants. The police would become more directly involved in the surveillance of baker-merchant relations

---

122. Unlike Poussot, who wanted to shift all credit risks back to the merchants, Lenoir seems to have wanted the broker in effect to buy the merchants' goods and pay for them on the spot. This is how the Javanese market brokers *(bakuls)* operated. The Ibadan cattle brokers had to guarantee their merchants against butcher default by formally promising to bear all credit losses, but in practice they made their dealers share the burden. Alice G. Dewey, *Peasant Marketing in Java* (New York, 1962), pp. 79–80; Cohen, "Social Organization of Credit," pp. 10–11.

on a day-to-day basis, because the brokers were to be obliged to give a copy of this daily declaration to the senior commissaire.[123]

Lenoir predicted that his reform would meet with warm endorsement from the vast majority of flour merchants, whose "interest dictated approval," and from those brokers who were "honest and public-spirited." In fact only 45 (or 46) merchants and 6 brokers offered their support to Lenoir's ordinance. Either 104 or 150 mealmen, depending on the source used, and 8 brokers joined in a passionate appeal against the measure. According to these appellants, "all the basest methods of the Police have been deployed" in order to gain the adhesion of the merchants, including promises of rewards and psychological and physical intimidation. Initially, the pro-Lenoir group consisted of only 35 merchants, but 11 others were "pressured" into changing sides. The appellants charged that between one-third and one-half of the original 35 partisans of the police were creditors of a few brokers who had recently declared failure, and were motivated by a crass desire to obtain preferential treatment for their claims. Morally weak and devoid of principle, the pro-Lenoir faction was of little significance to the provisioning of Paris, argued their adversaries. The appellants calculated that while the 46 "police" mealmen supplied only 20,300 sacks of flour a year, they (150 strong) furnished 107,200 sacks, to which should be added another 36,900 sacks marketed by 33 other dealers who had not joined the issue but were reputed to be sympathetic to the appellant cause. The appellants hoped that the lieutenant general of police would recoil at the prospect of jeopardizing fully seven-eighths of the annual Parisian supply.[124]

The pro-Lenoir merchant group was recruited from throughout the supply zone, with a concentration of about one-third of its members in the Gonesse area, which was dominated by relatively small-scale mealmen. The appellants were likewise widely dispersed, but their stronghold was the Pontoise-Beaumont-Chambly-Presles-Persan region, home of some of the most aggressive merchant-millers, where they outnumbered their opponents by 47 to 7. This western flour zone had a long history of resistance to the Paris police on such issues as price controls and sale by weight. As for the brokers, the appellants were almost all veterans with many years of experience. The majority if not all of the pro-Lenoir brokers had only recently received appointments (though two of their wives were members of the Huet family, which had deep roots in the Halle's grain and flour business).

The appellant brokers had no doubt that they were the victims of a plot mounted to do them in. Lenoir does not appear to have been considered a conscious party to it; rather, he was manipulated by the conspirators, led by one of his commissaires, Serreau. The latter, in league with a judge from the

123. AN, Y 15392, 3 April 1779; arrêt du parlement, 19 June 1779, AN, AD XI 40.
124. For the above paragraph and the following discussion of the appeal, see "Mémoire pour les marchands de farines et leurs facteurs" (1779), BN, 4 FM 25012.

consular court and other influential businessmen, allegedly wanted to replace the veteran brokers with a "company" of venal officeholders in which they would have a hidden financial interest. They would arrange for the posts to be sold to their friends, just as Serreau had already managed to have several of his protégés named as brokers in the last year or so.

While Serreau used his influence to win Lenoir's support, his "subalterns" and his merchant and broker protégés began a "campaign of denigration" throughout the supply zone geared to discredit the old-line brokers. Even as Serreau told Lenoir that the brokers had amassed opulent riches as a result of sordid business practices, his agents spread the word that the brokers "had no fortune, that they could not meet their obligations [to their flour merchants]." These rumors became self-fulfilling prophecies, contended the brokers, for "they destroyed the confidence that the merchants had in several of us and precipitated them to the brink of ruin." Obliged to file for failure, these several brokers found themselves in the hands of Serreau's confederate at the consular court. According to the brokers, the court refused widow Pellerin's perfectly legitimate request for a determination by a mediator of exactly how much she owed. Although the court generously accorded time to Pellerin's baker clients to repay their debts, despite her urgent cash hunger, it denied any grace to the baker debtors of broker Pontois, Serreau's favorite. Meanwhile the judge and the commissaire were said to have "stirred up" the creditors of Pellerin and Mabille, who was also in failure, making it impossible for them to arrange "amicable terms."

There is some independent evidence that Serreau treated Pellerin and Mabille (who had been Poussot's creature) with unwonted harshness. On the suspicion that Pellerin was attempting to conceal certain of her assets, which may have been true, Serreau conducted a degrading and exhaustive search of her lodgings. Everything was placed under seals to underline the lack of public trust in her comportment. The homes of her son and daughter were similarly searched and sealed.[125] Yet the fate of the Pellerin family seems mild compared to what befell Mabille. Once chosen for his high moral character to collaborate with the police, this broker was thrown into jail upon the issuance of a lettre de cachet, while the police rummaged and sealed his house.[126] Even if certain creditors had been willing to consider accepting terms before the police intervened, it is extremely unlikely that they would have agreed to take the risk afterward. In most cases the police and the consular jurisdiction did everything they could to facilitate the recovery of businessmen whose failure was by definition innocent rather than fraudulent (a *faillite* rather than a *banqueroute*). In this instance, however, it is clear that they wanted the brokers to go under.

Serreau pointed to these failures as evidence that the brokerage was

125. AN, Y 15388, 19 December 1778, and Y 15389, 29 January and 26 February 1779.
126. AN, Y 15388, 13 December 1778.

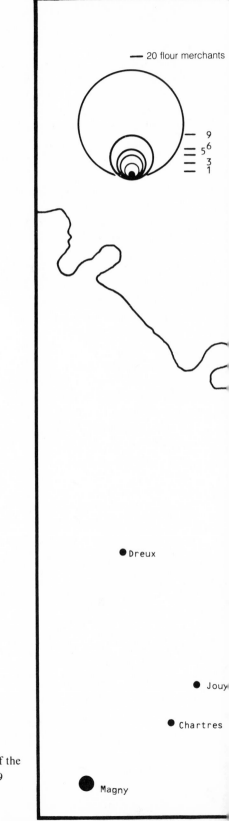

MAP 6 Geographical distribution of the flour merchants supplying Paris, 1779

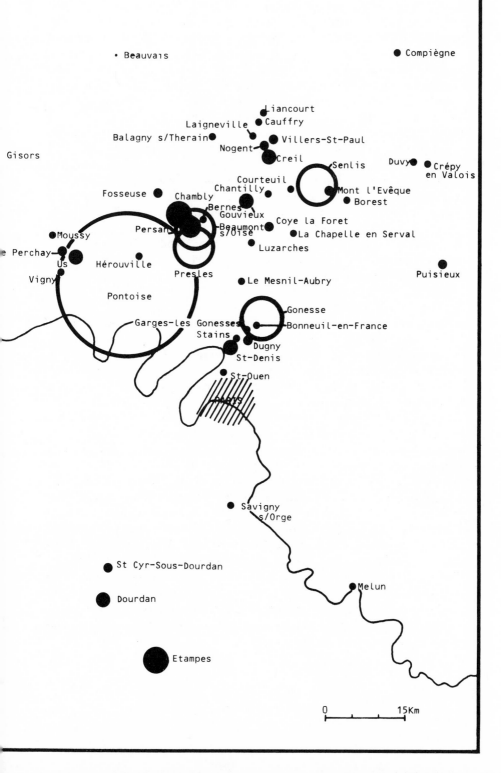

- Beauvais
- Compiègne

Liancourt
Cauffry
Laigneville
Balagny s/Therain
Nogent
Villers-St-Paul
Creil
Senlis
Duvy
Crépy en Valois
Gisors
Courteuil
Chantilly
Fosseuse
Chambly
Mont l'Evêque
Bernes
Borest
Gouvieux
Persan
Beaumont s/Oise
Coye la Foret
Moussy
La Chapelle en Serval
e Perchay
Us
Luzarches
Vigny
Hérouville
Puisieux
Presles
Pontoise
Le Mesnil-Aubry
Gonesse
Garges-Les Gonesses
Bonneuil-en-France
Stains
Dugny
St-Denis
St-Ouen
PARIS

Savigny s/Orge

St Cyr-Sous-Dourdan

Dourdan
Melun

Etampes

0   15Km

flawed, if not corrupt, and could not be trusted to mediate transactions so crucial to the survival of the capital's inhabitants. The brokers retorted that even if the Pellerin and Mabille failures were in some sense warranted, they were relatively trivial episodes. During the past decade there had been failures amounting to 72 million livres at the central markets, a figure that presumably included all the sellers as well as the factors and must also have encompassed other trades. The combined debts of Pellerin (24,000 livres) and Mabille (68,000) represented an infinitesimally small percentage of this sum. The brokers had little more to say about the Pellerin case because it struck them as the most banal and innocuous of affairs. They were, however, outraged over the way that Mabille had been treated (the same Mabille who had once aroused their jealousy in Poussot's time). He was an innovative and enterprising businessman, "universally esteemed," who would surely have succeeded in righting his affairs had he not been imprisoned. He was not simply a broker. He was also a grain and flour trader and a mill and bakery operator—so much for the traditional "incompatibilities," unable to withstand the inexorable logic of vertical integration. True, Mabille's bakers owed him over 150,000 livres, conceded his broker friends, but he had already made arrangements to collect a large part of these accounts receivable; moreover, he had other resources.

The brokers criticized the text of the ordinance as well as the context in which it was prepared. They denounced the entrance requirement of 50,000 livres as an "illusory" test that would only mean "subjecting them continually to inquisitorial investigations that had no purpose." The obligation to pay the merchants immediately was equally ill conceived. The bulk of merchants themselves did not demand immediate payment—they understood that it was not realistic. Without any official constraints, brokers contended, the merchants almost invariably received payment within two to four weeks. The ordinance's avowed aim was to accelerate and facilitate commercial exchange, yet it was strangely silent on the question of baker payments. If the brokers were supposed to pay the merchants immediately, why were the bakers ordinarily granted such liberal terms by the consular jurisdiction— sometimes up two years? Given the difficulties that the brokers experienced in recovering baker debts for flour, it was absurd, they contended, to fix the commission that they were allowed to levy at 21 sous 6 deniers. Ordinarily, commercial commissions were at least 4 percent: 2 percent for the work actually performed in the commercial operation and 2 percent for the risk. The fee set by the ordinance represented about 2.5 percent in raw terms, even less if one allowed for the trickling return of accounts receivable. Moreover, the brokers affirmed, such authoritarian regulation of commercial relations was gratuitous, "for, if the merchant voluntarily gives them a larger fee, what check can an ordinance impose on their will?"

This last objection pointed to the underlying principle of the entire broker brief. The police were inherently "incompetent" to control commercial relations. Their effort was "dangerous" and "useless" because it violated the laws of nature. Those laws prescribed that a person's property and his right to dispose of that property freely were sacred. To transgress those laws was not merely to trammel and gradually stifle trade, but also to undermine the very social order, to prevent it from enjoying prosperity and growth, and to deliver it to corruption and tyranny. Another blow struck by the marketplace against the market principle, the Lenoir ordinance was no trivial matter. With the universalizing exuberance of the physiocrats, the brokers attached their fate to the destiny of progress in France. Though one needed only to be a merchant, not a philosopher, in order to detect the flaws of regulation, physiocratic discourse clearly shaped the brokers' brief. Rebuffed twice in two decades by popular referenda-riots and stubbornly resisted by the police at all levels, grain and flour liberalism was alive and well in the Paris Halle ten years before the Revolution forever vindicated the ideology from which it sprung.

"All the evils that the People suffer in matters concerning their subsistence come from the Regulations," the brokers pronounced, "and they [the police] would still impose more Regulations!" In another formula redolent of the laissez-faire rhetoric of the *économistes,* the brokers asked: "Did they [the police regulations] produce one single grain of wheat?" Wistfully, the brokers recalled the liberal reforms of 1763 and 1774, which wisely "accustomed the people not to blame the inclemency of the weather [that is, short crops] on the Magistrate or the Administration" and to look to "the nature of things," that is, to the free play of market forces, for their subsistence. "This desire to administer that which takes care of itself as a function of the reciprocal interests of producers and consumers" was the fundamental defect in police doctrine and the chief threat to abundance in the marketplace.

The Lenoir ordinance, in the view of the brokers, betrayed the heavy hand of police at its worst. It presumed to do what it could not do. First, it claimed the right to create and revoke brokerships at its pleasure. This was beyond the power of the authorities: "They cannot confer as they please the right to sell someone else's property" nor could they "dismiss a broker who was agreeable to those [merchants] who gave him their confidence." Second, the brokers contested the right of the police to define and speak for something called the public interest. There was no such thing. There was only the interest of owners of property. The ordinance presumed to "order the disposition of another's property, which cannot be authorized by any sort of notion of public welfare." By placing "impossible obstacles to the exercise of their rights of property," the ordinance would only succeed in driving off the merchants ("who would find other outlets for their flour") and imperiling the provisioning of Paris. Such was the brazen message and warning the brokers conveyed to the parlement. Refusing to free them from "this [new] state of dependence," the magistrates approved Lenoir's text with virtually no changes.

In some ways the most telling point that the brokers made was not in their argument but in the list of merchant signatures appended to it. These 150 merchants (an uncertain but plausible figure) manifestly disproved Serreau's claim that the brokers had no commercial following and were thus no longer capable of sustaining the capital's flour provision. The only way to account for this astonishing mobilization of the majority of Parisian suppliers is to assume that they considered their vital interests to be at stake. I do not believe that it can be ascribed to the "increase" in commission ostensibly authorized by the ordinance.[127] The brokers had commonly been receiving as much as 20 sous a sack from the late fifties onwards. An increase of 7.5 percent over two decades seems eminently reasonable and unlikely to have provoked collective disaffection. Lenoir made a point of referring to memoranda that he received from various mealmen, who may nevertheless have felt that they ought to have been more frankly consulted. Serreau's unwillingness to establish a dialogue rankled: "Every time [that they talked] he treated them with a disdainful arrogance that he would not have shown to the *forts* of the Halle." Even though the ordinance provided the mealmen with certain of the guarantees that many of them had long sought, it appeared to them that they would have to accept an even more rigorous "subjugation" than they had heretofore known. No more than the brokers did the merchants want to be reduced to "dependence." A horror of the tightening police grip on the flour trade seems to have been the paramount incentive to merchant resistance to Lenoir's project. Solidarity with the brokers per se was of less significance, though many of the mealmen had excellent relations with their particular brokers, whose existence may have been jeopardized by the new conditions for practice.

Evidence concerning the impact of the Lenoir reform on the flour trade is sorely lacking, but the story of Marie-Catherine Maitre proves that it was implemented in at least some of its essential aspects.[128] Widow of a huissier at the Châtelet, Marie-Catherine apparently solicited a post as a broker hard upon the publication of Lenoir's ordinance, when the Halle was in a state of flux. Approved by the lieutenant general, she swore before a notary to pay her merchants promptly as ordered, and she arranged for her father, Jean-Baptiste Lointier, to stand surety. An affluent laboureur and fermier from the Pontoise area, worth at least 90,000 livres in land, buildings, and equipment, her father was happy to afford his widowed daughter "a chance to succeed."

127. This is the thesis of Biollay, *Origines du factorat*, p. 12.
128. Biollay wrote that the brokers resisted, that the most recalcitrant were arrested, and that others lost their posts. He adduces no documentation for these claims, however. *Origines du factorat*, p. 12.

Though they did not remain in close touch, Lointier had the impression that his daughter's affairs initially prospered. In fact, they had started to sour less than a year after she began, perhaps because she lacked commercial experience. Lointier did not get the bad news until the summer of 1781, when a group of creditors, led by a flour dealer named Gibert, took legal steps to have his property seized to cover his daughter's debts.

Widow Maitre owed Gibert 1,415 livres and had not paid him despite his friendly requests, followed by his invocation of Lenoir's ordinance requiring same-day remittance, followed by a sentence of condemnation to payment obtained from the consular court. After a sheriff's summons, Maitre solicited and received terms, but she failed to fulfill them. Gibert then joined with a number of creditors—according to Maitre's own reckoning, which may have been too low, she owed 26,324 livres to thirty merchants—to form a legal "union" in order to file a collective suit against her. She again sought terms, but her proposition served only to arouse "the indignation of all the creditors." She had the "arrogance" to demand ten years in which to pay, during the first two of which she would enjoy a total moratorium.

Gibert hoped to accelerate the civil action by bringing police pressure to bear. He warned Lenoir that the Maitre affair involved the public interest as well as the fortunes of a group of suppliers: "I witnessed a discouragement among the creditors who seem to have decided to send no more merchandise to the Halle. Moreover, I believe that I detected anxiety on their part regarding [the honesty and reliability] of the other brokers." Demoralization and alienation were spreading among other suppliers in the hinterland. The only way to "appease" the mealmen and at the same time to "frighten" the brokers into toeing the line, Gibert suggested, was to make an example of Marie-Catherine Maitre by "throwing her out of the Halle."

In fact the widow Maitre disappeared from the Halle at about this time. During the last several weeks that she was visible, she and her son pressed her baker clients, who owed her a total of 56,578 livres, ranging in amounts from 78 to 4,744 livres, to convert their flour debts into personal notes endorsed in her name. Clearly she was trying to anticipate the liens that would be placed on her accounts receivable and to pocket as much of those assets as she could.

Her own father suspected her of preparing "a coup" against her creditors. When he learned that he was being sued, he rushed to Paris "in order to take stock of his daughter's business." He was deeply hurt by her behavior. She had not kept him truthfully informed on the state of her affairs, despite his stake in her solvency. She refused him access to her books, however, and Lointier was obliged, like Gibert, to call upon Lenoir's help.[129]

The widow Maitre never returned to the Halle. Lenoir had not been

129. AN, Y 15392, July–August 1781.

bluffing. Her story helps to explain the striking contraction that took place in the brokerage corps in the last decade of the old regime, when business had become riskier and more difficult to sustain than ever before. According to the author of a comprehensive police dictionary, there were only six brokers assigned to the wholesale flour trade in the mid-eighties. Nine others were said to have operated a retail brokerage that sold small amounts of flour not only to the public but to "poor bakers" who could barely afford to buy more than a half-sack at a time. Fifteen brokers, presumably different brokers from the flour factors, were supposed to have handled all the grain and small grains.[130] A register of grain and flour entries for July 1789 listed seven wholesale brokers, six of whom had been among the fourteen brokers who had vainly filed suit to block Lenoir's reform in 1779.[131]

Surely the six or seven brokers did not lack for clients. Indeed, given their small number, they may even have been able to overcome their old rivalries by carving out and distributing among themselves commercial *chasses gardées.* Save for momentary lapses, a quasi-public brokerage system continued to function in Paris until the last quarter of the nineteenth century. Liberal ideology triumphed in many sectors of French life, but public authorities remained persuaded, as Delamare had been a hundred and seventy-five years earlier, that the provisioning of the capital was far too delicate an affair to entrust to unmediated, private commerce. As for the flour merchants who threatened to abandon Paris, there is no indication of mass defections in the wake of the reorganization of the brokerage.

The chief function of these brokers was to spare the merchant the burden of traveling to Paris to dispose of his goods and to collect sums that were due him. In return for a commission, the broker graded the merchandise, stored it, transported it, and of course sold it at the best price possible. He (or, as it frequently turned out, she) took responsibility for recovering the credit extended to baker buyers. The brokers also provided information on market conditions, banking services, and entertainment. They tried to cultivate close relations with both merchant (seller) and baker (buyer) clients. Frequently this dual courtship led them into the double pratik bind: they needed to appease impatient merchants who longed to be paid but feared alienating baker debtors by pressing too hard. Competition among brokers for clients, both sellers and buyers, was fierce: "professional jealousy" led to bitter and sometimes violent animosities.

A broker recognized no more infamous insult than to be called "bankrupt." The epithet was not a remote or abstract pejorative. A number of brokers failed—innocently, according to their testimony and the verdict of the

130. Des Essarts, *Dictionnaire universel de police,* 4:465–66. Cf. Albert Babeau, *Paris en 1789* (Paris, 1892), p. 332.

131. AN, H 2200, and arrêt du parlement, 19 June 1779, BHVP.

commercial court, but culpably in the eyes of certain observers of the Halle. No failure in the subsistence complex was more devastating, for the brokers spanned it more fully than any other agents. Despite their reputation for affluence, the brokers seem to have had surprisingly fragile fortunes.

The eighteenth-century brokers were the direct descendants of the de facto brokers who had long before set themselves up in the Paris markets in response to merchant and laboureur demand. The first generation in the eighteenth century appears to have been recruited largely outside the subsistence complex. General commercial experience seems to have been prized more highly at this juncture than expertise in provisioning affairs. Although they sought administrative legitimation in several ways, the brokers acted as if they owned their posts, selling and bequeathing them at will. Occasionally the police appropriated a place or created a new one: they did not play an active role in the organization of the brokerage until Poussot's arrival in the fifties. A surprisingly large number of brokers were women, who assumed managerial and financial responsibilities that were usually reserved for men. While their legal and professional status was ambiguous, in practical terms they exercised more or less independently a public and commercial function of capital importance.

Responding to accusations that the brokers were high-handed and corrupt intermediaries who cheated both their baker and merchant clients, harried independent dealers, operated various rackets, manipulated prices, and engaged surreptitiously in grain and flour speculation, Poussot resolved to impose a "new rule." Business procedures were to be rationalized and standardized, and made transparent. Far more rigorous books were to be kept and would be made available to anyone for verification. Poussot conceived of the brokerage as a public service, and was prepared to purge any broker who failed to live up to this ethic. Future recruitment would depend exclusively on merit and character. No one could operate a brokerage without a written commission from the lieutenant general of police, and all commissions would be revocable, dependent on good service and relative docility. Poussot foresaw the evolution of the reformed broker corps into a veritable corporation, the statutes of which would take their inspiration from the new rule, that would stand as collective guarantor of the business of each individual broker.

Judging from the chorus of complaints that surged forth in the seventies, Poussot was only partially successful in eliminating what he called the "bad habits" of the brokers. Prompted in part by a series of jolting failures, lieutenant general of police Lenoir struck a harsh blow in 1779 with the publication of an ordinance that treated the brokers as thieves and apostates, and imposed a new code of recruitment and accountability and a new set of procedures that promised the merchants more efficient service and better protection against loss. Like Poussot, Lenoir insisted that the broker had to act like a public servant. It was precisely on this point that eight of the brokers and a majority of the flour merchants who regularly supplied Paris took issue with Lenoir's new rule. They claimed that brokerage was a purely commercial affair between merchants and agents of their designation concerning private property. They denounced the lieutenant general's ordinance as a violation of natural law and as a gesture of despotism. Despite this vocal opposition, the evidence indicates that the ordinance was indeed executed. A considerably shrunken broker corps seems to have functioned to the satisfaction of the authorities during the last decade of the old regime.

CHAPTER 14

The Police of the Paris Markets:
Measurers and Porters

*T*he measurers and porters of grain and flour typified one of the contradictions of ostensibly rational absolute monarchy: they were charged with
serious administrative responsibilities, yet they owned the offices that they
exercised. They had a venal as well as a police interest in defending the
monopoly of the official marketplace. No officers were closer to everyday
provisioning affairs than the measurers and porters. They knew all the tricks
of the traders. Those who refused to become their clients they tended to treat
as adversaries. Assigned the task of smoothing transactions, in the eyes of
many buyers and sellers the measurers and porters made them more onerous.
Organized in corporations to protect their common interests, the measurers
and porters doggedly resisted attempts to discipline or to replace them.

The Police Functions of the Measurers

Assisted by a single inspector in the central marketplace and deprived of
any direct jurisdiction over the ports, theoretically under municipal aegis, the
police commissaire responsible for the provisioning of Paris could not have
exercised effective surveillance over the grain and flour trade without the
collaboration of the measurers and porters. Theoretically, no transaction
could take place without the intervention of these officers. Very little occurred in the provisioning trade to which they were not privy. They collected
the intelligence that informed short-term decisions and they gathered the

quantitative data that shaped long-term policy. Their relatively dense presence at the markets and on the streets was believed to deter sellers and buyers from illicit enterprises.

The measurers preferred to be perceived as "officers of police" and had stronger claims on the title than the porters, who tirelessly contested their preeminence.[1] Guardians of the very standards of exchange, measurers had occupied prestigious roles in a number of societies. Invoking the Roman model, Delamare argued that measuring could not be construed as merely manual labor, because it required an unusual dose of "probity and vigilance" as well as "a sort of authority."[2] The measurers had three main functions, according to Delamare: to act "as arbiters of justice and of good faith between sellers and buyers," to serve as "the watchdog of commerce, in order to denounce the abuses and the defects," and to keep a running record of prices and supply, a delicate task of enormous economic and political moment.[3]

The measurers opened, closed, and presided over the market, not only on market days, which saw the heaviest turnover, but every day of the week, for sales in Paris were suspended only on Sunday. They opened the sacks to invite inspection by prospective buyers and also to check on quality. They made a point of looking beneath the surface of the pile and plunging deeply into the sack in order to uncover suspect "mixtures," or adulteration.[4] The measurers were the only ones who could definitively close the sacks signifying a legitimate sale. The service that formally justified the remuneration they received was a mandatory act of measuring by which they verified the quantity exchanged and "guaranteed that neither buyer nor seller would be fooled."[5]

Yet their crucial role in the concourse between buyers and sellers was often much less tangible. They mediated transactions by matching, encouraging, and scrutinizing buyers and sellers—at least, this is what the most serious among them tried to do. They were instinctively *dirigiste,* though this was authority that they improvised on their own initiative. They aimed at a more or less even distribution among the bakers. They quashed transactions involving amounts they judged excessive or persons brandishing dubious credentials.[6] Measurer Delasalle compelled Dame Meunier, a flour dealer, to sell

1. Deliberations of the bureau of the Hôtel de Ville, 22 May 1758, AN, H* 1867, fol. 445. At least one measurer pressed the case to its logical conclusion by becoming a police inspector, a post he could not have attained had the authorities not recognized the efficacy of his previous training. Nicolas Beaubigny, AN, MC, XXXIX-342, 9 March 1731, and Archives Seine-Paris, fonds Feydeau, DE[1], article 4.

2. Delamare, *Traité de la police,* 2:607–8, 652, 660.

3. Ibid., p. 652. Duchesne developed this same theme in his *Code de la police,* p. 108. Le Camus plagiarized Delamare in the *Journal économique* (November 1753): 145–56.

4. See, for example, the case of flour dealer Fourcret, BN, Coll. Joly 1829, fol. 278. Cf. Diderot et al., eds., *Encyclopédie,* 10:427.

5. Arrêt du conseil, 21 November 1752, BN, Coll. Joly 1829, fol. 333.

6. See, for instance, AN, Y 11228, 11 January 1741.

to Dame Guillaume, the wife of a baker who needed merchandise to bake his next ovenful, despite his reputation as a poor payer.[7] "Good order" was the shibboleth of the measurers. That meant, inter alia, that buyers and sellers had to wait their turn. When a blatier name Farin, who had previously tried to sell without being measured, boisterously demanded immediate service, he was threatened with expulsion from the Halle. It also meant that merchants had to sustain their ordinary level of supply, or provide a cogent reason for failing to meet what imperceptibly became a quota. Thus the measurers recommended that port dealer Bocquet lose his accreditation for curtailing his shipments.[8]

Good order also precluded speculative or "artificial" price increases. Charged with the job of recording prices, the measurers also tried to make them, by cajolery and by pressure. They insisted on public haggling, warned buyers against settling for a price they considered too high, and refused to close the sacks of sellers who obtained a price significantly above the current. The least reticent measurers exercised a sort of coercive brokerage.[9] In the view of certain police officials, such as inspector Poussot, the measurers were far too authoritarian on price guidelines. This "supposed maximum [*prétendue taxe*]" was dangerous, Poussot maintained, for it "has always worked unfairly against the good qualities" in both wheat and flour, "driving off the good merchants and bringing down the levels of trade at the Halle."[10] Poussot always suspected venal self-seeking where he spotted zeal among the measurers. But the measurers regarded his plea for "a real liberty" as an invitation to abuse and disarray.

Nine measurers called controllers were permanently designated to collect price and sale data, seconded on official market days by five others. Assigned to the different ports and to the different categories of merchandise at the Halle (wheat, flour, oats, small grains), they kept registers containing the amount of merchandise placed for sale, the amount sold, the amount left for the next day, the range of prices, the names of buyers and sellers, and sometimes a transcription of the *lettre de voiture* or minage certificate authenticating the declared provenance of the grain and/or flour. Data were collected in several stages and in some cases different measurers gathered the same data, thereby providing the senior officers with a form of control. Each of the sedentary measurers charged with mediating and measuring was supposed to make a declaration of sale and price to the controller of his sector before passing on to a new operation. The most scrupulous measurers personally

7. AN, Y 11226, 21 July 1739.

8. AN, Y 11220, 30 May 1733; BN, Coll. Joly 1312, fol. 29 (1735).

9. See the striking similarities between the practices of the Paris measurers and those of the measurers in the pre–World War II markets of Hopei in China. Li and Tayler, "Grain Marketing in Hopei Province," p. 121.

10. Arsenal, ms. Bast. 10141, fol. 253 (28 September 1759).

noted down the information; others, less conscientious or pressed to move to the next transaction, merely submitted "bulletins" filled out by the sellers.[11]

This information gave the authorities an ongoing profile of the supply system. It informed them not only of aggregate movement but also of the quantity supplied by each area of the provisioning zone and the amounts furnished by each supplier. The commissaire was thus in a position to venture certain predictions about supply behavior, to pinpoint the origins of deficiencies, to establish normative levels of service, to penalize unreliable suppliers.

The measurers also constructed the mercuriale, the barometer of prices that so profoundly shaped the behavior of the police, the people, and the subsistence professionals. Few texts composed in the eighteenth century had greater direct impact on mass social life than the hundreds of individual declarations of the measurers that comprised the mercuriale. A measurer could virtually nullify the influence of high-priced transactions by not registering them. Or he could drive up the price of bread, perhaps in complicity with the bakers, by inflating the price maxima across the board. Complaints about the infidelity of measurer reporting abounded elsewhere, but seem to have been rare in Paris, perhaps because the commissaire or the inspector used independent sources to check on the rigor of price registration.[12] So important did the lieutenant of police consider the price archives that when controller-general Turgot abolished the post of measurer in 1776, he rushed to seize all their books. When the assembly of police sought expert testimony on the "reasonableness" of certain grain prices, it called upon those who were considered to know them best, a measurer and a porter.[13]

The police of the measurers was not confined to the ports and the Halle, because all grain and flour traffic did not pass through the markets. Complementing the "sedentary" officers assigned to measure at these markets were the "ambulatory" measurers who prowled the streets near the bakeshops and around the *barrières* or city entry gates in search of merchandise arriving en droiture.[14] The measurers were relentless enemies of droiture traffic because it drained the markets of their vitality and threatened to deprive them of revenue. They had always maintained that droiture trade was illegal, and continued to use that argument sporadically well after droiture had attained a structural role in the provisioning trade. Unable to prevent droiture, they resorted to other tactics. They tried to challenge every droiture shipment in

11. AN, H* 1870, fols. 91–106, 11 January 1763; AN, Y 9538, 10 November 1751, and Y 12606, 27 May 1758.

12. On the infidelities in London, see Thrupp, *Bakers of London,* pp. 23–24; in Rouen, see Miromesnil to Laverdy, 10 March 1768, *Correspondance politique,* p. 11. See also Baulant and Meuvret, *Prix des céréales,* 1:1ff.

13. Albert to Machurin, 12 March 1776, AN, Y 12626[A]; BN, ms. fr. 11356, fol. 372.

14. AN, Y 9622, 28 November 1759, and Y 9539, 26 May 1758.

the hope of finding a trade irregularity, such as a lack of a certificate authenticating the purchase or fraudulent or expired certificates, that would allow them to seize the merchandise. Often they stopped delivery wagons at random in the streets, but as a rule they were alerted to the entry of suspect merchandise by their clerks at the *barrières*.[15] These clerks, who may have worked simultaneously for the General Farm, examined and registered all grain and flour arrivals. When a driver failed to provide proper documentation, the clerk immediately summoned the measurer–duty officer, even in the middle of the night. The clerks were also empowered to collect measurer droits, but it is doubtful that many suppliers volunteered payment on entry.[16] Since many bakers bought illicitly off the market or by commission, it was not difficult for the measurers to find pretexts for procuring handsome indemnities. And when the droiture transaction was impeccable, the measurers tried to claim that they were owed duties in any case. We have seen how passionately the bakers resisted and resented the first tactic and contested the validity of the second.

Given their familiarity with the provisioning trade, the measurers were sometimes sent on mission to the supply zone by the lieutenant general. It was a logical extension of their vocation to impose order, for trading abuses in the countryside were a direct source of disorder in the capital. In 1740, for instance, lieutenant general Marville dispatched a measurer to check on and prod the laboureurs in the Beauce.[17] Construing their mandate in the broadest possible terms, the measurers stretched their police jurisdiction into the countryside around Paris without specific instructions from above. Measurers Alexandre and Cholet uncovered a large hoard in an inn at the hamlet of Point du Jour in 1757. Dufay and Jérome inspected public and private houses as well as wagons in their freewheeling rounds in the suburbs.[18] Occasionally the police chief asked the measurers to undertake delicate tasks within Paris. Pierre Buignet, a syndic of the measurers' corps, who was relied upon as an expert witness by both the assembly of police and the Hôtel-Dieu, assumed responsibility during the subsistence crises of 1725 and 1740 for receiving, stocking, reconditioning, and selling the king's grain, an enormously trying business.[19] Measurer Chapin fulfilled similarly demanding functions for the prévôt des marchands.[20]

The consular court deferred to the measurers by asking them to serve as

15. AN, Y 9538, 4 September 1756 and 6 September 1757; Hérault notes and *laissez-passer*, 20 May 1728, Arsenal, ms. Bast. 10274; BN, Coll. Joly 1829, fols. 317ff.

16. AN, Y 9539, 3 January 1761 and 19 August 1763; Y 9538, 6, 20 May 1757.

17. Arsenal, ms. Bast. 10141, fol. 261 (16 October 1759).

18. AN, Y 9538, 6 May 1757; Y 9474, 18, 25 January 1771.

19. AN, Y 11220, 8 October 1733 and Y 11227, 25 May 1740; assembly of police, 28 February 1732, BN, ms. fr. 11356, fol. 185; Archives Assistance publique, deliberations of the bureau of the Hôtel-Dieu, 13 October 1741, no. 110.

20. 23 January 1756, AN, F¹¹ 264.

arbiters in grain and flour conflicts opposing bakers and suppliers or brokers and merchants. Better known for opinionated trenchancy than for impartiality, as mediators the measurers ran true to form. Unlike the priest-mediators, who effaced themselves, listened quietly to all the parties, and sought a reconciliation through mutual understanding, the measurers tended to decide rapidly which party deserved to win, then openly shifted their weight to that side.[21]

The Police Functions of the Porters

Functionally, the porters were in many ways indistinguishable from the measurers. They spoke in the name of abundance, good order, and the public interest. They construed their task in the broadest police sense as "uncovering all violations concerning grain and flour" and insinuating themselves into the very structure of the provisioning trade to prevent such violations.[22] They became directly involved in transactions, specifically in order to guarantee their honesty, but more generally in order to be in a position to control them. To a fuming buyer who shouted, "It's not your business," porter Joseph Savadon serenely denied the right to purchase flour on the grounds that he refused to divulge the use he would make of it.[23] Porter Jean Marlet energetically supported a buyer's efforts to persuade a grain dealer to lower the price.[24] In addition to helping make prices, the porters also collected price data on the markets, thus providing the police authorities with a means of verifying the reports of the measurers.[25] As the traffic controllers of the marketplaces, responsible for the movement of merchandise to and from the concourse of transactions, the porters were in a better position than the measurers to keep track of daily grain and flour entries.[26]

Like the measurers, the porters had itinerant as well as fixed posts. They did not wait for the buyers and sellers to come to them. They were in the forefront of the war against droiture, generally motivated by the same kinds of concerns as the measurers. They set traps for dealers and bakers, halted them to check their papers and goods, and delivered oral summonses and proclaimed seizures, as a result of which they sometimes had to face angry crowds in the streets. When the porters were not on patrol, the clerks at the

21. See, for example, Aiserly v. Gasson, 21 January 1761, Archives Seine-Paris, D6B[6], carton 3, and Cheroux v. Houdan, 21 June 1773, D6B[6], carton 6.
22. AN, Y 9539, 26, 29 January 1762.
23. AN, Y 11220, 23 December 1733.
24. AN, Y 11223, 4 August 1736.
25. Duplessis to procurator general, 4 May 1726, BN, Coll. Joly 1118, fols. 137–38, and AN, Y 9533, April 1749 (porter Bourguignon, *rapporteur des farines*).
26. AN, Y 11220, 6 May 1733; police sentence, 28 June 1727, BN, ms. fr. 21633, fol. 283; "état des arrivages et des ventes," April 1731 (porter Robert), Arsenal, ms. Bast. 10270.

Grain and flour porters at the Paris markets, sixteenth century (Deutsches Brotmuseum)

city gates alerted them to the entry of suspect merchandise.[27] The lieutenant of police dispatched porters as well as measurers to investigate illicit selling and buying practices in the supply crowns.[28]

Their functions overlapped so much that many contemporaries saw no reason to distinguish between measurers and porters. An experienced flour merchant spoke of a measurer who "broke" his flour, a task that theoretically only porters could perform. The commissaire of the central markets department often treated them like members of a single corps of "officer measurers and porters." A commissaire affixing seals to the estate of a deceased porter referred to him in his text as a measurer and as a porter alternately; even his widow, in her petition to have the seals lifted, incorrectly called him a measurer. Poussot himself, who knew them better than anyone, got them confused on occasion.[29]

27. Police sentence, 7 February 1766, Archives Seine-Paris, 6 AZ 472; AN, Y 9538, 15 June 1725, and Y 9539, 1 October 1765.
28. Police sentence, 11 January 1737, BN, ms. fr. 21635, fol. 164.
29. AN, Y 11226, 3 September 1739; Y 9442, 20 January 1741; Y 9499, 17 February 1744;

The porters delighted in this conflation because it situated them on a plane of equality with the measurers, their rivals, and administrative role models. Some porters would have gone a step further toward enhancing their status (or rather obfuscating it) by suppressing the word *porter,* a degrading title that evoked the grossest sort of unskilled manual labor. Thus, Olivier Meusnier styled himself "officer for grain and flour"; his colleague J.-B. Touchard preferred "officer of the Halles."[30]

The measurers protested and resisted this effort on the part of their "inferiors" to occupy the lofty terrain of "police officer," over which they claimed exclusive command at the markets. The measurers scorned the porters as "mere beasts of burden," unfit to undertake delicate administrative tasks.[31] They complained tirelessly of porter misconduct. Measurers Durin and Beaubigny denounced porters Coupin and Marlet for "interfering in the making of prices, which is not at all your business." When porter Ligon attempted to confiscate twenty sacks of contraband flour just minutes before Latour, one of the measurers' syndics, arrived on the scene, Latour filed an official protest against "this encroachment on our department."[32] If they had wielded the necessary authority, the measurers would have confined the porters to what they considered their primary vocation: loading and unloading boats and wagons. They importuned the lieutenants general for injunctions prohibiting the porters from "troubling them in their police functions." So intense was the measurers' hostility that they joined their archenemies, the bakers, in a suit meant to exclude the porters from exercising police functions of any sort.[33]

The porters countered that, save for a few superficial details, their charge was essentially the same as the measurers'. Despite their name, the servile task of loading and unloading was not at all at the core of their professional activity. They tried to shift the focus to the role they played at the point of transaction—a role exactly parallel to that played by the measurers and organically bound up with it. The porters orchestrated the transaction by pouring the merchandise into receptacles that they provided and "breaking" the flour by discharging the sack and turning it in preparation for measuring. Like the measurers, they construed the manual labor involved in this process to be

Y 13099, 17 September 1746; Arsenal, ms. Bast. 10141 (2 May 1756). A baker elder differentiated between "the two communities" but suggested that they had virtually the same vocation. Deline, *Mémoire* (1726), p. 2, BN (factum).

30. AN, MC, XXVI-245, 27 May 1710, and AN, Y 11230, October 1743.

31. BN, Coll. Joly 1429, fol. 199. Poussot quite rightly spoke of "the enmity between measurers and porters." Cf. the symbolic act of execration performed by the porter's aide who defecated in the wig of a leading measurer. AN, Z^{1H} 646, 22 May 1733 (Coulbant v. Dragon).

32. AN, Y 11223, 4 August 1736, and Y 9539, 3 January 1761. A quarter-century earlier, another measurer had reviled Ligon for his "turbulence." Y 11223, 1 June 1736.

33. Ordonnance, 1 June 1725, BN 4° 35614; AN, H* 1873, fols. 608–27, June 1770.

incidental to the "police" they exercised by their vigilant and often not-so-discreet presence. At least once in the seventeenth century and again at the beginning of the eighteenth, the measurers vainly attempted to expel the porters from the arena of transaction by usurping their functions and thus undermining their claims to a copolice.[34] The porters contended that they provided the critical mediation at the transaction, that they were in closer touch with the buyers and sellers, that the measurers' contribution was largely symbolic and practically superfluous, and that they were generally negligent in the performance of their duty.[35] Like the measurers, in order to consecrate their administrative status, the porters tried to transform their payment from a remuneration for service into a sort of droit, collectable not only at the point of transaction at the Halle and the ports but also upon entry when shipped en droiture. When the measurers proved more successful than the porters in levying this fee at the city toll gates, the latter accused them of "setting up a true monopoly and an extortion racket."[36]

The *Forts*

To make their case for police status persuasive, the porters felt that they had to dissociate themselves as completely as possible from the abasement of manual labor. To do this, and at the same time offer a service that they were expected to provide and that was remunerated, the porters farmed out the work—and, they hoped, the stigma as well—to a group of sturdy subalterns called *forts* or *plumets*. The practice dated back at least to the sixteenth century, and it was controversial from the beginning.[37] While the porters continued to receive the fee fixed by law for each type of loading and unloading operation, they commissioned gagne-deniers from the army of unskilled day laborers who lived in and off the central markets to do the work for them. They paid them a wage that represented only a fraction of the fee they pocketed for their monopoly and that was incommensurate with the time and labor involved. The porters expected the *plumets* to obtain a supplement from the sellers and buyers. In at least one case in the eighteenth century, the porters negotiated a deal for the *plumets:* the mealmen agreed to pay them 10 sous per voie.[38] In most cases there was no such arrangement. The *plumets* did everything they could to extract a substantial pourboire. While they viewed it as an integral part of their wage, honestly earned, it was perceived by those who were invited, and often harassed, to pay it as a form of extortion, an obligation to pay twice for the same service.

34. AN, F[12] 94, fol. 245 (26 April 1747) and BN, Coll. Joly 1829, fol. 236.
35. "Réflexions," ca. 1730, AN, F[11] 264.
36. BN, Coll. Joly 1429, fol. 189.
37. Delamare, *Traité de la police,* 2:668.
38. Arsenal, ms. Bast. 10141 (2 February, 5 April 1756).

The *fort* cut an imposing figure, at once larger and lower than life. "I mean by this class of men," wrote the abbé Galiani, "the last of all, and so much the last that it almost strains the nuance between man and the beast of burden. I speak of this class of men . . . who substituted their backs for their heads and who for talent and occupation have only the strength of their muscles."[39] The portrait was harsh, but the *forts* themselves cultivated a reputation for ferocity and crudeness above and beyond the claims to which their nature and manner entitled them, for it increased their leverage in dealing with those who needed their services. Where Galiani was far wide of the mark was in underestimating their cleverness, their sense of place, and their insight into the complex operation of the market.

Little is known about their origin, geographic or social. Of sixty-four *forts* whose conduct Poussot examined at mid-century, fifty-two, or over 81 percent, were natives of Paris. A substantial number of them were "raised in the Halles": the Halles were their "pays," they succeeded one another "de père en fils," and they jealously regarded their posts as transmissible "heritages." "Although raised in the Halles," wrote Poussot of twenty-two-year-old Pierre Delarue, "he does not have the defects—he is good-natured, tranquil, not at all a drunkard, is a good worker and of sufficient strength." A flour broker's helper, Julien Desnoeud, whose older brother was a *fort,* demanded a similar place on the grounds that his brother-in-law, also a *fort,* had bequeathed him the right to succeed. (The *forts* behaved like robe nobles, with the difference that they had no *paulette* tax to acquit.) The de la Metairie family had dynastic ambitions: eighteen-year-old Jacques sought a place while his father and grandfather still worked as *forts.* Others, such as Charles Maillet or the three Mairet brothers, from lack of connections or cunning, never succeeded in penetrating the *fort* milieu. They remained "gagne-deniers à la halle au bled," mere casual laborers dependent on the leftovers or the tasks that the *forts* renounced. The ages of the *forts* ranged from nineteen to sixty-five. The average ages in four of the leading *bandes* were thirty-eight, thirty-four, thirty-six, and forty-nine.[40]

Work as a *fort* in grain and flour was rarely a full-time enterprise. Many of them also labored elsewhere in the central markets, while some exercised a second profession entirely outside the realm of the Halles. Among the latter were the *forts* who served simultaneously as soldiers, either in the French Guards or the Guard of Paris. Although the current state of our knowledge precludes such an analysis, if it *could* be demonstrated that a large portion of

39. Galiani, *Commerce des bleds,* pp. 210–11. The physical task was backbreaking, according to Poussot, who reported that two hundred forts were wounded on the job during his twenty years in the central markets, some of them mortally. Arsenal, ms. Bast. 10141 (2 February 1756).

40. Arsenal, ms. Bast. 10141 (28 July 1756, 16 April 1757, 22 November and 28 December 1760) and 10140, unnumbered pages on recruitment of the forts.

The *forts* in the early nineteenth century (private collection)

the *forts* fulfilled the two functions, we would have a sharper understanding of the legendary volatility attributed to the Parisian military and paramilitary contingents and of the perennial fears of violent eruption from within the halles, as well as a vivid illustration of the blurred line that separated the forces of order from those of disorder in the urban core.[41]

During and after the old regime it was often not so much the attitudes of consumers who were dispersed throughout the city as the opinion of the personnel of the Halles, the little people concentrated in the marketplace who were of course consumers as well as workers, that captured the attention of rulers and ministers. Until the twentieth century, the leaders of France always reserved or feigned to reserve for them a special solicitude. The romance between fishmonger and monarch had a political dimension. The royalists shrewdly used the "dames des Halles" as foils for their counterrevolutionary propaganda of nostalgia, while the *Révolutions de Paris* was quick to celebrate the "worthy *forts* of the Halle" who were "*forts* for their fatherland."[42]

The astuteness of the *forts* eluded Galiani, but their instinctive subversive proclivities, as he construed them, did not. "Sole authors of all the riots," he wrote, the *forts* were to be "very much feared by a good Prince."[43] Presumably, if the *fort*-soldier started the riot, the soldier-*fort* was unlikely to be very zealous or very effective in repressing it—at least not before the message got across. We know for a fact that the soldiers of the guards and their wives, who often worked in the central markets, played a prominent role in the disorders that buffeted the Halles in the last hundred years of the old regime.[44] On the other hand, the *fort*-soldier could change roles in the other direction as well. Inspector Poussot, not naive about matters of public tranquility, contended that he could best avoid disorder by placing the soldiers in the most delicate posts open to *forts*.[45] In any event, because he occupied such a sensitive place, the *fort* in grain or flour could not be treated with indifference by the authorities.

Prior to the reign of Louis XV, the *forts* had no recognized status as a professional group in the markets. Like many other elements of the urban laboring poor who were denied an autonomous place in the corporate work

41. Scores of soldiers were *forts,* but the evidence is too scattered to permit any rigorous counting. See Archives Assistance publique, Panneterie, 1755–61, unclassified, and Journal de l'économe de Scipion, 1768–70, Hôpital Général 105, Fosseyeux liasse 7; Arsenal, ms. Bast. 10141 (6 November 1759, 22 December 1760).

42. *Révolutions de Paris,* no. 106 (16–23 July 1791): 90. Cf. the alliance between "les forts de la halle" and "mesdames les harangères." Gazetins, 3 October 1729, Arsenal, ms. Bast. 10160, fol. 110.

43. Galiani, *Commerce des bleds,* pp. 211–12.

44. See Kaplan, *Famine Plot,* pp. 7–9.

45. Arsenal, ms. Bast. 10141 (27 January 1761). I hope to learn more about market-paramilitary interpenetration when Jean Chagniot publishes his thesis "Paris et l'armée au XVIIIe siècle," cited by Jean Meyer, *Etudes sur les villes en Europe occidentale (milieu du XVIIe siècle à la veille de la Révolution Française)* (Paris, 1983), p. 178.

structure—the journeymen are the most prominent example—the market laborers organized themselves, informally and semiclandestinely, for the purpose of enhancing their competitive position and protecting common interests. The police believed that these illicit "cabals" and "monopolies" encouraged the workers to replace police regulations with their own codes of behavior, to use violence to coerce buyers and sellers to rely exclusively on their services, and to prevent other laborers from obtaining work in their terrain. In 1698 lieutenant general of police d'Argenson expressly prohibited the *forts* from forming "any bands or societies among themselves" on pain of a fine of 500 livres and banishment from the markets. Yet the authorities betrayed an ambivalent attitude toward these illicit guilds, in part because they knew that these bodies would find a way to continue to exist in one form or another. It made more sense in the eyes of certain grass-roots police agents such as Poussot to infiltrate and appropriate these organizations and use them as vehicles of social and economic control.

As early as the twenties a number of "bands" in the markets were informally consecrated by the police. Theoretically, the authorities screened recruitment and imposed rules that were to serve as corporate statutes. A prospective *plumet* was to petition the porters for a place. The porters were supposed to solicit approval for each candidate from city hall or the lieutenant general's office. Each *plumet* received a numbered metal medallion that he was enjoined to wear whenever he was at work in order to make him easy to identify. No *fort* could work for the porters without a medallion and no authorized *plumet* could transfer his medallion to anyone else without penalty of exclusion.[46] The ultimate sanction against an intractable *plumet* was the withdrawal of his medallion, a measure tantamount to expulsion from the corporation.[47] To some extent the bands of *forts*, like any other corporation, were expected to assume responsibility for keeping their own house in order. Thus they had syndics, probably appointed by the police rather than elected, whose function was to communicate orders to the *forts* and transmit their complaints to the authorities as well as to maintain order within.[48]

The Origins and Uncertain Existence
of the Market Officers

The Paris measurers traced their origins "into the night of time." It is likely that they performed market service well before they received their first stat-

46. See the ordinances of 15 July 1724 and 18 December 1725, AN, AD XI 38; Arsenal, ms. Bast. 10141 (1 September 1756).
47. Police sentence of 18 October 1753, cited in Arsenal, ms. Bast. 10141 (13 November 1754).
48. See the "sindiques" in Poussot's listing of the bands, ibid., 10140.

utes in the thirteenth century. In the fifteenth century, they were divided into three "bands" functioning at the Halle, the Grève, and the Juiverie market in the Cité. They were required to take out a bond of surety, a practice that would have been applauded by the buyers and sellers had it survived into the eighteenth century.[49] The measurers were organized on the model of a guild in a "community" governed by rules approved by the king and registered by the parlement. Like most guilds, the measurers gave expression to their moral and spiritual dimension in a confrérie, consecrated to the Virgin.[50] By the early seventeenth century, the measurers had become venal hereditary officeholders.[51]

As an officially recognized community, the porters had a less venerable pedigree. Well before they became public officers, however, "they formed a sort of corps or society" that lobbied for recognition even as it tried to impose a de facto monopoly of service. In 1410 Charles VI granted legal status to the brotherhood organized by the porters of the Halle at the church of St.-Eustache. By the early sixteenth century, the porters of the Halle and the Ecole port were united in a single corporation. The porters of the Grève declined to join them, however, and the two groups quarreled bitterly over territory and prerogatives until the middle of the seventeenth century, when the royal government, after having transformed the porters in each community into officeholders, decreed their fusion.[52]

The 1670s inaugurated a century of uncertainty and instability for the measurers and the porters. Their existence was threatened alternately by fiscality and reformism, two apparently antagonistic policies that were imbricated in the system of royal government and were in some ways mutually dependent. Like many other corporations, the measurers and the porters were seriously weakened by more-or-less relentless royal fiscal pressure. The government partly compensated them and the other officers on the ports and markets by authorizing them to levy higher and higher fees on incoming merchandise.[53] These droits shifted a heavy burden to consumers, but *not* where they were most sensitive and vulnerable: bread grains and flours were almost invariably spared. Yet this rampant fiscal manipulation further confused the "public" stature of the measurers and porters and made it even more

49. Sylvestre, *Histoire des professions alimentaires,* pp. 34–38; Alfred Franklin, *La Vie privée d'autrefois,* vol. 3, *La Cuisine* (Paris, 1887–1902), p. 220; Antoine-Jean-Victor Leroux de Lincy, *Hôtel de Ville de Paris* (Paris, 1844), p. 55.

50. Lespinasse, *Métiers et corporations,* 1:240–41; François Olivier-Martin, *L'Organisation corporative de la France d'ancien régime* (Paris, 1938), pp. 109–11, 456.

51. Delamare, *Traité de la police,* 2:111.

52. Ibid., pp. 665–74; AN, F¹² 94, fol. 244 (26 April 1747).

53. Charles Louandre, *De l'alimentation publique sous l'ancienne monarchie française* (Paris, 1864), p. 542; Biollay, *Pacte de famine,* p. 61, and *Origines du factorat,* pp. 5–7. For a discussion of the droits involved, see Gustave Bienaymé and A. de Saint-Julien, *Histoire des droits d'entrée et d'octrois à Paris* (Paris, 1887), pp. 97–103.

difficult for them to pass as authentic police officials. The sporadic reformist impulse, a sort of knee-jerk expiation for the fiscal depredations, completed the work of discrediting them. By calling for the suppression of the measurers and porters, this reformism reinforced the idea that their offices were little more than fiscal contrivances to which the government turned in desperation, and that the functions exercised through them were at bottom gratuitous.

In 1674 Louis XIV quashed the posts of eighteen of the sixty-eight measurers, reserving their droits for collection by the General Farm. Since he lacked the funds to reimburse the value of the suppressed posts, it is likely that he aimed merely at extorting a tribute from the corporation, which the measurers promptly offered—36,000 livres. It appears that, in response to the same pressure, the porters ransomed sixty-eight of their offices for a much larger sum.[54] In 1690, the measurers agreed to pay 300,000 livres in order to preempt the creation of new posts that would dilute their authority and diminish their revenue.[55] In 1699 they were warned that they would not be allowed to subsist in their present form unless they showed more assiduity in exercising their functions. Specifically, they were reproached for failing to provide their superiors with information on market activities and to appear in court to testify when called.[56]

It would be wrong, however, to perceive the edict of July 1704 creating sixty offices of visitors and controllers of grain in each of the two corporations as an effort to purge the measurers and porters of their bad elements. It was meant only to bleed them. The porters did everything in their power to subvert the sale of the new posts: they spread the rumor that the new offices would shortly be assimilated to the old ones at a value considerably below the purchase price and they refused to reveal the accounts of their earnings to the prospective buyers. Nevertheless, the king magnanimously allowed the measurers and porters to purchase the new offices en bloc, provided they agreed to accept his financial terms immediately.[57]

Convinced that there was no market to make this royal blackmail credible, the two corporations refused the proposition. At the end of the year the king was forced to offer a compromise. He would suppress the posts of controller and in their place create thirty-two new offices of measurer and twenty-two of porter. The corporations would be able to acquire them, but to strengthen the royal bargaining position Louis XIV did everything he could to make the

---

54. Arrêt du conseil, 21 March 1674, and letters patent, May 1674, BHVP. The letters patent accorded the measurers a droit on all grain and flour entering the city, yet this fee was associated with the service of measuring and therefore was not entirely a droit. This ambiguity was to cause grave problems for both the authorities and the measurers throughout the eighteenth century.

55. Declaration, 20 June 1690, BHVP.

56. Declaration, 1 September 1699, BHVP. Cf. a sharp rebuke for similar negligence by lieutenant general of police La Reynie, 6 May 1667, Delamare, *Traité de la police,* 2:116.

57. Arrêt du conseil, 24 January 1705, BHVP.

posts attractive to individual buyers from the outside. Anyone could purchase one or more posts: all the traditional "incompatibilities" were suspended. A buyer-investor would not be obliged to exercise the office himself. The new measurers and porters were to enjoy the droits on oats and on small grains that had originally been bestowed upon the controllers. No corporate reception fee would be required and the new owners would have to pay only half of the standard "resignation" fee guaranteeing hereditary transmission of the post. Nor would the "old" officers be in a position to marginalize the "new" ones. The king intended to shape the internal administration of the corporation by reserving the (elected) posts of syndics, auditors, and examiners to the new buyers for four years and the position of treasurer to them forever. The new men were to have charge of assigning the measurers and porters to their daily tasks and of keeping all the books.[58]

Threatened with the loss of virtually all their power (the new officers would be "our masters," the veterans complained bitterly), with a shrinking of their income, and with a loss in the market value of their offices, the measurers and porters were forced to seek a deal. The king agreed to reduce the number of new posts in each corporation to twenty, to allow the measurers and porters collectively to acquire and incorporate them, to extend the new droits to each of the corporations, and to declare old and new offices equal in terms of prerogatives and functions. The measurers promised to pay 231,000 livres, plus a surcharge of 21,000 livres for the offices—less than the king initially demanded, but in a lump cash payment that he could not resist. The porters got off for substantially less.[59]

The government stung the measurers and porters again in 1706. Reminding them of an edict of November 1704 creating four "perpetual" officers-syndics in each of the "police corporations," it declared that it had attributed the functions of these syndics to the "new" measurers and porters "by inadvertence." In order to escape the consequences of the edict of 1704, the measurers agreed to pay a total of 90,000 livres.[60] Pleading straitened circumstances, the porters refused to absorb the offices. The royal government responded by initiating procedures to seize and sell their corporate property. Ensuing negotiations issued in a compromise: the king increased the special compensatory droits that he had originally offered the porters and they promised 108,000 livres, all of which they were authorized to borrow.[61]

In 1711 the king frightened the measurers and porters into submission with an old but still effective ploy. In return for an increase of 3,000 livres in gages and supplementary droits on oats and the small grains, the measurers were asked to pay 165,000 livres and the porters 198,000. When they rebuffed the

58. Edict, December 1705, ibid.
59. Edict, May 1706, AN, AD XI 38.
60. Declaration, 9 February 1706, BHVP.
61. Declaration of 17 July 1706 and edict of May 1708, ibid.

offer on the grounds that they could not raise the money, Louis XIV announced that he had found a financier ready to buy the package and thus to have a hand permanently in corporate affairs. The two corporations quickly asked for and were accorded a second chance to amass the funds and thus to protect their liberty.[62]

Apprehensive over sharp challenges to their prerogatives from both the measurers and the bakers, at the end of 1712 the porters took the exceptional step of *proposing* to the crown an increase in the official evaluation of their offices, tantamount to a low-interest loan, in exchange for an explicit confirmation of their powers. In particular, they sought the (re-)legitimation of such disputed prerogatives as the right to pronounce verbal summonses, to oblige suppliers and buyers to use their services, to verify the papers of all persons transporting grain or flour, and to collect certain droits at the city gates. To relieve their anxiety, the soi-disant impecunious porters offered 172,000 livres. It is not clear if this deal was consummated as the porters envisaged it.[63]

Nor did the royal government let the measurers and porters forget that the insurance premiums they purchased provided no more than short-run protection. Even as the king-fisc continued to hector them, in an edict of May 1715, the king-reformer committed himself to their liquidation, but at an indeterminate time in the future: when his finances would permit it. The following year the porters were required to help hasten that day by contributing yet again to the royal treasury. This time, however, there was no quid pro quo. The porters were condemned, by a chamber of justice impaneled to investigate "abuses and graft," to restitute 3,000 livres. Sharply critical of the porters' greed and irresponsibility, the judgment constituted a strong argument for the reformers, who maintained that suppression was the only solution. It denounced the porters for arbitrarily increasing their fees by 100 to 150 percent, wresting payment from small-scale suppliers who were legally permitted to unload their own horses and mules, encouraging their *plumets* to extort tribute by not compensating them fairly, and engaging surreptitiously in the grain trade through illicit association with bakers and merchants.[64]

The final blow, an edict abolishing their venal offices, struck the measurers and the porters, as well as other officers on the ports and markets, in 1719. To perform their daily tasks, the government authorized the lieutenant general and the prévôt des marchands to name *commis:* revocable employees remunerated by a fixed wage. The original aim was to eliminate any vestige of the porter office by confiding responsibility for flour breaking to the measurer *commis* and for other porter tasks to interested gagne-deniers. The authorities abandoned this idea when it became apparent that the competition for porter

62. Declaration, 13 October 1711, AN, AD XI 38.
63. BN, Coll. Joly 1312, fol. 102.
64. Arrêt of the chambre de justice, 18 August 1716, BN, ms. Clairambault 767, fols.

work failed to prevent "exactions" and in fact issued in "chaos in the market-places." An arrêt du conseil established sixty-eight porter *commis* who re-covered the right to break flour, much to the chagrin of the measurer agents, whose wages were proportionately reduced. Curiously, as if a formal suppres-sion of the venal posts satisfied the reform requirements, many of the ex-measurers and ex-porters managed to obtain commissions as *commis* while awaiting reimbursement of their charges.[65]

Whatever hope the government may have entertained of reimbursing all the officers was more or less rapidly dashed by the disarray that followed the fall of John Law. Confident that they would eventually recover their offices and their droits, a considerable number of officers never sought reimburse-ment, but instead pressed the government to reconsider its decision.[66] In 1730 the government reestablished the offices, fixing their number at eighty per corporation, ostensibly in order to aid these ex-officers "who, for lack of work, find themselves without subsistence," and to raise the level of job performance, now considered to be higher among operatives who had an instinctive appetite for "good order" than among workaday *commis*. In fact the government acted in order to turn a quick profit.[67] Former officeholders were granted a six-month most-favored-buyer period in which they could (re-) purchase an office (or several) in exchange for the government paper assigned to them in reimbursement of the old offices for six-sevenths of the price and cash for the remaining fraction. Thereafter, anyone could purchase a post provided he paid for at least one-sixth of it in cash. The reconstituted corpora-tions were also authorized to purchase offices for the purpose of reducing the number of measurers and porters.

Twenty-four "old" measurers resolved to acquire offices again. Even be-fore the procedure was established for (re-)purchase, these old hands for-mally revived the corporation and elected leaders. In fact, the corporation

---

239–40. In 1731 the municipal court condemned a former grain trader, now a porter, to a fine of 400 livres for "[illicitly] meddling in grain traffic." AN, F^{11} 264 (13 April 1731).

65. Edict of September 1719 and arrêts du conseil of 12 September 1719 and 15 October 1720, BN, Coll. Joly 1312, fols. 92, 96–97, and AN, AD XI 38.

66. For an example of paper reimbursement procedure that left the measurers with interest-bearing notes rather than cash, see Philippe Emery, AN, MC, XXXIX-342, 16 April 1731 (receipt from 30 June 1726). On the other hand, ex-measurer Louis Soret received cash—but only 15,000 livres in principal, significantly below the market value on which the revived measurers' corporation counted. AN, MC, C-536, 15 February 1731. The govern-ment apparently referred to the purchase price in order to determine the indemnity. Presum-ably Soret accepted the offer because he did not believe that the market could do better.

67. Edict, June 1730, BN, Coll. Joly 1312, fols. 138–42. Cf. Marcel Marion, *Histoire financière de la France depuis 1715* (Paris, 1914–27), 1:151. The Parlement of Paris sharply criticized the king for resorting to this onerous fiscal device and for pretending that venal officers were more efficient than commissioned agents. Remonstrance, 28 August 1730, Jules Flammermont, ed., *Remontrances du Parlement de Paris au 18e siècle* (Paris, 1888–98), 1:219–31.

had never ceased to function during the period between 1719 and 1730, though it had had no statutory existence. It had continued to serve as a clearinghouse for police operations even as it had become the lobbying agency for the dispossessed officers. This rump corporation proposed a deal that the government accepted. It would pay 3,200,000 livres for the eighty offices, 7,500 livres less per post than the edict demanded.[68] Only forty-eight "new" offices were to be sold by the corporation, making a total of seventy-two members; the eight others would be absorbed by the collectivity and suppressed. Each measurer, old and new, would pay 22,000 livres, the former drawing upon the indemnities for their pre-1719 offices. The remainder of the sum was to be borrowed. Among the first lenders to offer their funds were a number of measurers themselves, including Noel Besnard, who received an annuity of 1,000 livres in return for 28,000 livres in cash principal.[69] The porters' corporation also survived more or less intact. It is likely that the porters obtained a rebirth settlement similar to that of the measurers, though the details remain obscure.

An edict of September 1759 announced the suppression of the measurers yet again. "New needs," however, once more prevented the king from keeping his promise. This edict may have been motivated by political concerns linked to the introduction of the flour-weighing system at the Halle rather than by a genuine expectation that the measurer issue could finally be resolved, for it did not contain a realistic plan for reimbursement. Shortly we shall have occasion to see how profoundly this edict, in conjunction with inspector Poussot's reformist offensive, jarred the market officials. An edict of March 1760 "allowed" the measurers and porters to continue to exercise their offices and pledged to finance their extinction gradually between 1771 and 1782. By the end of 1768, however, the government realized that this program was too ambitious: it postponed the beginning of the projected reimbursement period to 1777.[70] The measurers trembled when Turgot came to power in 1774, for he made it clear that he regarded them as vicious anachronisms, the rudimentary instruments of the police that he was determined to destroy.[71] Nevertheless, the measurers and porters survived Turgot's and several other less energetic attempts to liquidate them in the last decade before the Revolution.

68. BN, ms. fr. 21632, fols. 236–37.

69. AN, MC, XXXIX-404, 7 August 1731.

70. Edicts of September 1759 and March 1760 and declaration, 5 December 1768, BN. The government also committed itself to the suppression of the measurers in the other market towns of the kingdom at the end of the sixties. See conseil secret, 21 January 1769, AN, X^{1B} 8957; Pierre Binet, *Réglementation du marché du blé en France au XVIIIe siècle et à l'époque contemporaine* (Paris, 1939), pp. 44. The reputation of the provincial measurers was very much like that of their Parisian counterparts: Vandoul to Saint-Priest, 9 May 1773, AD Hérault, C 2914, and Masson to intendant of Champagne, 9 September 1766, AD Aube, C 299.

71. Edicts of 1776, AN, AD XI 40.

Corporate Life

The measurers and the porters owed their survival in part to the tenacity of their corporate organizations. Each corporation vigorously defended the economic, social, and political interests of its members. It maneuvered to forestall suppression, to make the office market more lively, to increase fees and other income, to repel encroachments by other corporations on its jurisdiction, and to prevent its "clients" from escaping its jurisdiction. The "community," as the corporation was called in the language of the eighteenth century, protected the rights of its members when they fell ill, favored the succession of their sons to their posts, assisted widows materially for a year after the death of their spouses, and encouraged the confreres to establish links of solidarity through participation in baptismal, marriage, burial, and testamentary rites.

The measurers and the porters entrusted the administration of their communities to their *sanior pars:* an elite who imposed themselves by force of character and/or wealth or patronage. This elect provided for its own reproduction by coopting the leading figures in each cohort and for the reproduction of the corporation by carefully screening candidates, actively seeking out prospective buyers whose solidity would redound to both oligarchical and corporate advantage, and sometimes helping to arrange the financing for the purchase of an office. The corporate leadership—syndics, adjoints, receivers—arranged for the common treasury, into which all the earnings of the individual offices were supposed to flow, to be divided up equally among members after deduction of expenses, including various "gratifications and reimbursements" to the leaders. This financial management was the chief source of internal tension in the communities of the measurers and of the porters, as in virtually all the trade guilds. The authority of the corporate elders over money matters was all the more suspected and resented because they were also responsible for internal discipline and were thus in a position to reward confreres who supported them and to punish adversaries.

Beyond its stewardship of the private interests of the members and the collective interests of the group, the community exercised a public vocation. In this sense each of the two communities operated as a branch of the city administration and of the police. They served as bridges between the markets of the ports and the Halle, estranged by the rivalry between the jurisdictions of the Hôtel de Ville and the Châtelet, and helped to forge a more-or-less coherent and unified police posture. They coordinated all data collection and collation. Each community defined the specific jobs to be performed and assigned officers to them. It framed the criteria for the comportment of the officers and for the judgments that they would have to make in the field. The community was answerable for the moral character as well as the professional deftness of its members. It was the vehicle through which the authorities communicated with the measurers and porters.

No wonder that the matter of the control of the corporation tended to exercise measurers and porters alike. In the second half of the seventeenth century, a dissident group of measurers led by a former syndic tried to wrest control from the ruling oligarchy. The case made by these insurgents is redolent of the accusations characteristically leveled against the ruling elite of the trade corporations by their disaffected confreres: the current syndics and their partisans, many of whom were former and future syndics, refused to account to the membership either for their actions or for their allocation of funds. Inept and disorderly at best, at worst their stewardship was corrupt. It issued in widespread demoralization among the members, who no longer cared about their work. The measurer dissidents obtained the creation of a commission to study new statutes. It was disbanded, however, as a result of the sabotage .of one of its members, who specialized in "the commerce of substitutes" and who feared that the reformers would try to ban the practice of hiring replacements to perform the measurers' work. The leadership ultimately submitted a new charter for approbation when the prévôt des marchands announced that a reformist version drafted by the dissidents would be adopted within two weeks if it went unchallenged. If a majority of the corporation approved the new charter, the dissidents charged that it was because they were cajoled, fooled, or intimidated. According to the critics, the leadership statutes were tantamount to a codification of the status quo. Evasive, confusing, and uninformed by underlying "principles," they guaranteed that the oligarchy would "remain master for ever, [free] to do as it pleases."[72]

The rebirth of the measurers' corporation in 1730 was marred by conflict between the twenty-four old hands, who took control before the others arrived, and the forty-eight new officers. Excluded from the decision-making process, denied access to accounts, and refused a fair share of the fees collected by the old hands during the time that they held exclusive sway, the forty-eight new officers formed their own corporation, elected syndics, and instituted a suit against the twenty-four, whom they accused of mismanagement and misappropriation of funds. A sixteenth-century-style "peace" was worked out by government commissioners that resulted in the fusion of the corporations and the indemnification of the new officers for part of the sum allegedly misused by the old measurers and for their legal expenses. Pressured into endorsing the accord, the twenty-four veterans never admitted to any wrongdoing, and an undercurrent of tension lingered for many years to come.[73]

72. AN, F[11] 264.
73. AN, V[7] 371, 13 July 1736.

The corporation tried to heal the deep wounds of the early thirties by consecrating a new oligarchy composed of representatives of the old factions and the new. By and large this solution seems to have worked, for no major political disputes sundered the corporation during the remainder of the century. However, the measurers came close to an internal crisis at the time of the introduction of the flour-weighing station in the late fifties and early sixties. Fearing ruin, a number of measurers repudiated the corporate leadership and offered to serve inspector Poussot on his terms in the hope that they could conserve a role in the new market that he was laboring to forge. The syndics adjusted rapidly to the new situation, however, reestablishing a reasonably good working relationship with their police superiors and a relative harmony among the confreres.

The new charter that the measurers secured in 1763 differed rather little from the bitterly contested document of the reign of Louis XIV in terms of the relationship between the syndics and the membership. The syndics were not bound to consult the measurers on matters of policy; if they so decided, they could seek the counsel of an executive committee of eight recruited by them among former syndics. Nor were they constrained to provide specific kinds of information. Only one general assembly per year was required. There was no institutionalized system of internal appeal against their decisions: the statutes perpetuated the myth of immanent confraternal consensus. Like the earlier charters, the Louis XV statutes paid much more attention to technical matters of work assignments than to the exercise of authority. Great pains were taken to assure that the data so precious to the authorities would be properly collected and verified. No mention was made of hiring job replacements, but the penalties for absenteeism were light. (Drinking with a baker in a tavern during working hours was more severely punished.) Laconic on the question of internal accountability, the charter of 1763 also avoided confronting the issue of external control. The measurers remained subordinated within extremely imprecise guidelines to both the lieutenant general of police and the prévôt des marchands. They maintained offices on the rue de la Mortellerie, prevotal space par excellence, as well as at the Halle.[74]

Only a handful of measurers challenged the authority of the syndics, and they did so as a consequence of personal antipathy or case-specific confrontation rather than on grounds of general principle. Corporate justice branded Jean-Jacques Pochet a "rebel" and an "agitator." In June 1734 he reproached syndic Chatillon publicly for changing the assignment list for more or less sordid reasons and thus jeopardizing the efficacy of the services performed. Chatillon denounced Pochet for his "insolence," suggested that he belonged in the madhouse, and threatened to beat him "to a pulp."[75] Two years later

74. AN, H* 1870, pp. 91–106, 11 January 1763; Archives Seine-Paris, DQ[10] carton 606, no. 857.
75. AN, Y 11221, 9 June 1734.

Pochet ambushed and assaulted one of the historic leaders of the corporation, former syndic Jean-Isaac Delasalle. The motive was vengeance, according to the victim, for he had been obliged to castigate Pochet in front of everyone at the Halle for coming late to work and working in slovenly fashion. Haughtily announcing that "he was noble like the sword he brandished," Pochet had warned Delasalle on the spot "that someday he would pay."[76] Pochet got in trouble again in 1744 for treating the syndics "with contempt and violence." He contended that he was discriminated against in job assignments and that his remonstrances were never given a proper hearing. Fined 100 livres and excluded from work (and thus corporate revenue-sharing) for three months, Pochet begged for and obtained indulgence.[77]

Measurers Pingot and Beaulieu, also singled out as troublemakers, enjoyed disrupting corporate business meetings by heckling and insulting the officers in charge. They mocked the solemnity of procedures and the narcissism of the syndics. One day when Delasalle was reminiscing about his success in "arranging accommodations for the peace and union of the confreres," Pingot took the floor to denounce him and the other elders as "knaves" and "rascals." The syndics charged that Pingot and Beaulieu spent more time in the taverns than on the markets. Not content to avoid work themselves, they prevented other measurers from filing their declarations.[78] Conveniently labeled and disposed of as vicious drunkards, Pingot and Beaulieu were also critics of certain practices on which the syndics depended. In particular, they resented the system of mutual surveillance and denunciation that invited a measurer to place his own interests above his sense of fraternal solidarity.[79] Two other measurers were frequently embroiled with their fellow measurers, who regarded them as "rebels" and "men of fury." Jean-Baptiste Gouault, who described himself as "tender and compassionate," took umbrage at the proclivity of the syndics to slander everyone who disagreed with them. The other, Jean-Martin Cholet, was widely known as an overbearing and short-tempered man.[80]

With the approval of the prévôt des marchands, the porters kept their corporation alive during the suppression phase of the twenties. The *commis* elected syndics who were authorized to act "in the name of the community" for the purpose of effecting seizures of merchandise and conducting litigation. They were also permitted to set up a corporate office at the Ecole port.[81]

76. AN, Y 11223, 27 October 1736.
77. AN, Z^{1H} 417, 19 December 1744, and F^{11} 264, 27 November 1744. The fine was reduced to 20 livres and the exclusion penalty rescinded.
78. AN, Y 11222, 19 January 1735 and Y 11223, 11 September 1736.
79. See, for instance, Quesnel v. Clemenceau, AN, Y 11224, 21 March 1737.
80. AN, Y 13516, 27 January 1757, and Y 15260, 6 October 1752.
81. AN, F^{11} 264 (28 January 1724, 13 September 1725, 25 January 1726, and 8 October 1727). After 1730, the main porter office was located on the rue de la Mortellerie. Archives Seine-Paris, DQ^{16} 3943^A.

Despite the precarious existence of the corporation during the period of disestablishment, it was rocked by serious internal dissension. Six dissidents led a campaign to protest the election of Jacques-François Cousin and Simon Robert as syndics in 1727. Cousin had already held that position for fourteen years—despite the fact that the old statutes, apparently fallen into desuetude, expressly required a syndic to stand aside for four years before seeking a second *two-year* term. Robert had also served as syndic for a number of years before suppression. The insurgents charged Cousin with embezzlement of corporate funds and fraudulent bookkeeping practices. All of the other confreres, sixty strong, joined together in support of the two syndics.[82]

We do not know what transpired in the election of 1729. Perhaps there was none, the term having been exceptionally extended to four years. In any event the two incumbents won reelection in October 1731, and once again their installation was bitterly contested, this time by a larger camp of antagonists, including the third syndic, who had just been chosen for the first time. The critics charged that the veteran syndics had triumphed only by using techniques of "seduction" and "corruption." They warned of the "grave danger" of allowing corporate elders to perpetuate their rule. Preoccupied with their own power, they would transform syndical authority into instruments of personal aggrandizement. Such syndics would attempt to manipulate the members by threatening not to pay them unless they approved their accounting of corporate funds or by assigning them systematically to the least attractive jobs.[83]

Just as the dissidents petitioned for the quashing of the elections and the disqualification of the incumbents, so Cousin and Robert filed complaints with the police against "the cabal" of firebrands who refused to accept the untainted verdict of majority rule. Nor were these "rebels" content to await the decision of the authorities. They acted to disrupt the community's life and they tried to destroy the usefulness of the two syndics by subjecting them to harassment and calumny. In front of everyone in the corporate offices, the dissidents denounced them as "rogues who owe the community considerable sums" and who sought to retain office in order to avoid paying. Robert was called "a bugger of a thief" who had stolen 3,000 livres. Cousin was reviled as "a scoundrel who played at being *le gros seigneur.*" Refusing to recognize Cousin and Robert as legitimate chiefs, their adversaries ripped down the assignments and instructions they posted at the bureaux and attempted to reorganize the service in the markets, with whose operations, according to the embattled syndics, they were only superficially familiar.[84]

The envenomed atmosphere of the community became oppressive for everyone. Porters such as Denise and Brisbard, who had no special affection for the incumbents, assailed the insurgents for sapping morale and mutual

82. Arsenal, ms. Bast. 10153 (October 1727).
83. Memorandum, porters to prévôt des marchands, 1731, BN, F⁰ FM 1554.
84. AN, Y 11218, 13 November 1731.

trust. Nicolas Blavette, a dissident, found no better way of impugning the standing of Louis Fontaine, Robert's son-in-law and defender, than by telling the confreres that "he had screwed Fontaine's wife on the trading floor of the Halle."[85]

Under pressure from the lieutenant of police, the insurgents backed off. Speaking for him, de Courcy, the senior commissaire for subsistence affairs, warned them that they would be banned from work in the markets if they persisted in disturbing the peace of the community and the markets. Now and again one of them jumped up at a meeting to inveigh against the avidity and corruption of Cousin and Robert, but the "cabal" had lost its organizational impetus.[86]

The insurgents nourished grudges for many years to come. If they could not discharge them directly upon their foes, they found proxies on whom to avenge themselves. Cousin's son, for instance, whose swaggering manner did nothing to atone for his lineage, complained that he was mistreated by his father's enemies. The latter also made a point of "espousing the cause" of any confrere reprimanded by the two syndics.[87] Some of the dissidents appear to have mellowed over time. One of the most mutinous critics of the twenties and thirties, Nicolas Blavette spoke in the forties in favor of "the discipline of the community" and against those who would "perturb" its functioning.[88]

The municipality, after having refused to annul the election of 1731, overturned the vote of 1739, as a result of a dispute over the behavior of the *plumets*. As a consequence of continuing squabbling concerning the choice of syndics, the city fathers decided in 1757 that henceforth one of them was to be present at all electoral assemblies.[89] Cousin and Robert were still syndics at the end of the forties, though it is possible that one or both retired for a term at one point or another.[90] Beginning in the late thirties, a second-level corporate leader began to draw some of the ire that had been focused on the veteran syndics. He was Bourguignon, chief of flour transactions, whose Stakhanovite preoccupation with productivity caused him to treat porters who failed to "break" their daily quota of flour with unwonted brutality. By dismissing him, Cousin and Robert won a small measure of good will.[91]

Real tranquility never seems to have settled upon the porters' community. "Those who shout the loudest," wrote inspector Poussot in 1759, "are the masters."[92] Yet it is clear that there was less coordinated and politicized

85. AN, Y 11218, 7 January 1732; Y 15946, 11 December 1751; Y 11219, 7 January 1732.

86. AN, Y 11219, 3 May 1732.

87. E.g., AN, Y 11236, 18 March 1749.

88. AN, Y 11231, 21 April 1743.

89. AN, F[11] 264, 15 May 1739 and 16 December 1757.

90. "Enquête sur le passage entre la halle au bled et la rue de la Cordonnerie," AN, Y 9533, 1749.

91. AN, Y 11225, 10 March 1738.

92. Arsenal, ms. Bast. 10141 (11 April 1759).

dissidence in the forties and fifties than there had been earlier. Disputes turned on some of the familiar themes, but they were sporadic and ephemeral. Syndic Michel-Martin Le Roy denounced porter Bautry for trying "to render my conduct suspect" by telling the assembled community that he had plundered its funds.[93] How ironic in the eyes of certain old hands must have been the indignation of syndic Billouard, who had been in his youth one of the most vehement critics of Cousin and Robert, when he was informed that a porter was spreading the word that he was a "knave" and a "thief."[94] A porter's wife accused the leadership of wasting corporate funds by holding Sunday night banquets at corporate expense and then pressing the members to pay special levies or make loans to keep the community in the black.[95] More common than attacks on corporate leadership were eruptions of individual rivalry and tension in more or less petty affairs: altercations stemming from excessive hazing of new members (whitewashing with flour, for example); quarrels over small sums of money; disagreements escalating into vituperation ("Your wife will lay anyone for 20 sous").[96]

Threats did more to promote corporate cohesion than any sort of internal élan. First, the measurers persisted in their campaign to discredit and displace the porters. The porters had to respond to this challenge both in the courts and in the field, the major theaters of confrontation. Second, royal fiscal pressure continued to squeeze the community, albeit less frequently than before 1719. The relative dispatch with which the porters complied in 1748 to a levy of 90,000 livres was surely linked to their anxiety over the measurers' offensive, which quickened their desire to remain on good terms with the government.[97] In the years after their reestablishment, it appears that a considerable number of porters invested in their community's future by lending it money to meet royal demands.[98]

The porters received new statutes in 1759 that did not fundamentally change corporate practice. In some ways this charter seems more democratic than the one obtained by the measurers a few years later. It offered more procedural opportunities to make the leadership accountable for its administration. It provided no mechanism by which a clique of syndics and elders could dispose of virtually all corporate affairs without convoking the membership. Provision was made for holding general assemblies whenever extraordinary affairs arose. The municipality, to whom the new statutes had to be submitted for ratification, inserted a clause barring the syndics from acting in the name of the community without consulting it and, more specifically, from

93. AN, Y 12604, 31 May 1756.
94. AN, Y 12606, 27 October 1758.
95. Arsenal, ms. Bast. 10141 (30 November 1760).
96. AN, Y 11231, 6 August 1744; Y 12604, 24 October 1758. Cf. Y 11223, 25 July 1736.
97. Conseil secret, 20 July 1748, AN, X^{1B} 8925.
98. See, for instance, the large *rentes* subscribed by porters Marie and Pingore. AN, Y 15250, June 1742 (for 3 March 1738), and Y 15053, 28 June 1749 (for ca. 1738).

entering in the corporate minutes a resolution that was not actually passed by a plurality.

On the other hand, oligarchical momentum was reinforced. Syndics could be reelected for a second two-year term without any interval. Two of the four adjoints chosen each year to assist the syndics were automatically the outgoing syndics, who thus clung to the levers of power for at least another year. Subsequently they were eligible to be reelected adjoint from the general membership pool. The statutes did not clearly disqualify an ex-syndic from standing for reelection after tenure as adjoint or after a fallow period. The only specific qualification for the post of syndic was the ability to read and write (prospective porters were also required to be able to read and write, apparently for the first time in corporate history).

The statutes of the porters were less voluble than those of the measurers on the character of the various jobs to be performed. Beyond managing corporate finances and personnel assignments, the chief task of the syndics was to patrol the capital, especially near its periphery, in search of contraband merchandise. Individual porters had no constitutional recourse if they were dissatisfied with their assignments. Unwarranted absence was punished by light fines. The penalties for cheating on the report of fees collected were more severe. The charter enjoined the porters to behave "modestly," especially among themselves. The cost of insulting a confrere was 3 livres (more than the fine for missing a whole day's work); physical assault drew 12 livres the first time, 24 livres or more if it happened again. The porters fixed reception fees to be paid by new officers entering the community at 800 livres for the sons of confreres ("in order to favor their succession") and at 1,100 livres for outsiders. Considering this tribute unreasonably bloated, the municipality reduced it to 300 and 600 livres respectively.[99]

Recruitment

Little is known about the socio-professional origins of the measurers and of the porters. A number of them emerged more or less directly from the provisioning milieu. There was something to the charge made by the exasperated flour merchants that the measurers were "for the most part relatives or friends of the bakers of Paris."[100] Fleurent Ferry and Jean Dupuis were former master bakers who became measurers in mid-career.[101] Measurer Am-

99. AN, H* 1868, fols. 497–503 (23 January 1759). An arrêt du conseil of 5 December 1741 had fixed reception fees at 300 and 600 livres. AN, AD XI 39.

100. Petition to lieutenant general, 21 December 1725, Arsenal, ms. Bast. 10271; Fourcret's testimony, BN, Coll. Joly 1829, fol. 279.

101. AN, MC, LXXV-705, 13 January 1768; Archives Seine-Paris, DC⁶ 249, fol. 256; Delamare, *Traité de la police,* 2:936, 941. Cf. the Roman prohibition against bakers serving as measurers. Delamare, ibid., pp. 608, 711.

broise Richer's brother and brother-in-law were both master bakers, though, to balance the picture, it is worth adding that his niece was married to a flour dealer.[102] The porters were at least as thoroughly intertwined with the bakers. Porters Jean Parmentier, Claude Chaudron, and Eustache Felix came from the trade of baking.[103] Porter Roche Le Roy married the widow of a baker. The daughter of porter Denis Guérin became the wife of a master baker.[104] Several porters turned to baker friends for loans in order to purchase their offices.[105] Delasalle dabbled in the grain trade before he became a measurer and continued to deal in it on the side after he took office, despite the stern prohibition against this "confusion" of vocations. Similarly, porter Olivier Meusnier remained involved in the hay trade.[106] Son of a laboureur, Claude Lalouette seems to have tilled the soil before moving to the city. Porters Pierre Marie of Normandy and Jean Franchette of Picardy also came from peasant families.[107]

Yet a great many measurers and porters must have acquired their expertise in subsistence affairs on the job, for they betray no direct prior connection with the provisioning world. Among the measurers, Charles Pagot worked as a cabinetmaker, Noel Besnard was a harness maker (who also purchased an office of *planchéieur*), Jean-Baptiste Grandcolas sold vinegar. Pierre Doudemont kept a tennis court, Louis Jubeaux made carriages, Antoine Machary rented out carriages, Jacques Tavant called himself "business agent," and Guillaume de St.-Martin claimed he was a négociant and engaged in moneylending.[108] Of the porters, Pierre Regnaud was a clockmaker, Louis Fontaine a hatmaker, Laurent Florat a goldsmith, Guillaume Floque a second-hand-clothes dealer, and Pierre Magnac a merchant dealing in wines, horses, and printed textiles. Antoine Belancourt and Pierre Desbois acquired masterships in wigmaking before they became porters and Pierre-Paul d'Estienne and Charles Damerat traded in wines.[109] These master craftsmen and mer-

102. AN, Y 15950, 10 August 1754.

103. BHVP, ms. n.s. 33, 21 November 1661; AN, MC, XVII-533, 16 April 1714, and MC, LXXXIX-484, 19 March 1743.

104. AN, MC, XXVIII-45, 12 May 1699, and MC, LXXXIX-469, 14 July 1740.

105. AN, MC, XLIII-412, 29 September 1755; MC, VII-288, 21 July 1771; MC, LXXVII-118, 28 December 1710.

106. Arsenal, ms. Bast. 10150; AN, MC, XXCI-245, 27 May 1710. On the absolute "incompatibility" between the exercise of the office and grain commerce, see BN, Coll. Joly 1312, fol. 118, and Savary des Bruslons, *Dictionnaire portatif de commerce*, 4:314.

107. AN: Y 11221, 14 February 1734; Y 15250, June 1742 (marriage contract of 18 March 1691); MC, XXXVIII-97, 13 May 1711.

108. AN: Y 3808, 7 June 1769; MC, XXXIX-342, 16 April 1731, and MC, XX-581, 9 August 1743; Y 15953, 24 December 1756; MC, LXXV-705, 13 January 1768, MC, XXXIX-397, 13 October 1748, and MC, LXXXIX-580, 15 September 1758; X1B 9434, 18 August 1768; MC, XXIII-458, 17 November 1724.

109. AN: MC, VII-288, 6 July 1771; MC, XLVI-135, 30 June 1702; MC, CI-116, 2 March 1707; MC, XXIV-552, 10 February 1712; Y 11236, 26 March 1749; Y 11219, 7 January and 2 March 1732; Y 11229, 28 April 1742; Arsenal, ms. Bast. 10150 (August 1750) and 10141 (30 November 1760).

chants regarded the market office as a good investment, affording a reasonable return in interest on their capital and in public standing. So did seven bourgeois de Paris who purchased porter charges, in at least two cases as "establishments" for their sons.[110] For measurer Nicolas Beaubigny the office was a springboard to a police career as an inspector.[111] Others probably came to the post as a result of marriage. His bride's father, a measurer, promised Michel Boivin, a bourgeois de Paris, that he would help him to succeed to his office, a third of the value of which he would bestow upon his daughter in dowry.[112] The future wife of Nicolas Regnault arranged for him to be received in the measurer's office that her first husband had exercised, half the value of which she constituted as dowry.[113]

There was a market in measurer and porter offices, though it was somewhat confined by a web of relations and connections that tended to favor certain buyers. A buyer had to be approved not only by the corporation, usually a formality, but also by the lieutenant general or the prévôt des marchands.[114] Princesses and presidents of sovereign courts pressed these magistrates to recognize the special merits of their clients who sought offices.[115] Some measurers tried to control the future disposition of their offices by writing a repurchase option into the contract of sale, usually in the hope of recovering the post a generation later in order to place a grandson.[116] The widow of porter Jacques Chaudron retained ownership of her husband's charge through an elaborate fictional sale that, strictly following the corporate statutes, was illegal. Her aim was double: to provide for her young son's professional future while preserving as much of the office's current income as possible. She leased the office for fifteen years to Jean-Baptiste Pluot, the sixteen-year-old son of a syndic in the porter corporation whose patronage assured both parties that no objections would be raised to the arrangement. In return for a salary of 200 livres a year and one-half of certain emoluments, Pluot agreed to pay all the costs of his reception in the community (which his father would surely be in a position to moderate), to fulfill all the functions of the charge, to remit all revenues of the office in which he did not have a share

110. AN, MC, LXIX-311, 1, 6, 8 July and 7 August 1732; MC, LXIX-319, 7 July 1734.

111. Archives Seine-Paris, fonds Feydeau, DE¹ article 4 (2 November 1731). Cf. AN, MC, XXXIX-342, 9 March 1731.

112. AN, MC, VII-1002, 7 August 1733, and AN, Y 12730, 12 February 1734.

113. AN, MC, CII-324, 26 August 1740.

114. The officers initially depended exclusively on the prévôt des marchands. Delamare, *Traité de la police,* 2:656. But the lieutenant of police rapidly imposed his tutelage, not only on those working at the Halle, but on the officers on the ports as well. Cf. BN, Coll. Joly 1312, fol. 141.

115. Dubois to Madame la princesse de Bourbon, Arsenal, ms. Bast. 10271, and Langlois de La Fortelle to lieutenant general, ms. Bast. 10149.

116. See Linget v. Besnard, AN, MC, XXXIX-342, 16 April 1731. Linget had sold to Emery on the condition that the latter would eventually resell to his children or grandchildren. Instead, Emery sold to Besnard.

to the widow Chaudron, and to absorb all penalties for absence and/or job negligence. If Pluot were to be removed from office for any reason or to die before the end of the contract, widow Chaudron would owe him no compensation, not even for his admission expenses. If Chaudron wanted to replace him before the expiration of the lease and he agreed to relinquish the post, she would pay him an indemnity of 1,000 livres.[117]

A relatively brisk demand for the office of measurer kept prices over 20,000 livres in the thirties. In the forties the office barely commanded 15,000 livres, but the price began to climb back toward 20,000 livres in the fifties.[118] Critics of the measurers writing in the late sixties contended that the market price then was substantially below the 20,000-livre value that the government admitted for the office.[119] At the beginning of the century the price of a porter's charge fluctuated between 13,800 livres (1701) and 12,000 livres (1707).[120] The government set the reimbursement ceiling in 1721 at 15,000 livres, a price that had been reached in the market a few years before, though in light of successive monetary manipulations the face values are of little utility for comparison.[121] Though Charles Damerat and Jean Pingore both had paid 12,000 for their offices in 1707 and 1712 respectively, in 1721 the government paid Damerat an indemnity of 12,000 livres and Pingore 15,000 livres, presumably as a function of relative real values.[122] Had these porters waited a few years they would have been able to realize 21,000 livres on the open market, the current price in the wake of "re-creation."[123] Prices fell as low as 15,000 livres in the late forties, but rebounded to the range of 18,000 to 20,000 livres a decade later. In the early sixties, the government assessed the *finance* at 17,000 livres.[124]

It was quite common for future measurers and porters to purchase partly on credit. Measurer Delasalle put 7,500 livres down in cash and constituted a rente to the benefit of the seller for the remainder. Nicolas Beaubigny, also a measurer, borrowed 5,000 livres from a third party and reimbursed the bulk of it four years later, drawing on his savings and on a new loan advanced by a

117. AN, MC, LXXXIX-418, 15 March 1743.

118. AN, MC, XXXIX-397, 13 October 1748, and MC, LXXXIX-580, 15 September 1758. In 1695 the office sold for 12,000 livres, in 1710 for 16,000 livres, and in 1719 for 20,000 livres. BHVP, ms. série 114, 29 December 1695; AN, MC, LXVII-118, 6 October 1710; AN, Y 11869, 12 March 1764 (concerning a contract of 22 August 1719).

119. Bertin and Dambraine, "Mémoire," Arsenal, ms. 2588, p. 150.

120. AN, MC, XXVI-245, 27 May 1710 (for 1701); MC, XLVI-175, 30 June 1703; MC, CI-116, 2 March 1707.

121. Arrêt du conseil, 21 January 1721, AN, AD XI 38; AN, MC, XXIV-552, 10 February 1712.

122. AN, MC, LXXXIX-377, 20 September 1726.

123. AN, MC, LXIX-319, 7 July 1734; MC, LXIX-311, July and August 1732; MC, IV-483, 17 April 1734; AN, Y 15250, June 1742 (for 26 March 1734).

124. AN, Y 15056, June 1749 (compte Pingore); Arsenal, ms. Bast. 10279 and 10141 (11 April 1759); édit concernant les offices et les droits sur les ports, etc., March 1760, BHVP.

measurer colleague. Porter Jean Pingore paid 4,000 livres in cash, 1,100 livres in third-party notes, and the remainder in annuities. The full, immediate payment of 21,000 livres in cash, gold and silver, made by a bourgeois de Paris, was exceptional.[125] Credit linkages sometimes became extremely intricate, spanning several generations of officeholders and their families. The widow of measurer Louis Jubeaux sold his office to Jean-Baptiste Picard. The latter remitted 10,000 livres directly to the family of Gabeau, to whom the Jubeaux family still owed money for the purchase of the office. Antoine Machary bought the office from Picard's estate. Part of his purchase price went to reimburse friends and relatives of Gabeau who had extended credit to Picard.[126]

The turnover rate in both corporations appears to have been rather high in the second half of the century. Between June 1757 and August 1768, fifteen porters died and at least eight and perhaps as many as fifteen others renounced their posts. In only three cases did sons succeed fathers. The average length of tenure for the sixteen cases for which we have this information was 16.6 years.[127] Few porters could match the longevity record of the dominant syndics of the first half of the century, Cousin (at least thirty-five years) and Robert (over forty years).[128] Between August 1763 and August 1768, at least seven measurers voluntarily abandoned their posts, in addition to the ten who died in office.[129]

Fortune

One of Poussot's reproaches against the market officers was that they focused all their energies on extracting money rather than on performing service.[130] We have no hard data on the annual earnings of the measurers and only a handful of references to that of the porters. The "product and emoluments" of porter Pierre Marie's charge were as follows:

> 1737: 1,147 livres 15 sous
> 1738: 1,197 livres 10 sous
> 1739: 1,300 livres

125. AN, Y 11869, 12 March 1764; AN, MC, XXXIX-342, 9 March 1731; MC, XXIV-552, 10 February 1712; MC, LXIX-319, 7 July 1734.

126. AN, MC, XXXIX-397, 13 October 1748, and MC, LXXXIX-580, 15 September 1758.

127. AN, Z^{1H} 312.

128. "Enquête sur le passage entre la halle au bled et la rue de la Cordonnerie," AN, Y 9533, 1749.

129. AN, Z^{1H} 312.

130. Arsenal, ms. Bast. 10141 (29 May 1758).

1740: 1,053 livres 12 sous
1741: 816 livres.[131]

The last two years surely reflected the breakdown of the ordinary supply patterns, provoked by a grave subsistence crisis. Jean Pingore's office earned about 1,400 livres a year in the late forties. His widow complained that this income was "extremely limited."[132] Given the bourgeois horizons of many officeholders, her complaint was quite justified. Unlike Pingore, however, many porters did not depend more or less exclusively on their office for their incomes. By 1760, a porter could expect approximately 1,600 livres a year.[133]

Notarial records give us some insight into the cultural, material, and personal lives of the measurers, but the data base is too narrow for generalization concerning the whole group. Themselves of very different social origins (two were sons of laboureurs, one the son of a merchant from Béarn, another the son of a magistrate at Corbeil, a fifth the son of a master weaver from Savoy, still another the son of a Norman grocer), the measurers in our group married women of diverse backgrounds: daughters of bourgeois de Paris (two), a measurer, a master rope maker, a journeyman carpenter, and a gagne-denier.[134] Wagering in the mid-twenties on the reestablishment of the office for which he had refused to seek reimbursement, a measurer-father dowered his daughter with a third of its prospective value. To prepare the way for his son-in-law to be received in this office, he promised to undertake the "necessary steps and solicitations" (the costs of which he would share equally with the newlyweds) to have him named a measuring *commis*. The father agreed to lodge and nourish the couple as long as the commission lasted, and up to two years after it expired. The widow of a measurer arranged for her new husband to assume the office, half of the value of which, roughly 10,000 livres, constituted her marriage portion. The daughter of one of the bourgeois de Paris brought 6,600 livres and the other 6,000. These were substantial marriage contributions—considerably higher than, say, those attracted by bakers or millers—which, if matched by proportional male dowries, augured brilliantly for the launching of the household and the development of the career.[135] The most intriguing case is that of Jacques Tavant, a resourceful opportunist

131. AN, Y 15250, 7 June 1742. Extrapolating from figures in the *inventaire* of measurer Besnard for 1742, I obtain annual revenue of 627 livres. This figure strikes me as implausibly low. AN, MC, XXXIX-367, 21 March 1742.

132. AN, Y 16156, ca. June 1749 *(partage)*, and Y 15053, 28 June 1749 *(compte)*.

133. Arsenal, ms. Bast. 10279.

134. AN, Y 12730, 12 February 1734, Y 11869, 13 July 1724, and Y 11221, 4 June 1734. The following references are all from AN, MC: CII-324, 26 August 1740; XXVIII-56, 30 April 1701; VIII-964, 1 October 1724; XXX-147, 15 June 1698; XXIII-458, 17 November 1724; XXIII-558, 31 August 1748; XXIII-581, 13 June 1752; VIII-1002, 7 August 1733.

135. We know the *apport* only of Lalouette, the son of a laboureur, whose 1,500 livres in cash and land were slightly below the value of his wife's dowry of cash and trousseau, evaluated at 2,000 livres.

("agent d'affaires") who managed to acquire an office despite two very modest marriages, first to a journeyman's daughter (dowry of 300 livres) and then to a dayworker's daughter (dowry of 100 livres); marriages that clearly indicate that he himself was quite poor. His upward mobility was consecrated by a third marriage to the daughter of a royal engineer, who brought him about 4,600 livres in dowry and agreed to mother his six children.

We have record of only four porter marriages, all during the last part of the reign of Louis XIV. Taking into account discrepancies in the value of the livre, it is clear that with one exception the porters contracted far less opulent marriages than the measurers. The range of wealth is quite striking. Jean Franchette, son of a laboureur, and Marie Robbe, the widow of a bourgeois de Paris, each directed 5,000 livres to enter their legal matrimonial community, which suggests that their total marriage fortune was substantially greater.[136] The daughter of a deceased bourgeois de Paris brought Pierre Marie, another laboureur's son, only 760 livres in dowry, more than half of it in (unconvertible) trousseau.[137] Another bourgeois de Paris dowered his daughter with 2,100 livres in cash and notes, while the daughter of a Burgundian wood merchant brought 2,600 livres, 1,800 livres in cash and the rest in personal effects.[138]

Taken as a group, based on afterdeath inventory data for five to eight cases depending on the categories, the measurers appear quite well off at death compared, say, to most of the artisans and merchants on the ports and at the Halle. With mean total assets at 41,354 livres (median = 28,816 livres) and mean accounts payable at a mere 2,260 livres (median = 1,197 livres), average fortune amounted to 34,477 livres (median = 18,414 livres).[139] The value of their office alone, when it was mortgage free, guaranteed them a considerable estate. It loomed as the largest item in the assets column, worth 19,218 livres on the average (median = 20,000 livres). Next in order of magnitude were annuities, in some cases invested with the corporation, whose mean capitalized value amounted to 11,255 livres (median = 2,253 livres). Only two measurers possessed real property: one owned half a house in Paris assessed at 12,000 livres and the other some small parcels worth 1,000 livres near Pantin. None of the measurers in our inventory group, only one in the *scellé* group, and one in the testamentary group owned his own house. Nor were their rented lodgings spacious: the average apartment contained two rooms. For 1,500 livres a year Besnard occupied an elite first-floor flat near the Palais-Royal, but it contained only four rooms.

The mean value of household furnishings is surprisingly modest: 869 livres

136. AN, MC, XXXVIII-97, 13 May 1711. The douaire was listed as 10,000 livres!
137. AN, Y 15250, June 1742 (18 March 1691).
138. AN, MC, LXXVII-98, 23 January 1707; MC, LXIX-146, 19 April 1692.
139. For the documentation for measurer and porter fortune, see Appendix I.

(median = 485 livres). The measurers tended to put their money in more liquid forms of decoration, such as silver (average = 1,039 livres) and jewelry (282 livres). Some of them kept unusually large amounts of cash on hand, the average per capita for the group amounting to 2,270 livres. Husband and wife wore apparel of approximately the same value, averaging 161 and 167 livres respectively. Besnard, one of the wealthiest, and Lenormand, one of the poorest, each affirmed his burgherly penchant by keeping an array of fine wigs. Only Besnard stocked wine, a small cellar of Burgundy worth 218 livres.

One finds certain "cultural" ornaments or tools in the measurers' households. Ten of the eighteen measurers whose households I could enter hung paintings or engravings on their walls (average = 15, median = 12). The subjects were characteristically religious or historical, though there were a number of family portraits, still lifes, and landscapes. Two measurers displayed portraits of Louis XV. Four of the eighteen had libraries, the bulk of which were composed of devotional and historical titles. Tavant, whose life was an upward trajectory from extremely humble rural origins to a comfortable bourgeois third marriage, amassed two hundred books, along with fifty engravings and three paintings (an evangelist, a nun, and Saint Theresa). Besnard, who owned fifty-five paintings and eighteen engravings, had eighty-eight books on his shelves.[140] Louis Colin, who left only a fraction of Besnard's estate, possessed forty-two paintings and engravings and sixty books, along with an ivory Christ on a gilded wooden cross.

At least ten of the two dozen measurers in our sample employed domestic servants. Lalouette had two, perhaps because he also ran a rope-making business. Alexandre Barbet, a bachelor, bequeathed all of his furniture and his wine and half of his "savings" to his woman servant, as well as a substantial annuity worth 264 livres a year to her nephew. Several measurers died owing their servants considerable sums.

Boasting a net fortune of 133,368 livres, Jean-Noel Besnard was the richest measurer in the sample. In addition to the house in which he was principal tenant (and had among his lodgers lieutenant of police Hérault), Besnard maintained a second residence in the Porcherons, which featured a billiard room. He enjoyed a substantial annuity income, capitalized at 41,941 livres, which does not embrace the principal of six lifetime annuities whose value was not spelled out. Along with his measurer's post he owned an office of *garde-batteaux* assessed at 30,000 and a charge of *planchéieur,* the price of which was not indicated. Before he died he dowered his two children with

140. Among Besnard's paintings were a Virgin with Child, an Ecce Homo, a Resurrection, a Calvary, a chaste Suzanne, a Saint Peter, a Saint John, a Virgin, an Adoration, a dozen still-lifes and landscapes, a number of genre paintings (including a beggar), and several depictions of animals.

10,000 livres each. He left 10,998 livres in cash at his death. It is likely that Besnard derived the bulk of his fortune from his activity as a master harness maker.

A number of other measurers were quite well off. Jean-Isaac Delasalle, a former syndic, and Claude Lalouette both had net fortunes of over 30,000 livres. Delasalle's chances had been favored from the beginning, for his wife brought him a dowry of 6,000 livres, 5,000 of it in cash, whereas Lalouette had had to settle for a portion of 2,000 livres. Beyond their offices, their wealth was founded on very different bases. Delasalle had almost 9,000 livres worth of capitalized annuities, while Lalouette, who had a handful of *rentes* of derisory value, had a 9,000-livre investment in a rope-making atelier and in his son's harness-making business. Pierre Buignet, the doyen of the measurers' community, was also a controller-inspector of hay. He owned an elegantly furnished house and left a large capital in annuities. Alexandre Barbet may have had as much as 105,000 livres in the capitalized value of annuities, in addition to substantial savings, expensive jewelry, and over 10,000 livres in accounts receivable. Several other measurers, bachelors like Barbet, were able to live quite comfortably, in part because they were free of family obligations. Ambroise Richer and François Soret shared a small apartment for eighteen years, and each left hefty savings. Romain Belhomme bequeathed generous cash gifts to three of his confreres, "dear friends."

Less is known about the large number of measurers who had modest resources or about those who were frankly poor. In none of these instances could the measurer claim clear title to his office. Too poor to bother signing a marriage contract, Jean-Baptiste Picard and his wife worked as street merchants. Her death made available several thousand livres in liquid capital that Picard invested in a measurer's charge. He lived frugally for the rest of his life in a single room rented for 86 livres a year, devoting much of his income to paying for the post. Louis Argues died with assets consisting of 179 livres in furniture and 343 livres in silverware. At the time of his death, Michel Millot owed large sums of money to eight persons, including over 6,000 livres to an innkeeper who seems to have advanced him funds for the purchase of his office. Eight persons also filed claims upon the estate of Jacques Lenormand, who was less heavily burdened than Millot, but who lived *au jour le jour.*

The extremely fragmentary data that we have on the wealth of porters at mid-career or later suggest that many of them were well off, without, however, qualifying as affluent. Pingore's widow called her situation unenviable, yet her husband's fortune at death amounted to about 41,000 livres, a little more than half in the capitalized value of annuities, 15,000 livres for his office, and the rest in household effects and notes. Pierre Marie left two porter offices worth about 21,000 livres apiece, 19,200 livres in the principal of *rentes* owed by the porters' corporation, and a house and land near Caen. Guillaume Torselle inhabited fourteen rooms in a four-story house. The furnishings were not opulent but dense and sturdy, including thirteen beds (the bed often represented the single most expensive item in the home). Long-time syndic Simon Robert occupied an apartment barely equal in size to one of Torselle's floors, but it was superbly appointed. His wife's wardrobe contained a resplendent array of silks, satins, taffetas, velvets, and embroidered and printed fabrics, and he and his wife both wore gold and silver jewelry studded with diamonds. Olivier Meusnier, who owned an office of *courtier-chargeur de foin* as well as a porter's charge, decorated his apartment with eleven paintings, including a Christ and a Virgin, four engravings, two ivory crosses, and thirty-four pieces of faience. His library consisted of twenty volumes of historical and devotional works. The wife of Jean Monnestier was sufficiently prosperous to bequeath 4,000 livres to the fabrique of St.-Gervais to endow three low masses a week in perpetuity.[141]

On the other side of the spectrum were the porters who never succeeded in freeing their offices from mortgage. Lodged in a small, sparsely outfitted apartment, Pierre-Paul Josset was deeply indebted to at least seven individuals. Even after he sold his assets to meet his obligations, Denis Guérin, a retired porter, still owed 10,000 livres to his daughters. Henri Sallembier had few clothes, no silver or jewelry, and humble furnishings. The prized possessions of the widow of another porter who lived austerely in a single room were two paintings of Saint Catherine and two mirrors, articles of luxury for the laboring poor in the first part of the eighteenth century.[142]

The Case against the Measurers and Porters

This police of the measurers and porters was controversial less because it seemed to eddy against the tide of commercial rationalization and modernization than because of the vested interest that these officers had in its rigorous execution and the brusquerie and haughtiness with which they often proceeded. Merchants and bakers contended that, for base motives of personal aggrandizement, measurers and porters abused their legal authority, harassed them, and damaged the public interest by sapping the capital's supply lines. Using their police connection as leverage, the officers subjected buyers and sellers to "a veritable extortion." Like judges, yet arbitrarily and without any legitimate authority, the measurers and porters meted out fines and confiscations and other penalties. The bakers argued against the strict construction of the rules governing droiture trade, a policy that could be imple-

141. AN, Y 15056, June 1749, and Y 15053, 28 June 1749; Y 15250, June 1752; Y 11449, 7 May 1727; Y 15946, 11 December 1751; AN, MC, XXVI-245, 27 May 1710; Archives Seine-Paris, DC⁶ 256, fol. 185, 9 December 1775.

142. AN, Y 15955, 20 August 1758; MC, LXXXIX-469, 14 July 1740; Y 13099, 17 September 1746; Y 14669, 26 October 1749.

mented only by muzzling the officers. And if they had the right to inspect droiture shipments, they had no justification for demanding remuneration for work that they did not perform. Around mid-century the bakers offered the measurers a quid pro quo which in fact may have percolated into practice: they would concede a fee on droiture provided the measurers let all the droiture traffic pass.

Other groups joined the call for a chastening of the officers' gluttony. Civil and military assistance institutions such as the Hôtel-Dieu and the Invalides, educational establishments such as the collège du Plessis, and religious communities such as the abbaye de Ste.-Geneviève, the sisters of Charity, the nuns of St.-Catherine, and the convent of Picpus vehemently protested against the "pretended droits" and the badgering inspections to which the measurers and the porters tried to subject them. In a protracted lawsuit, the nuns of Val de Grace fought the efforts of the porters to make it legally mandatory for the convent to use their services. The porters are not "officers of coercion," contended the sisters; "they are no more than officers of convenience."[143] The master *grainiers,* or small-grain dealers, felt measurer aggressiveness in another way. Hitherto they had enjoyed a monopoly on retail sales in their shops. By introducing the retail bushel measure in the Halle, the measurers threatened "to drive the grainiers out of business."[144]

The suppliers, especially those serving the Halle, and the brokers denounced the measurers and porters as fomenters of disorder rather than guarantors of the proper operation of the market. These officers were too often absent, slow to respond to requests for service, lethargic and indifferent in their performance. Measurer Gombard spent the peak business hours in a tavern, promising earnestly to come after he finished his glass, yet managing somehow to keep it filled. Instead of attending to business personally in the transaction arenas, many officers directed things by remote control—"from the crossroads of the tavern," remarked Poussot. By refusing to work in the rain, measurer Jean-Claude Hubert also impeded the distribution process. A broker lost sales because the measurers pretended to be occupied while in fact "they sauntered about doing nothing." Anxiously awaiting an overdue porter assigned to her place in order to consummate a sale, broker widow Provost dispatched her daughter to fetch him at 1:30 in the afternoon at the corporate office, where she found him asleep. She tried to rouse him, but he

143. Demieux to Hérault, 24 April 1727, Arsenal, ms. Bast. 10274; "Mémoire" to police, 15 September 1725, ms. Bast. 10270; BN, Coll. Joly 1829, fol. 337, and 1312, fols. 53–85, 121–31, 159–61, 230–31; Trudaine to Sartine, 10 June 1769, AN, F^{12*} 153; Archives Assistance publique, deliberations of the bureau of the Hôtel-Dieu, 25 May 1728, no. 97; Archives Assistance publique, factum collection, "Mémoire pour les administrateurs de l'Hôtel-Dieu" (1758); Archives Seine-Paris, D5B^6 1814, June 1724.

144. Petition of the *grainiers,* 14 March 1731, and report of de Courcy, 11 March 1731, AN, Y 11218. Cf. the brutal insults which unforgiving mistress *grainières* hurled against the widow of a leading measurer. Y 11221, 14 February 1734.

refused to go to work. The senior porter in the flour service to whom the broker complained told her haughtily "that her daughter was an impudent creature to have dared to awake an *officer.*" In a similar instance, broker Marie de Monnery lost a large sale of 24 sacks and perhaps also a merchant client when porter Cousin *fils* refused to do any work after 3:30 P.M.

Although he was assigned to the place of broker Girard in the weekly list published by the syndic of his corporation, porter Jean-Baptiste Touchard preferred to work for Dame Lebrun, another broker. Girard heatedly complained that she was losing her best baker customers because they were unwilling to wait the two hours or more that it usually took her to find a substitute porter. Touchard claimed that he had switched assignments with a colleague for whose negligence he could not be held accountable, but Girard had no doubt in her mind that Touchard and Lebrun had "a secret understanding," at once commercial and sexual, the two poles of exchange around which life in the markets was articulated. Their absence and failure to perform the work did not prevent the porters from charging buyers and sellers whose transactions came to their attention. Poussot wanted to tax the porters for damages to indemnify suppliers who were delayed by the porters' failure to discharge their duties promptly.[145]

Twenty or more measurers, Poussot claimed, never actively exercised their charges at all, apparently settling for a reduced share of collective revenue. To the inspector, this sort of abuse was symptomatic of the general climate in the markets. The measurers and porters were as arrogant toward the police as they were brutal and brusque toward the buyers and sellers. No wonder they treated their clients contemptuously, when they showed no reluctance to defy the commissaire and the inspector. When Machurin told the measurers to serve a baker desperately short of flour before the official opening of the market, a syndic replied insolently that "the commissaire has no power to give such an order, it must come from above." The measurers and porters "have always played the role of both judge and party and do not accept the idea that they are in any way dependent on the police officials assigned to supervise them by the lieutenant general," observed Poussot.[146]

Disgusted with the lack of prompt and courteous service, grain dealer Charles Gonnet threatened to follow the example of other exasperated merchants and abandon his Paris provisioning. It is unacceptable, he maintained, that a reliable and substantial supplier such as he, furnishing six muids every week, should have to waste the whole day waiting for service. Measurer

145. AN, Y 11233, 16 February and 17 March 1746; Y 11223, 30 June 1735; Y 11237, 26 May 1756; Y 11229, 5, 15, 17 December 1742; Arsenal, ms. Bast. 10141 (1 September 1756 and 11 September 1760). Corporate penalties for absenteeism were relatively light. Police sanctions were harsher, but prosecution was rare. See the fine of 50 livres imposed on porter Pluot. AN, F[11] 264, 3 February 1758.

146. Arsenal, ms. 10141 (16 February 1756, 17 January 1757, 17 January 1758, 12 October 1759, 17 February 1760).

Tavant told Gonnet that "he didn't give a damn" how much he supplied and that he could very well wait until he got served. When Gonnet grabbed an empty measure and began to fill it to establish his claim to service, Tavant cursed him and punched his pregnant wife in the breast. Nine years later broker Chicheret complained that the same Tavant tried to force him to terminate his selling well before the market officially ended, and more generally that the measurers took no real interest in their responsibilities, farming them out to the gagne-deniers of their entourage. Chicheret also denounced the porters for refusing to "break" the flour at the bottom of the receptacles, a task only they were authorized to perform. The broker interpreted this attitude as part of the swagger of superiority affected by these officers, who passed on as much of their work as possible to gagne-deniers. Yet broker Denise Bardou found that porter Josset regarded the residue of several bushels of flour as his to keep, a reward for his solicitude. Josset pointedly warned her that if she resisted he would "have her driven from the Halle as a lout, a scoundrel, a wretch." To punish Bardou's sister Marie Collier, wife of a flour merchant, for her lack of deference, porter Langlois spread the damaging word that her husband had lost 400 livres in collection money not while attending a mass, as he claimed, but in a brothel.[147]

The brokers and the mealmen suffered from the preferential treatment that the market officers gave to certain supplier-protégés who were suspected of purchasing their protection. The flour merchants protested against the "heaping twelfth bushel" accorded the bakers by the measurers, "who were for the most part friends or relatives of the bakers."[148] The burning desire of most flour merchants to switch to a weighing system was in part a reflection of their impatience to escape the yoke of the measurers who gave them "no justice."

The mealmen charged that the measurers and porters "favored" certain bakers, delaying and arranging sales to reserve for them the best flour at the lowest prices of the day. The bakers confirmed these allegations.[149] Pressed by commissaire Regnard senior to account for the paltry amounts of bread that they offered for sale in their shops, four bakers from the faubourg St.-Jacques explained "that it was extremely difficult to obtain grain or flour, that to get any of it one needed recommendations to the measurers."[150]

Widow Aumont, a flour broker, accused measurer Delasalle of repeatedly preventing her from selling to bakers whom she knew to have "an extreme need" for flour in order to reserve it for "bakers of his acquaintance whom he

147. AN, Y 11236, 7 October 1749; Y 12606, 27 May and 21 August 1758; Y 9539, 21 August 1758; Y 11226, 3 February and 7 March 1739. On porter theft from the Halle, see also Y 11242, 8 October 1755. Cf. the "vile," double-dealing reputation of measurers in North African markets. Fogg, "Organization of a Moroccan Tribal Market," p. 56.

148. "Mémoire," 21 December 1725, Arsenal, ms. Bast. 10271.

149. See, for example, the complaint of flour dealer Fourcret in 1752, BN, Coll. Joly 1829, fol. 279.

150. Regnard to lieutenant general, ca. May 1726, Arsenal, ms. Bast. 10273.

wishes to protect." Delasalle, as the official in charge of the flour section, was indeed in a position to decide who should have access to which merchandise. In one instance, he violently drove off a baker from Aumont's place ("You shall have none of this flour," he screamed) because he wanted to hold that flour for "a baker friend who was not present at the market." When Aumont protested, Delasalle warned her that he would see that she lost her broker's permit if she did not cooperate.[151] Aumont's complaint was not an isolated one, for the following year three leading baker elders, speaking for "a great number" of fellow guildsmen, heatedly denounced "the injustices and evil maneuvers committed every day" by Delasalle. These bakers "cried out for vengeance" because Delasalle "has a dozen *rantiers* [*sic*] that is to say those who make him presents of gold or silver or girls of pleasure and who [in return] obtain the very top quality merchandise while three hundred honest bakers suffer the consequences of this outrageous injustice."[152]

The big bakers often fell victims to the officers' rigidity. "Chased from the Halle" before they could satisfy all their needs, they were forced to buy at Versailles and other neighboring markets, thus undermining Poussot's centralizing ambitions. A similar inflexibility "drove away the best merchants," who were prevented by the measurers and porters from obtaining the price their high quality merchandise merited.[153]

Irate bakers waited in ambush to avenge themselves against the measurers and porters who confiscated their merchandise.[154] Several times measurers were almost lynched by citizen posses mobilized by bakers and brokers.[155] Those who escaped physical abuse were publicly mocked and insulted by the bakers, as well as by brokers and their aides, who ignored numerous police sentences enjoining them "to show honor and respect" to the measurers and porters and "not to trouble them in their work."[156] Self-styled "officers of the king," the measurers and porters likened themselves to magistrates against whom an insult was a crime.[157]

The bumptious and bullying conduct of the *plumets* also incensed buyers and sellers. The *plumets* tried to impose their services where they were not wanted. Jean-François Michaud slapped the wife of master baker René Du-

151. AN, Y 13090, 8 November 1739.

152. Petition of baker elders to lieutenant general and procurator general, BN, Coll. Joly 1122, fol. 98 (ca. fall 1740), and assembly of police, 14 July 1740, BN, ms. fr. 11356, fol. 428.

153. Arsenal, ms. Bast. 10141 (28 September 1759, 4 April 1761).

154. See the case of Pierre Thory, AN, Y 11236, 12 September 1749.

155. AN, Y 12607, 3 December 1759; Y 9539, 22 May 1761; and Y 9474, 29 October 1771. Cf. Y 12608, 15 April 1760.

156. See the case of the Grezel brothers, AN, Y 9441, 20 May 1740, and Y 9621, 7 August 1739. See also BN, Coll. Joly 1829, fols. 317–23; police sentence, 11 October 1738, Archives de la Préfecture de Police, fonds Lamoignon, H^{32bis}, fols. 407–9; Arsenal, ms. Bast. 10149 (the case of Lentier in 1726 who "gave no more a damn for the measurers than he did for his cat").

157. See Hubert's discourse in AN, Y 11233, 17 March 1746.

breuil when she insisted that he refrain from helping her journeymen unload meal.[158] Other *forts* commandeered wagons that were waiting to transport grain or flour that had not passed through their hands, or signaled porters to delay the transactions of those who rejected their assistance. Buyers, sellers, and brokers who agreed under duress to employ these *forts* but refused the "bonuses" they demanded risked having to pay another price: verbal and physical abuse, slow and slovenly work, even sabotage. A *plumet* named Baume shoved and insulted a master baker. Villefranche, a *plumet* and soldier in the French Guards, assaulted the driver of a mealman. At the place of broker Pilloy, the *plumets* punctured a number of flour sacks and mixed dirt and mud into several others. In all but one of these cases the porters were not only indifferent to the protests of the victims, but seemed to approve of these violent actions.[159] In 1739 the municipal court suspended the porter syndics from work for six months and fined their corporation 1,000 livres for having tolerated exactions by the *plumets*.[160] While some clients perceived the *plumets* as working hand in hand with the porters to cheat and abuse the public, others saw them as victims of their employers, who lorded it over them and denied them an honest wage.[161]

The Reform of Market Police

Several years in the central markets convinced Poussot that most of the complaints against the measurers and the porters were well founded. They were enemies of "good order" and thus of "good police." A large number obtained their offices "for the revenue only" and either focused more or less exclusively on extracting as much money as possible from the position or evinced a *rentier*'s sublime indifference to the responsibilities of the office, provided it yielded a regular quarterly dividend. Many were "brutal and hot headed," mistreating their customers as well as their employees. Some were manifestly corrupt. Others applied the rules with a mindless rigor that discouraged buyers and sellers. Dissension and disorganization plagued both corporations; both lacked effective, public-spirited leadership. Established to facilitate transactions and increase abundance, the measurers and the porters performed in ways that impeded exchanges and diminished the supply.

The relations of the measurers and porters with the police were no better

---

158. AN, Y 11571, 16 January 1755.

159. AN, Y 11243, 22 March, 1 April 1756; Y 11220, 24 July 1733; Arsenal, ms. Bast. 10141 (5 February 1756). I have found only one instance in which the syndics filed charges against a grasping *plumet*. AN, Y 9538, 14 June 1724.

160. Prevotal sentence, 15 May 1739, AN, F[11] 264.

161. AN, Y 11242, 8 October 1755.

than their relations with the public. Preoccupied with increasing their authority even as they were determined to increase their profits, they pretended to be "completely independent" of the commissaire and the inspector. "These officers," observed Poussot, "see themselves as more important at the Halle than all the officers of the police; the commissaire has had many occasions to take issue with them, and if I have not complained as many times as he, it is merely to avoid pestering the Magistrate." They defied Machurin's orders regarding the operation of the market, they disputed Poussot's right to send his deputies into the Halle, and they dismissed employees whom they knew to be sympathetic to either the commissaire or the inspector. They acted as if the jurisdiction "belonged to them."[162] Had they been properly disciplined all along, Poussot contended, the measurers and the porters would not have become so incorrigibly insolent and refractory. Ties between them and certain prominent police officials, among whom surely stood Machurin's predecessor, de Courcy, had been "too cozy." The municipality occasionally punished the market officers for negligence or abuse, but in prosecuting its losing battle against the lieutenance générale de police, it just as often whitewashed measurers and porters who had received reprimands from the Châtelet.[163]

Tension between the police and the two corporations of officers reached a peak in 1759 around the time of the inauguration of the *poids,* the system of selling flour by weight whose establishment the measurers and porters had vainly sought to prevent. The *poids* conveyed with a powerful, institutional voice the message that Machurin and Poussot had inscribed in all of their projects for the reorganization of the central market: that the capital could be more copiously, more cheaply, more reliably, and more peacefully provisioned without the collaboration of the measurers and porters than with it.[164] Their insolent attempts to obstruct transactions once the *poids* began to function merely underscored the soundness and the urgency of the police diagnosis: these officers were agents of infection who had to be purged from the stomach of Paris. The commissaire and the inspector felt confident that a *régie* of clerks appointed by and accountable to the lieutenance générale could handle the needs of the Halle. A dozen of the most docile measurers and porters could be put to work by the *régie;* the others would be compensated for their offices and disbarred from any connection with the marketplace.[165]

Partly in response to pressure from the police, in September 1759 the royal council issued an arrêt suppressing all the measurer and porter offices. Although a lack of funds compelled the government to postpone liquidation and to reestablish the posts (more or less temporarily) within the year, the timing

162. Arsenal, ms. Bast. 10141 (29 August and 6 November 1759).
163. See, for example, AN, F^{11} 264, 4 June 1756 and 7 June 1757.
164. Arsenal, ms. Bast. 10141 (26 September and 5 October 1759).
165. Ibid. (5, 26 September and 12 October 1759).

and the tone of this arrêt sharply enhanced the prestige and the leverage of the commissaire and the inspector and sapped the will of many of the measurers and porters to resist.[166]

Well before the publication of the law, there were signs that certain market officers were prepared to "submit" to the police.[167] Even as he negotiated their capitulation, Poussot took a big step toward reclaiming ground-level police jurisdiction in the central markets by organizing a brigade of "little inspectors" composed of his brother, who had more than two decades of experience in police work, and two clerks, young men with "education" and apprenticeships in public administration. They were to undertake general surveillance, provide intelligence, assist in maintaining order and directing traffic, respond immediately to complaints, and take a special interest in the proper functioning of the flour-weighing station.[168]

During the panic following suppression, a score of market officers, anxious to be considered for appointment as commissioned agents to replace the measurers and porters, repented and offered their cooperation. The inspector cultivated them warmly, albeit with careful discrimination, assuring "the best subjects" among them (those who were "esteemed by sellers and buyers," "very honest," "enemies of rapine," "extremely hard workers," "gentle and meticulous") posts in the market and promising the rest other patronage considerations.[169]

Certain submissions seemed to be short-lived, as the pendulum swung the other way and the market offices were reestablished the following spring. "The measurers have resumed their old ways, which means that they believe that no one but themselves may police the market," noted Poussot in his journal. Herlaut, whom the inspector had "reduced to reason" and who had "loudly applauded the [new] arrangements," provided the most vivid illustration of this problem of reversion. Instead of performing the largely clerical functions to which he had been assigned, Herlaut "began [again] to parade in the flour arena, to question and challenge the sellers, buyers, brokers and others, and to harass them." Other officers "held councils" in the marketplace, delayed and disrupted exchanges, and boisterously savored their sweet revenge.[170]

Poussot permitted them to prance and prattle for a while but made it patently clear that the police would not tolerate a return to the status quo

166. Archives Seine-Paris, 2 AZ 2³⁶, pièces 3F and 6F; édit du roi concernant les offices, March 1760, BN; *Mercure historique et politique contenant l'état présent de l'Europe, ce qui se passe dans toutes les cours* 147 (November 1759): 442–44.

167. See, for instance, Bautray's demarche, Arsenal, ms. Bast. 10141 (11 April 1759).

168. Arsenal, ms. Bast. 10141 (23, 28 July, 29–31 August, and 5 October 1759); AN, Y 12612, 3 September 1763.

169. Arsenal, ms. Bast.10141 (12 October, 6 November 1759).

170. Ibid. (10 April 1760).

ante. Such a relapse would signify a rejection of progress, a return to the
"interest" and "inertia" that Poussot associated not only with venality in the
marketplace but also with outdated and/or pernicious marketing practices,
breakdowns in the supply, retrograde milling techniques, and poor quality
bread at gratuitously high prices. If he could not prevent the renascent market
officers from exercising any police authority at all—his idea was to confine
them to "collecting fees and declarations"—the inspector was determined
that henceforth they would do it according to the rules that he and the commissaire fashioned.

Supported directly by lieutenant general of police Sartine, who shared his
passion for improving the provisioning system, Poussot subjected the recalcitrant measurers and porters to tremendous pressure. Faced with the threat of
exclusion from the Halle, Herlaut had a profound change of heart. Convinced
this time that Herlaut was sincere, if only because he had no real choice,
Poussot made him his unofficial "inspector for the measurers." The effect was
stunning. "Since Herlaut has been charged with the management of the
[officers at the] Halle," observed Poussot, the market "has been in fine
shape." To drive the lesson home to those officers still tempted by defiance,
the inspector resorted to the sort of violence that was the idiom of the marketplace. Using a blank lettre de cachet, he arrested the porter Magnac, "a
libertine" with a fiery temper and "the strength of twenty men," whose ungov-
ernability was notorious. Kept incommunicado for a month—not in a prison
but in a secret hiding place, so that not even his wife could obtain official
notification of his status—Magnac underwent a moral transformation that
filled his captor-rehabilitator with enthusiasm. "He has renounced all the
faults of his youth," Poussot informed Sartine, "and he has a great desire to
win your confidence." Just as Magnac became Poussot's "man" among the
porters, so his friend Bourguignon, whom the inspector had once considered
the most mutinous and irresponsible porter, pledged his "desire" and his
"zeal" to work for the police. In addition to a vow of dutifulness, Poussot
extracted from Magnac a great deal of information about mismanagement and
malversation in the porter corporation that would help in the task of reform.
The police encouraged the younger members of both corporations, who felt
"cheated" and "excluded," to challenge the authority of the syndics and to
insist on strict accountability. The fear that the police would quite literally
annex or take possession of their corporations spurred a number of officers to
make their peace with them.[171]

The "fractious" and "licentious" behavior of the *forts* also preoccupied the
police. Poussot imputed a large measure of responsibility to the porters.
Instead of inculcating discipline and stressing service, the porters taught the

---

171. Ibid. (20 January, 7 April, 6 October, 28, 30 November, 4, 6 December 1760, and 27
January 1761).

plumets by example to defy the rules and abuse the public. By paying a wage at least a third below the level that Poussot deemed minimally reasonable, the porters virtually obliged their *plumets* to extort supplements, and sometimes even tried to recover a percentage in kickbacks.[172]

The other major source of difficulty lay in recruitment, for which the police themselves had to take the blame. De Courcy had commonly admitted children into the bands of *plumets,* beginning at age eight, in return for a few louis. He winked his eye at the traffic in places that removed control of the composition of the bands entirely from the hands of the police. The porters also made appointments to and dismissals from the bands without consulting the authorities, which enabled them to tighten the screws of dependency in which they held the *plumets.* As a result of this laxity, the bands were peopled with such men as twenty-three-year-old Rigaud the younger, who "does not work a day in a week, is a lazy drunkard, insults everyone . . . and has not been free of venereal disease in the past year and a half." Though he had been banished from the central markets by a police sentence, a *plumet* called the Rose returned to work there with impunity, sure of his corporate shelter.[173] Of the eighteen members of the band of the *petits forts* around 1755, half were either chronically indolent or inveterately drunk, or both. Four of the fifteen members of the *gros forts* were "brutal" and "drunkards," two of whom served simultaneously in the French Guards. Another soldier in the French Guards, Labasse, was the "enforcer" of the *gros forts.* He relished the task of beating up colleagues and clients who took issue with the will of the band. In Poussot's judgment he was "the wickedest man in the Halle."[174]

The process of "subordinating" the *forts* began with the imposition of a police monopoly on recruitment. Commencing in the late fifties, only the lieutenant general of police, on the advice of the senior commissaire of the department of the Halles, could name *forts* to work as *plumets* or to serve in other official capacities in the markets. Practically speaking, that assured Poussot of direct control. He filtered applications, approving only those of whose "submission" he was certain. He recommended André Dromont for the band of *chargeurs* because he was "a very honest man, a good worker, quiet, not at all a tippler, and full of good will." Dromont provided Poussot with "useful" and "faithful" reports on happenings in and around the central markets. "Gentle, well-behaved, obedient," twenty-seven-year-old Georges Collier won Poussot's patronage for a place in the band of the *savates.* Poussot expelled Bailly from the *petits forts* for having assaulted a woman who

172. Ibid. (26 August 1760).
173. Ibid. (13 May 1758, 12 April 1760, 27 May 1756) and Arsenal, ms. Bast. 10140 (listing of the bands).
174. Arsenal, ms. Bast. 10141 (1 August 1759). Cf. the case of Baptiste, a soldier and *fort* arrested for mugging and theft. AN, Y 10070, 1 July 1739.

rented carriages, with the prospect that he could be reinstated if he proved himself capable of good behavior over the next few months.[175]

While the porters remained nominally responsible for the discipline of the *plumets,* the police wrested effective control of all the activities of the various *forts.*[176] The commissaire and the inspector set up work rules and a variable scale of rates for different functions. Guaranteed henceforth a "just" wage, the *plumets* no longer had any justification to solicit tips; any such gesture could henceforth result in their immediate exclusion from the bands. The medallion that identified them endowed them with the exclusive right and responsibility of performing labor at the markets; they could no longer farm out their menial tasks to *garçons* as the porters had passed their tasks on to the *forts.* In case of disputes, the *forts* were to appeal directly to the arbitration of the police. They would be under the constant scrutiny of Poussot's "little inspectors." For the sake of economy, efficiency, and more effective control, Machurin and Poussot sought to consolidate the *forts* in a smaller number of functionally specialized bands. They enjoyed some success in the legumes, small grains, and dairy products, but it is not clear to what extent they were able to rationalize the bands that served in wheat and flour.[177] In order to strengthen his hand politically as well as administratively against the measurers and porters, Poussot strove to win the personal loyalty of each *fort* by showing them "that their interest was in it." He boasted, "All I had to say was one word," and all eighteen members of the band assigned to flour "came to see me this morning to pledge their obedience and fidelity, not only for the [market] work but for everything that I might order them to do for the sake of the public good."[178]

The reorganization of the *forts* stirred little overt opposition from the porters. They were too weak and vulnerable to offer serious resistance. Poussot mused that if they did not like the new arrangement, he might have no choice but "to compel these officers to do their [manual] labor themselves, as the law stipulated they should."[179] The inspector even suggested that some of the ablest *plumets* could themselves replace their erstwhile employers in

175. Arsenal, ms. Bast. 10141 (27 May 1756, 17 January 1757, 25 May 1757).

176. See evidence of the porter efforts to cling to control in the "regulation on the plumets" that they submitted to the municipality—but significantly, not to the Châtelet—shortly after their reestablishment. AN, AD XI 39, 8 July 1760.

177. Arsenal, ms. Bast. 10141 (8 July 1756, 5 June, 1 July, 1 August, 16 October 1759, 9 May, 29 June 1760).

178. Ibid. (26 September 1759).

179. Ibid. (9 September 1760). I have found one instance of a porter who actually unloaded grain—during which time the overcoat, jacket, and vest that he had removed were stolen. AN, Y 11382, 11 December 1770. If one takes seriously Ramazzini's inventory of the dreadful occupational illnesses to which porters were highly vulnerable, it is no wonder that they farmed out the tasks. *Diseases of Workers,* p. 311.

certain functions. More ominous murmurings, of a quasi-corporate character, came from the soldiers of the French Guards, who resented the new pattern of distribution and accountability that denied them autonomy and limited their job opportunities in the Halle theater. In the hope of appeasing them, Poussot tried to relocate them in other places in the central markets, but they continued to show their bad humor by taking over loads without authorization and wielding big sticks as they prowled the market arena.[180]

The reforms that resulted in the integration of the measurers and the porters, along with the *forts,* into the police apparatus on the terms defined by Poussot were part of his larger project to restructure and revitalize the central markets. Had he and Machurin not succeeded in bringing a new degree of order and responsibility to the administrative and operational base of the Halle, it would have been infinitely more difficult for them to realize durable changes in the way provisioning took place. "You must be told," the inspector warned the lieutenant of police, "that everything in the central markets that has some relation with the police is absolutely detested."[181] To be sure, hating the police was a way of life in the stomach of Paris, a bond between such natural enemies as buyers and sellers, bosses and employees, residents and strangers. To the extent, however, that police was detested for corruption, arbitrariness, and brutality, Poussot may have contributed toward moderating this sentiment somewhat. For, as a result of his and Machurin's efforts to purge, standardize, and regulate, grass-roots police became more coherent and more predictable.

The measurers and the porters exercised (and sometimes abused) ground-level police authority in the grain and flour markets of the capital. They were the custodians of the sacrosanct marketplace and the enemies of the market principle. In one way or another they mediated every transaction on the trading floor. They "opened" and "closed" sacks, verifying the quantity and quality of the merchandise and consecrating and recording the sale. In some cases they orchestrated exchanges, allocated supplies, and influenced price making. The data they gathered gave the authorities a continuous profile of the provisioning situation. Measurers and porters not assigned to the market-places patrolled the streets and outskirts of the city and even the hinterland in search of trading violations and contraband goods. Others undertook special missions for the lieutenant general of police or the commissaire. Traditionally there was jealousy and friction between the two communities, the measurers claiming a superior status to the porters. To free themselves of the stigma of manual labor, the porters passed most of the physical work to subalterns

180. Arsenal, ms. Bast. 10141 (6 November 1759).
181. Ibid. (27 January 1758).

called *forts* or *plumets,* many of whom were soldiers of the guard, which did not guarantee their good behavior.

Both corporations had a precarious existence. On the one hand, they were milked dry by royal fiscality; on the other hand they were constantly menaced with suppression by royal reformism. Their posts were abolished in 1719 and recreated in 1730. The government announced a "definitive" suppression in 1759 and again in 1774. The measurers and porters owed their survival in part to the tenacity of their corporations, which kept control of the posts even during the "suppression" period when the government commissioned agents to replace the venal officeholders. The corporations negotiated with the government to protect the investments of their members, repelled encroachment from rival groups, worked to sustain the value of their posts, and organized mutual-aid services in times of illness, economic distress, and death. Like the merchant and craft guilds, the measurer and porter corporations were controlled by an oligarchy that was periodically challenged by member insurgents, especially on the issue of internal financial management.

Recruitment was extremely diverse. A number of measurers and porters had close ties with baker families, but many acquired their expertise in grain and flour on the job. The range of fortune was similarly variable. Some quite affluent measurers and porters purchased their offices as straightforward investments and had little interest in exercising their charges. Others depended on the revenue from their posts for survival.

Merchants and bakers, seconded by institutional buyers, sharply criticized the behavior of the measurers and porters. They complained of haughtiness, harassment, favoritism, extortion, and indifferent or incompetent service. Suppliers threatened to discontinue furnishing the Halle if they were not spared this treatment, and bakers, who could not obtain sufficient quantities of grain and flour, threatened to meet the suppliers outside the marketplace. The Paris police authorities were persuaded that many of these complaints were justified. Commissaire Machurin and inspector Poussot tried to break the mutinous spirit of the measurers and porters, and were partly successful. Frightened by the specter of exclusion from the marketplaces, many of them "submitted" to new disciplinary standards. Machurin and Poussot took direct control over the recruitment of the forts and required the measurers and porters to seek their approbation before inducting a new member.

CHAPTER 15

Conclusion

*P*olice and provisioning formed an inseparable couple in old-regime society. Police embodied a conception of social organization that valued order above all else and a conception of social relations that made order contingent upon an adequate food supply. Police bespoke a political engagement in a society whose political culture was permeated and shaped by subsistence anxieties. To the extent that the consumer-people attributed the lapses of provisioning to the government, police was nothing less than a guarantee of its moral and political legitimacy.

The police representation of provisioning implied a world view that has an apocalyptical ring in retrospect but that more or less faithfully reflected the material and psychological environment of the old regime. It grew out of the following assumptions:

1. Fragility and dependence. Society was wholly dependent for its reproduction, in social as well as biological terms, on an adequate supply of grain.
2. Chronic insecurity. Despite the fertility of French arable, nothing was less certain at any given moment than the adequacy of the grain supply. Society was hostage to both the caprices of nature and the machinations of men.
3. Potential explosiveness. The mass of consumers, for whom there was no practical difference between *cherté* and famine, would not tolerate a situation of recurrent dearth. They would hold their leaders to account.

4. Imperative intervention. The government had to act to reduce its own
   vulnerability and the threat to society.

While the government had no control over nature, it was in a position to
check men's evil machinations.[1] Those vices, insofar as they manifested
themselves in the distribution of subsistence goods, led to odious antisocial
actions, but in a sense they too were rooted in nature—human nature. For
human nature was flawed by rapacity and self-regard, and self-interest was
the chief motivating force of commerce. To entrust provisioning wholly to
commerce, then, was unthinkable, for the gratification of commerce was
profit rather than public service, and substantial profit in the grain and flour
trade could only be made at public expense. Grain could not be treated as an
ordinary object of commerce, because it was different from any other item in
trade. As Galiani put it, "Bread . . . belongs to police and not to commerce."
Grain was a matter of life and death; demand for it was inelastic and always
pressing. "As the substance of first necessity and first concern in the civil
order of societies," Galiani went on, "it is a question to be resolved politically,
on the grounds of reason of state."[2]

The political solution to the subsistence problem did not entail the scrap-
ping of commerce, however. Not even at the peak of their absolutistic ambitions did the French kings envision transferring the burden of provisioning
from commerce to the state.[3] It was too vast, too complex an undertaking,
and too expensive. Commerce had serious defects, but its social function was
distribution, and it was the only agency equipped to perform that function.
Commerce had the strengths of its weaknesses. Self-interest inspired no
confidence, but no other force could move goods as efficiently across time
and space. The political solution was to draw upon the power of commerce
without accepting its premises. Commerce had to be conscripted into public

1. To help deal with nature, the government called upon the church to transform the
crowd into a congregation in order to seek heavenly intercession. The church of course
redirected the focus of responsibility upon the vices of men. See Steven L. Kaplan, "Religion, Subsistence and Social Control: The Uses of St. Genevieve," *Eighteenth-Century
Studies* 18 (Winter 1979–80): 142–68.

2. Galiani to Madame d'Epinay, 7 August 1773, in *Lettres de l'abbé Galiani à Madame
d'Epinay,* 2:77; Galiani, *Commerce des bleds,* pp. 30–31, 170–74.

3. Certain municipal governments, encouraged by the state, maintained "organizations
of abundance" meant to buffer the cities against shortage rather than to supply them on a
regular basis. Beginning around 1727, the Paris police established an emergency granary
system located in the religious communities, public-assistance institutions, and educational
establishments of the capital and its hinterland. It afforded the city a certain margin of
protection in the short run, but it could not be counted upon in a major scarcity. In the
second half of the century, the state supplemented this network with a modest reserve
situated at Corbeil that never represented more than about two weeks' supply. The government injected large doses of the "king's grain and flour" only when the ordinary supply
system had broken down and when the ordinary police had proven impotent to repair it.
Steven L. Kaplan, "Lean Years, Fat Years: The 'Community' Granary System and The
Search for Abundance in Eighteenth-Century Paris," *French Historical Studies* 10 (Fall
1977): 197–230, and *Bread, Politics and Political Economy,* 1:347–63.

service, without, however, demoralizing or crippling it. To enable and if necessary to compel commerce to fulfill the victualing mission in a socially responsible fashion, the police relied upon a congeries of regulations and controls that I have associated with the idea of the marketplace.

The aim of the marketplace was not to smother the market principle that animated commerce, but rather to set limits upon the way in which it could operate. In practice the police allowed commerce a large measure of liberty in its day-to-day business. As much as they ulcerated over liberty degenerating into license and monopoly, the authorities also worried that overpolice might destroy commerce and thus undermine the provisioning structure. Marketplace means mattered less than marketplace ends. The provisioning of Paris was the product of a give and take between the market principle and the marketplace. This did not always mean, however, that the authorities were on one side and the merchants on the other. Metropolitan provisioning was a collaborative as well as a conflictual enterprise, and the two camps often found it useful to switch sides. When the market principle promised to help Paris authorities to wrench supplies from local marketplaces in the hinterland, they paid warm homage to it. Nor did Paris merchants shrink from involving the prior claims of the Paris marketplace when the market principle threatened to place them in competition with "outsiders." The give and take was of course an equivocal relationship. Only a tremor of administrative anxiety over the subsistence situation was needed to unsettle the precarious balance, for in time of stress the marketplace abruptly put up roadblocks and the market principle lost its safe-conduct.

"The Ministry in the old regime," wrote an essayist in 1792, "afraid of the people in the big cities, tried to give them cheap bread in order to hold them in a sort of lethargy." For the most part, it is true that in exchange for a regular and accessible supply of cereals, the consumer-people offered their "cadaverous tranquility."[4] The state remained steadfastly committed to the consumer interest, with two spectacular exceptions, one in 1763–70 and another in 1774–76. (A third exception, in the eighties, proved more timid in inspiration and in resonance.) On these occasions the royal government broke radically with provisioning tradition and recanted its covenant with the consumer-people. Grain and flour were freed from all the controls that had inhibited their movement, spied on their whereabouts, and governed the conditions of their exchange. Virtually all the practices that had once been decried as antisocial monopoly were now legitimized in the name of natural law, laissez-faire efficiency, agricultural renewal, and commercial revitalization. Even as grain and flour were liberated, the hands of the police were manacled and the consumers were invited to fend for themselves.[5] On both occasions the old supply system disintegrated. In part because they were passionately resisted

---

4. "La Cherté du Pain" (1792), AN, T 644$^{1-2}$; Manuel, *Police de Paris*, 1:10.
5. The effort to quarantine Paris temporarily from the contagion of liberty in 1763–64 did not work. See Kaplan, *Bread, Politics and Political Economy*, 1:300–33.

by the police and the people, neither of these liberal regimes endured. Each experience seemed to confirm the basic premise of the police of provisioning: that unless the merchants were "contained," the people could not be "contained."

Voltaire understood perfectly that police in general and the police of provisioning in particular were strategies of social control. He joked that Paris needed only "bread and circuses" to flourish, but he mistakenly thought that any bread, rye or even barley, would do.[6] The Paris grain trade was almost exclusively confined to wheat. Consumers disdained the lesser cereals, which produced loaves darker in color, heavier and coarser in texture, less savory in taste—loaves that were at once unappetizing and demoralizing. Paris was located in a rich wheat-growing region. Buyers had a host of types from which to choose. They placed a great premium on high quality because it promised not only better flour and bread, but also more. Selecting the right wheat or flour required a knowledge of place and persons, a sharp eye, an acute nose, a sensitive hand, and an abiding residue of mistrust.

Grain transport was slow and costly, especially by land. Transportation improved in the course of the century, though no exhaustive study has yet enabled us to measure the changes. Certainly high freight costs were one of the major impediments to the development of a regional or a national market. The lack of public transport facilities hindered shipping. It was hard to predict when merchandise would arrive. Accidents, especially on the river, were not infrequent, and they were not covered by insurance of any sort. The slow diffusion of information, along with the slow circulation of capital and the lack of credit institutions, reinforced both the parochial character of everyday trade and the extremely nervous and speculative character of more ambitious undertakings. If tolls and fees of various sorts did not clutter the roads and rivers of the Paris area, the chaos of weights and measures obstructed exchanges. Underdeveloped means of communication and transportation encouraged the survival of an intense grain particularism and xenophobia. The subsistence world was a closed world. Grain traders from other communities were viewed as enemies. Locally cultivated grain was understood to belong to the local citizenry. There was little genuine sense of interdependence. High transport costs combined with the slow circulation of information were among the chief causes of the imperfect adjustment of supply to demand, which in turn resulted in significant price fluctuations.

Primitive conservation technology also hampered the grain trade. While it reassured the police to know that hoarders could not risk holding out indefinitely, the lack of reserve capacity limited the ability of commerce to attenuate price fluctuations. Grain suffered in travel, not only across vast distances, where it overheated and fermented in the holds of oceangoing

---

6. Voltaire to François de Chennevières, 22 October 1760, in *Correspondence,* 37: 156 (no. 7823); Voltaire to Suzanne Necker, 6 February 1770, ibid., 74:81 (no. 15144).

vessels, but also on the river barges, where it usually went uncovered. Information on "repairing" damaged grain was often unreliable or unavailable. The older methods of conservation were labor intensive and costly; the newer methods required substantial capital and time. Grain and flour merchants and bakers became much more sensitive to the problem of conservation in the course of the eighteenth century than they had ever been before. More care was taken to *prevent* deterioration. Elementary conservation procedures became an integral part of the trade. The newer techniques proved extremely successful, as a result of economies of scale, in international and colonial traffic, especially of flour.

The immediate hinterland around the capital consisted of a decommercialized sector, closed to all merchants, which extended for a radius of eight (later ten) leagues around the capital. It was established in order to compel all the laboureurs within its confines to furnish Paris directly and personally. The primary supply crown reached out to the Orléanais in the south, the Champagne in the east, Picardy in the north, and Normandy in the west. This zone was more or less officially consecrated and was reserved for the capital's use, though there was some infringement on the borders by merchants from other regions. It did not substantially change until well into the nineteenth century. In time of crisis, the supply area swelled to encompass as much of France as could be drained. It is significant, however, that the agents of this expansion were less often the regular suppliers acting on their own initiative than specially commissioned royal buyers.

The zone markets were not organized into a coherent system. Some served as feeder and relay markets for others that might be called entrepôt or concentration markets. For economic and political reasons, market towns were disinclined to accept secondary roles vis-à-vis neighboring markets. Nor was there a concerted effort to divide temporal and spatial responsibilities. Markets competed bitterly with each other for local and extralocal hegemony. At the same time, virtually all of them shared an ambivalent attitude toward the imperialistic capital. Local officials wanted desperately to focus the intensity of metropolitan demand on the market in order to profit from it, and at the same time wanted to shield their town from its excesses. Market successes depended on location, transport and milling facilities, institutional fees and other fiscal burdens, local police laxity or rigor, and buyer idiosyncracies. Paris-based merchants tended to favor certain markets from generation to generation. But the bakers and merchant-millers were increasingly scornful of the traditional spheres of influence, they evinced less fidelity to place, and they pushed out more deeply into the hinterland. Moreover, the Paris buyers—in some cases with authorization, in others illicitly—fled the established markets for the markets of the moment in the inns, granaries, and farmhouses. There were fewer important markets in the Paris supply zone on the eve of the Revolution than in the time of Delamare.

Historically, the political and economic efflorescence of Paris was intimately connected with river commerce. Appropriately, the port merchants were for centuries its chief victualers, led by the barons of the rue de la Mortellerie, a clan linked by bonds of kinship, marriage, neighborhood, and business. Though they walked the Grève with a swagger, the Mortellerie corps, like their protector, the Parisian municipality, steadily declined in influence in the course of the century. They fell victim to the rise of the flour trade, to the enterprise and vigor of the bakers and the merchant-millers, to a lack of control over their purchasing agents in the field, to a reputation of relatively inferior merchandise, to their unwillingness to adapt to changing commercial conditions, to their dependence on the patronage of the city fathers, and to their growing conviction that they no longer had the opportunity to make profits of satisfactory magnitude. The Halle merchants formed a far less homogeneous and cohesive group. They seemed to fare better, because they did not have the historical standard against which to suffer measure and because they were more supple in their trading practices and relations.

The striking fact about the Paris supply system was its fragmentation. Even in his halcyon days, Jean Delu did not play a truly predominant role in the provisioning of the city. Without the scores of forains, country dealers, and especially the hundreds of laboureurs and blatiers, the capital could not have met its needs. Whether as a result of the constraints of the police regime, which discountenanced commercial concentration and deterred merchants with capital from entering the grain trade, as the physiocrats contended, or as a consequence of the inherently uncertain and locally constricted character of the trade, a group of powerful and rich merchants never emerged to appropriate the major responsibility for provisioning Paris.

Briefly, when the market principle prevailed and the marketplace toppled in the wake of the radical reforms of 1763–64, a few "companies" materialized and flourished, at the cost of traumatizing consumers and discrediting the government that tolerated and even protected such "tentacular monsters." The constitution of companies proved, incidentally, that small firm size in the grain and flour trade was not technologically ineluctable. If the liberal experiment had any lasting effect on the character of the trading corps, however, it was in the other direction. Enticed by the prospect of easy profits in the rough-and-ready ambience of the mid-sixties, a horde of men (and some women) from all walks of life plunged feverishly into more-or-less petty grain and flour speculation. Many of them appear to have remained in the trade, at least on a part-time basis, even after the restoration of the police system.

Apart from the liberal interlude, the only times during which Paris benefited from the collaboration of traders capable of mobilizing huge amounts of capital and dealing across the vast stretches were the periodic subsistence crises. The trade fell apart in times of dearth, either because of the real shortage of merchandise and the soaring price schedule, or because of the panic that seized small traders no less than consumers (the "dearth of opinion"), or as a result of speculative maneuvers. The trading system was taxed with the greatest responsibilities precisely when it was least able to meet them. It is revealing of the character of Paris trade that the authorities felt obliged not only to seek out "extraordinary" resources, but to entrust the bulk of the task to négociants who had nothing to do with the Paris provisioning operation. The bankers Samuel Bernard and Isaac Thellusson spent millions of livres of the king's money to supplement the ordinary supply and save the capital from disaster during the crises of 1725–26 and 1738–41 respectively. Shipbuilders, slave traders, and international traders and trading companies also entered the fray, generally under direct commissions from the government.

Paris merchants were considered incapable of dealing beyond their bailiwick. They were denounced at first for allowing the crisis to occur by not maintaining their ordinary supply level as the crisis set in and thereby failing the capital in its moment of dire need. They were denounced a second time for further diminishing their supply once they realized that they were in competition with dei ex machina millionaire traders who were guaranteed against loss by the government. Liberal critics argued that it was exactly this sort of government intervention that perpetuated and exacerbated the underdevelopment and infirmities of the everyday grain and flour trade.

The most important long-term transformation in the structure of the Paris provisioning trade was the displacement of grain by flour. This change was largely wrought by the bakers, who saw an opportunity to save time and money by eliminating intermediary stages of exchange. Instead of buying wheat in Paris in conditions that they could not control, then shipping it to a miller who was more often than not located in the hinterland, and then returning it to their shops, the bakers began to go to the country in increasingly large numbers. Many bakers personally scoured the *plat pays,* on and off the markets, for grain, which they dropped off immediately at a mill. Others asked their millers to do the grain buying for them. Still others renounced the grain trade entirely in favor of direct purchase of flour from the merchant-millers whom they called into existence. Flour entries had definitively superseded grain entries in Paris by 1730, and flour continued to widen its lead during the course of the century. By 1760, certain Paris officials wanted to replace the grain mercuriale with a flour price schedule, on the grounds that flour was a truer guide to the state of provisioning, that bread followed flour more directly than it followed wheat, and that, as a consequence of the autonomy of the flour crisis, it was possible to have relatively moderate wheat prices and exorbitant flour prices simultaneously.

A second profound structural mutation, intimately connected to the first, was the commercialization of milling. The most ambitious millers abandoned custom milling in favor of speculative grain buying and flour manufacturing.

These millers became merchants, and the change implied a new kind of relationship with the market, with the buyers, and with the police. Unlike the custom miller, the merchant-miller and the flour merchant, who very frequently operated a mill, were keenly interested in the quality of the wheat they ground and the flour it yielded. They were eager to test out new technologies and to modernize their mills. They were not averse to making capital improvements. They were more alert to competition than ever before.

The merchant-miller aggressively sought out clients, extended credit, visited Paris frequently, and canvassed the countryside for grain. Culturally he underwent a certain kind of urbanization, or urban socialization: in the taverns around the Halle, at the hôtel of the commissaire, in the consular court, at the bakeshop. Sometimes he married his daughter or son to a Parisian, more likely than not recruited in the subsistence complex. When he amassed some capital, he considered investing in city *rentes* instead of buying a small piece of arable or vineyard.

The flour trade was supposed to be concentrated at the Halle. Flour merchants were invited to consign the merchandise for sale by a broker or to sell it personally on the *carreau.* Many mealmen, however, preferred to bypass the market and distribute their flour directly to the bakeshops. This direct sale, or droiture traffic, resulted from commission by the baker, who alerted the merchant to deliver a given quantity and quality of flour at a specified time, or from a speculative initiative by the mealman, who sought a baker willing to take the merchandise that he had to offer. Because it obscured the transaction from the regard of the police, reduced visible abundance (and thereby distorted the price-making machinery), and worried the public, the authorities tried to suppress or at least circumscribe droiture trading. They tried to make the Halle more attractive by instituting sales by weight (thereby insulating the sellers from the harassment and the bad faith of the porters and the measurers), by simplifying procedures for declaring entries and sales, by allowing home delivery after declaration, by establishing a sack-retrieval program, by building a new Halle and later covering it to improve its storage function, by reorganizing and disciplining the market laborers *(forts* or *plumets),* by purging the ranks of the porters and measurers, and by restructuring the brokerage system in order to protect the interests of the flour merchants. On the other hand, the police unleashed the market officers to prowl in the streets and to patrol the environs in search of contraband that remained subject to seizure.

The rate of growth of droiture traffic probably decreased in the early sixties, but there was no hope of eradicating a commerce that both flour merchants and bakers found so attractive. Neither in the hinterland nor in intramural Paris were the police successful in concentrating all the trade on the market. Or rather, the very notion of market had begun to change irreversibly, despite the strictures of the police regime and without the benefit of liberalizing legislation, in response to purely commercial pressures to rationalize relationships.

Had the port-based grain merchants been right about the adequacy of the milling industry in Paris and its suburbs, perhaps their business would not have slackened so sharply. In fact, bakers did have to look far into the hinterland, because there were too few mills nearby and they did not grind fast enough. Contemporaries tended to overestimate the *real* productive capacity of a mill in a given year. (As a result, their outrage at seemingly inordinate milling fees may have been in part unfounded.) Given the frequent, more-or-less predictable stoppages due to accidents of weather, repairs, and redressings, in addition to the inherent or mechanical limits on production, Paris required a rather vast pool of mills to satisfy its needs. A large number of these mills ground exclusively for the capital, which implied certain things about their location, their power sources, their stones, their bolting apparatus, their technology. Many others served both metropolitan and local urban demand. Still others aimed primarily at the local custom trade, but were prepared to grind for Paris when called upon. The small mill still predominated even in primary Paris service, but a number of genuine factories began to appear in the two decades before the Revolution. Malisset foreshadowed Darblay. Certain millers, or more likely baker-millers, began to practice a kind of vertical integration, controlling the whole process from cultivation of wheat through bread making and sales.

The Darblays of the eighteenth century were among the first to adopt the process called economic milling. Based on middling recovery and gradual reduction, this new technology prefigured the basic conception of modern milling. It was the product of two cultures, the one an unlettered culture of the métier, the other an elite culture of science and politics. The first culture developed and practiced the new process discreetly, if not clandestinely. The second culture articulated and refined its principles and drew out its implications. This innovation was unthinkable without the millers of Senlis and Corbeil, but it surely would not have been so widely publicized without the patronage of the subsistence scientists and of the political economists. The economists viewed the new technology as both an argument and a metaphor for the physiocratic program. The savants regarded it as a symbol of the waning of the dark ages in the practical arts that affected mankind most critically. To the chagrin of the professionals of the métier, the idea took root among the savants and the economists that subsistence making was too important to be left to the merchants, millers, and bakers, even as the police believed that distribution of grain, flour, and bread was too important to be left to commerce on its own.

Economic milling was exciting because it seemed capable of profoundly modifying the way in which the subsistence trade worked, or of reinforcing and accelerating structural transformations that had already begun to make

themselves felt. Thus, for example, economic milling demanded the commercialization of milling, the eclipse of the grain trade by the flour trade, the
liberty to export flour, the perfecting of conservation technology, the care and
cleansing of grain before grinding as well as the mixing and improving of flour
after grinding, the abandonment by the bakers of home bolting, the reevalua-
tion of traditional methods of calculating bread-price schedules, the introduction of new breadways, and the creation of institutional means for conducting
research and disseminating new information on subsistence matters. For the
police and the people, economic milling promised a greater margin of security, a kind of squaring of the Malthusian circle: the production of more
(and better) bread from the same amount of wheat. For the merchant-millers,
it was the beginning of the process of industrialization of flour production. To
be sure, economic milling did not revolutionize the subsistence world overnight. It ran into considerable resistance. Given the difficulties it faced, its
progress was quite astonishing. Even when it was not wholly adopted, it
impelled or compelled millers to improve their traditional techniques. It
redefined the very function of milling and it set new and irreversible standards
for excellence.

The old-regime miller is even less well known than the grain trader, despite
his abundant place in folklore. He had an unsavory and unsettling reputation.
Like the miller of the Frau, he feared that he was unlikely to be believed no
matter how earnestly he spoke the truth.[7] Yet he often occupied a pivotal role
in the rural community, a role that made him a notable, a man of social and
economic as well as occult power. The miller worked hard and long. If he
possessed no magic potion to spare him this toil, frequently he did have
Obélix's physique to put to the task. He ground when he had grain and good
weather, and the rest of the time he devoted to maintaining his machine.
Commercialization began to change things for him: he hired hands to do much
of the work and he became a businessman. Still, it was rare for a flour
merchant to distance himself from the mill and its operation. Millers tended to
marry within the subsistence universe, to constitute family dynasties, and to
live simply.

Along with creditor-debtor relationships, family ties enmeshed large numbers of traders in networks of interlocking connections. Within the subsistence complex perhaps as much as within any sector of old-regime life, sons
tended to follow fathers professionally and to marry women whose fathers
worked in the same milieu. Labyrinthine kinship ties united millers, bakers,
grain and flour merchants, and laboureurs (and stretched in some cases to
embrace brokers or market officers). These connections gave each "firm" a
much larger amount of social capital than it could have hoped to form on its
own. Further extended by friendships, these family linkages significantly low-

7. Eugène Le Roy, *Le Moulin du Frau.*

ered transaction costs by transmitting trustworthy information, reducing uncertainty, introducing parties who could count on each other, building exchange rules on mutual identity and confidence, and focusing on long-term relations. The social organization fashioned by these networks helped young members to launch careers, members in difficulty to recover, and widows and widowers to find new mates. It facilitated shifts from one side of the subsistence business to another, mergers leading to more rational enterprises, and innovations that required more capital or knowledge than a single person could muster. It acted in some ways like an old-regime corporation, though it was a far looser organization: it defended the group against external threats, it punished renegades in its midst, it formed an arena of sociability, it fell prey to internal dissension, it oscillated between periods of integration and disintegration. Family and friendship ties were like a honeycomb of pratik bonds, as solid and as brittle.

Virtually every seller sought to establish pratik relations with his buyers. Based on a reciprocal commitment in which the seller offered concessions on price, quality, quantity, or payment terms and the buyer pledged his fidelity, the pratik union represented a precious form of business capital. It meant earnings on which one could count plus an increment of moral authority that could enhance one's standing in the community. Pratik liaison theoretically spared the seller anxiety about his client, but the competition for customers was so intense that the courtship never abated. The most acrimonious quarrels in the markets involved recriminations over pratik seduction or betrayal.

Many merchant-millers called upon Paris brokers to market their flour. This spared them the need to visit Paris every week, but not the need to cultivate clients: this contact remained a necessity if they wanted to be sure of regular and rapid sales. In fact, some of them actually accompanied their shipments and rounded up clients to whom the brokers sold their merchandise. The major incentive to use brokers was probably the desire to avoid getting involved in the collection of accounts receivable. Theoretically, the broker was supposed to assume the risk of extending credit to the bakers and the responsibility of recovering it. An aggressive broker managed to pay his merchants within a month or six weeks. The problem was that when a broker began to fall behind, it was extremely hard to catch up. Once he got in trouble, a broker's instinct was to pass the accounts receivable on to the merchant in lieu of cash payment.

The broker's bind illustrates the great fragility of the entire subsistence nexus: the whole connection was built on a cascading foundation of private credit, and there were no institutional guarantees against collapse. Consumers bought bread on credit, offered by bakers; bakers bought flour on credit, offered by flour merchants or brokers; flour merchants bought grain on credit from grain merchants, or they bought directly from cultivators, many of whom were loath to accord terms. Bakers and merchants naturally tried to diversify their sources of supply as much as possible in order to multiply their lines of credit. Brokers tried to have as many sellers and as many buyers as possible, in order to maximize their juggling opportunities. One hesitated to press a debtor client for fear of losing his practice. When a creditor did put the squeeze on a debtor, a convulsive chain reaction often occurred—insults, brawls, litigation, failure, fraud, flight. Lack of a universal, rational, public or quasi-public credit mechanism was certainly the chief source of upheaval in the personnel of the subsistence trade and in everyday commercial relations. Not only failures failed—some of the most high-powered and inventive merchants (Nicolas-Louis Martin, Malisset, Bucquet) went under. One of the lessons of failure is that the provisioning business was extremely difficult and risky. Even the fortunes of the "successful" merchants were fragile. With some exceptions, one did not make a killing in this commerce—and keep it.

The authorities never faced the problem of credit in its totality, though late in the century they did try to tighten the obligations of the brokers. Brokerage was a critical institution from the police vantage point because it was the keystone of the marketplace system, the privileged agency of exchange. By the facilities he offered, the broker was supposed to focus supply and demand palpably on the market. Inspector Poussot's vision of a dynamic central subsistence market was built around the brokers. It was for that reason that he strained to reform recruitment and institute new rules of accountability on the part of the brokers to the sellers, buyers, and police.

Poussot himself is perhaps the best yardstick of what changed and what remained the same in everyday grain and flour trade in the eighteenth century. He was a police inspector, but he read Delamare critically. He understood that provisioning meant trade and that trade turned on private interests, and within certain limits he was willing to believe that the pursuit of private interests could redound to public advantage. He insisted on the absolute sanctity of the open market in Paris, but cared much less about the locus and character of transactions in the hinterland. Once goods were on the trading floor in the capital, Poussot was inclined to allow supply and demand to run their course. He combatted the authoritarian excesses of the measurers and the porters, who had more leverage over transactions than he liked. Based in the Halle, the inspector symbolized the eclipse of the ports. He was the leading patron of the flour trade, for he wanted to found the renaissance of the Halle on the dynamism of the flour trade. He instituted the flour-weighing station and he proposed a new, covered market building specifically to meet the needs of flour. Poussot introduced Malisset to the lieutenant general of police and was present at the first major tests of economic milling and of kiln conservation. He had a passion for data collection—like so many leading administrators of the time, he believed that knowledge was power. His goal was "constant abundance" and his pastoral vocation was to persuade commerce that abundance should never be lamented. Poussot struggled to resolve within himself the tensions between the marketplace and the market principle that characterized the workings of the provisioning trade.

Drastically improved communications and transportation in the first half of the nineteenth century did not change the highly speculative and volatile character of the grain and flour trade—it retained that character at least until the time of Frank Norris's *Pit*. The post-Napoleonic trade was conducted by fewer, bigger dealers, but high-price fever continued to call out swarms of little traders during shortages. The millers absorbed much of the grain trade and some of the bakery. They displaced the bakers, to whom they had long been subordinated, as the most dynamic force in the provisioning trade. Factory mills were no longer a rarity. Even modest-sized millers added one or more pair of stones and sometimes a waterwheel as well. Steam conquered little terrain—it was too costly and it broke down too often. The economic process became more refined, with the addition of purifiers and with greater differentiation in the break cycle.

The soi-disant modernization of the provisioning trade did not result in the modernization of attitudes. Technology was not corrosive of what the physiocrats maliciously called prejudice. The people and the police remained profoundly suspicious of provisioning merchants even in the age of steam and telegraphy, and the merchants indignantly complained of the stigma attached to their business. Monopoly evoked the same fears and described essentially the same phenomena in 1860 as in 1760. The people counted upon the state to protect their fundamental welfare as much as in the days of old-regime paternalism, or more, and they trusted it even less. The famine-plot motif was as deeply inscribed in the political culture (and not just in the popular political culture) as it had been in the days of Louis XV. Social organization became increasingly submerged in the market principle, yet the people continued to demand that their subsistence receive exceptional treatment. The people continued to act as if certain economic relations were (or should be) a function of social values rather than vice versa. Modernization drew a much sharper boundary between public and private, but in the subsistence domain it commanded only spasmodic respect. Whereas the law privileged the marketplace in the eighteenth century and usage accommodated the market principle, in the nineteenth century the relation was to some extent inverted, but the practical results remained very much the same. Modernization merely signified that marketplace and market principle were more clearly associated with organized socioeconomic interests and political parties.

By a sort of neo-Tocquevillean (or perhaps neo-Jacobin) extension, the marketplace and the market principle live on, sometimes in flagrant contradiction, always in uneasy tension, under the labels Equality and Liberty.

Appendixes: Sources

Appendix A

Mortellerie Merchants

1725–40

Albert, Institut, mss. 513–21 and BN, LK⁷ 6289
Bassery, Institut, mss. 513–21 and BN, LK⁷ 6289
Bayeux, AN, Y 13087, 20 July 1737
Blanchet, Archives Seine-Paris, DC⁶ 232, fol. 8
Michel Bourjot, AN, Y 13634, 13 March 1729
Cadiou, AN, Z¹ᴴ 239, 16 October 1726
Caillet, Institut, mss. 513–21 and BN, LK⁷ 6289
Jacques Chevalier, AN, Y 15247, 3 May 1740
Coppin, AN, Y 13643, 13 March 1729
Delu, Archives Assistance publique, no. 96, 14 January 1727
De Marine, Institut, mss. 513–21 and BN, LK⁷ 6289
Veuve Denis, Institut, mss. 513–21 and BN, LK⁷ 6289
Denise (Veuve Bégulle), AN, Z¹ᴴ 239, 1726
Derain [d'Herain], Institut, mss. 513–21 and BN, LK⁷ 6289
Germain Dumont, AN, MC, IV-487, 16 April 1735
Jean Dumont, AN, MC, IV-487, 16 April 1735
Fosseyeux l'ainé, Institut, ms. 513–21 and BN, LK⁷ 6289
Fosseyeux le jeune, Institut, mss. 513–21 and BN, LK⁷ 6289

Gautier, AN, Y 13634, 13 March 1729

Gibert, Institut, mss. 513–21 and BN, LK^7 6289

Glignard, AN, Z^{1H} 239, 25 September 1726

Guesnet, AN, Y 12575, 19 March 1731

Jubert [Gibert?], AN, Y 12575, 19 March 1731

Veuve Leblanc, Archives de la Préfecture de Police, AB/195, 19 July 1740 (écrou Trudet)

Legrais, Archives Assistance publique, no. 99, 2 November 1730

Legren, Institut, mss. 513–21 and BN, LK^7 6289

Le Sieur, AN, Y 13087, 20 July 1737

Masse, AN, Z^{1H} 646, 28 August 1734

Meunier, Institut, mss. 513–21 and BN, LK^7 6289

Mignard, AN, Z^{1H} 239, 1726

Moussier l'ainé, Institut, mss. 513–21 and BN, LK^7 6289

Moussier le jeune, Institut, mss. 513–21 and BN, LK^7 6289

Paillard, Institut, mss. 513–21 and BN, LK^7 6289

Picard, AN, Z^{1H} 239, 1726

Robert, Institut, mss. 513–21 and BN, LK^7 6289

Robin, AN, Z^{1H} 239, 16 October 1726

Rogier, AN, MC, IV-488, 8 August 1735

Rousseau, Arsenal, ms. Bast. 10270 (Bourlon to Hérault, October 1725)

Simonnet, Institut, mss. 513–21 and BN, LK^7 6289

Veuve Turlin, AN, Z^{1H} 239, 16 October 1726

Vassou, Institut, mss. 513–21 and BN, LK^7 6289

Vignard, AN, Y 14946, 8 July 1732 and Y 15934, 19 August 1734

Viquet, Institut, mss. 513–21 and BN, LK^7 6289

1741–60

Armet, AN, MC, VII-284, 4 July 1753

Etienne Aubert, AN, MC, XII-518, 21 May 1751

Bassery, Archives Seine-Paris, D2B^6 736, 24 April 1741

Baury, Archives Seine-Paris, D2B^6 802, 10 October 1746

Borde, Archives Seine-Paris, D2B^6 800, 12 August 1746

Boussat, Archives Seine-Paris, D2B^6 841, 14 January 1750

Carrier, Archives Seine-Paris, D4B^6 13-587, 21 August 1753 (faillite Mondinet)

Chalier, Archives Seine-Paris, D4B^6 16-763, 1 September 1756

Louis Chevallier, Archives Seine-Paris, D4B^6 6-287, 1 February 1746

Chevret, AN, Y 11228, 29 July 1741

Colinet, Archives Seine-Paris, D4B^6 14-653, 5 November 1754 (faillite M. Fleury)

Corneille, Archives Seine-Paris, D4B^6 14-653, 5 November 1754 (faillite M. Fleury)

Cuisnon, Archives Seine-Paris, D4B^6 6-287 (faillite Chevallier)

Marin Denise, AN, MC, V-456, 17 August 1750

Despreaux, Archives Seine-Paris, D4B^6 14-653, 5 November 1754 (faillite M. Fleury)

Duchenois, Archives Seine-Paris, D4B^6 14-653, 5 November 1754 (faillite M. Fleury)

Jean Dumont, AN, MC, XLIX-690, 6 July 1751

Pierre Dumont, BN, F 23673, no. 136 (arrêt of Paris Parlement, 17 January 1742)

Pierre-François Dumont, AN, MC, XLIX-690, 6 July 1751

Fleury, Archives Seine-Paris, D4B^6 22-1082, 19 August 1760

Didier Fosseyeux, Archives Seine-Paris, D4B^6 14-653, 5 November 1754 (faillite M. Fleury)

Jean-Baptiste Fosseyeux, Archives Seine-Paris, D4B^6 11-526

César Gilbert, AN, Y 13741, 11 May 1741 (scellé Leguay)

Granget, AN, Y 11229, 5 January 1742

Greban, Archives Seine-Paris, D4B^6 11-526

Goujart, AN, MC, LXXXIX-71, 29 January 1751

Guyot, AN, MC, XXVI-457, 10 April 1751

Harinet, Archives Seine-Paris, D4B^6 21-1029, 5 January 1760 (faillite Cottin)

Nicolas Jauvin, AN, Y 13926, 21 April 1741

Jauvin le jeune, Archives Seine-Paris, D4B^6 14-653, 5 November 1754 (faillite M. Fleury)

Veuve Leblanc, AN, Y 13741, 11 May 1741 (scellé Leguay)

Lefebvre, AN, Y 15603, 5 May 1742 (scellé Thevenet)

Lenain, AN, MC, VII-278, 13 April 1751 and AN, Y 15359, 16 April 1758

Pelletier, Archives Seine-Paris, D4B^6 4-211, 4 December 1742

Pinondel(le), Archives Seine-Paris, D4B^6 14-653, 5 November 1754 (faillite M. Fleury)

Quenet, Archives Seine-Paris, D2B^6, 25 October 1743

J. Rousseau, AN, MC, IV-568, 27 August 1750 and XXVI-459, 22 July 1751

Sovat l'ainé, Archives Seine-Paris, D4B^6 21-1029, 5 January 1760 (faillite Cottin)

1761–75

Armet, AN, Y 15072, 1 March 1769 and Archives Seine-Paris, DC^6 333, 14 September 1771

Bassery, AD Marne, C 422

Bastry, Archives Seine-Paris, D4B^6 24-1218, 11 August 1762 (faillite Tayret)

Boursier, Archives Seine-Paris, D4B^6 24-1218, 11 August 1762 (faillite Tayret)

Chauvin, AN, Y 13167, 21 July 1761

Dangin, Archives Seine-Paris, D4B^6 101-7116, 15 April 1778 (faillite Letellier)

Denise, Archives Seine-Paris, D4B^6 24-1218, 11 August 1762 (faillite Tayret)

Despreaux, AD Marne, C 422

Duhamel, AD Marne, C 422

Fosseyeux, AD Marne, C 422

Foucat, AN, Y 15269, 17 January 1761

Gratien, Archives Seine-Paris, D4B^6 44-2528, 1 April 1771 (faillite Dugrand)

Greban, AD Marne, C 422

Herbert, Archives Seine-Paris, D4B^6 74-4884, 1 October 1779

Hure, AD Marne, C 422

Jauvin, Archives Seine-Paris, D2B⁶ 986, 10 February 1762
Layne, Archives Seine-Paris, D4B⁶ 23-1185, 10 March 1762
Lefebvre, AD Marne, C 422
Lepinay, AD Marne, C 422
Lesergent, AD Marne, C 422
Letellier, Archives Seine-Paris, D4B⁶ 101-7116, 15 April 1788
Maheu, AD Marne, C 422 (same as J. Mahut, AN, Y 12619, 17 February 1770?)
Moignat, Archives Seine-Paris, 6 AZ 1447, 14 June 1770
M. Nicole, Archives Seine-Paris, D4B⁶ 51-796, 24 February 1776
Parme le jeune, Archives Seine-Paris, D4B⁶ 24-1218, 11 August 1762 (faillite Tayret)
Pinondel(le), Archives Seine-Paris, D4B⁶ 24-1218, 11 August 1762 (faillite Tayret)
Pluyette, AD Marne, C 422

Appendix B
Business Failures of Grain Merchants

Archives Seine-Paris, D4B⁶

6-287, 1 February 1746
8-403, 30 August 1749
16-763, 1 September 1756
22-1082, 19 August 1760
22-1133, 13 May 1761
23-1185, 10 March 1762
27-1446, 8 May 1765 and 17 May 1771
33-1491, 19 November 1768
35-1896, 29 July 1769
36-1951, 25 November 1769
36-1967, 2 January 1770
43-2425, 13 January 1772
43-2431, 18 January 1772
43-2482, 28 February 1772
44-2535, 11 April 1772 and 2 June 1775
44-2581, 20 May 1772
47-2845, 26 May 1773
49-2956, 2 October 1773
50-3057, 3 February 1774
50-3094, 9 March 1774
52-3196, 23 June 1774
52-3199, 8 July 1774 (Aubert fils)
52-3199, 27 August 1774 and 16 June
  1775 (Aubert père)
56-3521, 25 September 1775
56-3522, 25 September 1775

51-3601, 24 February 1776
61-3873, 10 December 1776
52-3199, 18 February 1777 (Veuve Aubert)
62-4004, 9 April 1777
63-4098, 4 July 1777
65-4205, 14 October 1777
68-4476, 10 August 1778
70-4630, 16 February 1779
71-4665, 10 March 1779
72-4725, 17 May 1779
73-4846, 26 August 1779
76-5015, 18 September 1779
74-4884, 1 October 1779
76-5015, 11 February 1780
82-5503, September 1781
83-5565, 13 December 1781
89-6089, 17 January 1784
90-6204, 28 May 1784
97-6766, 2 September 1786
85-5740, 16 October 1786
99-6955, 9 August 1787
99-6951, 30 September 1787
100-7066, 8 February 1788
101-7116, 15 April 1788

Appendix C
Master and *Forain* Baker-Millers

Master Baker-Millers

Archives Nationales, Minutier Central

XIII-134, 25 January 1699 (Lescureux)
XII-179, 15 April 1714 (Bacon)
XXXIV-501, 14 May 1725 (Denis Delamarre)
VII-402, 21 February 1732 (Grezel)
XII-412, 10 October 1740 (Sauval)
CII-367, 7 September 1751 (André Leroux)

VII-287, 14 June 1753 (Siméon Delamarre)
VII-291, 1 June 1754 (André Leroux)
VII-325, 12 March 1760 (Siméon Delamarre)
VII-381. 9 November 1768 (Siméon Delamarre)

Archives Nationales, Series Y

9619, 12 August 1737 (Jean Fleury)
12141, 3 July 1739 (Duval)

15247, 3 May 1740 (Tuillier)
11229, 23 February 1742 (Blanvillain)

Archives Seine-Paris

D4B⁶ 14-653, 5 November 1754 (Michel Fleury)
D4B⁶ 28-1476, 14 September 1765 (Herbert)

DC⁶ 24, fols. 100, 167: 1781 (Picot)
D4B⁶ 92-6394, 17 February 1785 (Deschamps)

Bibliothèque Nationale, Collection Joly de Fleury

1116, fol. 223: October 1725 (Jean Fleury)
1116, fol. 231: 1725 (Larue)
1116, fol. 230: 1725 (Thévenot)

Bibliothèque Historique de la Ville de Paris

ms. n.a. 173, fol. 400: 8 May 1782 (le Grand Moulin)

Forain Baker-Millers

Archives Nationales, Series Y

13499, 13 May 1733 (Martial)
12141, 30 June 1739 (Pellet)
9440, 4 September 1739 (Pellet)
9440, 4 September 1739 (Piochard)

9440, 11 September 1739 (Duval)
9441, 26 August 1740 (Lerouge)
18670, 30 September 1769 (Lamard)

Archives Seine-Paris

5 AZ 263, pièce 1, 17 February and 24 March 1740 (Landry)
D2B⁶ 950, 21 February 1759 (Lenain)
D4B⁶ 16-788 (Longpré)

Bibliothèque de l'Arsenal, mss. Bastille

10027, fol. 68, 1730 (Veret, Bresche, Bertheville)
10274, Divot to Hérault, 4 December 1748 (Betemont l'aîné)

Bibliothèque Nationale, Collection Joly de Fleury

1152, fols. 6–7, Clément to procurator general, 6 August 1770 (Boudier)

Archives Départementales Seine-et-Marne

80 E 249, 15 February 1770, notariat Halbou (Gaucher)

Appendix D
References to Mill Leases

Water Mills

Archives Nationales, Minutier Central

CIX-412, 3 November 1712
XXVIII-178, 19 May 1721
LXXXV-448, 10 February 1734
LXXXIX-445, 2 July 1737
LXXXIX-469, 3 August 1740
XXVI-453, 14 August 1750
XIII-292, 7 January 1751 (lease cited in
   marriage contract)
XCVIII-513, 4 March 1751
CIX-581, 12 March 1751
LXII-423, 23 March 1751
CVIII-493, 1 May 1751
XIV-341, 8 May 1751

XCIX-510, 10 May 1751
CII-366, 16 June 1751
XCII-571, 22 June 1751
LII-356, 28 June 1751
CXV-592, 16 July 1751
XLIV-398, 20 July 1751
CX-377, 11 August 1751
CXXI-350, September 1751 (Fremeau)
X-498, 9 October 1751
XXXV-668, 14 October 1751
LXX-367, 5 November 1751
CII-368, 15 December 1751

Archives Seine-Paris

D4B⁶ 92-6394, 17 February 1785

Archives Départementales Seine-et-Marne

H 563, 23 March 1747 and 11 May 1748

E 1247, 29 May 1750

B 411, pièces 75–77, 17 December 1750 (inventaire Ducellier)

H 198, 10 May 1756

H 559, 10 November 1764

H 448, fols. 1470–71 (moulin de Poncet, abbaye de Faremoutiers)

G 236, 1 May 1771 and 7 August 1789

H 61, 29 January 1772

H 38, 7 December 1776

H 730, 23 July 1782

G 255, 27 April 1784

H 338, 28 May 1788

E 719, 1 July 1789

H 396 (seigneurie de la Chapelle-Châtenay)

H 749 (grand prieur de France to Jean Obron)

H 559 (abbaye royale de Notre-Dame-de-la-Joye, Nemours)

Archives Départementales Seine-et-Oise

Tabellion de Brueil, notariat de Meulan, 23 December 1726 (Montalet-le-Bois)

Tabellion de Brueil, notariat de Meulan, 3 July 1731 and 8 January 1741 (Petit Moulin)

E 3397, 24 January 1735

Tabellion de Brueil, notariat de Meulan, 1 November 1737 (Moulin Neuf de Bonnival)

E Supplément 166, July 1742 and 26 November 1755

Tabellion de Brueil, notariat de Meulan, 19 May 1744 (moulin des Prez)

Tabellion de Brueil, notariat de Meulan, 20 May 1744 (moulin de Wy)

Tabellion de Brueil, notariat de Meulan, 1746 (Grand Moulin)

70 H 8, 12 October 1752

70 H 7, 7 October 1755, 1 April 1764, and 24 July 1771

E 3397, 2 April 1772

E 1855, 10 October 1782

Archives Départementales Yvelines

E Supplément 322, 1 December 1729, 5 August 1749, 29 June 1757, and 14 February 1758

E Supplément 166, 2 July 1742 and 26 November 1755

E Supplément 166, 16 November 1772

E Supplément 166, 27 June 1780

Archives Départementales Oise

G 41, 24 November 1728

H 1460, 20 July 1731

H 1229, 29 January 1737

H 1229, 19 April 1752

Archives Départementales Aube

G 3410, pièces 100-101, 18 September 1755

Archives Départementales Eure-et-Loir

H 81, 14 November 1705, 9 September
  1713, and 14 April 1758
E II 52, 7 April 1712
G 3005, 24 May 1726
E 1137, 28 May 1742 and 12 October
  1752
VIII E 1003, 6 June 1743
XVI E 309, 7 February 1746

XVI E 309, 18 May 1746
E 469, 10 January 1749
E 469, 23 June 1751
E 469, 27 October 1754
E 871, 27 September 1756
H 81, 14 April 1758
E 469, 23 April 1765
E II 84, 22 July 1774 and 21 April 1781

Bibliothèque Municipale, Chartres

NA 137, 24 April 1783
NA 137, 17 June 1786
NA 137, 5 November 1787
NA 137, 25 February 1788

NA 137, 12 March 1788
NA 137, 14 February 1789
NA 137, 22 April 1789

Bibliothèque Municipale, Mantes-la-Jolie

Inventaire, seigneurie de Sailly, liasse 49, 23 November 1750

Windmills

Archives Nationales, Minutier Central

III-808, 13 September 1708
LXVI-396, 26 February 1728
LXIX-316, 20 October 1733
XXVIII-241, 9 November 1735
V-421, 21 July 1745
LII-37, 14 April 1750
XLIV-395, 13 January 1751
XXIX-487, 27 February 1751
XXXVIII-388, 12 March 1751
LII-355, 6 April 1751

XXI-388, 31 July 1751
XVII-799, 10 August 1751
XVIII-618, 11 September 1751
LXXXI-331, 22 September 1751
LXXVI-332, 8 October 1751
LXVI-499, 3 November 1753
VII-307, 28 April 1757 (inventaire après
  décès)
VII-325, 12 March 1760
VII-381, 9 November 1768

Archives Nationales, Series Y

11229, 23 February 1742

Archives Seine-Paris

Faillite of master baker Michel Fleury, 5 November 1754, D4B^6 14-653 (moulin des
  Prunes and moulin dit La Marmite)

Archives Départementales Seine-et-Marne

E 851, 30 July 1777 and 9 February 1780
H 749, 24 July 1785

Archives Départementales Seine-et-Oise

E 2751, 9 November 1727
E 2751, 21 July 1729

Appendix E

Miller Marriages

Archives Nationales, Minutier Central

LXV-196, 2 July 1718
VII-307, 28 April 1757 (contract of 15
    June 1723)
LXXXIX-377, 13 July 1726
XXVIII-203, 17 October 1726
XXVIII-210, 12 August 1728
XIII-232, 23 May 1729
XCVIII-443, 20 July 1731
LXIX-319, 31 August 1734
XXXV-626, 18 October 1739
L-349, 19 October 1739
XXXV-627, 19 July 1741

XXVIII-290, 27 January 1745
CIX-555, 24 May 1746
XIII-292, 7 January 1751
II-529, 13 February 1751
LXXXV-528, 30 June 1751
II-532, 19 July 1751
CII-367, 23 September 1751
CV-1238, 28 November 1751
VII-287, 14 June 1753
VII-297, 31 July 1755
VII-369, 8 February 1767

Archives Nationales, Series Y

11571, 18 August 1755 (contract of 19 July 1725)

Archives Départementales Seine-et-Oise, notariat de Meulan

Tabellion de Jambville, 24 June 1677
Tabellion de Brueil, 11 August 1744

Appendix F

Baker-Miller Marriage Connections

Archives Nationales, Minutier Central

XXVIII-203, 17 August 1726 (Lepère)

XXVIII-210, 12 August 1728 (Porcherin)

LXXXIX-469, 17 July 1740 (Pariset)

LXXXIX-469, 17 July 1740 (Taboureau)

LXI-422, 30 July 1744 (Lavigne)

XXVIII-290, 27 January 1745 (Ducatelle-Flabbe)

CIX-580, 17 February 1751 (Brivant)

XCVIII-513, 4 March 1751 (Girard)

XXXVIII-388, 7 April 1751 (Richer)

XCIII-23, 24 July 1751 (Simon)

VII-287, 14 June 1753 (Goy)

VII-288, 9 August 1753 (Lapareillé)

VII-297, 31 July 1755 (Bleziman)

VII-307, 28 April 1757 (Devaux)

VII-369, 8 February 1767 (Lacour)

LXXXIX-655, 12 December 1767 (Taboureau)

VII-398, 21 June 1771 (Baron)

CI-602, 4 February 1775 (Plé)

Archives Nationales, Series Y

11571, 19 July 1725, 18 August 1755 (Lavigne)

13085, 17 April 1736 (Gaudet)

11232, 27 August 1745 (Lapareillé)

15257, 17 November 1749 (Masson)

15258, 10 December 1750 (Richer)

15940, 10 August 1754 (Richer)

11571, 18 August 1755, 13 December 1747 (Aubin)

10396, 26 March 1779 (Bleziman)

Archives Seine-Paris

V5E, extrait du registre des baptèmes de Nointel, 1738 (Tabar)

Appendix G

Baker Debts to Flour Merchants

Archives Seine-Paris, D2B[6]

689, 3 May 1787 (Etry and Verrier)

736, 28 April 1741 (Lalande)

736, 10 April 1741 (Gosset)

736, 3 April 1741 (Janse)

736, 17 April 1741 (Giboreau)

736, 10 April 1741 (Denis)

736, 19 April 1741 (Noret)

737, 10 May 1741 (Cosme)

737, 29 May 1741 (Denis)

754, 1 October 1742 (Lherittier)

754, 5 October 1742 (Godard)

754, 24 October 1742 (Godard)

766, 16 October 1743 (Vassal)

766, 2 October 1743 (Pachot)

768, 18 December 1743 (Segnin)

768, 2 December 1743 (Ferry)

798, 17 June 1746 (Picon)

800, 12 August 1746 (Denis)

801, 7 September 1746 (Denis and Chantard)

801, 12 September 1746 (Perinot)

802, 7 October 1746 (Noret and Mosny)

802, 12 October 1746 (Janse)

802, 17 October 1746 (Girardière)

809, 10 May 1747 (Vieuxbled)

809, 19 May 1747 (Ravault)

809, 31 May 1747 (Foucret and Douceur)

841, 9 January 1750 (Gibout)

841, 16 January 1750 (Desrues)

337, 16 January 1750 (Desrues)

841, 21 January 1750 (Horn)

950, 5 February 1759 (Fichot)

986, 17 February 1762 (Halle)

1009, 9 January 1764 (Guibert and Deline)

1019, 12 November 1764 (Oru and Leprince)

1034, 26 February 1766 (Flanée)

1034, 28 February 1766 (Lamoureux, Hamare and Raute)

1102, 11 October 1771 (Dupré and Desouge)

1103, 8 November 1771 (Daubigny)

1109, 15 May 1772 (Gentry and Quentin)

1126, 8 October 1773 (Faron, Pellerin, Farvis, de Souger, and Oudard)

1128, 1 December 1773 (Gibert and Touroux)

1128, 6 December 1773 (Penot and Jetain)

1128, 10 December 1773 (Noël)

Archives Nationales, Minutier Central

CXI-321, 13 July 1775 (inventaire Cousin and Delamarre)

Appendix H

Business Failures of Millers and Flour Merchants

Archives Seine-Paris, D4B⁶

1-15, 6 July 1695

27-1437, 19 April 1765

30-1626, 30 May 1767

43-2415, 30 December 1771 and 22 July 1777

46-2723, 16 December 1772

48-2869, 5 July 1773

48-2896, 2 August 1773

52-3225, 29 July 1774

53-3245, 3 August 1774

54-3331, 7 January 1775

54-3338, 12 January 1775

55-3480, 5 August 1775 and 30 December 1777

56-3545, 15 October 1775

58-3733, 10 July 1776

62-3958, 18 February 1777

64-4161, 28 August 1777

65-4227, 12 November 1777

66-4316, 20 February 1778

68-4429, 6 June 1778

68-4498, 4 September 1778

69-4510, 26 September 1778

75-4952, 15 December 1779

75-4975, 12 January 1780

75-4984, 20 January 1780

78-5235, 14 September 1780

82-5476, 7 August 1781

82-5487, 24 August 1781

83-5555, 1 December 1781

83-5559, 10 December 1781

92-6394, 17 February 1785

93-6425, 23 March 1785

93-6484, 8 July 1785

98-6904, 16 May 1787

112-8091, 1 March 1792

Appendix I
Measurer and Porter Fortunes

Inventaires après décès
Archives Nationales, Minutier Central

VIII-964, 13 October 1724   XXXIX-367, 21 March 1742
XIII-240, 23 November 1730   XXIII-581, 9 June 1752
XXVIII-224, 29 January 1731   XXXIX-441, 9 May 1757
VIII-1001, 18 April 1733   XXIII-558, 8 August 1758
VIII-1002, 7 August 1733

Comptes and partages
Archives Nationales

Y 12730, 12 February 1734
Y 15953, 24 December 1756
Y 11869, 9 September 1763

Scellés
Archives Nationale

Y 12138, 2 September 1736   Y 15953, 2 April 1756
Y 15340, 14 January 1744   Y 15956, 3 January 1759
Y 15950, 10 August 1754   Y 13121, 3 December 1769

Testaments
Archives Seine-Paris

DC⁶ 219, fol. 81, 5 October 1728   DC⁶ 237, fol. 130, 18 July 1754
DC⁶ 231, fol. 16, June 1744   DC⁶ 281, fol. 187, 21 November 1787
DC⁶ 235, fol. 149, 5 October 1751

Archives Nationales, Minutier Central

LXXV-705, 13 January 1768

Bibliography

Primary Sources

Archival Sources

Archives des Affaires Etrangères
France 1371

Archives de l'Assistance Publique
Hôtel-Dieu   Incurables
Hôpital Général   Scipion

Archives and Bibliothèque du Conservatoire National des Arts et Métiers

Archives Départementales
Aube   Haute-Garonne
Bouches-du-Rhône   Hérault
Calvados   Ille-et-Vilaine
Côte-d'Or   Indre-et-Loire
Doubs   Isère
Eure-et-Loir   Loire-Atlantique
Gironde   Marne

Nord   Seine-et-Marne
Oise   Seine-et-Oise
Orne   Somme
Puy-de-Dôme   Yvelines
Seine-Maritime

Archives du Département de la Seine et de la Ville de Paris

DC^6 $D7B^6$
DE^1 $D11\ U^3$
DQ   1 AZ
DQ^{10} 2 AZ
$D2B^6$ 3 AZ
$D4B^6$ 6 AZ
$D5B^6$ Etude Lhéritier, unclassified
$D6B^6$ Fonds Feydeau

Archives Municipales

Corbeil BB
Pontoise 5F4

Archives and Bibliothèque du Musée National des Arts et Traditions Populaires

Archives Nationales (by series)

AD O^{*1}
F^7 Q^1
F^{10} T
F^{11}, F^{11*} X^{1A}
F^{12}, F^{12*} X^{1B}
F^{20} X^{2B}
G^7 Y
H Z^{1H}
H^* Z^{1G}
K   BB
KK   Archives privées (AP): 127
NN   Plans
O^1

Minutier Central des Notaires (Archives Nationales)

Archives de la Préfecture de Police

AB
Fonds Lamoignon

Bibliothèque de l'Arsenal

Manuscrits
Manuscrits de la Bastille

Bibliothèque de l'Ecole Nationale de la Meunerie

Collection Marcel Arpin

Bibliothèque Forney

Bibliothèque Historique de la Ville de Paris

Arrêts du conseil
Arrêts du Parlement de Paris
Edits, déclarations, lettres patentes
Manuscrits
Manuscrits nouvelle série
Sentences and ordonnances de police

Bibliothèque de l'Institut

Manuscrits 513–21

Bibliothèque Municipale de Bordeaux

Bibliothèque Municipale de Chartres

Bibliothèque Municipale de Corbeil

Bibliothèque Municipale de Grenoble

Bibliothèque Municipale de Mantes-la-Jolie

Bibliothèque Municipale de Melun

Bibliothèque Municipale d'Orléans

Manuscrits Lenoir

Bibliothèque Municipale de Pontoise

Bibliothèque Municipale de Troyes

Bibliothèque Nationale

Arrêts du conseil

Arrêts du Parlement de Paris
Collection Joly de Fleury
Collection Vexin
Edits, déclarations, lettres patentes
Factums
Manuscrits français
Manuscrits nouvelles acquisitions
  françaises
Sentences and ordonnances de police

Bibliothèque Ste.-Geneviève, Paris

**Deutsches Brotmuseum, Ulm-Donau, Federal Republic of
  Germany**

Index of Christian Art, Princeton University

Musée du Bled et du Pain, Verdun-sur-le-Doubs

Musée Français du Pain (S. A. M.), Charenton-le-Pont

Musée des Moulins, Moulins

Contemporary Periodicals

Année littéraire. Amsterdam, 1754–69; Paris, 1770–75.

Bulletin de la Société d'encouragement pour l'industrie nationale. Paris, 1801–.

Ephémérides du citoyen, ou Bibliothèque raisonnée des sciences morales et politiques.
  Paris, 1765–.

Gazette d'agriculture, commerce, arts et finances. Paris, 1769–83.

Gazette du commerce. Paris, 1763–May 1765.

Gazette du commerce, de l'agriculture et des finances. Paris, June 1765–68.

Journal de l'agriculture, du commerce, des arts et des finances, or *Journal de l'agriculture, des arts et des finances.* Paris, 1765–83.

*Journal économique, ou Mémoires, notes et avis sur les arts, l'agriculture, et tout ce
  qui peut avoir rapport à la santé ainsi qu'à l'augmentation des biens de famille.*
  Paris, 1751–72.

Journal encyclopédique ou universel. Liège, 1756–59; Bouillon, 1760–93.

Journal historique et politique des principaux événements. Geneva, 1772–92.

Journal de Paris. Paris, 1777–1840.

Journal de physique. Paris, 1773–93.

Journal des sçavans. Amsterdam and Paris, 1725–75.

Mémoires pour servir à l'histoire des sciences et des beaux-arts [*Journal de Trévoux*].
  Paris, 1750–67.

Mercure de France. Paris, 1725–75.

Mercure historique et politique contenant l'état présent de l'Europe, ce qui se passe dans toutes les cours, l'intérêt des princes, et généralement tout ce qu'il y a de plus curieux . . . le tout accompagnée de réflexions politiques pour chaque état. The Hague, 1725–75.

Nouveau Journal helvétique. Neuchâtel, September 1769–80.

Nouvelles Ephémérides économiques. Paris, 1774–88.

Révolutions de Paris, dédiées à la nation et au district des Petits-Augustins. Paris, July 1789–February 1794.

Revue rétrospective: Recueil de pièces intéressantes et de citations curieuses. Paris, 1884–87.

Primary Printed Works (Anonymous)

Académie des sciences. *Machines et inventions approuvées par l'Académie royale des sciences.* 7 vols. Paris: G. Martin, 1735–77.

Almanach royal. Paris: D'Houry, 1734–91.

"Avis économique sur la boulangerie." *Journal économique* (July, September, and October 1757).

Détail sur quelques établissements de la ville de Paris demandé par sa majesté impériale la reine de Hongrie à M. Lenoir. Paris: n.p., 1780.

Dictionnaire de l'Académie françoise. 4th ed. 2 vols. Paris: Veuve de B. Brunet, 1762.

———. 5th ed. 2 vols. Paris: Bossange et Masson, Garnery, Henri Nicolle, 1811.

———. 7th ed. 2 vols. Paris: Firmin-Didot et Cie., 1884.

Dictionnaire universel françois et latin. New ed. 6 vols. Nancy: P. Antoine, 1740.

Dictionnaire universel françois et latin, vulgairement appelé Dictionnaire de Trévoux, contenant la signification & la définition des mots de l'une & de l'autre langue. Vols. 1, 2, 6. The Hague: n.p., 1690, 1701.

———. New ed. 8 vols. Paris: Compagnie des libraires associés, 1771.

Encyclopédie méthodique. 185 vols. Paris: Panckoucke, 1782–1832.

Enquête sur la boulangerie du département de la Seine. Paris: Imprimerie impériale, 1859.

Enquête sur la révision de la législation des céréales. Paris: Conseil d'Etat, 1859.

Lettre d'un gentilhomme des états de Languedoc à un magistrat du Parlement de Rouen, sur le commerce des bleds, des farines, et du pain. Amsterdam: n.p., 1768.

Manuel ou Vocabulaire des moulins à pot. Paris: Lejay, 1786.

Marcel Barbier: Meunier à Moutiers-en-Beauce (Groupe de Recherches sur les traditions en Beauce). St.-Denis: Le Vent du Ch'min, 1980.

Mémoire important par rapport au bien public et à la provision de farine pour la ville de Paris. Paris: n.p., 1733.

"Mémoire sur les moulins." *Journal économique* (September 1760).

"The Miller's Daughter," in *The Penguin Book of Ballads.* Ed. Geoffrey Grigson. Baltimore: Penguin Books, 1975.

"Objections et réponses sur le commerce des grains et des farines." *Ephémérides du citoyen* 1 (1769).

Rapport de M. l'abbé Bossut, de M. l'abbé Rochon et de M. le Mis de Condorcet, *membres de l'Académie des sciences, sur le canal que le gouvernement fait con-struire en Nivernais pour l'approvisionnement de Paris.* Paris: Imprimerie royale, 1786.

"Recette pour la conservation des bleds." *Journal économique* (May 1751).

Recueil des principales lois relatives au commerce des grains avec les arrêts, arrêtés, et remontrances du Parlement sur cet objet et le procès-verbal de l'assemblée générale de la police. Paris: n.p., 1769.

"Réflexions sur le commerce du pain." *Journal économique* (July 1761).

"Sur les moulins à vent," in *Histoire de l'Académie royale des sciences. Avec les mémoires de Mathématique & de Physique, 1711* (1714), pp. 92–100.

Tableau universel et raisonné de la Ville de Paris. Paris: J. P. Costard, 1760.

Printed Works (Author Known)

Acremant, Germaine. *Les Ailes d'argent.* Paris: Plon, 1933.

Alarcon, Pedro A. de. *El Sombrero de tres picos, or The Three-Cornered Hat.* Trans. M. Armstrong. London: Gerald Howe, 1927.

Allingham, William. "A Mill." *Irish Poets of the Nineteenth Century.* Ed. Geoffrey Taylor. London: Routledge & Kegan Paul, 1951.

Andersen, Hans Christian. "The Buckwheat," in *Tales from Hans Christian Andersen.* New York: Thomas Y. Crowell, 1897.

————. "The Ice Maiden," in *Stories and Fairy Tales.* Trans. H. Oskar Sommer. London: George Allen, 1907.

————. "The Windmill," in *Stories and Tales.* Boston: Houghton Mifflin, 1870.

Argenson, René-Louis de Voyer, marquis d'. *Journal et mémoires du marquis d'Argenson.* Ed. E.-J.-B. Rathery. Paris: Mme Vve J. Renouard, 1859–67.

Bachaumont, Louis Petit de. *Mémoires secrets pour servir à l'histoire de la République des lettres en France depuis 1762 jusqu'à nos jours, ou Journal d'un observateur.* 31 vols. London: John Adamson, 1777–89.

Barberet, Joseph. *Le Travail en France: Monographies professionnelles.* 7 vols. Paris: Berger-Levrault et Cie, 1886–90.

Barbier, Edmond-Jean-François. *Chronique de la régence et du règne de Louis XV (1718–1763), ou Journal de Barbier.* 8 vols. Paris: Charpentier, 1857–66.

Barrett, Walter. *More Tales from the Fens.* London: Routledge & Kegan Paul, 1964.

Baudeau, Abbé Nicolas. *Avis au peuple sur son premier besoin, ou Petits Traités économiques, par l'auteur des "Ephémérides du citoyen."* Amsterdam and Paris: Hochereau jeune, 1768.

————. *Avis aux honnêtes gens qui veulent bien faire.* Amsterdam and Paris: Desaint et al., 1768.

————. *Résultats de la liberté et de l'immunité du commerce des grains, de la farine, et du pain.* Amsterdam and Paris: Desaint et al., 1768.

————. "Suite des avis au peuple." *Ephémérides du citoyen* 10 (1769): 17–42.

Baulant, Micheline, and Jean Meuvret. *Prix des céréales, extraits de la Mercuriale de Paris (1520–1698).* 2 vols. Paris: S.E.V.P.E.N., 1960–62.

Bazin, René. "Le Moulin qui ne tourne plus," in *Contes de bonne Perrette.* Paris: C. Lévy, [1903].

Beckmann, John. *A History of Inventions and Discoveries.* Trans. William Johnston. 3d ed. 4 vols. London: Longman et al., 1817.

Béguillet, Edme. *Description historique de Paris et de ses plus beaux monuments.* 3 vols. Paris: n.p., 1779–81.

———. *Discours sur la mouture économique.* Paris: Panckoucke, 1775.

———. *Traité de la connoissance générale des grains et de la mouture par économie.* Dijon: L.-N. Frantin, 1778.

———. *Traité des subsistances et des grains qui servent à la nourriture de l'homme.* Paris: Prault fils, 1780.

Bellepierre de Neuve-Eglise, Louis-Joseph. *L'Agronomie et l'industrie, ou Les Principes de l'agriculture, du commerce et des arts.* 6 vols. Paris: P. Despilly, 1761.

———. *L'Art de battre, écraser, piler, moudre et monder les grains, avec de nouvelles machines.* Paris: J.-G. Merigot le jeune, 1769.

Belidor, Bernard Forest de. *Architecture hydraulique, ou L'Art de conduire, d'élever, et de ménager les eaux pour les différents besoins de la vie.* 4 vols. Paris: C.-A. Jombert, 1737–39.

Bielfeld, Jacob Friedrich von. *Institutions politiques.* 2 vols. The Hague: P. Gosse, Jr., 1760–62.

Boislisle, Arthur-Michel de, ed. *Correspondance des contrôleurs généraux des finances avec les intendants des provinces.* 3 vols. Paris: Imprimerie Nationale, 1874–97.

———. *Mémoires des intendants sur l'état des généralités dressés pour l'instruction du duc de Bourgogne.* Vol. 2, *Mémoire de la généralité de Paris (1700).* Paris: Imprimerie Nationale, 1881.

Bosc, Louis-Augustin-Guillaume. "Mouture," in *Encyclopédie méthodique.* Vol. 5, Agriculture. Paris: Panckoucke, 1813.

Botkin, B.A., ed. *A Treasury of American Folklore.* New York: Crown Publishing Company, 1944.

Bottrell, William. *Stories and Folklore of West Cornwall.* Penzance: F. Rodda, 1880.

———. *Traditions and Hearthside Stories of West Cornwall.* Penzance: W. Cornish, 1870.

Boullemer, L. de. "Traité sur les bleds." *Journal économique* (May 1772): 193–96.

Bourdon-Desplanches, L.-J. *Lettre à l'auteur des observations sur le commerce des grains.* Amsterdam: n.p., 1775.

Briggs, Katharine M. *A Dictionary of British Folktales.* Bloomington: Indiana University Press, 1930.

Brillon Duperron. *Considérations sur la mouture.* N.p., n.d.

———. *Observations sur la mouture des bleds.* N.p., n.d.

Brion de la Tour, Louis. *Etat actuel de la France.* Paris: Desnos, [1774?].

Brissot de Warville, J.-P. *New Travels in the United States of America, 1788.* Ed. D. Echeverria. Cambridge, Mass.: Belknap Press of Harvard University Press, 1964.

Bucquet, César. *Manuel du meunier et du constructeur de moulins à eau et à grains.* New ed. Paris: Onfroy, 1790.

———. *Mémoire sur les moyens de perfectionner les moulins et la mouture économique.* Paris: César Bucquet, 1786.

————. *Observations intéressantes et amusantes du Sieur Bucquet, ancien meunier de l'Hôpital Général, à MM. Parmentier et Cadet.* Paris: Chez les marchands de nouveautés, 1783.

————. *Traité pratique de la conservation des grains et des farines et des étuves domestiques.* Paris: Onfroy, 1783.

Cadet de Vaux, Antoine-Alexis. *Avis sur les blés germés par le comité de l'école gratuite de boulangerie.* Paris: Imprimerie de P.-D. Pierres, 1782.

————. *Moyens de prévenir le retour des disettes.* Paris: D. Colas, 1812.

————. *Traités divers d'économie rurale, alimentaire, et domestique.* Paris: D. Colas, 1821.

Campbell, John G., ed. *Superstitions of the Highlands and Islands of Scotland.* Glasgow: John MacGlehase and Sons, 1900.

Capuana, Luigi. "The Miller," in *Golden Feather.* Trans. Dorothy Emmrich. New York: E. P. Dutton, 1930.

Casona, Alejandro [Rodriguez-Alvarez, A.]. *La Molinera de Arcos,* in *Obras Completas.* Aguilar: España, 1963.

Cassini de Thury, César-François. *Tableau des 175 feuilles de la carte de France.* Paris: Veuve Gautier, 1768.

Catherwood, Mary Hartwell. "The Mill at Petit Cap," in *The Chase of Saint-Castin and Other Stories of the French in the New World.* Boston: Houghton Mifflin, 1894.

Cervantes, Miguel de. *Don Quixote.* New York: W. W. Norton, 1981.

Chamousset, P. de. *Œuvres complettes [sic] de P. de Chamousset . . . précédées de son éloge par l'abbé Cotton des Houssauges.* 2 vols. Paris: P.-D. Pierres, 1783.

Chassin, Ch.-L. *Les Elections et les cahiers de Paris en 1789, documents recueillis, mis en ordre et annotés.* 4 vols. Paris: Jouaust et Sigaux, 1888–89.

Chaucer, Geoffrey. *The Reeve's Prologue and Tale.* Ed. A.C. and J.E. Spearing. Cambridge and New York: Cambridge University Press, 1979.

Choiseul, Etienne-François, duc de. *Mémoires de M. le duc de Choiseul . . . écrits par lui-même et imprimés sous ses yeux, dans son cabinet, à Chanteloup, en 1778.* Ed. Soulavie. Chanteloup and Paris: Buisson, 1790.

Chomel, Abbé Noël. *Dictionnaire oeconomique.* 4th ed. 2 vols. Paris: Veuve d'E. Ganeau, 1740.

Condillac, Abbé Etienne Bonnot de. *Le Commerce et le gouvernement considérés relativement l'un à l'autre* (1766). *Collection des principaux économistes.* Ed. E. Daire and G. de Molinari. Vol. 14. 1847. Reprint. Osnabrück: Otto Zeller, 1966.

Condorcet, Jean-Antoine-Nicolas de Caritat, marquis de. *Lettre d'un laboureur de Picardie à M. N*** [Necker] auteur prohibitif* (1775). *Collection des principaux économistes.* Ed. E. Daire and G. de Molinari. Vol. 14. 1847. Reprint. Osnabrück: Otto Zeller, 1966.

Cotte, Louis. *Leçons élémentaires sur le choix et la conservation des grains, sur les opérations de la meunerie et de la boulangerie et sur la taxe du pain. Suivi d'un catéchisme à l'usage des habitants de la campagne, sur les dangers auxquels leur santé et leur vie sont exposées.* Paris: Frères Barbon, year III.

Cretté de Palluel, François. "Mémoire sur les moyens d'économiser la mouture des grains et de diminuer le prix de pain." *Mémoires d'agriculture, d'économie rurale et domestique publiés par la Société royale d'agriculture* (Fall 1788): 20–27.

Cuvier, G., ed. *Recueil des éloges historiques lus dans les séances publiques de l'Institut de France.* Paris: Firmin-Didot frères, fils et Cie, 1861.

Daudet, Alphonse. *Lettres de mon moulin.* Paris: G.P. Rouge, 1980.

———. *Letters from My Mill.* Trans. John P. MacGregor. New York: Taplinger, 1966.

Dégh, Linda, ed. *Folktales of Hungary.* Chicago: University of Chicago Press, 1965.

Delamare, Nicolas. *Traité de la police.* 4 vols. Paris: J. et P. Cot (J.-F. Hérissant), 1705–38.

Denisart, Jean-Baptiste. *Collection de décisions nouvelles et de notions relatives à la jurisprudence actuelle.* 9th ed. 48 vols. Paris: Desaint, 1777.

Desbordes, Jean-Michel, ed. *La Chronique villageoise de Varreddes (Seine-et-Marne): Un document sur la vie rurale des XVIIᵉ et XVIIIᵉ siècles.* Paris: Editions de l'Ecole, n.d.

Des Essarts, Nicolas-Toussaint L. *Dictionnaire universel de police.* 8 vols. Paris: Moutard, 1786–90.

Desmoulins, Camille. *Les Insignes Meuniers de Corbeil, ou La Compagnie des famines découverte, en présence de M. Necker, accusé, par M. Desmoulins.* Paris: Lefèvre, 1789.

Diderot, Denis. *Correspondance.* Ed. Georges Roth. 16 vols. Paris: Editions de Minuit, 1955–70.

———. "Principes philosophiques pour servir d'introduction à la connaissance de l'esprit et du coeur humain" (1769). *Oeuvres complètes.* Paris: Club français du livre, 1969.

——— et al. *Encyclopédie, ou Dictionnaire raisonné des sciences, des arts et des métiers, par une société de gens de lettres.* Ed. Diderot and D'Alembert. 35 vols. Paris: Briasson, David l'aîné, Le Breton, Durand, 1751–65.

Doudney, Sarah. "The Lesson of the Water-Mill," in *The Home Book of Verse.* Ed. Burton E. Stevenson. New York: Henry Holt, 1922.

Dransy. *Mémoire sur la construction des moulins à farine* (Paris, 1785), in Antoine-Augustin Parmentier. *Mémoire sur les avantages que la province de Languedoc peut retirer de ses grains. Avec le mémoire sur la nouvelle manière de construire les moulins à farine par M. Dransy.* Paris: Imprimerie des Etats de Languedoc, 1787.

Duchesne. *Code de la police, ou Analyse des règlements de police.* 4th ed. rev. and enl. Paris: Prault père, 1767.

Duhamel du Monceau, Henri-Louis. *A Practical Treatise of Husbandry.* London: n.p., 1756.

———. *Traité de la conservation des grains et en particulier du froment.* Paris: H.-L. Guérin et L.-F. Delatour, 1753.

Dumay, Gabriel, ed. *Une Emeute à Dijon en 1775.* Dijon: Darantière, 1886.

Dupâquier, Jacques, Marcel Lachiver, and Jean Meuvret. *Mercuriales du pays de France et du Vexin français, 1640–1792.* Paris: S.E.V.P.E.N., 1968.

Dupin, Claude. *Forces productrices et commerciales de la France.* Paris: Bachelier, 1827.

Dupont de Nemours, Pierre-Samuel. *Analyse historique de la législation des grains depuis 1692 à laquelle on a donné la forme d'un rapport à l'Assemblée nationale,* Paris: Petit, 1789.

———. *De l'Exportation et de l'importation des grains* (1764). *Collection des économistes et des réformateurs sociaux de la France.* Ed. Edgard Depitre. Paris: P. Geuthner, 1911.

———. "Observations sur la mouture." *Ephémérides du citoyen* 9 (1769): 149–58.

Dupré d'Aulnay, Louis. *Traité général des subsistances militaires.* Paris: Prault père, 1744.

Dupré de St.-Maur, Nicolas-François. *Essai sur les monnaies, ou Réflexions sur le rapport entre l'argent et les denrées.* Paris: J.-B. Coignard, 1746.

Dussausoy, Maille. *Le Citoyen désintéressé, ou Diverses idées patriotiques concernant quelques établissements et embellissements utiles à la ville de Paris.* Paris: Gueffier, 1767–68.

Dwight, H.G. "Mill Valley," in *Stamboul Nights.* New York: Doubleday, Page, 1923.

Eliot, George. *The Mill on the Floss.* Boston: Houghton Mifflin, 1961.

Emrich, Duncan, ed. *American Folk Poetry: An Anthology.* Boston: Little, Brown, 1974.

Evans, Oliver. *The Young Millwright and Miller's Guide.* 9th ed. Philadelphia: Carey, Lea & Blanchard, 1836.

Expilly, Abbé J.-J. *Dictionnaire géographique, historique et politique des Gaules et de la France.* 6 vols. Paris: Desaint et Saillant, 1762–70.

———. *Tableau de la population de France.* N.p., 1780.

Fabre, Jean-Antoine. *Essai sur la manière la plus avantageuse de construire les machines hydrauliques et en particulier les moulins à bled.* Paris: A. Jombert jeune, 1783.

Farjeon, Eleanor. *Martin Pippin in the Apple Orchard.* Philadelphia: J. B. Lippincott, 1949.

Flammermont, Jules, ed. *Remontrances du Parlement de Paris au 18ᵉ siècle.* 3 vols. Paris: Imprimerie Nationale, 1888–98.

Fréminville, Edme de la Poix de. *Dictionnaire ou traité de la police générale des villes, bourgs, paroisses et seigneuries de la campagne.* Paris: Gissey, 1758.

Galiani, Abbé Ferdinando. *Correspondance.* Ed. Lucien Perey and Gaston Maugras. 2 vols. Paris: Calmann-Lévy, 1881.

———. *Dialogues sur le commerce des bleds* (1770). Ed. Fausto Nicolini. Milan: R. Riccardi, 1959.

———. *Lettres de l'abbé Galiani à Madame d'Epinay.* Ed. Eugène Asse. 2 vols. Paris: G. Charpentier, 1881–1903.

Godwin, William. "The Miller, His Son, and His Ass," in *Fables Ancient and Modern.* Ed. David L. Greene. New York: Garland, 1976.

Graham, Sylvester. *A Treatise on Bread, and Breadmaking.* Boston: Light & Stearns, 1837.

Gray, Andrew. *The Experienced Millwright.* Edinburgh: n.p., 1806.

Grimm, Friedrich M., et al. *Correspondance littéraire, philosophique et critique par Grimm, Diderot, Raynal, Meister, etc. . . . .* Ed. Maurice Tourneux. 16 vols. Paris: Garnier frères, 1877–82.

Grivel. "Boulangerie," in *Encyclopédie méthodique,* Economie politique. Vol. 1. Paris: Panckoucke, 1784.

Hardy, Thomas. *The Trumpet-Major.* London: Macmillan, 1962.

Henderson, Bernard, and C. Calvert. "The Miller's Man Who Became an Ass," in *Wonder Tales of Alsace-Lorraine.* New York: Frederick A. Stokes, 1925.

Herbert, Claude-Jacques. *Essai sur la police générale des grains, sur leurs prix et sur les effets de l'agriculture* (1755). *Collection des économistes et des réformateurs sociaux de la France.* Ed. E. Depitre. Paris: P. Geuthner, 1910.

Heywood, John. *The Play of the Weather.* Eds. Maurice Hussey and Surendra Agarwala. New York: Theatre Arts Books, 1968.

Hurtado de Mendoza, Diego de. *The Life of Lazarillo de Tormes.* Trans. Clements Markham. London: Adam and Charles Black, 1908.

Jaucourt, Louis de. "Farine," in Diderot et al. *Encyclopédie, ou Dictionnaire raisonné des sciences, des arts et des métiers, par une société de gens de lettres.* Ed. Diderot and D'Alembert. Vol. 17. Paris: Briasson, David l'aîné, Le Breton, Durand, 1751–65.

Jefferson, Thomas. *The Writings of Thomas Jefferson.* Ed. Andrew A. Lipscomb. 20 vols. Washington, D.C.: Thomas Jefferson Memorial Association of the United States, 1903–1904.

Jousse, Mathurin. *L'Art de charpenterie.* Paris: n.p., 1702.

Lacombe d'Avignon, François. *Le Mitron de Vaugirard, dialogues sur le bled, la farine et le pain, avec un petit traité de la boulangerie.* New ed. Amsterdam: n.p., 1777.

La Condamine, Charles-Marie de. "Pain mollet," in *Almanach des Muses.* Paris: Delalain, 1770.

Lacroix, Paul [Jacob]. *Recueil de farces.* Paris: Adolphe Delahays, 1859.

La Fontaine. *Oeuvres complètes.* Paris: Seuil, 1965.

Le Camus. "Mémoire sur le bled." *Journal économique* (November 1753).

———. "Suite du mémoire sur le pain." *Journal économique* (December 1753).

Lee, F. H., ed. *Folktales of All Nations.* New York: Tudor Publishing, 1930.

Legrand d'Aussy, Pierre J.-B. *Histoire de la vie privée des françois* (1783). Ed. J.-B.-B. de Roquefort. Paris: Laurent-Beaupré, 1815.

Lemercier de la Rivière, P.-P.-F.-J.-H. *L'Intérêt général de l'Etat, ou La Liberté du commerce des blés, démontrée conforme au droit naturel, au droit public de la France, aux lois fondamentales du royaume, à l'intérêt commun du souverain et de ses sujets dans tous les temps, avec la réfutation d'un nouveau système publié en forme de "Dialogues sur le commerce des blés."* Amsterdam and Paris: Desaint, 1770.

Lenoir, Jean-Charles-Pierre. *Détail sur quelques établissemens de la ville de Paris demandé par sa majesté impériale la reine de Hongrie à M. Le Noir. . . .* Paris: n.p., 1780.

Le Roi. "Froment," in Diderot et al. *Encyclopédie, ou Dictionnaire raisonné des sciences, des arts et des métiers, par une société de gens de lettres.* Ed. Diderot and D'Alembert. Vol. 7. Paris: Briasson, David l'aîné, Le Breton, Durand, 1751–65.

Le Roy, Eugène. *Le Moulin du Frau.* Périgueux: Périgord, 1969.

Liébault, Jean. *L'Agriculture et maison rustique de MM. Charles Estienne et Jean Liébault.* Lyon: C. Carteron, 1689.

Linguet, Simon-Nicolas-Henri. *Réponse aux docteurs modernes, ou Apologie pour l'auteur de la "Théorie des loix," et des "Lettres sur cette théorie," avec la réfutation du système des philosophes économistes.* 2 vols. London and Paris: n.p., 1771.

———. *Théorie des loix civiles, ou Principes fondamentaux de la société.* London: n.p., 1767.

Macquer, Philippe. *Dictionnaire portatif des arts et métiers, contenant l'histoire, la*

description, la police des fabriques et manufactures de France et des pays étrangers.
2 vols. Paris: Lacombe, 1766.

―――. *Dictionnaire raisonné universel des arts et métiers, contenant l'histoire, la description, la police des fabriques et manufactures de France et des pays étrangers.*
Ed. Pierre Jaubert. New ed., rev. 4 vols. Paris: P. -F. Didot jeune, 1773.

Malisset, Pierre-Simon. "Mouture par économie." *Journal économique* (August 1761).

Malouin, Paul-Jacques. *Description des arts du meunier, du vermicelier, et du boulenger, avec une histoire abrégée de la boulengerie et un dictionnaire de ces arts.* N.p.,
1761.

―――. *Description des arts du meunier, du vermicellier, et du boulanger.* New ed. Ed.
Jean-Elie Bertrand. Neufchâtel: La Société typographique, 1771.

―――. *Description et détails des arts du meunier, du vermicelier et du boulenger.*
Paris: Saillant et Nyon, 1779.

―――. "Histoire des maladies épidémiques de 1750, observées à Paris." *Histoire de l'Académie royale des sciences. Avec les mémoires de Mathématique & de Physique,* 1750 (1754): 311–39.

[Manesse, L. C.] *Traité du droit de bâtir moulin et des bannalités en général.* Paris:
n.p., 1785.

Manuel, [Louis-]Pierre. *La Police de Paris dévoilée.* 2 vols. Paris: J.-B. Garnery,
year II.

Marville, F. de. *Lettres de M. de Marville, lieutenant général de police, au ministre Maurepas (1742–1747).* Ed. Arthur-Michel de Boislisle. 3 vols. Paris: E. Champion,
1896–1905.

Megas, Georgios, ed. *Folktales of Greece.* Chicago: University of Chicago Press, 1970.

Mercier, Louis-Sébastien. *L'An deux mille quatre-cent quarante, rêve s'il en fut jamais.*
New ed. London: n.p., 1785.

―――. *Tableau de Paris.* New ed. 12 vols. Amsterdam: n.p., 1782–88.

Mesange, Mathias. *Traité de charpenterie.* Paris: n.p., 1753.

Miromesnil, Armand-Thomas Hue de. *Correspondance politique et administrative de Miromesnil, premier président du Parlement de Normandie.* Ed. P. Le Verdier. 5
vols. Paris and Rouen: A. Picard, 1899–1903.

Model, Johann Georg. *Récréations physiques, économiques et chimiques.* Trans. and
ed. Antoine-Augustin Parmentier. 2 vols. Paris: Monory, 1774.

Moheau. *Recherches et considérations sur la population de la France* (1778). *Collection des économistes et des réformateurs sociaux de la France.* Ed. René Gonnard.
Paris: P. Geuthner, 1912.

Montchrétien, Antoyne de. *L'Economie politique patronale, traité de l'oeconomie politique dédié en 1615 au Roy et à la Reyne mère du Roy.* Ed. Theodore Funck-Brentano. Paris: Plon, Nourrit et Cie, 1889.

Morellet, Abbé André. *Théorie du paradoxe.* Amsterdam: n.p., 1775.

Müller, Wilhelm. "The Journeyman's Song," in *Anthology of German Poetry through the Nineteenth Century.* Eds. Alexander Gode and Frederick Ungar. New York:
Frederick Ungar, 1964.

Muret, Jean-Louis. *Mémoire sur la mouture des grains, et sur divers objets relatifs.*
Berne: La Société typographique, 1776.

Musset, Paul Edme de. *Monsieur le Vent et Madame la Pluie.* Paris: Hetzel, 1846.

Narbonne, Pierre de. *Journal des règnes de Louis XIV et Louis XV de l'année 1701 à l'année 1744 par Pierre Narbonne, premier commissaire de police de la ville de Versailles.* Ed. J.-A. Le Roi. Versailles: Bernard, 1866.

Necker, Jacques. *Sur la législation et le commerce des grains.* 2 vols. Paris: Pissot, 1775.

Nicodème, P.-J. "Dissertation économique." *Journal de l'agriculture, du commerce, des arts et des finances* (February 1773).

Norton, Grace Fallow. *The Miller's Youngest Daughter.* Boston: Houghton Mifflin, 1924.

Parent, Antoine. *Essais et recherches de mathématique et de physique.* Paris: J. de Nully, 1713.

Parmentier, Antoine-Augustin. *Avis aux bonnes ménagères des villes et des campagnes sur la meilleure manière de faire leur pain.* Paris: Imprimerie royale, 1772.

———. *Eloge de M. Model.* Paris: Monory, 1775.

———. *Examen chymique des pommes de terre: dans lequel on traite des parties constituantes du bled.* Paris: Didot, 1773.

———. *Expériences et réflexions relatives à l'analyse du bled et des farines.* Paris: Monory, 1776.

———. *Mémoire sur les avantages que la province de Languedoc peut retirer de ses grains.* Paris: Imprimerie des Etats de Languedoc, 1787.

———. *Le Parfait Boulanger, ou Traité complet sur la fabrication et le commerce du pain.* Paris: Imprimerie royale, 1778.

——— et al. *Traité théorique et pratique sur la culture des grains suivi de l'art de faire le pain.* 2 vols. Paris: Delalain, 1802.

Patissier, Philippe. *Traité des maladies des artisans et celles qui résultent des diverses professions, d'après Ramazzini.* Paris: J.-B. Baillière, 1827.

Pigeonneau, H., and A. de Foville, eds. *L'Administration de l'agriculture au contrôle général des finances. Procès-verbaux et rapports.* Paris: Guillaumin, 1882.

Pluche, Abbé Antoine. *Le Spectacle de la nature, ou Entretiens sur les particularités de l'histoire naturelle qui ont paru les plus propres à rendre les jeunes gens curieux et à leur former l'esprit.* 9 vols. Paris: Frères Estienne, 1755–64.

Pocock, Isaac. *The Miller and His Men: A Melo-drame, in Two Acts.* London: J. Dicks, n.d.

Poncelet, Polycarpe. *Histoire naturelle du froment.* Paris: G. Desprez, 1779.

———. *Mémoire sur la farine.* Paris: Pissot, 1776.

Pourrat, Henri. *A Treasury of French Tales.* Boston: Houghton Mifflin, 1954.

Preussler, Otfried. *The Satanic Mill.* Trans. Anthea Bell. New York: Macmillan, 1973.

Rabelais, François. *Pantagruel.* Paris: Gibert jeune, 1936.

Ramazzini, Bernardino. *Diseases of Workers.* Trans. W. C. Wright. New York: Hafner, 1964.

Reneaume, M. "Sur la manière de conserver les grains." *Mémoires de l'Académie des sciences,* 1708 (1709), pp. 63–86.

Restif de la Bretonne, Nicolas-Edme. *La Vie de mon père.* Ed. Gilbert Rouger. Paris: Garnier, 1970.

Rhys, Ernest, ed. *English Fairy and Other Folktales.* London: Walter Scott, 1890.

Robinson, Edward A. "The Mill," in *Chief Modern Poets of Britain and America.* Eds. Gerald De Witt Sanders, John H. Nelson, and M. L. Rosenthal. New York: Macmillan, 1970.

Roret, Nicolas-Edme. *Manuel du boulanger et du meunier . . . par A.-M. Dessables.* Paris: n.p., 1825.

Roubaud, Abbé Pierre-Joseph-André. *Récréations économiques, ou Lettres de l'auteur des "Représentations aux Magistrats" à M. le Chevalier Zanobi, principal interlocuteur des "Dialogues sur le commerce des blés."* Amsterdam and Paris: Delalain, 1770.

Rozier, Abbé François. *Cours complet d'agriculture théorique, pratique, économique, et de médicine rurale et vétérinaire.* 9 vols. Paris: Hôtel Serpente, 1781–96.

Rutledge, Jean-Jacques [James Rutlidge]. *Second Mémoire pour les maîtres boulangers, lu au bureau des subsistances de l'Assemblée nationale, par le chevalier Rutledge.* Paris: Baudouin [1789].

Sage, Balthasar-Georges. *Analyse des blés.* Paris: Imprimerie royale, 1776.

Savary, Jacques. *Le Parfait Négociant.* 2 vols. Paris: n.p., year II.

Savary des Bruslons, Jacques. *Dictionnaire portatif de commerce.* 7 vols. Copenhagen: C. & A. Philibert, 1761–62.

Saville, John F. *The Miller's Maid, a Melo-drama in Two Acts.* London: Longman, Hurst, Rees, Orme and Brown, 1821.

Schreber. "Observations," in Paul-Jacques Malouin. *Description des arts du meunier, du vermicellier, et du boulanger.* New ed. Ed. Jean-Elie Bertrand. Neufchâtel: La Société typographique, 1771.

Sitwell, Edith. "Spinning Song," in *Poems New and Old.* London: Faber & Faber, 1940.

Stern, James, ed. *Grimm's Fairy Tales.* Trans. Margaret Hunt. New York: Pantheon, 1944.

Stevenson, Robert Louis. "Will O' the Mill," in *The Works of Robert Louis Stevenson.* Vol. 11. New York: Scribner's, 1922.

Tennyson, Alfred. "The Miller's Daughter," in *Victorian Literature: Poetry.* Eds. Donald J. Gray and G. B. Tennyson. New York: Macmillan, 1976.

Tessier, Abbé Henri-Alexandre. "Blatier," in *Encyclopédie méthodique.* Agriculture. Vol. 2. Paris: Panckoucke, 1791.

———. "Le Commerce des grains," in *Encyclopédie méthodique.* Agriculture. Vol. 3. Paris: Panckoucke, 1793.

———. "Conservation," in *Encyclopédie méthodique.* Agriculture. Vol. 3. Paris: Panckoucke, 1793.

———. "Consommation de Paris," in *Encyclopédie méthodique.* Agriculture. Vol. 3. Paris: Panckoucke, 1793.

Tillet, Mathieu. *Précis des expériences qui ont été faites par ordre du Roi à Trianon sur la cause de la corruption des bleds et sur les moyens de la prévenir.* Troyes: Veuve Michelin, 1756.

———. "Projet d'un tarif." *Histoire de l'Académie royale des sciences. Avec les mémoires de Mathématique & de Physique,* 1781 (1784), pp. 107–68.

Turgenev, Ivan. *The Hunting Sketches.* Trans. B. G. Gurney. New York: New American Library, 1962.

Turgot, Anne-Robert-Jacques. *Oeuvres de Turgot et documents le concernant, avec biographie et notes.* Ed. Gustave Schelle. 5 vols. Paris: Félix Alcan, 1913–23.

Voltaire, François-Marie Arouet de. *Voltaire's Correspondence.* Ed. Theodore Besterman. 107 vols. Geneva: Institute et Musée Voltaire, 1953–65.

————. *Oeuvres complètes de Voltaire.* Ed. L. Moland. 52 vols. Paris: Garnier frères, 1877–85.

Wahlenberg, Anna. "The Mill and the Water-Nymphs," in *Old Swedish Fairy-Tales.* Trans. Antoinette De Coursey Patterson. Philadelphia: Penn Publishing Co., 1925.

Yeats, W. B., ed. *Fairy and Folktales of Ireland.* Gerrards Cross: Colin Smythe, 1973.

Young, Arthur. *Travels in France by Arthur Young during the Years 1787, 1788, 1789.* Ed. M. Betham-Edwards. 3d ed. London: G. Bell, 1890.

————. *Travels in France during the Years 1787, 1788 & 1789.* Ed. Constantia Maxwell. Cambridge: The University Press, 1929.

————. *Travels in France during the Years 1787, 1788 and 1789.* Ed. Jeffry Kaplow. Garden City, N.Y.: Doubleday, 1969.

Zola, Emile. *Le Ventre de Paris.* Paris: Gallimard, 1960.

Secondary Sources

Secondary Works (Anonymous)

Cent Ans: La Halle au blé en 1789, la Bourse de commerce en 1889. Paris: n.p., 1889.

Commission de recherche et de publication des documents relatifs à la vie économique de la Révolution. *Bulletin d'histoire économique de la Révolution,* 1913 (1915).

"Histoire des boulangers." *Magasin pittoresque,* 25th year (1857).

"L'Hiver de 1709." *Magasin pittoresque,* 24th year (1856).

Les Moulins: Technique, histoire, folklore. Lille: Musée régional de l'hospice comtesse, 1975.

"Pain au son ou pain trompeur." *Le Monde,* 15 October 1980, p. 15.

Secondary Works (Authors Known)

Addis, William Edward, and Thomas Arnold. *A Catholic Dictionary.* 15th ed. London: Routledge & Kegan Paul, 1951.

Afanassiev, Georges. *Le Commerce des céréales en France au dix-huitième siècle.* Trans. Paul Boyer. Paris: A. Picard, 1894.

Ammann, Louis. *Meunerie et boulangerie.* Paris: J.-B. Baillière, 1925.

Amos, Percy A. *Processes of Flour Manufacture.* London: Longmans, Green, 1912.

Anderson, Russell H. "The Technical Ancestry of Grain-Milling Devices." *Agricultural History* 12, no. 3 (July 1938): 256–70.

Armengaud, Jacques-Eugène. *Meunerie et boulangerie.* Paris: Armengaud aîné, 1882.

Arpin, Marcel. *Historique de la meunerie et de la boulangerie, depuis les temps préhistoriques jusqu'à l'année 1914.* 2 vols. Paris: Le Chancelier, 1948.

Ashley, W.J. *The Bread of Our Forefathers.* Oxford: Clarendon Press, 1928.

Ashton, John. *The History of Bread from Prehistoric to Modern Times.* London: Brooke House, 1901.

Avenel, Georges, vte. d'. "Paysans et ouvriers depuis sept siècles: Les frais de nourriture aux temps modernes." *Revue des deux mondes* 148 (15 July 1898): 424–51.

Babeau, Albert. *Paris en 1789.* New ed. Paris: Didot, 1892.

Bakhtin, Mikhail. *Rabelais and His World.* Trans. Helene Iswolsky. Cambridge, Mass.: M.I.T. Press, 1968.

Balland, Antoine. *La Chimie alimentaire dans l'oeuvre de Parmentier.* Paris: J.B. Baillière, 1902.

Barnes, Donald G. *A History of the English Corn Laws from 1600 to 1846.* London: G. Routledge, 1930.

Barrabé, E. *Le Pain à bon marché: Meuneries-boulangeries, nécessité de leur création.* Paris: Plon, 1876.

Bastié, Jean. *La Croissance de la banlieue parisienne.* Paris: Presses universitaires de France, 1964.

Bathe, Dorothy, and Greville Bathe. *Oliver Evans: A Chronicle of Early American Engineering.* Philadelphia: Historical Society of Pennsylvania, 1935.

Baulant, Micheline. "Le Prix des grains à Paris de 1431 à 1788." *Annales: Economies, sociétés, civilisations,* 23d year, no. 3 (May–June 1968): 520–40.

Beals, Ralph L. *The Peasant Marketing System of Oaxaca, Mexico.* Berkeley: University of California Press, 1975.

Beaujeu-Garnier, Jacqueline. *Atlas et géographie de Paris et de la région de l'Ile-de-France.* Paris: Flammarion, 1977.

———. *Le Relief de la France.* Paris: S.E.D.E.S., 1972.

Becker, Gary S. *The Economic Approach to Human Behavior.* Chicago: University of Chicago Press, 1976.

Beedell, Suzanne. *Windmills.* New York: Scribner's, 1975.

Belshaw, Cyril S. *Traditional Exchange and Modern Markets.* Englewood Cliffs, N.J.: Prentice-Hall, 1965.

Bennett, Adelaide. "The Windmill Psalter: The Historical Letter E of Psalm One." *Journal of the Warburg and Courtauld Institutes* 43 (1980): 59–63.

Bennett, Richard, and John Elton. *History of Corn Milling.* 4 vols. London: Simpkin, Marshall, 1898–1904.

Ben-Porath, Yoram. "The F-Connection: Families, Friends, and Firms and the Organization of Exchange." *Population and Development Review* 6 (March 1980): 1–30.

Benzacar, Joseph. *Le Pain à Bordeaux.* Bordeaux: Gounouilhou, 1905.

Bergeron, Louis. "Approvisionnement et consommation à Paris sous le premier empire." *Mémoires de la Fédération des sociétés historiques et archéologiques de Paris et de l'Ile-de-France* 14 (1963): 197–232.

Bernard, Maurice. *La Municipalité de Brest de 1750 à 1790.* Paris: Librairie ancienne Honoré Champion, 1915.

Berry, Brian J. L. *Geography of Market Centers and Retail Distribution.* Englewood Cliffs, N.J.: Prentice-Hall, 1967.

Bienaymé, Gustave. "La Fiscalité alimentaire et gastronomique à Paris." *Journal de la Société de statistique de Paris,* 31st year (1890): 40–60.

——— and A. de Saint-Julien. *Histoire des droits d'entrée et d'octrois à Paris.* Paris: P. Dupont, 1887.

Binet, Pierre. *La Réglementation du marché du blé en France au XVIIIe siècle et à l'époque contemporaine.* Paris: Librairie sociale et économique, 1939.

Biollay, Léon. "Les Anciennes halles de Paris." *Mémoires de la Société de l'histoire de Paris et de l'Ile-de-France* 3 (1876): 293–355.

————. *Etudes économiques sur le XVIIIe siècle. Le Pacte de famine: l'administration du commerce.* Paris: Guillaumin, 1885.

————. *Origines et transformations du factorat dans les marchés de Paris.* Paris: Berger-Levrault & Cie, 1880.

Biot, Jean-Baptiste. *Lettres sur l'approvisionnement de Paris et sur le commerce des grains.* Paris: Bachelier, 1835.

Bloch, Camille. *Le Commerce des grains dans la généralité d'Orléans (1768), d'après la correspondance inédite de l'intendant Cypierre.* Orléans: H. Herluison, 1898.

Bloch, Marc. "The Advent and Triumph of the Windmill," in *Land and Work in Medieval Europe.* Trans. J. E. Anderson. Berkeley: University of California Press, 1967. Pp. 136–68.

————. "La Transformation des techniques." *Journal de psychologie normale et pathologique* 41, no. 1 (January–March 1948): 104–15.

Bohannan, Paul, and George Dalton, eds. *Markets in Africa.* Evanston: Northwestern University Press, 1962.

Boislisle, Arthur-Michel de. "Le Grand Hiver et la disette de 1709." *Revue des questions historiques* 73 (1903): 442–509.

Boiteau, Pierre, Suzanne Urverg-Ratsimamanga, and Rakota Ratsimamanga. "Rôle éventuel de la malnutrition dans l'épidémiologie de la lèpre." *Actes du 93e Congrès national des sociétés savantes tenu à Tours* (1968). *Bulletin philologique et historique du Comité des travaux historiques et scientifiques* 1 (1971): 9–18.

Bollème, Geneviève. "Littérature populaire et littérature de colportage au 18e siècle," in G. Bollème et al., *Livre et société dans la France du 18e siècle.* 2 vols. Paris and The Hague: Mouton, 1965.

Bord, Gustave. *Histoire du blé en France. Le Pacte de famine, histoire, légende.* Paris: A. Sauton, 1887.

Bourde, André J. *Agronomie et agronomes en France au dix-huitième siècle.* 3 vols. Paris: S.E.V.P.E.N., 1967.

————. *The Influence of England on the French Agronomes, 1750–1789.* Cambridge: Cambridge University Press, 1953.

Bouteloup, Maurice. *Le Travail de nuit dans la boulangerie.* Paris: Recueil Sirey, 1909.

Braudel, Fernand. *Civilisation matérielle et capitalisme (XVe–XVIIIe siècles).* Paris: Armand Colin, 1967.

———— and Ernest Labrousse, eds. *Histoire économique et sociale de la France.* Vol. 2, *Des derniers temps de l'âge seigneurial aux préludes de l'âge industriel (1660–1789).* Paris: Presses universitaires de France, 1970.

Braverman, Harry. *Labor and Monopoly Capital: The Degradation of Work in the Twentieth Century.* New York: Monthly Review Press, 1974.

Bromberg, R. J. "Markets in the Developing Countries: A Review." *Geography* 56 (April 1971): 124–32.

———— and Richard Symanski. "Marketplace Trade in Latin America." *Latin American Research Review* 9 (Fall 1974): 3–38.

Brookfield, H. C., ed. *Pacific Market-places.* Canberra: Australian National University Press, 1969.

Brunot, Ferdinand. *Histoire de la langue française des origines à 1900.* 13 vols. Paris: Armand Colin, 1905.

Burnett, John. *Plenty and Want: A Social History of Diet in England.* London: Nelson, 1966.

Cahen, Léon. "A propos du livre d'Afanassiev. L'Approvisionnement de Paris en grains au début du XVIIIe siècle." *Bulletin de la Société d'histoire moderne,* 22d year (5 March 1922).

———. "L'Economie française à la veille de la Révolution française." *Annales d'histoire sociale* 1 (1939).

Camporesi, Pietro. *Le Pain sauvage: L'Imaginaire de la faim de la Renaissance au XVIIIe siècle.* Trans. Monique Aymard. Paris: Le Chemin vert, 1981.

Cancian, Frank. *Economics and Prestige in a Maya Community.* Stanford: Stanford University Press, 1965.

Canton, G. R., and P. Hainsselin. "Le Moulin de Bus-les-Artois et son exploitation à la fin du 18e siècle." *Bulletin trimestriel de la Société des antiquaires de Picardie* (1967).

Cardwell, Donald S. L. *From Watt to Clausius: The Rise of Thermodynamics in the Early Industrial Age.* Ithaca: Cornell University Press, 1971.

Cassady, Ralph. "Negotiated Price-Making in Mexican Traditional Markets: A Conceptual Analysis." *América Indígena* 28 (1968): 51–78.

Castan, Yves. *Honnêteté et relations sociales en Languedoc, 1715–1780.* Paris: Librairie Plon, 1974.

Cerne, Alfred. *Les Moulins à eau de Rouen.* Rouen: Lestringant, 1936.

Chabot, Georges. *Géographie régionale de la France.* Paris: Masson, 1966.

Chagniot, Jean. "La Criminalité militaire à Paris au XVIIIe siècle." *Annales de Bretagne et des Pays de l'Ouest* 89 (October 1981): 327–46.

Charlot, G. "Essai historique sur la meunerie et la boulangerie." *Annales de la Société d'agriculture, sciences, arts et belles-lettres du département d'Indre-et-Loire* 30 (1851).

Cherrière. *La Lutte contre l'incendie dans les halles, les marchés, et les foires de Paris sous l'ancien régime.* In Julien Hayem, ed. *Mémoires et documents pour servir à l'histoire du commerce et de l'industrie en France.* 3d ser. Paris: Hachette et Cie, 1913.

Chryssochoïdes, N. *Nouveau Manuel complet du meunier ou négociant en grains et du constructeur des moulins.* 2 vols. Paris: L. Mulo, 1910.

Clark, Colin, and Margaret Haswell. *The Economics of Subsistence Agriculture.* 3d ed. New York: St. Martin's Press, 1967.

Clark, John G. *The Grain Trade in the Old Northwest.* Urbana: University of Illinois Press, 1966.

Cobb, Richard. *Les Armées révolutionnaires: Instrument de la terreur dans les départements.* 2 vols. Paris: Mouton, 1961–63.

Cochut, André. "Le Pain à Paris." *Revue des deux mondes,* 33d year, 2d period, 46 (14 August 1863): 964–95; 47 (15 September 1863): 400–435.

Cohen, Abner. "The Social Organization of Credit in a West African Cattle Market." *Africa* 35 (January 1965): 8–19.

Cole, William Alan, and Phyllis Deane. *British Economic Growth.* 2d ed. London: Cambridge University Press, 1967.

Coles-Finch, William. *Watermills and Windmills.* Sheerness: n.p., 1933.

Combes-Marnes, Léon. *Histoire de Corbeil à travers les siècles.* Corbeil: n.p., 1950.

Constant, Jean-Marie. *Nobles et paysans en Beauce aux XVIᵉ et XVIIᵉ siècles*. Lille: Service de reproduction des thèses, Université de Lille III, 1981.

Cook, Scott. "Economic Anthropology: Problems in Theory, Method and Analysis," in *Handbook of Social and Cultural Anthropology*, ed. John J. Honigmann. Chicago: Rand McNally, 1973.

————— and Martin Diskin, eds. *Markets in Oaxaca*. Austin: University of Texas Press, 1976.

Crozet-Fourneyron, Marcel. *Invention de la turbine*. Paris: C. Béranger, [1924?].

Curmond, Henri. *Le Commerce des grains et l'école physiocratique*. Paris: A. Rousseau, 1900.

Dardel, Pierre. *Navires et marchandises dans les ports de Rouen et du Havre au XVIIIᵉ siècle*. Paris: S.E.V.P.E.N., 1963.

Darney, Georges. *La Ferté-sous-Jouarre*. Paris: H. Champion, 1910.

Daumard, Adeline, and François Furet. *Structures et relations sociales à Paris au milieu du 18ᵉ siècle*. Paris: Armand Colin, 1961.

Daumas, Maurice. *L'Archéologie industrielle en France*. Paris: Robert Laffont, 1980.

Davis, William G. *Social Relations in a Philippine Market: Self-Interest and Subjectivity*. Berkeley: University of California Press, 1973.

Dazelle, Gabriel. "Moulins et meuniers d'autrefois." *Bulletin de la Société historique et scientifique des Deux-Sèvres* 10 (1957).

Delivre, J., and R. C. Plancke. *Les Moulins à vent de la Brie*. N.p., 1976.

Delplanque, Maurice. *Le Moulin de Frevent: Essai de monographie d'un moulin à eau*. St.-Omer: n.p., 1936.

Desmarest, Charles. *Le Commerce des grains dans la généralité de Rouen à la fin de l'ancien régime*. Paris: Jouve et Cⁱᵉ, 1926.

Devarenne, Anatole. *Les Moulins de la Vallée de l'Esches*. Méru: n.p., 1943.

Dewey, Alice G. *Peasant Marketing in Java*. New York: Free Press of Glencoe, 1972.

Dubler, Anne-Marie. *Müller und Mühlen im alten Staat Luzern*. Lucerne: Rex-Verlag, 1978.

Duby, Georges, and Armand Wallon. *Histoire de la France rurale*. Paris: Seuil, 1975.

Dugarçon, A. "Le Blé et le pain. Coopération et intégration." *Revue d'économie politique* 27 (1914): 289–325, 421–50.

Dunlap, F. L. *White versus Brown Flour*. Newark: Wallace and Tiernan, 1945.

Dupâquier, Jacques. *La Population rurale du bassin parisien à l'époque de Louis XIV*. Paris and Lille: Editions de l'Ecole des Hautes Etudes en Sciences Sociales and Publications de l'Université de Lille III, 1979.

Durand-Vaugaron, Louis. "Le Moulin à vent en Bretagne." *Annales de Bretagne* 74, no. 2 (June 1967): 299–348.

Dussourd, Henriette. "Les Moulins qui donnèrent leur nom à la ville de Moulins." *Actes du 93ᵉ Congrès national des Sociétés savantes tenu à Tours* (1968). *Bulletin philologique et historique du Comité des travaux historiques et scientifiques* 2 (1971): 515–22.

Edgar, William C. *The Story of Grain and Wheat*. New York: Appleton, 1903.

Eperlding, Emile. "Les Pierres à moulins et à l'industrie meulière de la Ferté-sous-Jouarre." *Les Moulins* (Publication semestrielle de la Féderation Française des Amis des Moulines), no. 7 (1982–83): 83–111.

Epstein, T. S. *Economic Development and Social Change in South India.* Manchester: Manchester University Press, 1962.

Evrard, Fernand. *Versailles, ville du roi(1770–1789). Etude d'économie urbaine.* Paris: E. Leroux, 1935.

Facque, Robert. *Les Halles et marchés alimentaires de Paris.* Paris: Recueil Sirey, 1911.

Fance, W. J., and B. H. Wragg. *Up to Date Breadmaking.* London: n.p., 1968.

Feyeux. "Un nouveau livre des métiers." *La Science sociale,* 2d year, 4 (October 1887): 323–50.

Firth, Raymond. *Malay Fishermen: Their Peasant Economy.* London: Routledge & Kegan Paul, 1946.

——, ed. *Themes in Economic Anthropology.* London: Tavistock Publishers, 1967.

—— and B. S. Yang, eds. *Capital, Savings, and Credit in Peasant Societies.* Chicago: Aldine, 1964.

Fisher, F. J. "The Development of the London Food Market, 1540–1640." *Economic History Review* 5, no. 2 (April 1935): 46–54.

Fogg, Walter. "The Organization of a Moroccan Tribal Market." *American Anthropologist* 44 (1942): 47–61.

Fong, H. D. "Grain Trade and Milling in Tientsin." *The Chinese Social and Political Science Review* 17 (October 1933): 367–429 and (January 1934): 553–631.

Forman, Shepard, and Joyce Riegelhaupt. "Marketplace and Market System: Toward a Theory of Peasant Economic Integration." *Comparative Studies in Society and History* 12 (1970): 188–212.

Fournier, Edouard. *Le Vieux-neuf, histoire ancienne des inventions et découvertes modernes.* 2d ed. 3 vols. Paris: E. Dentu, 1877.

Fourquin, Guy. *Les Campagnes de la région parisienne à la fin du Moyen Age.* Paris: Presses universitaires de France, 1964.

Francqueville, A. de. "Les Vieux Moulins de Picardie." *Bulletin de la Société des antiquaires de Picardie* 23 (1907–1908): 27–115.

Franklin, Alfred. *Dictionnaire historique des arts, métiers et professions exercés dans Paris depuis le XIIIᵉ siècle.* Paris: H. Welter, 1906.

——. *La Vie privée d'autrefois.* Vol. 3, *La Cuisine.* Paris: E. Plon, Nourrit, 1887–1902.

Freese, Stanley. *Windmills and Millwrighting.* Cambridge: Cambridge University Press, 1957.

Friedmann, Karen J. "Victualling Colonial Boston." *Agricultural History* 47, no. 3 (July 1973): 189–205.

Gargadennec, R. "Notice sur nos vieux moulins à eau." *Bulletin de la Société archéologique du Finistère* 84 (1958): 207–17.

Gast, Marceau, and François Sigaut, eds. *Les Techniques de conservation des grains à long terme.* 2 vols. Paris: Centre National de la Recherche Scientifique, 1979–81.

Gautier, Marcel. "Un Type d'habitation rurale à fonction 'industrielle': Les Moulins de Bretagne et de Vendée." *Norois: Revue géographique de l'Ouest et des pays de l'Atlantique nord* (1969): 387–414.

Gazier, A., ed. "La Police de Paris en 1770, mémoire inédit, composé par ordre de Marie-Thérèse." *Mémoires de la Société de l'histoire de Paris et de l'Ile-de-France* 5 (1878).

Geertz, Clifford. *Peddlers and Princes: Social Change and Economic Modernization in Two Indonesian Towns.* Chicago: University of Chicago Press, 1963.

―――, Hildred Geertz, and Lawrence Rosen. *Meaning and Order in Moroccan Society.* New York: Cambridge University Press, 1979.

Geoffroy, R. *Guide du meunier.* Marseille: Chez l'auteur, 1971.

George, Pierre, and Pierre Randet. *La Région parisienne.* Paris: Presses Universitaires de France, 1959.

Gerschenkron, Alexander. *Bread and Democracy in Germany.* Berkeley and Los Angeles: University of California Press, 1943.

Gibbings, Chris. *Moulins à vent de Bourgogne,* in *Les Moulins de France* (1978).

Gibert, Urbain. "Moulins à vent et meuniers." *Folklore* 21, no. 1 (Spring 1968).

Gille, Bertrand. "Fonctions économiques de Paris," in Guy Michaud, ed. *Paris: Fonctions d'une capitale.* Paris: Hachette, 1962.

Gillispie, Charles C., ed. *Dictionary of Scientific Biography.* 16 vols. New York: Charles Scribner's Sons, 1970–80.

―――. *Science and Polity in France at the End of the Old Regime.* Princeton: Princeton University Press, 1980.

Gindin, Claude. "Aperçu sur les conditions de la mouture des grains en France, fin du XVIIIᵉ siècle," in Albert Soboul, ed. *Contributions à l'histoire paysanne de la révolution française.* Paris: Editions sociales, 1977.

―――. "Le Pain de Gonesse à la fin du dix-septième siècle." *Revue d'histoire moderne et contemporaine* 19 (July–September 1972): 414–34.

Ginzburg, Carlo. "Cheese and Worms: The Cosmos of a Sixteenth-Century Miller," in J. Obelkevich, ed. *Religion and the People, 1000–1700.* Chapel Hill: University of North Carolina Press, 1979.

Girod, P.-E. "Les Subsistances en Bourgogne et particulièrement à Dijon à la fin du XVIIIᵉ siècle, 1774–1789." *Revue Bourguignonne de l'enseignement supérieur* 16, no. 4 (1906): i–xxiii, 1–145.

Gottschalk, Alfred. *Le Blé, la farine et le pain.* Paris: Editions de la Tournelle, 1935.

Goubert, Jean-Pierre. "Le Phénomène épidémique en Bretagne à la fin du XVIIIᵉ siècle (1770–87)." *Annales: Economies, sociétés, civilisations,* 24th year, no. 6 (November–December 1969): 1562–88.

Graff, Harvey J. *The Literacy Myth: Literacy and Social Structure in the Nineteenth Century City.* New York: Academic Press, 1979.

Grimshaw, Robert. *The Miller, the Millwright, and the Millfurnisher.* New York: H. Lockswood, 1882.

Grodecki, Louis. "Les Vitraux allégoriques de Saint-Denis." *Art de France,* no. 1 (1961): 19–41.

Hamilton, Edward Pierce. *The Village Mill in Early New England.* Sturbridge, Mass.: Old Sturbridge Village, 1964.

Harrowven, Jean. *The Origins of Rhymes, Songs and Sayings.* London: Kaye and Ward, 1977.

Henry, Bernard. *Des métiers et des hommes à la lisière des bois.* Paris: Editions du Seuil, 1976.

Herlaut, Auguste-Philippe. "La Disette de pain à Paris en 1709." *Mémoires de la Société de l'Histoire de Paris et de l'Ile-de-France* 45 (1918): 5–100.

Hill, Polly. "Markets in Africa." *Journal of Modern African Studies* 1 (December 1963): 441–53.

Hillairet, Jacques. *Evocation du vieux Paris.* Vol. 1, *Rive droite.* Paris: Editions de Minuit, 1951.

Hirschman, Albert O. *Exit, Voice and Loyalty. Response to Decline in Firms, Organizations, and States.* Cambridge, Mass.: Harvard University Press, 1970.

———. *The Passions and the Interests: Political Arguments for Capitalism before Its Triumph.* Princeton: Princeton University Press, 1977.

———. "Rival Interpretations of Market Society: Civilizing, Destructive or Feeble." *Journal of Economic Literature* 20 (December 1982): 1463–84.

Horder, Thomas Jeeves, Charles Dodds, and T. Moran. *The Chemistry and Nutrition of Flour and Bread, with an Introduction to Their History and Technology.* London: Constable, 1954.

Hunter, Louis C. *A History of Industrial Power in the United States, 1780–1930.* Vol. 2, *Waterpower in the Century of Steam.* Charlottesville: University Press of Virginia, 1979.

Irons, J. R. *Breadcraft.* London: Virtue and Company, 1948.

Jacob, H.-E. *Six Thousand Years of Bread: Its Holy and Unholy History.* Trans. R. and C. Winston. Garden City, N.Y., 1944.

Jacquart, Jean. *La Crise rurale en Ile-de-France, 1550–1670.* Paris: Armand Colin, 1974.

Jobez, L.-E.-Alphonse. *La France sous Louis XV, 1715–1774.* 6 vols. Paris: Didier, 1864–73.

Jorré, Georges. "Le Commerce des grains et la minoterie à Toulouse." *Revue géographique des Pyrénées et du Sud-Ouest* 4 (1933): 30–72.

Jourdan, A. "La Ville étudiée dans ses quartiers: Autour des Halles de Paris au Moyen Age." *Annales d'histoire économique et sociale* 7 (1935): 285–301.

Kahane, Ernest. *Parmentier, ou la dignité de la pomme de terre. Essai sur la famine.* Paris: Albert Blanchard, 1978.

Kaplan, Steven L. *The Bakers of Paris and the Bread Question in the Eighteenth Century* (forthcoming).

———. *Bread, Politics and Political Economy in the Reign of Louis XV.* 2 vols. The Hague: Martinus Nijhoff, 1976.

———. *The Famine Plot Persuasion in Eighteenth-Century France. Transactions of the American Philosophical Society* 72, part 3 (1982).

———. "Lean Years, Fat Years: The 'Community' Granary System and the Search for Abundance in Eighteenth-Century Paris." *French Historical Studies* 10 (Fall 1977): 197–230.

———. "Réflexions sur la police du monde du travail, 1700–1815." *Revue historique* 261, no. 1 (January–March 1979): 17–77.

Katzin, Margaret F. "The Business of Higglering in Jamaica." *Social and Economic Studies* 9 (September 1960): 297–331.

Kent-Jones, Douglas W., and A. J. Amos. *Modern Cereal Chemistry.* London: Food Trades Press, 1967.

——— and John Price. *The Practice and Science of Bread-Making.* Liverpool: Northern Publishing Co., 1951.

Khuri, Fuad I. "The Etiquette of Bargaining in the Middle East." *American Anthropologist* 70 (August 1968): 698–706.

Kirkland, John. *Three Centuries of Prices of Wheat, Flour and Bread.* London: National Bakery School, 1917.

———. *The Modern Baker, Confectioner, and Caterer.* London: Gresham Publishing Co., 1934.

Kirschbaum, Engelbert, ed. *Lexikon der Christlichen Ikonographie.* Vol. 3. Freiburg: Herder, 1971.

Klingaman, David. "Food Surpluses and Deficits in the American Colonies, 1768–1772." *Journal of Economic History* 31 (September 1971): 553–69.

Kozmin, Natalie P. "The Aging of Wheat Flour and the Nature of the Process." *Cereal Chemistry* 12 (1935).

Kozmin, Peter A. *Flour Milling.* Trans. M. Falkner and T. Fjelstrup. New York: D. Van Nostrand, 1917.

Kuhlmann, Charles B. *The Development of the Flour-Milling Industry in the United States.* Boston and New York: Houghton Mifflin, 1929.

Labrousse, Ernest. *Esquisse du mouvement des prix et des revenus en France au dix-huitième siècle.* 2 vols. Paris: Presses universitaires de France, 1933.

Lamberton, D. M., ed. *Economics of Information.* Harmondsworth: Penguin Books, 1971.

Lanzac de Laborie, Léon de. *Paris sous Napoléon.* Vol. 5, *Assistance et bienfaisance. Approvisionnement.* Paris: Plon-Nourrit et Cⁱᵉ, 1908.

Larousse, Pierre, ed. *Grand Dictionnaire universel du 19ᵉ siècle.* 17 vols. Paris: Administration du "Grand Dictionnaire universel," 1865–90.

LeClair, Edward E. "Economic Theory and Economic Anthropology." *American Anthropologist* 64 (December 1962): 1179–1203.

Lefèvre, Pierre. *Le Commerce des grains et la question du pain à Lille de 1711 à 1789.* Lille: C. Robbe, 1925.

Le Goff, Jacques. *La Civilisation de l'occident médiéval.* Paris: Arthaud, 1967.

Le Lay, F. "Meuniers et moulins dans une région du Morbihan au dix-huitième siècle." *Revue morbihannaise* (September 1911): 269–78.

Lemarchand, Guy. "Les Troubles de subsistances dans la généralité de Rouen." *Annales historiques de la Révolution française,* 35th year, no. 174 (October–December 1963): 401–27.

La Paire, Jacques-Amédée. *Histoire de la ville de Corbeil.* 2 vols. Lagny: E. Colin, 1901–1902.

Leroux de Lincy, Antoine-Jean-Victor. *Hôtel de Ville de Paris.* Paris: Carilian-Goeury et V. Dalmont, 1844.

Le Roy Ladurie, Emmanuel. *Histoire du climat depuis l'an mil.* Paris: Flammarion, 1967.

——— and Joseph Goy. *Tithe and Agrarian History from the 14th to the 19th Century.* Cambridge: Cambridge University Press, 1981.

Lespinasse, René de, and François Bonnardot. *Les Métiers et corporations de la ville de Paris.* Vol. 1, *Ordonnances générales, métiers d'alimentation.* Paris: Imprimerie Nationale, 1886.

Letaconnoux, Jean. *Les Subsistances et le commerce des grains en Bretagne au XVIIIᵉ siècle, essai de monographie économique.* Rennes: Oberthür, 1909.

————. "La Transformation des moyens de transport," in Camille Bloch et al. *Les Divisions régionales de la France.* Paris: Félix Alcan, 1913.

————. "Les Transports en France au dix-huitième siècle." *Revue d'histoire moderne et contemporaine* 11 (1908–1909): 97–114, 269–92.

————. "Les Voies de communication en France au dix-huitième siècle." *Vierteljahrschrift für Sozial- und Wirtschaftsgeschichte* 7 (1909): 94–141.

Li, Y., and J. B. Tayler. "Grain Marketing in Hopei Province, an Interim Report." *The Chinese Social and Political Science Review* 17 (April 1933): 107–69.

Lockwood, William G. *Periodic Markets: Source Materials on Markets and Fairs in Peasant Society.* Council of Planning Librarians Exchange Bibliography, no. 341, November 1972.

Louandre, Charles. *De l'alimentation publique sous l'ancienne monarchie française.* Paris: P. Dupont, 1864.

Loutchisky, I. "Régime agraire et populations agricoles dans les environs de Paris à la veille de la Révolution." *Revue d'histoire moderne,* n.s. 8 (March–April 1933): 97–142.

Lublinsky, V. S. "Voltaire et la guerre des farines." *Annales historiques de la Révolution française,* 31st year, no. 156 (April–June 1959): 127–45.

McCance, R. A., and E. M. Widdowson. *Breads White and Brown: Their Place in Thought and Social History.* London: Pitman, 1956.

Maillard, Lydia. *Les Moulins de Montmartre et leurs meuniers.* Paris: Le Vieux Montmartre, 1981.

Main, Jackson Turner. *The Social Structure of Revolutionary America.* Princeton: Princeton University Press, 1965.

Mandonnet, Paul. *Moulins à vent en Anjou.* Paris: n.p., 1964.

Marcel-Robillard, Charles. *La Belle Histoire des moulins à vent.* Chartres: Musée de Chartres, 1960.

————. *Le Folklore de la Beauce.* Paris: Gustave-Paul Maisonneuve et Larose, 1965–71.

Marion, Marcel. *Dictionnaire des institutions de la France aux 17ᵉ et 18ᵉ siècles.* 1923. Reprint. Paris: A. J. Picard, 1969.

————. "Une Famine en Guyenne (1747–48)." *Revue historique* 46 (May–August 1891): 241–87.

————. *Histoire financière de la France depuis 1715.* 6 vols. Paris: A. Rousseau, 1914–27.

Marmay, Pierre. *Guide pratique de meunerie et de boulangerie.* Paris: E. Lacroix, 1863.

Martin, [Bon-Louis] Henri. *Histoire de France.* 4th ed. 17 vols. Paris: Furne, 1855–60.

Martin, Germain. *Associations ouvrières au 18ᵉ siècle.* Paris: Rousseau, 1900.

————. "Les Famines de 1693 et 1709 et la spéculation sur les blés." *Congrès des Sociétés savantes de 1908 tenu à Paris. Bulletin du Comité des travaux historiques et scientifiques, économiques et sociales* (1908): 150–72.

Martineau, Jean. *Les Halles de Paris, des origines à 1789.* Paris: Editions Montchrestien, 1960.

Martinet, Alfred. *Les Aliments usuels.* 2d ed. rev. and enl. Paris: Masson, 1910.

Matz, Samuel A., ed. *Bakery Technology and Engineering.* Westport, Conn.: Avi Publishing Company, 1960.

Maurizio, A. *Histoire de l'alimentation végétale depuis la préhistoire jusqu'à nos jours.* Trans. F. Gidon. Paris: Payot, 1932.

Meillassoux, Claude, ed. *The Development of Indigenous Trade and Markets in West Africa.* London: Oxford University Press, 1971.

Merle, Louis. *La Métairie et l'évolution agraire de la Gâtine poitevine de la fin du Moyen Age à la Révolution.* Paris: S.E.V.P.E.N., 1958.

Meuvret, Jean. "Le Commerce des grains et des farines à Paris et les marchands parisiens à l'époque de Louis XIV." *Revue d'histoire moderne et contemporaine* 3 (July–September 1956): 169–203.

———. *Le Problème des subsistances a l'époque Louis XIV. La Production des céréales dans la France du XVIIᵉ et XVIIIᵉ siècle.* 2 vols. Paris: Mouton, 1977.

Meyer, Jean. *Etudes sur les villes en Europe occidentale (milieu du XVIIᵉ siècle à la veille de la Révolution Française).* Paris: Société d'édition d'enseignement supérieur, 1983.

Mintz, Sidney W. *Caribbean Transformations.* Chicago: Aldine, 1974.

———. "Internal Market Systems of Social Articulation," in *Intermediate Societies, Social Mobility, and Communication.* Proceedings of the 1959 Annual Spring Meeting of the American Ethnological Society. Ed. Verne F. Ray. Seattle: University of Washington Press, 1959.

———. "The Jamaican Internal Marketing Pattern: Some Notes and Hypotheses." *Social and Economic Studies* 4 (March 1955): 95–103.

———. "Men, Women and Trade." *Comparative Studies in Society and History* 13 (July 1971): 247–69.

———. "Peasant Market Places and Economic Development in Latin America." Vanderbilt University: Graduate Center for Latin American Studies, occasional paper no. 4 (1964).

———. "Pratik: Haitian Personal Economic Relations," in Viola E. Garfield, ed. *Symposium: Patterns of Land Utilization and Other Papers.* Proceedings of the 1961 Annual Spring Meeting of the American Ethnological Society. Seattle: University of Washington Press, 1961.

Molinari, Gustave de. "Céréales," in Charles Coquelin and Guillaumin, eds. *Dictionnaire de l'économie politique.* 2 vols. Paris: Librairie de Guillaumin et Cⁱᵉ, 1873.

Mott, Luis, Robert H. Silin, and Sidney W. Mintz. *A Supplementary Bibliography of Marketing and Marketplaces.* Council of Planning Librarians Exchange Bibliography, no. 792 (May 1975).

Mousnier, Roland. *Paris au XVIIᵉ siècle.* Paris: Centre de documentation universitaire, 1961.

Musart, Charles. *La Réglementation du commerce des grains en France au XVIIIᵉ siècle: La théorie de Delamare, étude économique.* Paris: E. Champion, 1922.

Nelson, Phillip. "Information and Consumer Behavior." *Journal of Political Economy* 78 (March–April 1970): 311–29.

Neumann, Erich. *The Great Mother: An Analysis of the Archetype.* Trans. R. Manheim. Bollingen ser. 47. Princeton: Princeton University Press, 1955.

Neveux, Hugues. *Les Grains du Cambrésis (fin du XIVᵉ–début du XVIIᵉ siècle): Vie et déclin d'une structure économique.* Lille: Service de reproduction des thèses, Université de Lille III, 1974.

Norvell, Douglass G., and Marian K. Thompson. "Higglering in Jamaica and the

Mystique of Pure Competition." *Social and Economic Studies* 17 (December 1968): 407–16.

Olivier-Martin, François. *L'Organisation corporative de la France d'ancien régime*. Paris: Recueil Sirey, 1938.

Orsatelli, Jean. *Les Moulins*. Marseille: Jean Lafitte, 1979.

Ortiz, Sutti Reissig. *Uncertainties in Peasant Farming: A Colombian Case*. New York: Humanities Press, 1973.

Parker, William N., and Eric Jones. *European Peasants and Their Markets*. Princeton: Princeton University Press, 1975.

Parrain, Charles. "Rapports de production et développement des forces productives: l'exemple du moulin à eau." *La Pensée*, n.s. no. 119 (February 1965): 55–70.

Payen, Jacques. *Capital et machine à vapeur au XVIIIe siècle*. Paris: Mouton, 1969.

Payne, Lloyd. *The Miller in Eighteenth-Century Virginia*. Williamsburg, Virginia: Colonial Williamsburg, 1958.

Petitfils, Guy. *Le Livre de mon moulin*. Paris: Stock, 1975.

Peyronel, Alain. *Moulins bateaux*. In *Les Moulins de France*, nos. 7–8 (1979).

Picot, Henry. *Vieux Moulins de France: Moulins à vent*. Paris: n.p., n.d.

Piot, Auguste. *Traité historique et pratique sur la meulerie et la meunerie*. Paris: E. Lacroix, 1860.

Piton, Camille. *Comment Paris s'est transformé. Histoire de Paris, topographie, moeurs, usages. Origines de la haute bourgeoisie parisienne: Le Quartier des Halles*. Paris: J. Rothschild, 1891.

Piuz, Anne-Marie. "Alimentation populaire et sous-alimentation au 17e siècle: Le cas de Genève." In Jean-Jacques Hemardinquer, ed. *Pour une histoire de l'alimentation*. Paris: Armand Colin, 1970.

Poëte, Marcel. *Une Vie de cité: Paris de sa naissance à nos jours*. 3 vols. Paris: A. Picard, 1924–31.

Poitrineau, Abel. *La Vie rurale en Basse-Auvergne au XVIIIe siècle, 1726–1789*. Paris: Presses universitaires de France, 1965.

Polanyi, Karl. *The Great Transformation*. New York: Rinehart, 1944.

———. *The Livelihood of Man*. Ed. Harry W. Pearson. New York: Academic Press, 1977.

———. *Primitive, Archaic and Modern Economies*. Ed. George Dalton. New York: Doubleday, 1968.

———, Conrad M. Arensberg, and Harry W. Pearson, eds. *Trade and Market in the Early Empires*. Glencoe, Ill.: Free Press, 1957.

Pratt, D. B., Jr. "Chemical and Baking Changes Which Occur in Bulk Flour during Short-term Storage." *Cereal Science Today* 2 (1957).

Prentice, E. P. *Hunger and History. The Influence of Hunger on Human History*. New York: Harper, 1939.

Rambaud, Adrien. *La Chambre d'abondance de la ville de Lyon (1643–1677)*. Lyon: J. Poncet, 1911.

Reynolds, John. *Windmills and Watermills*. New York: Praeger, 1970.

Richard, Emile. *Histoire de l'hôpital de Bicêtre, 1250–1791*. Paris: G. Steinheil, 1889.

Richardson, Harry W. *Regional Economics: Location Theory, Urban Structure and Regional Change*. New York: Praeger, 1969.

Richet, Charles, and Antonin Mans. *La Famine*. Paris: Centre de recherches, Charles Richet, 1965.

Ricommard, Jean. *La Lieutenance générale de police à Troyes au XVIIIᵉ siècle*. Troyes: J. L. Paton, 1934.

Rivals, Claude. *Le Moulin à vent et le meunier*. Ivry: Editions S.E.R.G., 1976.

Roche, Daniel. *Le Peuple de Paris*. Paris: Aubier, 1981.

Rollet, Augustin. *Mémoire sur la meunerie, la boulangerie et la conservation des grains et des farines*. Paris: Carilian-Goeury et V. Dalmont, 1846.

Roover, Raymond de. "The Scholastic Attitude toward Trade and Entrepreneurship." *Explorations in Entrepreneurial History*, n.s. 1 (Fall 1963): 76–87.

———. "Scholastic Economics: Survival and Lasting Influence from the Sixteenth Century to Adam Smith." *Quarterly Journal of Economics* 69 (1955): 161–90.

Rose, R. B. "The French Revolution and Grain Supply." *Bulletin of the John Rylands Library* 39, no. 1 (1956–57): 171–87.

Rothschild, Michael. "Model Market Organization with Imperfect Information." *Journal of Political Economy* 81 (November–December 1973): 1283–1308.

Roy, Paule. "Moulins à vent de Picardie." *Bulletin trimestriel de la Société des antiquaires de Picardie* (1967): 19–118.

Russell, J. "Stone Dressing," in Rex Wailes, *The English Windmill*. London: Routledge & Kegan Paul, 1954.

Sahlins, Marshall D. "On the Sociology of Primitive Exchange," in *The Relevance of Models for Social Anthropology*. New York: Praeger, 1965.

Saint-Germain, Jacques. *La Vie quotidienne en France à la fin du grand siècle*. Paris: Hachette, 1965.

Sars, Maxime de. *Le Noir, lieutenant de police, 1732–1807*. Paris: Hachette, 1948.

Sébillot, Paul. *Légendes et curiosités des métiers*. Paris: E. Flammarion, 1894–95.

Sellier, Ch. "Les Moulins à vent du vieux Paris." *Bulletin de la Société des amis des monuments parisiens* 7 (1893): 5–23.

Shackleton, Margaret. *Europe: A Regional Geography*. London: Longmans, Green, 1950.

Sheppard, Ronald, and Edward Newton. *The Story of Bread*. London: Routledge & Kegan Paul, 1957.

Skinner, G. William. "Marketing and Social Structure in Rural China." *Journal of Asian Studies* 24 (November 1964): 3–43; 24 (February 1965): 195–228; 25 (May 1965): 363–99.

———, ed. *The City in Late Imperial China*. Stanford: Stanford University Press, 1977.

Smith, Robert H. T. *Periodic Markets in Africa, Asia and Latin America*. Council of Planning Librarians Exchange Bibliography no. 318 (September 1972).

Snyder, Harry. *Bread; a Collection of Popular Papers on Wheat, Flour and Bread*. New York: Macmillan, 1930.

Stigler, George J. "The Economics of Information." *Journal of Political Economy* 69 (June 1961): 213–25.

Storck, John, and Walter D. Teague. *Flour for Man's Bread—A History of Milling*. Minneapolis: University of Minnesota Press, 1952.

Stouff, Louis. *Ravitaillement et alimentation en Provence aux XIVᵉ et XVᵉ siècles*. Paris and The Hague: Mouton, 1970.

Subtil, Alphonse. "La Fabrication du pain dans le Vexin." *Mémoires de la Société Historique et Archéologique de l'arrondissement de Pontoise et du Vexin* 56 (1894).

Swanson, C. O. *Wheat and Flour Quality.* Minneapolis: Burgess, 1938.

Swetnam, John. "Oligopolistic Prices in a Free Market—Antigua, Guatemala." *American Anthropologist* 75 (October 1973): 1504–10.

Sylvestre, A.-J. *Histoire des professions alimentaires dans Paris et ses environs.* Paris: n.p., 1853.

Syson, Leslie. *British Water-Mills.* London: B. T. Batsford, 1965.

Szanton, Maria C. B. *A Right to Survive: Subsistence Marketing in a Lowland Philippine Town.* University Park: Pennsylvania State University Press, 1972.

Taton, René, ed. *Enseignement et diffusion des sciences en France au XVIIIᵉ siècle.* Paris: Hermann, 1964.

Tax, Sol. *Penny Capitalism: A Guatemalan Indian Economy.* Washington, D.C.: Smithsonian Institution, Institute of Social Anthropology Publication no. 16 (1953).

Thery, Adrien-Henri. *Gonesse dans l'histoire: Une vieille bourgade et son passé à travers les siècles.* Persan: Imprimerie de Persan-Beaumont, 1960.

Thompson, Charles T., and Marilyn Huies. "Peasant and Bazaar Marketing Systems as Distinct Types." *Anthropological Quarterly* 41 (1968): 218–27.

Thompson, E. P. "The Moral Economy of the English Crowd in the Eighteenth Century." *Past & Present,* no. 50 (February 1971): 76–136.

Thrupp, Sylvia. *A Short History of the Worshipful Company of Bakers of London.* Croydon: Galleon Press, 1933.

T'ien, Ju-Kang. *The Chinese of Sarawak: A Study of Social Structure.* London: London School of Economics and Political Science, Monograph on Social Anthopology, no. 12, n.d.

Tissier, André. *La Farce en France de 1450 à 1550.* 2 vols. Paris: Centre de documentation universitaire & Société d'édition d'enseignement supérieur réunis, 1976.

Touchard-Lafosse, Georges. *Histoire de Paris et de ses environs.* Vol. 3. Paris: n.p., 1851.

Tunis, Edwin. *Colonial Craftsmen and the Beginning of American Industry.* Cleveland: World, 1965.

Uchendu, Victor. "Some Principles of Haggling in Peasant Markets." *Economic Development and Cultural Change* 16 (October 1967): 37–50.

Usher, Abbot P. *The History of the Grain Trade in France, 1400–1710.* Cambridge, Mass.: Harvard University Press, 1913.

Van der Woude, Ad, and Anton Schuurman. *Probate Inventories: A New Source for the Historical Study of Wealth, Material Culture and Agricultural Development,* in *A.A.G. Bijdragen* 23 (1980).

Veyne, Paul. *Le Pain et le cirque: Sociologie historique d'un pluralisme politique.* Paris: Editions du Seuil, 1976.

Veyrier du Muraud, Paul, et al., eds. *Inventaire sommaire des archives communales antérieures à 1790.* Orléans: n.p., 1907.

Viala, Louis. *La Question des grains et leur commerce à Toulouse au dix-huitième siècle (de 1715 à 1789).* Toulouse: E. Privat, 1909.

Villey, Edmond. "La Taxe du pain et les boulangers de la ville de Caen en 1776. Documents." *Revue d'économie politique* 2 (1888): 178–92.

Vince, John. *Discovering Windmills.* Aylesbury: Shire Publications, 1973.

Vincent, François. *Histoire des famines à Paris.* Paris: Editions politiques, économiques et sociales, 1946.

Vogler, Bernard, ed. *Les Actes notariés, source de l'histoire sociale, XVIᵉ–XIXᵉ siècles.* Strasbourg: Librairie Istra, 1979.

Vovelle, Michel. "Les Taxations populaires de février–mars et de novembre–décembre 1792 dans la Beauce et sur ses confins." *Actes du 82ᵉ Congrès national des sociétés savantes,* Bordeaux, 1957. *Mémoires et Documents. Commission de recherche et de publication des documents relatifs à la vie économique de la Révolution* 13 (1958).

Wailes, Rex. "Discussion of H. O. Clark's 'Notes on French Windmills,'" in H.O. Clark, "Notes on French Windmills," *Transactions of the Newcomen Society* 9 (1928–29): 52–59.

———. *The English Windmill.* London: Routledge & Kegan Paul, 1954.

Ward, Barbara E. "Cash or Credit Crop? An Examination of Some Implications of Peasant Commercial Production with Specific Reference to the Multiplicity of Traders and Middlemen." *Economic Development and Cultural Change* 8 (January 1960): 148–63.

Waterbury, John. *North for the Trade: The Life and Times of a Berber Merchant.* Berkeley: University of California Press, 1972.

Webber, M. J., and Richard Symanski. "Periodic Markets: An Economic Location Analysis." *Economic Geography* 49 (July 1973): 213–27.

Weulersse, Georges. *Le Mouvement physiocratique en France de 1756 à 1770.* 2 vols. Paris: Félix Alcan, 1910.

———. *La Physiocratie à la fin du règne de Louis XV, 1770–1774.* Paris: Presses universitaires de France, 1959.

———. *La Physiocratie sous les ministères de Turgot et de Necker (1774–1781).* Paris: Presses universitaires de France, 1950.

Whitmore, Mary Ernestine. *Medieval English Domestic Life and Amusement in the Works of Chaucer.* New York: Cooper Square Publisher, 1972.

Williams, Alan. *The Police of Paris, 1718–1789.* Baton Rouge: Louisiana State University Press, 1979.

Wilson, Paul N. *Watermills: An Introduction.* London: Society for the Protection of Ancient Buildings, 1973.

Wolff, Roger. *Les Vieux Moulins à eau de la Montcien.* Mantes-la-Jolie: Centre régional d'études historiques, n.d.

Zimiles, Martha, and Murray Zimiles. *Early American Mills.* New York: Clarkson N. Potter, 1973.

Zupko, Ronald E. *A Dictionary of English Weights and Measures from Anglo-Saxon Times to the Nineteenth Century.* Madison: University of Wisconsin Press, 1968.

———. *French Weights and Measures before the Revolution: A Dictionary of Provincial and Local Units.* Bloomington: Indiana University Press, 1978.

Index

PREPARED BY

MARY ANN QUINN

This index is intended to double as a glossary, in supplying concise definitions for foreign terms. Millers, merchants, and other members of the Paris provisioning world have generally been included only if they appear repeatedly in the volume or are significant figures.

Library of Congress Cataloging in Publication Data

KAPLAN, STEVEN L.
    Provisioning Paris.

    Bibliography: p.
    Includes index.
    1. Grain trade—France—Paris Region—History—18th
century.   2. Flour and feed trade—France—Paris Region—
History—18th century.   3. Food supply—France—
Paris Region—History—18th century.   4. Millers—
France—Paris Region—History—18th century.   5. Bakers
and bakeries—France—Paris Region—History—18th cen-
tury.   6. Merchants—France—Paris Region—History—
18th century.   I. Title.
HD9042.8.P37K37   1984   381′.456647′094436   84-7004
ISBN 0-8014-1600-0 (alk. paper)